Remembering Joseph

Remembering Joseph

Personal Recollections of Those
Who Knew the Prophet Joseph Smith

Mark L. McConkie

DESERET BOOK

SALT LAKE CITY, UTAH

If you have an original story about the Prophet Joseph Smith
from your family history or your own research,
please visit http://deseretbook.com/remembering-joseph

Images courtesy of LDS Church Archives.

© 2003 Mark L. McConkie

All rights reserved. No part of this book may be reproduced in any form or by any means without permission in writing from the publisher, Deseret Book Company, P. O. Box 30178, Salt Lake City, Utah 84130. This work is not an official publication of The Church of Jesus Christ of Latter-day Saints. The views expressed herein are the responsibility of the author and do not necessarily represent the position of the Church or of Deseret Book Company.

DESERET BOOK is a registered trademark of Deseret Book Company.

Visit us at DeseretBook.com

Library of Congress Cataloging-in-Publication Data

Remembering Joseph : personal recollections of those who knew the prophet Joseph Smith / [edited by] Mark L. McConkie.
    p.   cm.
    Includes bibliographical references and index.
    ISBN 978-1-57008-963-3 (alk. paper)
    1. Smith, Joseph, 1805–1844.   I. Smith, Joseph, 1805–1844.   II. McConkie, Mark L. III. Title.

BX8695.S6R44 2003
289.3'092—dc21   2003013409

Printed in the United States of America
Publishers Printing, Salt Lake City, UT

10   9   8   7   6   5   4

Contents

Illustrations vi

Introduction vii

1 The Problems and Promise
   of Historical Memories 1

2 The Character and Personality
   of the Prophet Joseph Smith 27

3 The Gifts of the Spirit 111

4 Joseph Smith and the Scriptures 231

5 The Ordinances and the Church 269

6 Historical Items 289

   Selected Biographical Registry 425

   Bibliography 455

   Index 507

Illustrations

Illustrations can be found on an insert between pages 268–69. Images are arranged alphabetically by author's last name.

Truman O. Angell	1-1	Parley P. Pratt	1-9
Israel A. Barlow	1-1	Josiah Quincy	1-10
George Q. Cannon	1-1	Willard Richards	1-10
Oliver Cowdery	1-1	Orrin Porter Rockwell	1-10
Governor Thomas Ford	1-2	Emma Smith	1-10
Martin Harris	1-2	Hyrum Smith	1-11
Joseph L. Heywood	1-2	Joseph F. Smith	1-11
Mary I. Horne	1-2	Joseph Smith III	1-11
Edward Hunter	1-3	Lucy Mack Smith	1-11
Benjamin F. Johnson	1-4	Mary Fielding Smith	1-12
Mary Ellen Kimball	1-4	William Smith	1-12
Heber C. Kimball	1-5	Eliza R. Snow	1-12
Mary A. Lambert	1-6	Lorenzo Snow	1-13
Alfred B. Lambson	1-7	William C. Staines	1-13
Christopher Layton	1-7	Edward Stevenson	1-14
Mary Elizabeth Rollins Lightner	1-7	John Taylor	1-15
		Phoebe Carter Woodruff	1-16
Wandle Mace	1-8	Wilford Woodruff	1-16
Joseph S. Murdock	1-8	Brigham Young	1-16
Edward Partridge	1-8	Margaret P. Young	1-16
Orson Pratt	1-8		

Introduction

The world must deal with the question of Joseph Smith. Was he a prophet? Did he see the Father and the Son? Was he commissioned of God? Is his testimony true? Did he receive priesthood and keys from John the Baptist, from Peter, James, and John, and from Moses, Elias, and Elijah? Has every truth and every power held by the ancient prophets and necessary for salvation been restored in our day? Is the Book of Mormon a revelation from God? Is it scripture, like unto the Bible?

The questions Joseph Smith raises, and which continue to press our spirits, are no less numbered and no less important than they were when Joseph was alive. The testimonies here assembled contain answers—answers provided chiefly by Joseph's family, friends, and associates. Who better to assess Joseph Smith and his ministry and mission than those who knew him well? This volume contains the testimonies of those who knew his character: they sat at his table, dined in his hall, slept on his floor, worked in his fields at his side, walked thousands of miles in his company, rode horses, carriages, and even trains with him as a companion; these are those who schooled with him, endured poverty and persecution with him, built temples and cities at his side, raised children with his, and, with him, saw children born and loved ones die. They knew his wife and children. These are the testimonies of those who heard him teach and preach, who talked with him of things great and small, and who watched as he mingled and ministered. In this volume we have testimonies of those who laughed and cried with him, who felt the touch of his hand and the sound of his voice, who heard him pray, bless, admonish, correct, and be corrected. These are the people who were present when he received revelations or when he prophesied—sometimes to individuals, sometimes to groups, sometimes to the world, and

Introduction

sometimes to a dispensation. These are the people who saw him heal the sick, speak wisdom such as they had never heard, and speak in and interpret tongues. These are the people who, with him, saw visions, angels, and more. These are the people who saw his faith turn farmers, carpenters, and artisans into apostles and prophets who performed miracles and became teachers and preachers whose words have been quoted unto our present generation, with the promise that they would be quoted a thousand years and more. These are the people who knew him well—as well as any mortal might know another. They knew him in every particular and in every detail. Who then is better qualified to answer the weighty questions about Joseph Smith, his mission and ministry?

Critics will claim that the very closeness of these people to Joseph disqualifies them from bearing an objective witness. But where is the objectivity of Peter, James, or John with regard to Jesus? They were the more qualified to testify of him precisely because they knew him as well as they did. Lazarus, the man born blind, and the ten lepers were perfect witnesses, but hardly objective. And in the realm of spiritual truth—that realm where prophets reside—let it be said that the Great Jehovah himself has a bias, a preference, and even favorites (see 1 Samuel 2:30; JST, Psalm 11:5; 1 Nephi 17:35, 40; Helaman 15:4; D&C 76:1–19). It is the resounding testimony of the hundreds cited herein that Joseph Smith was divinely appointed, and they speak from the strength of being expert witnesses. The Holy Ghost, they repeatedly certify, gave them testimony of Joseph Smith, testimony that is strengthened and emboldened by their personal interactions with the Prophet.

The sheer weight of these testimonies demands a hearing. Consider but one illustration: more than one hundred separate witnesses (about twenty-five are included in chapter 6) were present on August 8, 1844, when Brigham Young was transfigured and assumed both the voice and appearance of Joseph Smith—and they so testify. It is a miracle which is biblical in proportion, with astounding evidential implications. Similarly, hundreds and hundreds heard Joseph prophesy or exercise spiritual gifts; and when so many testimonies converge on the same conclusion, spiritually sensitive souls know that in honesty they must attend to that testimony and that conclusion. Even the doubter should be impelled to at least *hope* that the frequent and compelling testimony of these people is true, for it brings with it so much promise.

And thus the motive for this compilation.

INTRODUCTION

Organization of the Work

A word about format: This work is divided into two parts, a compact disc that contains all the materials assembled, and the text itself, containing selections taken from the disc. In this book, the materials are arranged under broad topical headings. On the CD, the materials are arranged alphabetically by author and then are generally listed chronologically under an author's surname, beginning with the older entries first and working toward the more recent. This sometimes creates tiny confusions, as some documents lack dates, sometimes events are told in ways that cause dates to overlap or become artificial, and sometimes memory conflicts, even on occasion giving accounts of the same events in different years. As a general rule, however, advancing alphabetically and chronologically is quite workable. On the CD, entries are preceded by brief summaries of what the entries contain; these are my summaries and are not a part of the original manuscript from which the entries are copied. All entries are verbatim transcripts of the originals from which they were taken. Generally, the author given is the one who recorded or dictated the reminiscence; in a number of cases, however, a third party recorded or retold the story in third person. On occasion I have included personal experiences that Joseph Smith recorded himself (or dictated for inclusion in his history); these add a needed extra dimension to some of the stories.

The printed bibliography includes materials found in both the CD and the printed text. Individual quotations are referenced to the bibliography by a simple code. Interested readers will find the original source in the bibliography by going to the author's name and then to the specific year noted at the end of the quote. Where the author had more than one source in a given year, the sources are differentiated by the use of a suffix (*a* or *b* or *c,* and so forth). There are four exceptions to this rule: when the source is the *Journal of Discourses, History of the Church, Collected Discourses,* or Conference Report, these sources are identified by the abbreviations JD, HC, CD, and CR, respectively.

Because this work contains so many secondary sources, readers must read with both eyes open, holding themselves accountable for the usage made of the materials contained herein. Secondary sources have significant deficits. Family histories typically emphasize the roles of ancestors, and thus are more prone to color history than are many other sources. In their very nature, family histories tend to be less objective, less balanced,

Introduction

less concerned about such historical minutia as dates, contexts, and related events. On the other hand, such histories often convey a feeling for ancestors, and frequently for the Prophet Joseph Smith, that is far more compelling than what most historians are able to achieve. In that sense family histories may be more accurate. We must ever remember that there is beauty and power in innocence. After all, Matthew, Mark, Luke, and John were not professional historians, and there is much family history in the Book of Mormon.

My intent is to be comprehensive, but not exhaustive. Some things I have deliberately excluded, such as those accounts which we know to be historically inaccurate, false, or maliciously prejudicial. These include items available elsewhere and involve such things as stories about the Three Nephites, seeing the Urim and Thummim after Joseph had returned it to the custody of the angel, mythologies about the ten tribes, and disingenuities about plural marriage, for instance. At the same time, I have included more of "stories" than "sayings," though often some of what Joseph said is encased in the stories people told about him. Since memory and recall are affected by such things as the age of the author, I have included on the CD the birth dates, wherever possible, of those quoted. As a general rule, in the text presented in this book I have made some modifications in spelling, capitalization, punctuation, grammar, and paragraphing to enhance readability. I have also Americanized and modernized spellings: *blest* becomes *blessed, were* is inserted for the *was* common to our ancestors, and *valour, honour,* and *endeavour* become *valor, honor,* and *endeavor*. In contrast, original grammar and spelling are typically retained on the CD (unless otherwise noted). Where original authors used numbers (1, 2, 3, etc.), I have typically written those numbers out—one, two, three, and so forth.

If you need help using the CD, or if you have an original story about Joseph Smith from your family history or your own research that you would like to share, please visit http://deseretbook.com/remembering-joseph.

A Word of Thanks

In the process of compiling these materials, I have incurred many debts, none more obvious than that to the multiple scores of Latter-day Saints, scattered throughout the country, who over the years have shared from their own family histories and memorabilia. Sheri Dew, president of

INTRODUCTION

Deseret Book Company, has been a believer in this project for over a decade, and she has always encouraged its publication. Her encouragement and support have made the whole thing possible. The idea of putting materials on a compact disc was hers. Her colleague Cory Maxwell has been both friend and supporter and is a model of the Christian gentleman. In terms of bringing materials together, no one has been more helpful than Stephen R. Sorenson, director of the archives division of the Church Historian's Office. From his staff over the years I have received more help than I deserve; they include Ronald G. Watt, April Williamson, Ronald O. Barney, William "Bill" Slaughter, Pauline Musig, W. Randall Dixon, Linda Haslam, Michael Landon, and others more invisible. The patient labors of Jay Parry and Lisa Mangum at Deseret Book still claim my admiration—and appreciation. I am also grateful for the contributions of others at Deseret Book, including Matt McBride, Richard Erickson, and Kent Minson. Bonnie Jean Thornley provided very helpful editing assistance; and to my brother Joseph Fielding McConkie I send a giant embrace for years of coaching and counseling, patient reading, reacting, and kindly yet penetrating insight. He is an example of what God intended brothers to be. What he is as a brother, my sister, Vivian Adams, is as a sister. Her insights are tucked away in places she has forgotten exist; her very existence is evidence that God loves his sons. Our sons Mark Jr., Taylor, Matthew, and David and daughter Rebecca (my "Executive Director") provided more computer help than it should be lawful for one man to need. Over the years this has become a family project, and I have received varied help from our other children: Ann Marie, Sara, Michael, and Daniel. And, more than any other, my wife, Mary Ann, claims a place in my eternities by her constant example and kindness—and the patience to let me spend so much time with Joseph Smith.

1

The Problems and Promise of Historical Memories

Joseph Smith's Friends

Who were these men and women who gathered around Joseph Smith? They were largely men and women with calloused hands and strong backs, farmers, carpenters, joiners, millwrights and wheelwrights, tanners and shoemakers, who stood beside women who could spin and sew, milk a cow, and bake bread over the open fire; these were men and women who knew how to carve a livelihood out of the land, how to turn a forest into fertile farmland, and how to barter goods. They lived with mud on their boots and sweat on their brows; the horse, the cow, and the ox were not only their servants, but their friends, on whom they depended for a livelihood. When the family cow died, the family wept; when she gave birth, the family rejoiced. These were men and women possessed of the skills to build cities out of wilderness: Kirtland grew out of the Ohio woods; Far West, Independence, and Adam-ondi-Ahman spread over the grassy plains of Missouri; and Nauvoo was built out of swampland into the largest, most prosperous, and most politically influential city in the state. Joseph Smith's Nauvoo outshone Abraham Lincoln's Springfield like the sun outshines the moon. These were a vibrant people who built vibrant cities, and when they left them none could restore them to their former luster. These same disciples went on to colonize the West, making the desert blossom as the rose.

In lesser numbers, these people had professional skills. John Bernhisel, Willard Richards, and Frederick G. Williams were physicians, as were Warren Cowdery and Luke S. Johnson—but Cowdery and Johnson also farmed. William W. Phelps was a newspaper editor, and Orson Hyde clerked, taught school, ran a business, and practiced law. William E. McLellin was a schoolteacher, and Lorin Farr and Eliza R. Snow tutored the Prophet's children in his home. George W. Robinson was a merchant, and Algernon Sidney Gilbert teamed with Newel K. Whitney to operate a store in Kirtland. These professional people were fewer in number than the farmers and artisans, but they left a profound impress, reaching out and touching the many.

Joseph Smith surrounded himself with people from every walk and used their talents, large and small, to build the Lord's kingdom. He took men trained to farm and paint and turned them into master managers and great leaders. Brigham Young was a carpenter, a painter, and a glazier who took the principles Joseph taught him and became the greatest entrepreneur and colonizer in American history. Heber C. Kimball, a blacksmith and potter, opened missionary work in Great Britain and later stood as Brigham's right-hand man. John Page, a farmer, became a master missionary who baptized over six hundred converts, and another farmer, Wilford Woodruff, baptized thousands. Dan Jones, a riverboat captain, was instrumental in the baptism of some six thousand more. In the less noticed corners of the kingdom, Phoebe Chase was set apart to heal the sick, and Jane Johnston Black was set apart as a midwife. Sister Black then proceeded to deliver over three thousand babies, some in the most primitive of settings, without ever losing either a mother or a child. Elizabeth Kendall, whose mother washed and ironed clothes for the Prophet's family, received a blessing from the Prophet that she would be a great nurse and care for many; she too, as a midwife, safely delivered hundreds of babies. Ann Green Carling, another midwife, had a similar story, and Harriet Johnson, whom the Prophet also set apart as a midwife, delivered about four thousand more. These were men and women of capacity who, in large and small ways, joined hands in subordination to the principles Joseph Smith taught and in the process built a great empire.

These were a people who differed from their fellows because of what they carried in their hearts and in their souls. They saw truth where others were blind, and they felt things others could hardly imagine. Joseph Smith Sr. testified to Fayette Lapham about inspired visions and angels, and Lapham concluded the Smiths were an "illiterate" people involved with "witchcraft and other supernatural things" (Lapham, 1870, p. 306). Jonathan Lapham agreed with his cousin Fayette. Stephen S. Harding courteously turned aside. Peter Ingersoll scoffed, as did the whole of the Chase and Stafford families. But when Father Smith bore that same testimony to Solomon Chamberlain, Parley P. Pratt, Orrin Rockwell, and Thomas B. Marsh, they heard with their souls and knew in ways that words only inadequately explain that God had once again communed with man. Sanford Porter, John Pulsipher, and Samuel Turnbow reported visions similar to Joseph Smith, all of which pointed them to Joseph Smith. Robert Mason prophesied that his young friend Wilford Woodruff would be a "conspicuous actor" in a great and forthcoming work to be established by God, and John Taylor beheld a vision in which he saw "an angel in the heavens, holding a trumpet to his mouth, sounding a message to the nations" (Roberts, 1963, p. 28). The voice of the Lord directed him to leave England and come to America, where he heard the gospel taught in its fulness. George Spilsbury heard that same voice, telling him he would be a minister of the gospel. First, however, he was baptized. Along with thousands of others, these witnesses were having experiences that the E. D. Howes and Orsimus Turners of the world could neither understand nor appreciate, but these experiences were binding them together as one.

These people who followed Joseph came from all over, for Joseph was quick to send missionaries to every reach of the American nation. New England Puritan blood readily joined with the settlers of the Ohio Valley; missionaries harvested modern Israelite wheat from the fields of Tennessee and the South. The Canadian missionary adventure became the seed ground that stretched into Victoria's England. Joseph, remembered Brigham Young (1845), told the early converts to take the message to their families, and they thus quickly wrote, visited, and talked with their own blood. Joseph himself visited his grandfather and cousins in upstate New York; he took his brother Hyrum and his parents to preach to his mother's family in Pontiac, Michigan. Families brought families into the fold: the Smiths and the Kimballs were related by marriage, and Newell Kimball Whitney, as his name implies, was related to Heber C. Kimball; the Youngs and the Kimballs were related; and the Greens and the Youngs were also related. Mary Ann Angell gave a copy of the Book of Mormon to her cousin Joseph Holbrook, who read with avidity and was baptized. Heber C. Kimball and George P. Billings were cousins, as were Brigham Young, Willard Richards, and Albert P. Rockwood. William and Zerubbabel Snow were the first of the Snow family to be baptized; then came their brother Erastus and soon thereafter their cousin Gardner Snow. Smith cousins abounded. Parley P. Pratt preached to his brothers, William and Orson, and both were baptized; on a mission to Toronto, Parley baptized Joseph Fielding, whose sisters, Mary and Mercy, were also baptized. They in turn wrote to their brother in England, the Reverend James Fielding, thus preparing him for the later arrival of the missionaries. Eliza R. Snow testified to her brother Lorenzo, who was soon converted; Abel Butterfield wrote to his mother saying he had worked for Joseph Smith, that Joseph was a good man, and then he testified of the coming of the angel Moroni, adding, "I can say of a truth that I have not seen anything but what is according to the Bible." Joseph Smith Sr. gave Wilford Woodruff a patriarchal blessing, promising that he would take the gospel to his father's family—and he did. They came "one of a city, and two of a family," just as Jeremiah had promised they would (Jeremiah 3:14). In Palmyra the Church grew up around the Smiths, in Colesville around the Knights, and in Fayette, where the Church was organized, around the Whitmers. When the Church moved to Kirtland, the families of Newel K. Whitney, William Huntington, John Johnson, Ezekiel Johnson, and Isaac Morley, among others, stabilized the growing gospel tree. Intermarriage followed, and the Partridges married into the Young family, the Cowderys and the Whitmers were joined, and the Johnsons and the Hydes were also linked. Their descendants would preside throughout all Israel.

Mid-nineteenth century America, of course, is hard to capture in a paragraph, but those converts who were shaped by it were largely literate. They were familiar with the literature of the day, most particularly the Bible, but because they preceded the standardization of spelling and the penetration of Webster's dictionary into cultural usage, their spelling was often phonetic. When Frederick Kesler first met the Latter-day Saints in 1839 he wrote as he spoke: "This strange people as I thought they must be ware located in a place cald commerce, a place 20 miles distant from whare I lived." He met Joseph Smith and some of the leading brethren, and was "greatly surprised in finding them a verry intelegant people & that they believed in & taught the same Doctorn & princaples That was taught by Christ & His apostles & that all thare doctrons was founded on the Bible" (Kesler, 1988, p. 57). In July of 1844 Susan Fairbanks wrote to her sister telling of conditions in Nauvoo: "i can boast on one thing i have been heare more than a week and i have not heard one Oath since I come" (Fairbanks, 1844). When Philemon C. Merrill (ca. 1890) told of Joseph

Smith being kidnapped by two Missourians, he wrote that it occurred when Joseph and his wife "went to visit her relations"—where we would likely say "relatives"—and when the Prophet's mother spoke in the October conference of 1845, she spoke of the organization of the Church, saying that "angels fluttered over us that time" (Lucy Mack Smith, 1845). We are not surprised when Jacob Butterfield wrote to his mother that he had "swoped [swapped] horses with Spaulding Smith," that "we had to hury to git our things on board the boat," and that he had "not but a small appertunity" to survey his new surroundings (Butterfield, 1836). Neither is it surprising to hear James Houston describe his conversion by saying he felt the convincing power of the Holy Ghost "run through me from head to foot" (Houston, n.d.)—but we must in truth admit that while these extracts show personality, even vibrancy, they are as much the exception as the rule. These Saints who followed Joseph Smith were products of their time and reflected the speech patterns and peculiarities of their day, but they wrote well, with feeling and discernment, and communicated artfully what they felt. Some of them wrote with a sloppy or hasty hand, but others, like George Q. Cannon, wrote with an elegant and very readable calligraphy. They were perhaps more educated in the processes of maintaining a living than in the "book learning" of the day, but they still wrote with clarity and exactness. In reviewing what they wrote, only occasionally does one wrestle to understand their meaning.

The bond that held them together was religious; they were joined by the conviction that Joseph Smith was a prophet and the foremost spokesman for Christ since Jesus himself walked the earth. Some recognized gospel truth the moment they heard it; others wrestled upon hearing the testimony of the Restoration. Some came with inspired dreams or visions; others with the certainty of what they felt when they heard missionaries testify. They knew the Book of Mormon was a revelation from God and, with regard to its message, that no middle ground was acceptable: "God or the devil has had a hand in that book," said Willard Richards, "for man never wrote it"—and within ten days he had read the book twice (Richards, 1997, p. 242). George Cannon, the father of George Q. Cannon, concluded that no man could have written the Book of Mormon, for an evil man could not write so good a book, and an honest man would never lie about having done so. And with all the conviction the Book of Mormon generated, it was the Bible that prepared people to receive the Book of Mormon. Warren Foote, for example, had read the

Bible three times before the age of sixteen, when he first read the Book of Mormon. Rachel Ridgeway was so entrenched in Bible study she at first thought it a sin to attend Mormon meetings, yet converts like her followed the Book of Mormon into the waters of baptism by the thousands. It was the book that changed lives and emboldened these early Saints with the willingness to suffer the persecutions of the mob, the hardships of frontier life, and the enmity of the world. It was also the book that brought the Holy Ghost into people's lives, and thus sanctified souls and filled them with the fires of testimony.

Still, they were, in all their greatness, very human. Sometimes they quarreled, and sometimes they were annoyed one with another. In crossing the plains, Eliza R. Snow and Stephen Markham voiced strong differences (Gifford, 1975); during Zion's Camp, an erupting and quarrelsome spirit prompted the Prophet to warn that if the brethren did not repent, they would be visited with a scourge—and cholera followed, killing as many as thirteen, and some accounts say eighteen. Algernon Sidne Gilbert said he would rather die than preach the gospel to the gentiles, and the Lord soon took him at his word (HC, 1:118). But for all their failings, they were a record-keeping people. They kept journals and diaries, wrote letters, and filled the newspapers they published with anecdotes and experiences that have preserved, perhaps better than any people in American history, what they thought, experienced, and believed. At the same time, so central to their lives were their contacts with the Prophet Joseph Smith that they recalled with surprising consistency their interactions with him, sometimes decades after his death. In a culture that told stories, stories of Joseph Smith were repeated and then repeated again, and children inherited stories from parents, grandparents, and others. Children told the stories they inherited with the same degree of conviction as the primary storytellers.

The Problems of Memory

Both the problems and the promise of recording memories, and the memories of others, are captured in an editorial written by Joseph F. Smith in the *Improvement Era* of March 1898.* In response to the question of

---

* *I personally own the bound copy of the* Improvement Era *for 1898 that belonged to President Joseph F. Smith. At the end of the editorials from which the above quotation comes, either he, or Joseph Fielding Smith, from whom I inherited the volume, enscribed*

whether it was advisable "to gather individual testimony from our aged brethren who have been faithful in the cause of truth, and also from our elders who return home from time to time from missions, and who are full of the spirit of their callings," Joseph F. Smith wrote:

> We see no impropriety in brethren gathering individual testimonies concerning the truth, either from the aged brethren or from the elders returning from missions. On the contrary, we believe that the testimonies of our aged brethren who knew the Prophet Joseph Smith, and other early elders and leaders of the church, ought to be secured, and carefully recorded; provided, of course, that the circumstances are well authenticated and carefully and accurately stated. *We fear that many things that are reported as coming from the Prophet Joseph Smith, and other early elders in the church, by not being carefully recorded or told with strict regard for accuracy, have lost something of their value as historical data, and unwarranted additions have sometimes been made to the original facts, until it is difficult to determine just how far some of the traditions which have come to us may be accepted as reliable representations of what was said or what was done.* Let those who feel impressed to make a record of facts, as they become acquainted with them, do so; but let them exercise the greatest care in obtaining accuracy of statement and in giving the authority for the statements they record (Smith, 1898, p. 372; emphasis added).

What Joseph F. Smith says about careful recording of historical data is compounded by the problems of memory, and these warnings apply to the enthusiastic believer as well as to the critical nonbeliever. I illustrate from my own experience. As a young missionary I wrote to my father, Elder Bruce R. McConkie, asking about the events associated with his call to the First Council of Seventy. He wrote back in September 1968 and said:

the initials "J.F.S." The article is lodged in the "Editor's Table," as it was called, and Joseph F. Smith and Brigham H. Roberts were the editors of the Improvement Era *at that time. At the end of the "Editor's Table" for the November 1897 (p. 56) issue, which is part of the same leather-bound volume, in what appears to be the handwriting of Joseph F. Smith, are the initials "J.F.S.," once again suggesting he wrote that editorial as well. Without the aid of Joseph F. Smith's personal volumes, historian Davis Bitton has also drawn the conclusion that Joseph F. Smith is the author of the above statement (see Bitton, 1996, p. 83).*—MLM

> Before telling you the historical details of how I was called to the First Council of the Seventy, however, I think I better offer a word of caution relative to stories in general. It is very common for people to be misquoted. This applies with particular force to the general authorities. Almost everywhere I go, including almost every stake conference I attend, someone comes to me and says that at such and such a time and place I said such and such to them or to someone else. Now I ordinarily have no independent recollection as to what was said on the indicated occasion. In the great majority of cases, however, I am confident I would not have said the thing attributed to me. Very often the language and approach in the quoted material is such that I can identify it in my mind as having come from some other one of the brethren. . . .
>
> It is also not uncommon for a member of a Stake Presidency to get up in a general session of conference and say that Brother McConkie said such and such last night in the leadership session and in his recitation to totally and completely misconstrue and misquote what I had said. This matter of quoting the brethren falsely is of such general concern and creates such a problem that even the *Church Handbook* contains a statement that church members should not quote the brethren where extravagant or unusual things are concerned unless they have the matter in writing.

My father then continued, detailing some of his thoughts on the telling of stories and the recording of history:

> There are two ways to tell a story. One is to recite factually what took place, leaving the hearer or reader to make what interpretations where feelings and other things are concerned that he desires to make. Another way to tell a story is to do it symbolically or figuratively: that is, to tell stories of events which are intended to leave the feeling as to what really was involved. This latter way is not historically accurate. [One of the Brethren] used to tell me and others that the way to write history was not to make a recitation of the facts and events that took place, but to comment about them in such a way as to give people a feeling of what was involved with the people about whom the data were being written. There are people who have this idea where storytelling is concerned. It is personally very objectionable to me. I

think that stories should recite what happened and not some fairy-tale type dissertation about the events. To my mind one presentation is history and the other is mythology. It must be understood, however, that the people who talk in this mythological way, in their own minds at least, are not being dishonest. They are simply making a presentation in the dramatized way they think it should be made. It does not accord with how I think things should be done, but then other people have different ideas and are entitled to their views.

He then picks up on one of the dangers—and temptations!—of storytelling:

> There is another thing about stories. Even those who attempt to tell them accurately soon begin to twist and change or to enlarge. I tell an occasional story in my sermons. . . . It would be very easy for me to amplify and expand, to put words in the mouths of people, in order to get the effect over. I could for instance, greatly improve upon the statements made by some of the people in the conversations. It would get the points over better. . . . President Heber J. Grant was a storyteller in his sermons and he is one of the few men who has ever done this who has stuck religiously and strictly to the actual facts involved, reciting them always in almost the verbatim language. It takes an exceedingly high degree of integrity and honesty to tell stories accurately like this. . . . When stories are recited for historical reasons they are told in one way, and when they are recited for entertainment they are presented in another.

Joseph Smith was aware of these kinds of problems, and thus Jesse Crosby quotes him as saying that he (Joseph) did not enjoy the gift promised "every American citizen; that of free speech." Joseph, Crosby said, could not give his private opinions, for "on any subject of importance his words were often garbled and their meaning twisted and then given out as the word of the Lord because they came from him" (Crosby, n.d. [b]). But Joseph could not control what was said when he was not present, or for that matter, after he died, when so many of the stories about him reached the public ear.

The problems of exaggeration and distorting perceptions are mammoth. So also is the temptation to intrude personal bias or preference upon a text, an event, or a memory. This is nowhere more evident than in the case of Jesus Christ, who has the single most misquoted, misapplied, and misunderstood voice in the history of the earth. The Bible, for its part, is the single most misquoted and misunderstood book. It is not surprising, then, that prophets would be similarly misquoted. Even the saintliest of the Saints can be so tempted, and religious recusants for reasons ranging from vanity to malice make professions of witting and unwitting distortions.

Knowing that we easily err, Joseph Smith warned that "a prophet was only a prophet when he was acting as such" (HC, 5:265). Thus it is that prophets are entitled to *personal* opinions just like any other man (Alma 40:20; 1 Corinthians 7:25), and sometimes have differences among themselves. They even make mistakes (Galatians 2:11). Orson Hyde, for instance, once preached a sermon that contained some false sentiments. Joseph Smith was present, and following the meeting said, "I told Elder Hyde that I was going to offer some corrections to his sermon this morning," and, to Elder Hyde's eternal credit, Elder Hyde replied, "They shall be thankfully received." In the afternoon meeting Joseph spoke and "then corrected Elder Hyde's remarks, the same as I had done to him privately" (Nelson, 1979, pp. 215–16). Similarly, we have in our history an account of Brigham Young preaching something in the morning session of a conference and returning in the afternoon session of the same conference and saying "this morning you heard what Brigham Young thinks about this subject, and now I would like to tell you what the Lord thinks about it." He then reversed the position he had taken in the morning session (McConkie, 1966a). Who is to be surprised, then, that men and women who do not hold the prophetic mantle, and who have less experience and exposure, would make mistakes as well? This would particularly be the case when they operated from memory, without notes.

This very human proclivity to read personal preferences, biases, and even prejudices into a memory or a text is so deeply rooted in our perception processes that we generally do not even see it unfolding. One simple illustration will suffice: the journals of the early Saints are filled with instances in which Joseph wrestled, always coming off the winner, as when he whipped the bully from LaHarpe (Moore, 1892, p. 255) or when he selected the best wrestler among the crowd and "threw him several times in succession" (Burnett, 1946, p. 41), for Joseph "never found his match" (Johnson, 1974, p. 89). In what is likely a more accurate assessment, James Henrie saw his father (William Henrie) wrestle Joseph, but he admitted that while his "father could throw the Prophet frequently" Joseph generally came out ahead (William Henrie, n.d., p. 2). In an age of heroes, the wrestling prowess of the hero Joseph Smith might easily be exaggerated.

This propensity to read a bias or a preference into an experience is particularly alarming when doctrinal interpretations are concerned. We have in the Church Historian's Office, for example, a statement made by one who knew the Prophet well, wherein he describes a question-and-answer session some of the early brethren are said to have had with Joseph. In that meeting Joseph is reputed to have taught that some of the less courageous souls in premortality approached the Father and pled not to come to this earth, reasoning that they lacked the faith to endure mortal testing. Joseph is also quoted as saying that Adam came from another planet as "an immortalized being" and that those who were fence-sitters and "neutral spirits" were sent to earth cursed with a darker skin (Anson Call, n.d.). These statements are all false. They are contrary to what the revelations say, are at odds with what Joseph himself taught, and in one instance even contradict a formal proclamation of the First Presidency (Joseph F. Smith et al., 1909, pp. 75–81). Written on this document, in the readily recognizable handwriting of President Joseph Fielding Smith, is the statement "Not to be considered Church doctrine." Joseph Fielding Smith then wrote his initials next to his statement. Yet somehow these musings carved their way into the aged imagination of a very good man whom the Prophet loved and trusted. It is important to note, in this connection, that this particular error on these particular items does not annul this man's testimony on other items. A man can be an expert witness on one thing but an unqualified witness on another, and we are sometimes at a loss to explain the thought processes involved. David Whitmer, to drive the point home, was always clear and consistent when he testified of seeing Moroni and the gold plates; he never wavered on those issues to his dying day. But on other issues he was not a competent witness, and on some doctrinal and historical issues he was an unreliable witness, even writing that Joseph Smith himself fell into apostasy after the publication of the Book of Mormon (Whitmer, 1887).

Some of the recollections contained in this volume were given when the storytellers were quite old. Memory, of course, often dims with age. One classic illustration of this problem comes from the remembrances of

David Lewis, who at age ninety sat down with five members of the Church Historian's staff and shared his recollections of his early days in the Church, including his involvement in the organization of the Church on 6 April 1830, when he was twelve years of age. At some points in the interview he forgets a point or cannot recall another, and members of the Historian's staff volunteer information which he then confirms. Is that his memory at play or the memory of one of the Church historians? And what would have happened had the Historian's staff not been there to prod that ninety-year-old memory? And, more to the point, what does this episode suggest in the instances of aging memories of people who lacked the beneficial prod of the Church Historian's office? What was lost? Or altered?

Just as old age can affect memory, so also can youth. Again, a personal family experience illustrates. My own mother was two-and-one-half years old when President Joseph F. Smith passed away. She remembers going to the viewing. But what does she remember? Exactly what one expects from a two year old—the ankle-high buttoned boots the women wore in that day, and her father picking her up, holding her in his arms, and looking down into the casket, which was covered with a glass shield. Many of the entries in this collection come from people who met and knew the Prophet in their childhood and youth. Thus Wilford Woodruff Jr., born in 1840, remembers what a child of his age might be expected to remember about Joseph Smith—that he visited the Woodruff home, played with the children, and was always kind (Woodruff, 1901, p. 616). Many are the children that remember sitting on Joseph's lap; perhaps every child here recorded remembers that Joseph was kind and that he loved children. The teens, for their part, remember "teen things"—Elam Cheny, Enoch Dodge, Mary Dunn Ensign, and Edwin Holden, for example, all remember Joseph playing ball with them or his playing ball with other teens; Mary Jane Robey Epperson remembers when Joseph came and administered to her; and Goudy Hogan, for his part, sat on the stand behind Joseph when he preached the King Follett discourse and seems best to have remembered what Joseph wore. Alvah Alexander was somewhat of an exception, for he says he preferred hearing Joseph preach to playing ball with him. Still, when we read Alexander's self-assessment, written as he looked back through long years, we wonder if he was reinterpreting his teenage experience.

Sometimes right-spirited and well-intended memories leave challenging interpretive problems. Solomon Hancock, for instance, tells a touching story of being with his pregnant wife and meeting the Prophet on his way to Carthage, and of giving Joseph five dollars on that occasion to buy food. The historical record, however, shows no Hancock births in the year of the martyrdom. Was a child stillborn and thus unmentioned, or had time distorted Hancock's memory? Both Philo Dibble and Mosiah Hancock tell of lightning hitting the flagpole at the celebration held by the Saints in Independence, Missouri, on the Fourth of July, 1838. The pole was splintered. Dibble quotes Joseph as saying, "As that pole was splintered, so shall the nations of the earth be!" (Dibble, 1968, p. 88), while Hancock remembers Joseph said, "There goes the liberty of the people" (Mosiah Hancock, n.d., p. 7). Are they referring to the same expression? Did Joseph say both things? Is one or both of them interpolating?

Of a more serious nature are memories that touch upon the doctrines Joseph taught. On what has become a famous quote about the U.S. Constitution hanging by a thread, Brigham Young said: "Will the Constitution be destroyed? No: it will be held inviolate by this people; and, as Joseph Smith said, 'The time will come when the destiny of the nation will hang upon a single thread. At that critical juncture, this people will step forth and save it from the threatened destruction.' It will be so" (JD, 7:15). Jedediah M. Grant, a year later, quoted the same prophecy a little differently: "What did the Prophet Joseph say? When the Constitution shall be tottering, we shall be the people to save it from the hand of the foe" (see Bitton, 1996, p. 95). Orson Hyde, however, remembers what Joseph said quite differently: "It is said that Brother Joseph in his lifetime declared that the elders of this Church should step forth at a particular time when the Constitution should be in danger, and rescue it, and save it. This may be so; but I do not recollect that he said exactly so. I believe he said something like this—'that the time would come when the Constitution and the country would be in danger of an overthrow; and' said he, 'if the Constitution be saved at all, it will be by the elders of this Church.' I believe this is about the language, as nearly as I can recollect it" (JD, 6:152).

Thus we have contradictory memories. In this instance, the puzzle seems easy to solve, for the preponderance of those who refer to Joseph's original quote remember it in substance the way Brigham Young reported it, and the leading Brethren have done the same in our own day. John

Taylor, for his part, does not try to quote Joseph verbatim; rather he gives us the substance of what Joseph said in a paraphrase: "This nation abounds with traitors who ignore that sacred palladium of liberty [the Constitution] and seek to trample it under foot. Joseph Smith said they would do so, and that when deserted by all, the elders of Israel would rally around its shattered fragments and save and preserve it inviolate" (JD, 21:31). He reverbalized the same concept some years later (JD, 20:138; 21:349–50), but was nonetheless true to his original memory. What he illustrates, however, is another problem: sometimes in quoting Joseph, the early Brethren quoted the concept Joseph taught, putting that concept in their own words. This is both a help and a hindrance. It helps in the sense that we focus on doctrines, ideas, and issues rather than becoming rabbinic about word meanings. It hinders because perfect certainty about Joseph's exact words is lost. It also leaves unanswered the question, "Where does what Joseph said leave off, and what John Taylor interpreted Joseph to mean begin?"

Sometimes the Brethren would paraphrase a verse or more from the revelations Joseph received, and attribute the content to Joseph. For instance, George Q. Cannon quotes the Prophet as saying, "Let us not go up against Zion, for the inhabitants of Zion are terrible" (JD, 8:302), which is a paraphrase of Doctrine and Covenants 45:70: "Let us not go up to battle against Zion, for the inhabitants of Zion are terrible." No substantive meaning has been changed, but it is helpful to know where the original quote is found. Others of the early Brethren were equally adept at quoting from the Doctrine and Covenants and attributing their expressions to Joseph Smith—which, in a very real sense, they were (see, for example, Orson Pratt, JD, 16:5 and D&C 64:36).

Other problems also attract our attention. Sometimes it is difficult to know if a speaker is actually quoting Joseph from memory or placing such words in Joseph's mouth as he likely would have spoken (see, for instance, Orson Pratt, JD, 14:141). We have instances where one person quotes a second who in the original instance was quoting Joseph Smith, which in turn affects how we interpret what has been said. Nonetheless, the context in which the quotes occur generally reveal not only Joseph's intent, but the accuracy with which the speaker conveys what Joseph intended.

As the cumulative weight of all the weaknesses of memory presses upon our own minds, what confidence can we have in the recollections of these faithful Saints? How do we discern what to accept and what to reject? Several truths stand out. First, that soul who has filled his mind with truth will instinctively resonate to the voice of truth. Those familiar with gospel patterns and doctrines will have feelings about what is written by the early Saints and others that more accurately describe what is involved than academic scholarship can generally yield. Historical scholarship is important for it disciplines our thought, exposing us to alternatives and sometimes to better views. In the final analysis, however, it in no way compares to the simple expedient of filling one's mind with truth as a precursor to discerning truth. Students of the scriptures are always more discerning than those who do not study the scriptures. One compelling illustration, from our own history, comes from what has been dubbed "The Whitehorse Prophecy," an account of dubious historicity that purports to be a statement the Prophet Joseph Smith made concerning the wars, turmoils, and other difficulties that would exist in the last days. It became prominent enough in Latter-day Saint lore that President Joseph F. Smith was prompted to give corrective instructions with regard to it, and did so explaining that when people fill their minds with truth they are far less subject to errors of discernment and at the same time less prone to chase the extravagant, the marginal, the obscure, and the less reliable. They are simultaneously more inclined to judge by the doctrines and instructions in the standard works and the teaching of the living seers (see Joseph F. Smith, 1918).

In a similar vein, while speaking of the doctrines of the Church, President Joseph Fielding Smith said something that applies with equal force to our history and historical recollections:

> It makes no difference what is written or what anyone has said, if what has been said is in conflict with what the Lord has revealed, we can set it aside. My words, and the teachings of any other member of the Church, high or low, if they do not square with the revelations, we need not accept them. Let us have this matter clear. We have accepted the four standard works as the measuring yardsticks, or balances, by which we measure every man's doctrine.
>
> You cannot accept the books written by the authorities of the Church as the standards of doctrine, only insofar as they accord with the revealed word in the standard works.
>
> Every man who writes is responsible, not the Church, for what he writes. If Joseph Fielding Smith writes some thing which

is out of harmony with the revelations, then every member of the Church is duty bound to reject it. If he writes that which is in perfect harmony with the revealed word of the Lord, then it should be accepted (1967, 3:203–4).

Thus, where we have stories that illustrate false principles or draw false conclusions, such stories should be summarily rejected. We have, for instance, some who claim Joseph Smith said the ten tribes were hidden under the polar ice cap, or living together in the "north countries," or even that they were on a planet on the opposite side of the moon and hidden from our view by the rotational patterns of the earth and moon. Because these so clearly violate what the revelations say, we rightly conclude that if Joseph said anything on those subjects, it has been so distorted in transmission that what has come down to us is so inaccurate that it makes no sense to pay any attention to it. The same may be said of those who attribute to Joseph statements that men live on the moon who dress much like Quakers and who live to be nearly a thousand years old. Similar statements, for the same reasons, warrant no attention.

A second helpful standard in determining the accuracy and historicity of different statements and stories is that of comparing, where available, the testimonies of multiple witnesses. There is a richness that comes to historical detail by gleaning the insights and perceptions of multiple witnesses. For example, in the materials contained herein (including the accompanying CD), there are more than one hundred accounts of different people who were present on August 8, 1844, when Brigham Young was transfigured, sounding and appearing like the Prophet Joseph Smith. By comparing and contrasting those different accounts, a marvelous picture is drawn of what took place, and it is a picture that no single account conveys. Similarly, the multiple accounts of the First Vision add measurably to what the Prophet Joseph Smith has said as recorded in the Pearl of Great Price. Dozens of people left accounts of the kidnapping of the Prophet in Dixon, Illinois, in 1843, and some accounts add to or clarify that which other accounts leave less well described. Sometimes we have people who make historical errors that are readily corrected by comparison to other accounts, and in some few instances, we have some who have sought to falsify the historical record because of doctrinal or other differences. We have, for example, some journals written by people who apostatized; some such accounts are contradicted by so many other witnesses that it becomes clear that the bitter spirit that governed the writing also governed the interpretation of the data. Similarly, some have denied that Joseph ever preached the plurality of wives, in spite of the overwhelming number of people who heard him do so and made note of their recollections—sometimes in affidavits.

The Promise

What, then, is the value of these recollections, particularly in view of the potential for error in historical transmission? Several answers immediately come to mind. First, the memories of those not so frequently mentioned in existing histories of the Church enlarge, enrich, and add color and flavor to what has already been written. The classic experience illustrating the additive power of multiple witnesses comes from Joseph Smith and Oliver Cowdery, each of whom were present when the Aaronic Priesthood was restored and each of whom made a different emphasis in the written accounts they left. Joseph was direct, succinct, and to the point; he grasped the essence of the experience, and told no more. Oliver, for his part, was much more descriptive, adding enlivening and expanding detail that Joseph neglected. Oliver, for instance, reminds us of the important Book of Mormon translation process out of which the experience grew, and then notes that they heard the "voice of the Redeemer," something Joseph does not mention, and that when the Baptist spoke, his voice "dispelled every fear." He also adds that the Aaronic Priesthood was restored "that the Sons of Levi may yet offer an offering unto the Lord in righteousness!" thereby teaching that this was a part of the restoration of all things. For emphasis, he repeats the testimony, "we heard the voice of Jesus." What Joseph does in one verse, Oliver takes a page and one half to do—and we are deeply enriched by the additional information he shares (see Joseph Smith–History 1:71n).

Another important illustration is found in the enlarged view that multiple witnesses provide of the importance of the First Vision, about which a good deal has been written. Joseph Smith gave several accounts of the vision during his lifetime, and several contemporary accounts were also produced before the Prophet's death. The picture painted by these additional, secondhand accounts helps us to see that Joseph told the story of his experience in the grove much more than had previously been imagined. The pattern that emerges is one of constant retelling of the First Vision and of Joseph deliberately using it as an aid to missionary work.

Lorenzo Snow, for example, makes specific mention of hearing Joseph tell of the Father and the Son appearing, when Lorenzo heard Joseph speak at the John Johnson farm in 1831. This accords with the pattern we see in what has already been printed, but the picture is now much more insistent: Joseph wanted to tell that story, and others wanted to hear it.

The same may be said of his experiences with the angel Moroni—Joseph told that story over and over in order to bear witness of the restoration of the gospel and of his role in that restoration. When we read the accounts of converts coming into the Church, there are repeated accounts of Joseph telling of his own experiences, including the First Vision and Moroni coming. Mary Isabella Horne recalls that there was such power in the telling of these experiences that the Saints asked Joseph to tell them, which he did. The pattern that emerges of Joseph as a missionary is that of Joseph being a constant witness of his own experiences. In January 1840, William W. McGuire heard Joseph preach in the home of Edward Hunter, who was then living in Chester County, Pennsylvania. Joseph emphasized, "Brothers and Sisters, I will not tell you much of what the Lord told Paul, or of what He told Peter, but I will tell you what the Lord told me" (McGuire, 1886). The emphasis was on *his own* experiences, not those of the biblical prophets. This is important, for it accords with the instructions given in the Doctrine and Covenants on how the gospel should be taught, and it shows, once again, that Joseph was submissive to the Lord's will in all things. Some have written and spoken of Joseph's biblical background—which was mammoth!—and have gone so far as to suggest that his approach was "Pauline," meaning it was filled with and patterned after the teachings of the apostle Paul. The many, many witnesses who told of their conversion experiences refute the "biblical and Pauline thesis" and emphatically demonstrate that Joseph was "a restoration man"—he spoke about and from his own experiences, and when he quoted biblical texts, as he often did, he interpreted them in terms of the revelations he had received and the experiences he had obtained. In effect, Joseph used the biblical text to showcase the doctrines he had learned from Nephi, Alma, Mormon, and Moroni.

Lydia Knight was touched by the powerful testimony Joseph bore of the coming forth of the Book of Mormon and the restoration of the priesthood—she could now receive an authorized baptism! (Knight, 1974, p. 44). The Reverend George Moore, though he never joined the Church, remembered Joseph for teaching of the Book of Mormon plates and noted that Joseph's doctrines stood independent of all existing religious teachings (Moore, 1982, pp. 10–11). When Mary A. Noble heard Joseph speak of the Book of Mormon, she said, "Never did I hear preaching sound so glorious to me as that did. I realized it was truth from heaven" (Mary Noble, n.d., pp. 18–19). David Osborn was overwhelmed when Joseph spoke of the keys held by "Adam, Enoch, Noah, Moses, the patriarchs and some of the prophets," and he was impressed by Joseph's averral that he would be held accountable at the day of judgment for how he treated his testimony of the Book of Mormon (Osborn, 1892, p. 173). James Palmer was struck with the force of Joseph's conviction and his declaration that he "did translate the Book of Mormon . . . and all the powers of earth and hell can never rob me of the honor of it" (Palmer, n.d.). Parley P. Pratt, Eliza R. Snow, Jesse N. Smith, and others echo these sentiments, as do John Taylor, Lorenzo Snow, George Vogel, and Helen Mar Whitney. And the list goes on! And in so doing, it gives us a much enlarged view of Joseph as a missionary and of the fact that he was a firsthand witness, never beholden to the testimony of others, but reliant on his own experiences. It is a powerful display.

In addition to what these secondary accounts tell of Joseph, they tell a good deal about the people who followed Joseph Smith. What kind of people were they? They were men and women of extraordinary courage. When the mob burned Nauvoo and drove the Saints from their homes, Louisa Hall Harris remembered she had left a pewter teapot in her house and rushed back exclaiming, "I am going to get that tea pot. Damn them, they can't have that to melt into bullets to kill us with!" (Louisa H. Harris, n.d.). When that same mob came to Jane Johnston Black, demanding she hand over her firearms, she drew from her bosom a small six-shooter, pointed it at the leader of the mob and said, "Do you want it?" "Indeed I do," was the reply. "Captain, I am serving notice on you that I intend using it before giving it to you. Now do you think you want it?" With a piercing glance he replied, "I guess not" and rode on (Jane Black, n.d. [a], p. 7).

These people who interacted with Joseph possessed the same virtues he possessed. They showed the faith to follow, the hardiness to survive, and the spiritual sensitivity to know. Many came to Joseph because of inspired dreams and visions; others felt the testimony of missionaries; all came because the Spirit of the Lord directed them to. Illustrations abound: "Aunt" Jane James walked a thousand miles to meet the Prophet, wore out her shoes and stockings in the walk, but continued anyway, barefooted (James, 1905, p. 552). Hannah Simmonds Philips was seventeen when she joined the Church and secured permission from her parents to leave them and her native England and travel to Nauvoo. Her mother left her bonnet hanging on a peg in the hall next to the stairs and oft cried when she saw it—a reminder of the daughter she had lost to Mormonism but at the same time a symbol of a young girl's faith (Philips, n.d.). Rachel Ridgeway Grant read the Book of Mormon "nearly all the night," knew it was true, and knew that she would not be happy unless she gathered with the Saints. She left New Jersey for Nauvoo (Grant, 1905, p. 550). Andrew Jackson Stewart was teaching at a Methodist camp meeting about baptism and was accused by one of his fellow exhorters of preaching "Old Joe Smith's doctrines." He was stunned, for he thought he was simply teaching what the Bible taught. Soon thereafter Elders William Coray and William G. Rule came and taught him the gospel. After he was baptized they told him they had been sent by Joseph Smith to him and that Joseph had instructed them not to return to Nauvoo until they had baptized Stewart (Stewart, n.d., p. 149). Thousands upon thousands of similar stories were unfolding in the lives of people everywhere the missionaries went and sometimes in places where they did not.

The same faith that attracted people to Joseph's side kept them there, even amidst the trials and poverty that were so pervasive. Caroline Butler was too poor to help with the construction of the Nauvoo Temple, but with the faith typical of these early gatherers, she earnestly wanted to help. One day while riding in the wagon with her children, she spotted two dead buffalo. She and her children pulled the long hair from the buffalo manes, took it home, washed it, carded it, and spun it into a coarse yarn from which she knitted eight pairs of heavy mittens, which were then used by the temple rock cutters in the winter. She had nothing to give, but gave her all (Butler, 1993, p. 113). Caroline Butler is but one of the thousands, and the recollections in this volume tell of their interactions with the Prophet and demonstrate that gifts of the Spirit had been restored to the earth and were exercised by many—not just by Joseph Smith and his immediate associates.

In spite of the occasional interpretive problems associated with memory and recall, there is much to be trusted in these accounts. In the scholarly world, students of memory are taught that we remember longer and more exactly when recall is associated with strong emotions—fear, anxiety, anger, or frustration, or, on the positive side, joy, excitement, anticipation, even love. It is unsurprising therefore that these early Saints had such deep, lasting, and uniform memories of Joseph Smith: they confronted the same mobs, personally saw him surrounded by the blood-hungry and the hateful; some three hundred or more were part of the kidnapping at Dixon, Illinois, for example. They shared in his joys; he spoke to crowds large and small. Margaret Pierce Young (n.d., pp. 1–3) remembered Joseph speaking until about 2 o'clock in the morning to her father's family in her father's home, while on the other hand Parley P. Pratt (1985, p. 298) told of Joseph speaking to a crowd of about three thousand in Philadelphia. Of Joseph's remarks, Parley said, "The effect was electric." People were touched! And crowds of thousands frequently gathered to hear Joseph speak in Nauvoo, and they remembered with unstrained consistency the events involved.

This brings us to an issue which the scholarly world cannot understand: that the Spirit of the Lord can leave an impress far more indelible than any other agent, and that when people heard Joseph speak by the power of the Holy Ghost, which Joseph so fully did, the impress upon their souls was infinitely more indelible than any human emotion can etch. One of the gifts of the Spirit is the gift of memory, and the consistency with which these early Saints and pioneers record their memories suggest they were more influenced by that gift than even they knew. Martha Thomas quotes Joseph as saying, "When a true spirit makes known anything to you, in the daytime, we call it a vision. If it is a true spirit it will never leave you, every particular will be as plain fifty years hence as now" (Thomas, 1927, pp. 23–24). Joseph knew the Spirit of the Lord caused people to remember what he said. When speaking from the stand in Nauvoo, the police sought to usher a group of teenage boys away. "Let the boys alone," Joseph told the police. "They will hear something they will never forget" (Harvey Cluff, n.d.). What Joseph said of visions and speeches is true of other gifts as well. In his own case, for instance, he received one revelation in 1831 but did not record it until 1843. When the written account of that revelation was destroyed, Joseph simply dictated it anew (JD, 6:281–82), much as Jeremiah had done in a very similar case thousands of years before him (Jeremiah 36:1–32).

Joseph knew he was speaking, writing, and behaving not just for those within his immediate reach, but that he was speaking to an entire dispensation, and that those who heard him would repeat what he said for generations yet unborn. He knew he would die before most of the Twelve, for instance, and thus promised them that after he died, they would be able to recall that which he had taught while yet alive. Brigham Young later testified that he remembered things Joseph had taught, even though he had not thought of them since he heard Joseph teach them (Kelley, 1938, pp. 81–82). In this context it is no accident, as so many of the entries in this collection testify, that on the day Brigham Young was transfigured before the Saints, so many youth and children were not only in attendance, but participant in the spiritual manifestations of the day. They were destined to tell the story of the transfiguration of Brigham Young for more than sixty years, for their testimonies, like Joseph's, were binding upon an entire dispensation. Sometimes Joseph even took specific occasion to counsel a particular Saint to teach to future generations what Joseph had taught. To Benjamin F. Johnson he said, "Benjamin, in regard to those things I have taught you privately, that are not yet for the public, I give you the right when you are so led, to commit them to others, for you will not be wrong in discerning those worthy of your confidence" (Johnson, 1903). Many are the Saints who said such things as "I shall never forget" or "I will ever remember." In short, the Savior's promise to his disciples that the Holy Ghost would "bring all things to [their] remembrance" (John 14:26) is hardly more applicable in one dispensation than another.

These early Saints collected strong memories, sometimes by the power of the Holy Ghost, which they wanted to have preserved long after they were gone. Mary Goble Pay tells of the struggles to get across the plains, which cost her own mother and two siblings their lives; Mary's frostbitten toes were amputated using a saw and a butcher's knife. She recorded her memories because "it is wise for our children to see what their parents passed through for the gospel, yes, I think it is" (Pay, 1974, p. 150). These people wrote and spoke because they wanted their recollections preserved as testimonies to their children and future generations. While in England in 1877, President Joseph F. Smith purchased a set of the *Journal of Discourses.* In volume eighteen he enscribed his name and address. Then he wrote: "Let my children value these volumes as Scripture. I treasure them for their [his children's] sake." It was a measure of his confidence in his brethren, and in what they said, that he would so speak.

It is too much to claim scriptural status for the stories recorded in this volume, but our feelings are akin to those of Joseph F. Smith with regard to what his brethren said. There is much of the sacred in these memories, and they give a much enlarged view of Joseph Smith. We see the very personable, human side of Joseph, hugging children, laughing and joking with teens, embracing his brethren, weeping with them and their wives. We see his mind expanding—in Hebrew, Latin, Greek, German, and even, we are told, in Chaldean (Aramaic). Through the eyes of Joseph F. Smith we see the Prophet kneeling upon the floor, with the Egyptian manuscripts spread before him, studying, pondering, and notetaking. Through the ears of Eunice Billings Snow we hear Joseph sing his favorite hymns, and we stand with William Holmes Walker outside Joseph's house during the family's evening prayers, when with Emma and the children he sang the sweetest and most heavenly music Walker had ever heard. We sit on a rail fence and listen to the tale of one whose house had burned down, and we watch Joseph take five dollars from his pocket and say to those assembled, "I feel sorry for this brother to the amount of five dollars; how much do you feel sorry?" (Workman, 1892, p. 641). We see the hundreds—or was it thousands?—stand in the rain just to hear him preach; and with Wilford Woodruff, we are transfixed as Joseph speaks with such power that his face shone as amber.

We see how the Saints loved him and shared life's experiences with him in personal, intimate settings. We see him dining in the Johnson home, where he sat at the head of the table, after first having carved the turkey. In the same way we see Sister Myra Henrie put out hot potatoes and buttermilk for the Prophet; and we hear his grateful and gracious response when he was given food at the home of Mary Isabella Horne: "Sister Horne, if I had a wife as small as you, when trouble came I would put her in my pocket and run" (Horne, 1982, p. 64). He provides a banquet for the poor, and they speak of it for generations. They then take pride in having given him a meal, a knife, an article of clothing, a saddle, or a book. Immanuel Masters Murphy visited him in prison and was honored to give him a handshake with a five-dollar gold piece in it. Israel Barlow felt it an honor simply to hold his stirrup or the bridle of his horse.

More profoundly, however, are we touched by the number of memories that show us Joseph exercising spiritual gifts, for he healed the sick, prophesied of things great and small, spoke in tongues and interpreted the same, discerned the character of men, commanded the elements, dreamed inspired dreams, and saw great visions, and, through it all, exercised a greater number of spiritual gifts, and exercised them with greater regularity and frequency than any prophet of whom we have record. When poisoned and afflicted with projectile vomiting, he had the faith to be healed; he laid hands upon the unconscious Benjamin Brown, who had been sick for weeks, and Brown was immediately healed. Clint Harris had a crippling fever sore; Joseph spoke, and Harris was healed. On Zion's Camp the brethren were weary and parched with thirst; Joseph called for a shovel, dug a small hole in the prairie, and water sprang forth. As early as 1832 he prophesied that Brigham Young would be his successor; soon thereafter he prophesied that the Saints would go to the Rocky Mountains. He did so again in 1842. He promised Benjamin F. Johnson that his family would never leave the Church, notwithstanding mobbings, persecutions, and trials. Some thirty-five years before the event, he told Eliza R. Snow that she would visit Palestine, and he wept as he gave Andrew Lamoreaux an inspired blessing predicting that he would go on a mission to France, learn another language, do much good, and die a martyr before he returned to his family—all of which came to pass. He invited men to meetings with the promise that, when they attended, they would see visions. John Murdock and Zebedee Coltrin attended one such meeting and testified that they saw the Christ. Others did the same. In yet another moment, Zebedee Coltrin, in Joseph's company, saw Father Adam and Mother Eve; and Joseph B. Noble reports that Joseph confided to him that he knew the angels so well he recognized them by the sound of their voices even before he saw their faces.

Joseph Smith was a man who knew how to bring people to Christ, and that was his compelling emphasis. The Book of Mormon, which the world both hated and feared, is the most Christ-centered book in print, and its message haunted and yet haunts those who profess a conviction in Christ but are more wedded to their own traditions than to the humble Nazarene. The Pearl of Great Price contains accounts of people who saw the Christ anciently, and the Doctrine and Covenants contains accounts of those who have seen him in our day. It also contains the promise that all who are humble and pure may receive that same blessing. In the realm of Joseph's own experience there were those who did. We think of Oliver Cowdery, Sidney Rigdon, Newel Knight, John Murdock, Zebedee Coltrin, and others, and we are gladdened that they left such faith-building testimonies. Every healing Joseph performed, and there were hundreds if not thousands, was performed in the name of Christ; every prophecy he spoke, and there were multiple thousands, was spoken in the name of Christ; every sermon he preached, every blessing he gave, and every ordinance he performed, and again there were thousands, were done in the name of Jesus Christ. Given these experiences, and the host of faith-promoting accounts which a generation of faithful souls have given us through their suffering, how can we help but to be encouraged, strengthened, and bettered by what they gave? And how can we fail to be more grateful to a kindly God for restoring his work through the Prophet Joseph Smith. The recollections and memories in this volume tell but a part of that great eternal drama. Because of the effects these recollections produce in our lives, and the Spirit they bring to us, we are awed. Surely, eternal good comes from remembering Joseph.

2

The Character and Personality of the Prophet Joseph Smith

Joseph in His Youth

Mrs. Palmer

The Spirit of the Lord remained with Joseph Smith from the time at which he received his first vision. Mrs. Palmer, a lady advanced in years came to Utah with her daughter, who was a teacher in the Presbyterian schools of our state. The daughter taught in Montrose, Sevier Co., died there, and is buried in the Monroe cemetery.

Mrs. Palmer's father, according to a story told by her, owned a farm near to that of the Smith family in New York. Her parents were friends of the Smith family, which she testified was one of the best in that locality, honest, religious, and industrious, but poor. The father of the family, she said, was above the average in intelligence. She had heard her parents say he bore the appearance of having descended from royalty. Mrs. Smith was called "Mother Smith" by many. Children loved to go to her home.

Mrs. Palmer said her father loved young Joseph Smith and often hired him to work with his boys. She was about six years old, she said, when he first came to their home. She remembered going into the field on an afternoon to play in the corn rows while her brothers worked. When evening came she was too tired to walk home and cried because her brothers refused to carry her. Joseph lifted her to his shoulders and with his arm thrown across her feet to steady her and her arm about his neck he carried her to their home.

She remembered the excitement stirred up among the people over the boy's first vision, and of hearing her father contend that it was only the sweet dream of a pure minded boy. She stated that one of their church leaders came to her father to remonstrate against allowing such close friendship between his family and the "Smith Boy," as he called him. Her father, she said, defended his own position by saying that the boy was the best help he had ever found. He told the churchman that he always fixed the time of hoeing his large field to that when he could secure the services of Joseph Smith, because of the influence that boy had over the wild boys of the neighborhood, and explained that when these boys worked by themselves much time would be spent in arguing and quarreling, which often ended in a ring fight. But when Joseph Smith worked with them the work went steadily forward, and he got the full worth of the wages he paid. She remembered the churchman saying in a very solemn and impressive tone that the very influence the boy carried was the danger they feared for the coming generation, that not only the young man, but all who came in contact with him would follow him, and he *must be put down*.

Not until Joseph had a second vision, and began to write a book which drew many of the best and brightest people of the churches away from them, did her parents come to a realization of the fact that their friend, the churchman, had told them the truth. Then her family cut off their friendship for all the Smiths, for all the family followed Joseph. Even the father, intelligent man that he was, could not discern the evil he was helping to promote. Her parents then lent all the aid they could in helping to crush Joseph Smith; but it was too late, he had run his course too long. He could not be put down. Mrs. Palmer recognized the picture of Joseph Smith placed among other pictures as a test, and said of him that there was never a truer, purer, nobler boy than he before he was led away by superstition (n.d.).

General Descriptions of Joseph

Peter H. Burnett

Joseph Smith, Jr., was at least six feet high, well-formed, and weighed about one hundred and eighty pounds. His appearance was not prepossessing, and his conversational powers were but ordinary. You could see at a glance that his education was very limited. He was an awkward but vehement speaker. In conversation he was slow, and used too many words to express his ideas, and would not generally go directly to a point. He possessed the most indomitable perseverance, and was a good judge of men, and deemed himself born to command, and he did command. His views were so strange and striking, and his manner was so earnest, and apparently so candid, that you could not but be interested. There was a kind, familiar look about him that pleased you. He was very courteous in discussion, readily admitting what he did not intend to controvert, and would not oppose you abruptly, but had due deference to your feelings. He had the capacity for discussing a subject in many different aspects, and for proposing many original views, even of ordinary matters. His illustrations were his own. He had great influence over others. As an evidence of this I will state on Thursday, just before I left to return to Liberty, I saw him out among the crowd, conversing freely with every one, and seeming to be perfectly at ease. In the short space of five days he had managed so to mollify his enemies that he could go unprotected among them without the slightest danger. Among the Mormons he had much greater influence than Sidney Rigdon. The latter was a man of superior education, an eloquent speaker, of fine appearance and dignified manners; but he did not possess the native intellect of Smith, and lacked his determined will. Lyman Wight was the military man among them. There are several others of the prisoners whose names I have forgotten (1946, pp. 40–41).

Elam Cheney

Brother Joseph was a man weighing about two hundred pounds, fair complexion, light brown hair. He was about six feet tall, sound bodied, very strong and quick—no breakage about his body. He most always wore a silk stock, and was smooth faced. He was very sympathetic and would talk to children and they liked him. He was honest, and was liked by everybody who knew him (1906, p. 540).

Note: A "silk stock" is a stiff, close-fitting neck cloth, somewhat like a scarf; it was a common dress item worn in the Prophet's day.

Thomas Ford

Thus fell Joe Smith, the most successful impostor in modern times; a man who, though ignorant and coarse, had some great natural parts, which fitted him for temporary success, but which were so obscured and counteracted by the inherent corruption and vices of his nature that he never could succeed in establishing a system of policy which looked to permanent success in the future. His lusts, his love of money and power, always set him to studying present gratification and convenience, rather than the remote consequences of his plans. It seems that no power of intellect can save a corrupt man from this error. The strong cravings of the animal nature will never give fair play to a fine understanding; the judgment is never allowed to choose that good which is far away, in preference to enticing evil near at hand. And this may be considered a wise ordinance of Providence, by which the counsels of talented but corrupt men are defeated in the very act which promised success.

It must not be supposed that the pretended Prophet practiced the tricks of a common impostor; that he was a dark and gloomy person, with a long beard, a grave and severe aspect, and a reserved and saintly carriage of his person; on the contrary, he was full of levity, even to boyish romping, dressed like a dandy, and at times drank like a sailor and swore like a pirate. He could, as occasion required, be exceedingly meek in his deportment; and then again rough and boisterous as a highway robber; being always able to satisfy his followers of the propriety of his conduct. He always quailed before power, and was arrogant to weakness. At times he could put on the air of a penitent, as if feeling the deepest humiliation for his sins, and suffering unutterable anguish, and indulging in the most gloomy forebodings of eternal woe. At such times he would call for the prayers of the brethren in his behalf, with a wild and fearful energy and earnestness. He was full six feet high, strongly built, and uncommonly well muscled. No doubt he was as much indebted for his influence over an ignorant people, to the superiority of his physical vigor, as to his greater cunning and intellect (1854, pp. 354–55).

Note: While intellectually gifted, Governor Thomas Ford was politically motivated, and his estimations of Joseph Smith were born in his own anti-Mormon prejudices. Much of what he wrote is a justification for his own behavior, which includes certain complicity in the murder of Joseph Smith.

Rachel R. Grant

I guess you have seen the picture where Brother Joseph was preaching to the Indians. I was there at that time. The Indians were all kneeling down on the grass in front of the Mansion, and if you have seen that picture, that just describes the way everything was, though it is a miserable picture of the Prophet. He was a fine, noble-looking man, always so neat. There are some of the pictures that do not look a particle like him (1905, p. 550).

Jane James

I could not begin to tell you what he was, only this way, he was tall, over six feet; he was a fine, big, noble, beautiful man! He had blue eyes and light hair, and very fine white skin (1905, p. 553).

Jacob Jones

The Prophet weighed about 150 pounds, had nice brown hair, was always jovial and could crack a joke. He could sing well and loved music, loved to dance, and would leave a meal at any time to wrestle with anyone. He was nimble as a cat and he was fond of us boys and would often play with us. Anyone could not help but love him and he loved everybody. He always shook hands with all, even the babes. He had a very fine gray horse that he always rode whenever there was a parade (n.d. [a]).

Lydia B. Knight

Many were the curious glances that I cast at this strange man who dared to call himself a prophet. I saw a tall, well-built form, with the carriage of an Apollo; brown hair, handsome blue eyes, which seemed to dive down to the innermost thoughts with their sharp, penetrating gaze; a striking countenance, and with manners at once majestic yet gentle, dignified yet exceedingly pleasant (1883, p. 14).

Newel Knight

The business in which my father was engaged often required him to have hired help, and among the many he from time to time employed was a young man by the name of Joseph Smith, Jun., to whom I was particularly attached. His noble deportment, his faithfulness, and his kind address could not fail to win the esteem of those who had the pleasure of his acquaintance. One thing I will mention, which seemed to be a peculiar characteristic with him in all his boyish sports and amusements: I never knew any one to gain advantage over him, and yet he was always kind and kept the goodwill of his playmates (1969, p. 47).

John D. Lee

Joseph Smith was a most extraordinary man; he was rather large in stature, some six feet two inches in height, well built though a little stoop shouldered, prominent and well-developed features, a Roman nose, light chestnut hair, upper lip full and rather protruding, chin broad and square, and eagle eye, and on the whole there was something in his manner and appearance that was bewitching and winning; his countenance was that of a plain, honest man, full of benevolence and philanthropy and void of deceit or hypocrisy. He was resolute and firm of purpose, strong as most men in physical power, and all who saw were forced to admire him, as he then looked and existed (1881, p. 76).

Note: Because of John D. Lee's involvement in the Mountain Meadows Massacre, some may worry about his credibility. Most of the materials taken from his journal and quoted herein were written prior to the massacre, which occurred in 1857. His diaries, as they relate to Joseph Smith, appear historically sound in what they report.

Lyman O. Littlefield

The opportunity [to meet the Prophet] came, and I first beheld him a tall, well-proportioned man, busily mingling with the members of Zion's Camp, shaking hands with them, meeting them with friendly greetings, and carefully seeing to their comforts. His familiar, yet courteous and dignified manner, his pleasant and intelligent countenance, his intellectual and well-formed forehead, the expressive and philanthropic facial lineaments, the pleasant smile, and the happy light that beamed from his mild blue eyes; all these were among the attractive attributes that at once awakened a responsive interest in the mind of every kindly beholder, which increased in intensity as the acquaintance continued. With his most familiar friends he was social, conversational, and often indulged in harmless jokes; but when discoursing upon complicated topics that pertained to the welfare of individuals or the progressiveness of communities, his elucidations were clear and so full of common sense and genuine philosophy that the candid and fair-minded felt interested by his views, though they might decline to entertain or promulgate all of the self-evident truths he originated.

Such is a brief though imperfect pen picture of this celebrated man; he was all this when I first beheld him in this traveling camp, and is it any wonder that I, so young in years, should be filled with sensations of intense pleasure and respect for him when I first met him . . . ? (1892a, pp. 56–57).

James Palmer

[Joseph Smith] looked and had the appearance of one that was heaven born while preaching, or as though he had been sent from the heavenly worlds on some divine mission. He was a man of fine form and stature measuring over six feet in height, he was of a light complexion, his hair was of a flaxen color, he wore no whiskers, his chin was a little tipped, his nose was long and straight, his mouth was rather massive, and his upper lip rather long and a little inclined to be thick. He had a large full chest and intelligent eyes and fine limbs; altogether he presented a very formidable appearance, being a man of gentlemanly bearing (n.d., pp. 69–70).

Parley P. Pratt

President Joseph Smith was in person tall and well built, strong and active, of a light complexion, light hair, blue eyes, very little beard, and of an expression peculiar to himself, on which the eye naturally rested with interest, and was never weary of beholding. His countenance was ever mild, affable, beaming with intelligence and benevolence, mingled with a look of interest and an unconscious smile, or cheerfulness, and entirely free from all restraint or affectation of gravity; and there was something connected with the serene and steady penetrating glance of his eye, as if he would penetrate the deepest abyss of the human heart, gaze into eternity, penetrate the heavens, and comprehend all worlds.

He possessed a noble boldness and independence of character; his manner was easy and familiar; his rebuke terrible as the lion; his benevolence unbounded as the ocean; his intelligence universal, and his language abounding in original eloquence peculiar to himself—not polished—not studied—not smoothed and softened by education and refined by art, but flowing forth in its own native simplicity, and profusely abounding in variety of subject and manner. He interested and edified, while, at the same time, he amused and entertained his audience; and none listened to him that were ever weary with his discourse. I have even known him to retain a congregation of willing and anxious listeners for many hours together, in the midst of cold or sunshine, rain or wind, while they were laughing at one moment and weeping the next. Even his most bitter enemies were generally overcome, if he could once get their ears.

I have known him when chained and surrounded with armed

murderers and assassins who were heaping upon him every possible insult and abuse, rise up in the majesty of a son of God and rebuke them, in the name of Jesus Christ, till they quailed before him, dropped their weapons, and, on their knees, begged his pardon, and ceased their abuse.

In short, in him the characters of a Daniel and a Cyrus were wonderfully blended. The gifts, wisdom, and devotion of a Daniel were united with the boldness, courage, temperance, perseverance, and generosity of a Cyrus. And had he been spared a martyr's fate till mature manhood and age, he was certainly endowed with powers and ability to have revolutionized the world in many respects, and to have transmitted to posterity a name associated with more brilliant and glorious acts than has yet fallen to the lot of mortals. As it is, his works will live to endless ages, and unnumbered millions yet unborn will mention his name with honor, as a noble instrument in the hands of God, who, during his short and youthful career, laid the foundation of that kingdom spoken of by Daniel, the prophet, which should break in pieces all other kingdoms and stand forever (1985, pp. 31–32).

Josiah Quincy

A fine-looking man is what the passer-by would instinctively have murmured upon meeting the remarkable individual who had fashioned the mold which was to shape the feelings of so many thousands of his fellow-mortals. But Smith was more than this, and one could not resist the impression that capacity and resource were natural to his stalwart person. I have already mentioned the resemblance he bore to Elisha R. Potter, of Rhode Island, whom I met in Washington in 1826. The likeness was not such as would be recognized in a picture, but rather one that would be felt in a grave emergency. Of all men I have met, these two seemed best endowed with that kingly faculty which directs, as by intrinsic right, the feeble or confused souls who are looking for guidance. This it is just to say with emphasis; for the reader will find so much that is puerile and even shocking in my report of the Prophet's conversation that he might never suspect the impression of rugged power that was given by the man (1883, p. 381).

Jane S. Richards

The first time I ever saw Joseph Smith I recognized him from a dream I had had. He had such angelic countenance as I never saw before. He was then thirty-seven years of age, of ordinary appearance in dress and manner, a child-like appearance of innocence. His hair was of a light brown, blue eyes, and light complexioned. His natural demeanor was quiet, his character and disposition was formed by his life work, he was kind and considerate, taking a personal interest in all his people, considering every one his equal. We were regular in our attendance at the meetings, and [I] was always anxious to hear Brother Joseph (1880, p. 11).

Jane S. Richards

[Joseph Smith] was one of the most engaging personalities it has ever been my good fortune to meet. As Prophet he seemed to understand, and was able to foretell the mysteries of the future with a marked degree of accuracy, and nearly as much readiness as the ordinary individual could relate the happenings of the past. As Seer and Revelator he was fearless and outspoken, yet humble, never considering that he was more than the mouthpiece through whom God spoke. As the leader of his people he was ever active and progressive but always modest and considerate of them and their trying circumstances. Socially he was an ideal of affability and always approachable to the humblest of his acquaintants (1905, p. 550).

Herbert S. Salisbury

My grandmother, Catherine Smith Salisbury, told me that her brother Joseph was six feet tall, athletic and fair, and loved to wrestle. She said that he was not in the least snobbish, but treated all he met with kindness, consideration, and respect. Once when a noted wrestler from New England visited him in Nauvoo, he challenged the wrestler to "take a fall" with him. In the ensuing bout he threw the wrestler three times, and the man then refused to take any more "falls." From what she told me, I think the Prophet must have been as affectionate with his relatives as President George Albert Smith. She said that on her rare visits to Nauvoo the Prophet treated her and her family with great kindness and generosity and sent her home laden with food, money, and clothing (1945).

Asa Searles

Mr. Asa B. Searles was a native of Chenango County, New York, and was born January 27, 1810. Later in life he was for several years in South

Bainbridge, New York. He there attended a school which his brother taught, and had for a schoolmate Joseph Smith, the future Mormon Prophet, whom he described as being kind-hearted and possessed of much brain, which was supported by a large, strong body (1893, p. 53).

John Smith

He was twelve years of age at the time his father and Joseph the Prophet were martyred. Speaking of the current pictures of the Prophet, he agreed with Sister Bathsheba W. Smith. The Prophet Joseph stood even six feet high in his stocking feet and weighed 212 pounds. The speaker's Father, Hyrum Smith, stood five feet eleven and a half inches high and they weighed in the same notch, varying from 210 to 212 pounds (CD, 5:33).

Eunice B. Snow

Some of the most impressive moments of my life were when I saw the Nauvoo Legion on parade with the Prophet (then General Joseph Smith) with his wife, Emma Hale Smith, on horseback at the head of the troops. It was indeed an imposing sight. He so fair, and she so dark, in their beautiful riding-habits. He in full military suit, and she with her habit trimmed with gold buttons, a neat cap on her head, with a black plume in it, while the Prophet wore a red plume in his, and a red sash across his breast. His coat was black, while his white pants had red stripes on the outside seams. He also wore a sword at his side. His favorite riding-horse was named Charlie, a big black steed (1910b).

Lorenzo Snow

Soon after arriving in Kirtland [about June 1836] I was on the street with my sister, Eliza. Joseph Smith came along. He was in a great hurry and stopped just long enough to be introduced and shake hands. He turned to my sister and said: "Eliza, bring your brother over to the house to dinner." She was then boarding at his home and teaching his private school. As he left us I watched him just as far as I could see him and then turned to my sister and said: "Joseph Smith is a most remarkable man; I want to get better acquainted with him. Perhaps, after all, there is something more to Joseph Smith and to Mormonism than I have ever dreamed."

Accordingly, the next time I saw the Prophet was at his own house in Kirtland following his invitation to me to take dinner with him. I remember this meeting and conversation as if it were but yesterday. He sat down at one end of the table and I sat next to him. Eliza sat on the other side. He seemed to have changed considerably in his appearance since I first saw him at Hiram, four and a half years before. He was very ready in conversation, and had apparently lost that reserve and diffident feeling that he seemed to have before. He was free and easy in his conversation with me, making me feel perfectly at home in his presence. In fact, I felt as free with him as if we had been special friends for years. He was very familiar (1937, p. 83).

George W. Taggart

[September 10, 1843] Now something concerning Old Jo, so called. He is a young looking man of his age, which is near thirty-eight years and one of the finest looking men there is in the country and he does not pretend to be a man without failings and follies. He is a man that you could not help liking as a man, setting aside the religious prejudice which the world has raised against him. He is one of the warmest patriots and friends to his country and laws that you ever heard speak on the subject. Neither is he puffed up with his greatness as many suppose but on the contrary is familiar with any decent man and is ready to talk up any subject that anyone wishes. And I assure you it would make you wonder to hear him talk and see the information which comes out of his mouth and it is not in big words either but that which anyone can understand (2001, pp. 172–73).

General Character Descriptions

Aroet L. Hale

Left there [Portage, Ohio,] in company with Elder Thomas B. Marsh and David W. Patten, thence to Palmyra to the home of Elder Martin Harris, thence to the Hill Cumorah. All went on to the hill and offered up our thanks to the Most High God for the records of the Nephites and other blessings. Then went about from house to house to inquire the character of Joseph Smith in previous to his receiving the book of the plates of Mormon. The answer was that his character was as good as young men in general. This was on the 30th day of May, 1835 (n.d., pp. 1–2).

John W. Hess

In the autumn of 1838 my father lived in Ray County, Missouri, near the Richmond Landing. Joseph the Prophet, in company with his brothers Hyrum and William and eleven others whose names I do not remember, had been up to Caldwell County to lay out the city of Far West. When they got to the Missouri River on their return to Kirtland, they found that the boats did not run on regular time on account of the river being low, and as they were compelled to wait for a steamer, they came to my father's house near the landing and stayed there thirteen days. Father was the only Mormon in that part of the country.

At that time Joseph was studying Greek and Latin, and when he got tired studying he would go and play with the children in their games about the house, to give himself exercise. Then he would go back to his studies as before. I was a boy then about fourteen years old. . . .

I relate this to show the kindness and simplicity of his nature. I never saw another man like Joseph. There was something heavenly and angelic in his looks that I never witnessed in the countenance of any other person. During his short stay I became very much attached to him, and learned to love him more dearly than any other person I ever met, my father and mother not excepted.

The next time I saw the Prophet was at the Richmond courthouse, in chains, after the surrender of the city of Far West. I used to walk six miles every day to see him during his stay in Richmond Jail. Although a boy of about fourteen years, I became convinced beyond doubt that he was a prophet of God, and that testimony has never left me (1892, pp. 302–3).

Goudy E. Hogan

I very frequently went with my Father from where we lived eight miles to Nauvoo to meeting and back home the same day on foot to hear the Prophet Joseph Smith and the Patriarch Hyrum and others preach with great power. I was then fourteen years old, but I was very anxious to go to meeting and listen to what the servants of the Lord had to say. On one occasion when I went with my Father to Nauvoo to meeting on April 6th, the same year of the martyrdom, while they held meeting in the grove not far from the temple, a very large congregation was gathered having

The Character and Personality of the Prophet Joseph Smith

come a long way on foot. I with a few other boys climbed up on some boards behind the stand that was temporary so that I could hear every word that was said. I was sitting close behind the Prophet Joseph Smith so that I nearly touched his clothes. I had not been long in the church and was somewhat superstitious and took particular notice of his manner of dress and action. I remember that he had on a light colored linen coat with a small hole in each elbow of his coat sleeve. I remember thinking that he was not a proud man and that his very noble experience inspired me with great confidence and faith that he was a great prophet of the Lord. I also remember while one was preaching the Prophet Joseph spoke to the elder that was preaching to stop speaking for a minute. Joseph the Prophet rose from his seat and said in a loud voice, owing to the large congregation that was assembled, saying he wished some of those young men on the outside of the congregation that were making disturbance by talking loud to the young ladies would not do so but wait and go to their homes and speak to them by the consent of their parents. The speaker continued his discourse and after a while the Prophet walked down from the stand and walked through the further side of the congregation where the disturbance was. Although the alley was densely crowded with people standing up, the way opened up so that he walked through and back without any hindrance where it would seem impossible for any other man to do so. Such was the respect of the people for Joseph Smith, so you can see that he was not above acting in the capacity of a deacon when it was really necessary. There was no more disturbance in that meeting. In this meeting he said that North and South America would become Mount Zion and that the constitution would hang on a single untwisted thread and that the Latter Day Saints would save it (1945).

Illinois Democratic Press

[This newswriter tells of visiting Nauvoo in 1843, shortly after the Dixon kidnapping, and then of returning in 1852. Beginning with the earlier visit:] While in the city, we visited JOE SMITH and SIDNEY RIGDON at their houses. The former was a fine-looking man—tall and portly, with an expressive countenance and florid complexion. We found him at first reserved; but after telling him who we were, and what was the object of our visit, he became communicative, and seemed to be pleased with the notice we paid him. One little incident occurred while we were at his house, which proved conclusively that the Prophet appreciated fully the importance of turning everything to personal account. We had not been seated more than half an hour when his mother entered the room, and informed us that in the next apartment there were some very interesting ancient records which she would be glad to show us. We accepted her invitation, when we were introduced to some half a dozen Egyptian mummies, who, we were informed, constituted the family of Pharaoh. We were then shown a large number of framed sheets of papyrus covered with hieroglyphics, which had been taken from the bandages about the mummies, and these were the "interesting records," which the old lady had invited us to see, and which—Gideon-like—she undertook to explain to us. We soon found that the thread of her discourse was simply a rehearsal of the Bible history of the creation and the end of man, the deluge, and the subsequent history of the Israelites. As we were all more or less familiar with this, we soon wearied of the discourse, and, to our great scandal in the good woman's estimation, begged her to excuse us from hearing more. Just as we were on the point of retiring, however, our eyes fell upon a placard, inscribed as follows: "EGYPTIAN MUMMIES AND ANCIENT RECORDS TO BE SEEN HERE—PRICE 24 CENTS." Of course, we paid the score without a word, and bowed ourselves out of the residence of the Prophet. . . .

A distinguished writer observed that a man should be estimated not so much by what he knows as by what he accomplishes. Judged by this standard, the leaders of the Mormons—the founder of the sect, his immediate co-workers, and those upon whom his mantle fell at a time when their star seemed destined to set in disaster and blood, but who guided them safely in their wonderful exode (sic.) into the wilderness, and have so shaped their subsequent movements, that seeming disaster has been turned into success, must be counted among the remarkable men of the times. It is folly to call them ignorant—it is not more wise to call them fanatics and enthusiasts. These epithets may properly apply to a large number of their followers. But the leaders are men of mind, possessed of rare powers of invention, great capacity for execution, wonderful judgment, and felicity in determining upon the means to a given end. Bad men they undoubtedly are, but they are not fools (1852, p. 6).

Eunice B. Snow

During the persecution of the Prophet, especially when he was in hiding, he would sometimes be allowed to visit his family for an evening, and would request my father and mother to come to sing for him. They would take me with them, and when Joseph found that I could sing a part alone he requested them to bring me. We would sing his favorite hymns: "When Joseph His Brethren Beheld," "Redeemer of Israel," "The Spirit of God," and several others. He would become so inspired with the spirit of the music that he would clap his hands and shout hosanna to the Lord (1910a).

Specific Characteristics of the Prophet

Attentive to Temporal Concerns

Jesse W. Crosby

Brother J. W. Crosby, a prominent man in early Dixie and an early preacher of the gospel, lived a close neighbor to the Prophet in Nauvoo. Being a very observing man, he learned much of that great man's home life, and he used to tell us many interesting things about it. He said the Prophet had great ability as a financier, and that had his enemies left him he would have become one of the wealthiest men in America. Everything his hand touched seemed to prosper. His fields were always in good condition and yielded well. When people came to see him, and he had many visitors, their teams were fed the best of hay and his barn was full. No other orchard had as fine fruit as his did. If an inferior cow was by any means shoved on to him, it would be but a short time before she became a first-class milker. Many men sought his advice when in financial difficulty, and none failed to profit by it if they followed the counsel he gave. A period of great prosperity for [Joseph], Brother Crosby said, would seem to induce a raid upon him. One trial after another would be launched until he was left penniless and perhaps in debt. On one of these occasions, when the Prophet had been absent from home for some time, Brother Crosby went to his home to see if he might render some assistance. When he made the purpose of his visit known, the [Prophet's] wife burst into tears and said that if the persecution would cease they could live as well as any other family in the land. They could even have the luxuries of life.

Bro. Crosby related the following items of interest concerning the Prophet. He was strong and active, and could build more rods of good fence in one day than most men could do in two, and he always left his fence clear of everything that might gather fire, such as underbrush, loose limbs, and tall strong weeds. He was orderly. His wood yard was an example of order. Logs were neatly piled and all trash cleared away. If he did not finish the log on which he was chopping the remnant was laid back on the pile and not left on the ground for a stumbling block. The chips he made he picked up himself into a basket and put them in a wooden box which stood in the wood yard to [be] carried them into the house to be burned.

Bro. Crosby confessed this: During a period of financial depression for the Prophet, the ax was stolen from his wood yard, and Brother Crosby contributed to loan him the ax belonging to himself because of the unfailing habit of the Prophet to always sharpen the ax he had been using before it left his hand. People in that section burned hard wood and to keep the ax in good shape required much time and energy. Some of the home habits of this best friend, however, such as building kitchen fires, carrying out ashes, carrying in wood and water, assisting in the care of the children, etc., were not in accord with Brother Crosby's idea of a great man's duty (n.d. [b]).

Edwin Holden

In 1838 Joseph and some of the young men were playing various outdoor games, among which was a game of ball. By and by they began to get weary. He saw it, and calling them together he said: "Let us build a log cabin." So off they went, Joseph and the young men, to build a log cabin for a widow woman. Such was Joseph's way, always assisting in whatever he could (1892, p. 153).

Bold and Forthright

William E. Jones

I was not intimately acquainted with the Prophet, but I have many times listened to his inspired words; and I never shall forget the words he spoke on the first Sunday after I came to Nauvoo. The temple was built a few feet above the ground. While preaching he pointed towards it and said, "The Lord has commanded us to build that temple. We want to build it, but we have not the means. There are people in this city who have the means, but they will not let us have them. What shall we do with such people? I say damn them!" and then he sat down. On the following day several persons came forward with their means, and this averted the curse which would doubtless otherwise have followed them (1892, p. 66).

Characteristics As a Friend

Margaret Clawson

I have heard mother [Margaret Clawson] tell a little incident about the Prophet: Soon after we went to Nauvoo, she had occasion to do a little shopping, and on her way to the store, she passed the Mansion House. The Prophet was standing on the lawn conversing quite earnestly with several very elegant Gentile gentlemen. As she passed along, very naturally she looked at the Prophet. She knew him, but he did not know her. All at once he reached his arm over the fence, grasped her by the hand, and gave her a hearty shake. He did not hesitate in his conversation with the gentlemen but kept right on talking, and mother passed on. I need not say she was delighted. I am sure he divined what a noble-spirited woman she was (1919b, p. 317).

Howard Coray

In the following June [1840] I met with an accident, which I shall here mention: The Prophet and myself, after looking at his horses, and admiring them, that were just across the road from his house, we started thither, the Prophet at this same time put his arm over my shoulder. When we had reached about the middle of the road, he stopped and remarked, "Brother Coray, I wish you were a little larger, I would like to have some fun with you." I replied, "Perhaps you can as it is," not realizing what I was saying, Joseph a man of over 200 pounds weight, while I scarcely 130 pounds, made it not a little ridiculous for me to think of engaging with him in anything like a scuffle. However, as soon as I made this reply, he began to trip me; he took some kind of a lock on my right leg, from which I was unable to extricate it, and throwing me around, broke it some three inches above the ankle joint. He immediately carried me into the house, pulled off my boot, and found at once that my leg was decidedly broken; then he got some splinters and bandaged it. A number of times that day did he come in to see me, endeavoring to console me as much as possible. The next day when he happened in to see me after a little conversation, I said, "Brother Joseph, when Jacob wrestled with the angel and was lamed by him, the angel blessed him; now I think I am also entitled to a blessing." To that he replied, "I am not the patriarch, but my father is, and when you get up and around, I'll have him bless you." He said no more for a minute or so, meanwhile looking very earnestly at me, then said, "Brother Coray, you will soon find a companion, one that will be suited to your condition and whom you will be satisfied with. She will cling to you, like to cords of death, and you will have a good many children." He also said some other things, which I can't so distinctly remember.

In nine days after my leg was broken, I was able to get up and hobble about the house by the aid of a crutch and in two weeks thereafter, I was about recovered, nearly as well as ever, so much so that I went to meeting on foot, a distance of a mile. I considered this no less than a case of miraculous healing. For nothing short of three months did I think it would be ere I should be around again, on my feet, able to resume work. . . .

Subsequent, some three or four weeks, to getting my leg broken, and while at meeting, the blessing of the Prophet came into my mind, viz: "that I should soon find a companion, etc. etc." So I thought I would take a square look at the congregation, and see who there was, that possibly the fair one promised me might be present. After looking and gazing awhile at the audience, my eyes settled upon a young lady sitting in a one-horse buggy. She was an entire stranger to me and a resident of some other place. I concluded to approach near enough to her to scan her features well and thus be able to decide in my own mind whether her looks would satisfy my taste. She had dark brown eyes, very bright and penetrating, at least they penetrated me, and I said to myself, she will do. The fact is, I was decidedly struck.

After the dismissal of the meeting, instead of going for my dinner, I remained on the ground and presently commenced promenading about to see what I could see. I had not gone far before I came square in front of the lovely miss, walking arm in arm with a Mrs. Harris, with whom I was well acquainted. They stopped and Mrs. Harris said, "Brother Coray, I have the honor of introducing you to Miss Martha Knowlton, from Bear Creek." I, of course, bowed as politely as I knew how, and she curtsied, and we then fell into somewhat familiar conversation. I discovered at once that she was ready, offhand, and inclined to be witty; also, that her mind took a wider range than was common for young ladies of her age. This interview, though short, was indeed very enjoyable, and closed with the hope that she might be the one whom the Lord had picked for me; and thus it proved to be.

I shall not go into all the details of our courtship; suffice it to say, every move I made, seemed to count one in the right direction. I let Brother Joseph into the secret and showed him a letter that I had written, designed for her. He seemed to take uncommon interest in the matter and took pains to see her and talk with her about me, telling her that I was just the one for her. A few letters passed between us; I visited her at her home, proposed, was accepted, and on the 6th day of February, 1841, we were married at her father's house. Brother Robert B. Thompson performed the ceremony.

I will say in this connection that what the Prophet said in regard to the companion which I should soon find has been fully verified. A more intelligent, self-sacrificing, and devoted wife and mother, few men have been blessed with (n.d., pp. 10–12).

Wandle Mace

One day Joseph rode upon the [Nauvoo] temple grounds as we stood together talking after our day's work and called out, "Boys, has Bonaparte any friends in the French Army?" Of course we were all attention to know his meaning. He then told us he had learned from the mother of O. P. Rockwell, that for the sum of [one] hundred dollars she could obtain Porter's release from prison. Joseph said he had not sufficient money himself so he wanted the brethren to assist him. All present responded heartily. Some could give five dollars, others various amounts. Those who had money with them gave it to him; some went to their homes for the money.

While waiting for the brethren to return, Joseph dismounted from his horse and engaged in a friendly wrestle with some of the "boys," as he called them. He often tried to get me to wrestle with him but I never would. I was a strong man as well as he was. Often when we met and shook hands he would pull me to him for a wrestle and say, slapping my shoulder with his hand, "If you are not a strong man, there is no use of putting a man upright."

Joseph obtained the necessary funds and soon afterward O. P.

Rockwell was allowed his freedom after many weary months of imprisonment. He made his way on foot across the state of Missouri, which swarmed with his enemies, who had sworn to take his life if only they could get their eyes on him. The Lord preserved him in his journey and he reached Nauvoo and the house of the Prophet on 25 December 1843. Joseph and all the Saints rejoiced in his safe return to liberty and friends (n.d. [b], pp. 92–93).

Joseph Smith

I took dinner in the north room, and was remarking to Brother Phelps what a kind, provident wife I had—that when I wanted a little bread and milk, she would load the table with so many good things, it would destroy my appetite. At this moment Emma came in, while Phelps, in continuation of the conversation said, "You must do as Bonaparte did—have a little table, just large enough for the victuals you want yourself."

Mrs. Smith replied, "Mr. Smith is a bigger man than Bonaparte: he can never eat without his friends." I remarked, "That is the wisest thing I ever heard you say" (HC, 6:165–66).

William Taylor

I always carry with me my old copy of the Doctrine and Covenants, the second edition of that work, and printed in Nauvoo, 1844—and in section 105 of that book, I read:

"Forasmuch as the Lord has revealed unto me that my enemies, both in Missouri and this State, were again in the pursuit of me; and inasmuch as they pursue me without a cause, and have not the least shadow or coloring of justice or right on their side in the getting up of their prosecutions against me; and inasmuch as their pretensions are all founded in falsehood of the blackest dye, I have thought it expedient and wisdom in me to leave the place for a short season, for my own safety and the safety of this people. . . . When I learn that the storm is fully blown over, then I will return to you again" [D&C 127:1].

This was all that was made public in regard to the Prophet's hiding place, few ever knew where it was, but it was at my father's home on the Henderson River.

My first acquaintance with the Prophet Joseph Smith began in this way. It was on my nineteenth birthday, he appeared at my father's house in the woods, accompanied by my brother, John Taylor, [afterward President

John Taylor,] S. Roundy, and J. D. Parker, about the middle of the night, September 2, 1842. How they ever found their way in the darkness is a mystery, for I, who was very familiar with the country, could not have come by so circuitous a route even in the daylight.

Late in the night the Prophet had gone to my brother John's house in Nauvoo and said to him:

"I want you to go with me to your father's."

My brother said: "But I can't go, Brother Joseph; I am sick in bed!"

The Prophet replied:

"I'll come in and help you dress, and you'll find no inconvenience from going out."

So Brother John got up, dressed, and started out with him, and by the time they reached our home, none of us could tell that he had been the least sick.

The four stayed at our house a few days and then the Prophet sent the other three back to Nauvoo to see if anything was going wrong at that place. In a few days they returned. During their absence the Prophet and I spent most of our time during the day in the woods, near our house on the Henderson bottom, walking around, shooting squirrels sometimes, or doing anything we could to amuse ourselves. I was the Prophet's only companion in these tramps through the woods, and I have often thought it strange, that though there were many people in that part of the country we never met anyone when we were out.

During the stay of Brother Joseph at my father's, Brother William Clayton came to see him, and reported the revelations which the Prophet had at this time, and they were some of the grandest that ever were given to him. Section 106, old edition; section 128, present edition. Every word of this divine revelation is full of doctrine and a completeness of the Holy Spirit. And it is such a perfect expression of the glad tidings of joy that the everlasting gospel brings; verse 23:

"Let the mountains shout for joy, and all ye valleys cry aloud; and all ye seas and dry lands tell the wonders of your Eternal King! And ye rivers, and brooks, and rills, flow down with gladness. Let the woods and all the trees of the field praise the Lord; and ye solid rocks weep for joy! And let the sun, moon, and the morning stars sing together, and let all the sons of God shout for joy! And let the eternal creations declare his name forever and ever! And again I say, how glorious is the voice we hear from heaven, proclaiming in our ears, glory, and salvation, and honor, and immortality, and eternal life; kingdoms, principalities, and powers!"

I do not remember exactly how long the Prophet remained at our home, but it seems to me it was about two weeks, but in this short period, owing to the nature of the circumstances surrounding us, I had more real close association with him than I would have had in a lifetime under different conditions. It is impossible for me to express my feelings in regard to this period of my life. I have never known the same joy and satisfaction in the companionship of any other person, man or woman, that I felt with him, the man who had conversed with the Almighty. He was always the most companionable and lovable of men—cheerful and jovial! Sometimes on our return home in the evening after we had been tramping around in the woods, he would call out:

"Here, mother, come David and Jonathan."

Much has been said of his geniality and personal magnetism. I was a witness of this—people, old or young, loved him and trusted him instinctively.

I said to him once:

"Brother Joseph, don't you get frightened when all those hounding wolves are after you?"

And he answered:

"No, I am not afraid; the Lord said he would protect me, and I have full confidence in his word."

I knew the danger, and whatever happened to him would happen to me, but I felt no more fear than I now feel. There was something superior to thoughts of personal safety. Life or death was a matter of indifference to me while I was the companion of the Lord's anointed!

He said to me often:

"I'll never forsake you, William," and I knew he wouldn't (1906, pp. 547–48).

Characteristics As a Leader

Truman O. Angell

After the endowment, I was ordained a member of the 2nd Quorum of Seventies, and the following spring I commenced making arrangements to go on a mission. While I yet had a day or two more work, and while at work, Joseph Smith, Jr., the Prophet and Seer came to me and asked me to build a store. I answered that in consequence of being a seventy I was about to go out into the vineyard to preach. "Well," he said, "Go ahead," and I continued my work. The next day I looked up and saw the First Presidency of the Church together, distant about forty rods. I dropped my head and continued my work.

At this time a voice seemed to whisper to me, "It is your duty to build that house for President Smith," and while I was meditating, I looked up and Brother Joseph Smith, Jr., was close to me. He said, "It is your duty to build that house." I answered, "I know it." Accordingly I changed my determination and yielded obedience. The numerous and continued calls to do this and that job soon plunged me in business so deep that I asked Brother Joseph if it was my calling to work at home. He said, "I'll give you work enough for twenty men." I then began work on an extensive scale and laid my plans to go ahead. Among the multiplicity of buildings under my charge, I had the supervision of finishing the second, or middle wall of the temple, including the stands, etc. (1967, p. 197).

Howard Coray

Stephen A. Douglas called to see [Joseph Smith to] ask him some questions. One thing he desired to know was how he managed to govern a people so diverse, coming from so many different countries with their peculiar manners and customs. "Well," he said, "I simply teach them the truth, and they govern themselves," was his ready answer. Among other great men who called to see him was Cyrus Walker—a lawyer of much note; he tried to sound the Prophet, and see how deep he was. Well, it was with Walker, as it had been with all the others, he soon got enough, found Joseph too deep . . . and gave up the enterprise. Thus it was in every instance that came under my observation: how could we expect it to be otherwise? For any man who had never peered into heaven and seen heavenly things, [to] be a match for one who had half a score or more heavenly messengers for teachers.

[As his secretary] I continued the work of copying his letters until I finished the same. He then desired me to write up the Church history, saying that he would furnish all the material. I declined, telling him that I did not [consider] myself competent for such a work. He said, if I would undertake it, I would be thankful for it as long as I lived. Having more confidence in him than I had in myself, I engaged in the business of a historian. He placed in my hands some items and scraps of history for me to arrange chronologically and fix up as best I could. We had now moved into his new office, a two-story building arranged to do the office work in the upper story. John C. Bennett was occupying a portion of the room, engaged in writing the Nauvoo Charter. Joseph dictated much of the Charter. I could overhear the instructions he gave Bennett, and know it was gotten up mainly as Joseph required (1977, pp. 343–44).

Mary I. Horne

I first met the Prophet Joseph Smith in the fall of 1837, at my home in the town of Scarborough, Canada West.

When I first shook hands with him I was thrilled through and through and I knew that he was a prophet of God, and that testimony never left me, but is still strong within me, and has been a monitor to me, so that I can now bear a faithful testimony to the divinity of the mission of that great man of God.

During the three days series of meetings held in a new barn which my husband had built, the Prophet made his home with us. The use of this barn became a necessity because the Methodists, who were bitterly opposed to us, refused to let [rent] their churches to the Prophet and saints.

As an example of Brother Joseph's humility, as well as his respect for authority, I mention the following: As soon as he reached Toronto, Canada, he inquired who the presiding officer was. On learning that it was the late President John Taylor, the Prophet said, "Send for him, as I desire to hold a meeting with the people." When President Taylor arrived, Brother Joseph said, "Brother Taylor, I am the Prophet Joseph. I want you to call a meeting, as I would like to talk to the saints."

While in Canada he visited all the branches of the Church, and gave the saints instructions on the organization and order of the priesthood, respect for proper authority, corrected some of the mistranslations of the Bible, and took pleasure in answering questions pertaining to the gospel and the organization of the Church. Brother and Sister Taylor, my husband, and I enjoyed the privilege of accompanying the Prophet on these visits (1951, p. 158).

Joseph Smith

At this place I discovered that a part of my company had been served with sour bread, while I had received good, sweet bread from the same cook. I reproved Brother Zebedee Coltrin for this partiality, for I wanted my brethren to fare as well as I did (HC, 2:75; see also George A. Smith, JD, 13:20; n.d., p. 17).

Joseph Smith

On returning to my office after dinner, I spoke the following proverb: For a man to be great, he must not dwell on small things, though he may enjoy them; this shows that a prophet cannot well be his own scribe, but must have someone to write for him (HC, 5:298).

Joseph Smith

Elder Noah Rogers, of the Seventies, was blessed by the same brethren, Elder Kimball being mouth. It was said that he might have power to discern between good and evil, be filled with the power of God, have faith to heal the sick, cast out devils, and cause the lame to walk, and have the heavens opened, and have an appointment from on high, even from God, if he was faithful. "Except thou art willing to be led, thou shalt never lead. Thou shalt return to this place." He was set apart to accompany Brother Addison Pratt to the Pacific Islands (HC, 5:405).

Joseph Smith

The Mayor [Joseph Smith] said that if anyone offered a bribe to a policeman, the city will pay that policeman twice the amount offered for the information, when reported to the Mayor (HC, 6:153).

John Taylor

What is it that will enable one man to govern his fellows aright? It is just as Joseph Smith said to a certain man who asked him, "How do you govern such a vast people as this?" "Oh," says Joseph, "it is very easy." "Why," says the man, "but we find it very difficult." "But," said Joseph, "it is very easy, for I teach the people correct principles and they govern themselves;" and if correct principles will do this in one family they will in ten, in a hundred, and in ten hundred thousand. How easy it is to govern the people in this way! (JD, 10:57–58; see also Erastus Snow, JD, 24:159).

Brigham Young

Joseph laid out as much work as we can do for twenty years. I have no disposition to seek more till I see those we have obeyed.

... When we have the Spirit of the Lord we work together in oneness and we shall accomplish the designs sooner or later. Joseph used to say, "Don't be scared. I have not apostatized yet!" And he did not! I say brethren, I have not apostatized, and there are a good many who have not (1850b; see also Brigham Young, JD, 5:331).

Brigham Young

Now I am going to tell a dream that I had, which I think is as applicable, to the people to-day—the 21st day of June, 1874, as when I had it. There were so many going to California, and going this way and that way, and they did not know what they wanted, and said I—"Stay here, we can raise our food here, I know it is a good stock country, a good sheep country, and as good a country for raising silk as there is in the world, and we shall raise some of the best of wheat. There stands a man—Burr Frost, and there is Truman O. Angell, who were present at the time." Said I, "We can raise all we want here, do not go away, do not be discouraged." That was when the pioneers came; the next year, it was California, California, California, California. "No," said I, "stay here."

After much thought and reflection, and a good deal of praying and anxiety as to whether the people would be saved after all our trouble in being driven into the wilderness, I had a dream one night, the second year after we came in here. Captain Brown had gone up to the Weber, and bought a little place belonging to Miles Goodyear. Miles Goodyear had a few goats, and I had a few sheep that I had driven into the Valley, and I wanted to get a few goats to put along with the sheep. I had seen Captain Brown and spoken to him about the goats, and he said I could have them. Just at that time I had this dream, which I will now relate.

I thought I had started and gone past the Hot Springs, which is about four miles north of this city. I was going after my goats. When I had gone round the point of the mountain by the Hot Springs, and had got about half a mile on the rise of ground beyond the Spring, whom should I meet but Brother Joseph Smith. He had a wagon with no bed on, with bottom boards, and tents and camp equipage piled on. Somebody sat on the wagon driving the team. Behind the team I saw a great flock of sheep. I heard their bleating, and saw some goats among them. I looked at them and thought—"This is curious, Brother Joseph has been up to Captain Brown's and got my goats." There were men driving the sheep, and some of the sheep I should think were three and a half feet high, with large, fine beautiful white fleeces, and they looked so lovely and pure; others were of moderate size, and pure and white; and in fact there were sheep of all sizes, with fleeces clean, pure, and white. Then I saw some that were dark and spotted, of all colors and sizes and kinds, and their fleeces were dirty, and they looked inferior; some of these were a pretty good size, but not as large as some of the large fine clean sheep, and altogether there was a multitude of them of all sizes and kinds, and goats of all colors, sizes, and kinds mixed among them.

Joseph stopped the wagon, and the sheep kept rushing up until there was an immense herd. I looked in Joseph's eye, and laughed, just as I had many a time when he was alive, about some trifling thing or other, and said I—"Joseph, you have got the darndest flock of sheep I ever saw in my life; what are you going to do with them, what on earth are they for?" Joseph looked cunningly out of his eyes, just as he used to at times, and said he—"They are all good in their places." When I awoke in the morning I did not find any fault with those who wanted to go to California; I said, "If they want to go let them go, and we will do all we can to save them; I have no more fault to find, the sheep and the goats will run together," but Joseph says, "they are all good in their places" (1874, pp. 340–41).

Lorenzo D. Young

I returned to Kirtland, and in a short time was requested to attend a council of the First Presidency, which consisted of the Prophet, S. Rigdon, and F. G. Williams. I was requested by Joseph Smith to make a report of my mission, and particularly that part of it connected with Dr. Avard, and the branch of the Church over which he presided. The impressions I had received of him were not flattering to his character for honesty and integrity. Without bringing any accusation against him, in a moderate way I expressed my views to the council. Elder Rigdon manifested his displeasure by animadverting rather sharply on my remarks. After he was through expressing his views the Prophet Joseph said, "Brother Young, I wish you to express your views of Dr. Avard without fear or favor." I expressed a wish not to do so, to which he replied that he really desired that I should. I then more fully gave my opinion that Dr. Avard was a dishonest, hypocritical man. I said to Elder Rigdon, "Give Dr. Avard time and he will prove my estimate of his character to be correct" (1946, pp. 51–52).

Characteristics As a Teacher

Joseph Smith

We crossed the Embarras River and encamped on a small branch of the same about one mile west. In pitching my tent we found three massasaugas or prairie rattlesnakes, which the brethren were about to kill, but I said, "Let them alone—don't hurt them! How will the serpent ever lose his venom, while the servants of God possess the same disposition, and continue to make war upon it? Men must become harmless before the brute creation; and when men lose their vicious dispositions and cease to destroy the animal race, the lion and the lamb can dwell together, and the sucking child can play with the serpent in safety." The brethren took the serpents carefully on sticks and carried them across the creek. I exhorted the brethren not to kill a serpent, bird, or an animal of any kind during our journey unless it became necessary in order to preserve ourselves from hunger.

I had frequently spoken on this subject, when on a certain occasion I came up to the brethren who were watching a squirrel on a tree, and to prove them and to know if they would heed my counsel, I took one of their guns, shot the squirrel and passed on, leaving the squirrel on the ground. Brother Orson Hyde, who was just behind, picked up the squirrel, and said, "We will cook this, that nothing may be lost." I perceived that the brethren understood what I did it for, and in their practice gave more heed to my precept than to my example, which was right (HC, 2:71–72).

Compassionate and Kind

Mary F. Adams

While [Joseph] was acting as mayor of the city, a colored man called Anthony was arrested for selling liquor on Sunday, contrary to law. He pleaded that the reason he had done so was that he might raise the money to purchase the freedom of a dear child held as a slave in a southern state.

He had been able to purchase the liberty of himself and wife and now wished to bring his little child to their new home. Joseph said,

"I am sorry, Anthony, but the law must be observed, and we will have to impose a fine."

The next day Brother Joseph presented Anthony with a fine horse, directing him to sell it, and use the money obtained for the purchase of the child.

Sister Adams says how well she remembers the feeling of sorrow that pervaded the city, when the two brothers were lying dead in the Mansion House. She, with the rest of the children, were not permitted to go in the streets owing to the crowd of people who thronged the city, coming and going by steamboat and carriages, and all with grieving hearts for the departed loved ones (1906; see also Walker, 1943, pp. 8–9, for a similar account of these events).

Schuyler Everett

At Nauvoo he saw the Prophet Joseph Smith many times on a beautiful white horse. They were staying with an aunt, (Mrs. Redfield), and saw a little calf for the first time. They went out to pet and examine the animal, but it became frightened and broke the rope. Time and again Schuyler got it into a corner, but each time it came near Adelaide [his younger sister], she became frightened and ran in the opposite direction. Finally Schuyler lost his temper and shouted:

"You darn fool! Why don't you head it?" At that moment Joseph Smith happened to be riding by. He got off his horse, tied up the calf, and then petting Adelaide on the head, said, "You are not a little fool, are you sissy?" He never even looked at Schuyler. This was a lesson the boy never forgot. Often in his later years, he related the story to his grandchildren, and his eyes always filled with tears (n.d.).

Celia A. Keys

One time shortly after they moved to Brush Creek, Celia was working in her garden. She looked up; there were several Indians coming toward their little sod house. She hurried to the house—for she had a small baby in the cradle. The Indians came in without knocking. They kept saying, "Beeskit! Beeskit!" meaning bread. Celia had very little bread, but when she refused, the leader of the group menaced the baby with a knife. For a minute she thought she would throw a kettle of hot water. Then she remembered:

Several years before when she was a little child in Nauvoo, she was alone on the street. A large group of Indians rode down the street yelling. She was crying with fright when the Prophet Joseph Smith picked her up and set her before him on his large white horse. He told her not to be afraid of the Indians. He said, "I promise you that if you will never harm the Indians, they will never harm you, nor any of your descendants."

Celia gave them the bread she had, and they left in peace (n.d.).

Joseph Knight Sr.

One day the Prophet saw his elderly friend hobbling along without a cane. The Prophet approached him and, putting his arm around him, pressed Father Knight's fingers onto the top of his cane and said, "Brother Knight, you need this cane more than I do." The Prophet then told him to keep it as long as he needed it, and then to pass it on to descendants with the first name Joseph. The cane has been passed down through several descendants until the present day (1997, p. 167).

Calvin W. Moore

There is one thing more, which I witnessed, I will relate: It was at the time Porter Rockwell was in jail in Missouri. His mother went to see him at the jail, and the Missourians told her that if she would raise a certain amount of money and give them they would let her son go. Joseph started out to get the money. He came to a large crowd of young men who were wrestling, that being the popular sport in those days. Among the boys there was a bully from La Harpe, I believe. He had thrown down everyone on the ground who took hold of him. When Joseph came to the crowd he told them what he wanted, passed around the hat, raised what money he could, and then went into the ring to take part with the young men and boys in their games. So he was invited to wrestle with this bully. The man was eager to have a tussle with the Prophet, so Joseph stepped forward and took hold of the man. The first pass he made Joseph whirled him around and took him by the collar and seat of his trousers and walked out to a ditch and threw him in it. Then, taking him by the arm, he helped him up and patted him on the back and said. "You must not mind this. When I am with the boys I make all the fun I can for them" (1892, p. 255; see also Mace, n.d. [b], pp. 92–93).

Ephraim H. Nye

E. H. Nye, who was President of the California Mission of the Latter-day Saints Church, 1898, tells of meeting and spending the evening with an aged gentleman who was, as a boy, a stage driver between Nauvoo and Keokuk, with Carthage as a halfway station. On the fateful twenty-seventh of June 1844, he came rattling into Carthage with the stage. Driving past the old jail, the man said he saw the mob gathered around it; as his passengers were getting out, the shooting commenced; and while driving to the stable, the Prophet jumped out of the window. He saw him fall; but as soon as the stableman took charge of the team, he jumped off and ran, frightened as he states, half out of his wits.

"This man," says Elder Nye, "speaks in the highest terms of commendation and praises of the Prophet and his family. He says that he arrived in Nauvoo at night a stranger, about a year prior to the death of Joseph Smith, without money or friends, a boy fourteen years of age, having understood that his brother lived there. On inquiring for his brother, he learned that it was eight miles to his home, with snow on the ground and very cold. The gentleman of whom he inquired took him over to a large house that he thought was a hotel and told the man of that house of the situation, who said, "Come in, son, we'll take care of you." He was taken in, warmed, fed, and lodged. The next day was bitter cold and the man of the house, who he learned was Joseph Smith, told him to content himself in peace, it was too cold for him to go out to his brother's place alone; some teams would be in from there and then he could go out. The boy said he had no money but he was told not to worry about that; they would take care of him. After this incident, he became well acquainted with Joseph Smith, who always called him "Sonny," and after the boy obtained the position of stage driver Joseph Smith rode with him repeatedly" (n.d.).

Joseph F. Smith

One day during cold weather, my father took me by my hand and led me down the road to a little brick building. It was not much larger than what you would call a beehive house, a little beehive, but it was the best they had at that time, and in it was a little sheet-iron stove. I remember the looks of it just as well as if I had seen it yesterday. There I remember the Prophet Joseph, my father, Brigham Young, Sidney Rigdon, and

Willard Richards and there were a number of others. I remember these more particularly for the reason that I became better and better acquainted with them as I grew up. I remember them all the way through. They met in that hovel to consider what they should do with the obligations that rested in their hands, from those that had been despoiled of all they possessed in the world.

"What will we do with them?" they said. "They are impoverished; they are without everything or anything and they cannot pay their debts. What shall we do with these obligations? Shall we hold them against those people that have been robbed and plundered and despoiled of all they had and wait until they are able to pay and then collect it with usury? No, I guess not."

That is my conclusion, for I saw them sit there and talk together for quite a long while and these piles of papers lay on a little table before the Prophet, and my father and others. By and by, I saw the Prophet gather them up one after another, a bundle here and a bundle there, and put them together; he opened the door of the stove and stuck them in, and I saw them burn. Now, I understand that the brethren did that to cancel the debts, the debts and obligations of those that were rendered incapable of meeting their obligations because of the persecution and robbery and plunder. I think now that it was a mighty fine thing to do. There was forgiveness in it, there was charity in it, there was mercy in it, for those that were helpless at the time. Many of them, I believe, grew up well furnished, well fitted, in later years. Some of them, of course fell away because of the persecutions that were brought upon them. Well, that was an incident that I remember very well (1916, p. 56).

Mercy Rachel Thompson

I saw him by the bedside of Emma, his wife, in sickness, exhibiting all the solicitude and sympathy possible for the tenderest of hearts and the most affectionate of natures to feel. And by the deathbed of my beloved companion, I saw him stand in sorrow, reluctantly submitting to the decree of Providence, while the tears of love and sympathy freely flowed. Joseph took charge of the funeral ceremonies, strictly adhering to my husband's wish that there should be no military or other display at his burial as had been but a short time before on the occasion of the burial of Joseph's brother, Don Carlos, both having been officers in the legion.

Don Carlos died August 7th, 1841, Joseph's little son, Don Carlos, died about August 18th, now, Robert B. Thompson, his faithful secretary, on the 27th of the same month, so that Joseph could feel the import of the lines of Dr. Young addressed to death:

Thy shafts flew thrice and thrice my peace was slain; Yea thrice, ere thrice yon moon had filled her horn.

This indeed was a time of sorrow, but I can never forget the tender sympathy and brotherly kindness he ever showed toward me and my fatherless child. When riding with him and his wife Emma in their carriage I have known him to alight and gather prairie flowers for my little girl (1892, p. 399).

Lorenzo D. Wasson

[In a letter to Emma Smith's brother, David Hale, her nephew Lorenzo Wasson wrote:] Aunt Emma received a letter from you and was much pleased with it, as well as Uncle Joseph. I was pleased with the respect you showed to Uncle Joseph, for I think it is no more than he merits from those that should be his friends, as he never has injured us or laid a straw in our way as I know of, but has ever expressed the greatest degree of friendship. He offers to each of you brothers eighty acres of land if you will come to the City of Nauvoo. The land is in Iowa Territory, in what is called the "Half Breed Tract"; it is said to be of superior quality of both timber and prairie, well watered; and I have no doubt that he feels a little pride in being situated in affluent circumstances that he can offer the benevolent hand to the relatives of his that are most dear to him. When I came to Nauvoo, and finally always ever since I knew Uncle Joseph, I have entertained a strong irreligious unprovoked prejudice against him—and no doubt we all have. But since I came here my prejudice has left me like the chaff before the wind. The doctrine that the Mormons promulgate, and their construction of the scriptures is, I think, correct as far as I have become acquainted with it. Where is the man that knows that he is propagating a religion that is false and founded on hypocrisy, that will not forsake it when placed at the point of fifty bayonets and summoned to renounce his faith or die imprisoned for months, and fed on human flesh seasoned with arsenic and tarred and feathered and various other fiendish devilish tortures inflicted up on him? I ask where is the man that will stand the torture of fire and fagot if he is not sure he is doing the works of righteousness? There is not a man in Christendom among all the sons and daughters of Adam, I will venture to say. I have heard recapitulated the bloody tragedy that was enacted in Missouri by a drunken and inhuman mob. Picture to yourself women and children wandering houseless and homeless in the bleak prairies in cold winter weather, robbed of all their worldly treasures, without food, and scarcely clothes to cover their backs. It is enough to melt the hardest heart that is susceptible of feeling. But I must close my epistle. Were I to follow the Mormons through all their scenes of prosperity and adversity it would swell the pages of a volume like that of Josephus. But the Mormons have found shelter in Illinois; they have settled on the banks of the Mississippi in Illinois and Iowa. They are now in a prosperous condition.

[To this letter, the Prophet wrote the following addendum:] As Lorenzo and Emma have given me space for a few lines, I gladly embrace it, to send to you and yours my sincere and heartfelt respects, and I do honestly think if you come to this country, and settle it would be much to your advantage. I will do what Lorenzo has stated and even more, I will help you to improve the land; also, we want to see you all very much settled in this country (1841).

Andrew Workman

A few days after this I was at Joseph's house; he was there, and several men were sitting on the fence. Joseph came out and spoke to us all. Pretty soon a man came up and said that a poor brother who lived out some distance from town had had his house burned down the night before. Nearly all of the men said they felt sorry for the man. Joseph put his hand in his pocket, took out five dollars, and said, "I feel sorry for this brother to the amount of five dollars; how much do you feel sorry?" (1892, p. 641).

Brigham Young

A great many inquire, saying, "Why does not our Church keep a store here?" Many can answer that question, who have lived here for some years past; and you who make such an inquiry, would have known the reason, had you also lived here. You that have lived in Nauvoo, in Missouri, in Kirtland, Ohio, can you assign a reason why Joseph could not keep a store, and be a merchant? Let me just give you a few reasons, and there are men here who know how matters went in those days. Joseph goes to New York and buys 20,000 dollars' worth of goods, comes into Kirtland, and commences to trade. In comes one of the brethren, "Brother Joseph, let me have a frock pattern for my wife." What if Joseph says, "No, I cannot, without the money." The consequence would be, "He is no prophet," says James. Pretty soon Thomas walks in. "Brother Joseph, will you trust me for a pair of boots?" "No, I cannot let them go without the money." "Well," says Thomas, "Brother Joseph is no prophet; I have found that out, and I am glad of it." After awhile, in comes Bill and Sister Susan. Says Bill, "Brother Joseph, I want a shawl, I have not got the money, but I wish you to trust me a week or a fortnight." Well, Brother Joseph thinks the others have gone and apostatized, and he [doesn't] know but these goods will make the whole Church do the same, so he lets Bill have a shawl. Bill walks off with it and meets a brother. "Well," says he, "what do you think of Brother Joseph?" "O he is a first-rate man, and I fully believe he is a prophet. See here, he has trusted me this shawl." Richard says, "I think I will go down and see if he won't trust me some." In walks Richard. "Brother Joseph, I want to trade about 20 dollars." "Well," says Joseph, "these goods will make the people apostatize; so over they go, they are of less value than the people." Richard gets his goods. Another comes in the same way to make a trade of 25 dollars, and so it goes. Joseph was a first-rate fellow with them all the time, provided he never would ask them to pay him. In this way it is easy for us to trade away a first-rate store of goods, and be in debt for them (JD, 1:215).

Courageous

Joseph Smith

Wednesday, 27 [November 1839]—About 1 o'clock this morning the wind arose, when Elder Brigham Young went on deck, prayed to the Father in the name of Jesus, when he felt to command the wind and the waves to cease, and permit them to proceed on their journey in safety. The winds abated, and he gave glory, honor, and praise to the God who rules all things. Arriving in Buffalo in the morning, they took the stage for Batavia.

While on the mountains some distance from Washington, our coachman stepped into a public house to take his grog, when the horses took fright and ran down the hill at full speed. I persuaded my fellow travelers to be quiet and retain their seats, but had to hold one woman to prevent her throwing her infant out of the coach. The passengers were exceedingly agitated, but I used every persuasion to calm their feelings;

and opening the door, I secured my hold on the side of the coach the best way I could, and succeeded in placing myself in the coachman's seat, and reining up the horses, after they had run some two or three miles, and neither coach, horses, or passengers received any injury. My course was spoken of in the highest terms of commendation, as being one of the most daring and heroic deeds, and no language could express the gratitude of the passengers, when they found themselves safe, and the horses quiet. There were some members of Congress with us, who proposed naming the incident to that body, believing they would reward such conduct by some public act; but on inquiring my name, to mention as the author of their safety, and finding it to be Joseph Smith the "Mormon Prophet," as they called me, I heard no more of their praise, gratitude, or reward (HC, 4:23–24; see also Wandle Mace, n.d. [b], pp. 51–55).

John Taylor

I am reminded of a circumstance that occurred in Missouri, which I will mention to show the kind of feeling that Joseph Smith was possessed of. Some twenty-five years ago, in Far West, a mob—one of those semi-occasional occurrences—had come against us with evil intent, placing themselves in position to give us battle; and there were not more than about 200 of us in the place. We had one fellow who was taken with a fit of trembling in the knees, and he ordered our people to retreat. As soon as Joseph heard this sound, he exclaimed, "Retreat! where in the name of God shall we retreat to?" He then led us out to the prairie facing the mob and placed us in position; and the first thing we knew a flag of truce was seen coming towards us. The person bearing it said that some of their friends were among our people, for whose safety they felt anxious. I rather think it was a case in which the wife was in the Church but not the husband, and the mob wished these parties to come out as they, he said, were going to destroy every man, woman, and child in the place. But these folks had a little "sand" in them, as the boys say; they sent word back, that if that was the case they would die with their friends. Joseph Smith, our leader, then sent word back by this messenger, said he, "Tell your general to withdraw his troops or I will send them to hell." I thought that was a pretty bold stand to take, as we only numbered about 200 to their 3,500; but they thought we were more numerous than we really were; it may be that our numbers were magnified in their eyes; but they took the hint and left; and we were not sorry (JD, 23:37).

Encouraged Learning

Joseph B. Noble

As we were about ready to start, a learned gentleman by the name of Seixas came to Kirtland and wished to teach a Hebrew class and other languages, if wanted. President Joseph Smith called the leaders together and said to us it was a favorable opportunity to get a knowledge of the Hebrew and other languages. The hand of God was in it. We [immediately] went to school. The next six months I gained considerable information on the Hebrew and Chaldee language, so I could read and translate tolerably well. I had at this time no knowledge of the English grammar. That was against me in making progress (n.d. [b], pp. 7–8).

Free in Conversation

Wandle Mace

Such was Joseph the great prophet of the last days as he often joined us on the temple grounds, when we were sure of a rare treat if we could get him to talk to us. Someone present being in a hurry to hear him would say, "Brother Joseph talk to us." He would say, "What do you want me to talk about, start something." Soon a conversation would bring out some question for Joseph to answer, and then I could lean back and listen. Ah, what pleasure this gave me; he would unravel the scriptures and explain doctrine as no other man could. What had been mystery he made so plain it was no longer mystery (n.d. [b], pp. 102–3).

Grateful

Benjamin F. Johnson

Previous to the dedication of the temple on the 27th of March, 1836, all who had labored upon it were called together, and in the public congregation received their blessings under the hands of the First Presidency. I had attended all the meetings, listened to the blessings given, and felt a great joy in these prophetic words that filled and thrilled me. Yet all the time I was thinking that these blessings would only be for those who had labored with their hands upon the temple, and as I had not myself worked upon it, not being strong enough for such labor, I would not receive any blessing, and it grieved me exceedingly to think that perhaps through my neglect I was to be deprived of that which to me appeared of more worth than all earthly things. When on the last day of blessings, I was standing by the door in the crowded congregation, and oh! how I did yearn for a blessing! And as the last blessing, apparently, was given, the Prophet earnestly looked towards the door where I was standing, and said to his brother Hyrum, "Go and see if there is not one more yet to be blessed." Brother Hyrum came to the door, and seeing me, put his hand upon my shoulder and asked me if I had not worked upon the temple. I said, "No sir," but it seemed like passing a sentence upon my fondest hopes. He then asked if I had done nothing towards it. I then thought of a new gun I had earned and given as a donation, and of the brick I had helped to make. I said, "I did give often." "I thought," he said, "there was a blessing for you," and he almost carried me to the stand. The Prophet blessed me, with a confirmation of all his father had sealed upon me, and many more also. I felt then that the Lord had respect for my great desire. Even to be the youngest and last to be blessed seemed to me a high privilege. When the Prophet had looked towards the door, I felt as though he would call for me, though I could not see how I had merited so high a privilege. But so it was, and my joy was full (1947, pp. 22–23).

CATHERINE M'GUIRE KNIGHT

On February 10, 1844, Sister Catherine M. Knight and her sister were baptized by Caleb Baldwin. Their father then gave the two girls a five-dollar gold piece, and asked if they would like to give it to the Prophet. They were pleased to do that and he took them to the home of the Prophet. The Prophet shook hands with the father and said, "How are you, Brother McGuire?" The father said, "Brother Joseph, my little girls wish to give you a small present." He reached his hand to her and said, "So you want to give the Prophet a present, do you?" She said, "Yes," and laid the gold in his hand and he laid his hand on her head and said, "God bless you with a double blessing." Then her sister gave her gold piece and he laid his hand upon her head and said, "God bless you with a double blessing" (1918, pp. 554–55).

Joseph Smith

Spent the day in studying as usual. A man called to see the House of the Lord, in company with another gentleman. On entering the door they were politely invited, by the gentleman who had charge of the house, to take off their hats. One of them replied with the request unhesitatingly, while the other observed that he would not take off his hat nor bow to "Jo Smith," but that he had made "Jo" bow to him at a certain time. He was immediately informed by Elder Morey, the keeper of the house, that his first business was to leave, for when a man insulted Joseph Smith he, Brother Morey, was himself insulted. The man manifested much anger, but left the house. For this independence and resolution of Elder Morey, I respect him, and for the love he manifested towards me; and may Israel's God bless him, and give him an ascendency over all his enemies (HC, 2:401).

Honest

Jesse W. Crosby

One day when the Prophet carried to Brother Crosby's house a sack of flour he had borrowed, the wife remarked that he had returned more than he had received. He answered that it should be so. That anything borrowed should be returned always with interest to the lender. "Thus," said he, "the borrower, if he be honest is a slave to the lender." Brother Crosby felt it to be an opportune time to give to the man he loved so well some corrective advice, which he had desired for a long time to do.

He reminded him of every phase of his greatness and called to his mind the multitude of tasks he performed that were too menial for such as he. And to fetch and carry flour, he told him, was too great a humiliation. "Too terrible a humiliation," Brother Crosby repeated, "for you who are the head, and you should not do it." The Prophet listened quietly to all he had to say; then made answer in these words: "If there be humiliation in a man's house who but the head of that house should or could bear that humiliation?" (n.d. [b]).

Edward Hunter

Brother Hunter, at Joseph's request, visited Springfield to interview Governor Ford and represent matters in their proper light, and ask him to use his influence to allay the excitement and hostility which had now set in like a flood in the direction of Nauvoo and the "Mormons." Joseph's parting words to him were: "You have known me for several years; say to the governor, under oath, everything good and bad you know of me." Brother Hunter was accompanied on his errand by J. Bills and P. Lewis. They were followed for miles by officers whose intention was to arrest them, but having the promise of God's prophet that they should accomplish their journey and return in safety, they were not overtaken, and in due time arrived at their destination (1971, p. 230).

Joseph S. Murdock

[In a letter to a friend:] As for the Prophet, we have had some dealings with him, and we find him to be a man of his word; he is very punctual in all his dealings and there is no doubt in my mind but he is a prophet of God and as much called to guide the people in this day as Moses was in his day. And as for his taking the property of the Saints and converting it to his own use, it is not so. It is like a good many other stories that are told about him. I wish you could be here and see for yourself and know and understand for yourself and not from another (1844).

Sarah M. Pomeroy

My father, Thomas Colborn, a member of Zion's Camp and well acquainted with the Prophet Joseph, moved from the state of New York to Nauvoo with his family in the spring of 1843. I was then in my ninth year. Upon arriving there, we camped down by the river in a little log cabin, near the Hilbert stone house. The day after our arrival, I was out in the yard when a gentleman rode up and inquired for Thomas Colborn. Of course I did not know who it was, but there was something so noble and dignified in his appearance that it struck me forcibly.

My father soon came out and shook him cordially by the hand, and called him Brother Joseph. I knew then it was the Prophet. Father invited him in and he alighted and followed him into the house. He soon told his errand.

It was quite an exciting time just then. The Prophet had been falsely accused of an attempt to murder Governor Boggs of Missouri. The mobbers had tried every means to take him, and had made their boast that if they got him, he never should return alive. Porter Rockwell, a firm friend of Joseph's, had been kidnapped and taken to Missouri as an accomplice, and was about to have his trial, but money was scarce wherewith to pay the lawyers' fees. Joseph requested my father to lend him $100.00 to pay the lawyer who defended Porter Rockwell. He explained the situation, and father freely counted out the money. "This shall be returned within three days, if I am alive," said the Prophet, and departed.

My aunt, father's sister, who was camped with us, was quite wrathy, and called my father very foolish and unwise.

"Don't you know, Thomas," said she, "you will never see a cent of that money again. Here are your family without a home, and you throw your money away."

"Don't worry, Katie," father replied, "if he cannot pay it, he is welcome to it."

This conversation was held before us children, and I thought seriously about it. Would he pay it, or would he not? But I had strong faith that he would.

The day came when it was to be paid. A cold, wet, rainy day. The day passed. Night came; 9 o'clock, 10 o'clock, and we all retired for the night. Shortly after there was a knock at the door. Father arose and went to it, and there in the driving rain stood the Prophet Joseph.

"Here, Brother Thomas, is the money." A light was struck, and seated at the table, he counted out the $100.00 in gold.

He said, "Brother Thomas, I have been trying all day to raise this sum, for my honor was at stake. God bless you."

My aunt had nothing to say. She afterwards left the Church.

My testimony is that Joseph Smith was truly a prophet of God. This incident I have related strengthened my testimony (1906, p. 539).

Humble

William F. Cahoon

I wish to mention one circumstance which I shall never forget. I was called and ordained to act as a ward teacher to visit the families of the

Saints. I got along very well until I was obliged to pay a visit to the Prophet. Being young, only seventeen years of age, I felt my weakness in the capacity of a teacher. I almost felt like shrinking from my duty.

Finally, I went to the door and knocked, and in a minute the Prophet came to the door. I stood there trembling and said to him; "Brother Joseph, I have come to visit you in the capacity of a ward teacher, if it is convenient for you." He said, "Brother William, come right in. I am glad to see you. Sit down in that chair there and I will go and call my family in." They soon came in and took seats. The Prophet said, "Brother William, I submit myself and family into your hands," and took his seat. "Now, Brother William," said he, "Ask all the questions you feel like."

By this time my fears and trembling had ceased and I said, "Brother Joseph, are you trying to live your religion?" He answered, "Yes." I then said, "Do you pray in your family?" He answered, "Yes." "Do you teach your family the principles of the gospel?" He replied, "Yes, I am trying to do it." "Do you ask a blessing on your food?" He said he did. "Are you trying to live in peace and harmony with all your family?" He said that he was.

I turned to Sister Emma, his wife, and said, "Sister Emma, are you trying to live your religion? Do you teach your children to obey their parents? Do you try to teach them to pray?" To all these questions she answered, "Yes, I am trying to do so." I then turned to Joseph and said, "I am now through with my questions as a teacher, and now if you have any instructions to give, I shall be happy to receive them." He said, "God bless you, Brother William," and if you are humble and faithful you shall have power to settle all difficulties that may come before you in the capacity of a teacher." I then left my parting blessing upon him and his family, as a teacher, and departed (1892, pp. 492–93; 1960, p. 80).

Heber C. Kimball

I recollect often hearing Brother Joseph say that many times his legs trembled like Belshazzar's when he got up to speak before the world, and before the Saints (JD, 2:220).

Joseph Smith

About January 16, 1838, being destitute of money to pursue my journey, I said to Brother Brigham Young: "You are one of the Twelve who have charge of the kingdom in all the world; I believe I shall throw myself upon you, and look to you for counsel in this case." Brother Young thought I was not earnest, but I told him I was. Brother Brigham then said, "If you will take my counsel it will be that you rest yourself, and be assured you shall have money in plenty to pursue your journey."

There was a brother living in the place who had tried for some time to sell his farm but could not; he asked counsel of Brother Young concerning his property; Brother Young told him that if he would do right, and obey counsel, he should have an opportunity to sell. In about three days Brother Tomlinson came to Brother Brigham and said he had an offer for his place; Brother Brigham told him that this was the manifestation of the hand of the Lord to deliver Brother Joseph Smith from his present necessities. Brother Brigham's promise was soon verified, and I got three hundred dollars from Brother Tomlinson, which enabled me to pursue my journey (HC, 3:2; see also Brigham Young, 1968, pp. 24–26).

Industrious

JOSEPH HOLBROOK

May 3rd [1833]—We [Joseph Holbrook and Truman O. Angell] traveled thirty miles and called a number of times, but the people were unwilling to hear of Mormonism. We took dinner in the town of Manchester where the Book of Mormon was found. The gentleman did not believe that Joseph Smith was the author of said book, as he was well acquainted with him and did not know any harm of him until the Book of Mormon came forth, but he believed the Smith family were honest, industrious farmers (n.d., p. 27).

EDWARD PARTRIDGE

In December of the same year (1830), Joseph appointed a meeting at our house. While he was preaching, Sidney Rigdon and Edward Partridge came in and seated themselves in the congregation. When Joseph had finished his discourse, he gave all who had any remarks to make, the privilege of speaking. Upon this, Mr. Partridge arose, and stated that he had been to Manchester, with the view of obtaining further information respecting the doctrine which we preached; but, not finding us, he had made some inquiry of our neighbors concerning our characters, which they stated had been unimpeachable, until Joseph deceived [them] relative to the Book of Mormon. He also said that he had walked over our farm, and observed the good order and industry which it exhibited; and, having seen what we had sacrificed for the sake of our faith, and having heard that our veracity was not questioned upon any other point than that of our religion, he believed our testimony, and was ready to be baptized, "if," said he, "Brother Joseph will baptize me."

"You are now," replied Joseph, "much fatigued, Brother Partridge, and you had better rest today, and be baptized tomorrow."

"Just as Brother Joseph thinks best," replied Mr. Partridge, "I am ready at any time."

He was accordingly baptized the next day (December 11, 1830). (1958, pp. 191–92).

William Smith

"Well," said Brother Briggs, "it is said that Joseph and the rest of the family were lazy and indolent."

"We never heard of such a thing until after Joseph told his vision, [William Smith responded,] and not then by our friends. Whenever the neighbors wanted a good day's work done they knew where they could get a good hand and they were not particular to take any of the other boys before Joseph either. We cleared sixty acres of the heaviest timber I ever saw. We had a good place. We also had on it from twelve to fifteen hundred sugar trees, and to gather the sap and make sugar and molasses from that number of trees was no lazy job. We worked hard to clear our place and the neighbors were a little jealous. If you will figure up how much work it would take to clear sixty acres of heavy timber land, heavier than any here, trees you could not conveniently cut down, you can tell whether we were lazy or not, and Joseph did his share of the work with the rest of the boys.

"We never knew we were bad folks until Joseph told his vision. We were considered respectable till then, but at once people began to circulate falsehoods and stories in a wonderful way" (1891).

Loving Toward Children and Youth

Margarette Burgess

Another time my older brother and I were going to school, near to the building which was known as Joseph's brick store. It had been raining the previous day, causing the ground to be very muddy, especially along that street. My brother Wallace and I both got fast in the mud, and could not get out, and of course, childlike, we began to cry, for we thought we would have to stay there. But looking up, I beheld the loving friend of children, the Prophet Joseph, coming to us. He soon had us on higher and drier ground. Then he stooped down and cleaned the mud from our little, heavy-laden shoes, took his handkerchief from his pocket and wiped our tear-stained faces. He spoke kind and cheering words to us, and sent us on our way to school rejoicing. Was it any wonder that I loved that great, good, and noble man of God? As I grew older I felt to honor and love him, for his mission to earth in restoring the gospel of our Lord and Savior Jesus Christ.

I will relate another incident which occurred. Joseph's wife, Sister Emma, had lost a young babe. My mother having twin baby girls, the Prophet came to see if she would let him have one of them. Of course it was rather against her feelings, but she finally consented for him to take one of them, providing he would bring it home each night. This he did punctually himself, and also came after it each morning. One evening he did not come with it at the usual time, and Mother went down to the mansion to see what was the matter, and there sat the Prophet with the baby wrapped up in a little silk quilt. He was trotting it on his knee, and singing to it to get it quiet before starting out, as it had been fretting. The child soon became quiet when my mother took it, and the Prophet came up home with her. Next morning when he came after the baby, Mother handed him Sarah, the other baby. They looked so much alike that strangers could not tell them apart; but as Mother passed him the other baby he shook his head and said, "This is not my little Mary." Then she took Mary from the cradle and gave her to him, and he smilingly carried her home with him. The baby Mary had a very mild disposition, while Sarah was quite cross and fretful, and by this my mother could distinguish them one from the other, though generally people could not tell them apart. But our Prophet soon knew which was the borrowed baby. After his wife became better in health he did not take our baby anymore, but often came in to caress her and play with her. Both children died in their infancy, before the Prophet was martyred (1892, pp. 66–67).

Evaline B. Johnson

When I was very young my parents moved to Kirtland, Ohio, where we lived on the same block as the Prophet Joseph Smith.

I remember my mother was cleaning house, her quilts were hanging on the line, the bedding was lying on the lawn; there were two or three steps at the front door; it was open. I saw a man as he came up the steps. I was sitting on the floor. He came and picked me up and sat me on his left arm and crossed the room to a large mirror. We both looked into the glass. He then turned and sat me down and asked where father was. When he went out of the room mother called me to her and told me he was the prophet of the Lord, and what a good man he was.

I was then about three years old, but very small for my age. This is the truth as my memory serves me (1906, p. 545).

Lyman O. Littlefield

[During the Zion's Camp march], I was then so very young I was naturally enough not made acquainted with the intricate or minute order in which the camp was organized for traveling; but I remember that they were classed into messes of tens for purposes of cooking, washing our clothing, eating, sleeping, etc. While there the men were paraded outside of the camp for exercise and instruction. This created within me, as I remember, some lonesome reflections. I sat down upon a rock where the men were passing, the better to observe their movements. While thus seated, the Prophet Joseph Smith, who happened to be passing by in quite a hurry, noticed me. He stepped to where I sat alone. It might have been my isolated position that attracted him. I knew not the motive; but that man, who to me appeared so good and so godlike, really halted in his hurry to notice me—only a boy. Placing one of his hands upon my head, he said: "Well, bub, is there no place for you?"

This recognition from the man whom I then knew was a prophet of God created within me a tumult of emotions. I could make him no reply. My young heart was filled with joy to me unspeakable. He passed on and left me in my lonely attitude, for he was then in quite a hurry to accomplish something pertaining to the movements of the men which could not be delayed.

I mention this circumstance as it illustrates a trait of his character, which in after years he has often been seen to exemplify. He was naturally fond of the young—especially little children. He did not like to pass a child, however small, without speaking to it. He has been know to actually cross a street if he saw a child alone on the opposite side, to speak to it or to inquire if it had lost its way (1892c, pp. 108–9).

Joseph H. Moesser

The Prophet Joseph Smith was a frequent visitor at our house. He used to take me on his knee and talk and play with [us] children. My mother would sometimes reprove me for this, but he would say, "I love the children." I saw [him] and his brother after the martyrdom and when they were laid out in the old Mansion House. One of the brethren lifted me up so I could see them, and now at the age of eighty-six years . . . I can remember it as though it was yesterday. I also remember him taking my father and mother and [us] children through the Nauvoo Temple, [and I] remember the oxen that held up the font, then as we went on the top I looked over the railing that was around there. It seemed so far down that I became very frightened (n.d.).

Lucy Meserve Smith

The little children were very much attached to the Prophet, as he used to play with them as one of their equals. Indeed he was loved best by those who were the most acquainted with him. His daughter, Julia, told me that her papa talked to her before he left, and told her to be a good girl; and he particularly enjoined it upon her to never mistreat any of her playmates, and then he should be happy to meet her again. "Oh," said she, "how bad I should feel if I thought I should not be prepared to meet my dear papa!"

My two brothers, Freeborn and David Smith, came to Nauvoo in the fall of 1842. They were very much attached to the Prophet Joseph Smith. My brother David was passing his store one day and he said the man of God ran out, took him by the hand, and said, "God bless you, Brother Smith." He said it made him feel so good to have the prophet of God take so much pains to come out to shake his hand and bless him, he felt it through his whole system (1892, p. 470).

Charles H. Stoddard

As a boy [Charles Stoddard] was employed by the Prophet Joseph Smith, in Nauvoo, Illinois. While the Prophet was in hiding, he carried food to the Prophet and delivered messages to and from the Prophet. The

Prophet trusted him implicitly. Upon one occasion, when in the street fixing a kite with other boys, a man came up and inquired where the Prophet was, to which Charles replied, "He went to heaven on Hyrum's white horse, and we are fixing this kite to send his dinner to him." No one suspected his important duties because of his youth.

While employed by the Prophet Joseph, William Law requested Charles to come and work for him. He did not want to. After consulting with the Prophet, he decided to do so. During his employment with William Law, many private matters were talked of by Law and his associates in the presence of the boy, without any hesitation, perhaps thinking that the boy would not pay any attention to what was said. The boy was nevertheless on the alert and took full cognizance of what was going on.

Upon retiring one evening, in a lean-to attached to a building which was partly vacant and partly used for storage purposes, the lad was awakened by conversation being held in the vacant portions of the building. This building was a rendezvous of the bitter apostates and enemies of the Prophet, among whom was William Law, who seemed to be a ringleader. The lad listened through a hole in the leg structure through which light was also emerging, and learned that these men were plotting against the Prophet's life. He heard Law tell this group of apostates that he would have Charles clean, oil, and load his gun, which was one of his regular duties. After the group had disbanded and had all left the building, the lad dressed and hurried to the home of the Prophet and told him all that he had seen and heard and asked the Prophet what he should do. The Prophet told him to return and act as nothing had happened, and to do as his employer requested, and admonished him to load the gun well. He told the boy that they could not hurt him until his time had arrived. The boy did as requested. The next morning Mr. Law requested him to clean, oil, and load his six-shooter, which was faithfully done as the Prophet advised. When the opportune time arrived, Law aimed the revolver at the Prophet with the intention of killing him. He pulled the trigger but the gun misfired as did all of the other five loads in the six-shooter. He cursed because the gun did not discharge, and blamed the boy for not loading the weapon properly. The boy replied that he had done it to the best of his ability. Law then aimed at a post and all six loads were discharged. (1949, p. 1).

Loving Toward the Saints

Jesse Hale

[In a letter:] I have received favors from you [i.e., Emma Smith] which I believe were bestowed from the pure motive of regard and friendship. I shall not soon forget them neither shall I forget the very friendly visit we received from Joseph Smith and his family one year ago last summer. The lively interest your husband manifested at that time in our welfare by voluntarily offering to let me have money to enter land and save our improvements when the land should come into market evinced a friendship unexpected and his memory will long be cherished (1845).

Mary Ellen Kimball

I first met the Prophet in the fall of 1843, at meeting, on the temple ground. I believed him to be a true prophet of God, and have never had a doubt, but feel more positive daily. I heard him preach often, and was highly gratified with his teaching.

I was never intimately acquainted with him, as our family lived five miles out of the city of Nauvoo, that is my mother and stepfather, Joseph Dunlap. But I spent a part of my time in the city at the house of Sister Clawson, mother of Bishop Hyrum Clawson.

The last time I saw the Prophet he was on his way to Carthage Jail. Himself and his brother Hyrum were on horseback, also Brothers John Taylor and Willard Richards. They stopped opposite Sister Clawson's house, at the house of Brother Rosecrans. We were on the porch. The streets of Nauvoo were narrow, and we could hear every word he said. He asked for a drink of water. They all took a drink. Some few remarks passed between them which I do not remember; but one sentence I well remember: after bidding good-bye, he said to Brother Rosecrans, "if I never see you again, or if I *never come back,* remember that I love you." This went through me like electricity. I went in the house and threw myself on the bed and wept like a whipped child. And why this grief for a person I had never spoken to in my life, I could not tell. I knew he was a servant of God, and only think of the danger he was in! and how deeply he felt it, for I could see that he looked pale!

But what could I do—only pour out my soul in fervent prayer to our

Father that He would take him under His kind care and protection as He had hitherto done; for in over thirty cases, he, the Prophet, had been liberated and set free, and why not as this time? But his enemies had ripened in wickedness and he in goodness (1892).

James Leech

After arriving in Nauvoo [circa late May or early June 1841] we were five or six weeks looking for employment, but failed to get any. One morning I said to my brother-in-law, "Let us go and see the Prophet. I feel that he will give us something to do." He considered a short time, then consented to go. On arriving at his house we inquired for the Prophet. We were told he was over the road. So we went over, and found him in a little store selling a lady some goods. This was the first time I had had an opportunity to be near him and get a good look at him. I felt there was a superior spirit in him. He was different to anyone I had ever met before; and I said in my heart, he is truly a prophet of the most high God.

As I was not a member of the Church I wanted Henry [Nightengale, my companion,] to ask him for work, but he did not do so, so I had to. I said, "Mr. Smith, if you please, have you any employment you could give us both, so we can get some provisions?"

He viewed us with a cheerful countenance, and with such a feeling of kindness said, "Well, boys, what can you do?"

We told him what our employment was before we left our native land.

Said he, "Can you make a ditch?"

I replied we would do the best we could at it.

"That's right, boys," and picking up a tape line he said, "Come along with me."

He took us a few rods from the store, gave me the ring to hold, and stretched all the tape from the reel and marked a line for us to work by.

"Now, boys," said he, "can you make a ditch three feet wide and two and a half feet deep along this line?"

We said we would do our best, and he left us. We went to work, and when it was finished I went and told him it was done.

He came and looked at it and said, "Boys, if I had done it myself it could not have been done better. Now come with me."

He led the way back to his store, and told us to pick the best ham or piece of pork for ourselves. Being rather bashful, I said we would rather he would give us some. So he picked two of the largest and best pieces of meat and a sack of flour for each of us, and asked us if that would do. We told him we would be willing to do more work for it, but he said, "If you are satisfied, boys, I am."

We thanked him kindly, and went on our way home rejoicing in the kindheartedness of the prophet of our God.

In November of the same year I was baptized into the Church, and from that time until the martyrdom of our prophet, I often had the privilege of seeing his noble face lit up by the Spirit and power of God, as he taught the Saints the principles of eternal life (1892, pp. 152–53).

Catherine T. Leishman

We all ate breakfast at the [Nauvoo] landing, but father said he would fast until he had seen the Prophet Joseph, to whose place he started. When within two blocks of the house the Prophet, seeing father, crossed the street and gave his hand saying, "How are you, Brother?" Father saying, "I do not know you," the Prophet then said, "I am the man you are looking for," all the time holding father's hand. Father then put a piece of gold in the Prophet's hand. Joseph said, "God bless you, brother, you shall never want for bread." He never did. The Prophet then said, "Bring your family down to my house," but father, thanking him, said that owing to our long journey I must first get a place where we can set ourselves in order.

Then the Prophet told him he had an empty house, which father rented at once. We remained at the Prophet's house until we bought a home of our own, near where the Prophet lived. All of these things were a strong testimony to my father which lasted him until his death in September 1867, aged eighty-seven years.

Once while Father was building a storehouse for the purpose of merchandizing, the Prophet said, "Brother, I fear you are building too extensive," which proved to be true, for trouble soon began. The Saints were persecuted and driven, and our store and nearly all of our possessions were left behind (n.d., pp. 1–3).

Mary Elizabeth Rollins Lightner

One morning [circa 1831] Joseph came while we were eating breakfast of cold mush. It was after we had lost most of our things and we were very poor; but my stepfather liked cold mush so [he] had told Mother not to fix anything else. When Joseph came in, Mother and I looked at each other and must have shown it for he asked for some, first saying "Brother Burk, that mush looks good. I like mush." Of course he was asked to have some. He ate heartily but we thought he did it to lessen our embarrassment (1936, p. 4).

Mentally Quick and Alert

Josiah Quincy

"General Smith," said Dr. Goforth, when we had adjourned to the green in front of the tavern, "I think Mr. Quincy would like to hear you preach." "Then I shall be happy to do so," was the obliging reply; and, mounting the broad step which led from the house, the Prophet promptly addressed a sermon to the little group about him. Our numbers were constantly increased from the passers in the street, and a most attentive audience of more than a hundred persons soon hung upon every word of the speaker. The text was Mark 16:15, and the comments, though rambling and disconnected, were delivered with the fluency and fervor of a camp-meeting orator. The discourse was interrupted several times by the Methodist minister before referred to, who thought it incumbent upon him to question the soundness of certain theological positions maintained by the speaker. One specimen of the sparring which ensued I thought worth setting down. The prophet is asserting that baptism for the remission of sins is essential for salvation. *Minister.* Stop! What do you say to the case of the penitent thief? *Prophet.* What do you mean by that? *Minister.* You know our Savior said to the thief, "This day shalt thou be with me in Paradise," which shows he could not have been baptized before his admission. *Prophet.* How do you know he wasn't baptized before he became a thief? At this retort the sort of laugh that is provoked by an unexpected hit ran through the audience; but this demonstration of sympathy was rebuked by a severe look from Smith, who went on to say: "But that is not the true answer. In the original Greek, as this gentleman (turning to me) will inform you, the word that has been translated paradise means simply a place of departed spirits. To that place the penitent thief was conveyed, and there, doubtless, he received the baptism necessary for his admission to the heavenly kingdom." The other objections of his antagonist were parried with a similar adroitness, and in about fifteen minutes the Prophet concluded a sermon which it was evident that his disciples had heard with the heartiest satisfaction.

In the afternoon we drove to visit the farms upon the prairie which this enterprising people had enclosed and were cultivating with every appearance of success. On returning, we stopped in a beautiful grove, where there were seats and a platform for speaking. "When the weather permits," said Smith, "we hold our services in this place; but shall cease to do so when the temple is finished." "I suppose none but Mormon preachers are allowed in Nauvoo," said the Methodist minister, who had accompanied our expedition. "On the contrary," replied the Prophet, "I shall be very happy to have you address my people next Sunday, and I will insure you a most attentive congregation." "What! do you mean that I may say anything I please and that you will make no reply?" "You may certainly say anything you please; but I must reserve the right of adding a word or two, if I judge best. I promise to speak of you in the most respectful manner." As we rode back, there was more dispute between the minister and Smith. "Come," said the latter, suddenly slapping his antagonist on the knee, to emphasize the production of a triumphant text, "if you can't argue better than that, you shall say all you want to say to my people, and I will promise to hold my tongue, for there's not a Mormon among them who would need my assistance to answer you." Some backthrust was evidently required to pay for this; and the minister, soon after, having occasion to allude to some erroneous doctrine which I forget, suddenly exclaimed, "Why, I told my congregation the other Sunday that they might as well believe Joe Smith as such theology as that." "Did you say Joe Smith in a sermon?" inquired the person to whom the title had been applied. "Of course I did. Why not?" The Prophet's reply was given with a quiet superiority that was overwhelming: "Considering only the day and the place, it would have been more respectful to have said Lieutenant-General Joseph Smith." Clearly, the worthy minister was no match for the head of the Mormon Church (1883, pp. 391–92).

Note: While the Prophet was intellectually quick and perceptive, some of what Quincy records is clearly faulty, for the Prophet never taught that baptisms could be performed in the world of the spirits, as Quincy quotes him as having suggested.

Open and Approachable

WILLIAM A. HICKMAN

I spent a year in Hancock County and then went to Nauvoo and stayed another year, then moved back to the country and stayed until the spring of 1844. Going to Nauvoo frequently, I heard Joseph Smith several times. I considered his preaching Bible doctrine. I heard him speak of the United States government several times, which he always did in the highest terms. I heard him say once in a public audience that the Constitution of the United States was part of his religion and a good part, too. He said we were a cried-down people and misrepresented, but should there come war in his day, he would show to the people who was true and loyal to their government. Said he, "I would call on the able-bodied men and go at their head and the world should know what we could do." Such assertions were often made by him. He said that he was satisfied there would be war in which the United States would be engaged, but he did not expect to live to see it. Now, said he, "Brethren and friends if any of you have anything against me, come and tell me, and I will make it right. Do not be backward. Come publicly or privately and see if I do not satisfy you, or anyone that has anything against me" (n.d., p. 2).

Patient in Shouldering Burdens

EMILY PARTRIDGE YOUNG

My soul is harrowed up when I let my mind revert back to those days of sorrow and persecution that followed the Prophet Joseph all his life. His troubles at home were more sad and harder to bear than all the troubles that could be heaped upon him by outside.

I was intimately acquainted with him for several years. More acquainted with his home life than with his public—or rather, his private life outside of his home. I have known him to come in with his head bowed. He would walk the floor back and forth, with his hands clasped behind him (a way he had of placing his hands when his mind was deeply troubled), his countenance showing that he was weighed down with some terrible burden. Many times my heart has ached for him. He did not often speak to his family of his outside troubles.

Joseph was a prophet of God, and a friend of man. His was a noble character. All who knew him can testify to that assertion. He was all that the word *gentleman* would imply—pure in heart, always striving for right, upholding innocence, and battling for the good of all (1897).

Persevering

BRIGHAM YOUNG

I started from Kirtland on a mission to the east, accompanying the Prophet Joseph, his brother Hyrum, David W. Patten, Sidney Rigdon, and Thomas B. Marsh on their way to Canada. When we arrived at Painesville, the Prophet was arrested by an officer for some pretended debt. Joseph immediately entered into trial before the court, which found no cause of action. After his release he was again arrested and brought before the court, when he was again dismissed. He was arrested the third time, and on examination was held over to trial. Brother Anson Call, who had lately joined the Church, stepped forward and proffered to become his bail.

The sheriff, who was personally acquainted with Brother Call, took him to one side and advised him strongly against being bail for the Prophet, asserting the Prophet would be sure to abscond, and he would lose his farm; but Brother Call willingly became his bail. On being released [Joseph] was arrested a fourth time, for a debt of a few dollars, which was paid forthwith, and the fifth time he was arrested, which cause was soon disposed of, and he concluded to return to Kirtland for the night. As he got into his buggy, an officer also jumped in, and catching the lines with one hand, put his other hand on Joseph's shoulder and said, "Mr. Smith, you are my prisoner."

Joseph inquired what was the cause of action. The officer informed him that a gentleman, a few months previous, had left a stove with him, for the price of which he was sued. Brother Joseph replied, "I never wished to purchase the stove, but the gentleman insisted on putting it up in my house, saying it would bring him custom." Joseph left his watch and other property in security, and we returned home to Kirtland.

Next day we started again, and traveled by land as far as Ashtabula, shunning Painesville and other places where we suspected our enemies were laying in wait to annoy Joseph. We tarried in Ashtabula through the day, wandering over the bluffs, through the woods, and on the beach of the lake, bathing ourselves in her beautiful waters, until evening, when a steamboat arrived from the west. We went on board and took passage for Buffalo. I gave the Prophet my valise for a pillow, and I took his boots for mine, and we all laid down on the deck of the vessel for the night.

We arrived in Buffalo early the next morning. Joseph and the brethren proceeded to Canada (1968, pp. 17–18).

Playful and Fun-Loving

Mosiah Hancock

This summer I played my first game of ball with the Prophet. We took turns knocking and chasing the ball, and when the game was over the Prophet said, "Brethren, hitch up your teams"; which we did, and we all drove to the woods. I drove our one-horse wagon standing on the front bolster, and Brother Joseph and father rode on the hounds behind. There were thirty-nine teams in the group and we gathered wood until our wagons were loaded. When our wagon was loaded, Brother Joseph offered to pull sticks with anyone—and he pulled them all up one at a time—with anyone who wanted to compete with him. Afterwards, the Prophet sent the wagons out to different places of people who needed help; and he told them to cut the wood for the Saints who needed it. Everybody loved to do as the Prophet said, even though we were sickly, and death was all around us, folks smiled and tried to cheer everyone up (n.d., pp. 22–23).

James W. Phippen

I have seen him on the playground with "the boys," as he called them, ball playing, wrestling, jumping, and helping to roll up logs on buildings for the widows. I have seen him in public and in private talking with the Saints on various occasions, so kind, so charitable, a prophet in very deed, so noble in appearance. He loved the Saints. He was willing to suffer for them and die if necessary. Old members of the Church never tire of talking of Joseph, what he said and did. May his memory be fresh in their minds forever and with the children of the Saints (1906, p. 540; see also Lucy D. Allen, 1906, p. 538).

Edward Stevenson

I have often seen the Prophet indulge in a game of checkers. He was cheerful—often wrestling with Sidney Rigdon. One time he had his pants torn badly, but had a good laugh over it. In Missouri, when mob forces oppressed the Saints, we were encamped in Adam-ondi-Ahman, mostly around campfires without tents. One night the snow fell four or five inches. The Prophet, seeing our forlorn condition, called on us to form into two parties—Lyman Wight at the head of one line and he (Joseph) heading the other line—to have a sham battle. The weapons were snowballs. We set to with a will full of glee and fun (1974, p. 86).

Positive in Nature

Heber C. Kimball

Now let us go to work, every one of us, and pull together, and put means into the hands of the Trustee-in-trust, pay up our tithing, and then if we have a surplus which we do not want to put out to usury now, put it in the hands of the Trustee-in-trust. Go to work, not only next spring, but now make preparations, and let us build a temple. What say you? I do not want you to say yes, unless you calculate to do it, but, as Brother Joseph used to say, "Yankee doodle do it." Now go to work, and do the thing right up, and when next fall comes to pass, let us see the walls of the temple erected, and the roof on it. What say you? (JD, 1:357).

George A. Smith

Cousin Joseph [Smith] came to see me. I told him I was almost discouraged, being afraid that my joints would be drawn out. He told me I should never get discouraged, whatever difficulties might surround me. If I were sunk into the lowest pit of Nova Scotia and all the Rocky Mountains piled on top of me I ought not to be discouraged, but hang on, exercise faith, and keep up good courage, and I should come out on top of the heap (n.d., p. 36).

Quick to Bless Others

Benjamin F. Johnson

About the middle of October [1839] a letter came to say that my dear mother and young sister were apparently near to death, in Springfield, Illinois, and were anxious for my return. And in my anxiety again to see my mother, I procured quinine, which was just becoming known as an antidote for fevers and, taking it in large doses, my fever soon abated, and under its tonic influence I fancied I had become well, and in joy and hope hastened preparation to start [for] the house of my mother and kindred at Springfield. My horse was in the yard ready to mount, but I wished to take leave of the Prophet, with the hope again to receive his blessing. Of the whole sum I had obtained with which to pay for an outfit and passage to England, with the twelve, when they should start, to which I had been called by the June Conference at Quincy, I had but one ten dollar bill, I said, "As this is all I have left, I want to pay a tithe of it." He saw I was weak in body and that my heart was sad in leaving him, so thinking to cheer and arouse me, when putting the nine silver dollars in my hand he playfully knocked my hand upward, and scattering the money all over the room. My heart was so full of tears, and my emotions must have vent, so forgetting all but the feeling that we were boy companions playing together, I sprang at and grappled him, as though to teach him a lesson, but the lesson was all to me, for on making one grand effort to throw him, I found myself in strength no more than a bulrush as compared with him, and as my strength was fictitious and my real recovery was but illusion, collapsed and fainted in his arms. He placed me in repose, and did all necessary for my restoration and comfort. Then gathering up the scattered money, and after a period of delay, weak, trembling, and desolate, yet determined to start, I led my horse to the other gate and as I was passing through, with the bridle on my arm, his hand detained me, and placing his hands upon my head, he seemed to pour out his soul in blessing me. He told the Lord I had been faithful to care for others, that I was now worn and sick, and that on my journey I would need his care, and he asked that a special guardian might go with me from that day and stay with me through all my life. And oh! my dear brother, how often have I seen through life [the] footprints of that angel, and knew that his hand had drawn me back from death (1903).

Mary Elizabeth Rollins Lightner

Before or about the time I finished the last chapter [of the Book of Mormon], the Prophet Joseph Smith arrived in Kirtland, and moved into a part of Newel K. Whitney's house (Uncle Algernon's partner in the Mercantile Business), while waiting for his goods to be put in order. Brother Whitney brought the Prophet Joseph to our house and introduced him to the older ones of the family. (I was not in at the time.) In looking around he saw the Book of Mormon on the shelf, and asked how that book came to be there. He said, "I sent that book to Brother Morley." Uncle told him how his niece had obtained it. He asked, "Where is your niece?" I was sent for; when he saw me he looked at me so earnestly, I felt almost afraid. After a moment or two he came and put his hands on my head and gave me a great blessing, the first I ever received, and made me a present of the book, and said he would give Brother Morley another. He came in time to rebuke the evil spirits, and set the church in order. We all felt that he was a man of God, for he spoke with power, and as one having authority in very deed (1926, pp. 194–95).

Witty, with Good Humor

Caroline S. Callister

[Caroline] was very intimate with the Prophet's family, often staying there several days at a time. Her mother was a very fleshy woman. One day the Prophet came to this house and said he believed he weighed as much as aunt Clarissa but when they were weighed she weighed the most. He went in the house and got a piece of bread and butter in each hand, then he got on the scales and said, "Come down, come down" (n.d.).

Mary I. Horne

Brother Joseph and several of the brethren came to Quincy. They came to [my] house, partook of refreshments and scattered. Brother Joseph was in the best of spirits. He said laughingly: "Sister Horne, if I had a wife as small as you, when trouble came I would put her in my pocket and run" (1982, p. 64).

Benjamin F. Johnson

The Prophet often came to our town, but after my arrival, he lodged in no house but mine, and I was proud of his partiality and took great delight in his society and friendship. When with us, there was no lack of amusement; for with jokes, games, etc., he was always ready to provoke merriment, one phase of which was matching couplets in rhyme, by which we were at times in rivalry; and his fraternal feeling, in great degree did away with the disparity of age or greatness of his calling (1947, p. 92).

Heber C. Kimball

Heber's first visit to Commerce was on Sunday, the 12th of May [1839]. On the 25th he again went up the river, with several others of the Twelve, and spent the day in council with Joseph and the brethren. While on the water, standing by the railing of the boat, gazing in admiration at the beautiful site of Nauvoo, Heber observed: "It is a very pretty place, but not a long abiding home for the Saints."

This remark was carried to the ears of Elder Rigdon and his family, who were comfortably quartered in a nice stone house built by Dr. Isaac Galland, from whom the Saints had purchased some of their lands. Heber's reputation as a prophet was by this time pretty well established in Israel, and Sidney who had had about as much persecution as he could stand, and was in nowise hankering after a repetition of the Missouri scenes, was considerably alarmed at his words, dreading their prophetic potency. At the council, which was held at the house of the Prophet Joseph, Sidney remarked that he had some feelings against Elder Kimball, and then, referring to the prediction of the latter in relation to the city of the Saints, said, petulantly:

"I should suppose that Elder Kimball had passed through sufferings and privations and mobbings and drivings enough, to learn to prophesy good concerning Israel."

With a mixture of meekness and humor, Heber replied:

"President Rigdon, I'll prophesy good concerning you all the time—if you can get it."

The retort amused Joseph, who laughed heartily with the brethren, and Elder Rigdon yielded the point (1945, pp. 256–57).

Susan Martineau

As a child I often saw the Prophet in the Sunday meetings in the [Kirtland] temple, and also at the house of my father, Joel H. Johnson, but my more distinct recollections begin about 1841, when we lived in Ramus, afterward named Macedonia, about twenty miles from Nauvoo, where father was presiding elder. The Prophet frequently came to our house and sometimes stayed overnight. On one occasion Joseph, with Heber C. Kimball, Jedediah M. Grant, and some others from Nauvoo, whose names I do not now remember, partook of a Christmas dinner at my father's, and standing at the head of the table, carved the turkey. Fearing that his clothing might accidentally be soiled, my stepmother, Susan Bryant Johnson, tied a long apron upon him. He laughed and said it was well, for he did not know what might happen to him. My brother Seth and I were in the room, admiring, in our childish way, him whom we thought the greatest man on earth (1906, p. 541).

Frederic G. Mather

Smith was in the habit of announcing from his lofty pulpit, "The truth is good enough without dressing up, but Brother Rigdon will now proceed to dress it up" (1880, p. 210).

Daniel D. McArthur

When he first spoke to me I was in the woods, about half a mile south of Kirtland. He was on his horse and I was chopping wood. Said he, "Good afternoon." I returned the compliment. He had a smile on his face, and I felt that he was going to say something else. "You are not the young man who sold his wife for a bull-eye watch the other day, are you?" he asked. I replied, "No, sir," and he went on laughing. There was a man who had sold his wife for a bull-eye watch a day or two before, and there was quite a talk about it in the neighborhood, so I suppose he thought he would have a little fun with me (1892, pp. 128–29).

George C. Riser

Joseph and Elder Orson Hyde, who had then lately returned from Jerusalem, called into the adjoining rooms where a Brother Albert Brown and a Sister Knight (wife of Bishop Vinson Knight) lived. The door being left open, I could hear the conversation. Elder Hyde spoke of some things relative to his mission—said that while in company with some of the leading Jews they became somewhat merry: exhilarated, drinking wine, and smoking. They said to him, "Mr. Hyde, [we'd] be damned if we won't do anything you may tell us." Brother Joseph told Brother Hyde that that was the time he ought to have gathered the Jews. The jocose conversation so contrary to my notions of the character of a prophet and saints caused me to think soberly; but upon reflection I could not think of anything they had said but what was innocent, and I felt that a prophet had a right to enjoy himself innocently as well as any other person (n.d.).

Edwin Rushton

On or about the 6th of May 1843 a grand review of the Nauvoo Legion was held in Nauvoo. The Prophet Joseph Smith complimented them for the good discipline and evolutions performed. The weather being hot, he called for a glass of water. With the glass in his hand he said, "I will drink you a toast, to the overthrow of the mobocrats," which he did in language as follows:

"Here's wishing they were in the middle of the sea in a stone canoe, with iron paddles, and a shark swallow the canoe, and the devil swallow the shark, and him locked up in the northwest corner of hell, the key lost, and a blind man looking for it" (n.d.).

Mary Ann Winters

Brothers Joseph and Hyrum and a large company of people were at the landing to meet us [when we arrived at Nauvoo]. Brother Pratt had introduced him to the company, and a general handshaking followed with the friends who had come to take them to their various homes and destinations. Then Brother Joseph came on the boat and into the cabin where our family were. After cordial greetings, he took a seat, and taking the little boys, Parley and Nathan, upon his knees, seemed much affected, Brother Pratt remarking, "We took away three children and have brought back five." Then Brother Joseph said, "Well, well, Brother Parley, you have returned bringing your sheaves with you," the tears streaming down his face.

Brother Pratt, seeing the general emotion this caused, said, in a tender, jesting fashion, "Why, Brother Smith, if you feel so bad about our coming home, I guess we will have to go back again," tears of joy filling his own eyes. This broke the spell—smiles returned, and joy unbounded filled every heart. It was indeed a time of rejoicing, that two boat loads of Saints had arrived in one day.

Brother Joseph arose saying, "Come, Brother Parley, bring your folks right up to my house; it is only a little way, and you can be more comfortable after your long journey." My mother was placed in a big chair, and Brother Hodge, with others of Brother Joseph's bodyguard, carried her up to the Mansion, Brother Pratt carrying the baby—the rest of us following along, listening to all that Brother Joseph had to say. Some of our friends insisted on having part of our family, so Aunt Olive and we children were taken up to Mother Sessions, where she nursed us up to good health again—the little ones that were not quite over the effects of the measles—and I had chills and fever while on the boat (1916b, p. 577).

The Prophetic Character of Joseph Smith

Behavior As a Prophet

Edward Stevenson

Twelve days after the Prophet escaped from Missouri, a general conference of the Church was held at Quincy, Illinois. His soul was filled with emotion, and it seemed as though he could not utter his feelings, only with a flood of tears. He looked calm, however, and a halo of brightness hovered about him. He was of a tender heart, as well as of a stern and firm disposition when occasion required it. I have known the Prophet to weep with tender affection, and have seen him with his sword drawn, as a military officer, when he was mighty as well as powerful.

After the Prophet had looked over the congregation, he said, "To look over this congregation of Latter-day Saints who have been driven from their homes and are still in good faith, without homes, as pilgrims in a strange land, and to realize that my life has been spared to behold your faces again, seemed to be so great a pleasure that words were only a vague expression of my soul's gratitude."

I have heard the Prophet say that he did not claim perfection, but possessed human weaknesses. He said, "When I speak as a man it is Joseph only that speaks. But when the Lord speaks through me, it is no more Joseph Smith who speaks; but it is God, and let all Israel hear" (1974, pp. 86–87).

Corrected Others

Benjamin Ashby

While in Nauvoo I was living so near to Joseph Smith that I was enabled to see him in his daily life as well as in his public administrations, though at this time his life was sought, and considerable of his time was spent in seclusion to avoid his enemies. Like all boys I used to play in the streets. He once spoke to me, giving me an invitation to make less noise. It was in front of his house and he was setting out in the porch talking to some gentleman and I presume, I disturbed them (n.d. [a], p. 8).

Parley P. Pratt

In one of those tedious nights we had lain as if in sleep till the hour of midnight had passed, and our ears and hearts had been pained, while we had listened for hours to the obscene jests, the horrid oaths, the dreadful blasphemies, and filthy language of our guards, Colonel Price at their head, as they recounted to each other their deeds of rapine, murder, robbery, etc., which they had committed among the "Mormons" while at Far West and vicinity. They even boasted of defiling by force wives, daughters, and virgins, and of shooting or dashing out the brains of men, women, and children.

I had listened till I became so disgusted, shocked, horrified, and so filled with the spirit of indignant justice that I could scarcely refrain from rising upon my feet and rebuking the guards; but had said nothing to Joseph, or anyone else, although I lay next to him and knew he was awake. On a sudden he arose to his feet, and spoke in a voice of thunder, as the roaring lion, uttering, as near as I can recollect, the following words:

"SILENCE, ye fiends of the infernal pit. In the name of Jesus Christ I rebuke you, and command you to be still; I will not live another minute and bear such language. Cease such talk, or you or I die THIS INSTANT!"

He ceased to speak. He stood erect in terrible majesty. Chained, and without a weapon; calm, unruffled, and dignified as an angel, he looked upon the quailing guards, whose weapons were lowered or dropped to the ground; whose knees smote together, and who, shrinking into a corner, or crouching at his feet, begged his pardon, and remained quiet till a change of guards.

I have seen the ministers of justice, clothed in magisterial robes, and criminals arraigned before them, while life was suspended on a breath, in the courts of England; I have witnessed a Congress in solemn session to give laws to nations; I have tried to conceive of kings, of royal courts, of thrones and crowns; and of emperors assembled to decide the fate of kingdoms; but dignity and majesty have I seen but once, as it stood in chains, at midnight, in a dungeon in an obscure village of Missouri (1985, pp. 179–80).

Joseph Smith

Martin Harris having boasted to the brethren that he could handle snakes with perfect safety, while fooling with a black snake with his bare feet, he received a bite on his left foot. The fact was communicated to me, and I took occasion to reprove him, and exhort the brethren never to trifle with the promises of God. I told them it was presumption for any one to provoke a serpent to bite him, but if a man of God was accidentally bitten by a poisonous serpent, he might have faith, or his brethren might have faith for him, so that the Lord would hear his prayer and he might be healed; but when a man designedly provokes a serpent to bite him, the principle is the same as when a man drinks deadly poison knowing it to be such. In that case no man has any claim on the promises of God to be healed (HC, 2:95–96).

Joseph Smith

Spent the forenoon in reading. About twelve o'clock a number of young persons called to see the Egyptian records. My scribe exhibited them. One of the young ladies who had been examining them was asked if they had the appearance of antiquity. She observed, with an air of contempt, that they had not. On hearing this, I was surprised at the ignorance she displayed, and I observed to her that she was an anomaly in creation, for all the wise and learned that had examined them, without hesitation pronounced them ancient. I further remarked that it was downright wickedness, ignorance, bigotry, and superstition had caused her to make the remark; and that I would put it on record. And I have done so, because it is a fair sample of the prevailing spirit of the times, showing that the victims of priestcraft and superstition would not believe though one should rise from the dead (HC, 2:329–30).

Joseph Smith

Elder William O. Clark preached about two hours, reproving the Saints for a lack of sanctity, and a want of holy living, enjoining sanctity, solemnity, and temperance in the extreme, in the rigid sectarian style.

I reproved him as Pharisaical and hypocritical and not edifying the people; and showed the Saints what temperance, faith, virtue, charity, and truth were. I charged the Saints not to follow the example of the adversary in accusing the brethren, and said, "If you do not accuse each other, God will not accuse you. If you have no accuser you will enter heaven, and if you will follow the revelations and instructions which God gives you through me, I will take you into heaven as my back load. If you will not accuse me, I will not accuse you. If you will throw a cloak of charity over my sins, I will over yours—for charity covereth a multitude of sins. What many people call sin is not sin; I do many things to break down superstition, and I will break it down;" I referred to the curse of Ham for laughing at Noah, while in his wine, but doing no harm. Noah was a righteous man, and yet he drank wine and became intoxicated; the Lord did not forsake him in consequence thereof, for he retained all the power of his priesthood, and when he was accused by Canaan, he cursed him by the priesthood which he held, and the Lord had respect to his word, and the priesthood which he held, notwithstanding he was drunk (HC, 4:445).

Joseph Smith

Last night, Arthur Milliken had a number of books stolen, and found them this afternoon in Brother Hyrum's hayloft. Two boys, Thomas Morgan and Robert Taylor, were arrested on suspicion and brought before me for examination. After a brief investigation, the court adjourned until ten o'clock tomorrow morning.

While the court was in session, I saw two boys fighting in the street, near Mills' Tavern. I left the business of the court, ran over immediately, caught one of the boys (who had begun the fight with clubs,) and then the other; and, after giving them proper instruction, I gave the bystanders a lecture for not interfering in such cases, and told them to quell all disturbances in the street at the first onset. I returned to the court, and told them that nobody was allowed to fight in Nauvoo but myself (HC, 5:282; see also Lyon, 1977–78, p. 144).

Joseph Smith

At ten A.M. went to meeting. Heard Elder Orson Hyde preach, comparing the sectarian preachers to crows living on carrion, as they were more fond of lies about the Saints than the truth. Alluding to the coming of the Savior, he said, "When He shall appear, we shall be like Him, &c. He will appear on a white horse as a warrior, and maybe we shall have some of the same spirit. Our God is a warrior. (John 14:23.) It is our privilege to have the Father and Son dwelling in our hearts, &c."

We dined with my sister Sophronia McCleary, when I told Elder Hyde that I was going to offer some corrections to his sermon this morning. He replied, "They shall be thankfully received" (HC, 5:323).

Brigham Young

Brother Hyde was upon this same theory once, and in conversation with Brother Joseph Smith advanced the idea that eternity or boundless space was filled with the Spirit of God, or the Holy Ghost. After portraying his views upon that theory very carefully and minutely, he asked Brother Joseph what he thought of it? He replied that it appeared very beautiful, and that he did not know of but one serious objection to it. Says Brother Hyde, "What is that?" Joseph replied, "it is not true" (JD, 4:266; see also Wilford Woodruff, CD, 2:60, 85).

Counsel Was Prophetic and Inspired

John L. Butler

I concluded to ride over to Far West some fourteen miles from where we lived and I saw Brother Joseph Smith. He resided there. He asked me if I had removed my family. I told him no, I had not. "Then," said he, "go and move them directly and do not sleep another night there." "But," said I, "I don't like to be a coward." "Go and do as I tell you," said he. So I started back again and got home about two hours after dark. I then said to my wife, "We must pack up our things and leave here directly, for Brother Joseph has told me to." My wife was very glad for she had been wanting to move for a long time. So we loaded up one wagon load and took it down to Brother Taylor's about one mile and a half and my wife and Malinda Porter, a young woman that was boarding with us, who was keeping school. They packed up another wagon load by the time I got back and we all started off just about the break of day.

Now about sunrise, or a little while after, Brother Gee saw in the distance a large body of men. He said that he thought there was about thirty-odd. He watched them come toward the house and surround it. He then ran down to Taylor to tell them that we were all killed, I suppose, and when he saw us, he said, "Oh, I am so glad that you are here for there are about thirty men around your house to kill you all." I then saw the hand of the Lord guiding Brother Joseph Smith to direct me to move my family away. If he had not, why in all probability we should all have been murdered, and I felt to thank God with all my heart and soul (1993).

Introspective and Humble

Jesse W. Crosby

Bro. Crosby told us he went one day with a sister to the Prophet. She had a charge to make against one of the brethren for scandal. When her complaint had been heard the Prophet asked her if she was quite sure that what the brother had said of her was utterly untrue. She was quite sure that it was. He then told her to think no more about it, for it could not harm her. If untrue it could not live for nothing, but the truth will survive. Still, she felt she should have some redress. Then he offered her his method for dealing with such cases for himself. When an enemy had told a scandalous story about him, which had often been done, before he rendered judgment he paused and let his mind run back to the time and place of setting of the story to see if he had not by some unguarded word or act laid the block on which the story was built. If he found he had done so, he said that then in his heart he forgave his enemy, and felt thankful that he had received warning of a weakness that he had not known he possessed. Then he said to the sister that he would have her to do the same: search her memory thoroughly and see if she had not herself all unconsciously laid the foundation for the scandal that annoyed her. Brother Crosby said the sister thought deeply for a few moments and then confessed that she believed that she had. Then the Prophet told her that in her heart she could forgive that brother who had risked his own good name and her friendship to give her this clearer view of herself. The sister, Brother Crosby said, thanked her advisor and went away in peace (n.d. [b]).

"Like unto Other Men"

JOHN LOVELL

John went to see the Prophet at Mr. Lawrence's home. When he first saw the Prophet he was telling how he obtained his horse in Kirtland, Ohio. The other brethren were washing and blacking their shoes. In his journal, John says: "I had been brought up so strict to the religion of the day that I thought it impossible for a prophet to talk about horse trades on Sunday. But their preaching overbalanced any bad effects this may have made" (n.d., p. 3).

JOHN OAKLEY

When we arrived at Nauvoo, Brother Joseph Smith invited us to the upper room of the Public Store. He shook hands with us and informed us that his enemies had been hunting him. He greeted us warmly and told us that we must not look for perfection in him. If we did he would look for perfection in us (n.d.).

PARLEY P. PRATT

Some of the neighboring citizens visited us next morning—it being Sunday. One of the ladies came up and very candidly inquired of the troops which of the prisoners the "Mormons" worshipped? One of the guards pointing to Mr. Smith with a significant smile, said, "This is he." The woman, then turning to Mr. Smith, inquired whether he professed to be the Lord and Savior?

Do not smile, gentle reader, at the ignorance of these poor innocent creatures, who, by the exertions of a corrupt press and pulpit, are kept in ignorance and made to believe in every possible absurdity in relation to the Church of the Saints. Mr. Smith replied that he professed to be nothing but a man, and a minister of salvation, sent by Jesus Christ to preach the gospel. After expressing some surprise, the lady inquired what was the peculiar nature of the gospel, as held by himself and his Church? At this the visitors and soldiers gathered around, and Mr. Smith preached to them faith in the Lord Jesus Christ, repentance towards God, reformation of life, immersion in water, in the name of Jesus Christ, for remission of sins, and the gift of the Holy Ghost by the laying on of hands.

All seemed surprised, and the lady, in tears, went her way, praising God for the truth, and praying aloud that the Lord would bless and deliver the prisoners (1985, pp. 164–65).

Joseph Smith

I was this morning introduced to a man from the east. After hearing my name, he remarked that I was nothing but a man, indicating by this expression, that he had supposed that a person to whom the Lord should see fit to reveal His will must be something more than a man. He seemed to have forgotten the saying that fell from the lips of St. James, that Elias was a man subject to like passions as we are, yet he had such power with God, that He, in answer to his prayers, shut the heavens that they gave no rain for the space of three years and six months; and again, in answer to his prayer, the heavens gave forth rain, and the earth gave forth fruit. Indeed, such is the darkness and ignorance of this generation, that they look upon it as incredible that a man should have any intercourse with his Maker (HC, 2:302).

Joseph Smith

This morning, I read German, and visited with a brother and sister from Michigan, who thought that "a prophet is always a prophet;" but I told them that a prophet was a prophet only when he was acting as such (HC, 5:265).

Brigham Young

I remember Joseph Smith's saying, "If I were as pure and holy as you wish me to be, I could not stay with you; I should not be here to guide and direct you, for the Lord would take me from you." He did take him; the people were not worthy of him (JD, 8:189).

Missionary Minded

Ebenezer Robinson

All the other hands in the printing office were members of the Church, but none of them ever made any attempt at proselyting [me]. On one occasion when boarding at Joseph Smith's, he said to [me], "When you are baptized I want to baptize you," on another occasion, as we were walking together after dinner, from his house to the printing office, he said to [me], "you will help me build Zion, won't you?" [I] do not recollect of making any reply at either time.

. . . At dinner that day, (October 16, 1835) Joseph Smith, Jr., finished his meal a little before the others at the table, and went and stood in the doorway (the door being open, it being a warm pleasant day), with his back to the door jamb, when [I] arose and went and stood before him, and looking him in the face said, "Do you know what I want?" when he replied, "No, without it is to go into the waters of Jordan." [I] told him that was what [I] wanted, when he said he would attend to it that afternoon. We then went to the printing office together, he to his council room which adjoined the room where [I] worked, and [I] to [my] work in the printing office. [I] worked until well on to the evening, feeling very anxious all the time, for it seemed that [I] could not live overnight without being baptized; after enduring it as long as [I] could, went to the door of [his] room, and gently opened it, (a thing [I] had never presumed to do before). As soon as Mr. Smith saw [me] he said, "Yes, yes, brethren, Brother Robinson wishes to be baptized, we will adjourn and attend to that."

We repaired to the water, (the Chagrin River which flows through Kirtland) and, after a season of prayer, Brother Joseph Smith, Jr., baptized [me] by immersion, and as [I] arose from the water it seemed that everything [I] had on left [me], and [I] came up a new creature, when [I] shouted aloud, "Glory to God." [My] heart was full to overflowing, and [I] felt that [I] had born again in very deed, both of water and of the Spirit.

In going up from the water Brother Joseph Smith said to the brethren, "I am not afraid of Brother Robinson ever denying the faith." [I] thank our Heavenly Father that a doubt of the truth of the glorious gospel of our Lord and Savior, Jesus Christ, which [I] then obeyed, has never found lodgement in this poor heart from that day to this (April 25, 1889), for one single moment. [My] soul rejoices in it still, and [I] trust it will, by his grace assisting [me], while our Heavenly Father gives us breath (1890, p. 58).

Pious and Devout

William H. Walker

[About the spring of 1840 my father, John Walker,] sent me to Nauvoo on some business with President Joseph Smith, the Prophet. I arrived at his house about nine o'clock, just as his family was singing, before the accustomed evening prayer. His wife, Emma, leading in the singing. I thought I had never heard such sweet, heavenly music before. I was equally interested in the prayer offered by the Prophet. Much pleased with my visit, and business accomplished satisfactorily, I returned home in a few days (1943, p. 8).

Powerful in Testimony

Lyman O. Littlefield

Sidney Rigdon was a fine-looking man, polished in address, and powerful in oratory; but he was far behind Joseph in the possession of those magnetic powers of the mind which attracted the multitude, and chained the attention of his auditors. In comparison, Rigdon's eloquence was delightful, like the ripple of the merry brooklet that glides over its pebbled bed or dashes down a narrow declivity; but the testimony of Joseph struck through the heart, and, like the thunder of the cataract, declared at once the dignity and matchless supremacy of the Creator (1888, pp. 35–36).

Prophetic Promises

John L. Butler

March [1840], Joseph and Hyrum moved up to Commerce, and I went up just after them to look at the place and see how I should like it. Brother Joseph asked me if I was coming to live there. I told him that I wanted to live where he did. "Well," said he, "you have not got your family here yet, have you?" I told him no, I had not moved them up yet, but that I had come up just to look at the place. Brother Joseph then said, "You will come over to my house and stay while you are here, and until you move your family up." I thanked him for his kind offer, and when I got over to the house, I found a whole lot of folks sick. It was a very sickly place indeed. I asked Brother Joseph what kind of a place it was. He said it was a low, marshy, wet, damp, and nasty place, but that if we went to work and improved it, it would become more healthy and the Lord would bless it for our sakes (1993).

Restraint in Prophetic Office

Jesse W. Crosby

Brother Crosby said that he with some other brethren once went to the Prophet and asked him to give them his opinion on a certain public question. Their request was refused. He told them he did not enjoy the right vouchsafed to every American citizen, that of free speech. He said to them that when he ventured to give his private opinion on any subject of importance his words were often garbled and their meaning twisted and then given out as the word of the Lord because they came from him (n.d. [b]).

Righteous Indignation

William H. Walker

On August 31st [1843] the Mansion House was finished, and furnished, which was commenced the year before, and the Prophet and his family moved into the Mansion. I had charge of the House under his direction. An incident occurred which would go to show how detestable he felt towards, and the contempt he had for any person of questionable character. In regard to his private life, as to purity, honesty, virtue, charity, benevolence, liberality, refined and sensitive feelings, and nobility of character, his superior did not exist on earth.

On the 15th of September the Mansion was opened as a hotel. Not long after the opening of the House, one afternoon a stranger came and registered his name. Just before supper he insulted one of the hired girls. The Prophet heard of it after the stranger had retired. The next morning he was in the bar room to meet him as he came down from his room. Mr. Smith said to him, "Sir: I understand that you insulted one of the employees of this house last evening." He began to make all kinds of apologies, but nothing of this kind would answer the purpose. He told the stranger to get his baggage and to get away from there as soon as possible, in such unmistakable language, and in a tone of voice that almost made his hair stand straight on his head. The man offered to pay his bill. "I want you to get. I want none of your money, or any other man's of your stamp." Upon this the stranger cut a lively exit (1943, p. 10).

Spiritually Sensitive

John M. Chidester

We continued our [Zion's Camp] journey until we reached the Wakandaw River, having traveled twenty-five miles without resting or eating. We were compelled to ferry this stream; and we found on the opposite side of it a most desirable place to camp, which was a source of satisfaction to the now weary and hungry men. On reaching this place the Prophet announced to the camp that he felt impressed to travel on; and taking the lead, he invited the brethren to follow him.

This caused a split in the camp. Lyman Wight and others at first refused to follow the Prophet, but finally came up. The sequel showed that the Prophet was inspired to move on a distance of some seven miles. It was reported to us afterwards that about eight miles below where we crossed the river a body of men was organized to come upon us that night.

When we reached Salt Creek, Missouri, Allred settlement had prepared a place to hold meeting in. Joseph and Hyrum Smith and others were on the stand at the meeting when some strangers came in and were very anxious to find out which of them were Joseph and Hyrum, as they had pledged themselves to shoot them on sight. But the Prophet and his brother slipped away unobserved, being impressed that there was danger of their lives being taken (1892, p. 151).

Mary I. Horne

In compliance with a revelation from the Lord commanding him to lay our grievances before the judges, governors, and even the President of the United States, the Prophet Joseph, in company with a number of the brethren, came to Quincy, and the Prophet laid the condition of the affairs of the Church before Governor Carlin.

On his return from his visit to Governor Carlin, the Prophet sent the brethren ahead on their return trip, telling them he would follow later. When he reached Lima, where they intended to remain overnight, he found officers of the law awaiting him. They arrested him and brought him back to Quincy. This was Friday evening. About noon the next day the Prophet came to our house and said, "Sister Horne, the Spirit always draws me to your home." "Brother Joseph," I said, "you are always welcome. But how it is you are here when I thought you were almost home?" "Haven't you heard that I have been in court all morning?" he asked. I replied that I had not. "Well, I have," he said. "I told the officers that I would be forthcoming at any hour in the morning they might name, if they would let me go, so here I am. What am I to do? They won't let me have my trial in Nauvoo, but they are going to take me to Walla Walla. I thought I should be at home by this time where my wife would look after my clothing, as it is in need of attention." "I will wash your clothing," I answered. "Indeed, Sister Horne, you do not look able to do it." I insisted, and he finally consented, as I told him my Saturday's work was all done. I prepared his clothing that afternoon, so he was ready for his journey in the morning.

Sister Cleveland, who had heard of the Prophet's arrest, came to see him, and met him at the door just as he was leaving. As she shook hands with him, she began speaking in tongues. Brother Joseph listened until she had finished, then turned to us and said, "You need have no fears for me, as Sister Cleveland says, I shall have my trial and be acquitted" (1951, pp. 159–60).

Benjamin F. Johnson

At this time there was living in one of the Prophet's homes, Father G. W. Harris, then, I think, President of the High council, who had married the widow of Wm. Morgan of Free Mason fame, and who left two children, Lucinda and Thomas. Lucinda, then sixteen years of age, appeared to be very lovable, both in purity and beauty, and being often companions naturally drew us together in feeling. The Prophet, seeing our partiality for each other told me to make her my wife, seeming to enjoin it upon me. I at once moved to that object, and found there was a mutuality of feeling between us, and we soon pledged our vows to each other (1947, p. 11).

Tested the Faith of the Saints

Edwin D. Woolley

[Woolley] engaged in the mercantile business [in Nauvoo]. While thus engaged the Prophet called upon him one day and said, "Brother Woolley, we want all your goods for the building up of the Kingdom of God;" or words to that effect. Elder Woolley went to work at once and packed up ready for removal all the goods in his store, with the exception of some which were held on commission from different mercantile firms; he then went to Joseph and said, "Brother Joseph, I wish to know, if you also want the goods I hold on commission, and will pay the houses in St. Louis and other places from where I obtained them; and also whether you will send teams to take the goods away, or wish me to deliver them." The Prophet answered by asking, "And you have packed all your goods except those you hold on commission and are ready ᴛ deliver them, or haul them over?" "Yes," was the answer. "Then," said the Prophet, with deep feeling, at the same time putting his hand affectionately on Brother Woolley's shoulder, "Take your goods, replace them on your shelves, and go on with your business." The Prophet had probably only been testing him and found that he was willing to make any sacrifice necessary for the cause he had espoused, and that the property was doing as well in his hands as it would in some other way, and that anything needed could be had at any time it might be called for (1971, 1:283).

Some Political Sentiments and Insights

Josiah Quincy

I should not say quite all that struck me about Smith if I did not mention that he seemed to have a keen sense of the humorous aspects of his position. "It seems to me, General," I said, as he was driving us to the river, about sunset, "that you have too much power to be safely trusted to one man."

"In your hands or that of any other person," was the reply, "so much power would, no doubt, be dangerous. I am the only man in the world whom it would be safe to trust with it. Remember, I am a prophet!"

The last five words were spoken in a rich, comical aside, as if in hearty recognition of the ridiculous sound they might have in the ears of a Gentile. I asked him to test his powers by naming the successful candidate in the approaching presidential election.

"Well, I will prophesy that John Tyler will not be the next president, for some things are possible and some things are probable; but Tyler's election is neither the one nor the other."

We then went on to talk of politics. Smith recognized the curse and iniquity of slavery, though he opposed the methods of the Abolitionists. His plan was for the nation to pay for the slaves from the sale of the public lands. "Congress," he said, "should be compelled to take this course, by petitions from all parts of the country; but the petitioners must disclaim all alliance with those who would disturb the rights of property recognized by the Constitution and foment insurrection."

It may be worthwhile to remark that Smith's plan was publicly advocated, eleven years later, by one who has mixed so much practical shrewdness with his lofty philosophy. In 1855, when men's minds had been moved to their depths on the question of slavery, Mr. Ralph Waldo Emerson declared that it should be met in accordance "with the interest of the South and with the settled conscience of the North. It is not really a great task, a great fight for this country to accomplish, to buy that property of the planter, as the British nation bought the West Indian slaves." He further says that the "United States will be brought to give every inch of their public lands for a purpose like this." We, who can look back upon the terrible cost of the fratricidal war which put an end to slavery, now say that such a solution of the difficulty would have been worthy a Christian statesman. But if the retired scholar was in advance of his time when he advocated this disposition of the public property in 1855, what shall I say of the political and religious leader who had committed himself, in print, as well as in conversation, to the same course in 1844? If the atmosphere of men's opinions was stirred by such a proposition when war-clouds were discernible in the sky, was it not a statesmanlike word eleven years earlier, when the heavens looked tranquil and beneficent?

General Smith proceeded to unfold still further his views upon politics. He denounced the Missouri Compromise as an unjustifiable concession for the benefit of slavery. It was Henry Clay's bid for the presidency. Dr. Goforth might have spared himself the trouble of coming to

Nauvoo to electioneer for a duelist who would fire at John Randolph, but was not brave enough to protect the Saints in their rights as American citizens. Clay had told his people to go to the wilds of Oregon and set up a government of their own. Oh yes, the Saints might go into the wilderness and obtain justice of the Indians, which imbecile, time-serving politicians would not give them in the land of freedom and equality.

The prophet then talked of the details of government. He thought that the number of members admitted to the lower house of the national legislature should be reduced. A crowd only darkened counsel and impeded business. A member to every half million of population would be ample. The powers of the President should be increased. He should have authority to put down rebellion in a state, without waiting for the request of any governor; for it might happen that the governor himself would be the leader of the rebels. It is needless to remark how later events showed the executive weakness that Smith pointed out—a weakness which cost thousands of valuable lives and millions of treasure; but the man mingled Utopian fallacies with his shrewd suggestions. He talked as from a strong mind utterly unenlightened by the teachings of history. Finally, he told us what he would do, were he President of the United States, and went on to mention that he might one day so hold the balance between parties as to render his election to that office by no means unlikely.

Who can wonder that the chair of the National Executive had its place among the visions of this self-reliant man? He had already traversed the roughest part of the way to that coveted position. Born in the lowest ranks of poverty, without book-learning and with the homeliest of all human names, he had made himself at the age of thirty-nine a power upon earth. Of the multitudinous family of Smith, from Adam down (Adam [Smith] of the "Wealth of Nations," I mean), none had so won human hearts and shaped human lives as this Joseph. His influence, whether for good or for evil, is potent today, and the end is not yet.

I have endeavored to give the details of my visit to the Mormon prophet with absolute accuracy. If the reader does not know just what to make of Joseph Smith, I cannot help him out of the difficulty. I myself stand helpless before the puzzle (1883, pp. 396–400).

First Meetings with Joseph Smith

Israel A. Barlow

At this time two Mormon elders, names unknown, visited the Barlow family in Mendon and told them about the restored gospel. No doubt the Book of Mormon was purchased and read, and the life of the young latter-day prophet discussed, for Israel has been quoted by his son, Israel II, as having said, "If I could just see this Joseph Smith I think I could detect if he is a prophet." Israel was to make that opportunity come about, for Israel II also said that shortly thereafter his father drove in a buggy 200 miles and visited with the Prophet for a few days. After he talked with him two or three hours he said he knew that he was a prophet of God (1968, pp. 97–98).

Note: Another version of this story reads: "I shall see this man and know for myself if he is a prophet." See Barlow, 1968, p. 119.

George Q. Cannon

It was the author's privilege thus to meet the Prophet for the first time. The occasion was the arrival of a large company of Latter-day Saints at the upper landing at Nauvoo. The general conference of the Church was in session and large numbers crowded to the landing place to welcome the emigrants. Nearly every prominent man in the community was there. Familiar with the names of all and the persons of many of the prominent elders, the author sought with a boy's curiosity and eagerness to discover those whom he knew, and especially to get sight of the Prophet and his brother Hyrum, neither of whom he had ever met. When his eyes fell upon the Prophet, without a word from anyone to point him out, or any reason to separate him from others who stood around, he knew him instantly. He would have known him among ten thousand. There was that about him, which, to the author's eyes, distinguished him from all the men he had ever seen (1964, pp. 20–21).

Mary A. Lambert

I first saw Joseph Smith in the spring of 1843. When the boat in which we came up the Mississippi River reached the landing at Nauvoo, several of the leading brethren were there to meet the company of Saints that had come on it. Among those brethren was the Prophet Joseph

Smith. I knew him the instant my eyes rested upon him, and at that moment I received my testimony that he was a prophet of God, for I never had such a feeling for mortal man as thrilled my being when my eyes first rested upon Joseph Smith. He was not pointed out to me. I knew him from all the other men, and, child that I was (I was only fourteen), I knew that I saw a prophet of God (1905, p. 554).

Mary A. Noble

The next season I taught school in the neighborhood of my father. This was 1833, in the fall and winter of the same year. I commenced keeping company with Mr. Noble, and in a year, the spring of 1834, Brother Joseph Smith came from Kirtland, Ohio, to my father's New York estate, Avon, Livingston County. This was the first time I ever beheld a prophet of the Lord, and I can truly say at the first sight that I had a testimony within my bosom that he was a man chosen of God to bring forth a great work in the last days. His society I prized, his conversation was meat and drink to me. The principles that he brought forth bind the testimony that he bore of the truth of the Book of Mormon and made a lasting impression upon my mind. While he was there, Sidney Rigdon and Joseph and Brigham Young, Luke and Lyman Johnson, and twelve or fourteen of the traveling elders had a council to my father's. I, in company with my sisters, had the pleasure of cooking, and serving the table, and waiting on them, which I considered a privilege and blessing (n.d., pp. 18–19).

Amasa Potter

In the year 1842 I was moving with my parents from Indiana to Nauvoo, Illinois, and one bright sunny day as we came within three miles of that city we met a buggy with two men in it. The buggy turned out of the road and stopped.

My father was driving our team, and he stopped the horses. The man in the buggy asked if we were moving to Nauvoo. Father replied that we were.

The gentleman in the buggy said, "No doubt you have heard of Joseph Smith the Prophet."

Mother then answered, "We have come five hundred miles to see him."

"I am that man," replied the person in the buggy who acted as spokesman, and then called us all up to the side of the buggy and shook hands with us, and gave father some instructions about where to go to purchase some land, and to settle near the city.

But one thing I remember was, when the Prophet took hold of my hand and said to me, "May God bless you, my little man," I felt a thrill through my whole body like a current of electricity, and I can say that the recollections of my feelings on that occasion have followed me through life, and when dangers on sea and land threatened my destruction, I have thought of the Prophet Joseph Smith, and all perils have been removed from me (1894, pp. 131–32).

Lucy Meserve Smith

I was born February 9th, 1817, at Bethel, Oxford County, Maine, and I was baptized August 12th, 1837. I first met the Prophet Joseph Smith on a steamboat, when I landed at the ferry in Nauvoo. The first words he said to our company were: "I guess you are all Latter-day Saints here, by the singing I heard when the boat landed." He then shook hands with each one in the company, and then took his sister, Lucy Millikan's seven months' old boy in his arms and sat down and wept for joy, as his sister was thought to be in a decline when she left home the year before with her husband. She was indeed the picture of health when she returned, which gave the Prophet double joy on meeting her with her son.

President Joseph Smith, the Prophet, looked the same to me when I met him as I saw him in a dream before I left home (1892, p. 470).

William C. Staines

I arrived in Nauvoo, April 12th, 1843. The next day the Prophet Joseph preached to us and blessed us. I had seen him in a vision while crossing the sea, and when I saw him that day he had on the same hat and coat that I saw him in when at sea. I heard him preach a number of times and saw him in and around the city, giving counsel, and I always believed in him from my first seeing him until his death, that he was the leader of this dispensation and God Almighty's prophet (1891, p. 122).

Emmeline B. Wells

Journeying from my home in Massachusetts to Nauvoo, Illinois, with a company of Latter-day Saints, we were joined in Albany by some elders returning from missions in the eastern states. Among them was the late

Jacob Gates, who was accompanied by his wife, with whom I became well acquainted en route. Sister Gates talked a great deal about the Prophet Joseph, whom she knew intimately, and when she saw that I was specially interested in him, promised me that she would introduce me to him on our arrival in Nauvoo. She also told me many things concerning his life and mission that I had not known before; and I listened carefully to all the elders' conversation, for they were full of zeal and the spirit of the Latter-day work, and of love for the Prophet Joseph. To me it was a continuous revelation, although Sister Gates seemed to think it impossible for one so young and inexperienced to realize the greatness and wonderful power of the Prophet Joseph Smith; in time I came to understand the feeling when I tried to explain to others the power he possessed that impressed the people with whom he came in contact.

As we neared our destination in sailing up the Mississippi, the elders, there were eight of them now (four more who had been laboring in Kentucky having joined us at Louisville), were full of enthusiasm at the thought of seeing the Prophet again. But not once in all the conversation did I hear a description of his personal appearance. There were no photographs in those days, and I had not formed any idea of him except of his wonderful power. I think in looking back upon that time, I must have been in a state of mingled emotions of astonishment and awe, not knowing what I should do or say on my arrival.

At last the boat reached the upper landing, and a crowd of people were coming toward the bank of the river. As we stepped ashore the crowd advanced, and I could see one person who towered away and above all the others around him; in fact I did not see distinctly any others. His majestic bearing, so entirely different from anyone I had ever seen (and I had seen many superior men) was more than a surprise. It was as if I beheld a vision; I seemed to be lifted off my feet, to be as it were walking in the air, and paying no heed whatever to those around me. I made my way through the crowd; then I saw this man whom I had noticed, because of his lofty appearance, shaking hands with all the people, men, women, and children. Before I was aware of it he came to me, and when he took my hand, I was simply electrified, thrilled through and through to the tips of my fingers, and every part of my body, as if some magic elixir had given me new life and vitality. I am sure that for a few minutes I was not conscious of motion. I think I stood still, I did not want to speak, or be spoken to. I was overwhelmed with indefinable emotion.

Sister Gates came to me and said, "I'll introduce you to the Prophet Joseph now, he is here."

I replied, "I don't want to be introduced to him."

She was astonished, and said curtly, "Why, you told me how desirous you were of meeting him."

I answered, "Yes, but I've seen him and he spoke to me."

"But he didn't know who you were!"

I replied, "I know that but it don't matter," and Sister Gates walked away without another word of explanation. I was in reality too full for utterance. I think had I been formally presented to the Prophet, I should have fallen down at his feet, I was in such a state of ecstacy. The one thought that filled my soul was, I have seen the prophet of God, he has taken me by the hand, and this testimony has never left me in all the "perils by the way." It is as vivid today as ever it was. For many years, I felt it too sacred an experience even to mention (1905, p. 555).

Newel K. Whitney

When Joseph Smith arrived in Kirtland in February, 1831, his sleigh, containing himself, his wife Emma, and one or two other persons, drew up in front of the store of Gilbert and Whitney, and the youthful prophet, alighting and entering, thus addressed the junior partner: "Newel K. Whitney, thou art the man," at the same time extending his hand as if to an old and familiar acquaintance. "You have the advantage of me," said the one addressed, mechanically taking the proffered hand, a mystified look overspreading his countenance. "I could not call you by name as you have me." "I am Joseph the Prophet," said the stranger, smiling. "You've prayed me here, now what do you want of me?"—referring to a vision in which he had seen the merchant and his wife praying for his coming to Kirtland. This was Newel K. Whitney's introduction to the founder of Mormonism. He cordially welcomed the Prophet and his wife; and of their entertainment at his home Joseph says: "We were kindly received and welcomed into the house of Brother N. K. Whitney. I and my wife lived in the family of Brother Whitney several weeks, and received every kindness and attention that could be expected, and especially from Sister Whitney (1904, p. 234; see also Elizabeth Ann Whitney 1878a, p. 51; Joseph Smith tells this same story, saying he arrived in Kirtland "about the first of February" 1831; see HC, 1:145–46).

Wilford Woodruff

I went with Brother Parley through Jefferson County to the North, and then immediately prepared to go to Kirtland. I started to Kirtland on the 11th day of April, 1834, and arrived in Kirtland on the 25th day of the same month. I then for the first time had an interview with the Prophet Joseph. He invited me to his house. I rejoiced to behold his face and to hear his voice. I was fully satisfied that Joseph was a prophet before I saw him. I had no prejudices on my mind against him, but I expected to see a prophet.

My first introduction to him was rather singular. I saw him out in the field with his brother Hyrum: he had on a very old hat and was engaged shooting at a mark. I was introduced to him, and he invited me home with him.

I accepted the invitation, and I watched him pretty closely, to see what I could learn. He remarked, while passing to his house, that this was the first hour he had spent in recreation for a long time.

Shortly after we arrived at his house, he went into an adjoining room, and brought out a wolf-skin, and said, "Brother Woodruff, I want you to help me to tan this;" so I pulled off my coat, went to work and helped him, and felt honored in so doing. He was about going up with the brethren to redeem Zion, and he wanted this wolf-skin to put upon his wagon seat, as he had no buffalo robe.

This was my first introduction to the Prophet Joseph Smith, the great Seer of this last dispensation.

I was not there long before I heard him talk about going to Zion, and it did my soul good to hear him speak of many things concerning Zion, the gathering of Israel, and the great Latter-day work; and I felt truly satisfied with what I saw and heard.

I recollect that in the evening after I got there, several of the brethren came in and talked with Brother Joseph, and asked what they should do, for they had not means to bear their expenses from there to Missouri. Brother Joseph said, "I am going to have some money soon;" and the next morning he received a letter containing a hundred and fifty dollars, sent to him by Sister Voce, of Boston (JD, 7:101).

3

The Gifts of the Spirit

"The Word of Knowledge"

Howard Coray

While thus engaged [as Joseph Smith's secretary], I had many very precious opportunities, great and small, [for] almost every day, [people] were calling on him, some for one thing, and some for another—politicians and preachers and of different persuasions—some with the view of testing the depth of his knowledge and, if possible, confounding him and putting [him] to shame. Well, what did I discover—that he was equal to every occasion, that he had a ready answer for all questions. I heard him say that God had given him the key of knowledge by which he could trace any subject through all its ramifications. I had heard it remarked that Joseph Smith was Sidney Rigdon's cat's paw. Soon after he returned from the East he came to see Joseph, and the thought went through my mind: "Now I will see, who the cat's paw is." Well, I did see. After passing the usual compliments, Rigdon said to Joseph: "When I was preaching in Philadelphia after I had finished my discourse a man stepped up to me and desired me to explain something in John's Revelation," mentioning at the same time what it was. "Well, I could not do it, how is it Joseph?" Joseph cited him at once right off hand to a passage in Ezekiel and something in some other book of the Old Testament, saying that they explained all about it. I thought to myself, "That don't look much like Joseph's being a cat's paw" (1977, pp. 343–44).

Note: A "cat's paw" is a nineteenth-century colloquialism meaning "dupe" or "fool; a person used by another to accomplish some purpose."

Edward Stevenson

I very well remember the Prophet on one occasion dining at our house, and recollect some of his conversation. He was looking over a copy of the Book of Martyrs, which was in the house. In doing so he remarked, "Many of those who suffered death at the fiery stake were honest, true Christians according to the light they possessed." He requested to have the loan of the Book of Martyrs, which he said he would return to us in Zion. He did return it at Far West, Missouri, remarking as he did so, "I have seen those martyrs by aid of the Urim and Thummim; God has a salvation for them."

His words of sympathy increased my love, which was already strong, for him.

Opening the Bible to the Apocrypha, he said, "There are many precious truths in these books—just as true as any of the Bible—but it requires much of the Spirit of God to divide the truths from the errors which have crept into them." He also spoke of a great work to be done in England, "for," said he, "there are many of the house of Ephraim in that land, who are waiting for the fullness of the gospel." This was several years before any missionaries were sent to England, where afterwards the elders met with such great success.

While he was quietly relating his experience, visions, trials, and heavenly communion, we felt greatly blessed and favored, and felt honored in imparting to him of our hospitality in return for his rich and comforting words, knowing that we were entertaining one of the greatest prophets of God that ever graced His footstool. Although but a lad, I was pleased to see and hear him, and going into our garden I plucked some of our best apples for him. After dinner the Prophet walked about the premises and much admired our home, particularly the clear, mirror-like lake, with its surroundings, which was a part of our homestead.

. . . The Prophet instructed us that he received command from heaven that baptism by immersion was the only acceptable mode (1894b, p. 570; see also 1974, pp. 85–86).

Note: Joseph Smith returned the Urim and Thummim he used in translating the Book of Mormon to Moroni long before Stevenson's 1834 visit to Michigan. But because "a Urim and Thummim consists of two special stones called seer stones or interpreters" (McConkie, 1966b, p. 818), it is entirely possible that Joseph used a seer stone in this instance.

The Gift of Faith

Caroline S. Callister

One time when his enemies were hounding him he came to her father's house to get away from them. When the meal was ready he sat down to the table, bowed his head and said, "O God, may their bread never fail," and it never did even in the scarce time in the Valleys, [Father] always had a little bread. One day [the Prophet] came in with a pint-cup of flour [and] said, "Father Smith I had a little flour and I wanted to divide it with you" (n.d.).

Elias Cox

I attended many meetings where [Joseph Smith] presided; and can testify to the world that he was a true prophet of God. I call to mind one prophecy which I saw immediately fulfilled. It was in regard to the Saints who had assembled at the usual gathering place in Nauvoo grove. A severe storm arose. We grew very frightened and were preparing for home. Joseph told us to just arise to our feet, and the storm wouldn't hurt us. We obeyed. The storm soon passed away, the sun shone warm and the President resumed his speaking (1906, p. 544).

Philo Dibble

When Joseph first came to Nauvoo, then called Commerce, a Mr. [Hugh] White, living there, proffered to sell him his farm for twenty-five hundred dollars, five hundred dollars of the amount to be paid down, and the balance one year from that time. Joseph and the brethren were talking about this offer when some of them said: "We can't buy it, for we lack the money." Joseph took out his purse, and, emptying out its contents, offered a half dollar to one of the brethren, which he declined accepting, but Joseph urged him to take it, and then gave each of the other brethren a similar amount, which left him without any. Addressing the brethren, he then said: "Now you all have money, and I have none; but the time will come when I will have money and you will have none!" He then said to Bishop [Vinson] Knight: "You go back and buy the farm!"

Brother Knight went to White, but learned from him that he had raised the price one hundred dollars, and returned to Joseph without closing the bargain. Joseph again sent him with positive orders to purchase, but Brother Knight, finding that White had raised the price still another hundred dollars, again returned without purchasing. For the third time then Joseph commanded him to go and buy the farm, and charged him not to come back till he had done so.

When Bishop Knight got back to White, he had raised another hundred on the place, making the whole amount twenty-eight hundred dollars. However, the bargain was closed and the obligations drawn up, but how the money was going to be raised neither Brother Knight nor the other brethren could see. The next morning Joseph and several of the brethren went down to Mr. White's to sign the agreement and make the first payment on the land. A table was brought out with the papers upon it, and Joseph signed them, moved back from the table, and sat with his head down, as if in thought for a moment. Just then a man drove up in a carriage and asked if Mr. Smith was there. Joseph hearing it, got up and went to the door. The man said, "Good morning, Mr. Smith; I am on a speculation today. I want to buy some land, and thought I would come and see you." Joseph then pointed around where his land lay, but the man said: "I can't go with you today to see the land. Do you want any money this morning?"

Joseph replied that he would like some, and when the stranger asked, "How much?" he told him, "Five hundred dollars."

The man walked into the house with Joseph, emptied a small sack of gold on the table, and counted out that amount. He then handed to Joseph another hundred dollars, saying: "Mr. Smith, I make you a present of this!"

After this transpired, Joseph laughed at the brethren and said: "You trusted in money; but I trusted in God. Now I have money and you have none" (1968, p. 96).

Jedediah M. Grant

I used once to be troubled with dyspepsia, and had frequently to call upon the elders to administer, and on one occasion, Brother Joseph Smith says to me, "Brother Grant, if I could always be with you, I could cure you." How is it that Brother Brigham is able to comfort and soothe those who are depressed in spirit, and always make those with whom he associates so happy? I will tell you how he makes us feel so happy. He is happy himself, and the man who is happy himself can make others feel so, for the light of God is in him and others feel the influence, and feel happy in his society (JD, 3:12).

Heber C. Kimball

A certain number were appointed to speak at each meeting. On one occasion I was called upon to speak on the principle of faith. Several brethren spoke before me, and quoted every passage mentioned in the Scriptures on the subject. I referred to an original circumstance which took place in my family. My daughter had broken a saucer; her mother promised her a whipping, when she returned from a visit on which she was just starting; she went out under an apple tree and prayed that her mother's heart might be softened, and when she returned she might not whip her; although her mother was very punctual when she made a promise to her children to fulfill it, yet when she returned she had no disposition to chastise her child. Afterwards the child told her mother that she had prayed to God that she might not whip her.

Joseph wept like a child on hearing this simple narrative and its application (1864c, p. 568).

Orson Pratt

I heard Brother Joseph, when speaking of those that were sick in Nauvoo, make remarks similar to those that I have now made. He said that those who would not, when in good health, call upon the Lord, and acknowledge His hand in all things, and remember him, would not have faith when it was needed—he said that those individuals would have but very little faith in the days of their calamities and affliction.

Then seek to get faith and spirit sufficient to assist us in the days of our afflictions, that we may be prepared for all the vicissitudes of life. We ought to know that we are well off at the present, but all do not realize this fact.

How often I have thought of the remark made by the Prophet; nothing can be more true than that remark; it carries its own evidence with it, that those individuals who have wealth and riches in abundance, but do not remember the Lord, when troubles come, they will be in the greatest distress, generally speaking (JD, 3:15).

John L. Smith

In my early years I used to often eat at the table with Joseph the Prophet. At one time he was called to dinner. I being at play in the room with his son Joseph, he called us to him, and we stood one each side of him. After he had looked over the table he said, "Lord, we thank Thee for this Johnny cake, and ask Thee to send us something better. Amen." The corn bread was cut and I received a piece from his hand.

Before the bread was all eaten, a man came to the door and asked if the Prophet Joseph was at home. Joseph replied he was, whereupon the visitor said, "I have brought you some flour and a ham."

Joseph arose and took the gift, and blessed the man in the name of the Lord. Turning to his wife, Emma, he said, "I knew the Lord would answer my prayer" (1892, p. 172).

Joseph Smith

June 24 [1834]—This night the cholera burst forth among us, and about midnight it was manifested in its most virulent form. Our ears were saluted with cries and moanings and lamentations on every hand; even those on guard fell to the earth with their guns in their hands, so sudden and powerful was the attack of this terrible disease. At the commencement, I attempted to lay on hands for their recovery, but I quickly learned by painful experience, that when the great Jehovah decrees destruction upon any people, and makes known His determination, man must not attempt to stay His hand. The moment I attempted to rebuke the disease I was attacked, and had I not desisted in my attempt to save the life of a brother, I would have sacrificed my own. The disease seized upon me like the talons of a hawk, and I said to the brethren: "If my work were done, you would have to put me in the ground without a coffin" (HC, 2:114).

Note: In the third Lecture on Faith, the Prophet taught that it is impossible to exercise faith contrary to the will of God. This vignette seems to illustrate this principle.

William Somerville

William Somerville served as a bodyguard to the Prophet Joseph Smith, and, with side arms in hand, lay on the floor of the bedroom in the Nauvoo House in which Joseph slept, placing his feet against the door, which opened inwards toward the bedroom, so that anyone entering would have to waken him before being able to reach the Prophet.

On one occasion, while on a guard duty assignment, the Prophet came to him and told him that on that particular night his guard service would not be needed, as it had been revealed to him that the little children had been praying for his welfare and the Lord had heard their prayers and would honor their faith by protecting him (n.d. [b]; see also Jane S. Richards, 1905, p. 550).

Mary C. Westover

I was very small when we lived in Nauvoo, but I must have seen Joseph Smith many times, for I always attended the meetings. The most striking thing I remember of him was a prophecy he made, which I saw fulfilled immediately. I was at the funeral service of King Follet [Follett], which was held in the Nauvoo Grove. There was a heavy thunderstorm arose and as it increased the people became frightened and started to go home; but before anyone left the Prophet arose and told the multitude if they would remain still and pray in their hearts the storm would not molest them in their services.

They did as they were bidden, the storm divided over the grove. I well remember how it was storming on all sides of the grove, yet it was as calm around us as if there was no sign of a storm so nearby.

I thought as I sat there that the Lord was speaking through Joseph. My testimony of the truthfulness of the gospel has grown as my years have increased, and I hope to retain it till the end of my life and even till the end of the world. I can testify that I have seen Joseph Smith and he was a true prophet of God and the gospel he established is the same as that of Jesus Christ (1906, p. 545; see also Westover and Westover, n.d.; Amasa Potter, 1894).

Brigham Young

One day while crossing a large prairie, six or eight miles from any house, we crossed a small stream. The ground was frozen deep on each side, and we sprung one of the axletrees of Brother Barnard's carriage. Brother Barnard said we could not travel with it any farther. Brother Joseph looked at it and said, "I can spring that iron axletree back, so that we can go on our journey." Brother Barnard replied, "I am a blacksmith, and used to work in all kinds of iron, and that axletree is bent so far round that to undertake to straighten it would only break it." Brother Joseph answered, "I'll try it." He got a pry, and we sprung it back to its place, and it did not trouble us anymore till we arrived at Far West, March 14, 1838. Brother Barnard, seeing this done, concluded that he would never say again that a thing could not be done when a prophet said it could (1968, pp. 24–26).

Brigham Young

I recollect many times when Brother Joseph, reflecting upon how many would come into the Kingdom of God and go out again, would say, "Brethren, I have not apostatized yet, and don't feel like doing so." Many of you, no doubt, can call to mind his words. Joseph had to pray all the time, exercise faith, live his religion, and magnify his calling, to obtain the manifestations of the Lord, and to keep him steadfast in the faith (JD, 2:257).

Brigham Young

Joseph said, years ago, that he had all hell on his back, and all the world. All the evil influences that knew anything about him were combined to crush him; but, said he, "I will rise above them all, and bear off the kingdom;" and so he did, until he was slain (JD, 4:352).

"Faith to Be Healed"

Jared Carter

About this time [June 1831] there was some displays of the power of God . . . miraculously in the Church in Thomson, by the instrumentality of Brother Joseph, the seer, one in my own family which took place as follows:

It was my youngest child that was distressingly sick, at which time Joseph came to my house and I told him that I had faith that the babe might be healed. He then spoke in the name of the Lord that it should be according to my faith. The child was healed immediately. The same day there was one of our sisters healed from blindness by his instrumentality (n.d.).

John Harper

In the month of December [1843] I became very bad with a violent pain in my right side; it was excruciating. I had been bad from the 26th to the evening of the 27th, when through solicitation of my dear wife and the help of a cane I went out to get some of the Twelve to administer to me. I came to the Mansion House where the Prophet lived. I went into the bar room and asked Brother Loren Walker if Brother Joseph Smith was in, and he said "yes" and he went up stairs and told him to come down; I told him that I was very sick with a pain in my side; he said: "Sit down," and he laid his hands on my head and rebuked the pain in the name of the Lord and when he took his hands off my head I was healed and went home rejoicing in the name of the God of my salvation and have never been troubled with it since that time (n.d.).

Parley P. Pratt

After the gush of feelings consequent on our happy meeting had subsided, I accompanied Joseph Smith over the Mississippi in a skiff to visit some friends in Montrose. Here many were lying sick and at the point of death. Among these was my old friend and fellow servant, Elijah Fordham, who had been with me in that extraordinary work in New York City in 1837. He was now in the last stage of a deadly fever. He lay prostrate and nearly speechless, with his feet poulticed; his eyes were sunk in their sockets; his flesh was gone; the paleness of death was upon him; and he was hardly to be distinguished from a corpse. His wife was weeping over him, and preparing clothes for his burial.

Brother Joseph took him by the hand, and in a voice and energy which would seemingly have raised the dead, he cried: "BROTHER FORDHAM, IN THE NAME OF JESUS CHRIST, ARISE AND WALK." It was a voice which could be heard from house to house and nearly through the neighborhood. It was like the roaring of a lion, or the heavy thunderbolt. Brother Fordham leaped from his dying bed in an instant, shook the poultices and bandages from his feet, put on his clothes so quick that none got a chance to assist him, and taking a cup of tea and a little refreshment, he walked with us from house to house visiting other sick beds, and joining in prayer and ministrations for them, while the people followed us, and with joy and amazement gave glory to God. Several more were called up in a similar manner and were healed.

Brother Joseph, while in the Spirit, rebuked the elders who would continue to lay hands on the sick from day to day without the power to heal them. Said he: "It is time that such things ended. Let the elders either obtain the power of God to heal the sick or let them cease to minister the forms without the power" (1985, p. 254).

Joseph Smith

On the 6th of May [1832] I gave the parting hand to the brethren in Independence, and, in company with Brothers Rigdon and Whitney, commenced a return to Kirtland, by stage to St. Louis, from thence to Vincennes, Indiana; and from thence to New Albany, near the falls of the Ohio River. Before we arrived at the latter place, the horses became frightened, and while going at full speed Bishop Whitney attempted to jump out of the coach, but having his coat fast, caught his foot in the wheel, and had his leg and foot broken in several places; at the same time I jumped out unhurt. We put up at Mr. Porter's public house, in Greenville, for four weeks, while Elder Rigdon went directly forward to Kirtland. During all this time, Brother Whitney lost not a meal of victuals or a night's sleep, and Dr. Porter, our landlord's brother, who attended him, said it was a pity we had not got some "Mormon" there, as they could set broken bones or do anything else. I tarried with Brother Whitney and administered to him till he was able to be moved. While at this place I frequently walked out in the woods, where I saw several fresh graves; and one day when I rose from the dinner table, I walked directly to the door and commenced vomiting most profusely. I raised large quantities of blood and poisonous matter, and so great were the muscular contortions of my system, that my jaw in a few moments was dislocated. This I succeeded in replacing with my own hands, and made my way to Brother Whitney (who was on the bed), as speedily as possible; he laid his hands on me and administered to me in the name of the Lord, and I was healed in an instant, although the effect of the poison was so powerful, as to cause much of the hair to become loosened from my head. Thanks be to my Heavenly Father for His interference in my behalf at this critical moment, in the name of Jesus Christ. Amen (HC, 1:271).

Joseph Smith

John Corrill entered a complaint against Lyman Wight for teaching that "all disease in this Church is of the devil, and that medicine administered to the sick is of the devil; for the sick in the Church ought to live by faith."

Elder Wight acknowledged that he had taught the doctrine, and rather believed it to be correct.

The President decided that it was not lawful to teach the Church that all disease is of the devil, but if there is anyone who has this faith, let him have it to himself; and if there are any who believe that roots and herbs administered to the sick, and all wholesome vegetables which God has ordained for the use of man—and if any say that such things applied to the sick, in order that they may receive health, and this medicine is applied by any member of the Church—if there are any among you that teach that these things are of Satan, such teaching is not of God (HC, 2:147; see also HC, 2:288, where Joseph practices what he preaches by administering mild herbs to his sick father).

"Faith to Heal"

Benjamin Brown

My family, with myself, were also taken sick, and I laid so for two or three weeks. I was so far gone that I was quite senseless, and all thought I was dying. Doubtless I should have died, but one day Joseph Smith was passing by my door, for I had managed to procure a house, and was called in, and, as I was afterwards informed, laid his hands upon me, and commanded me to rise and walk in the name of the Lord. The first thing I knew was that I found myself walking on the floor, perfectly well, and within ten minutes afterwards I was out of the house visiting my daughter, whom I had not seen for nearly a month. I felt so full of joy and happiness, that I was greatly surprised that everyone else was not as full of praise as myself. This was the second time that I had been healed instantly by the power of God, through his servants.

This man, Joseph Smith, was the one that the world says was an impostor, and a false prophet, and either deny that he ever performed any miracle, or, if any are too well attested to be denied, attribute them to the power of the imagination over the body. Was it the power of imagination over the body, that cured me, when I did not even hear Joseph's voice or know that any operation on my behalf was going on, until I found myself well? The honest in heart will judge righteously (1853, p. 12).

Sylvia Chase

The change of climate brought on a sickness which was known as winter fever. Sylvia, a daughter of Isaac, was very sick, and father Chase sent for the Prophet to come and administer to her. There was so much sickness and the Prophet was so in demand that he could not come, but taking a handkerchief out of his jacket he said, "Take this and give it to her. Tell her to hold it in her hand. It shall be the same as an administration." This was done and the fever left her and she began to improve from that time" (Tanner, 1926).

William Clayton

Brother Samuel Rolfe being present, and being seriously afflicted with a felon [a deeply infected area] on one hand, President Joseph instructed him to wash in the font, and told him he would be healed, although the doctors had told him it would not be well before spring, and advised him to have it cut. He washed his hands in the font and in one week afterwards his hand was perfectly healed. After this time baptisms were continued in the font, and many realized great blessings, both spiritually and bodily (1845).

Philo Dibble

When Joseph came to Kirtland his fame spread far and wide. There was a woman [Elsa Johnson] living in the town of Hiram, forty miles from Kirtland, who had a crooked arm, which she had not been able to use for a long period. She persuaded her husband, whose name was [John] Johnson, to take her to Kirtland to get her arm healed.

I saw them as they passed my house on their way. She went to Joseph and requested him to heal her. Joseph asked her if she believed the Lord was able to make him an instrument in healing her arm. She said she believed the Lord was able to heal her arm.

Joseph put her off till the next morning, when he met her at Brother [Newel K.] Whitney's house. There were eight persons present, one a Methodist preacher, and one a doctor. Joseph took her [Elsa Johnson] by the hand, prayed in silence a moment, pronounced her arm whole, in the name of Jesus Christ, and turned and left the room.

The preacher asked her if her arm was whole, and she straightened it out and replied: "It is as good as the other." The question was then asked if it would remain whole. Joseph hearing this, answered and said: "It is as good as the other, and as liable to accident as the other."

The doctor who witnessed this miracle came to my house the next morning and related the circumstance to me. He attempted to account for it by his false philosophy, saying that Joseph took her by the hand, and seemed to be in prayer, and pronounced her arm whole in the name of Jesus Christ, which excited her and started perspiration, and that relaxed the cords of her arm. I subsequently rented my farm and devoted all my time to the interest of the Church, holding myself in readiness to take Joseph wherever he wished to go (1968, p. 78; see also Hayden, 1875; Oliver B. Huntington, 1891a, pp. 225–26; 1891d, pp. 411–12).

Clinton Harris

Clinton Harris, Principal Proprietor of the Harrisburg and Oston Railroad in Texas, made the following statement in the presence of William Gamall, James Gamall, Elinor McLean and Doctor Blank of Uden, vizt.

That Joseph Smith in the year 1830 called upon him and invited him to go down and see them baptize, saying, "Come Clint, go down and see us baptize,"—Clinton answered—"I cannot walk, for I have had a fever sore on my leg for many years"—Joseph replied, "Come go down, are you going to be lame all your days, come start and go down, and you'll do well enough." Clinton started, straightened his leg, and could walk and has been able to walk ever since. This Clinton is one of the wealthiest men in Texas.

Doctor Blank said "O, that is nothing, it is all owing to Mesmerism." Clinton replied, "Not so, Sir, he (Joseph Smith) never touched me, and I verily believe I should have been a cripple unto this day had I not been healed at that time. I believe in Mormonism, tho' I am not a Mormon."

This account was received by George A. Smith from the mouth of James Gamall at the Head of Echo Canyon on Oct. 18, 1857 (1857).

Note: Mesmerism, a not uncommon practice of Joseph Smith's day, was a doctrine or system of healing which suggested that a hypnotic state, usually accompanied by an insensibility to pain and muscular rigidity, could be induced through an influence exercised by an operator over the will and nervous system of the patient.

Heber C. Kimball

July 22nd [1839]—The Prophet Joseph arose from his bed of sickness, when the power of God rested upon him, and he went forth administering to the sick. He commenced with the sick in his own house, then visited those who were camping in tents in his own door yard, commanding the sick in the name of the Lord Jesus Christ to arise from their beds and be whole; when they were healed according to his words. He then went from house to house, and from tent to tent, upon the bank of the river, healing the sick by the power of Israel's God, as he went among them. He did not miss a single house, wagon or tent, and continued this work up to "the upper stone house," where he crossed the river in a boat, accompanied by

Parley P. Pratt, Orson Pratt, John E. Page, John Taylor, and myself, and landed at Montrose. He then walked into the cabin of Brother Brigham Young, who was lying very sick, and commanded him in the name of the Lord Jesus Christ to arise and be made whole. He arose, healed of his sickness, and then accompanied Joseph and his brethren of the Twelve, and went into the house of Brother Elijah Fordham, who was insensible, and considered by his family and friends to be in the hands of death. Joseph stepped to his bedside, looked him in the eye for a minute without speaking, then took him by the hand and commanded him in the name of Jesus Christ to arise from his bed and walk. Brother Fordham immediately leaped out of his bed, threw off all his poultices and bandages, dressed himself, called for a bowl of bread and milk, which he ate, and then followed us into the street. We then went into the house of Joseph B. Noble, who was also very sick, and he was healed in the same manner.

Joseph spoke with the voice and power of God.

When he had healed all the sick by the power given unto him he went down to the ferry boat, when a stranger rode up almost breathless, and said that he had heard that Joseph Smith was raising the dead, and healing all of the sick, and his wife begged him to ride up and get Mr. Smith to go down and heal her twin children, about three months old. Joseph replied, "I cannot go, but will send someone." In a few minutes he said to Elder Woodruff, "You go and heal those children, and take this pocket handkerchief, and when you administer to them, wipe their faces with it, and they shall recover." Brother Woodruff did as he was commanded, and the children were healed.

The mob spirits, when they saw men whom they thought were dying, arise from their beds, and pray for others, stood paralyzed with fear; yet those same men would have killed Joseph and his brethren if they had had an opportunity. Joseph recrossed the river to his own home and I returned to mine, rejoicing in the mercies and goodness of God. This was a day never to be forgotten by the Saints; nor by the wicked; for they saw the power of God manifest in the flesh (1945, pp. 262–64; see also Wilford Woodruff, 1865, p. 326; Brigham Young, 1968, pp. 49–50; Heber C. Kimball, JD, 2:233–34; Wandle Mace, n.d. [b], pp. 41–42).

Artemus Millet

I was taken sick with cholera and we sent for Joseph Smith Sen. and John his brother, who said the sickness was not unto death. And when they administered it did not have the desired effect. I suffered such excruciating pain that my groaning was heard at Joseph Smith Jun. a distance of 250 yards. I was afterwards told that when in agony I called out "Let Joseph Smith Jun. come and lay his hands on me and I shall be healed and I know it," not knowing what I said. He pressed his way through the crowd, for the house was filled with people, and came forward, and laying his hands upon my head asked God the Father in the name of Jesus Christ to heal me. The vomiting and purging ceased and I began to mend from that very moment (n.d.).

Parley P. Pratt

About this time a young lady, by the name of Chloe Smith, being a member of the Church, was lying very low with a lingering fever, with a family who occupied one of the houses on the farm of Isaac Morley, in Kirtland. Many of the Church had visited and prayed with her, but all to no effect; she seemed at the point of death, but would not consent to have a physician. This greatly enraged her relatives, who had cast her out because she belonged to the Church, and who, together with many of the people of the neighborhood, were greatly stirred up to anger, saying, "These wicked deceivers will let her lie and die without a physician, because of their superstitions; and if they do, we will prosecute them for so doing." Now these were daily watching for her last breath, with many threats.

Under these circumstances, President Smith and myself, with several other elders called to see her. She was so low that no one had been allowed for some days previous to speak above a whisper, and even the door of the log dwelling was muffled with cloths to prevent a noise.

We kneeled down and prayed vocally all around, each in turn; after which President Smith arose, went to the bedside, took her by the hand, and said unto her with a loud voice, "In the name of Jesus Christ arise and walk!" She immediately arose, was dressed by a woman in attendance, when she walked to a chair before the fire, and was seated and joined in singing a hymn. The house was thronged with people in a few moments, and the young lady arose and shook hands with each as they came in; and from that minute she was perfectly restored to health (1985, pp. 51–52).

Joseph Smith

This afternoon I was called, in company with President David Whitmer, to visit Angeline Works. We found her very sick, and so much deranged that she did not recognize her friends and intimate acquaintances. We prayed for her and laid hands on her in the name of Jesus Christ, and commanded her in His name to receive her senses, which were immediately restored. We also prayed that she might be restored to health; and she said she was better (HC, 2:328).

Joseph Smith

Sunday, 5 [September 1841]—I preached to a large congregation at the stand on the science and practice of medicine, desiring to persuade the Saints to trust in God when sick, and not in an arm of flesh, and live by faith and not by medicine, or poison; and when they were sick, and had called for the elders to pray for them, and they were not healed, to use herbs and mild food (HC, 4:414).

Joseph Smith

As a great number of brethren lay sick in the town, on Tuesday, 23rd July, 1839, I told Don Carlos and George A. Smith to go and visit all the sick, exercise mighty faith, and administer to them in the name of Jesus Christ, commanding the destroyer to depart, and the people to arise and walk; and not leave a single person on the bed between my house and Ebenezer Robinson's, two miles distant; they administered to over sixty persons, many of whom thought they would never sit up again; but they were healed, arose from their beds, and gave glory to God; some of them assisted in visiting and administering to others who were sick (HC, 4:398–99).

Lorenzo D. Young

The task [of finishing the outside walls of the Kirtland Temple] was completed on the 8th of January, 1836, but Lorenzo was sick the last two days. He had caught a bad cold accompanied with a very severe cough, and in a few days was confined to his bed. His disease was pronounced "quick consumption," and he sank rapidly. When for two weeks he had been unable to walk, Dr. Williams, one of the brethren, came to see him. Considering his case a bad one, he returned the next day and brought with him Dr. Seeley, an old practicing physician, and another doctor whose name is forgotten.

They examined the patient and Dr. Seeley asserted that he had not as much lungs as would fill a tea saucer. He appeared a somewhat rough, irreligious man. With what he probably considered a good-natured fling at the belief of the Saints in miracles, he said to Father Young, "Unless the Lord makes your son a pair of lungs there is no hope for him." Again we will let the subject of our narrative tell his experience, when his life seemed to hang only on a thread:

I was so low and nervous that I could scarcely bear any noise in the room. The next morning after the visit of the doctors, my father came to the door of the room to see how I was, and I recall his gazing earnestly at me with tears in his eyes. As I afterwards learned, he went from there to the Prophet Joseph and said to him: "My son, Lorenzo, is dying: can there not be something done for him?" The Prophet studied a few moments and replied, "Yes, of necessity I must go away to fill an appointment which I cannot put off. But you go and get my brother Hyrum, and with him get together twelve or fifteen good faithful brethren; go to the house of Brother Lorenzo and all join in prayer; one by mouth and the others repeat after him in unison. After prayer divide into quorums of three. Let the first quorum who administer anoint Brother Young with oil, then lay hands on him, one being mouth, and the other two repeating in unison with him. When all the quorums have, in succession, laid their hands on Brother Young and prayed for him, begin again with the first quorum by anointing, continuing the administration in this way until you receive a testimony that he will be restored."

My father came with fifteen of the brethren and these instructions were strictly followed. The administrations were continued until it came the turn of the first quorum the third time. Brother Hyrum Smith led. The Spirit rested mightily upon him and he was full of blessing and prophecy. He said that I should regain my health, live to go with the Saints into the bosom of the Rocky Mountains to build up a place there, and that my cellar should overflow with wine and fatness.

At that time I had not heard about the Saints going to the Rocky Mountains; possibly Brother Smith had. After he was through the administration he seemed surprised at some things he had said, and wondered at the manifestations of the Spirit. I coughed no more and rapidly recovered. I had been pronounced by the best physicians in the country past all human aid. I am now a living witness of the powers of God through the administration of the elders (1946, pp. 45–46).

"Working of Miracles"

William F. Cahoon

This [Zion's] camp marched through a population of tens of thousands of people like lambs among wolves, but no man among them opened his mouth to say, "Why do you do so?" On we marched, singing our favorite song, "Hark, Listen to the Trumpeters."

[The following was related by William F. Cahoon and Father Cole.] While traveling across the vast prairie, treeless and waterless, they camped at night after a long and wearisome day's march. They had been without water since early morning, and men and animals suffered greatly from thirst, for it had been one of the hottest days of June. Joseph sat at his tent looking out upon the scene. All at once he called for a spade. When it was brought, he looked about him and selected a spot, the most convenient in the camp for men and teams to get water. Then he dug a shallow well, and immediately the water came bubbling up into it and filled it, so that the horses and mules could stand and drink from it. While the camp stayed there, the well remained full, despite the fact that about two hundred men and scores of horses and mules were supplied from it (1960, pp. 81–82; see also Oliver B. Huntington, n.d. [b], pp. 23–24; 1902, pp. 20–21).

Levi Curtis

About the month of August, 1856, William D. Huntington and I went into Hobble Creek Canyon to get a tree or log suitable for making drums. After we had finished our labor and started for home, both of us riding on the log, our conversation naturally turned upon the doctrines of the Church and experiences of the past, when the life and labors of the Prophet Joseph were touched upon. This subject aroused into more than usual earnestness the mind and conversation of my associate.

He said that in Nauvoo he lived in the family of and worked for Joseph Smith at the time the Prophet had such a wonderful time with the sick, when nearly everybody was stricken down and he himself was among the afflicted, and was one of those who were healed by Joseph. He said he had been sick some weeks and kept getting weaker, until he became so helpless that he could not move. Finally he got so low he could not speak, but had perfect consciousness of all that was passing in the room. He saw friends come to the bedside, look at him a moment, and commence weeping, then turn away.

He further stated that he presently felt easy, and observing his situation found that he was in the upper part of the room near the ceiling, and could see the body he had occupied lying on the bed, with weeping friends, standing around as he had witnessed in many cases where people had died under his own observation.

About this time he saw Joseph Smith and two other brethren come into the room. Joseph turned to his wife Emma and asked her to get him a dish of clean water. This she did; and the Prophet with the two brethren accompanying him washed their hands and carefully wiped them. Then they stepped to the bed and laid their hands upon the head of his body, which at that time looked loathsome to him, and as the three stretched out their hands to place them upon the head, he by some means became aware that he must go back into that body, and started to do so. The process of getting in he could not remember; but when Joseph said "amen," he heard and could see and feel with his body. The feeling for a moment was most excruciating, as though his body was pierced in every part with some sharp instruments.

As soon as the brethren had taken their hands from his head he raised up in bed, sitting erect, and in another moment turned his legs off the bed.

At this juncture Joseph asked him if he had not better be careful, for he was very weak. He replied, "I never felt better in my life," almost immediately adding, "I want my pants."

His pants were found and given him, which he drew on, Joseph assisting him, although he thought he needed no help. Then he signified his intention to sit in a chair at or near the fireplace. Joseph took hold of his arm to help him along safely, but William declared his ability to walk alone, notwithstanding which, the help continued.

Astonishment had taken the place of weeping throughout the room. Every looker-on was ready to weep for joy; but none were able or felt inclined to talk.

Presently William said he wanted something to eat. Joseph asked him what he would like, and he replied that he wanted a dish of bread and milk.

Emma immediately brought what he called for; as one may easily comprehend, every hand was anxious to supply the wants of a man who, a few moments before was dead, really and truly dead! Brother Huntington ate the bowl of bread and milk with as good a relish as any he ever ate.

In a short time all felt more familiar, and conversation upon the scene that transpired followed. William related his experiences, and the friends theirs.

Joseph listened to the conversation and in his turn remarked that they had just witnessed as great a miracle as Jesus did while on the earth. They had seen the dead brought to life.

At the close of his narrative to me William Huntington remarked:

"Now I have told you the truth, and here I am a live man, sitting by the side of you on this log, and I testify that Joseph Smith was a prophet of God" (1892, pp. 385–86).

Addison Everett

In the conversation between Joseph and Hyrum, Oliver Cowdery was spoken of—Joseph said "Poor boy!" and went on to state that at Colesville he and Oliver were under arrest on charges of deceiving the people. When they were at the justice's house for trial in the evening, all were waiting for Mr. Reid, Joseph's lawyer. And while waiting the justice asked Joseph some questions, among which was this:

"What was the first miracle Jesus performed?"

Joseph replied, "He made this world, and what followed we are not told" (1890, pp. 75–76).

Amasa Potter

I recollect the Prophet arising to speak at another time in the grove in Nauvoo. I think it was on the occasion of the funeral of Elder King Follett, who was crushed to death in a well. The subject of baptism for the dead was dwelt upon, and when he had spoken about thirty minutes there came up a heavy wind and storm. The dust was so dense that we could not see each other any distance, and some of the people were leaving when Joseph called out to them to stop and let their prayers ascend to Almighty God that the winds may cease blowing and the rain stop falling, and it should be so. In a very few minutes the winds and rain ceased and the elements became calm as summer's morning. The storm divided and went on the north and south of the city, and we could see in the distance the trees and shrubs waving in the wind, while where we were it was quiet for one hour, and during that time one of the greatest sermons that ever fell from the Prophet's lips was preached on the great subject of the dead (1894, p. 132).

Harriet A. Preston

I remember sitting on the stone steps which led up to the entrance of the temple, and with what reverent admiration I looked upon it, although too young to sense its significance. I recall having gone to a well which our beloved prophet had blessed to the end that all those who should drink of it should receive health (1920, p. 19).

Joseph Smith

In the evening, Bishop Whitney, his wife, father, mother, and sister-in-law, came and invited me and my wife to go with them and visit Father Smith and family. My wife was unwell, and could not go, but my scribe and I went.

When we arrived, some of the young elders were about engaging in a debate on the subject of miracles. The question—"Was it, or was it not, the design of Christ to establish His gospel by miracles?" After an interesting debate of three hours or more, during which time much talent was displayed, it was decided, by the President of the debate, in the negative, which was a righteous decision.

I discovered in this debate, much warmth displayed, too much zeal for mastery, too much of that enthusiasm that characterizes a lawyer at the bar, who is determined to defend his cause, right or wrong. I therefore availed myself of this favorable opportunity to drop a few words upon this subject, by way of advice, that they might improve their minds and cultivate their powers of intellect in a proper manner, that they might not incur the displeasure of heaven; that they should handle sacred things very sacredly, and with due deference to the opinions of others, and with an eye single to the glory of God (HC, 2:317–18).

"Given to Prophesy"

William F. Cahoon

On May 5, 1834 the [Zion's] camp left [for] Missouri. It was truly a solemn morning; we left our wives, children, and friends, not knowing whether we would see them again, as we were threatened by enemies that would destroy and exterminate us from the land. We were facing the "lion in his den."

Joseph Smith had made this pledge to us, "If you will go with me to Missouri and keep my counsel, I pledge that I will lead you there and back and not a hair of your head shall be hurt" (1960, p. 81).

George Q. Cannon

The last time the Prophet addressed the people he predicted that peace should be taken from the earth, and that terrible calamities would come upon its inhabitants, and particularly upon our own nation. He predicted what the results would be of the spirit of mobocracy which then raged, and which had caused our expulsion from our homes, if allowed to prevail. Already, the prediction had been recorded by him, twelve years previous to his death, that there would be a rebellion break out in South Carolina, and a fratricidal war commence between the South and the North. The revelation upon this subject had been written [see D&C 87]; it had been published. It was well known to the great bulk of the Latter-day Saints years previous to this. I, when quite a child heard it, and looked for its fulfillment until it came to pass. And this was the case with the body of the people who were familiar with the predictions which had been uttered by the Prophet Joseph Smith (JD, 22:135).

Jared Carter

[From Kirtland I] commenced a mission to the east on [the] 22nd day of September 1831, with Brother Ebensar Page. We traveled to Hiram, in the first place, where we attended meeting where Brother Joseph and Sidney live. Brother Joseph, after I had come there, asked me if I was willing to preach to them. I told him that I was; accordingly I endeavored to on Sunday, the 25th. In the afternoon, we had a meeting and Brother Joseph, the Prophet and Seer, before the meeting closed, had the spirit of prophecy come on him while he was looking upon me and I saw that the form of his countenance was changed; he while looking upon me said, "Bless the Lord" and after this prophesied relative to the mission that I had commenced and expressed what should take place on conditions I was faithful, and in this I found him of the truth and to predict the truth for the whole was fulfilled (n.d.).

Isaac Decker

In 1836, soon after the dedication of the Kirtland Temple, and while the brethren were holding meetings from house to house, breaking bread, consecrating and drinking wine and prophesying, I attended one of the meetings where Joseph Smith, Martin Harris, and John Smith were present. Martin said there would not be a living Gentile on the earth in four years. Joseph reproved him and said, "Brother Martin, you are too fast; after messages are sent with lightning speed, with iron carriages drawn by iron horses snorting fire and smoke, with less speed than the messages were carried, *then,* it may do to talk about the time for the destruction of the Gentiles. But before that takes place they will make wonderful improvements in machinery of every kind, especially implements of husbandry for the working of the land and raising grain, saving a great deal of labor to the saints in building up the kingdom. The Lord will inspire the Gentiles to do this, but they will not acknowledge his hand in it, nor give him the glory, but will take the glory to themselves, and when their destruction comes the wicked will slay the wicked; the saints will not destroy the Gentiles, they will be divided among themselves and destroy one another. But the time is with the Lord. The benefits of all their ingenuity and inventions will be the means of advancing the building up of Zion with greater speed. The Lord will have the glory" (1870).

Note: Some may feel Joseph alludes to trains—"iron carriages drawn by iron horses snorting fire and smoke." Note, however, that trains existed in Joseph's day; indeed, the earliest and most primitive trains existed even before his birth, and some were in commercial operation during his lifetime. He himself rode on a train in July 1836 (HC, 2:436). Perhaps this is a reference to cars and trucks, or for that matter, something not yet invented. The significant dimension of what Decker mentions, it seems, is the timing of the destruction of the Gentiles as something which follows dramatic technological advancement, and the fact that they will not be destroyed by the Saints but that "they will destroy one another."

Philo Dibble

On the 11th of February, 1841, I married a second wife [Dibble's first wife had died]—a widow Smith of Philadelphia, who was living in the family of the Prophet. He performed the ceremony at his house, and Sister Emma Smith insisted upon getting up a wedding supper for us. It was a splendid affair, and quite a large party of our friends were assembled.

I then rented a house of Hyrum [Hiram] Kimball on the river bank for ten dollars per month, and kept a warehouse, and also boarders and a bakery. While there in business, I saw in vision my grave before me for two weeks; it mattered not whether my eyes were open or shut it was there, and I saw no way of escape. One day Brother Joseph came and took dinner with us, and as we arose from the table I walked out upon the porch and sat down on a bench. Joseph and my wife followed me, and he came before me and said: "Philo, you must get away from here or you will die, as sure as God ever spoke by my mouth!" He then turned to my wife and said: "And you will hardly escape by the skin of your teeth!"

I immediately stepped into Joseph's carriage and rode with him to the south part of town and rented another place, after which I settled up my business as fast as I could, and made arrangements to remove. Many hearing of Joseph's prediction about me, said if they had been in my place they would have remained where I was and tested the truth of it, but I assured them if they had been in my place they would have done just as I did.

After I had settled my business and removed my family, we were one day at Joseph's house, when he said to my wife: "You didn't believe what I told Philo the other day! Now, I will tell you what the Lord told me; He told me to go and tell Philo to come away from there, and if he obeyed he should live; if not he should die; and I didn't want to see you a widow so soon again. If Philo had remained there fourteen days longer, he would have been a corpse" (1968, p. 93).

Mary D. Ensign

[Joseph Smith] was also a man of great faith. On one occasion my father was very sick and sent for the Prophet to come. He shook hands with father and asked him if he had ever had the measles. Father said, "No." The Prophet then said, "You will have them," and before he took his hands off, father was broken out with the measles as thick as could be (n.d.; see, for comparison, Exodus 4:6–7; Numbers 12:10–16).

Jesse W. Fox

Speaking about Russia brings to mind a prophecy which is accredited to the Prophet Joseph Smith, concerning this country. Elder Jesse W. Fox Sr. received the narration from Father Taylor, the father of the late President John Taylor. The old gentleman said that at one time the Prophet Joseph Smith was in his house conversing about the Battle of Waterloo, in which Father Taylor had taken part. Suddenly the Prophet turned and said, "Father Taylor, you will live to see, though I will not, greater battles than that of Waterloo. The slave question will cause a division between the North and the South, and in these wars greater battles than Waterloo will occur. But," he continued, with emphasis, "when the great bear (Russia) lays her paw on the lion (England) the winding up scene is not far distant."

These words were uttered before there was any prospect of war with Mexico, and such a thing as division in the United States was never contemplated. Yet these fierce struggles came, and though Joseph himself was slain before they occurred, Father Taylor lived to witness some of the world's most remarkable battles. [He died May 27, 1870, in Salt Lake City, Utah.]

The struggle between the bear and the lion has not yet happened, but as surely as Joseph the Prophet ever predicted such an event, so surely will it not fail of its fulfillment (1890, p. 162; see also Jesse W. Crosby, n.d. [b]; Oliver B. Huntington, n.d. [b], p. 34).

Lillie Freeze

We should post ourselves regarding the prophecies that have been predicted. I will mention one in particular that was uttered by the Prophet Joseph Smith; he said the time would come when none but the women of the Latter-day Saints would be willing to bear children (1890, p. 81).

Catherine Greer

My mother belonged to the Methodist Church. Brother Joseph told her, "Sister Camp, you will come into the church and be one of the best Latter-day Saints," but my mother did not believe it, but when she went to Nauvoo next time, she investigated and was baptized by Brother John Taylor (n.d.).

Aroet L. Hale

The Prophet Joseph predicted a curse on John C. Bennett. He told him if he did not repent of his sins and sin no more, the curse of God Almighty would rest upon him, that he would die a vagabond upon the face of the earth, without friends to bury him. He told him that he stunk of women. In the year 1850, President Young was speaking about the matter. He said that he had watched the life of John C. Bennett. Bennett went to California in the great gold fever excitement, that Bennett died in one of the lowest slums of California, that he was dragged out with his boots on, put into a cart, hauled off, and dumped into a hole, a rotten mass of corruption. This prediction or prophecy came to pass as well as many others that I heard the Prophet Joseph make (n.d., pp. 6–7).

Levi W. Hancock

I was living with Joseph Smith Jr. and had completed the translating room and had seen many new brethren, and had heard Joseph speak many things concerning them, but no observation sunk with such weight on my mind as the one that he made about Brigham Young and Joseph Young. Some time in the month of Nov. 1832, these men came to Joseph Smith in the evening and sung and prayed with us. After they had gone from there Joseph Smith said to me, "How do you like the men?" or something near it. After he had got my answer he said, "These are good men," and "There is Brigham Young; [he] is a great man and one day the whole kingdom will rest upon him; and there is the smaller one, he is a great man, but his brother [Brigham] is greater" (n.d. [a]).

Jesse P. Harmon

He [Uncle Appleton] was baptized in Nauvoo. He and grandfather [Jesse Perse (Pierce) Harmon] were both very active in church and civic affairs. They were policemen and grandfather was a bodyguard of the Prophet Joseph Smith. He was also a major and later a colonel in the Nauvoo Legion. When the *"Nauvoo Expositor,"* a paper, was issued by the enemies of the Church, . . . the City Council declared it a misdemeanor and ordered the police to destroy it. The Prophet promised them that not one of them would be harmed; although it caused great excitement and many threats from the mob, no one was injured (n.d.).

Oliver B. Huntington

I will relate a testimony that Joseph Smith was a prophet, which was borne by a gentile as witnessed by Brother Packard and told to us that evening, or night. He said that he was in a saloon in the Sweet Water, when gold was first found there, and a very tall lank westerner came in finely dressed in the best broadcloth and everything on him corresponding. He looked rather out of place among a lot of rough miners, and one of his old comrades meeting him asked where he got such fine clothes, or how he could afford to wear such?

The tall man replied that it was because they cost him nothing. His comrade asked how that happened.

The reply was "because Joseph Smith was a true prophet."

"What has that to do with your getting that suit of clothes?"

The tall man said, "[I] will tell you. I went into a store in Carson; an old friend of mine kept it. I was dead broke and had on next to nothing, and the storekeeper asked me why I didn't wear better clothes? I told him I'd like to."

He said for me to "pick out the best suit I could find in the store and pay him when Stephen A. Douglas was elected President." Now that occurred when Douglas was running for President of the U.S.

A little before the election I told the storekeeper I'd take two suits on them terms, but he said one was all he proposed to let me have.

The interlocutor asked how he dare take them on that condition. "Well, you see, Joe Smith told Douglas before he thought of trying to be President that he would try it some day, and that if he used his influence against the Mormons he should never set in the President's chair, and I kept watch and kept thinking of that prophecy, just to see if Joe was a true prophet. When I see Douglas trying to be President I knew Joe Smith was a true prophet and that Douglas would not be elected because he had turned against the Mormons. I have watched Joe's prophecies and never seen one of them fail (n.d. [b], pp. 16–17).

Oliver B. Huntington

Joseph Smith the Prophet once undertook to plead law. I have the name of the man who was under arrest, in my journal somewhere, but it would be a *job* to find it, and the name matters but little—the story of the Prophet acting as a prosecuting attorney is impressed upon my mind never to be blotted out or dimmed by time, it will be fresh while reason lasts, not so much for the law he quoted, but for the great prophecy he uttered and the divine appearance of the man while he spoke the word of the Lord.

Soon after we left Nauvoo and settled in Commerce, three of our brethren were kidnapped by Missourians, taken to Missouri and starved and whipped until they were hardly able to run at all, but they managed to get away and returned home.

One of the men who did that wicked, cruel deed was found years after in disguise parading the streets of Nauvoo, and was recognized by old Father James Allred as the very man who took him forcibly from Illinois back into Missouri and there treated him worse than a . . . man should treat his dog.

The Prophet was mayor, but the kidnapper was brought before an alderman for trial and Joseph acted as prosecuting attorney. When he had just fairly started to set forth the crime that the defendant was arraigned for, he suddenly left the law and declared the word of God with regard to the state of Missouri and its inhabitants. He told what the Saints had suffered at the hands of Missouri and the injustice and cruelty of their sufferings, and he went on to tell what Missouri should be called to endure in order to pay the penalty of wrongs inflicted and for the blood of the Saints they had shed.

A portion of the words of the prophecy I will quote verbatim: "She shall drink out of the same cup, the same bitter dregs we have drunk, poured out, out, out! And that by the hand of an enemy—a race meaner than themselves."

All the time he was delivering the word of the Lord his face shone as if there was a light within him and his flesh was translucent.

The time occupied was considerable, for he pronounced two other very remarkable prophecies.

When he had done prophesying he stopped speaking entirely, while he wiped a flood of perspiration from his face and gave vent to his pent-up breath with a long blow, kind of a half-whistle, and after a minute or two he remarked, "Well, where that meaner race is coming from God only knows. It is not the (slaves), for they don't know enough, and are gentlemen by the side of their masters. It is not the Indians, for they are the chosen people of God and a noble race of men, but as sure as God ever spoke by me that shall come to pass."

I lived to see that prophecy literally fulfilled in the Rebellion, when every family in that part of the state that the Saints used to occupy was killed or compelled to leave their homes by the Bushwackers or Guerrillas under Quantrell—a generation of vipers raised mostly after that prophecy was uttered (1890b, pp. 124–25).

Oliver B. Huntington

My father was living in a good hewed log house in 1840 when one morning as the family all sat at breakfast old Father Joseph Smith, the first Patriarch of the Church and father of the Prophet Joseph, came in and sat down by the fireplace, after declining to take breakfast with us, and there he sat some little time in silence looking steadily in the fire. At length he observed that we had been driven from Missouri to this place [Nauvoo]; with some passing comments, he then asked this question: "And how long, Brother Huntington, do you think we will stay here?" As he asked this question I noticed a strange, good-natured expression creep over his whole being—an air of mysterious joy.

Father answered, after just a moment's hesitation, "Well, Father Smith, I can't begin to imagine."

"We will just stay here seven years," he answered. "The Lord has told Joseph so—just seven years," he repeated. "Now this is not to be made public; I would not like to have this word go any further," said the Patriarch, who leaned and relied upon his son Joseph in all spiritual matters as much as boys generally do upon their parents for temporalities. There were then two or three minutes of perfect silence. The old gentleman with more apparent secret joy and caution in his countenance said, "And where do you think we will go to when we leave here, Brother Huntington?"

Father did not pretend to guess; unless we went back to Jackson County.

"No," said the old Patriarch, his whole being seeming to be alive with animation. "The Lord has told Joseph that when we leave here we will go into the Rocky Mountains; right into the midst of the Lamanites."

This information filled our hearts with unspeakable joy, for we knew that the Book of Mormon and this gospel had been brought to light more for the remnants of Jacob upon this continent than for the Gentiles.

Father Smith again enjoined upon us profound secrecy in this matter and I don't think it was ever uttered by one of Father Huntington's family.

The history of Nauvoo shows that we located in Nauvoo in 1839 and left it in 1846.

The Church did move to the Rocky Mountains into the midst of the Indians or Lamanites—or more properly speaking the Jews—and here expect to live until we move to the spirit land or the Lord moves us somewhere else (1891b, pp. 314–15; see also Bathsheba W. Smith, 1905, pp. 549–50; Eliza R. Snow, 1884, p. 76).

Oliver B. Huntington

On one occasion while the Prophet was waiting for his boots to be repaired by my brother Dimick in Nauvoo he indulged in recounting personal services rendered him by Dimick; he exhibited his gratitude and greatness of soul in this way.

He said, "Now, Dimick, in return for such acts, you may ask of me what you will and it shall be given you, even if it be to the half of my kingdom."

Dimick told it to me, and said that in thinking what he should ask for, decided he would not ask for anything that would impoverish Joseph, nor would he ask for worldly honors or goods, but made this request:

"Brother Joseph, I want that where you and your father's house are (having reference to eternity) there I and my father's house may be also."

Joseph sat in meditation but a moment, and then said, "Dimick, in the name of Jesus Christ it shall be even as you ask" (1891d, p. 466).

Oliver B. Huntington

A few days after Joseph arrived from Missouri, Dimick [Oliver's brother] went in to see the beloved prophet, to whom he was devotedly attached. Joseph remarked to him in their conversation, "Dimick, there is a very important mission for you among the Indians."

Dimick soon went home and told his wife that Joseph had a mission for him among the Indians, and he wanted to be ready in the morning. So the poor wife was up most of the night mending and preparing his clothing for an absence of an indefinite period of time. The devoted followers of the Prophet apparently had no limits to service nor bounds to possibilities.

After breakfast Dimick, with valise in hand, went to report to the Prophet, and said: "Well, Brother Joseph, I am ready to go now."

"Go where?" asked the Prophet.

"To the Indians," was the reply.

Joseph smiled in a lovingly, dignified way peculiar to himself, and remarked: "You are not to go now, Dimick, but after awhile you will do a great work among the Lamanites."

To go or not to go made no difference to Dimick, so long as he yielded obedience to the Prophet's call.

When we came into Salt Lake Valley Dimick Huntington was the first man that learned to talk with the Indians; he was the "first man" among them and to them to the end of his life. His name among the Indians was Ne-oam-bahds, which in Ute means "Good Talk." All the tribes in the mountains gave him credit for always telling them the truth. His influence was great among all the tribes that knew him and many that knew his name only.

I traveled among various tribes and bands of Indians from here to the Sierras, and invariably found his name familiar with them.

He was interpreter for Territorial Superintendent of Indian Affairs while Brigham Young was Governor, and remained interpreter and manager of Indians for the Church until his death. . . .

Thus we see that he truly filled the mission given him by the Prophet (1896, pp. 84–85).

Orson Hyde

Something near eight years ago [about 1832] Joseph Smith, a prophet and servant of the Most High God, did predict upon my head that I should yet go to the city of Jerusalem, and be a watchman unto the house of Israel, and perform a work there which would greatly facilitate the gathering together of that people (1913, p. 55).

Orson Hyde

Now I look around this congregation, and contemplate that there are, perhaps, some ten or twelve thousand persons, and it may be more, I do not know; there is a very large number; then when I think that numerous as we are here we are but the representatives—not more than a tithing of those left behind, of the same stripe, it reminds me of the words of Joseph the Prophet, when he said, "Brethren, remember that the majority of this people will never go astray; and as long as you keep with the majority you are sure to enter the celestial kingdom" (JD, 13:367).

Orson Hyde

I remember once, in Nauvoo, when we felt ourselves happy and fortunate if we could get half a bushel of meal to make mush of, the Prophet Joseph Smith, talking to some of us at the house of Brother John Taylor, said—"Brethren, we are pretty tight run now, but the time will come when you will have so much money that you will be weary with counting it, and you will be tried with riches;" and I sometimes think that perhaps the preface to that time has now arrived, and that the Saints will soon be tried with riches; but if riches would kill our prospects of eternal life by alienating us from the priesthood and kingdom of God, I say it would be far better for us to remain like Lazarus, and that all our fine things should perish like the dew, and we come down to the bedrock of faith, and trust in the true and living God (JD, 17:5).

Andrew Jenson

I will now refer you to another most remarkable prophecy and its fulfillment. Among the prominent men of Illinois, who befriended the Saints when they were expelled from Missouri, was Stephen A. Douglas, afterwards know as the "Little Giant," and who became one of the great statesmen of our nation. This man continued friendly to the Saints for many years, and especially to Joseph Smith, in whose case he, as an Illinois district judge, rendered a fair and impartial decision at Monmouth, June 10, 1841, at a time when the Missourians were endeavoring to get Joseph Smith into their power. After that he and the Prophet exchanged visits, and on one occasion when Joseph dined with him in Carthage, Illinois, May 18, 1843, he listened to a lengthy explanation from the Prophet about the Missouri persecutions. Winding up the conversation, Joseph spoke of the dire effects that would flow to the nation if the United States should refuse to redress the wrongs of murder, arson, and robbery committed against the Saints in Missouri and the crimes committed upon the Saints by officers of the government. Turning to Judge Douglas he said:

"You will aspire to the presidency of the United States, and if ever you turn your hand against me or the Latter-day Saints, you will feel the weight of the hand of the Almighty upon you; and you will live to see and know that I have testified the truth to you, for the conversation of this day will stick to you through life."

This remarkable prophesy concerning Judge Douglas personally has had a literal fulfillment. Judge Douglas continued to raise in prominence in the nation as long as he remained a friend to the Saints. But, finally he turned against them, and at the time the excitement ran high against the "Mormons" in 1857, and preparations were being made to send an army against the people of Utah, Judge Douglas thought he would add a little to the great popularity he had already achieved by doing the most popular thing that could be done at the time, namely, denounce the "Mormons." Hence, in a political speech which he delivered in Springfield, Ill., June 12th, 1857, and which was published in the *Missouri Republican* of June 18th following and partly republished with comments in the *Deseret News* of September 2nd, 1857, Senator Douglas attacked the Saints in Utah in a most fierce and unwarranted manner, and among many other bitter expressions which he made, he called "Mormonism a loathsome, disgusting ulcer," to which he recommended that Congress apply the knife and cut it out. In the *Deseret News* of the date mentioned, the prophecy of Joseph

Smith was republished with warning remarks directed to Mr. Douglas, who at that time, in fulfillment of Joseph's words, was already aspiring to the presidency of the United States.

In the campaign of 1860 he became the candidate of the Independent Democratic party for that position. It is asserted that no man ever entered into a campaign with brighter prospects of success than did Senator Douglas on that occasion. His friends viewed him as sure to be seated in the Presidential chair, because of his great popularity. But, alas, he and his friends had reckoned without Divine interposition. He had lifted his hands against the Saints of the Most High God and denounced the people whom he knew to be innocent and whom he ought to have defended. The result was that he was sadly defeated at the election, as he only received two electoral votes against seventeen cast for Abraham Lincoln (Republican) and eleven cast for J.C. Breckenridge (Democrat).

When the result of the election became known in Utah, Apostle Orson Hyde published the following in the *Deseret News* of December 12, 1860:

Ephraim, Utah Ter., Nov. 27, 1860.

"Will the judge now acknowledge that Joseph Smith was a true prophet? If he will not, does he recollect a certain conversation had with Mr. Smith at the house of Sheriff Backenstos, in Carthage, Illinois, in the year 1843, in which Mr. Smith said to him: 'You will yet aspire to the presidency of the United States. But if you ever raise your hand, or your voice against the Latter-day Saints, you shall never be President of the United States.'

"Does Judge Douglas recollect that in a public speech delivered by him in the year 1857, at Springfield, Illinois, of comparing the Mormon community, then constituting the inhabitants of Utah Territory, to a 'loathsome ulcer on the body politic,' and of recommending the knife to be applied to cut it out?

"Among other things the judge will doubtless recollect that I was present and heard the conversation between him and Joseph Smith, at Mr. Backenstos' residence in Carthage, before alluded to.

"Now, Judge, what think you about Joseph Smith and Mormonism?"

A few months later, or in June, 1861, Judge Douglas died in disappointment and grief. Never has the saying of any prophet of God been more literally and minutely fulfilled than the prediction made by the Prophet Joseph Smith concerning this man (CD, 2:161–63).

Elizabeth C. Kendall

"Mother" Clements [Elizabeth's mother] washed and ironed for the Prophet Joseph Smith's family, and Elizabeth and her brothers delivered the finished articles in a little wagon. Many times they took popcorn and apples with them to give to members of the Smith family, which seemed to please them very much. On one of these deliveries the Prophet asked Elizabeth if she would like to see the "mummies" which were kept in the attic. Naturally, she was thrilled and curious. At first Elizabeth was frightened when she saw them, but Joseph, noticing this, came to her side and, laying his hand on her shoulder, said, "If you will touch them you will never be afraid of the dead." This she did and he then placed his hand on her head and gave her a blessing. He told her she would be a great nurse and would care for and administer to many, and that she would accomplish various other needed services during her lifetime (1960, p. 112).

Note: Elizabeth became a plural wife of Levi Newell Kendall on 7 November 1852. In the next twenty-five years, twelve children were born to them. "They moved to Springville in 1858, and true to the Prophet's blessing, Elizabeth, besides rearing her own large family, was called to do nursing, and also to help prepare the dead for burial. She became a midwife and delivered hundreds of babies, for which service she usually received farm produce in lieu of money" (Kendall, 1960, p. 113).

Heber C. Kimball

It seems that prior to starting on this mission, Heber had been promised by the Prophet that he should see the Queen of England. The fulfillment occurred as follows: On the 26th of January [1841] Victoria opened the British Parliament. Apostles Kimball and Woodruff, with Dr. Copeland and several other friends, started out for the purpose of witnessing the royal pageant. Arriving at St. James' Park at 10 A.M., they beheld an immense concourse of people, extending in two unbroken lines from Buckingham Palace to the House of Lords. It was estimated that from three to four hundred thousand people were assembled. Through the courtesy of one of the Queen's life-guards—and no small favor was it on that day—Heber and his party succeeded in getting a place in the front line, past which the grand procession was to move. The royal cortege passed within ten feet of where they stood, so that they obtained a fair view of Her Majesty, both going to and returning from the Houses of Parliament. The Queen sat in a gorgeous state carriage, drawn by eight cream-colored horses, richly caparisoned. At her left hand sat Albert, the

Prince Consort. Following were six carriages, each drawn by six horses, containing members of the royal family, lords and nobles.

Says Heber: "We saw her, as the Prophet Joseph had told us. She made a low bow to us, and we returned the compliment. She looked pleasant, small of stature, with blue eyes, an innocent looking woman. Prince Albert is a fine looking man. All things went on pleasantly. No accidents" (1945, pp. 304–5).

Heber C. Kimball

I heard Joseph say twice that Brother Brigham and I should be in that council in Jerusalem, when there should be a uniting of the two divisions of God's government (JD, 9:27).

Alfred B. Lambson

I thought I was a bigger infidel than Robert Ingersoll, and read the Bible for spite, the better to find fault with. . . .

[Yet] something kept drawing me west, farther and farther west. With St. Louis as my objective point, I went to Nauvoo to visit my uncle. I put up at the Mansion House, curious to see the Prophet, and was sitting watching for him to enter. Presently, he came in and sat down. Lorin Walker put a towel about the Prophet's shoulders and dressed his hair for him, after which he got up and came over to me, lifting me bodily out of the chair, and asked: "Young man, where are you from and where are you going?" I told him where I hailed from and that I was bound for St. Louis to join a fur company going to Oregon, to which he said: "When you join a fur company at St. Louis to go to Oregon, I will take Nauvoo on my back and carry it across the Mississippi, and set it down in Iowa," adding, "I have use for you."

The Prophet made a deep impression upon me; I felt that he was superior to any man I had ever seen. In fact, if any other man had asked me those questions I should have very soon told him it was none of his business—but what use the Prophet could have for me I could not see (1915, pp. 147–48).

Note: Col. Robert G. Ingersoll, a self-announced agnostic, made a career in the latter half of the nineteenth century debating with clergy and others on religious themes, most of which he considered silly superstitions. He thought God was a man-made invention, Jesus often less inspiring than Confucius and others, hell an invention of fear-filled clerics and an "infamous lie," Moses a man of more mistakes than inspiration, the existence of an afterlife uncertain and unprovable, and religion in general a flight from accepting responsibility for self. See, for example, The Complete Lectures of Col. R. G. Ingersoll *(Chicago: Rhodes & McClure, 1897, 1900).*

Note: That Joseph did "have use" for Alfred B. Lambson is illustrated in a letter which Lambson, a wheelwright, wrote telling of his experiences crossing the plains: "On one occasion with the organized help of the camp, and one or two skilled assistants, under my direction, we measured, cut, welded, and set eighty-five tires in one day" (see Kesler, 1952, p. 103).

Andrew Lamoreaux

I have just learned from the family of the late Andrew L. Lamoreaux that Joseph Smith, during his tour to Washington in 1839, stopped with them in Dayton, Ohio, and before leaving laid his hands on Elder Lamoreaux and blessed him, and prophesied upon his head, that he would go on a mission to France, learn another tongue, and do much good, but that he would not return to his family, as he would fall by the way as a martyr. The Prophet wept as he blessed him and told him these things, adding that it was pressed upon him and he could not refrain from giving utterance to it. Elder Lamoreaux talked with his family about it when he left them in 1852, and endeavored to persuade them that this was not the time and mission upon which he should fall, but to believe that he would at this time be permitted to return again. When the "Luminary" [a periodical published in the interest of the Church in St. Louis] brought the tiding of his death, they exclaimed, "Surely, Brother Joseph was a prophet, for all his words have come to pass." Thinking this incident should not be lost, I have penned it from the mouth of his eldest daughter and submit it to you, and would add that his excessive labor and toil in providing for the company under his charge during the hot weather in June, in the unhealthy climate of St. Louis, predisposed him to that terrible scourge that laid him low, and thus he fell a sacrifice for his brethren (1971, 3:666).

Note: On returning from the French Mission in 1855, Elder Lamoreaux stopped in St. Louis, where, at a camp of the Saints, he spent his energies in instructing and counseling the Saints under his charge. On the evening of June 10 he addressed the congregation in a large church. Having suffered with diarrhea for several days, he remarked that the usual remedies had not worked. He continued to worsen and was overtaken by cramps, which caused a steady decline until he died of what was called the Asiatic cholera.

George Laub

Now I will relate some of the prophecies that I heard our beloved Brother Joseph Smith declare while filled with the Spirit of the living God in the name of Jesus Christ that if they put him in for ruler of this nation, he would save them and set them at liberty, but if they refused they shall and will be swept off, that there will not be any more than a grease spot of them left.

Also, while filled with the Spirit he prophesied in the name of Jesus Christ that if the Missourians would not redress the wrongs of the Saints that the red hot wrath of Almighty God would be poured out upon them and the rulers of this nation also, and the Missourians should be destroyed of a meaner people than themselves. This now we can see, cities on fire all over the United States, which plainly fills this prophecy. . . . [T]hey refused to give him the rule of the nations and refused to redress the wrongs of the Missourians, but killed the man of God (n.d., pp. 30–31).

Sarah S. Leavitt

There was an Englishman who bought a farm from Joseph, adjoining ours, and when his land was surveyed, it took in our field of wheat. When the wheat was ripe, my husband took his cradle and went in to cut it. The man, Fox, I think was his name, forbid his cutting the wheat. He said it was on his land and he should have it. My husband went down to Joseph and asked him what he should do. Joseph told him to let Fox have the wheat, but he should be cursed; that the law would bear him out in keeping the wheat, but not to grieve for it, that he (Joseph) would pay him it in flour.

And the curses of God did overtake him so much that he did not live to eat the wheat. He and his wife would brag of their gold and how much money and every good thing they had, that they had enough to last for years. They would take me to her bureau and show me her nice things, but though I was very poor, I did not covet anything she had. Fox said nobody would dare to come around his house to steal his gold, for he had $50,000 in the house. When he told me that, I had a very curious feeling that he had come among the Saints and had brought deadly weapons to defend his gold and his great treasures. I told him he need be under no fear among the Saints, for if they could take his money without his knowing it, they would feel as Moses said, "Thou God seeth me," and to him that has fed and clothed us all of our lives we have got to give an account.

Not long after this we were sent for to his house. He was dying. He did not speak after we went in and soon breathed his last. His goods he had laid up for many years he had to leave behind. How hard it is for those who trust in riches to be saved in the kingdom of God. His wife did not live long after (1919, pp. 19–20).

Mary Elizabeth Rollins Lightner

My husband could get no work, and I commenced teaching painting to Julia Murdock Smith, to Steven Mark's daughter, and to Sarah Ann Whitney. I also procured a lot a block below the Prophet Joseph Smith's mansion; but as we could get no more work in Nauvoo, Mr. Lightner found a job cutting cord wood, fifteen miles up the river, at a place called Pontusuc. He got a little log room with a floor made of logs split in two, and very rough. The Prophet Joseph, on learning that we were going to leave there, felt very sad, and while the tears ran down his cheeks, he prophesied that if we attempted to leave the Church we would have plenty of sorrow; for we would make property on the right hand and lose it on the left, we would have sickness on sickness, and lose our children, and that I would have to work harder than I ever dreamed of; and, "At last when you are worn out, and almost ready to die, you will get back to the Church." I thought these were hard sayings and felt to doubt them. But the sequel proved them true. Before leaving Nauvoo on the 4th of July there was a general parade of the Legion; about noon Emma came to me to borrow my dining table, as the officers were to dine with her, and the Prophet Joseph came also; he said the Lord commanded him to baptize us that day. Emma asked, "Why is this? They have always been good members in the Church, and another thing, dinner will be ready soon and you certainly won't go in those clothes?" "No," he told us, and he wanted us to be ready by the time he was, for he would not wait for dinner; as we lived on the bank of the river, we were soon ready. Brother Henry and wife, Aunt Gilbert, and myself were baptized and confirmed. The Prophet Joseph tried hard to get Mr. Lightner to go into the water, but he said he did not feel worthy, but would, some other time. Joseph said to me that he never would be baptized, unless it was a few moments before he died.

It was with sorrowful feeling that I went to Pontusuc to live, but by my taking in sewing we made out to live, and that was all. A lady called on me and asked me if we had a cow. I said, "No." She said if I would let her have my bedstead she would give me a cow and two pigs. I gladly accepted her offer, and slept on the floor until we could nail up a substitute. In a short time George was taken sick and died. I was alone with him at the time; my husband had gone to a neighbor's for assistance. An old lady helped me dress him, and Mr. Lightner had to make the coffin, as he was the only carpenter in the place. The two men that dug the grave, and a little girl, were all that went to help bury my darling. I felt that the Prophet's words were beginning to be fulfilled (1926, pp. 202–3).

Mary Elizabeth Rollins Lightner

These are things I can testify to as the living truth, and I have told it to the Josephites [those who claimed Joseph Smith III was the rightful successor to Joseph Smith Jr.]. There is a great deal said about this church and the Josephites. I never knew of Joseph appointing him [Joseph Smith III] to be the prophet. I have never known him to say it, and I have known the boy ever since he was twelve years of age. I heard Joseph say this: "I have rolled this kingdom off of my shoulders onto the shoulders of the Twelve and they can carry out this work and build up His kingdom." Said he, "I am tired. I have been mobbed, I have suffered so much from outsiders and from my own family. Some of the brethren think they can carry out this work better than I can, far better. I have asked the Lord to take me away. I have to seal my testimony to this generation with my blood. I have to do it, for this work will never progress until I am gone, for the testimony is of no force until the testator is dead. People little know who I am when they talk about me, and they never will know until they see me weighed in the balance in the Kingdom of God. Then they will know who I am, and see me as I am. I dare not tell them and they do not know me." These words were spoken with such power that they penetrated the heart of every soul that believed on him (1905a, p. 3).

Mary Elizabeth Rollins Lightner

One day after asking about the Golden Bible he [Joseph Smith] told me if I lived thirty years after his death I would see and read things to prove the book true. I said: "Are you going to die?" (and) he answered: "I must seal my testimony with my blood, the testimony is of no force until the testator is dead. They say I am a fallen prophet, but I am more in favor with my God this day than ever before in my life. They know (not) who I am, and I dare not tell. They will not know until they see me at the bar of God" (1936, p. 3).

Asa Lyman

Asa Lyman, son of Richard and Philomena Lyman, born Lebanon, Grafton Co., N.Y., Nov. 26, 1785, was drowned in the Missouri River, near Winter Quarters, on the 11th of September 1844. His body not found. He had been a faithful member of the Church of Jesus Christ of Latter day Saints, and was a high priest. He was baptized in Matildaville, St. Lawrence County, in 1832. He was one of the stonemasons who built the Kirtland Temple. He had been afflicted with epileptic fits for two years. The Prophet Joseph told him if he went to work on that temple he should not be afflicted with a fit. He accordingly went to work, when it was six feet high, and continued until the top stone, fifty feet high, was put on, and all the time did not have one fit. At the time of his death he was catching fish to distribute among the poor (1847).

Paulina Lyman

United States of America
State of Utah
County of Salt Lake

Paulina E. Lyman, being first duly sworn, says, I am the daughter of Morris and Laura Clark Phelps, and was born in Lawrenceville, Lawrence County, Illinois, on the 20th of March, 1827. My present place of residence is Parowan, Iron County, Utah.

My father became a member of the Church of Jesus Christ of Latter-day Saints in 1831, and moved, with his family, to Jackson County, Missouri, in 1832. I was a little girl when the Prophet Joseph came to Jackson County, and distinctly remember attending a meeting at the house of Lyman Wight, at which he was present. At this meeting the Prophet Joseph blessed the children who were present, and I was one of them. In blessing me he said that I should live to go to the Rocky Mountains. I did not know at the time what the term "Rocky Mountains" meant, but I supposed it to be something connected with the Indians. This frightened me for the reason that I dreaded the very sight of an Indian, and it was this circumstance that impressed this prediction made in my blessing, upon my mind. I have always retained this circumstance in my memory, and now remember it as though it happened yesterday.

(signed) Paulina E. Lyman

Subscribed and sworn to me, this 31st day of July, 1902

(signed) James Jack, Notary Public (1902; see also Kate B. Carter, 1963, 6:432; Wandle Mace, n.d. [a], pp. 131–32; Joseph Smith, HC, 5:85; Brigham Young, JD, 3:257–58).

Daniel D. McArthur

Then we sat down to our mush and milk, and after eating, the men went out to hitch up their teams, and Joseph took his hat and stepped out into the yard. We boys followed close at his heels, and he turned around and said, "Boys, you think I am a prophet, and want to hear all I have to say. Now," said he, "if I should tell you all I know that will come to pass within twelve years, perhaps there would not one of you believe it, and would apostatize from the Church. But I shall let you learn things as they happen, then most likely you will all stand in the Church."

This saying of course caused me to watch what transpired in the following twelve years. About the first thing that took place after that was the great apostasy in 1837; next we were driven out of Kirtland; and Joseph was obliged to flee for his life; next Joseph and his brethren and the whole Church were driven out of Missouri; next Joseph and Hyrum were murdered; afterwards the entire Church were driven from Nauvoo, which history you are familiar with; all this inside of twelve years, and ten thousand other things besides! (1892, p. 129).

Henry W. Miller

At this time Henry W. Miller gave the church four thousand (4,000) dollars toward its [the temple's] construction. This was March 20, 1841. On his moving to Nauvoo, he was made a member of the building committee of the temple, and in the fall of 1841 he was called to go into the pineries and get out timber for the temple and the Nauvoo House. On this trip they encountered stormy weather. Grandmother relates in her journal how the men had to go ahead of the teams (oxen) and break trails so the oxen would follow. At night they would shovel away the snow, fixing a place to make their beds. During the winter they ran out of provisions and were out of bread for some time.

At one time, Joseph Smith made her the promise her children should never cry for bread. Through this ordeal, they lived up to this promise.

She had cooked and cared for the extra men. When flour finally came the children asked for dough before it was baked (n.d. [b]).

John Murdock

(On the 3rd day of April 1833, Bro. [Brother] Zebedee Coltrin and myself started on a mission to the eastern country.) During the winter that I boarded with Bro. [Brother] Joseph, as just mentioned, we had a number of prayer meetings, in the Prophet's chamber, in which we obtained great blessings. In one of these meetings the Prophet told us if we could humble ourselves before God, and exercise strong faith, we should see the face of the Lord. And about midday the visions of my mind were opened, and the eyes of my understanding were enlightened, and I saw the form of a man, most lovely, the visage of his face was sound and fair as the sun. His hair a bright silver grey, curled in most majestic form, his eyes a keen, penetrating blue, and the skin of his neck a most beautiful white, and he was covered from the neck to the feet with a loose garment, pure white, whiter than any garment I have ever before seen. His countenance was most penetrating, and yet most lovely. And while I was endeavoring to comprehend the whole personage from head to feet it slipped from me, and the vision was closed up. But it left on my mind the impression of love, for months, that I never felt before to that degree (n.d.).

John Neff

[John Neff Sr.] was a man of great faith, dedicated to the restored gospel. While visiting at the Mansion House in Nauvoo, six weeks before the martyrdom of Joseph and Hiram, the Prophet Joseph said, "I shall not live long." Sadly Brother Neff inquired, "Brother Joseph, then what shall we do?" The answer was, "There will be someone in my place" (n.d.).

William G. Nelson

In the summer of 1836 the Prophet stopped overnight with my father. We were then living in Missouri. This was the first time I had ever seen him. Some time after this we moved to Nauvoo, where we lived until starting west with the Saints. During the four years I saw the Prophet quite often. Father and he were personal friends, and he came to our home many times and talked with father in the presence of the family.

One day he rode up to the gate and called to my mother:

"Where is Brother Nelson today?"

Mother told him he was on the island cutting wood.

"I should like to have seen him. Is your family well?"

Mother answered that one of the boys was sick with chills and fever.

"Tell Brother Nelson that the boy will get well, and you will not have any more sickness in your family as long as you live in Nauvoo," the Prophet said.

This prophecy was literally fulfilled (1906, p. 543).

David Osborn

On another occasion he preached and chastised the rich, or those who had money, for buying land at government price and selling it in small lots to their poor brethren at a high price. He said the Lord was not pleased with their conduct. "You say I am a prophet. Well, then, I will prophesy, and when you go home write it down and remember it. You think you have been badly treated by your enemies; but if you don't do better than you are now doing, I prophesy that the state of Missouri will not hold you. Your sufferings have hardly commenced."

I think about eighteen months after this we all left the state (1892, p. 173).

Amasa Potter

[Joseph Smith] called [Amasa] to him on one occasion, taking him by the hand and said: "Young man, you have a great mission to perform, and when you are in danger think upon me and you will be delivered," and he could testify that prediction had been fulfilled many times, when his life hung on a thread as it were. It thrilled him to see the Prophet riding on his beautiful white horse at the head of the Nauvoo Legion, giving commands as their general; he seemed so kingly and noble. Even the horse seemed to sense the greatness of his mount (n.d.).

Orson Pratt

In that early day the prophet Joseph said to me that the Lord had revealed that twelve men were to be chosen as Apostles. A manuscript revelation to this effect, given in 1829—before the rise of this Church—was laid before me, and I read it. Joseph said to me, although I was young, weak, inexperienced, especially in public speaking, and ignorant of many important things which we now all understand, that I should be one of this Twelve. It seemed to me a very great saying. I looked upon the Twelve Apostles who lived in ancient days with a great deal of reverence—as being almost super-human. They were, indeed, great men—not by virtue of the flesh, nor their own natural capacities, but they were great because God called them. When Joseph told me that I would be one of the Twelve, I knew all things were possible with God, but it seemed to me that I would have to be altogether changed to occupy such a great position in the Church and Kingdom of our God (JD, 12:85–86).

Parley P. Pratt

As we arose and commenced our march on the morning of the 3rd of November [1839], Joseph Smith spoke to me and the other prisoners, in a low, but cheerful and confidential tone; said he: "Be of good cheer, brethren; the word of the Lord came to me last night that our lives should be given us, and that whatever we may suffer during this captivity, not one of our lives should be taken." Of this prophecy I testify in the name of the Lord, and, though spoken in secret, its public fulfillment and the miraculous escape of each one of us is too notorious to need my testimony (1985, p. 164).

Franklin D. Richards

The words of the Prophet Joseph have been and are being verified, those words he uttered before he went to Carthage. Said he: "I call for the four winds of heaven, the thunderings, lightnings, earthquakes, whirlwinds, the hailstorms, pestilence, and the raging seas to come forth out of their hiding places, and bear testimony of the truth of those things which I have taught to the inhabitants of the earth, as is promised in the revelations that have been given." These were some of his last words among the people. And what have we seen? Scarcely a week last summer without a cyclone or hurricane happening somewhere in the states, destroying towns and villages, or parts thereof (JD, 24:283).

Ebenezer Robinson

At the conclusion of the oration [by Sidney Rigdon] the vast multitude shouted, Hosanna! Hosanna!! Hosanna!!! three times, in confirmation of the declaration of independence made by the speaker. But to show the displeasure of our Heavenly Father, as [I] verily believe, a few days after, a thunderstorm arose, and passing over the place, a shaft of lightning struck the liberty pole and rived it into more than a thousand atoms. This struck dismay into the hearts of some, but [I was] told at the time, that Joseph Smith, Jr., walked over the splinters and prophesied that as he "walked over these splinters, so we will trample our enemies under our feet." This gave encouragement to the fearful and timid (1890, p. 149).

Orrin Porter Rockwell

[Following Rockwell's release from a Missouri jail and arrival in Nauvoo, Joseph said,] I prophesy, in the name of the Lord, that you—Orrin Porter Rockwell—so long as ye shall remain loyal and true to thy faith, need fear no enemy. Cut not thy hair and no bullet or blade can harm thee! (1966, p. 109).

Note: In recording this prophecy, Schindler says: "The story of Joseph's prophecy spread throughout Nauvoo within days, but the Prophet's exact words were never recorded. Rockwell himself mentioned the prophecy to his friends and family on many occasions. A journal notation made the following morning which refers to the incident can be found in James Jepson 'Memoirs and Experiences.' MS. Pp. 9–10. For additional evidence see [T. B. H.] Stenhouse Rocky Mountain Saints: A Full and Complete History of the Mormons, From the First Vision of Joseph Smith to the Last Courtship of Brigham Young. *[New York, 1873], p. 140n; [George W.] Bean, Autobiography, [compiled by Flora Diana Bean Horne. Salt Lake City, 1945,] p. 175, and Mrs. Elizabeth D. E. Roundy's letter to the LDS Church explaining her part in writing Rockwell's life history at his request. Letter on file in the Church Historian's Library."*

Catherine Smith Salisbury

[Catherine Salisbury] told me that she was one of the first eight members baptized into the Church. She said the first six members were, Joseph Smith, Jr., Oliver Cowdery, Samuel H. Smith, Hyrum Smith, David Whitmer, and Peter Whitmer, Jr.

. . . She said that when they [were] driven from their lands in Missouri the Prophet told General Doniphan, his attorney, not to invest in the lands, as the time would come when all improvements would be destroyed and not one building stone would be left standing upon another.

This prophecy was literally fulfilled during the Civil War when Gen. Ewing ordered the Missourians to vacate several counties, including the very ones where these same Missourians and their fathers robbed, murdered, and exiled the Mormons. . . . The Missourians speak of Gen. Ewing's Order No.

11, as the acme of the worst persecution in all history. They were made to take their movable property and leave those counties while the Union Army pushed them out and burned every house, barn, and stack so that Joseph Smith's prophecy to General Doniphan was literally fulfilled (1945).

Jacob Scott

When I was living so to all human appearance almost at the point of death, Joseph Smith the Prophet and Elder William Law came to see me; I was reduced to a skeleton. Joseph predicted openly that I would recover, and it was the common Town talk that Father Scott would not die at that time, although the report had been circulated often that I was dead; and the first time I went to Town in our wagon I met Brother Joseph in one of the streets, and the words with which he first accosted me were, "Well, Father Scott, did not God tell the truth that time?" He also hinted to my family and Elder Law in my hearing that perhaps an old friend of yours might go on the Lord's business to Ireland yet!!! But to shame I confess that, his words seemed to me as idle tales, and I believed him not.—The "cold clammy sweat" came out in me at intervals, and I expected to die in a very few days at most (1842a).

Bathsheba W. Smith

Joseph Smith attended one of our Relief Society meetings in the lodge room. He opened the meeting by prayer. His voice trembled very much, after which he addressed us. He said: "According to my prayer I will not be with you long to teach and instruct you; and the world will not be troubled with me much longer" (1892, p. 345).

George A. Smith

Joseph prophesied that if they would let us alone, we would spread the gospel all over the world, and if they did not let us alone, we would spread it anyhow, only a little quicker (JD, 2:219).

George A. Smith

I feel a little sorry this morning that our meeting house is so small; really it seems too bad that we have not a little more room, but it fulfills very clearly the early predictions of the first President of the Church,

(Joseph Smith,) that we may build as many houses as we would, and we should never get one big enough to hold the Saints (JD, 2:360).

George A. Smith

The very first thing that Joseph told the brethren, when they were going out to preach, was that their salary would be tar and feathers, abuse, and persecution—"You will be driven from house to house, and from country to country, and be hated of all men because of your religion;" and this has been fulfilled, and that too by the people in free America (JD, 2:331).

Job F. Smith

It was, I think, in the same discourse delivered near the tannery that, referring to the mobbers of Missouri, he prophesied that some of them should suffer in a manner emblematically as shown by the Irish fable of "the Killkenny cats which fought one another so viciously that they each ate the other up so that nothing was left but the ends of their two tails." Perhaps it may be thought that this prediction could never by any possibility ever be realized. But let them read the unbiased account of the Donner party (which perished in the Sierra Nevada in 1846–7) in Bancroft's *History of California;* they will arrive at the conclusion that the picture drawn by the Prophet was well taken. They started fighting among themselves and ended up by eating one another in the very deep snows of the Sierras. About half of them were rescued by parties from the western side of the mountains, and only a few of the remainder survived, having lived through the winter on human flesh.

Referring again to the discourse on the stand in front of the tannery, I remember it commenced to rain, and he stopped his discourse and asked the congregation if he should stop and dismiss the meeting, but many cried out "No, go on, go on," to which he replied then, "I will go on, let it rain or shine." Which he did (n.d. [b]).

John L. Smith

When [the Prophet was] playing in the yard of the old white mansion in Nauvoo, with Joseph and Frederick, two of his sons, a gentleman drove to the gate and asked if the Prophet Joseph Smith was at home; when he (the Prophet) sprang up from the grass plat, and, shaking the dust from his clothing, replied that he was. The gentleman then drove his one horse up to a tie post and left the lines lying loose, and got out and came into the house. When about halfway to the house Joseph said, "Mr., I think you would do well to tie your horse; he might get a scare and run away and break your carriage."

The gentleman replied, "I have driven that horse for some years and never tie him. I am a doctor and cannot afford to tie up at every place I call."

Joseph repeated, "You had better tie, all the same. Your horse might get a scare and run away."

The doctor replied, "No fear."

Joseph seemed quite uneasy, and got up several times from his chair on the porch or stoop. Suddenly the horse started up the street and struck a wheel against a post and scattered the pieces for a block or more. The doctor sprang to his feet, and looking after the horse, cried out to Joseph, "I'll be d—d if you ain't a prophet!" (1892, pp. 172–73).

Joseph Smith

Father Johnson's son, Olmsted Johnson, about this time came home on a visit, during which I told him if he did not obey the gospel, the spirit he was of would lead him to destruction, and when he went away, he would never return or see his father again. He went to the southern states and Mexico; on his return he took sick and died in Virginia (HC, 1:260).

Joseph Smith

We forded the Miami River with our baggage wagons, most of the men wading through the water. On the 17th of May [1834] we crossed the state line of Ohio, and encamped for the Sabbath just within the limits of Indiana, having traveled about forty miles that day. Our feet were very sore and blistered, our stockings wet with blood, the weather being very warm. At night a spy attempted to get into our camp, but was prevented by our guard. We had our sentinels posted every night, on account of spies who were continually striving to harass us, steal our horses, etc.

This evening there was a difficulty between some of the brethren and Sylvester Smith, on occasion of which I was called to decide in the matter. Finding a rebellious spirit in Sylvester Smith, and to some extent in others, I told them they would meet with misfortunes, difficulties, and hindrances, and said, "and you will know it before you leave this place," exhorting them to humble themselves before the Lord and become united, that they might not be scourged.

A very singular occurrence took place that night and the next day, concerning our teams. On Sunday morning, when we arose, we found almost every horse in the camp so badly foundered that we could scarcely lead them a few rods to the water. The brethren then deeply realized the effects of discord. When I learned the fact, I exclaimed to the brethren, that for a witness that God overruled and had His eye upon them, all those who would humble themselves before the Lord should know that the hand of God was in this misfortune, and their horses should be restored to health immediately; and by twelve o'clock the same day the horses were as nimble as ever, with the exception of one of Sylvester Smith's, which soon afterwards died (HC, 2:68–29; see also Heber C. Kimball, 1845a, p. 772; 1845b, p. 778; 1864a, p. 536; Charles L. Walker, 1980, 1:349).

Joseph Smith

During our travels we visited several of the mounds which had been thrown up by the ancient inhabitants of this country—Nephites, Lamanites, etc., and this morning I went up on a high mound, near the river, accompanied by the brethren. From this mound we could overlook the tops of the trees and view the prairie on each side of the river as far as our vision could extend, and the scenery was truly delightful.

On the top of the mound were stones which presented the appearance of three altars having been erected one above the other, according to the ancient order; and the remains of bones were strewn over the surface of the ground. The brethren procured a shovel and a hoe, and removing the earth to the depth of about one foot, discovered the skeleton of a man, almost entire, and between his ribs the stone point of a Lamanitish arrow, which evidently produced his death. Elder Burr Riggs retained the arrow. The contemplation of the scenery around us produced peculiar sensations in our bosoms; and subsequently the visions of the past being opened to my understanding by the Spirit of the Almighty, I discovered that the person whose skeleton was before us was a white Lamanite, a large, thick-set man, and a man of God. His name was Zelph. He was a warrior and chieftain under the great prophet Onandagus, who was known from the Hill Cumorah, or eastern sea to the Rocky mountains. The curse was taken from Zelph, or, at least, in part—one of his thigh bones was broken by a stone flung from a sling, while in battle, years before his death. He was killed in battle by the arrow found among his ribs, during the last great struggle of the Lamanites and Nephites (HC, 2:79–80).

Joseph Smith

While we were refreshing ourselves and teams about the middle of the day [June 3, 1834], I got up on a wagon wheel, called the people together, and said that I would deliver a prophecy. After giving the brethren much good advice, exhorting them to faithfulness and humility, I said the Lord had revealed to me that a scourge would come upon the camp in consequence of the fractious and unruly spirits that appeared among them, and they should die like sheep with the rot; still, if they would repent and humble themselves before the Lord, the scourge, in a great measure, might be turned away; but, as the Lord lives, the members of this camp will suffer for giving way to their unruly temper (HC, 2:80; see also Harrison Burgess, 1969, pp. 66–67).

Joseph Smith

Saturday, 9 [May 1840]—Elder Theodore Turley was released from Stafford jail, where he had been confined since his arrest on the 16th of March last, at the instigation of John Jones, a Methodist preacher, on the pretense of a claim arising under a partnership with another man fifteen years ago, before he left England; but the real object was to stop his preaching. He was without provisions for several days, but the poor Saints in the Potteries, on learning his condition, supplied his wants, some of the sisters actually walking upwards of twenty miles to relieve him. He preached several times to the debtors, was visited by Elders Woodruff, Richards, George A. Smith, A. Cordon, and others, and was dismissed from prison on his persecutors ascertaining their conduct was about to be exposed. This rather encouraged than disheartened the elders, as I had told them on their leaving Nauvoo, to be of good courage, for some of them would have to look through grates before their return (HC, 4:127–28).

Joseph Smith

I prophesy, in the name of the Lord God of Israel, anguish and wrath and tribulation and the withdrawing of the Spirit of God from the earth await this generation, until they are visited with utter desolation. This generation is as corrupt as the generation of the Jews that crucified Christ; and if He were here to-day, and should preach the same doctrine He did then, they would put Him to death. I defy all the world to destroy the work of God; and I prophesy they never will have power to kill me till my work is accomplished, and I am ready to die (HC, 6:58).

Joseph Smith

Evening, I attended prayer-meeting in the assembly room. We prayed that "General Joseph Smith's Views of the Powers and Policy of the United States" might be spread far and wide, and be the means of opening the hearts of the people. I gave some important instructions, and prophesied that within five years we should be out of the power of our old enemies, whether they were apostates or of the world; and told the brethren to record it, that when it comes to pass they need not say they had forgotten the saying (HC, 6:225).

Mary Fielding Smith

I must now give you an account of a very affecting event which took place in Kirtland Sunday before last. You will of course remember a Mr. [Wycom?] Clarke, a miller who has been a great opposer of our church. As he and his wife with some of their children and other friends were returning from the Presbyterian meeting house in a very nice carriage, about one minute after they passed the house of the Lord their horses took fright and started off the side of the hill, overthrew the carriage, and hurt Mr. C. [Clark] and one child considerably, but Mrs. C. [Clark] so seriously as to prove fatal. She was buried on the Wednesday following. She has left six weeping children and a mourning husband indeed. On the day preceding the accident she was heard to speak very unfavorably of our church but is now gone to prove whether it is the church of Christ or not. I greatly desire that the visitation may be sanctified to the family.

. . . I believe it is not quite a year since Bro. J. [Joseph] told Mr. C. [Clark] that the curse of God would be upon him for his conduct towards him and the Church. You may remember that our people wished to purchase his place, but he would not sell it on any reasonable terms and therefore kept it, and has been a trouble in the place but has prospered in business so much as to say he never prospered better, and told a person some time ago that he was ready for another of Joseph Smith's curses. I feel inclined to think he will never be heard to utter such words again. May the Lord forgive and save him and all others who raise their hand against the Lord's anointed, for I see more clearly than ever that this is no trifling sin in the sight of God. No, it is as great as ever it was in any age of the world. I sincerely wish that all the members of the Church had a proper sense of their duty and privilege in this respect (ca. 1837a, p. 67).

Eliza R. Snow

Some years before the death of the Prophet Joseph Smith, and long before the thought had entered the mind of President [Brigham] Young to propose a visit to the "Holy Land," the Prophet said to me, "You will yet visit Jerusalem." I recorded the saying in my Journal at the time, but had not reviewed it for many years, and the, to me, strange prediction had entirely gone from my memory.

Even when invited to join the Tourist-party, although the anticipation of standing on the sacredly celebrated Mount of Olives inspired me with a feeling no language can describe, Joseph Smith's prediction did not occur to me until within a few days of the time set for starting, when a friend brought it to my recollection, and then by reference to the long neglected Journal, the proof was before us. While on the tour, the knowledge of that prediction inspired me with strength and fortitude. (1944c, p. 504).

Note: Eliza's record tells of leaving Salt Lake City in October of 1872 with a small group led by President George A. Smith, and of visiting "Europe, Asia, Africa, Egypt, Greece, Turkey" and the Holy Land, including Jerusalem, and of returning home in July 1873, having fulfilled the prophecy of Joseph Smith.

Eliza R. Snow

Eliza R. Snow remembered hearing Joseph Smith say "that the time would come when the people would come to Zion to buy the finest of fabrics" (1978, p. 378).

John Tanner

At the April conference, 1844, Father Tanner was called to take a mission to the eastern states. Before starting, he went to Nauvoo to see the Prophet Joseph Smith, whom he met in the street. He held the Prophet's note for $2,000, loaned in 1835, to redeem the Kirtland Temple farm, and in the course of the conversation he handed the Prophet his note. The Prophet, not understanding what he meant by it, asked what he would have him do with it, and Father Tanner replied, "Brother Joseph, you are welcome to it." The Prophet then laid his right hand heavily upon Father Tanner's shoulder and said, "God bless you, Father Tanner, your children shall never beg bread." He went upon his mission, and was in the East when the Prophet and Patriarch were assassinated; he returned early in the fall of that year (n.d.).

Joseph Taylor

When I first saw him I believed he was one of God's noblemen; and as I grew older I became thoroughly convinced that he was a true prophet of God.

. . . In February, 1841, my brother John was in jail, in the hands of the Missourians, about two hundred miles from home, and my dear widowed mother was very much concerned about his safety. On one occasion she was crying and fretting about him.

When I saw her in trouble, I asked what was the matter.

She replied that she was afraid the Missourians would kill her dear son John, and she would never see him again.

I was strongly impressed to have her let me go to the Prophet Joseph and ask him if my brother would ever come home. She was very desirous for me to do so.

As the Prophet Joseph only lived about three miles from our house I got on a horse and rode to his home. When I reached there, Sister Emma Smith said that he and his son Joseph had just gone up the river near Nauvoo to shoot ducks. I rode up to them, when the Prophet inquired about my mother's welfare.

I told him that Mother was very sad and downhearted about the safety of her son John; and she had requested me to come and ask him as a man of God whether my brother would ever return home.

He rested on his gun, and bent his head for a moment as if in prayer or deep reflection. Then, with a beautiful beaming countenance, full of smiles, he looked up and told me to go and tell Mother that her son would return in safety inside of a week. True to the word of the Prophet, he got home in six days after this occurrence. This was a great comfort to Mother for her son had been absent about six months (1892, pp. 202–3).

Daniel Tyler

I will mention one prophecy among the many predictions of the Prophet Joseph Smith that was literally fulfilled.

During the persecutions in the fall of 1838, one of the brethren happened to be a stranger in Richmond, Ray Co., Missouri, a distance of some thirty or forty miles from Far West, in Caldwell County, where the Saints dwelt. About sundown he saw men loading guns into a carriage, and learned that they were to be taken that night to the mob in Daviess County, to fight the "Mormons." He feigned to be traveling in the opposite direction, and took a circuitous route to Far West, but did not arrive there until about eight o'clock the next morning. He related what he had seen of the actions of the mob, and a call was immediately made for ten volunteers to accompany Captain Allred, of the militia, to intercept and take the arms. To do this we had about twenty miles to ride across a trackless prairie, to reach the road leading from Richmond to Daviess County, where the mob was quartered. The man [driving the carriage] with the guns had a good, smooth road, free from rocks or obstruction of any kind, and, to all human appearance, might have reached his destination before we obtained the news of his having the arms.

When all were mounted, the Prophet Joseph said to Brother Allred, "I want you to ride as fast as your horses can carry you," (pointing the direction, that he might not reach the road in rear of the carriage) "and you will get those arms." These last words inspired faith in the little band, and even the horses did not seem to become weary.

When we neared the road, we cast our eyes towards Richmond, and at a distance of about half a mile we discovered a black-covered carriage standing in the road, without any team attached to it. On nearing it, we saw that it was empty. We examined and found that one of the axles was newly broken in two. Here was the carriage described, but where were the guns? We soon discovered a trail in the high grass where something heavy had been dragged from near the carriage. We followed this train a short distance and found a wooden box, containing seventy-four United States yagers [rifles]. While consulting how to get them to the town, we looked in the direction of the mob and discovered two men coming, about as fast as they could drive, in a lumber wagon. When they discovered us, supposing us to be mobs, they swung their hats and shouted "hurrah!" two or three times, and our little troop responded in the same way.

They got very near before they discovered their mistake. Brother

Allred directed the teamster to drive along side of the box. He then told the two men to get out and put it into the wagon, and then follow him. We returned the way we came, and reached our destination about sundown, when, after the guns were taken from the wagon, the men and team were released. The prediction of the Prophet was fulfilled, and the long-range guns, which were the best then known, designed for our destruction, were in our hands.

Joseph, knowing that the guns were government property, sent a dispatch immediately to notify General Atchison and Colonel Doniphan of Clay County, what had been done. They directed that the arms should be delivered over to them, they pledging their honor that they should not be used against our people.

The prophet's patriotism would not allow him to retain government property, although it had been obtained by our enemies for our destruction. If this was not a test of loyalty, I fail to see an opportunity where a test could be given (1969, pp. 33–34).

Daniel Tyler

At a conference in Nauvoo, Illinois, in the afternoon, while Sidney Rigdon was preaching one of his most powerful and eloquent sermons, the heavens began to gather blackness. He observed this and said to the Prophet, "Is it going to rain?" He answered, "Yes, and we had better dismiss the meeting, and let the people go home and not get wet." The conference was held under a large tree. The speaker replied, "I wish you to know I am not through, for I am as full of preach as my skin can hold," and sat down.

President Smith said to the audience. "You had better hurry home as soon as the meeting is dismissed, or you will get wet. We are going to have a heavy rain." The services were dismissed without singing, I think, when all started for their homes. Those who lived nearby reached their residences, while those from the suburbs had either to run into neighboring houses or take the pelting wind and rain.

The writer, with several others, who resided in the eastern part of the city, while running at the top of their speed, reached an empty cabin just as the rain began to pour, where we remained fully a half hour, until the clouds moved away. The next day being fair, Elder Rigdon finished his discourse (1892b, p. 128).

Daniel Tyler

On [one] occasion, when the Nauvoo Legion was on parade, the heavens began to blacken as if to rain. The people began to get uneasy, and some were preparing to leave. Joseph arose in his saddle and shouted, "Attention, Legion! Don't break the ranks—it is not going to rain. If it rains enough to wet through your shirt sleeves, the Lord never spoke by my mouth!"

It had already begun to sprinkle rain, but it ceased, the clouds passed away and drill continued as long as it was desirable. There are probably many living now who will remember these latter circumstances (1892b, p. 128).

Elizabeth Ann Whitney

My husband traveled with Joseph the Prophet through many of the eastern cities, bearing testimony and collecting means toward building temple in Kirtland, and also toward purchasing lands in Missouri. During this journey the Prophet Joseph often prophesied of the destruction that ultimately would come upon the cities of the eastern states, and especially New York, that in that city there would not be left a vestige of its grandeur. He said that wars would soon commence in our own land, which last has since transpired. He said to my husband, "If they reject us they shall have our testimony, for we will write it and leave it upon their doorsteps and window sills." He prophesied of the desolation by fire, by storms, by pestilence, and by earthquakes. After their return from the East, they traveled together up to Missouri, and while upon this journey my husband had his ankle broken. Through the power of the administration of the gospel ordinance and faith, he was relieved from all pain; but by Joseph's counsel returned home (1878b, p. 71).

Orange L. Wight

Now while in the coach with Joseph he asked me a great many questions about my mission and about the other elders in my travels, more particular about the Grants and Apostle John E. Page. Page had charge of the Pennsylvania mission and I was in Pittsburgh, Pennsylvania, with him part of the winter and with my father who was on a mission in New York State. While in conversation in the carriage I told the Prophet that a man by the name Brank was coming to Nauvoo. He looked troubled for a moment and said he had trouble enough with that man; Brank was an apostate. Then his countenance changed to one of inspiration and he said, "Orange, he will not come," and he never did come. That was a prophecy which seeing him and hearing the words I can never forget. It was proof to me that he was inspired (1903, pp. 8–9).

Wilford Woodruff

[In 1834] I arrived in Kirtland on Saturday and there met with Joseph and Hyrum Smith in the street. I was introduced to Joseph Smith. It was the first time that I had ever seen him in my life. He invited me home to spend the Sabbath with him, and I did so. They had meeting on Sunday.

On Sunday night the Prophet called us all who held the priesthood to gather into the little log school house they had there. It was a small house, perhaps fourteen feet square. But it held the whole of the priesthood of the Church of Jesus Christ of Latter-day Saints who were then in the town of Kirtland, and who had gathered together to go off in Zion's Camp. That was the first time I ever saw Oliver Cowdery, or heard him speak; the first time I ever saw Brigham Young and Heber C. Kimball, and the two Pratts, and Orson Hyde, and many others. There were no Apostles in the Church then except Joseph Smith and Oliver Cowdery. When we got together the Prophet called upon the elders of Israel with him to bear testimony of this work. Those that I have named spoke, and a good many that I have not named bore their testimonies. When they got through the Prophet said, "Brethren, I have been very much edified and instructed in your testimonies here tonight, but I want to say to you before the Lord, that you know no more concerning the destinies of this Church and kingdom than a babe upon its mother's lap. You don't comprehend it." I was rather surprised. He said, "It is only a little handful of priesthood you see here tonight, but this Church will fill North and South America—it will fill the world." Among other things he said, "It will fill the Rocky Mountains. There will be tens of thousands of Latter-days Saints who will be gathered in the Rocky Mountains, and there they will open the door for the establishing of the gospel among the Lamanites, who will receive the gospel and their endowments and the blessings of God. This people will go into the Rocky Mountains; they will there build temples to the Most High. They will raise up a posterity there, and the Latter-day Saints who dwell in these mountains will stand in the flesh until the coming of the Son of Man. The Son of Man will come to them while in the Rocky Mountains" (CR, April 1898, p. 57).

Wilford Woodruff

The Twelve Apostles were called by revelation to go to Far West, Caldwell County, to lay the foundation of the cornerstone of the temple. When that revelation was given, this Church was in peace in Missouri. It is the only revelation that has ever been given since the organization of the Church, that I know anything about, that had day and date given with it. The Lord called the Twelve Apostles, while in this state of prosperity, on the 26th day of April, 1838, to go to Far West to lay the cornerstone of the temple; and from there to take their departure to England to preach the gospel. Previous to the arrival of that period the whole Church was driven out of the state of Missouri, and it was as much as a man's life was worth to be found in the state if it was known that he was a Latter-day Saint; and especially was this the case with the Twelve. When the time came for the cornerstone of the temple to be laid, as directed in the revelation, the Church was in Illinois, having been expelled from Missouri by an edict from the Governor. Joseph and Hyrum Smith and Parley P. Pratt were in chains in Missouri for the testimony of Jesus.

As the time drew nigh for the accomplishment of this work, the question arose, "What is to be done?" Here is a revelation commanding the Twelve to be in Far West on the 26th day of April, to lay the cornerstone of the temple there; it had to be fulfilled. The Missourians had sworn by all the gods of eternity that if every other revelation given through Joseph Smith were fulfilled, that should not be, for the day and date being given they declared that it should fail. The general feeling in the Church, so far as I know, was that, under the circumstances, it was impossible to accomplish the work; and the Lord would accept the will for the deed. This was the feeling of Father Smith, the father of the Prophet. Joseph was not with us; he was in chains in Missouri, for his religion. When President Young asked the question of the Twelve, "Brethren, what will you do about this?" the reply was, "The Lord has spoken, and it is for us to obey." We felt that the Lord God had given the commandment and we had faith to go forward and accomplish it, feeling that it was His business whether we lived or died in its accomplishment.

We started for Missouri. There were two wagons. I had one and took Brother Pratt and President Young in mine; Brother Cutler, one of the building committee, had the other. We reached Far West and laid the cornerstone according to the revelation that had been given to us. We cut off apostates and those who had sworn away the lives of the brethren. We ordained Darwin Chase and Norman Shearer into the Seventies. Brother George A. Smith and myself were ordained into the Quorum of the Twelve on the cornerstone of the temple; we had been called before, but not ordained. We then returned, nobody having molested or made us afraid. We performed that work by faith, and the Lord blessed us in doing it (JD, 13:160).

Wilford Woodruff

August 8 [1839] I laid my hands upon my wife and children, blessed them, committed them into the hands of God, and started upon my English mission, leaving my family sick, and with not more than four days' provisions. Brother Brigham Young rowed me across the Mississippi in a boat; I was sick and feeble. When I landed, I laid down upon the bank of the river on a side of sole leather. The Prophet Joseph [Smith, Jr.] came along and looked at me, and said, "You are starting on your mission." I said, "Yes, but I look like a poor instrument for a missionary; I look more fit for a hospital or dissecting room than a mission." He replied, "What do you say that for? Go ahead in the name of the Lord, and you shall be healed and blessed on your mission." I thanked him. A brother came along with a wagon, carried me a few miles on my road. I started without purse or scrip, and passed by Parley P. Pratt, who was hewing logs for a house; he was barefooted, bareheaded, without coat or vest on. He said, "I have no money, but I have an empty purse; I will give you that." I went a few rods, and found Elder H. [Heber] C. Kimball building a log cabin. He said, "I have one dollar, I will give you that to put in your purse." He blessed me, and I went my way, accompanied by Elder John Taylor. I had a shake of the ague every other day, and lay on the bottom of the wagon while I traveled (1865, pp. 326–27).

Note: Joseph Smith's promise was fulfilled. In his ensuing mission, Wilford Woodruff baptized several thousand souls, including some six hundred of the United Brethren, who later immigrated to Nauvoo and the West.

Brigham Young

We proceeded to Kirtland and stopped at John P. Greene's, who had just arrived there with his family. We rested a few minutes, took some refreshment, and started to see the Prophet. We went to his father's house and learned that he was in the woods, chopping. We immediately repaired to the woods, where we found the Prophet, and two or three of his brothers chopping and hauling wood. Here my joy was full at the privilege of shaking the hand of the prophet of God, and received the sure testimony, by the spirit of prophecy, that he was all that any man could believe him to be, as a true prophet. He was happy to see us, and bid us welcome. We soon returned to his house, he accompanying us.

In the evening a few of the brethren came in, and we conversed together upon the things of the kingdom. He called upon me to pray; in my prayer I spoke in tongues. As soon as we arose from our knees the brethren flocked around him, and asked his opinion concerning the gift of tongues that was upon me. He told them it was the pure Adamic language. Some said to him they expected he would condemn the gift Brother Brigham had, but he said, "No, it is of God, and the time will come when Brother Brigham Young will preside over this Church." The latter part of this conversation was in my absence (1968, pp. 4–5).

Brigham Young

[During the winter and spring of 1834,] while the Prophet Joseph was gathering up the elders of Israel [Zion's Camp] to go up to Missouri and assist the brethren that had been driven from Jackson County, I was preaching and laboring for the support of my family. My brother, Joseph Young, arrived, and I requested him to go with me to Missouri. He hesitated; but while walking together a few days afterwards we met the Prophet, who said to him, "Brother Joseph, I want you to go with us up to Missouri." I informed the Prophet that my brother was doubtful as to his duty about going, to which the Prophet replied, "Brother Brigham and Brother Joseph, if you will go with me in the camp to Missouri and keep my counsel, I promise you, in the name of the Almighty, that I will lead you there and back again, and not a hair of your heads shall be harmed," at which my Brother Joseph presented his hand to the Prophet, as well as myself, to confirm the covenant. The brethren continued to come in from various parts of the country to Kirtland, and on the 5th of

May we started for New Portage, the place appointed for organization (1968, pp. 8–9).

Brigham Young

26th [November 1842]—I was suddenly attacked with a slight fit of apoplexy. Next morning I felt quite comfortable; but in the evening, at the same hour that I had the fit the day before, I was attacked with the most violent fever I ever experienced. The Prophet Joseph and Elder Willard Richards visited and administered unto me; the Prophet prophesied that I should live and recover from my sickness. He sat by me for six hours, and directed my attendants what to do for me. In about thirty hours from the time of my being attacked by the fever, the skin began to peel from my body, and I was skinned all over. I desired to be baptized in the river, but it was not until the fourteenth day that Brother Joseph would give his consent for me to be showered with cold water, when my fever began to break, and it left me on the eighteenth day. I laid upon my back, and was not turned upon my side for eighteen days.

I laid in a log house, which was rather open; it was so very cold during my sickness, that Brother Isaac Decker, my attendant, froze his fingers and toes while fanning me, with boots, greatcoat, and mittens on, and with a fire in the house from which I was shielded by a blanket.

When the fever left me on the eighteenth day, I was bolstered up in my chair, but was so near gone that I could not close my eyes, which were set in my head—my chin dropped down, and my breath stopped. My wife, seeing my situation, threw some cold water in my face; that having no effect, she dashed a handful of strong camphor into my face and eyes, which I did not feel in the least, neither did I move a muscle. She then held my nostrils between her thumb and finger, and placing her mouth directly over mine, blew into my lungs until she filled them with air. This set my lungs in motion, and I again began to breathe. While this was going on I was perfectly conscious of all that was passing around me; my spirit was as vivid as it ever was in my life, but I had no feeling in my body (1968, pp. 124–25).

Note: Shortly after this experience, Brigham Young was restored to his health and returned to his ministry.

Brigham Young

When I left my family to start for England, I was not able to walk one mile; I was not able to lift a small trunk, which I took with me, into the wagon. I left my wife and my six children without a second suit to their backs, for we had left all our property in possession of the mob. Every one of my family were sick, and my then youngest child, who has spoken before you to-day, was but ten days old at the time I left for England. Joseph said, "If you will go, I promise you, that your family shall live, and you shall live, and you shall know that the hand of God is in calling you to go and preach the gospel of life and salvation to a perishing world." He said all he could say to comfort and encourage the brethren. This was our situation, and I say, with regard to the remainder of the Twelve, they had all been driven like myself, and we were a band of brethren about equal. My family lived (JD, 2:19).

Brigham Young

The waste of life in the ruinous [Civil War] now raging is truly lamentable. Joseph the Prophet said that the report of it would sicken the heart; and what is all this for? It is a visitation from heaven, because they have killed the prophet of God, Joseph Smith, jun. Has not the nation consented to his death, and to the utter destruction of the Latter-day Saints, if it could be accomplished? But they found that they could not accomplish that.

. . . Joseph said that if they succeeded in taking his life, which they did, war and confusion would come upon the nation, and they would destroy each other, and there would be mob upon mob from one end of the country to the other (JD, 10:255).

Brigham Young

My name is had for good and evil upon the whole earth, as promised me. Thirty years ago Brother Joseph, in a lecture to the Twelve, said to me, "Your name shall be known for good and evil throughout the world," and it is so. The good love me, weak and humble as I am, and the wicked hate me (JD, 10:297).

Brigham Young

I heard Joseph say many a time, "I shall not live until I am forty years of age" (JD, 18:361).

John R. Young

One day my father [Lorenzo Dow Young, Brigham's brother] took me for a walk, to give me air and sunshine. We met Joseph and Hyrum Smith and Sidney Rigdon. Father shook hands warmly with Joseph and Hyrum, but he merely bowed to Brother Rigdon. Joseph asked if I was the child father had requested the elders to pray for. Being answered in the affirmative, the Prophet removed my hat, ran his fingers through my curly locks, and said, "Brother Lorenzo, this boy will live to aid in carrying the gospel to the nations of the earth."

His words thrilled me like fire; and from that hour I looked forward to the day when I should be a missionary.

Not long after that, Joseph was martyred at Carthage. I remember how my mother wept, and how shocked and prostrated everybody was, when the bloodstained bodies of the Prophet and his brother were brought home. Father was away doing missionary work when that fearful tragedy took place (1920, pp. 9–10).

John R. Young

Mr. Horner told me that when he was a boy Joseph the Prophet and Oliver Cowdery had called on the Horner family. John M. [Horner] wanted to visit with the young prophet; but his father insisted that he finish hoeing a piece of corn given him as a stint. Joseph, on learning of it, took off his coat, asked for a hoe, and helped finish the task. The sequel: John M. Horner was baptized by Oliver Cowdery, and confirmed and blessed by Joseph Smith, who predicted that the earth should yield abundantly at Brother Horner's behest. In California, Brother Horner at one time paid a tithe of twenty thousand dollars, the fruit of agriculture (1920, p. 142).

Joseph Young

As Uncle Haven expressed it, we visited the eastern states, and the Prophet Joseph prophesied before we went, that we should see the fruit of our labors in converting them to the gospel. Brother Phineas Young went with us to the Richards family, and after we had spent a short time with them, we went on to the East and saw my uncles and aunts, and preached to them. They looked on us as strange beings and our doctrine was strange to them. We preached to Uncle and Aunt Haven; we stayed but a little while with them and then went on to Albert P. Rockwood's, for this was according to the promise of the Prophet (1845, p. 108).

The Gift of Discernment

William H. Hickenlooper

In the year 1842, William paid a visit to Nauvoo, purchased a lot, and had a house built on it. Here he first saw the Prophet Joseph Smith. One day the Prophet met him and said, "You're the man I want to see. I want some money to send up the river for lumber for the temple." William loaned the amount desired, which was all he had with him, and went off wondering how the Prophet knew he had any money. Some of the people tried to discourage him, saying he would never get it back, but it was returned according to agreement (1971, 1:609).

Heber C. Kimball

He [Joseph Smith] took me for a walk by the river side and requested me to relate the occurrence at the Bozier house. I did so, and also told him the vision of evil spirits in England on the opening of the gospel to that people. After I had done this, I asked what all these things meant and whether or not there was anything wrong in me. "No, Brother Heber, at that time when you were in England, you were then nigh unto the Lord. There was only a veil between you and Him, but you could not see Him. When I heard it, it gave me great joy, for I then knew that the work of God had taken root in the land; it was this that caused the Devil to make a struggle to kill you." Joseph then said the nearer a person approaches the Lord, a greater power would be manifest by the Devil to prevent the accomplishment of the purposes of God. He then gave me a relation of many contests that he had had with Satan, and his power had been made manifest from time to time since the commencement of bringing forth the Book of Mormon (1880, p. 18; see also 1945, pp. 258–59; JD 3:229–30).

Mary Elizabeth Rollins Lightner

The Smith family was driven from New York, and a small church had been organized. Oliver Cowdery, Peter Whitmer, and Ziba Peterson were members. Well, I being anxious, though young, to learn about the plates from those who knew all about it, my mother and I went up to the Smith family the next night after they came to Kirtland. As I went in, there were two or three others present. They were all there, from the old gentleman and his wife to all the sons and daughters. As we stood there talking to them, Joseph and Martin Harris came in. Joseph looked around very solemnly. It was the first time some of them had ever seen him.

Said he, "There are enough here to hold a little meeting." They got a board and put it across two chairs to make seats. Martin Harris sat on a little box at Joseph's feet. They sang and prayed. Joseph got up and began to speak to us. As he began to speak very solemnly and very earnestly, all at once his countenance changed, and he stood mute. Those who looked at him that day said there was a search light within him, over every part of his body. I never saw anything like it on the earth. I could not take my eyes off him; he got so white that anyone who saw him would have thought he was transparent. I remember I thought I could almost see the cheek bones through the flesh. I have been through many changes since, but that is photographed on my brain. I shall remember it and see in my mind's eye as long as I remain upon the earth.

He stood some moments. He looked over the congregation as if to pierce every heart. He said, "Do you know who has been in your midst?" One of the Smiths said, "An angel of the Lord." Martin Harris said, "It was our Lord and Savior, Jesus Christ." Joseph put his hand down on Martin and said: "God revealed that to you. Brethren and sisters, the Spirit of God has been here. The Savior has been in your midst this night and I want you to remember it. There is a veil over your eyes, for you could not endure to look upon Him. You must be fed with milk, not with strong meat. I want you to remember this as if it were the last thing that escaped my lips. He has given all of you to me and has sealed you up to everlasting life that where he is, you may be also. And if you are tempted of Satan say, 'Get behind me, Satan.'"

These words are figured upon my brain and I never took my eye off his countenance. Then he knelt down and prayed. I have never heard anything like it before or since. I felt that he was talking to the Lord and that power rested down upon the congregation. Every soul felt it. The Spirit rested upon us in every fiber of our bodies, and we received a sermon from the lips of the representative of God (1905a, p. 1; see also 1905b, pp. 556–57).

Wandle Mace

[Joseph Smith] had been feeding us deliciously with spiritual food, his discourses were becoming better every time he addressed the Saints, and we anticipated a continuance of these things. We had known for a good while that certain men were plotting with the enemies of Joseph at Carthage and with the Missourians, for his death, at the same time professing to be his friends. One of these was no other than William Law, who had been his counselor. Joseph found him to be a wicked, corrupt, and treacherous man, which was plainly shown by the following incident, which is only one of many.

Late one night a steamboat landed some of their ilk, who waited while William Law went to Joseph's house and waking him—Joseph—asked him to come out, as he had something important to tell him. Joseph answered him, saying, "Brother Law, you know you have no business with me at this time of night." Law went off disappointed, his intention being to get Joseph down to the landing and onto the steamboat, which would land him in Missouri (n.d. [b], pp. 129–30).

Parley P. Pratt

While laboring here [i.e., the region surrounding Kirtland], letters were received from W. W. Phelps, then president of the Church in Missouri, suspending my papers because I had gone away in debt; which debt had been contracted in behalf of my sick wife while I had been away in the service of the conference. . . . I had once offered the money on the same, but the person to whom it was due, in view of my public services, refused to take it; nevertheless, President Phelps now censured me severely, observing in his letter that such conduct was not the way of the pure in heart. Under this censure I ceased to officiate, at which both the Church and people in general in and about New Portage were much grieved. In the forepart of February, 1835, I repaired to Kirtland, laid the case before President Smith, with my defense in writing, in which is stated the true circumstances. I proceeded to plead the injustice of the accusation, when the President arose to his feet, lifted his hand to heaven, and with a voice, and energy, and power of the Holy Spirit which thrilled the inmost soul, and would have raised the dead, he exclaimed: "Brother Parley, God bless you, go your way rejoicing, preach the gospel, fill the measure of your mission, and walk such things under your feet; it was a trick of Satan to hinder your usefulness; God Almighty shall be with you, and nothing shall stay your hand."

I was comforted, encouraged, filled with new life, thanking God that there was one noble spirit on the earth who could discern justice equity, appreciate the labors of others, and had boldness of soul to judge and act accordingly (1985, pp. 96–97).

George A. Smith

When the Church of Jesus Christ of Latter-day Saints was first founded, you could see persons rise up and ask, "What sign will you show us that we may be made to believe?" I recollect a Campbellite preacher who came to Joseph Smith; I think his name was Hayden. He came in and made himself known to Joseph, and said that he had come a considerable distance to be convinced of the truth. "Why," said he, "Mr. Smith, I want to know the truth, and when I am convinced, I will spend all my talents and time in defending and spreading the doctrines of your religion, and I will give you to understand that to convince me is equivalent to convincing all my society, amounting to several hundreds."

Well, Joseph commenced laying before him the coming forth of the work, and the first principles of the gospel, when Mr. Hayden exclaimed, "O this is not the evidence I want, the evidence that I wish to have is a notable miracle; I want to see some powerful manifestation of the power of God; I want to see a notable miracle performed; and if you perform such a one, then I will believe with all my heart and soul, and will exert all my power and all my extensive influence to convince others; and if you will not perform a miracle of this kind, then I am your worst and bitterest enemy."

"Well," said Joseph, "what will you have done? Will you be struck blind, or dumb? Will you be paralyzed, or will you have one hand withered? Take your choice, choose which you please, and in the name of the Lord Jesus Christ it shall be done."

"That is not the kind of miracle I want," said the preacher.

"Then, sir," replied Joseph, "I can perform none; I am not going to bring any trouble upon anybody else, sir, to convince you. I will tell you what you make me think of—the very first person who asked a sign of the Savior, for it is written, in the New Testament, that Satan came to the Savior in the desert, when he was hungry with forty days' fasting, and said, 'If you be the Son of God, command these stones to be made bread.' And now," said Joseph, "the children of the devil and his servants have been asking for signs ever since; and when the people in that day continued asking him for signs to prove the truth of the gospel which he preached, the Savior replied, 'It is a wicked and an adulterous generation that seeketh a sign,'" &c.

But the poor preacher had so much faith in the power of the Prophet that he daren't risk being struck blind, lame, dumb, or having one hand withered, or anything of the kind (JD, 2:326–27).

Joseph Smith

April 18 [1834]—In company with Elders Sidney Rigdon, Oliver Cowdery, and Zebedee Coltrin, I left Kirtland for New Portage, to attend a conference; dined at W. W. Williams', in Newburg, and continuing our journey, after dark, we were hailed by a man who desired to ride. We were checked by the Spirit, and refused. He professed to be sick, but in a few minutes was joined by two others, who followed us hard, cursing and swearing; but we were successful in escaping their hands, through the providence of the Lord, and stayed that night at a tavern, where we were treated with civility (HC, 2:50).

Joseph Smith

Friday, May 16 [1834]—About nine o'clock, while I was riding in a wagon with Brother Hyrum, Ezra Thayer, and George A. Smith, we came into a piece of thick woods of recent growth, where I told them that I felt much depressed in spirit and lonesome, and that there had been a great deal of bloodshed in that place, remarking that whenever a man of God is in a place where many have been killed, he will feel lonesome and unpleasant, and his spirits will sink (HC, 2:66; see also George A. Smith, n.d., pp. 12–13).

Joseph Smith

When I was preaching in Philadelphia, a Quaker called out for a sign. I told him to be still. After the sermon, he again asked for a sign. I told the congregation the man was an adulterer; that a wicked and adulterous generation seeketh after a sign; and that the Lord had said to me in a revelation, that any man who wanted a sign was an adulterous person. "It is true," cried one, "for I caught him in the very act," which the man afterwards confessed, when he was baptized (HC, 5:268).

Daniel Tyler

A short time prior to his arrival at my father's house my mother, Elizabeth Comins Tyler, had a remarkable vision. Lest it might be attributed to the evil one, she related it to no person, except my father, Andrews Tyler, until the Prophet arrived, on his way to Canada, I think. She saw a man sitting upon a white cloud, clothed in white from head to foot. He had on a peculiar cap, different from any she had ever seen, with a white robe, underclothing, and moccasins. It was revealed to her that this person was Michael, the Archangel. She was sitting in the house drying peaches when she saw the heavenly vision, but the walls were no bar between her and the angel, who stood in the open space above her.

The Prophet informed her that she had had a true vision, and it was of the Lord. He had seen the same angel several times. It was Michael, the Archangel, as revealed to her (1892a, p. 93).

John Woodland

After joining the Church, Jefferson Hunt became dissatisfied and wanted to sell his place and go to Missouri to the Mormons, and John Woodland bought it. That night after buying the place an angel appeared to him and showed him his future home and told him to go search it out. Next morning Brother Jefferson Hunt came to John Woodland's home. And John Woodland told Brother Jefferson Hunt that if he would wait a few days that he would accompany him to Missouri. He told Brother Jefferson Hunt about the dream and that the angel had shown him his home and that he would know this home by a tree that was about twenty-five feet higher than the other trees in the grove. And that he (John Woodland) was to go to that tree, place his back against it, and step twenty-five steps west, and he would find a spring with white sand boiling up, and he would know this was his home.

In a few days they saddled their horses, placed blankets and an ax on their saddles, and traveled into Missouri. After looking a few days Brother Jefferson Hunt then asked Brother John Woodland which way he was going to find his home. Brother John Woodland said that "the Spirit impressed me to go due north." They started and went north across a prairie about two miles, and they saw a grove with a tall tree in it, and Brother John Woodland exclaimed, "There is the tree I saw in my dream." They rode to the grove. Brother Jefferson Hunt held the horse while

Brother John Woodland went to the tree. Brother John Woodland placed his back against the tree and stepped twenty-one steps west and found the spring just as he had seen in the dream. He then called to Brother Hunt to come and have a drink. Brother Hunt laughed because he did not think there was water in existence. But when he came to Brother John Woodland he saw a beautiful spring, where they both had a good drink.

They then built a house to comply with the law and returned to their families. Brother John Woodland sold his house and moved to the new home which the Lord had shown him. After living and improving his new home for about one year, the Prophet Joseph Smith came to visit them. He looked on the place and then said, "Oh, Brother John, what a pretty place you have here. What would you take for it for a stake of Zion?" Brother John Woodland said, "If it is the will of the Lord, take it, and give me another place built as good."

Brother Joseph stood a minute, dropped his chin on his bosom, turned pale, and a bright light shone around him—after standing in this attitude for about fifteen minutes he raised and placed his hand on Brother John's shoulders and said, "Brother John, I won't have your place, for the Lord showed it unto you, and you had faith enough to seek it out." He then placed his hands upon Brother John's head and sealed the place unto him and his posterity for life and all eternity; he told him never to sell the place. After, he was offered a great amount of money for the place but would not sell it, and forbid all his posterity ever to sell it. Brother John Woodland and family remained on the place until they were driven away by the mob. They then went to Adam-ondi-Ahman (n.d.).

Note: Readers will note that once Woodland says he was to take "25 steps" and later that he took "21 steps." While the numbers do not match, this is how they are recorded in the original. Woodland provides no explanation.

Wilford Woodruff

President Woodruff relates an occurrence . . . which happened on his first visit to Kirtland after his baptism. He was in company with the Prophet and his brother, Hyrum, and a number of other leading elders when two preachers called to see President Joseph Smith. After some conversation, the Prophet made a mark on the ground, and standing with his toes against it, jumped, and, making another mark where he alighted, said to the brethren, "Boys, I don't think any of you can beat that." This happened to be on Sunday, and the two preachers broke out in condemnation of his conduct, because he, professing to be a prophet of God, should be guilty of such conduct on the Sabbath day. After they had given vent to their feelings, he said to them, "I knew what was in your hearts and that you had come to seek for iniquity" (1894b, p. 746).

Wilford Woodruff

I remember what Joseph said, a short time before he was slain in one of the last sermons I ever heard him preach. Said he, "Men are here today who are seeking my blood, and they are those who have held the priesthood and have received their washings and anointings; men who have received their endowments." I saw the faces of those men at that time, and they had a hand in slaying the Prophet (JD, 4:149).

Rebuking Evil Spirits

Zebedee Coltrin

[I] first saw the Prophet Joseph at a prayer meeting at the house of Father Morley. He was then a beardless young man. During the meeting the powers of darkness were made manifest in a remarkable degree, causing some to make horrid noises, and others to throw themselves violently around. One man by the name of Leman Copley, standing at the back side of the house, was taken by a supernatural power, and thrown into the window. Then Joseph said to Lyman [Wight], "Go and cast the devil out of Leman." He did so, and the devil entered into a brother by the name of Harvey Green and threw him upon the floor in convulsions. Then Joseph laid hands upon him and rebuked the spirit from him and from the house, upon which the spirit left him, and went outside among a crowd of men standing near the door, and made a swath among them several feet wide, throwing them violently to the ground.

Joseph said this was a fulfillment of the scriptures, where it says that the man of sin should be revealed (1866–1898, pp. 250–51; see also Lucy D. Allen, 1906, p. 537; Philo Dibble, 1892b, p. 303; Levi W. Hancock, n.d. [b], pp. 33–34).

Joseph Smith

Amongst those who attended our meetings regularly was Newel Knight, son of Joseph Knight. He and I had many serious conversations on the important subject of man's eternal salvation. We had got into the habit of praying much at our meetings, and Newel had said that he would try and take up his cross, and pray vocally during meeting; but when we again met together, he rather excused himself. I tried to prevail upon him, making use of the figure, supposing that he should get into a mud-hole, would he not try to help himself out? And I further said that we were willing now to help him out of the mud-hole. He replied that provided he had got into a mud-hole through carelessness, he would rather wait and get out himself than to have others help him; and so he would wait until he could get into the woods by himself, and there he would pray. Accordingly, he deferred praying until next morning, when he retired into the woods; where, according to his own account afterwards, he made several attempts to pray, but could scarcely do so, feeling that he had not done his duty, in refusing to pray in the presence of others. He began to feel uneasy, and continued to feel worse both in mind and body, until, upon reaching his own house, his appearance was such as to alarm his wife very much. He requested her to go and bring me to him. I went and found him suffering very much in his mind, and his body acted upon in a very strange manner; his visage and limbs distorted and twisted in every shape and appearance possible to imagine; and finally he was caught up off the floor of the apartment, and tossed about most fearfully.

His situation was soon made known to his neighbors and relatives and in a short time as many as eight or nine grown persons had got together to witness the scene. After he had thus suffered for a time, I succeeded in getting hold of him by the hand, when almost immediately he spoke to me, and with great earnestness requested me to cast the devil out of him, saying that he knew he was in him, and that he also knew that I could cast him out.

I replied, "If you know that I can, it shall be done," and then almost unconsciously I rebuked the devil, and commanded him in the name of Jesus Christ to depart from him; when immediately Newel spoke out and said that he saw the devil leave him and vanish from his sight. This was the first miracle which was done in the Church, or by any member of it; and it was done, not by man, nor by the power of man, but it was done by God, and by the power of godliness; therefore, let the honor and the praise, the dominion and the glory, be ascribed to the Father, Son, and Holy Spirit, for ever and ever. Amen.

This scene was now entirely changed, for as soon as the devil had departed from our friend, his countenance became natural, his distortions of body ceased, and almost immediately the Spirit of the Lord descended upon him, and the visions of eternity were opened to his view. So soon as consciousness returned, his bodily weakness was such that we were obliged to lay him upon his bed, and wait upon him for some time. He afterwards related his experience as follows:

"I now began to feel a most pleasing sensation resting on me, and immediately the visions of heaven were opened to my view. I felt myself attracted upward, and remained for some time enwrapt in contemplation, insomuch that I knew not what was going on in the room. By and by, I felt some weight pressing upon my shoulder and the side of my head, which served to recall me to a sense of my situation, and I found that the Spirit of the Lord had actually caught me up off the floor, and that my shoulder and head were pressing against the beams."

All this was witnessed by many, to their great astonishment and satisfaction, when they saw the devil thus cast out, and the power of God, and His Holy Spirit thus made manifest. As may be expected, such a scene as this contributed much to make believers of those who witnessed it, and finally the greater part of them became members of the Church (HC, 1:82–84).

Note: In his account of these events, Newel Knight adds that a vision was opened to his view, in which he saw "Jesus Christ seated on the right hand of the Majesty on High" (see Newel Knight, n.d.).

Speaking in Tongues

Jacob Jones

At one time the Prophet Joseph spoke to a group of Indians who had come to see him about the Book of Mormon, and he spoke to them in their own language, although he never had learned it. And he did many wonderful things that an ordinary man cannot do (n.d. [b]).

Lydia B. Knight

That evening (the seventh day the Prophet had been there) the family were all seated around the wide, old-fashioned fireplace in the parlor, listening to the Prophet's words and full of rejoicing.

"I would be so glad if someone who had been baptized could receive the gift of tongues as the ancient saints did and speak to us," said Moses Nickerson.

"If one of you will rise up and open your mouth it shall be filled, and you shall speak in tongues," replied the Prophet.

Everyone then turned, as by a common instinct, to me and said with one voice, "Sister Lydia, rise up."

And then the great glory of God was manifested to this weak but trusting girl. I was enveloped as with a flame, and, unable longer to retain my seat, I arose and my mouth was filled with the praises of God and His glory. The spirit of tongues was upon me, and I was clothed in a shining light, so bright that all present saw it with great distinctness above the light of the fire and the candles (1974, p. 45).

Amasa Potter

I remember the Prophet arising to preach to a large congregation in the grove west of the temple in Nauvoo. He stated that he would preach on spiritual gifts, as he said his Heavenly Father had given him power or a gift of other language. He took a large Bible that was on the stand, and read from Paul on spiritual gifts about half the chapter; and then said that we would exercise his gift and would read the same in German, so he read it and then asked the congregation if there were any that understood what he read, and two Germans arose in the congregation and said that it was read correctly. Then Joseph stated that every Latter-day Saint had a gift, and by living a righteous life, and asking for it, the Holy Spirit would reveal it to him or her (1894, p. 132).

Joseph Smith

About the 8th of November [1832] I received a visit from Elders Joseph Young, Brigham Young, and Heber C. Kimball of Mendon, Monroe County, New York. They spent four or five days at Kirtland, during which we had many interesting moments. At one of our interviews, Brother Brigham Young and John P. Greene spoke in tongues, which was the first time I had heard this gift among the brethren; others also spoke, and I received the gift myself (HC, 1:295–97; see also Heber C. Kimball, 1864a, p. 535; 1945, p. 92).

Joseph Smith

On the 22nd day of January [1833], I spoke to the conference in another tongue, and was followed in the same gift by Brother Zebedee Coltrin, and he by Brother William Smith, after which the Lord poured out His Spirit in a miraculous manner, until all the elders spake in tongues, and several members, both male and female, exercised the same gift. Great and glorious were the divine manifestations of the Holy Spirit. Praises were sung to God and the Lamb; speaking and praying, all in tongues, occupied the conference until a late hour at night, so rejoiced were we at the return of these long absent blessings (HC, 1:322–23).

"Interpretation of Tongues"

Mary Elizabeth Rollins Lightner

On one occasion after interpreting something [someone had said in tongues] about the saints going to be driven, there was a great cry raised by the High Council. They wrote to the Prophet and said I was talking with an evil spirit. Joseph answered: "What she has said is true and correct. Interpretation right belongs to the priesthood, but you did not ask for it, she did and received it." I lost the gift after we were driven. I was well acquainted with all those who saw the plates and all who handled them, even those who saw Moroni (1936, p. 3).

Visions

Israel A. Barlow

The following Wednesday, 30 March 1836, at Kirtland was an important day in the life of Israel Barlow. He was a bodyguard, at times, of the Prophet, who visited often in the Barlow home and spoke freely to Israel, Watson, and other members of the family. It was, perhaps, just about dusk of that mid-week day when Israel, on his horse, was passing the Kirtland Temple and saw the Prophet Joseph and Oliver Cowdery coming out of the temple door and down the walk to the east. Israel drew up at the gate to speak to them. He was greatly impressed, for the Prophet had on, so he thought, a very white suit while that of Oliver was black. Oliver was leaning heavily on the arm of Joseph and as he neared the gate Israel noticed that Oliver seemed very pale. At the same time he also noticed that Joseph's suit was not white but also black. Joseph, addressing Israel, said, "Brother Barlow, Oliver has just been blessed with a great manifestation and he is not used to this as I am, so it has been almost too much for him."

. . . In another version of this story the Prophet is said to have added to Israel, that they had just seen a heavenly vision and that on the next Sunday, April 3, he [Joseph] would deliver the "greatest sermon of my life" (1968, pp. 113–14).

Harrison Burgess

I will here relate a vision which was shown me. It was near the close of the endowments—I was in a meeting for instruction in the upper part of the temple, with about a hundred of the high priests, seventies, and elders. The Saints felt to shout, "Hosanna," and the Spirit of God rested upon me in mighty power and I beheld the room lighted up with a peculiar light such as I had never seen before, [soft and clear, and] the room looked to me as though it had neither roof nor floor to the building, and I beheld Joseph [Smith the Prophet] and Hyrum Smith [the Prophet's brother], and Roger Orton enveloped in the light. Joseph exclaimed aloud, "I behold the Savior, the Son of God." Hyrum exclaimed, "I behold the angels of heaven." Brother Orton exclaimed, "I behold the chariots of Israel." All who were in the room felt the power of God to that degree that many prophesied, and the power of God was made manifest [to all these in the assembly], the remembrance of which I shall never forget while I live upon the earth (1969, p. 103; see also Coltrin, 1883a, pp. 56–58).

Zebedee Coltrin

At Kirtland, we were called to the school of the prophets, and at one time when Joseph was in the translating room, myself and others were talking about the gift of tongues, when the spirit of tongues fell upon me and I [Zebedee Coltrin] spoke under its influence. Joseph came into the room and said, "God bless you, Brother Zebedee, that is the Spirit of God." He told me to continue, and the gift of tongues and of prophesying rested on the greater part of the brethren present and we continued speaking in tongues and prophesying through that day and the greater part of the following night.

At another time after fasting and prayer, Joseph told us that we should see the glory of God, and I saw a personage passing through the room as plainly as I see you now. Joseph asked us if we knew who it was, and answered himself. "That is Jesus, our elder brother, the Son of God." Again, I saw passing through the same room a personage whose glory and brightness was so great that I can liken it to nothing but the burning bush that Moses saw, and its power was so great that had it continued much longer, I believe it would have consumed us (1878, p. 103).

Zebedee Coltrin

Once after returning from a mission, he [Zebedee Coltrin] met Brother Joseph in Kirtland, who asked him if he did not wish to go with him to a conference at New Portage. The party consisted of Presidents Joseph Smith, Sidney Rigdon, Oliver Cowdery, and myself [Zebedee Coltrin]. Next morning at New Portage, he noticed that Joseph seemed to have a far-off look in his eyes, or was looking at a distance, and presently he, Joseph, stepped between Brothers Cowdery and Coltrin and taking them by the arm, said, "Let's take a walk." They went to a place where there was some beautiful grass and grapevines and swamp beech interlaced. President Joseph Smith then said, "Let us pray." They all three prayed in turn—Joseph, Oliver, and Zebedee. Brother Joseph then said, "Now brethren, we will see some visions." Joseph lay down on the ground on his back and stretched out his arms and the two brethren lay on them. The heavens gradually opened, and they saw a golden throne, on a circular foundation, something like a lighthouse, and on the throne were two aged personages, having white hair, and clothed in white garments. They were the two most beautiful and perfect specimens of mankind he ever saw. Joseph said, "They are our first parents, Adam and Eve." Adam was a large, broad-shouldered man, and Eve as a woman, was large in proportion (1883a, pp. 66–67; see also Oliver B. Huntington, n.d. [b], p. 25).

Note: In a different account of this same vision, Coltrin said of Adam and Eve that "their heads were white as snow, and their faces shone with youth" (see Coltrin, 1866–1898).

Levi W. Hancock

The Fourth of June [1831] came and we all met in a little string of buildings under the hill near Isaac Morley's in Kirtland, Geauga County, Ohio. Then we all went to a schoolhouse on the hill about one fourth of a mile, ascending nearly all the way. The building was built of logs. It was filled with slab benches. Here the elders were seated and the meeting was opened as usual. Joseph Smith began to speak; he said that the kingdom of Christ that he spoke of that was like a grain of mustard seed was now before him and some should see it put forth its branches and the angels of heaven would someday come like birds to its branches just as the Saviour had said. "Some of you shall live to see it come with great glory. Some of you must die for the testimony of this work" and he looked at Lyman White [Wight] and said to him, "You shall see the Lord and meet him near the corner of the house" and laid his hands upon him and blessed him with the visions of heaven.

Joseph Smith then stepped out on the floor and said, "I now see God, and Jesus Christ at his right hand, let them [his enemies] kill me, I should not feel death as I am now."

Joseph put his hands on Harvey Whitlock and ordained him to the high priesthood. He turned as black as Lyman was white. His fingers were set like claws. He went around the room and showed his hands and tried to speak; his eyes were in the shape of oval O's. Hyrum Smith said, "Joseph, that is not of God." Joseph said, "Do not speak against this." "I will not believe," said Hyrum, "unless you inquire of God and he owns it." Joseph bowed his head, and in a short time got up and commanded Satan to leave Harvey, laying his hands upon his head at the same time. At that very instant an old man said to weigh two hundred and fourteen pounds sitting in the window turned a complete somersault in the house and [fell with] . . . his back across a bench and lay helpless. Joseph told Lyman to cast Satan out. He did. The man's name was Leman Coply [Copley], formally a Quaker [Shaker]. The evil spirit left him and as quick as lightning Harvey Green fell bound and screamed like a panther. Satan was cast out of him. But immediately entered someone else. This continued all day and the greater part of the night.

But to return to the meeting, Joseph said, "Now if you elders have sinned it will do you no good to preach if you have not repented. Heamon [Heman] Bassett, you sit still; the Devil wants to sift you . . ." Then he ordained Jacob Scott and some others to the High Priesthood. He came to Zebidee [Zebedee] Coltrin and myself and told us that we had another calling as high as any man in the house. I was glad for that, for I was so scared I would not stir without his liberty for all the world. I knew the things I had seen was not made [that is, were not false.] . . .

After this we went down to the house and heard Harvey Whitlock say when Hyrum Smith said it was not God, he disdained him in his heart, and when the Devil was cast out he was convinced it was Satan that was in him and he knew then it. I also heard Harvey Green say that he could not describe the awful feeling he experienced while in the hands of Satan (n.d. [b], pp. 33–34).

Oliver B. Huntington

Monday, Sept. 27th [1897]—I met that day, at the Hall of Relicks, Hopkins G. Pendar an old Nauvoo Mormon, and from him learned that Joseph Smith, just before he was killed, made a sketch of the future home of the saints in the Rocky Mountains, and their route or road to that country as he had seen in vision; a map or drawing of it (n.d. [b], p. 50).

Heber C. Kimball

While these things [i.e., the endowment of the First Presidency and the Twelve] were being attended to, the beloved disciple John was seen in our midst by the Prophet Joseph, Oliver Cowdery, and others. After this all the quorums arose in order, together with the three Presidencies; and the Twelve then presented themselves separately and individually before the First Presidency, with hands uplifted towards heaven, and asked of God whatever they felt to desire; and after each individual petition the whole of the quorums answered aloud Amen! Hosanna! Hosanna! Hosanna! To God and the Lamb, forever and ever, amen and amen! (1945, p. 92).

Heber C. Kimball

Three days before the Prophet Joseph started for Carthage, I well remember his telling us we should see the fulfillment of the words of Jesus upon the earth, where he says the father shall be against the son, and the son against the father; the mother against the daughter, and the daughter against the mother; the mother-in-law against the daughter-in-law, and the daughter-in-law against the mother-in-law; and when a man's enemies shall be those of his own household.

The Prophet stood in his own house when he told several of us of the night the visions of heaven were opened to him, in which he saw the American continent drenched in blood, and he saw nation rising up against nation. He also saw the father shed the blood of the son, and the son the blood of the father; the mother put to death the daughter, and the daughter the mother; and natural affection forsook the hearts of the wicked; for he saw that the Spirit of God should be withdrawn from the inhabitants of the earth, in consequence of which there should be blood upon the face of the whole earth, except among the people of the Most High. The Prophet gazed upon the scene his vision presented, until his heart sickened, and he besought the Lord to close it up again.

When we hear of war in foreign lands—when we hear of the revolutions among nations afar off, we necessarily infer that distresses incident to war and the hottest of the battle will not come nigh unto us. It is natural for man to make favorable conclusions as to his own safety, when danger threatens, but the Prophet saw in the vision that war and distress of nations will not only occur in Europe, in Asia, and in the islands of the sea, but he saw it upon the American Continent—in the region of country where he first introduced the doctrine of the Son of God; so we may look for calamity in our own borders, in our own nation, as well as in the nations of foreign climes (JD, 2:147; see also, for comparison, Wandle Mace, n.d. [b], p. 85; Wilford Woodruff, JD, 22:235).

Orson Pratt

When we came to Kirtland the Lord gave us further commandments, and He revealed a great many things through His servant Joseph. Among others, He gave one that the Latter-day Saints in Kirtland, Ohio, should go to with their might and build a house to His name, wherein He promised to bestow great and choice blessings upon His people. He revealed the pattern according to which that house [Kirtland Temple] should be built, pointing out the various courts and apartments, telling the size of the house, the order of the pulpits, and in fact everything pertaining to it was clearly pointed out by revelation. God gave a vision of these things, not only to Joseph, but to several others, and they were strictly commanded to build according to the pattern revealed from the heavens (JD, 13:357; see also Orson Pratt, JD, 19:16; Truman O. Angell, n.d.).

Joseph Smith

I saw the Twelve Apostles of the Lamb, who are now upon the earth, who hold the keys of this last ministry, in foreign lands, standing together in a circle, much fatigued, with their clothes tattered and feet swollen, with their eyes cast downward, and Jesus standing in their midst, and they did not behold Him. The Savior looked upon them and wept. I also beheld Elder M'Lellin in the south, standing upon a hill, surrounded by a vast multitude, preaching to them, and a lame man standing before him supported by his crutches; he threw them down at his word and leaped as a hart, by the mighty power of God. Also, I saw Elder Brigham Young standing in a strange land, in the far south and west, in a desert place, upon a rock in the midst of about a dozen men of color, who appeared hostile. He was preaching to them in their own tongue, and the angel of God standing above his head, with a drawn sword in his hand, protecting him, but he did not see it. And I finally saw the Twelve in the celestial kingdom of God. I also beheld the redemption of Zion, and many things which the tongue of man cannot describe in full (HC, 2:381; see also Heber C. Kimball, 1845b, p. 788; also Heber C. Kimball, 1945, pp. 93–94, where he tells of hearing Joseph report this same vision, adding that Joseph said he also saw Adam in this vision, and that Adam admitted the Twelve into the presence of the Father).

Joseph Smith

I would just say to Brother Marks, that I saw in a vision while on the road, that whereas he was closely pursued by an innumerable concourse of enemies, and as they pressed upon him hard, as if they were about to devour him, and had seemingly obtained some degree of advantage over him, but about this time a chariot of fire came, and near the place, even the angel of the Lord put forth his hand unto Brother Marks and said unto him, "Thou art my son, come here," and immediately he was caught up in the chariot, and rode away triumphantly out of their midst. And again the Lord said, "I will raise thee up for a blessing unto many people." Now the particulars of this whole matter cannot be written at this time, but the vision was evidently given to me that I might know that the hand of the Lord would be on his behalf (HC, 3:12).

Joseph Smith

In the afternoon, Elder William Weeks (whom I had employed as architect of the temple,) came in for instruction. I instructed him in relation to the circular windows designed to light the offices in the dead work of the arch between stories. He said that round windows in the broad side of a building were a violation of all the known rules of architecture, and contended that they should be semicircular—that the building was too low for round windows. I told him I would have the circles, if he had to make the temple ten feet higher than it was originally calculated; that one light at the center of each circular window would be sufficient to light the whole room; that when the whole building was thus illuminated, the effect would be remarkably grand. "I wish you to carry out *my* designs. I have seen in vision the splendid appearance of that building illuminated, and will have it built according to the pattern shown me" (HC, 6:196–97).

Martha Thomas

There were a great many questions asked Brother Joseph about how he kept the pattern of the temple in his mind so perfect, etc. He said I will answer these questions today.

[He said,] When a true spirit makes known anything to you, in the daytime, we call it a vision. If it is a true spirit it will never leave you, every particular will be as plain fifty years hence as now (1927, pp. 30–31).

Inspired Dreams

Levi W. Hancock

About this time Joseph called on me to go to Rome with a hired girl by the name of Clarissa Reed, who had been living with him. I went and returned with her in about two weeks. He then said I must go with Evin Green. We started by the way of Chardon and preached by the way. The snow came and it began to get [too] cold to travel, but we went as far as we could get and returned back. Joseph talked plain to me for not pressing forward into Pennsylvania. I told him that I was to blame for I had had a [bad] dream. [He said, "I have had as bad a dream] as you ever had. You do as I now tell you to and you will come out alright." He gave me to understand how the Comforter would comfort the mind of man when asleep whether it meant anything or not, and Satan accused good people. He said go again and we started forthwith for Pennsylvania. We went as far as Painesville and stayed the night (n.d. [b], pp. 51–52).

Joseph Smith

After our departure from Colesville, after the trial, the Church there were very anxious, as might be expected, concerning our again visiting them, during which time Sister Knight, wife of Newel Knight, had a dream, which enabled her to say that we would visit them that day, which really came to pass, for a few hours afterwards we arrived; and thus was our faith much strengthened concerning dreams and visions in the last days, foretold by the ancient prophet Joel; and although we this time were forced to seek safety from our enemies by flight, yet did we feel confident that eventually we should come off victorious, if we only continued faithful to Him who had called us forth from darkness into the marvelous light of the everlasting gospel of our Lord Jesus Christ (HC, 1:101).

Joseph Smith

[In my dream] I was standing on a peninsula, in the midst of a vast body of water where there appeared to be a large harbor or pier built out for boats to come to. I was surrounded by my friends, and while looking at this harbor I saw a steamboat approaching the harbor. There were bridges on the pier for persons to cross, and there came up a wind and drove the steamboat under one of the bridges and upset it.

I ran up to the boat, expecting the persons would all drown; and wishing to do something to assist them, I put my hand against the side of the boat, and with one surge I shoved it under the bridge and righted it up, and then told them to take care of themselves. But it was not long before I saw them starting out into the channel or main body of the water again.

The storms were raging and the waters rough. I said to my friends that if they did not understand the signs of the times and the spirit of prophecy, they would be apt to be lost.

It was but a few moments after when we saw the waves break over the boat, and she soon foundered and went down with all on board.

The storm and waters were still very rough; yet I told my friends around me that I believed I could stem those waves and that storm, and swim in the waters better than the steamboat did; at any rate I was determined to try it. But my friends laughed at me, and told me I could not stand at all, but would be drowned.

The waters looked clear and beautiful, though exceedingly rough; and I said I believed I could swim, and I would try it anyhow. They said I would drown. I said I would have a frolic in the water first, if I did; and I drove off in the raging waves.

I had swum but a short distance when a towering wave overwhelmed me for a time; but I soon found myself on the top of it, and soon I met the second wave in the same way; and for a while I struggled hard to live in the midst of the storm and waves, and soon found I gained upon every wave, and skimmed the torrent better; and I soon had power to swim with my head out of water: so the waves did not break over me at all, and I found that I had swum a great distance; and in looking about, I saw my brother Samuel by my side.

I asked him how he liked it. He said, "First rate," and I thought so too. I was soon enabled to swim with my head and shoulders out of water, and I could swim as fast as any steamboat.

In a little time it became calm, and I could rush through the water, and only go in to my loins, and soon I only went in to my knees, and finally could tread on the top of the water, and went almost with the speed of an arrow.

I said to Samuel, "See how swift I can go!" I thought it was great sport and pleasure to travel with such speed, and I awoke (HC, 6:194).

"The Ministering of Angels"

Anonymous

Speaking of beautiful things brings to mind something the Prophet Joseph Smith once said when in conversation with some of his intimate friends.

They were remarking on the differences in people and their modes of living, and he said this: "If we knew how often the angels are prevented from visiting us, by day or by night by the bad smells around, we would labor hard to have everything sweet and clean as possible."

These may not be the exact words he used, but they convey his meaning. I often think of this (1897, p. 612).

Note: When Martha Smith Harris, the sister of Joseph F. Smith, saw in vision both her father and mother, and conversed with them, she said, "Their breath smelled like sweet ointment" (see Martha Ann Harris, 1991, p. 4). By way of contrast, Parley P. Pratt speaks of evil spirits, and observes: "Some of these foul spirits, when possessing a person, will cause a disagreeable smell about the person thus possessed, which will be plainly manifest to the senses of those about him, even though the person thus afflicted should be washed and change his clothes every few minutes" (1965, p. 117).

Joseph B. Noble

In 1833 I went to Kirtland. [Illegible] where I saw for the first time Joseph Smith. I went with him to a field and helped him mow some hay. While there he gave me much information in relation to the Book of Mormon, etc., etc. He told me that the voices of the angels became so familiar that he knew their names before he saw them (n.d. [a]).

Parley P. Pratt

I was chiefly engaged as a recruiting officer, and, not being much with the camp [Zion's Camp], can give but little of its history. I visited branches of the Church in Ohio, Indiana, Illinois, and Missouri, and obtaining what men and means I could, fell in with the camp from time to time with additional men, arms, stores and money. On one occasion, I had traveled all night to overtake the camp with some men and means, and having breakfasted with them and changed horses, I again started ahead on express to visit other branches, and do business to again overtake them. At noon I had turned my horse loose from the carriage to feed on the grass in the midst of a broad, level plain. No habitation was near; stillness and repose reigned about me; I sank down overpowered with a deep sleep, and might have lain in a state of oblivion till the shades of night had gathered about me, so completely was I exhausted for want of sleep and rest; but I had only slept a few moments till the horse had grazed sufficiently, when a voice, more loud and shrill than I have ever before heard, fell on my ear, and thrilled through every part of my system; it said: "Parley, it is time to be up and on your journey." In the twinkling of an eye I was perfectly aroused; I sprang to my feet so suddenly that I could not at first recollect where I was, or what was before me to perform. I related the circumstance afterwards to Brother Joseph Smith, and he bore testimony that it was the angel of the Lord who went before the camp, who found me overpowered with sleep, and thus awoke me (1985, pp. 93–94).

Parley P. Pratt

About the time of the arrival of the camp [Zion's Camp] at Fishing River, the mob of Jackson County sent a committee to twelve of their leaders, to confer with the authorities of the exiled Church in Clay County, to make proposals for the settlement of the whole matter, by purchasing the lands from which they had been driven. The Saints would not sell their lands to their murderers and the land pirates who had driven and plundered them; therefore, the mob's representatives were unsuccessful.

As this committee of twelve returned, and were crossing the Missouri River at evening, their boat sank in an instant in the middle of the stream, and only about half of the committee ever reached the shore alive. Brother Joseph said it was the angel of the Lord who sank the boat (1985, p. 95).

John Riggs

Dr. [John] Riggs saw Joseph the Prophet on his first arrival in Kirtland, and became immediately acquainted with him. He worked on the [Kirtland] Temple before he came into the Church, was at its first dedication, and heard Dr. Frederick G. Williams bear his testimony that while Sidney Rigdon was making his first prayer, he saw an angel enter the window, and take a seat between Father Smith and himself and remain there during the prayer (1884, p. 282).

Joseph Smith

There have also been ministering angels in the Church which were of Satan appearing as an angel of light. A sister in the state of New York had a vision, who said it was told her that if she would go to a certain place in the woods, an angel would appear to her. She went at the appointed time, and saw a glorious personage descending, arrayed in white, with sandy-colored hair; he commenced and told her to fear God, and said that her husband was called to do great things, but that he must not go more than one hundred miles from home, or he would not return; whereas God had called him to go to the ends of the earth, and he has since been more than one thousand miles from home, and is yet alive. Many true things were spoken by this personage, and many things that were false. How, it may be asked, was this known to be a bad angel? By the color of his hair; that is one of the signs that he can be known by, and by his contradicting a former revelation (HC, 4:581).

Joseph Smith

A man came to me in Kirtland, and told me he had seen an angel, and described his dress. I told him he had seen no angel, and that there was no such dress in heaven. He grew mad, and went into the street and commanded fire to come down out of heaven to consume me. I laughed at him, and said, "You are one of Baal's prophets; your God does not hear you; jump up and cut yourself;" and he commanded fire from heaven to consume my house (HC, 5:267–68).

Wilford Woodruff

Brother Kimball, Brother George A. Smith and myself had a similar experience in London, at a house where we were stopping. It seemed as if there were legions of spirits there. They sought our destruction; and on one occasion, after Brother Kimball had left, these powers of darkness fell upon us to destroy our lives, and both Brother Smith and myself would have been killed, apparently, had not three holy messengers come into the room and filled the room with light. They were dressed in temple clothing. They laid their hands upon our heads and we were delivered, and that power was broken, so far as we were concerned. Why did the Lord send these men to us? Because we could not have lived without it; and, as a general thing, angels do not administer to anybody on the earth unless it is to preserve the lives of good men, or to bring the gospel, or perform a work that men cannot do for themselves. That is the reason Moroni and other angels of God visited and taught Joseph Smith. They quoted to him whole chapters in the Bible—in Isaiah, Jeremiah, and Ezekiel—and told him what must come to pass in the last days. It was necessary for these angels to give him the priesthood. There was no mystery at all with regard to what was taught him. He knew it was of God. These very principles sustained Joseph Smith from the hour the gospel was delivered to him until he sealed his testimony with his blood (CD, 1:218).

Preaching

Angus M. Cannon

On one occasion especially do I remember Brother Joseph as he addressed an assembly of the Saints, in the spring of 1844. It was under some large oak trees, in a hollow south of the temple, near to Parley Street. He was discoursing upon the fact that God, in establishing His Church, had provided that only one man was authorized, of God, to receive revelations that should be binding upon the Church. At the time his counselor, [William] Law, was exercising a baneful influence upon the minds of the Saints and assuming to have light and possess knowledge, that the Prophet Joseph was not justified in giving certain revelations which Law claimed were not inspired of the Lord. It was on this same occasion that I heard the Prophet declare he had received the Melchizedek Priesthood, under the administration of Peter, James, and John.

The impression created upon my young mind in the inspired utterances of Joseph Smith have accompanied me throughout my subsequent life; and when darkness would otherwise have beclouded my mind, his testimony has come up vividly before me, giving me evidence that the Church of Jesus Christ of Latter-day Saints has been established and governed by the manifest power and authority of God. It has been as a beacon light, that shone forth, amidst the greatest darkness, my mind ever experienced, accompanied by a power and heavenly influence, indescribable.

Aside from seeing him at the head of the Legion, when he has lifted his hat in saluting his associates in arms, I never heard him speak in public, except as before mentioned. Neither was I ever permitted to approach sufficiently close to touch his person. But with the greatest veneration I viewed him (1906, pp. 546–47).

Sarah T. Clark

The last sermon I heard the Prophet preach impressed me so that I resolved to never quit praying. I was at the meeting when he told the people that the hounds were after him and that "He was going like a lamb to the slaughter!" I heard him say those words, and Oh the silence and sobbing and tears, and lamenting of the saints gathered in that room that beautiful Sunday morning when these touching, solemn words were uttered! It was a blessing to me that I went to that meeting. It was a blessing to me and my tribe that I heard that last sermon. It impressed me so, and I try to impress my children and others with the values of prayer and trust in our good Heavenly Father (n.d.).

Howard Coray

I soon went to Nauvoo—became acquainted with the Prophet—heard him preach and saw him conduct the April Conference of 1840. The power and wisdom that he displayed on this occasion was more evidence. . . . I have studied the gospel as revealed by Joseph Smith and wondered if it were possible for any one unaided by the Spirit of God to have revealed such a system of salvation and exaltation for man. My conclusion is in the negative. I sat and listened to his preaching at the stand in Nauvoo a great many times when I have been completely carried away with his indescribable eloquence—power of expression—speaking as I have never heard any other man speak (1889).

Joseph L. Heywood

I left my native state [of Massachusetts] in the spring of 1831 and became a citizen of Illinois; I spent some time in Alton and Springfield, Ill., and moved to Quincy, Adams County, Ill., in the fall of 1839. Engaging in the mercantile business in partnership with my brother-in-law, Oliver Kimball, I remained there until the fall of 1845, when I moved with my family to the city of Nauvoo, Hancock County, Ill. In December, 1842, I visited the Prophet Joseph Smith in Nauvoo, and after listening to his preaching by the gift and power of the Holy Ghost, I was converted and asked for baptism the same hour. I was baptized by Elder Orson Hyde in the Mississippi River, the Prophet Joseph assisting in cutting the ice. I was then confirmed a member of the Church of Jesus Christ of Latter-day Saints under the hands of Elders Orson Hyde, Joseph Smith, and Jedediah M. Grant (1971, 1:646).

Heber C. Kimball

On the 21st [of June, 1834] Colonel Sconce and two other leading men from Ray County came to see us, desiring to know what our intentions were, "for," said he, "I see that there is an almighty power that protects this people, for I started from Richmond, Ray County, with a company of armed men, having a fixed determination to destroy you, but was kept back by the storm and was not able to reach you." When he came into camp he was seized with such a trembling that he was obliged to sit down in order to compose himself. When he desired to know what our intentions were, Brother Joseph arose and began to speak; and the power of God rested upon him. He gave a relation of the sufferings of our people in Jackson County, and also many of our persecutions and what we had suffered from our enemies for our religion; and that we had come one thousand miles to assist our brethren, to bring them clothing, and to reinstate them upon their own lands; that we had no intentions to molest or injure any people, but only to administer to the wants of our afflicted brethren; and that the evil reports which were circulated about us were false, and were circulated by our enemies to get us destroyed.

After he had finished speaking, the power of which melted them into compassion, they arose and offered him their hands, and said they would use their influence to allay the excitement which everywhere prevailed against us. They accordingly went forth and rode day and night to pacify the people. They wept because they saw we were an afflicted people, and that our intentions were pure (1945, p. 53–54).

Lydia B. Knight

As evening drew near, Mr. Nickerson became anxious to hear something of the newcomer's faith.

"Oh," said he to his wife, "just let him talk; I'll silence him, if he undertakes to talk about the Bible. I guess I know as much about the scriptures as he does."

As soon as supper was over, he invited his visitors and family to go upstairs to the parlor, where he said they would have some talk. "Now Mr. Smith," he said, "I wish you and Mr. Rigdon to speak freely. Say what you wish and tell us what you believe. We will listen."

Turning to his wife, he whispered, "Now you'll see how I shall shut him up. "

The Prophet commenced by relating the scenes of his early life. He told how the angel visited him, of his finding the plates, and the translation of them, and gave a short account of the matter contained in the Book of Mormon.

As the speaker continued his wonderful narrative, I was listening and watching him intently. I saw his face become white and a shining glow seemed to beam from every feature.

As his story progressed, he would often allude to passages of scripture. Then Mr. Nickerson would speak up and endeavor to confound him. But the attempt was soon acknowledged even by himself to be futile.

The Prophet bore a faithful testimony that the priesthood was again restored to the earth, and that God and His Son had conferred upon him the keys of the Aaronic and Melchizedek Priesthoods. He stated that the last dispensation had come, and the words of Jesus were now in force: "Go ye into all the world and preach the gospel to every creature. He that believeth and is baptized shall be saved; but he that believeth not shall be damned."

The Gifts of the Spirit

Elder Rigdon spoke after the Prophet ceased. He related some of his early experiences, and told those present that he had received a testimony for himself of the truth of what Joseph had said. "God," said Elder Rigdon, "is no respecter of persons, but will give to all that ask of Him a knowledge of the things Joseph Smith has declared unto you, whether they are true or false, of God or of man."

After both men were through speaking, many questions were asked by all present, for information. The listeners were honest-hearted people, and when truth is told to such they are constrained to accept and believe.

"And is this, then," said Mr. Nickerson, "the curious religion the newspapers tell so much about? Why, if what you have said is not good sound sense, then I don't know what sense is."

A feeling of agreeable disappointment was felt by Mr. Nickerson and family, that these strange men were so different from the various representations of them.

Next day, notice was sent out that there would be public preaching in the Nickerson Brothers' new store-house. A large and attentive audience was present. Elder Sidney Rigdon spoke to the people with great clarity on the first principles of the gospel, and closed with a strong testimony to the truth of so-called "Mormonism."

The Prophet then arose and poured forth a golden stream of words, many of which were verily pearls without price, setting forth the restoration of the gospel and the great work that had commenced on the earth. With power he exhorted everyone who was present to seek for the truth of his and his companion's words from the source of all light, all truth, and all religion, and a knowledge of the truth of the same should surely follow.

Great was the excitement among the peaceful dwellers in Mount Pleasant.

The day following, a meeting was again held, and after it was over the Prophet baptized twelve persons, including myself, Mr. Nickerson and all of his household. I, who was always sober and full of reflection, received the glad message with trembling joy. I was filled with a bright, peaceful influence and was full of gratitude that God had spared me to hear and accept His glorious gospel. As a lonely girl, I had thought of death and its rest with a longing heart. But here was life—life eternal. After I was baptized, I was constrained to cry aloud, "Glory to God in the highest. Thanks be to His holy name that I have lived to see this day and be a partaker of this great blessing" (1974, pp. 42–44).

Dudley Leavitt

Though I was but fourteen years old when [Joseph Smith] was martyred, I then felt I would very willingly have laid down my life for him, and have ever since felt my all is ready to be used in sustaining the divine work established by the Almighty through the instrumentality of His servant Joseph.

One of my most vivid impressions respecting the Prophet occurred in my father's family. The night following our arrival in Kirtland from Canada, some persons came and spoke to my parents censuring Joseph Smith, whom my parents had not yet seen. I heard my father declare if such things were true such a man could not be a prophet of God. My father afterwards appeared quite dejected. The next day, being Sunday, my father and mother and the older children attended divine service, and saw and heard the Prophet Joseph. On my father's return from meeting all his dejection had vanished, and I heard him declare Joseph Smith to be a prophet of the Most High God (1893, p. 16).

Wandle Mace

Meetings in Nauvoo were held in a Jack Oak Grove, in the open air, and here I listened to the words of inspiration as they fell from the lips of the Prophet, as he taught the congregations of the Saints.

Who could listen to these words of inspiration and honestly say Joseph Smith is an imposter? No one, not even his bitter enemies.

Who among all the so-called Christian Churches, with all their learning, could explain the order of the priesthood? No one.

Who among them could explain *any* of the principles of life and salvation, with the ordinances necessary thereto? Not one.

I have listened to the Prophet Joseph in public, and in private, in sunshine and shower—as many others have done as he taught from the stand. At my own house, and at his house, I have been familiar with him, from the time he escaped from prison in Missouri in 1839 until his martyrdom in 1844, and [I] do know that no man could explain the scripture—throw them wide open to view, so plain that none could misunderstand their meaning—except he had been taught of God.

I have felt ashamed myself sometimes, having studied the scriptures so much, that I had not seen that which was so plain when he touched them. He, as it were, turned the key, and the door of knowledge sprang wide open, disclosing precious principles, both new and old.

I have many times been pondering upon a subject, and seemed to come to a stand-still, not knowing how to gain farther information relating to it, when upon going to meeting on the Sabbath, the key would be touched by Joseph and the subject would be so plain I wondered why I had not seen it before (n.d. [b], p. 46).

William H. Maughan

William had the privilege and blessing, as a youth, of gazing upon the countenance of the great prophet of God, Joseph Smith, and listening to his inspired utterances. To quote his language . . . concerning this experience, he said, "The impression left upon my youthful mind no lapse of time can ever efface. I have heard his voice. I have seen his face literally shine, illuminated from within by the effulgence of the Holy Spirit, and I testify to you that he was in very deed, a prophet of God" (1986, p. 6).

William W. McGuire

[I] heard Joseph Smith preach at the house of Edward Hunter in Chester Co., Pennsylvania, January 25, 1840. Joseph said: "Brothers and Sisters, I will not tell you much of what the Lord told Paul, or of what He told Peter, but I will tell you what the Lord told me" (1886).

Parley P. Pratt

While visiting with Brother Joseph in Philadelphia, a very large church was opened for him to preach in, and about three thousand people assembled to hear him. Brother Rigdon spoke first, and dwelt on the gospel, illustrating his doctrine by the Bible. When he was through, Brother Joseph arose like a lion about to roar; and being full of the Holy Ghost, spoke in great power, bearing testimony of the visions he had seen, the ministering of angels which he had enjoyed; and how he had found the plates of the Book of Mormon, and translated them by the gift and power of God. He commenced by saying: "If nobody else had the courage to testify of so glorious a message from heaven, and of the finding of so glorious a record, he felt to do it in justice to the people, and leave the event with God."

The entire congregation was astounded, electrified, as it were, and overwhelmed with the sense of the truth and power by which he spoke, and the wonders which he related. A lasting impression was made; many souls were gathered into the fold. And I bear witness, that he, by his faithful and powerful testimony, cleared his garments of their blood. Multitudes were baptized in Philadelphia and in the regions around; while, at the same time, branches were springing up in Pennsylvania, in Jersey, and in various directions (1985, pp. 260–61).

Ebenezer Robinson

In the afternoon of the 30th of October, 1838, a large body of armed men were seen approaching Far West, whom [I] supposed were mobbers coming to attack the city, as at that time [I] did not know of the governor's order calling out the militia, consequently felt it our duty to make as successful a resistance as possible.

Our men were collected upon the public square, where President Joseph Smith, Jr., delivered an address, in which he endeavoured to inspire the hearts of his hearers with courage, and deeds of valor, in defense of our families, our homes, and our firesides, in which he made this declaration that if the mob persisted in coming upon us, "We will play h—l with their apple cart" (1890, p. 206).

Joseph L. Robinson

The Prophet's voice was like the thunders of heaven, yet his language was meek and his instructions edified much. There was a power and majesty that attended his words and preaching that we never beheld in any man before. He truly had been educated pertaining to the kingdom of God. He was highly charged with the Holy Ghost, which was his constant companion (1974, p. 164).

Jacob Scott

Joseph preaches far oftener than formerly; the brethren and sisters are not so well pleased with any other, and no wonder, for he is a scribe well instructed, and he brings out of his treasures things new and old. In the winter there is preaching in different parts of the city every first day of the week, and in the country also we have preaching in our neighborhood in winter likewise (1844).

THE GIFTS OF THE SPIRIT

GEORGE A. SMITH

Sunday, June 1 [1834]—At ten-thirty this morning our trumpet, a common brass French horn, sounded in the camp for preaching. There were some two hundred or three hundred of the people from Jacksonville and the surrounding country gathered under the trees within our camp. A chest was brought out for the accommodation of the speakers. When Squire Cook (Joseph Smith) took standing professing to be a liberal free thinker, he spoke to the people very freely about one hour on his particular views. His manner and style were very unassuming and affable. He was listened to with great attention and those present remarked that he was one of the greatest reasoners they ever heard. The free thinker was followed by Elder John S. Carter, who delivered a very eloquent address on "Practical Piety." [Then others, including Joseph Young, Brigham Young, Hyrum E. Johnson, also spoke] (n.d., p. 18).

Note: To protect themselves from the harassment of their enemies, the brethren in Zion's Camp sometimes spoke in their camp meetings under pseudonyms. In this instance, Joseph Smith called himself "Squire Cook." In addition, they sometimes highlighted the doctrines of the Restoration by contrasting them with those of other denominations; hence, Joseph spoke as if he were a "liberal free thinker," in order to dramatize the differences between himself and others.

JOB F. SMITH

I had but limited personal acquaintance with him, living as I did outside of the city, but I always heard his public discourses and noticed his personality, his manner and earnestness. The stand from which he spoke was, I think, between twenty and thirty feet long, and it was his custom in addition to his arm gesture to walk the stand from one end to the other and sometimes call upon the audience for an expression of approval which was usually answered by a loud "Aye" from the congregation. I have never but once since heard a preacher or lecturer exercise the mental power and earnestness manifested by that great man. He was large in stature and powerful in invective, and occasionally sarcastic. Other elders, chiefly the apostles such as P. P. Pratt, Orson Hyde, E. T. Benson, and others, preached with great earnestness. I heard Sidney Rigdon once but his talk was very tame (n.d. [a], p. 6).

JOSEPH F. SMITH

My earliest recollection of a place of worship was in a little grove of trees in Nauvoo close to the site of the temple. This was the first place I remember where Latter-day Saints met together for the worship of God. In this grove I remember attending a large number of meetings, and it seemed to me then that the Sabbath day came around pretty frequently. I used to go, in company with my mother and the rest of the children to the grove, and we used to sit on benches and listen to the speeches of such men as Brigham Young, Orson Pratt, Parley P. Pratt, Orson Hyde, and others of the Twelve Apostles; and also the Prophet Joseph Smith, and his brother, Hyrum Smith. In connection with those whom I have named, I recall having seen the bishop of that day, Brother George Miller, and other men of prominence.

A little incident that was of interest to me I recall occurred on one occasion when I attended a meeting at Nauvoo. The Prophet Joseph Smith, while holding services, stood in a wagon, where he delivered a discourse. During its delivery the rain began to fall, and it was not long before it became a regular deluge. Those who had umbrellas climbed into the wagon and held them over the speaker, and none left the grove until the services were over (1910, pp. 7–8).

Lorenzo Snow

The first time I saw Joseph Smith, the prophet of the Lord, I was seventeen years of age. It was in 1831, in the fall of the year. It was rumored that he was going to hold a meeting in Hiram, Portage County, Ohio, about four miles from my father's home, where I was born and brought up. Having heard many stories about him, my curiosity was considerably aroused, and I thought I would take advantage of this opportunity to see and hear him. Accordingly, in company with some of the members of my father's family, I rode over to Hiram in our carriage.

When we reached there the people were already assembled in a small bowery; there were about two hundred and fifty or two hundred people present. I had heard something about the "Mormon" prophet and felt some anxiety to see him and judge for myself, as he was generally believed to be a false prophet. The meeting had already commenced and Joseph Smith was standing in the door of Father Johnson's house, looking into the bowery, and addressing the people.

I made a critical examination as to his appearance, his dress, and his manner as I heard him speak. He was only twenty-five years of age and was not, at that time, what would be called a fluent speaker. His remarks were confined principally to his own experiences, especially the visitation of the holy angel, giving a strong and powerful testimony in regard to these marvelous manifestations. He simply bore his testimony to what the Lord had manifested to him, to the dispensation of the gospel which had been committed to him, and to the authority that he possessed. At first he seemed a little diffident and spoke in rather a low voice, but as he proceeded he became very strong and powerful, and seemed to affect the whole audience with the feeling that he was honest and sincere. It certainly influenced me in this way and made impressions upon me that remain until the present day.

As I looked at him and listened, I thought to myself that a man bearing such a wonderful testimony as he did, and having such a countenance as he possessed, could hardly be a false prophet. He certainly could not have been deceived, it seemed to me, and if he was a deceiver he was deceiving the people knowingly; for when he testified that he had had a conversation with Jesus, the Son of God, and had talked with Him personally, as Moses talked with God upon Mount Sinai, and that he had also heard the voice of the Father, he was telling something that he either knew to be false or to be positively true.

I was not at that time what might be called a religious boy, but I was interested in what I saw and heard there. However, being busy in other directions, it passed measurably out of my mind until some three or four years later. After completing my classical studies at Oberlin College I went to Kirtland to continue my study of Hebrew with Dr. Joshua Seixas (1937, pp. 82–83).

Lorenzo Snow

I heard the Prophet discourse upon the grandest of subjects. At times he was filled with the Holy Ghost, speaking as with the voice of an archangel, and filled with the power of God; his whole person shone and his face was lightened until it appeared as the whiteness of the driven snow. . . . Finally my prayers were answered and I was convinced of the truth sufficiently to want to be baptized to get a knowledge for myself of the testimony that Joseph Smith had seen God. . . .

On Sunday, June 19, 1836, in the Kirtland Temple, Joseph arose in the pulpit just before the meeting closed and said: "A young man by the name of Lorenzo Snow wishes to be baptized, and Brother John Boynton (who was then one of the Twelve Apostles) will baptize him." After the meeting I was baptized in the stream that ran through Kirtland, and I was confirmed by Hyrum Smith who, with some others, laid hands upon me (1937, p. 84).

James P. Terry

At another time when he was speaking, a flock of wild geese flew over in close proximity to the meeting, when all eyes were turned to them. The Prophet said: "If you think more of the quacking of a flock of geese than of my preaching, all right," and sat down. If my memory serves me right, the meeting was dismissed immediately (1893, p. 331).

Zilpha Williams

We were here in season to see the Prophet before he fell a martyr for his religion. . . . I am ever thankful that I was permitted to hear from his own lips some of the great things of God which he is doing in these last days, and I could truly say they were not the words of him who hath a devil. Could you have seen him as I did, standing before the great congregation with a frank, open countenance beaming with intelligence, while his whole frame seemed animated with it and filled with love to his flock who hung with intense interest upon all he had to say to them. Could you have witnessed the strong attachment of those who were best acquainted with him, you would have said, "surely he cannot be that wicked man they have represented him to be" (1845).

Mary Ann Winters

I stood close by the Prophet while he was preaching to the Indians in the grove by the temple. The Holy Spirit lighted up his countenance till it glowed like a halo around him, and his words penetrated the hearts of all who heard him, and the Indians looked as solemn as eternity (1905, p. 558).

Margaret P. Young

In January 1840, word came that the Prophet Joseph Smith was to visit our branch on his way from Philadelphia. It was announced in the papers, and Father said, "Let us get our carriage and go to meet him." So James Downing, Levi Riter, Jacob Weiler, and Father, Robert Pierce, brought him to our house.

My mother served a splendid supper, and then the neighbors gathered to hear the Prophet discourse. I wish that I might describe my feelings at that meeting. Though they are fresh in my memory today, I cannot fall short of expressing myself. So animated with loving kindness, so mild and gentle, yet big and powerful and majestic was the Prophet, that to me he seemed more than a man; I thought almost, that he was an angel. We were all investigating, none of my people had yet entered the waters of baptism. However, it was a great joy to us to entertain the Prophet Joseph Smith, and hear his wonderful words of wisdom. It was 2 o'clock in the morning before we permitted him to retire. We wanted to listen to him all night.

After he had gone from the room, my mother said, "I don't see how anyone can doubt that he is a prophet of God. They can see it in his countenance, which is so full of intelligence." "Yes, truly!" my father replied. "He is a prophet of God." The very next day my mother was ready for baptism. The ice was six (6) inches deep, but was cut, and the way was prepared, and Mother entered the waters of baptism. She was baptized by Elder Lorenzo Barnes, and was confirmed a member of the Church of Jesus Christ of Latter-day Saints by the Prophet Joseph Smith.

My sister, Mary, followed, but Mother made me wait until the weather was milder, so it was not until April that I became a member of the Church. My father was baptized the following day.

We kept "open house" for the missionaries. Among those who visited us were Brother and Sister Erastus Snow, who had with them their first baby. They were indeed sweet singers, and we enjoyed their society very much. Brother Snow, afterwards, became one of the powerful leaders in Utah. Hyrum Smith, the Patriarch, also came to our home. His object was to borrow money for the Church. Father had sold his property with the fixed purpose of gathering with the Saints, so he freely loaned what was asked of him.

The Patriarch was like his brother Joseph, a very great gentleman, handsome, splendid, serious, and yet extremely polite and full of blessings.

One lovely day in harvest time, September 22, 1843, accompanied by William Smith, the brother of the Prophet, we bade farewell to our land of Quaker parentage, and traveling by rail and steamboat we soon landed in the beautiful city of Nauvoo, Illinois. At the landing, who should we meet but the Prophet and his wife, who took us to their home and entertained us most hospitably. Their family was always very friendly to us, seeming never to forget my father's hospitality in Pennsylvania, as well as his generosity in lending money that was needed (n.d., pp. 1–3).

Revelation

Lorenzo Brown

[Brown remembers hearing Joseph say:] After I got through translating the Book of Mormon, I took up the Bible to read with the Urim and Thummim. I read the first chapter of Genesis and I saw the things as they were done. I turned over the next and the next, and the whole passed before me like a grand panorama; and so on chapter after chapter until I read the whole of it. I saw it all! (1880).

Martha C. Cox

"Uncle" Allen Stout, Lizzie's uncle, used to come to live with us while he worked in the temple.... We all liked "Uncle Allen" and was glad to have him stay with us. He had used coffee for many years, but when he came to work in the temple he would not drink it anymore. He was in Nauvoo a bodyguard to the Prophet, and when asked to tell something about the days of Nauvoo he would tell it, but he was not much of a talker unless asked to do so. He gave me much information about the early history of the Church because I asked him many questions.

One day he said in answer to a statement I made that I thought it could not be possible for one to see a heavenly being, that I might see one without recognizing it as such—as happened once with him. I immediately became anxious to know all about it. He told me he was once walking with the Prophet on the west side of the Mississippi River on the road to Montrose, I think. They saw a man walking along a road leading in from the south and coming towards them. The Prophet told Allen to remain where he was while he stepped over to speak with this pedestrian. Allen turned his back towards them and for a time forgot the Prophet and became engaged with his own thoughts, while he stood whipping a low bush with the cane he carried.

The hand of the Prophet upon his shoulder aroused him. The Prophet said, "We must return immediately to Nauvoo." They walked silently and rapidly. Allen became very sorrowful over his recreancy to his duty and could not refrain from weeping. The prophet asked him why he wept. Allen confessed, "I am an insufficient bodyguard—criminally neglectful of your welfare. I allowed that man you met to speak with you without even being ready to defend if he attacked you. He could have killed you and made his escape without my knowing who he is, which way he went or what he even looks like. You will have to dispense with my services and take a guard on which you can depend. Your life is too precious to be trusted to my care."

The prophet then said, "That man would not harm me. You saw John the Revelator."

Some years afterwards I referred to this instance while speaking with the grandson of "Uncle Allen," and was surprised that he had never heard of it before. On further investigation we found that the old man had never told that story to his children, so we let valuable history slip by us (n.d., p. 139).

Heber C. Kimball

I have heard Joseph say many times that he was much tempted about the revelations the Lord gave through him—it seemed to be so impossible for them to be fulfilled. I do not profess to be a prophet; but I know that every man and woman can be, if they live for it. To enjoy this blessing they must walk in the channel of the priesthood, being subject to the order and government of heaven (JD, 3:112).

Heber C. Kimball

To refer again to what I know, what I have seen and experienced in my travels and my associations with the Prophet of the living God, I will remark that you have here with you a few of us that have traveled with him from the beginning, and we know his trials and sufferings, and we know that the greatest torment he had and the greatest mental suffering was because this people would not live up to their privileges. There were many things he desired to reveal that we have not learned yet, but he could not do it. He said sometimes that he felt pressed upon and as though he were pent up in an acorn shell, and all because the people did not and would not prepare themselves to receive the rich treasures of wisdom and knowledge that he had to impart. He could have revealed a great many things that we could not receive because we lacked that diligence and faithfulness that were necessary to entitle us to those choice things of the kingdom. He revealed the doctrine of celestial marriage, and the abuse of this holy principle caused many to stumble and fall away from the Church of the living God, but that was their own fault and they have nobody else to blame (JD, 10:166–67; see also John Taylor, JD, 10:147–48).

Mary Elizabeth Rollins Lightner

He (Joseph Smith) said, "John the Revelator was caught up to the third heaven, but I know one who was caught up to the seventh heaven, and saw and heard things not lawful for me to utter" (1936, p. 14).

Note: If Lightner's memory is correct in saying it was John who was caught up, then Joseph Smith is adding something to our knowledge not contained in the scriptures. If she is confusing John with Paul, who said he was caught up to the third heaven, the account is found in 2 Corinthians 12:2; see also Joseph Smith, 1976, p. 247).

Amasa M. Lyman

The Prophet Joseph once took me by the arm in the street, and said, "I have so many blessings, and there is nothing but what you can enjoy in your time and place the same as I do, and so can every man" (JD, 10:89).

Franklin D. Richards

Do not let us think that we have got all the revelation there is. In the last great revelation which the Lord gave to Joseph, He told him that He had not revealed all to him, but that there were many laws pertaining to His priesthood which He would reveal hereafter (JD, 26:169).

George A. Smith

There is a statement coming through George A. Smith, cousin of the Prophet and the Patriarch, to the effect that Joseph Smith the Prophet once declared that he was related to Captain John Smith, English explorer and colonizer of Virginia. This statement is said to be based on heavenly inspiration. If this is true, then the Smith family came out of Lincolnshire, for Captain John Smith was born at Willoughby, Lincolnshire. What little we know of Robert Smith would lend color to this statement, for the record shows that Robert left Boston in Lincolnshire by boat for London when he contemplated his migration to the United States (1938, pp. 15–16).

George A. Smith

The question is frequently asked, "How did you ever find this place [the Salt Lake Valley]?" I answer we were led to it by the inspiration of

God. After the death of Joseph Smith, when it seemed as if every trouble and calamity had come upon the Saints, Brigham Young, who was the president of the Twelve, then the presiding Quorum of the Church, sought the Lord to know what they should do and where they should lead the people for safety, and while they were fasting and praying daily on this subject President Young had a vision of Joseph Smith, who showed him the mountain we now call Ensign Peak, immediately north of Salt Lake City, and there was an ensign fell upon that peak, and Joseph said, "Build under the point where the colors fall and you will prosper and have peace."

The pioneers had no pilot or guide, none among them had ever been in the country or knew anything about it. However, they traveled under the direction of President Young until they reached the valley. When they entered it, President Young pointed to that peak and, said he, "I want to go there." He went up to the point and said, "This is Ensign Peak. Now, brethren, organize your exploring parties, so as to be safe from Indians; go and explore where you will, and you will come back every time and say this is the best place." They accordingly started out exploring companies and visited what we now call Cache, Malad, Toole, and Utah Valleys, and other parts of the country in various directions, but all came back and declared that this was the best spot (1869a, p. 248).

Joseph F. Smith

I want to tell you another thing: Our Heavenly Father has never yet to my knowledge revealed to this Church any great principle through a woman. Now, sisters, do not cast me off or deny the faith, because I tell you that God has never revealed any great and essential truth for the guidance of the Latter-day Saints through any woman. "Oh! but," says one, "what about Eliza Snow's beautiful hymn, 'O my Father, Thou that dwellest,' etc? Did not the Lord reveal through her that great and glorious principle that we have a mother as well as a father in heaven?" No. God revealed that principle to Joseph Smith; Joseph Smith revealed it to Eliza Snow Smith, his wife; and Eliza Snow was inspired, being a poet, to put it into verse. If we give anybody on earth credit for that, we give it to the Prophet Joseph Smith. But first of all we give it to God, who revealed it to His servant the Prophet. God reveals Himself and His truths through the channels of the priesthood (CD, 4:229).

John Taylor

I remember Joseph Smith speaking to me upwards of thirty years ago. Says he: "Brother Taylor, you have received the Holy Ghost. Now follow its teachings and instructions. Sometimes it may lead you in a manner that may be contrary almost to your judgment; never mind, follow its teachings, and if you do so, by and by it will become in you a principle of revelation, so that you will know all things as they transpire" (JD, 14:366–67; see also John Taylor, JD, 19:153–54; 22:314; Wilford Woodruff, CD, 2:266; 5:238).

Martha Thomas

I now speak of a sermon the Prophet preached in 1843. I think it was on celestial marriage, though he did not give it a name. He commenced with the old Bible, and clear through showing what they had done and how they were blessed. He said we were good people and loved him and he loved us, and the Lord had made known many great and marvelous things to him. We were anxious to know what they were. He said, "If I were to tell you, the best friends I have, apparently, would shed my blood," and so they did; that is, they joined hands with the ungodly and were murderers (1927, p. 31; see also James P. Terry, 1893, p. 331).

William H. Walker

It was quite a common occurrence, in those days, for officers to suddenly appear with an arrest for "Old Joe Smith," on some flimsy, trumped up charge. One day in the summer of 1842, I was sitting at the dinner table with the Prophet, when, without a word being spoken by any person present, he arose suddenly from the table, and went out of the room. No sooner had he closed the door than an officer entered by another door, having come up the river bank. He (Joseph) walked some twenty rods across the block, in a path leading to the brick store, in full view of another officer. Then he disappeared, without being discovered by either.

On another occasion some officers came into the city and put up at the hotel, just above his residence. Joseph gave me directions to take his horse, "Joe Dunkin" (named after Governor Dunkin), put on his military bridle, saddle, and portmanteaus (this article costing $100.00), and ride up Main Street to the upper-landing, cross on the ferry boat to Montrose, [and go] from there to Keokuk. From that, the report started that I had taken the horse to Joe Smith, and he had gone on west. Meantime I returned to Nauvoo with the horse, but no one knew that the horse had returned, neither friend or foe (1943, p. 9).

Wilford Woodruff

He remarked on several occasions when conversing with his brethren: "Brethren, you do not know me, you do not know who I am." As I remarked at our priesthood meeting on Friday evening, I have heard him in my early days while conversing with the brethren, say (at the same time smiting himself upon the breast), "I would to God that I could unbosom my feelings in the house of my friends." Joseph Smith was ordained before he came here, the same as Jeremiah was (JD, 21:317).

Wilford Woodruff

One morning, while we were at Winter Quarters, Brother Brigham Young said to me and the brethren that he had had a visitation the night previous from Joseph Smith. I asked him what he said to him. He replied that Joseph had told him to tell the people to labor to obtain the Spirit of God; that they needed that to sustain them and to give them power to go through their work in the earth.

Now I will give you a little of my experience in this line. Joseph Smith visited me a great deal after his death, and taught me many important principles. The last time he visited me was while I was in a storm at sea. I was going on my last mission to preside in England. My companions were Brother Leonard W. Hardy, Brother Milton Holmes, Brother Dan Jones, and another brother, and my wife and two other women. We had been traveling three days and nights in a heavy gale, and were being driven backwards. Finally I asked my companions to come into the cabin with me, and I told them to pray that the Lord would change the wind. I had no fears of being lost; but I did not like the idea of being driven back to New York, as I wanted to go on my journey. We all offered the same prayer, both men and women; and when we got through we stepped on to the deck, and in less than a minute it was as though a man had taken a sword and cut that gale through, and you might have thrown a muslin handkerchief out and it would not have moved it.

The night following this, Joseph and Hyrum visited me, and the Prophet laid before me a great many things. Among other things, he told me to get the Spirit of God; that all of us needed it. He also told me what the Twelve Apostles would be called to go through on the earth before the coming of the Son of Man, and what the reward of their labors would be; but all that was taken from me, for some reason. Nevertheless, I know it was most glorious, although much would be required at our hands.

Joseph Smith continued visiting myself and others up to a certain time, and then it stopped. The last time I saw him was in heaven. In the night vision I saw him at the door of the temple in heaven. He came and spoke to me. He said he could not stop to talk with me because he was in a hurry. The next man I met was Father Smith; he could not talk with me because he was in a hurry. I met half a dozen brethren who had held high positions on earth, and none of them could stop to talk with me because they were in a hurry. I was much astonished.

By and by I saw the Prophet again, and I got the privilege to ask him a question. "Now," said I, "I want to know why you are in a hurry. I have been in a hurry all through my life; but I expected my hurry would be over when I got into the kingdom of heaven, if I ever did."

Joseph said: "I will tell you, Brother Woodruff. Every dispensation that has had the priesthood on the earth and has gone into the celestial kingdom has had a certain amount of work to do to prepare to go to the earth with the Savior when He goes to reign on the earth. Each dispensation has had ample time to do this work. We have not. We are the last dispensation, and so much work has to be done, and we need to be in a hurry in order to accomplish it."

Of course, that was satisfactory to me, but it was new doctrine to me.

Brigham Young also visited me after his death. On one occasion he and Brother Heber C. Kimball came in a splendid chariot, with fine white horses, and accompanied me to a conference that I was going to attend. When I got there I asked Brother Brigham if he would take charge of the conference. "No," said he, "I have done my work here. I have come to see what you are doing and what you are teaching the people." And he told me what Joseph Smith had taught him in Winter Quarters, to teach the people to get the Spirit of God. He said, "I want you to teach the people to get the Spirit of God. You cannot build up the Kingdom of God without that" (CD, 5:237–38).

Wilford Woodruff

The Prophet Joseph Smith taught the Twelve Apostles in my day and time with regard to the principle of revelation. The Prophet said the elders of Israel would have their minds moved upon by the Spirit of God concerning various things which they might not always understand, but if they would follow out that principle and practice upon it, it would very soon become a principle of revelation to them. This is a true principle and by observing it I have been blessed all my life (CD, 5:316).

Brigham Young

Joseph Smith said to this people, that all the wisdom he had was received from the hand of the Lord. All the knowledge, wisdom, economy, and every business transaction pertaining to human life in connection with the spiritual kingdom of God on the earth, is given unto us as individuals, or as a community, from the liberal hand of God (JD, 1:78).

Brigham Young

Joseph said, twenty-two years ago, "Brother Brigham, if I were to tell this people all the revelations I have, every man would leave me." I do not want to know things faster than I can obey. Everything that is received must be lived up to by the people, and when this people are ready to receive further light, I promise you in the name of Israel's God it will be given every son and daughter (1855).

Brigham Young

Many years ago, the Prophet Joseph observed that if the people would have received the revelations he had in his possession, and wisely acted upon them, as the Lord would dictate, they might, in their power to do and understand, have been many years ahead of what they then were. Experience has taught us that it requires time to acquire certain branches of mechanism, also all principles and ideas that we wish to become masters of. The closer people apply their minds to any correct purpose the faster they can grow and increase in the knowledge of the truth (JD, 6:94).

Brigham Young

We have received these bodies for an exaltation, to be crowned with those who have been crowned with crowns of glory and eternal life. Yes, Joseph Smith said, the Lord whispers to the spirit in the tabernacle the same as though it were out of it. That is correct and true (JD, 9:287).

Brigham Young

Joseph said to me in Kirtland, "Brother Brigham, if I was to reveal to this people what the Lord has revealed to me, there is not a man or a woman would stay with me." In the day of prosperity now the people are slow to follow the Lord. If he were now to bless this people with gold and silver, houses and lands, with everything to make them wealthy and comfortable here in Deseret or Utah, a great many would turn away from him to worship their idols (JD, 9:294).

Seership

Israel A. Barlow

My grandfather, Israel Barlow, was a very trusted bodyguard to the Prophet Joseph Smith. Shortly before the martyrdom (the exact date not being available), the Prophet called upon him and requested that he make a journey of many miles on horseback and deliver a message from the Prophet to a certain man who lived in a neighborhood of enemies to the Prophet and to the Latter-day Saints. He was asked to make special observations of what he might see and hear while on this mission.

It was a hazardous time in the history of the Church, and the Prophet was constantly in jeopardy, not only from enemies without but within the Church. The Prophet told him to leave on this errand on a certain day early in the morning and ride to a certain man's home and there deliver the message. He was instructed to accept of their hospitality, which the Prophet Joseph assured him they would extend to him. "But," said the Prophet, "let them put your horse up for you and eat supper with them, but when it becomes sundown saddle your horse and leave. They will be insistent and try to persuade you to remain overnight, but if you value your life do not stay, but leave, and listen to the direction of the Spirit."

He left promptly at sundown and rode along the country road until it became dark. Just before he came to the river bridge, a voice said to grandfather, "Ride faster." He sped up his horse and the voice repeated again, and with more emphasis, "Ride faster." And again he increased the speed of the animal when the voice said to him, "Ride for your life." He then sped for all the animal's strength. As the horse's feet clattered across the bridge he could hear the mob, which had gathered in the brush to intercept him, cursing at the top of their voices. He had crossed the bridge but a short distance when the voice said to him: "Turn to the right," and he turned his horse off the road into the brush toward the river. There he stood in silence as the mob, who had mounted their horses, came racing over the bridge at break-neck speed, and down the road they went, supposedly after him.

After they had gone by he wound his way from the river's edge to the bed of the stream, and on through the willows. In the darkness he made his way along the river in the opposite direction from which the mob had expected him to go. Finally, when he thought it was safe, several miles away, he emerged from the river and made his way over the country back into Nauvoo, just as the day was breaking.

There he saw the Prophet Joseph walking up and down the street in front of his home. As grandfather approached and alighted from his horse, he began to tell the Prophet of his experience. The Prophet stopped him and told him he need not tell him for he already knew. The Prophet told him that he had been up all night waiting for his return, and stated, "I saw it all; you have no need to tell me." Thereupon the Prophet laid his hand upon grandfather's shoulder and gave him a blessing and said: "Thee and thine shall never want" (1968, pp. 194–95).

Caroline B. Crosby

It was a general time of rejoicing for several months among the Saints. They frequently met from house, to house, to break bread, and drink wine and administer to the poor and afflicted. We also would attend a [meeting] at Dr Frederick G. Williams. His eldest daughter had been lately married, and was about to leave for Missouri: he therefore blessed her family previous to their leaving. He laid his hands upon each of their heads, and the scribe wrote them [the blessings]. The Prophet Joseph was present and had a vision of their journey, saw their wagon turn over, but no one was injured. It came to pass even as he said (1982, p. 51).

Ira S. Hatch

About this time the construction of the Kirtland Temple had started. Ira Stearns Hatch, although not a member of the Church, and Wealtha [his wife] decided to make a contribution to its construction. Ira was very anxious to visit the Prophet, Joseph Smith, and feel the spirit of the man. So they prepared to make the trip, and upon arriving at Kirtland Ira inquired for the Prophet. Being informed that he would be found in the grove where they were cutting timber for the temple, Ira made his way to that place. As he approached the workmen, one of them struck his axe into a tree and came toward him. When close enough, he shook the hand of Ira Stearns Hatch and said, "Brother Hatch, I have been expecting you for three days; the money which you have brought will be used to help build the pulpit in the temple." This left Ira Stearns Hatch with no chance for doubt that Joseph Smith was indeed a true Prophet. Ira's testimony of the truthfulness of the gospel remained steadfast the remainder of his life (1988, pp. 3–5).

James H. Rollins

As early as February, 1831, I first met Joseph Smith in my Uncle Sidney Gilbert's house. This was the first day he arrived in Kirtland, and while he was in the house conversing with my uncle and aunt, I, being at the front gate, saw a wagon turn over as it was coming down the slippery hill, and heard a woman and two or three children screaming. This was Joseph's family. I ran in and told Joseph and Uncle about it, and Joseph ran to assist them without his hat. My first impression was that if any of the occupants were hurt seriously that Joseph could heal them, but none of them were hurt. Joseph and my uncle returned to the house. He asked my uncle if I was his son. He said, "No, I was his wife's nephew," "Well," [Joseph] said, "the Lord has shown him great things." I truly had seen Joseph and Hyrum in my vision in December 1830 (n.d., p. 2).

Joseph Smith

Brother Whitney had not had his [broken] foot moved from the bed for nearly four weeks, when I went into his room after a walk in the grove and told him if he would agree to start for home in the morning, we would take a wagon to the river, about four miles, and there would be a ferry-boat in waiting which would take us quickly across, where we would find a hack which would take us directly to the landing, where we should find a boat in waiting, and we would be going up the river before ten o'clock, and have a prosperous journey home. He took courage and told me he would go. We started next morning, and found everything as I had told him, for we were passing rapidly up the river before ten o'clock, and, landing at Wellsville, took stagecoach to Chardon, from thence in a wagon to Kirtland, where we arrived some time in June (HC, 1:272).

Joseph Smith

I have often felt a whispering since I received your letter, like this: "Joseph, thou art indebted to thy God for the offering of thy Sister Vienna, which proved a savor of life as pertaining to thy pecuniary concerns. Therefore she should not be forgotten of thee, for the Lord hath done this, and thou shouldst remember her in all thy prayers and also by letter, for she oftentimes calleth on the Lord, saying, O Lord, inspire thy servant Joseph to communicate by letter some word to thine unworthy handmaiden, and say all my sins are forgiven, and art thou not content with the chastisement wherewith thou hast chastised thy handmaiden?" Yea, sister, this seems to be the whispering of a spirit, and judge ye what spirit it is (HC, 1:408).

Joseph Smith

During this night the visions of the future were opened to my understanding, when I saw the ways and means and near approach of my escape from imprisonment, and the danger that my beloved Brother Markham was in. I awoke Brother Markham, and told him if he would rise very early and not wait for the judge and lawyers, as he had contemplated doing, but rise briskly, he would get safe home, almost before he was aware of it; and if he did not the mob would shoot him on the way; and I told him to tell the brethren to be of good cheer, but lose no time in removing from the country.

Friday, April 1 [1839]—This morning Brother Markham arose at dawn of day, and rode rapidly towards Far West where he arrived before nine A.M. The mobbers pursued to shoot him, but did not overtake him (HC, 3:316).

Prayer

Henry W. Bigler

Speaking about praying to our Father in Heaven, I once heard Joseph Smith remark, "Be plain and simple and ask for what you want, just like you would go to a neighbor and say, I want to borrow your horse to go to the mill." I heard him say to some elders going on missions, "Make short prayers and short sermons, and let mysteries alone. Preach nothing but repentance and baptism for the remission of sins, for that was all John the Baptist preached" (1892, pp. 151–52).

George A. Smith

[Saturday, May 24, 1834, on Zion's Camp] Joseph counseled us through life to cultivate a modest and graceful demeanor, avoiding vulgarity. He said that many of the camp, when they kneeled to pray would take unseemly positions which was not right. "When we kneel to pray, we should be in a graceful position, such as would not cause a disgusting impression to arise in the mind of any spectator" (n.d., p. 15).

George A. Smith

May 30, 1835—I was appointed on a mission to preach the gospel in the east. My circumstances were so reduced that I could not procure clothes to go in. Joseph and Hyrum gave me some grey cloth to make me a coat and snuff colored vest and pantaloons. [Others gave him other assistance, as well. Then] . . . I called to see Cousin Joseph; he gave me a Book of Mormon, shook hands with me, and said, "Preach short sermons, make short prayers, and deliver your sermons with a prayerful heart." This advice I have always denominated my "College Education" (n.d., p. 29).

Joseph Smith

Brother Richards asked if I wanted a wicked man to pray for me? I replied, Yes; if the fervent, affectionate prayer of the righteous man availeth much, a wicked man may avail a little when praying for a righteous man. There is none good but one. The better a man is, the more his prayer will avail. Like the publican and the Pharisee, one was justified rather than the other, showing that both were justified in a degree. The prayer of a wicked man may do a righteous man good, when it does the one who prays no good (HC, 5:208).

Joseph Smith

The Lord once told me that what I asked for I should have. I have been afraid to ask God to kill my enemies, lest some of them should, peradventure, repent.

I asked a short time since for the Lord to deliver me out of the hands of the governor of Missouri, and if it needs must be to accomplish it, to take him away; and the next news that came pouring down from there was that *Governor Reynolds had shot himself.* And I would now say, "Beware, O earth, how you fight against the Saints of God and shed innocent blood; for in the days of Elijah, his enemies came upon him, and fire was called down from heaven and destroyed them" (HC, 6:253).

John Taylor

It is right for heads of families to get their families together every morning and evening, and pray with them. Every man and woman to dedicate themselves to God; and in their secret prayers to ask God's care over them during the day. That will not hurt any of you. That was the doctrine that Joseph Smith taught me; and I have always appreciated it (JD, 26:112).

Daniel Tyler

At the time William Smith and others rebelled against the Prophet, as recorded in his history, when the walls of the Kirtland Temple were raised but a few feet above the ground, I attended a meeting "on the flats," where "Joseph" presided. Entering the schoolhouse a little before meeting opened, and gazing upon the man of God, I perceived sadness in his countenance and tears trickling down his cheeks. I naturally supposed the all-absorbing topic of the difficulty must be the cause. I was not mistaken. A few moments later a hymn was sung and he opened the meeting by prayer. Instead, however, of facing the audience, he turned his back and bowed upon his knees, facing the wall. This, I suppose, was done to hide his sorrow and tears.

I had heard men and women pray—especially the former—from the most ignorant, both as to letters and intellect, to the most learned and eloquent, but never until then had I heard a man address his Maker as though He was present listening as a kind father would listen to the sorrows of a dutiful child. Joseph was at that time unlearned, but that prayer, which was to a considerable extent in behalf of those who accused him of having gone astray and fallen into sin, that the Lord would forgive them and open their eyes that they might see aright—that prayer, I say, to my humble mind, partook of the learning and eloquence of heaven. There was no ostentation, no raising of the voice as by enthusiasm, but a plain conversational tone, as a man would address a present friend. It appeared to me as though, in case the veil were taken away, I could see the Lord standing facing His humblest of all servants I had ever seen. Whether this was really the case I cannot say; but one thing I can say, it was the crowning, so to speak, of all the prayers I ever heard. After the prayer another hymn was sung.

When Joseph arose and addressed the congregation, he spoke of his many troubles, and said he often wondered why it was that he should have so much trouble in the house of his friends, and he wept as though his heart would break. Finally he said: "The Lord once told me that if at any time I got into deep trouble and could see no way out of it, if I would prophesy in His name, he would fulfill my words," and added: "I prophesy in the name of the Lord that those who have thought I was in transgression shall have a testimony this night that I am clear and stand approved before the Lord." The next Sabbath his brother William and several others made humble confessions before the public. What their testimonies were, I never knew (1892b, pp. 127–28).

The Gift of Memory

John D. Lee

Winter Quarters, Tues., Feb. 16th, 1847—[President Brigham Young said:] "Brother Joseph [Smith] said that he had taught the Twelve all he knew concerning the order of the kingdom but the difficulty was that they could not remember it as he could then, but when it was necessary they would not be at a loss for understanding, and I bear record of the truth of his words before God this day, that I always had an understanding and everything was brought to mind just as he taught them to us. All the ordinances of the temple and building of the altar, etc., came to me just right when they were to be done" (1938, pp. 81–82).

Obedience

Israel A. Barlow

Upon another occasion my grandfather was assisting in the building of the temple at Nauvoo and was driving a pair of beautiful high-spirited black mares. One day while [grandfather was] backing his wagon in at the quarry which was down by the river's edge, the Prophet came over to him and said: "Israel, on your next trip, stop and buy yourself a buggy whip," to which grandfather assented. On his next trip up town he bought a buggy whip and returned for another load of rock. Backing the team in this time, he attempted to stop them as usual by saying, "Whoa," to which they paid no attention, but kept backing until Israel, in excitement, [he] was compelled to use the whip which the Prophet had told him to buy. The horses jumped forward and the wagon stopped right at the edge of the quarry, beyond which they would have plunged below.

Grandfather frequently told this story as an illustration of what obedience means. Grandfather accepted everything the Prophet Joseph Smith told him and never questioned "why?" Some would call this blind obedience, but not so. Israel Barlow knew full well the divine calling of the Prophet and bore that testimony to the day of his death (1968, pp. 195–96).

John D. Lee

In the sports of the day, such as wrestling, etc., he was over an average. Very few of the Saints had the strength needed to throw the Prophet in a fair tussel; in every gathering he was a welcome guest, and always added to the amusement of the people, instead of dampening their ardor. During the time that we were camping at Adam-ondi-Ahman, waiting to see what would be the result of the quarrel between our Church and the Gentiles, one Sunday morning (it had rained heavily the night before and the air was cold) the men were shivering over a few fire-brands feeling out of sorts and quite cast down. The Prophet came up while the brethren were moping around, and caught first one and then another and shook them up, and said, "Get out of here, and wrestle, jump, run, do anything but mope around; warm yourselves up; this inactivity will not do for soldiers." The words of the Prophet put life and energy into the men. A ring was soon formed, according to the custom of the people. The Prophet stepped into the ring, ready for a tussel with any comer. Several went into the ring to try their strength, but each one was thrown by the Prophet, until he had thrown several of the stoutest of the men present. Then he stepped out of the ring and took a man by the arm and led him in to take his place, and so it continued—the men who were thrown retiring in favor of the successful one. A man would keep the ring so long as he threw his adversary. The style of wrestling varied with the desires of the parties. The Eastern men, or Yankees, used square hold, or collar and elbow; those from the Middle States side hold, and the Southern and Western men used breeches hold and old Indian hug or back hold. If a man was hurt he stood it without a murmur; it was considered cowardly and childish to whine when thrown down or hurt in the fall.

While the sport was at its height Sidney Rigdon, the mouthpiece of the Prophet, rushed into the ring, sword in hand, and said that he would not suffer a lot of men to break the Sabbath day in that manner. For a moment all were silent, then one of the brethren, with more presence of mind than the others, said to the Prophet, "Brother Joseph, we want you to clear us from blame, for we formed the ring by your request. You told us to wrestle, and now Brother Rigdon is bringing us to account for it."

The Prophet walked into the ring and said, as he made a motion with his hand: "Brother Sidney, you had better go out of here and let the boys alone; they are amusing themselves according to my orders. You are an old man. You go and get ready for meeting and let the boys alone." Just then catching Rigdon off his guard, as quick as a flash he knocked the sword from Rigdon's hand, then caught him by the shoulder, and said: "Now, old man, you must go out, or I will throw you down." Rigdon was as large a man as the Prophet, but not so tall. The prospect of a tussel between the Prophet and the mouthpiece of the Prophet was fun for all but Rigdon, who pulled back like a crawfish, but the resistance was useless, the Prophet dragged him from the ring, bareheaded, and tore Rigdon's fine pulpit coat from the collar to the waist; then he turned to the men and said: "Go in, boys, and have your fun. You shall never have it to say that I got you into any trouble that I did not get you out of."

Rigdon complained about the loss of his hat and the tearing of his coat. The Prophet said to him: "You were out of your place. Always keep your place and you will not suffer; but you got a little out of your place and you have suffered for it. You have no one to blame but yourself." After that Rigdon never countermanded the orders of the Prophet, to my knowledge—he knew who was the boss (1881, pp. 76–78).

Daniel Tyler

Everyone has probably heard or read of the terrible martyrdom at Haun's Mill. At this late date some may be led to inquire why did not the Prophet foresee this and avert the terrible calamity. The older Saints, or those of long standing in the Church, understand all of the particulars, but there are our young folks and future generations who, not understanding some unpublished facts, would be liable and almost certain to marvel, as some already do. This is not strange, as the history of the Church shows that the man of God was in Far West, only about twenty miles distant.

Well, my young brethren and sisters, the following are a few of the facts. Brother Haun owned the mill, a grist mill, which took his name. From two to four days prior to the massacre, the citizens of the little settlement assembled in a mass meeting, and appointed Brother Haun a committee of one to go to the city for advice to know what to do. The whole country was under arms and excitement. The Apostle David W. Patten, with Brothers Gideon Carter and O'Banion, had already sealed their testimony with their blood. Under these circumstances it was quite natural that small settlements should begin to inquire what was best for them to do.

Brother Haun repaired to the city, and as the Prophet was but a private citizen and minister of the gospel, in the legal sense, he first went to Captain John Killian, of the Caldwell County militia, informed him of his appointment, and inquired what he and his brethren should do.

"Move into the city was the prompt reply."

Brother H.—"What! and leave the mill?"

Captain K.—"Yes, and leave the mill."

Brother H.—"What! to the mob?"

Captain K.—"Yes, to the mob."

Brother Haun then left the captain and went to "Brother Joseph," as the Prophet was familiarly called. He asked him the same questions, and received the same answers, word for word.

"But," responded the selfish mill-owner, "Brother Joseph, we think we are strong enough to defend the mill and keep it in our own hands."

"Oh, well," replied he, "if you think you are strong enough to hold the mill you can do as you think best."

What more could he say? His method had always been when his counsel was asked to give it freely and leave parties to receive or reject it. He could not, nor would not if he could, take away people's agency.

Brother Haun returned and reported that Brother Joseph's counsel was for them to stay and protect or hold the mill. The rest the reader knows, or can become acquainted with by reading the published account of the terrible tragedy. The foregoing facts I had from the late Captain Killian in person (1892a, pp. 94–95).

The Gift of Forgiveness

Daniel Tyler

One scene, I was informed after it occurred, was particularly touching, and showed the goodness of the good man's heart. A man who had stood in high in the Church while in Far West was taken down with chills or ague and fever. While his mind as well as body was weak, disaffected parties soured his mind and persuaded him to leave the Saints and go with them. He gave some testimony against the Prophet. While the Saints were settling in Commerce, having recovered from his illness, he removed from Missouri to Quincy, Illinois. There he went to work chopping cordwood to obtain means to take himself and family to Nauvoo and present to the injured man of God if, peradventure, he would forgive and permit him to return to the fold as a private member. He felt that there was salvation nowhere else for him, and if that was denied him all was lost as far as he was concerned. He started with a sorrowful heart and downcast look. While on the way the Lord told Brother Joseph he was coming. As soon as he turned to open the gate the Prophet sprang up from his chair and ran and met him in the yard, exclaiming "O Brother _____, how glad I am to see you!" He caught him around the neck and both wept like children. Suffice it to say that proper restitution was made and the fallen man again entered the Church by the door, received his priesthood again, went upon several important missions, gathered with the Saints in Zion, and died in full faith (1892c, p. 491).

Loyalty to Zion

Wilford Woodruff

When we went upon our first foreign mission, Joseph said to us, "No matter what may come upon you, round up your shoulders and bear it, and always sustain and defend the interests of the Church and Kingdom of God." When we took our departure his demeanor in parting was something that I had never noticed or experienced before. After crossing the Mississippi River, I crawled to the side of a house and lay down upon a side of sole leather, while suffering from the chills and fever. While [I was] resting there the Prophet Joseph came along and saw me. He gave me some parting advice in answer to some remarks made, and then told me to get up and go on, and all would be well with me. That is the way I parted with him upon that occasion (JD, 24:53).

4

Joseph Smith and the Scriptures

Writing Scriptures

John Taylor

In speaking with the Prophet Joseph once on this subject [of the restoration of priesthood and keys], he traced it from the first down to the last, until he got to the Ancient of Days. He wished me to write something for him of this subject, but I found it a very difficult thing to do. He had to correct me several times. We are told that the "judgment shall sit and the books be opened." He spoke of the various dispensations and of those holding the keys thereof, and said there would then be a general giving up or accounting for. I wrote that each one holding the keys of the several dispensations would deliver them up to his predecessor, from one to another, until the whole kingdom should be delivered up to the Father, and then God would be "all in all." Said he, "That is not right." I wrote it again, and again he said it was not right. It is very difficult to find language suitable to convey the meaning of spiritual things. The idea was that they should deliver up or give an account of their administrations, in their several dispensations, but that they would all retain their several positions and priesthood (JD, 18:330).

Daniel Tyler

On one occasion he read, among other scriptures, Hebrews, 6th chapter, 1st and 2nd verses, as follows:

"Therefore, leaving the principles of the doctrine of Christ, let us go on unto perfection; not laying again the foundation of repentance from dead works, of faith toward God,

"Of the doctrine of baptisms, and of laying on of hands, and of resurrection of the dead, and eternal judgment."

The Prophet said the first verse should read: "Therefore, *not* leaving the first principles of the doctrine of Christ, etc." This explanation not only made the entire subject of the two verses clear but reconciled them with other scriptures. Notwithstanding Paul is made to say "leaving," etc., the inference is clear that if the foundation of repentance, baptism, and the laying on of hands should be relaid they would have to perform those works over again, as every careful reader of the text must see. This also corroborates a revelation to the church of Ephesus: "Remember, therefore, from whence thou art fallen, and repent and do the first works." All Latter-day Saints know that the first works after repentance are baptism and the laying on of hands for the reception of the Holy Ghost. Here we find a presiding elder of a branch or ward of the Church commanded to perform these works over again, under pain of removal if he failed to obey the divine behest. Many more passages might be quoted to the same effect, but these are sufficient for my purpose. Joseph's translation not only reconciles the text with itself, but also with other scriptures, as already shown, and as was explained by the Prophet (1892a, p. 94).

Brigham Young

27th [December 1841]—I met with the Twelve at Brother Joseph's. He conversed with us in a familiar manner on a variety of subjects, and explained to us the Urim and Thummim which he found with the plates, called in the Book of Mormon the Interpreters. He said that every man who lived on the earth was entitled to a seerstone, and should have one, but they are kept from them in consequence of their wickedness, and most of those who do find one make an evil use of it. He showed us his seerstone (1968, p. 112).

Note: In Joseph's summary of this meeting, he says nothing of the Urim and Thummim, or of seerstones (see HC, 4:486).

Coming Forth of the Book of Mormon (1824–1829)

John H. Gilbert

I am a practical printer by trade. I have been a resident of Palmyra, New York, since about the year 1824, and during all that time have done some typesetting each year. I was aged ninety years on the 13th day of April 1892, and on that day I went to the office of the *Palmyra Courier* and set a stickful of type.

My recollection of past events, and especially of the matters connected with the printing of the "Mormon Bible" [Book of Mormon], is very accurate and faithful, and I have made the following memorandum at request, to accompany the photographs of "Mormon Hill," which have been made for the purpose of exhibits at the World's Fair in 1893.

In the forepart of June, 1829, Mr. E. [Egbert] B. Grandin, the printer of the *Wayne Sentinel*, came to me and said he wanted I should assist him in estimating the cost of printing 5,000 copies of a book that Martin Harris wanted to get printed, which was called the "Mormon Bible." It was the second application of Harris to Grandin to do the job—Harris assuring Grandin that the book would be printed in Rochester if he declined the job again.

Harris proposed to have Grandin do the job, if he would, as it would be quite expensive to keep a man in Rochester during the printing of the book, who would have to visit Palmyra two or three times a week for manuscript, etc. Mr. Grandin consented to do the job if his terms were accepted.

A few pages of the manuscript were submitted as a specimen of the whole, and it was said there would be about 500 pages.

The size of the page was agreed upon, and an estimate of the number of ems in a page, which would be 1,000, and that a page of manuscript would make more than a page of printed matter, which proved to be correct.

The contract was to print, and bind with leather, 5,000 copies for $3,000. Mr. Grandin got a new font of small pica, on which the body of the work was printed.

When the printer was ready to commence work, [Martin] Harris was notified, and Hyrum Smith brought the first installment of manuscript, of 24 pages, closely written on common foolscap paper—he had it under his vest, and vest and coat closely buttoned over it. At night [Hyrum] Smith came and got the manuscript, and with the same precaution carried it away. The next morning with the same watchfulness, he brought it again, and at night took it away. This was kept up for several days. The title page was first set up, and after proof was read and corrected, several copies were printed for Harris and his friends. On the second day—

[Martin] Harris and [Hyrum] Smith being in the office—I called their attention to a grammatical error, and asked whether I should correct it? [Martin] Harris consulted with [Hyrum] Smith a short time, and turned to me and said, "The Old Testament is ungrammatical, set it as it is written."

After working a few days, I said to [Hyrum] Smith on his handing me the manuscript in the morning, "Mr. [Hyrum] Smith, if you would leave this manuscript with me, I would take it home with me at night and read and punctuate it, and I could get along faster in the daytime, for now I have frequently to stop and read half a page to find how to punctuate it." His reply was, "We are commanded not to leave it." A few mornings after this, when [Hyrum] Smith handed me the manuscript, he said to me, "If you will give your word that this manuscript shall be returned to us when you get through with it, I will leave it with you." I assured Smith that it should be returned all right when I got through with it. For two or three nights I took it home with me and read it, and punctuated it with a lead pencil. This will account for the punctuation marks in pencil, which is referred to in the Mormon Report, an extract from which will be found below.

Martin Harris, Hyrum Smith, and Oliver Cowdery were very frequent visitors to the office during the printing of the Mormon Bible [Book of Mormon]. The manuscript was supposed to be in the handwriting of [Oliver] Cowdery. Every chapter, if I remember correctly, was one solid paragraph, without a punctuation mark, from beginning to end.

Names of persons and places were generally capitalized, but sentences had no end. The character or short "&" was used almost invariably where the word "and" occurred, except at the end of a chapter. I punctuated it to make it read as I supposed the author intended, and but very little punctuation was altered in proofreading. The Bible [Book of Mormon] was printed sixteen pages at a time, so that one sheet of paper made two copies of sixteen pages each, requiring 2,000 sheets of paper for each form of sixteen pages. There were thirty-seven forms of sixteen pages each—570 pages in all.

The work was commenced in August 1829, and finished in March 1830—seven months. Mr. J. H. Bortles and myself did the presswork until December, taking nearly three days to each form.

In December Mr. Grandin hired a journeyman pressman, Thomas McAuley, or "Whistling Tom," as he was called in the office, and he and

Bortles did the balance of the presswork. The Bible [Book of Mormon] was printed on a "Smith" Press, single pull, and old-fashioned "Balls" . . . were used—composition rollers not having come into use in small printing offices.

The printing was done in the third story of the west end of "Exchange Row," and the binding by Mr. Howard, in the second story; the lower story being used as a bookstore by Mr. Grandin, and now—1892—by Mr. M. Story as a dry goods store.

[Oliver] Cowdery held and looked over the manuscript when most of the proofs were read. Martin Harris once or twice, and Hyrum Smith once, Grandin supposing these men could read their own writing as well, if not better, than anyone else; and if there are any discrepancies between the Palmyra edition and the manuscript these men should be held responsible.

Joseph Smith, Jr., had nothing to do whatever with the printing or furnishing copy for the printers, being but once in the office during the printing of the Bible [Book of Mormon], and then not over fifteen or twenty minutes.

Hyrum Smith was a common laborer, and worked for anyone as he was called on.

[Oliver] Cowdery taught school winters—so it was said—but what he did summers, I do not know.

Martin Harris was a farmer, owning a good farm, of about 150 acres, about a mile north of Palmyra village, and had money at interest. Martin—as everybody called him—was considered by his neighbors a very honest man; but on the subject of Mormonism, he was said to be crazy. Martin was the main spoke in the wheel of Mormonism in its start in Palmyra, and I may say, the only spoke. In the fall of 1827, he told us what wonderful discoveries Jo [Joseph] Smith had made, and of his finding plates in a hill in the town of Manchester (three miles south of Palmyra), also found with the plates a large pair of "spectacles," by putting which on his nose and looking at the plates, the spectacles turned the hieroglyphics into good English. The question might be asked here whether Jo [Joseph] or the spectacles was the translator?

Sometime in 1828, Martin Harris, who had been furnished by someone with what he said was a facsimile of the hieroglyphics of one of the plates, started for New York. On his way he stopped at Albany and called on Lieutenant Governor Bradish—with what success I do not know. He proceeded to New York, and called on Professor C. Anthon, made known his business, and presented his hieroglyphics.

This is what the professor said in regard to them.

"The paper in question was, in fact, a singular scroll.

"It consisted of all kinds of singular characters, disposed in columns, and had evidently been prepared by some person who had before him, at the time, a book containing various alphabets; Greek and Hebrew letters, crosses and flourishes, Roman letters inverted or placed sidewise, arranged and placed in perpendicular columns, and the whole ended in a rude delineation of a circle, divided into various compartments, arched with various strange marks, and evidently copied after the Mexican Calendar, given by Humboldt, but copied in such a way as not to betray the source whence it was derived. I am thus particular as to the contents of the paper, inasmuch as I have frequently conversed with my friends on the subject since the Mormon excitement began, and well remember that the paper contained anything else but 'Egyptian Hieroglyphics.'"

Martin [Harris] returned from this trip east satisfied that "Joseph" was a "little smarter than Professor Anthon."

Martin was something of a prophet—he frequently said that "Jackson would be the last president that we would have; and that all persons who did not embrace Mormonism in two years' time would be stricken off the face of the earth." He said that Palmyra was to be the New Jerusalem, and that her streets were to be paved with gold.

Martin was in the office when I finished setting up the testimony of the Three Witnesses—([Martin] Harris, [Oliver] Cowdery, and [David] Whitmer). I said to him, "Martin, did you see those plates with your naked eyes?" Martin looked down for an instant, raised his eyes up, and said, "No, I saw them with a spiritual eye" (1893).

Joseph Knight Jr.

My father bought three farms on the Susquehanna River, in Broome County, New York. In 1827, he hired Joseph Smith, Jr. Joseph and I worked and slept together. My father said that Joseph was the best hand he ever hired. We found him a boy of truth. He was about twenty-one years of age.

I think it was in November, 1827, he made known to my father and me that he had seen a vision, that a personage had appeared to him and told him where there was a gold book of ancient date buried, and if he would follow the directions of the angel he could get it. We were told it in secret. My father and I believed what he told us. I think we were the first after his father's family.

At last he got the plates, and rode in my father's wagon and carried them home.

Joseph then commenced to translate the plates. Father and I often went to see him, to carry him some things to live upon. After many trials and troubles, he got the plates translated. By this time, my mother and many of my relations believed.

Joseph and Oliver came to Colesville, in May, 1830, where we lived, and Oliver baptized my father's family, and a few of my relatives. When we were going from the water, we were met by many of our neighbors, who pointed at us and asked if we had been washing our sheep. Before Joseph could confirm us, he was taken by the officers to Chenango County for trial, for saying that the Book of Mormon was a revelation from God.

My father employed two lawyers to plead for him, and they cleared him. That night our wagons were turned over and wood piled on them, and some sunk in the water. Rails were piled against our doors, and chains sunk in the stream, and a great deal of mischief done. Before Joseph got to my father's house, he was taken again to be tried in Broome County. Father employed the same lawyers, who cleared him there.

Four weeks passed before Joseph could get a chance to confirm us. Then we had the greatest time I ever saw. The house was filled with the Holy Ghost, which rested upon us (1974, pp. 5–6).

Sally Parker

I lived by his [Joseph Smith's] mother, and [she] was one of the finest women—always helping them that stood in need. She told me the whole story. The plates was in the house and sometimes in the woods for eight months on account of people trying to get them. Once they hid them under the hearth. They took up the brick and put them in and put the bricks back. The old lady told me this herself with tears in her eyes, and they ran down her cheeks too. She put her hand upon her stomach and said she has the peace of God that rested upon us, all that time. She said it was a heaven below. I asked her if she saw the plates. She said no, it was not for her to see them, but she hefted and handled them, and I believed all she said, for I lived by her eight months, and she was one of the best of women (1996, pp. 218–19).

Catherine Smith Salisbury

Catherine Smith Salisbury told me she was present at home when her brother, Joseph Smith, came in nearly exhausted, carrying the package of gold plates from which the Book of Mormon was translated. He was carrying the package clasped to his side with his left hand and arm, and his right hand was badly bruised from knocking down at least three men who had leaped at him from behind bushes or fences as he ran until out of breath. She said he entered the house running and threw himself on a couch panting from his extraordinary exertion.

She told me Joseph allowed her to "heft" the package but not to see the gold plates, as the angel had forbidden him to show them at that period. She said they were very heavy.

She told me that she was one of the first eight members baptized into the Church. She said the first six members were Joseph Smith, Jr., Oliver Cowdery, Samuel H. Smith, Hyrum Smith, David Whitmer, and Peter Whitmer, Jr. (1945).

Lucy Mack Smith

The next day [following Moroni's visit], my husband, Alvin, and Joseph, were reaping together in the field, and as they were reaping, Joseph stopped quite suddenly, and seemed to be in a very deep study. Alvin, observing it, hurried him, saying, "We must not slacken our hands or we will not be able to complete our task." Upon this Joseph went to work again, and after laboring a short time, he stopped just as he had done before. This being quite unusual and strange, it attracted the attention of his father, upon which he discovered that Joseph was very pale. My husband, supposing that he was sick, told him to go to the house, and have his mother doctor him. He accordingly ceased his work, and started, but on coming to a beautiful green, under an apple tree, he stopped and lay down, for he was so weak he could proceed no further. He was here but a short time, when the messenger whom he saw the previous night visited him again, and the first thing he said was, "Why did you not tell your father that which I commanded you to tell him?" Joseph replied, "I was afraid my father would not believe me." The angel rejoined, "He will believe every word you say to him."

Joseph then promised the angel that he would do as he had been commanded. Upon this, the messenger departed, and Joseph returned to the field, where he had left my husband and Alvin; but when he got there, his father had just gone to the house, as he was somewhat unwell. Joseph then desired Alvin to go straightway and see his father, and inform him that he had something of great importance to communicate to him, and that he wanted him to come out into the field where they were at work. Alvin did as he was requested, and when my husband got there Joseph related to him all that had passed between him and the angel the previous night and that morning. Having heard this account, his father charged him not to fail in attending strictly to the instruction which he had received from this heavenly messenger.

[Joseph later visited the Hill Cumorah.] While Joseph remained here, the angel showed him, by contrast, the difference between good and evil, and likewise the consequences of both obedience and disobedience to the commandments of God, in such a striking manner that the impression was always vivid in his memory until the very end of his days; and in giving a relation of this circumstance, not long prior to his death, he remarked that ever afterwards he was willing to keep the commandments of God.

Furthermore, the angel told him at the interview mentioned last, that the time had not yet come for the plates to be brought forth to the world; that he could not take them from the place wherein they were deposited until he had learned to keep the commandments of God—not only till he was willing but able to do it. The angel bade Joseph come to this place every year, at the same time of the year, and he would meet him there and give him further instructions.

The ensuing evening, when the family were altogether, Joseph made known to them all what he had communicated to his father in the field, and also of his finding the record, as well as what passed between him and the angel while he was at the place where the plates were deposited.

Sitting up late that evening in order to converse upon these things, together with over-exertion of mind, had much fatigued Joseph; and when Alvin observed it, he said, "Now, brother, let us go to bed, and rise early in the morning, in order to finish our day's work at an hour before sunset, then, if mother will get our suppers early, we will have a fine long evening, and we will all sit down for the purpose of listening to you while you tell us the great things which God has revealed to you."

Accordingly, by sunset the next day, we were all seated, and Joseph commenced telling us the great and glorious things which God had manifested to him; but, before proceeding, he charged us not to mention out of the family that which he was about to say to us, as the world was so wicked that when they came to a knowledge of these things they would try to take our lives; and that when we should obtain the plates, our names would be cast out as evil by all people. Hence the necessity of suppressing these things as much as possible, until the time should come for them to go forth to the world.

After giving us this charge, he proceeded to relate further particulars concerning the work which he was appointed to do, and we received them joyfully, never mentioning them except among ourselves, agreeable to the instructions which we had received from him.

From this time forth, Joseph continued to receive instructions from the Lord, and we continued to get the children together every evening for the purpose of listening while he gave us a relation of the same. I presume our family presented an aspect as singular as any that ever lived upon the face of the earth—all seated in a circle, father, mother, sons, and daughters, and giving the most profound attention to a boy, eighteen years of age, who had never read the Bible through in his life; he seemed much less inclined to the perusal of books than any of the rest of our children, but far more given to meditation and deep study.

We were now confirmed in the opinion that God was about to bring to light something upon which we could stay our minds, or that would give us a more perfect knowledge of the plan of salvation and the redemption of the human family. This caused us greatly to rejoice, the sweetest union and happiness pervaded our house, and tranquility reigned in our midst.

During our evening conversations, Joseph would occasionally give us some of the most amusing recitals that could be imagined. He would describe the ancient inhabitants of this continent, their dress, mode of traveling, and the animals upon which they rode; their cities, their buildings, with every particular; their mode of warfare; and also their religious worship. This he would do with as much ease, seemingly, as if he had spent his whole life among them.

On the twenty-second of September, 1824, Joseph again visited the place where he found the plates the year previous; and supposing at this time that the only thing required, in order to possess them until the time for their translation, was to be able to keep the commandments of God—and he firmly believed he could keep every commandment which had been given him—he fully expected to carry them home with him. Therefore, having arrived at the place, and uncovering the plates, he put forth his hand and took them up, but, as he was taking them hence, the unhappy thought darted through his mind that probably there was something else in the box besides the plates, which would be of some pecuniary advantage to him. So, in the moment of excitement, he laid them down very carefully, for the purpose of covering the box, lest some one might happen to pass that way and get whatever there might be remaining in it. After covering it, he turned round to take the record again, but behold it was gone, and where, he knew not, neither did he know the means by which it had been taken from him.

At this, as a natural consequence, he was much alarmed. He kneeled down and asked the Lord why the record had been taken from him; upon which the angel of the Lord appeared to him, and told him that he had not done as he had been commanded, for in a former revelation he had been commanded not to lay the plates down, or put them for a moment out of his hands, until he got into the house and deposited them in a chest or trunk, having a good lock and key, and, contrary to this, he had laid them down with the view of securing some fancied or imaginary treasure that remained.

In the moment of excitement, Joseph was overcome by the powers of darkness, and forgot the injunction that was laid upon him.

Having some further conversation with the angel on this occasion, Joseph was permitted to raise the stone again, when he beheld the plates as he had done before. He immediately reached forth his hand to take them, but instead of getting them, as he anticipated, he was hurled back upon the ground with great violence. When he recovered, the angel was gone, and he arose and returned to the house, weeping for grief and disappointment.

As he was aware that we would expect him to bring the plates home with him, he was greatly troubled, fearing that we might doubt his having seen them. As soon as he entered the house, my husband asked if he had obtained the plates. The answer was, "No, Father, I could not get them."

His father then said, "Did you see them?"

"Yes," replied Joseph, "I saw them, but could not take them."

"I would have taken them," rejoined his father, with much earnestness, "if I had been in your place."

"Why," returned Joseph, in quite a subdued tone, "you do not know what you say. I could not get them, for the angel of the Lord would not let me."

Joseph then related the circumstances in full, which gave us much uneasiness, as we were afraid that he might utterly fail of obtaining the record through some neglect on his part. We, therefore, doubled our diligence in prayer and supplication to God, in order that he might be more fully instructed in his duty, and be preserved from all the wiles and machinations of him "who lieth in wait to deceive" (1958, pp. 79–85).

Lucy Mack Smith

Not long subsequent to his [Joseph's] return [from Pennsylvania], my husband had occasion to send him to Manchester on business. As he set off early in the day, we expected him home at most by six o'clock in the evening, but when six o'clock came he did not arrive. We always had a peculiar anxiety about him whenever he was absent, for it seemed as though something was always taking place to jeopardize his life. But to return. He did not get home till the night was far spent. On coming in he threw himself into a chair, apparently much exhausted. My husband did not observe his appearance and immediately exclaimed, "Joseph, why are you so late? has anything happened to you? we have been much distressed about you these three hours." As Joseph made no answer he continued his interrogations, until, finally, I said, "Now, Father, let him rest a moment—don't trouble him now—you see he is home safe and he is very tired, so pray wait a little."

The fact was I had learned to be a little cautious about matters with regard to Joseph, for I was accustomed to see him look as he did on that occasion, and I could not easily mistake the cause thereof.

Presently he smiled and said in a calm tone, "I have taken the severest chastisement that I have ever had in my life."

My husband, supposing that it was from some of the neighbors, was quite angry and observed, "I would like to know what business anybody has to find fault with you!"

"Stop, Father, stop," said Joseph, "it was the angel of the Lord. As I passed by the hill of Cumorah, where the plates are, the angel met me and said that I had not been engaged enough in the work of the Lord; that the time had come for the record to be brought forth; and that I must be up and doing and set myself about the things which God had commanded me to do. But, Father, give yourself no uneasiness concerning the reprimand which I have received, for I now know the course that I am to pursue, so all will be well" (1958, pp. 99–100).

Lucy Mack Smith

The following day one Mr. Warner came to him and told him that a widow by the name of Wells, who was living in Macedon, wanted some labor done in a well, for which she would pay the money, and that she was anxious to have him (Joseph) do this labor for her. As this afforded us an opportunity to pay the cabinet-maker for the chest, Joseph went immediately to the house of Mrs. Wells and commenced work.

The next day after he left home, one of the neighbors asked Mr. Smith many questions concerning the plates. I will here observe that no one ever heard anything from us respecting them, except a confidential friend whom my husband had spoken to about them some two or three years previous. It appeared that Satan had now stirred up the hearts of those who had gotten a hint of the matter from our friend to search into it and make every possible move towards thwarting the purposes of the Almighty.

My husband soon learned that ten or twelve men were clubbed together, with one Willard Chase, a Methodist class leader, at their head, and what was still more ridiculous, they had sent sixty or seventy miles for a certain conjurer to come and divine the place where the plates were secreted.

We supposed that Joseph had taken the plates and hid them somewhere, and we were apprehensive that our enemies might discover their place of deposit. Accordingly, the next morning after hearing of their plans, my husband concluded to go among the neighbors to see what he could learn with regard to the plans of the adverse party. The first house he came to he found the conjuror and Willard Chase, together with the rest of the clan. Making an errand, he went in and sat down near the door, leaving it a little ajar in order to overhear their conversation. They stood in the yard near the door and were devising plans to find "Joe Smith's gold Bible," as they expressed themselves. The conjuror seemed much animated although he had traveled sixty miles the day and night previous.

Presently the woman of the house, becoming uneasy at the exposures they were making, stepped through a back door into the yard and called to her husband, in a suppressed tone, but loud enough to be heard distinctly by Mr. Smith, "Sam, Sam, you are cutting your own throat." At this the conjuror bawled out at the top of his voice, "I am not afraid of anybody—we will have them plates in spite of Joe Smith or all the devils in hell."

When the woman came in again, Mr. Smith laid aside the newspaper he had been holding in his hand and remarked, "I believe I have not time to finish reading the paper now." He then left the house and returned home.

Mr. Smith, on returning home, asked Emma if she knew whether Joseph had taken the plates from their place of deposit, or if she was able to tell where they were. She said she could not tell where they were, or whether they were removed from their place. My husband then related what he had both seen and heard.

Upon this, Emma said that she did not know what to do, but she supposed if Joseph was to get the record, he *would* get it and that they would not be able to prevent him.

"Yes," replied Mr. Smith, "he will, if he is watchful and obedient; but remember that for a small thing, Esau lost his birthright and his blessing. It may be so with Joseph."

"Well," said Emma, "if I had a horse I would go and see him."

Mr. Smith then said, "You shall have one in fifteen minutes, for although my team is gone, there is a stray on the place and I will send William to bring him immediately."

In a few minutes William brought up the horse with a large hickory withe around his neck (for it was according to law to put a withe around the neck of a stray before turning it into an enclosure), and Emma was soon underway for Macedon.

Joseph kept the Urim and Thummim constantly about his person, by the use of which he could in a moment tell whether the plates were in any danger. Just before Emma rode up to Mr. Wells', Joseph, from an impression that he had had, came up out of the well in which he was laboring and met her not far from the house. Emma immediately informed him of what had transpired, whereupon he looked in the Urim and Thummim and saw that the record was as yet safe; nevertheless, he concluded to return with his wife as something might take place that would render it necessary for him to be at home where he could take care of it.

He then told Mrs. Wells that business at home rendered it necessary for him to return. To this she did not agree at first, but finally consented. She then sent a boy for a horse, which Joseph mounted in his linen frock, and with his wife by his side on her horse decorated as before with a hickory withe around his neck, he rode through the village of Palmyra, which was on the way home.

On arriving at home he found his father pacing the ground near his door in great anxiety of mind. Joseph spoke to him, saying, "Father, there is no danger—all is perfectly safe—there is no cause of alarm."

When he had taken a little refreshment, he sent Carlos, my youngest son, to his brother Hyrum's, to have him come up immediately as he desired to see him. When he came, Joseph requested him to get a chest, having a good lock and key, and to have it there by the time he (Joseph) should return. And after giving these instructions, Joseph started for the plates.

The plates were secreted about three miles from home, in the following manner: Finding an old birch log much decayed, excepting the bark, which was in a measure sound, he took his pocket knife and cut the bark with some care, then turned it back and made a hole of sufficient size to receive the plates, and, laying them in the cavity thus formed, he replaced the bark; after which he laid across the log, in several places, some old stuff that happened to lay near, in order to conceal as much as possible the place in which they were deposited.

Joseph, on coming to them, took them from their secret place, and, wrapping them in his linen frock, placed them under his arm and started for home.

After proceeding a short distance, he thought it would be more safe to leave the road and go through the woods. Traveling some distance after he left the road, he came to a large windfall, and as he was jumping over a log, a man sprang up from behind it and gave him a heavy blow with a gun. Joseph turned around and knocked him down, then ran at the top of his speed. About half a mile farther he was attacked again in the same manner as before; he knocked this man down in like manner as the former and ran on again; and before he reached home he was assaulted the third time. In striking the last one, he dislocated his thumb, which, however, he did not notice until he came within sight of the house, when he threw himself down in the corner of the fence in order to recover his breath. As soon as he was able, he arose and came to the house. He was still altogether speechless from fright and the fatigue of running.

After resting a few moments, he desired me to send Carlos for my husband, Mr. Knight, and his friend Stoal, and have them go immediately and see if they could find the men who had been pursuing him. And after Carlos had done this, he wished to have him sent to Hyrum's, to tell him to bring the chest.

I did as I was requested, and when Carlos arrived at Hyrum's, he found him at tea with two of his wife's sisters. Just as Hyrum was raising a cup to his mouth, Carlos touched his shoulder. Without waiting to hear one word from the child, he dropped the cup, sprang from the table, caught the chest, turned it upside down, and emptying its contents on the floor, left the house instantly with the chest on his shoulder.

The young ladies were greatly astonished at his singular behavior and declared to his wife—who was then confined to her bed, her eldest daughter, Lovina, being but four days old—that he was certainly crazy.

His wife laughed heartily and replied, "Oh, not in the least; he has just thought of something which he has neglected; and it is just like him to fly off on a tangent when he thinks of anything in that way."

When the chest came, Joseph locked up the record, then threw himself upon the bed and, after resting a little so that he could converse freely, he arose and went into the kitchen, where he related his recent adventure to his father, Mr. Knight, and Mr. Stoal, besides many others who had by this time collected, with the view of hearing something in regard to the strange circumstance which had taken place. He showed them his thumb, saying, "I must stop talking, Father, and get you to put my thumb in place, for it is very painful."

I will here mention that my husband, Mr. Knight, and Mr. Stoal went in pursuit of those villains who had attempted Joseph's life, but were not able to find them.

When Joseph first got the plates, the angel of the Lord stood by and said:

"Now you have got the record into your own hands, and you are but a man, therefore you will have to be watchful and faithful to your trust, or you will be overpowered by wicked men; for they will lay every plan and scheme that is possible to get it away from you, and if you do not take heed continually, they will succeed. While it was in my hands, I could keep it, and no man had power to take it away! But now I give it up to you. Beware, and look well to your ways, and you shall have power to retain it, until the time for it to be translated."

That of which I spoke, which Joseph termed a key, was indeed nothing more nor less than the Urim and Thummim, and it was by this that the angel showed him many things which he saw in vision; by which also he could ascertain, at any time, the approach of danger, either to himself or the record, and on account of which he always kept the Urim and Thummim about his person (1958, pp. 104–10).

William Smith

I well remember the effect produced upon my father's family when he [Joseph] told them he was to receive the plates; how they looked forward with joy, and waited until the time should come. The circumstances that occurred, and the impressions made on my mind at that time, I can remember better than those which occurred two years ago. We were all looking forward for the time to come, father, mother, brothers, and sisters. He did not receive the plates at the time he expected, but some four years afterward. He had not lived as directed. When he went to get the plates he found them as he was told he should. He took them from the stone box in which they were found, and placed them on the ground behind him, when the thought came into his mind that there might be a treasure hidden with them. While stooping forward to see, he was overpowered, so that he could not look farther. Turning to get the plates, he found they had gone; and on looking around found that they were in the box again; but he could not get them, and cried out, "Why can't I get the plates as Moroni told me I could?" The angel then appeared to him, and told him it was because he had not done as directed. That the plates could not be had for the purpose of making money. That he could not have them for four years (1884, pp. 643–44; see also 1883, pp. 9–11).

The Book of Mormon

Martin Harris

This calls to my mind a little incident or two that he [Martin Harris] related to me [Edward Stevenson] while we were on our journey from Ohio to Utah. He said that Joseph Smith, the Prophet, was very poor, and had to work by the day for his support, and that he [Harris] often gave him work on his farm, and they had hoed corn together many a day, Brother Harris paying him fifty cents per day. Joseph, he said, was good to work and jovial and they often wrestled together in sport, but the Prophet was devoted and attentive to his prayers. Brother Harris gave Joseph $50.00 on one occasion to help translate the Book of Mormon. This action on the part of Martin Harris so displeased his wife that she threatened to leave him. Martin said that he knew this to be the work of God, and that he should keep the commandments of the Lord, whatever the results might be. His wife, subsequently, partially separated from him, which he patiently endured for the gospel's sake (1886, p. 389).

Abram Hatch

[In 1867 Hatch] visited Sidney Rigdon and family at Friendship, western New York. During his interview with the once-famous leader, whom he describes as a "grand looking old man, large and portly," who impressed him with his "intellectual importance," Mr. Hatch said, "Elder Rigdon, it is reputed that you wrote the Book of Mormon; did you or did you not? What is your testimony—your dying testimony?" The answer came without hesitation, "I did *not* write the Book of Mormon. It is the revelations of Jesus Christ." Mr. Rigdon still felt bad towards President Young, whom he accused of supplanting him and by his shrewdness depriving him of his rights as the lawful successor to Joseph Smith. Mr. Hatch regarded Rigdon as "an intellectual giant of a certain type," as "a man of extraordinary spiritual aspirations," yet "lacking in the elements of a great leader" (1904, 4:167).

Oliver B. Huntington

Sunday, June 13, 1897—I conversed with one old lady eighty-eight years old who lived with David Whitmer when Joseph Smith and Oliver Cowdery were translating the Book of Mormon in the upper room of the house, and she, only a girl, saw them come down from [the] translating room several times when they looked so exceedingly white and strange that she inquired of Mrs. Whitmer the cause of their unusual appearance, but Mr. Whitmer was unwilling to tell the hired girl the true cause, as it was a sacred, holy event connected with a holy, sacred work which was opposed and persecuted by nearly everyone who heard of it.

The girl felt so strangely at seeing so strange and unusual appearance, she finally told Mrs. Whitmer that she would not stay with her until she knew the cause of the strange looks of these men.

Sister Whitmer then told her what the men were doing in the room above and that the power of God was so great in the room that they could hardly endure it; at times angels were in the room in their glory, which nearly consumed them.

This satisfied the girl and opened the way to embracing the gospel (n.d. [b], pp. 49–50).

Note: The "hired girl" here referred to was Sally Heller Conrad, who later became the wife of David Edwin Bunnell, and the mother of Stephen Ithamar Bunnell, "an active elder of the Lake View Ward, Utah County, [who] was born Feb. 1, 1834, in Detroit, Michigan" (Andrew Jenson, 1971, 2:600). Stephen Bunnell died in Provo, Utah, on 23 July 1925 (Susan Easton Black, Membership of the Church of Jesus Christ of Latter Day Saints, 1830–1848, *BYU Religious Studies Center). Sally was born 19 September 1810 in Elmira, Tioga County, New York (LDS Family Search: Ancestral File), and thus would have been about 18½ years of age when working in the Whitmer home, for Joseph and Oliver arrived there about 1 June 1829 and stayed until the translation was completed 1 July 1829 (Conkling, 1979, p. 12); she would have been almost eighty-seven in June 1897, when Huntington recorded this memory. She died 23 July 1903 in Provo, Utah.*

Vilate M. Kimball

On the night of the 22nd of September, 1827, while living in the town of Mendon, after we retired to bed, John P. Green, who was then a traveling Reformed Methodist preacher, living within one hundred steps of our house, came and called my husband to come out and see the sight in the heavens. Heber awoke me, and Sister Fanny Young (sister of Brigham), who was living with us, and we all went out-of-doors.

It was one of the most beautiful starlit nights so clear we could see to pick up a pin. We looked to the eastern horizon, and beheld a white smoke arise towards the heavens. As it ascended, it formed into a belt, and made a noise like the rushing wind, and continued southwest, forming a regular bow, dipping in the western horizon.

After the bow had formed, it began to widen out, growing transparent, of a bluish cast. It grew wide enough to contain twelve men abreast. In this bow an army moved, commencing from the east and marching to the west. They continued moving until they reached the western horizon. They moved in platoons, and walked so close the rear ranks trod in the steps of their file leaders, until the whole bow was literally crowded with soldiers.

We could distinctly see the muskets, bayonets, and knapsacks of the men, who wore caps and feathers like those used by the American soldiers in the last war with Great Britain. We also saw their officers with their swords and equipage, and heard the clashing and jingling of their instruments of war, and could discern the form and features of the men. The most profound order existed throughout the entire army. When the foremost man stepped, every man stepped at the same time. We could hear their steps.

When the front rank reached the western horizon, a battle ensued, as we could hear the report of the arms, and the rush.

None can judge of our feelings as we beheld this army of spirits as plainly as ever armies of men were seen in the flesh. Every hair of our heads seemed alive.

We gazed upon this scenery for hours, until it began to disappear.

After we became acquainted with Mormonism, we learned that this took place the same evening that Joseph Smith received the records of the Book of Mormon from the angel Moroni, who had held those records in his possession.

Father Young, and John P. Green's wife (Brigham's sister Rhoda), were also witnesses of this marvelous scene. Frightened at what we saw, I said, "Father Young, what does all this mean?" He answered, "Why it is one of the signs of the coming of the Son of Man."

The next night a similar scene was beheld in the west, by the neighbors, representing armies of men engaged in battle (1877, pp. 107–9).

Emma Hale Smith

[In the winter of 1856 Emma] remarked of her husband Joseph's limited education while he was translating the Book of Mormon, and she was scribe at the time, "He could not pronounce the word Sariah." And one time while translating, where it speaks of the walls of Jerusalem, he stopped and said, "Emma, did Jerusalem have walls surrounding it?" When I informed him that it had, he replied, "O, I thought I was deceived" (1884, p. 397).

Brigham Young

I lived right in the country where the plates were found from which the Book of Mormon was translated, and I know a great many things pertaining to that country. I believe I will take the liberty to tell you of another circumstance that will be as marvelous as anything can be. This is an incident in the life of Oliver Cowdery, but he did not take the liberty of telling such things in meeting as I take. I tell these things to you, and I have a motive for doing so. I want to carry them to the ears of my brethren and sisters, and to the children also, that they may grow to an understanding of some things that seem to be entirely hidden from the human family.

Oliver Cowdery went with the Prophet Joseph when he deposited these plates. Joseph did not translate all of the plates; there was a portion of them sealed, which you can learn from the book of Doctrine and Covenants. When Joseph got the plates, the angel instructed him to carry them back to the Hill Cumorah, which he did.

Oliver says that when Joseph and Oliver went there, the hill opened, and they walked into a cave, in which there was a large and spacious room. He says he did not think, at the time, whether they had the light of the sun or artificial light; but that it was just as light as day. They laid the plates on a table; it was a large table that stood in the room. Under this table there was a pile of plates as much as two feet high, and there were altogether in this room more plates than probably many wagon loads; they were piled up in the corners and along the walls. The first time they went there the sword of Laban hung upon the wall; but when they went again it had been taken down and laid upon the table across the gold plates; it was unsheathed, and on it was written these words: "This sword will never be sheathed again until the kingdoms of this world become the kingdom of our God and his Christ."

I tell you this as coming not only from Oliver Cowdery, but others who were familiar with it, and who understood it just as well as we understand coming to this meeting, enjoying the day, and by and by we separate and go away, forgetting most of what is said, but remembering some things. So is it with other circumstances in life. I relate this to you, and I want you to understand it. I take this liberty of referring to those things so that they will not be forgotten and lost. Carlos Smith was a young man of as much veracity as any young man we had, and he was a witness to these things. Samuel Smith saw some things, Hyrum saw a good many things, but Joseph was the leader (JD, 19:38).

The Doctrine and Covenants

Adeline K. Belnap

How well [Adeline] remembers one day before her father [Vinson Knight] died, of a little excitement in school. The children were busy when the school room door was carefully opened and two gentlemen entered, carrying the limp form of Joseph Smith. The children all sprang to their feet, for Brother Joseph lay helpless in their arms, his head resting on his brother's shoulder, his face pale as death, but his eyes were open, though he seemed not to see things earthly. The teacher quieted them by telling them that Brother Joseph was in a revelation, and they were carrying him to his office above the schoolroom. That same revelation is recorded in section 124 of the Doctrine and Covenants and was a comfort to Adeline all during her [subsequent] life, as it speaks of her father and his family; tells his family to rejoice, for their father's sins are forgiven; he is chosen and anointed and shall be honored in the midst of his house (see D&C 124:74, 141).

Some of Adeline's fondest recollections all her life are of the Prophet Joseph Smith, for she saw him nearly every day in the early part of her life. She grew up under his teachings. She could always feel the influence of a Holy Spirit when near him, and realized that he was a man who was continually communing with heavenly beings (n.d., p. 2).

Zebedee Coltrin

[Zebedee] testified of seeing the Prophet come from the translating room after receiving the revelation known as the Word of Wisdom. "His face shone with brilliance," Zebedee later said (1878).

Philo Dibble

The vision which is recorded in the book of Doctrine and Covenants [D&C 76; Feb. 16, 1832] was given at the house of "Father Johnson," in Hiram, Ohio, and during the time that Joseph and Sidney were in the Spirit and saw the heavens open, there were other men in the room, perhaps twelve, among whom I was one during a part of the time—probably two-thirds of the time. I saw the glory and felt the power, but did not see the vision.

The events and conversation, while they were seeing what is written (and many things were seen and related that are not written,) I will relate as minutely as is necessary.

Joseph would, at intervals, say: "What do I see?" as one might say while looking out the window and beholding what all in the room could not see. Then he would relate what he had seen or what he was looking at. Then Sidney replied, "I see the same." Presently Sidney would say,

"What do I see?" and would repeat what he had seen or was seeing, and Joseph would reply, "I see the same."

This manner of conversation was repeated at short intervals to the end of the vision, and during the whole time not a word was spoken by any other person. Not a sound nor motion [was] made by anyone but Joseph and Sidney, and it seemed to me that they never moved a joint or limb during the time I was there, which I think was over an hour, and to the end of the vision.

Joseph sat firmly and calmly all the time in the midst of a magnificent glory, but Sidney sat limp and pale, apparently as limber as a rag, observing which, Joseph remarked, smilingly, "Sidney is not used to it as I am" (1892b, pp. 303–4).

Benjamin F. Johnson

I can now see, as President George A. Smith afterwards said, that I was then really "the bosom friend and companion of the Prophet Joseph." I was as welcome at the Mansion as at my own house, and on one occasion when at a full table of his family and chosen friends, he placed me at his right hand and introduced me as his "friend, Brother B. F. Johnson, at whose house he sat at a better table than his own." Sometimes when at my house I asked him questions relating to past, present, and future; some of his answers were taken by Brother William Clayton, who was then present with him, and are now recorded in the Doctrine and Covenants; the one as to what the Lord told him in relation to seeing his face at eighty-five years of age; also the one as to the earth becoming as a sea of glass, molten with fire [D&C 130:9, 14–17]. Other questions were asked when Brother Clayton was not present (1947, pp. 92–93).

Joel H. Johnson

I was with Joseph Smith, the Prophet, when the Word of Wisdom [D&C 89] was given by revelation from the Lord, February 27, 1833, and, I think, I am the only man now living who was present.

I was then thirty-one years of age, and had used tobacco somewhat extravagantly for fifteen years. I always used some strong drink, and tea and coffee.

I knew that God had spoken and condemned the use of these things, and, being determined to live by every word that proceeded from His mouth, I laid them all aside, and have not used them since.

I well remember that, soon after the publication of the Word of Wisdom, the same excuse was made, by some of the people, for drinking tea and coffee that is now made—that hot drinks did not mean tea and coffee.

On a Sabbath day, in the July [1833] following the giving of the revelation, when both Joseph and Hyrum Smith were in the stand, the Prophet said to the Saints:

"I understand that some of the people are excusing themselves in using tea and coffee, because the Lord only said 'hot drinks' in the revelation of the Word of Wisdom.

"The Lord was showing us what was good for man to eat and drink. Now, what do we drink when we take our meals?

"Tea and coffee. Is it not?

"Yes; tea and coffee.

"Then, they are what the Lord meant when He said 'hot drinks.'"

Brother Hyrum Smith spoke to the same effect (1881, p. 12).

HEBER C. KIMBALL

Here [Jackson County, Missouri,] Brother Thayre was taken sick with the cholera, and also Brother Hayes. We left them there, and also Brother Hancock who had been taken with the cholera during the storm. Brother Joseph called the camp together, and told us that in consequence of the disobedience of some who had not been willing to listen to his words, but had been rebellious, God had decreed that sickness should come upon us, and we should die like sheep with the rot; and said he, "I am sorry, but I cannot help it." When he spoke these things it pierced me like a dart, having a testimony that so it would be. In the afternoon of this day, we began to receive the revelation known as the "Fishing River revelation" [D&C 105, given June 22, 1834; see HC, 2:108–11] (1845c, p. 804).

KIRTLAND COUNCIL MINUTE BOOK

[Kirtland, December 27, 1832] Brother Joseph arose and said to receive revelation and the blessing of heaven, it was necessary to have our minds on God and exercise faith and become of one heart and one mind. Therefore, he recommended all present to pray separately and vocally to the Lord for [him] to reveal his will unto us concerning the upbuilding of Zion and for the benefit of the saints and for the duty and employment of the elders. Accordingly, we all bowed down before the Lord, after which each one arose and spoke in his turn his feelings and determination to keep the commandments of God. And then [he] proceeded to receive a revelation [D&C 88] concerning the duty [not legible] of our above stated. [At] 9 o'clock P.M., the revelation not being finished, the conference adjourned and commenced by prayer [and] thus [Joseph] proceeded to receive the residue of the above revelation. And it being finished and there being no further business before [the council], the conference closed the meeting by prayer, in harmony with the brethren and gratitude to our Heavenly Father for the great manifestation of His Holy Spirit during the setting of the conference (n.d.).

Newel Knight

In the beginning of August 1830, I, in company with my wife, went to make a visit to Brother Joseph Smith, Jun., who then resided at Harmony, Pennsylvania. We found him and his wife well and in good spirits. We had a happy meeting. It truly gave me joy to again behold his face. As neither Emma, the wife of Joseph Smith, nor my wife had been confirmed, we concluded to attend to that holy ordinance at this time, and also to partake of the sacrament before we should leave for home. In order to prepare for this, Brother Joseph set out to procure some wine for the occasion. But he had gone only a short distance when he was met by a heavenly messenger who informed him that it did not matter what the Saints ate and drank when they partook of the sacrament, but that they should not purchase wine or strong drink from their enemies [see D&C 27; see also HC, 1:106–8].

In obedience to this revelation, we prepared some wine of our own make and held our meeting, consisting of only five persons namely, Joseph Smith and wife, John Whitmer, and myself and wife. We partook of the sacrament, after which we confirmed the two sisters into the Church, and spent the evening in a glorious manner. The Spirit of the Lord was poured out upon us. We praised the God of Israel and rejoiced exceedingly (1974, p. 13).

William E. McLellin

[From Kirtland] I went home with [Joseph] on Saturday 29th [October 1831]. Early in the morning we reached there having stayed Friday night in the Nelson church. This day the Lord condescended to hear my prayer and give me a revelation of his will, through his prophet or seer (Joseph). And these are the words which I wrote from his mouth, saying [then follows D&C 66] (1994, p. 45).

WILLIAM E. MCLELLIN

I [William McLellin], as scribe have written revelations from the mouth of both the revelators, Joseph Smith and David Whitmer. And I have been present many times when others wrote for Joseph; therefore, I speak as one having experience. The scribe seats himself at a desk or table, with pen, ink, and paper. The subject of inquiry being understood, the Prophet and revelator inquires of God. He spiritually sees, hears, and feels, and then speaks as he is moved upon by the Holy Ghost, the "thus saith the Lord," sentence after sentence, and waits for his amanuenses to write and then read aloud each sentence. Thus they proceed until the revelator says Amen at the close of what is then communicated. I have known both those men mentioned above to seat themselves, and without premeditation, to thus deliver in broken sentences some of the most sublime pieces of composition which I ever perused in any book (1848, 1:98–99).

WILLIAM E. MCLELLIN

I [William Kelley] gleaned from him [William E. McLellin] and the records in his possession, the following items: He was present when the preface to the Book of Commandments [D&C 1] was given, and says that Sidney Rigdon wrote it down as it was dictated by Joseph [Smith]. A committee had been appointed to draft a preface, consisting of himself, O. [Oliver] Cowdery and I think Sidney Rigdon, but when they made their report, the conference then requested Joseph to inquire of the Lord about it, and he said that he would if the people would bow in prayer with him. This they did, and Joseph [Smith] prayed.

When they arose, Joseph dictated by the Spirit the preface found in the book of Doctrine and Covenants while sitting by a window of the room in which the conference was sitting [in the John Johnson home in Hiram, Ohio]; and Sidney Rigdon wrote it down. Joseph would deliver a few sentences and Sidney [Rigdon] would write them down, then read them aloud, and if correct, then Joseph [Smith] would proceed and deliver more, and by this process the preface was given.

In reply to the question, "Did Joseph [Smith] seem to be inspired at the time? that is, did any thing of unusual character appear to be moving him?" He said, "There was something ahold of him" (1882, p. 67).

Orson Pratt

In October 1830, I traveled westward over two hundred miles to see Joseph Smith, the Prophet. I found him in Fayette, Seneca County, New York, residing at the house of Mr. Whitmer. I soon became intimately acquainted with this good man, and also with the witnesses of the Book of Mormon. By my request, on the 4th of November, the Prophet Joseph inquired of the Lord for me, and received the revelation published in the Doctrine and Covenants, section 56 [now section 34] (1975, p. 9).

Parley P. Pratt

Feeling our weakness and inexperience, and lest we should err in judgment concerning these spiritual phenomena, myself, John Murdock, and several other elders, went to Joseph Smith, and asked him to inquire of the Lord concerning these spirits or manifestations.

After we had joined in prayer in his translating room, he dictated in our presence the following revelation: [D&C 50]. Each sentence was uttered slowly and very distinctly, and with a pause between each, sufficiently long for it to be recorded, by an ordinary writer, in long hand.

This was the manner in which all his written revelations were dictated and written. There was never any hesitation, reviewing, or reading back, in order to keep the run of the subject; neither did any of these communications undergo revisions, interlinings, or corrections. As he dictated them so they stood, so far as I have witnessed; and I was present to witness the dictation of several communications of several pages each (1985, p. 48).

Joseph Smith

Shortly after we had received the above revelations [D&C 25 and 26], Oliver Cowdery returned to Mr. Peter Whitmer's, Sen., and I began to arrange and copy the revelations, which we had received from time to time; in which I was assisted by John Whitmer, who now resided with me.

Whilst thus employed in the work appointed me by my Heavenly Father, I received a letter from Oliver Cowdery, the contents of which gave me both sorrow and uneasiness. Not having that letter now in my possession, I cannot of course give it here in full, but merely an extract of the most prominent parts, which I can yet, and expect long to, remember.

He wrote to inform me that he had discovered an error in one of the commandments—book of Doctrine and Covenants: "And truly manifest by their works that they have received of the Spirit of Christ unto a remission of their sins" [D&C 20:37].

The above quotation, he said, was erroneous, and added: "I command you in the name of God to erase those words, that no priestcraft be amongst us!"

I immediately wrote to him in reply, in which I asked him by what authority he took upon him to command me to alter or erase, to add to or diminish from, a revelation or commandment from Almighty God.

A few days afterwards I visited him and Mr. Whitmer's family, when I found the family in general of his opinion concerning the words above quoted, and it was not without both labor and perseverance that I could prevail with any of them to reason calmly on the subject. However, Christian Whitmer at length became convinced that the sentence was reasonable, and according to scripture; and finally, with his assistance, I succeeded in bringing, not only the Whitmer family, but also Oliver Cowdery to acknowledge that they had been in error, and that the sentence in dispute was in accordance with the rest of the commandment. And thus was this error rooted out, which having its rise in presumption and rash judgment, was the more particularly calculated (when once fairly understood) to teach each and all of us the necessity of humility and meekness before the Lord, that He might teach us of His ways, that we might walk in His paths, and live by every word that proceedeth forth from His mouth (HC, 1:104–5).

Joseph Smith

After the foregoing [D&C 67] was received, William E. M'Lellin, as the wisest man, in his own estimation, having more learning than sense, endeavored to write a commandment like unto one of the least of the Lord's, but failed; it was an awful responsibility to write in the name of the Lord. The elders and all present that witnessed this vain attempt of a man to imitate the language of Jesus Christ, renewed their faith in the fullness of the gospel, and in the truth of the commandments and revelations which the Lord had given to the Church through my instrumentality; and the elders signified a willingness to bear testimony of their truth to all the world (HC, 1:226).

Joseph F. Smith

I want to tell you another little circumstance connected with Brother Joseph C. Kingsberry. He is the man that made the first copy of the revelation on celestial marriage, and is a man in whom the Prophet Joseph had absolute confidence as an honorable, honest man, and entrusted to him the personal care of a branch of his family. He is a man who never betrayed a trust that was ever imposed in him by the Prophet Joseph Smith, and I do not believe he ever betrayed a trust that any man ever imposed in him; and that is the kind of a man that will stand the test, and will obtain eternal life. Such as he are the type of men that will endure in the faith to the end, because they have integrity, and because when they know the truth they will do it, and they will not waver to the right or the left, if it should take their lives to keep in the straight path.

Lest there should be a misunderstanding, I will say it was William Clayton who wrote the revelation on celestial marriage, as the Prophet's scribe, as it flowed from the mouth of the Prophet Joseph. A copy of that document was placed in the hands of Bishop N. K. Whitney, and Brother Joseph C. Kingsberry made a copy of it (CD, 5:30).

The Pearl of Great Price

Jerusha W. Blanchard

What fun we had with Aunt Emma's [i.e., Emma Smith] boys, Joseph, Frederick, Alexander, and David. How we raced through the house playing hide and seek. My favorite hiding place was in an old wardrobe which contained the mummies, and it was in here that I would creep while the others searched the house. There were three mummies: The old Egyptian king, the queen, and their daughter. The bodies were wrapped in seven layers of linen cut in thin strips. In the arms of the Old King lay the roll of papyrus from which our prophet translated the Book of Abraham (1922, p. 9).

Anson Call

While at Far West I happened in John Corls [Corrill's] or the Church store and my attention was called by Vincent Knights [Vinson Knight] who was opening some boxes of goods. Says he, "Joseph will be much pleased with these. He has been very uneasy about the translation of the Bible and the Egyptian records. Here they are." Placing them on the table, he said to me, "If you will take one of these, I will the other, and we will carry them over to Joseph's office." There we found Joseph and six or seven other brethren. Joseph was much pleased with the arrival of the books, and said to us, "Sit down and we will read to you from the translation of the Book of Abraham." Oliver Cowdery then read until he was tired when Thomas Marsh read, making altogether about two hours. I was most interested in the work (1838, p. 98).

Warren Foote

[May 13, 1837] The rest of our company being somewhat anxious to see the Prophet Joseph and the temple, [they] concluded to accompany father and myself to Kirtland. We hired a man to take us to that place for $5.00—distant twelve miles. We arrived there about noon. In the afternoon we went into the [Kirtland] Temple, and saw the mummies and the records which were found with them. (We went to the Prophet's house to see him. This is the first I saw him, and shook hands with him.) Joseph Smith Sen. explained them to us, and said the records were the writings of Abraham and Joseph, Jacob's son. Some of the writing was in black, and some in red. He said that the writing in red was pertaining to the priesthood. We were also shown through the temple (n.d. [a], pp. 5–6).

Sarah S. Leavitt

We stayed at Kirtland about a week and had the privilege of hearing Joseph preach in that thing the Baptist said they called a meetinghouse [temple], which proved to be a very good house. We went into the upper rooms, saw the Egyptian mummies, the writing that was said to be written in Abraham's day, Jacob's ladder being pictured on it, and lots more wonders that I cannot write here, and that were explained to us (1919, p. 7).

William W. Phelps

The last of June, four Egyptian mummies were brought here; there were two papyrus rolls, besides some other ancient Egyptian writings with them. As no one could translate these writings, they were presented to President Smith. He soon knew what they were and said they, the "rolls of papyrus," contained the sacred record kept of Joseph in Pharaoh's court in Egypt, and the teachings of Father Abraham. God has so ordered it that these mummies and writings have been brought in the Church and the sacred writing I had just locked up in Brother Joseph's house when your letter came, so I had two consolations of good things in one day. These records of old times, when we translate and print them in a book, will make a good witness for the Book of Mormon. There is nothing secret or hidden that shall not be revealed, and they come to the Saints (1835b, p. 529).

Orson Pratt

The Lord brought to light sacred records from the catacombs of Egypt. After several hundred men had wrought and toiled for many months in digging down one of these vast structures, they entered into its interior; they found a great number of mummies—the bodies of persons that had been preserved since the catacomb was built, and some eleven of these mummies, well preserved, were taken out by these men, and they finally fell into the hands of a person named M. [Michael] H. Chandler. They were sent from Egypt to Ireland, where it was supposed he resided, but learning that he resided in America, they were sent to him. After receiving the mummies he began to take off some of the ancient covering or wrapping, and to his astonishment he found upon the breast of one of these mummies a record written upon ancient papyrus in plain characters, written both in black and red inks, or stains, or colors. And the mummies and the records were exhibited by Mr. Chandler, in New York, Philadelphia, and many of the eastern states of our Union; and thousands of people saw them, and among them many learned men; and these characters were presented to them, and not infrequently was Mr. Chandler referred to "Joe" [Joseph] Smith as they used to term him, who, they said, pretended to have translated some records that he found in the western part of New York, and that if Mr. Chandler would go and see him perhaps he would translate those ancient characters.

Many of these references were made with the intention of ridiculing Mr. Smith; but it so happened that in traveling through the country, he visited Kirtland, Ohio, where the Prophet Joseph Smith resided, bringing the mummies and the ancient papyrus writings with him. Mr. C. [Chandler] had also obtained from learned men the best translation he could of some few characters, which however, was not a translation, but more in the shape of their ideas with regard to it, their acquaintance with the language not being sufficient to enable them to translate it literally. After some conversation with the Prophet Joseph, Mr. Chandler presented to him the ancient characters, asking him if he could translate them. The Prophet took them and repaired to his room and inquired of the Lord concerning them. The Lord told him they were sacred records, containing the inspired writings of Abraham when he was in Egypt, and also those of Joseph, while he was in Egypt; and they had been deposited, with these mummies, which had been exhumed. And he also inquired of the Lord concerning some few characters which Mr. Chandler gave him by way of a test, to see if he could translate them. The Prophet Joseph translated these characters and returned them with the translation to Mr. Chandler; and who, in comparing it with the translation of the same few characters by learned men, that he had before obtained, found the two to agree.

The Prophet Joseph having learned the value of these ancient writings was very anxious to obtain them, and expressed himself wishful to purchase them. But Mr. Chandler told him that he would not sell the writings, unless he could sell the mummies, for it would detract from the curiosity of his exhibition; Mr. Smith inquired of him the price, which was a considerable sum, and finally purchased the mummies and the writing, all of which he retained in his possession for many years; and they were seen by all the church that saw proper to visit the house of the Prophet Joseph and also by hundreds of strangers.

The Prophet translated the part of these writings which, as I have said is contained in the Pearl of Great Price, and known as the Book of Abraham (JD, 20:64–65).

John Riggs

When Mr. Chandler arrived in Kirtland with his mummies to exhibit, he put up at the hotel of Father Riggs, who, at the request of Chandler, sent his son to the Prophet's house to invite him and family to attend the exhibition that evening, but Joseph was engaged to attend a meeting and could not come. Young Riggs was again sent, with a note asking when Mr. Chandler could have an interview with the Prophet, who replied that he would come in the morning at 8 o'clock, which he did; and young Riggs was present when the Prophet first saw the papyrus from which is translated the Book of Abraham. Joseph was permitted to take the papyrus home with him, Father Riggs vouching for its return, and the morning following Joseph came with the leaves which he had translated, which

Oliver Cowdery read, and Mr. Chandler then produced the translation of Professor Anthon as far as the professor could translate it. Dr. Riggs, who was present at the reading, says that the translation agreed so far, but "there was one language Professor Anthon could not translate which the Prophet did" (1884, pp. 282–83).

Joseph Smith

The public mind has been excited of late by reports which have been circulated concerning certain Egyptian mummies and ancient records, which were purchased by certain gentlemen of Kirtland last July. It has been said that the purchasers of these antiquities pretend they have the bodies of Abraham, Abimelech (the king of the Philistines), Joseph, who was sold into Egypt, &c., &c., for the purpose of attracting the attention of the multitude, and gulling the unwary; which is utterly false. Who these ancient inhabitants of Egypt were, I do not at present say. Abraham was buried on his own possession "in the cave of Machpelah, in the field of Ephron, the son of Zohah, the Hittite, which is before Mamre," which he purchased of the sons of Heth. Abimelech lived in the same country, and for aught we know, died there; and the children of Israel carried Joseph's bones from Egypt, when they went out under Moses; consequently, these could not have been found in Egypt in the nineteenth century.

The record of Abraham and Joseph, found with the mummies, is beautifully written on papyrus, with black, and a small part red, ink or paint, in perfect preservation. The characters are such as you find upon the coffins of mummies—hieroglyphics, etc.; with many characters of letters like the present (though probably not quite so square) form of the Hebrew without points.

The records were obtained from one of the catacombs in Egypt, near the place where once stood the renowned city of Thebes, by the celebrated French traveler, Antonio Lebolo, in the year 1831. He procured license from Mehemet Ali, then Viceroy of Egypt, under the protection of Chevalier Drovetti, the French Consul, in the year 1828, and employed four hundred and thirty-three men, four months and two days (if I understand correctly)—Egyptian or Turkish soldiers, at from four to six cents per diem, each man. He entered the catacomb June 7, 1831, and obtained eleven mummies. There were several hundred mummies in the same catacomb; about one hundred embalmed after the first order, and placed in niches, and two or three hundred after the second and third orders, and laid upon the floor or bottom of the grand cavity. The two last orders of embalmed were so decayed that they could not be removed, and only eleven of the first, found in the niches. On his way from Alexandria to Paris, he put in at Trieste, and, after ten days' illness, expired. This was in the year 1832.

Previous to his decease, he made a will of the whole to Mr. Michael H. Chandler (then in Philadelphia, Pa.), his nephew, whom he supposed to be in Ireland. Accordingly, the whole were sent to Dublin, and Mr. Chandler's friends ordered them to New York, where they were received at the Custom House, in the winter or spring of 1833. In April of the same year, Mr. Chandler paid the duties and took possession of his mummies. Up to this time, they had not been taken out of the coffins, nor the coffins opened. On opening the coffins, he discovered that in connection with two of the bodies, was something rolled up with the same kind of linen, saturated with the same bitumen, which, when examined, proved to be two rolls of papyrus, previously mentioned. Two or three other small pieces of papyrus, with astronomical calculations, epitaphs, &c., were found with others of the mummies. When Mr. Chandler discovered that there was something with the mummies, he supposed or hoped it might be some diamonds or valuable metal, and was no little chagrined when he saw his disappointment.

"He was immediately told, while yet in the custom house, that there was no man in that city who could translate his roll: but was referred, by the same gentleman (a stranger) to Mr. Joseph Smith, Jun., who, continued he, possesses some kind of power or gifts, by which he had previously translated similar characters. I was then unknown to Mr. Chandler, neither did he know that such a book or work as the record of the Nephites had been brought before the public. From New York, he took his collection on to Philadelphia, where he obtained the certificate of the learned, and from thence came on to Kirtland, as before related, in July.

Thus I have given a brief history of the manner in which the writings of the fathers, Abraham and Joseph, have been preserved, and how I came in possession of the same—a correct translation of which I shall give in its proper place (HC, 2:348–51).

Joseph F. Smith

The idea that "the translation [of the Abraham papyrus] came to him very largely as the result of persistent study" is borne out in a story that the late Preston Nibley used to tell of how in 1906 he visited the Nauvoo House in company with President Joseph F. Smith. President Smith (as Elder Nibley recollected with his remarkable memory) recalled with tears the familiar sight of "Uncle Joseph" kneeling on the floor of the front room with Egyptian manuscripts spread out all around him, weighted down by rocks and books, as with intense concentration he would study a line of characters, jotting down his impressions in a little notebook as he went (1968, pp. 17–18).

Wilford Woodruff

Joseph the Seer has presented us some of the Book of Abraham which was written by his own hand but hid from the knowledge of man for the last four thousand years, but has now come to light through the mercy of God. Joseph has had these records in his possession for several years, but has never presented them before the world in the English language until now, but he is about to publish it to the world or parts of it by publishing it in the *Times and Seasons,* for Joseph the Seer is now the editor of that paper, and Elder Taylor assists him in the writing, while it has befallen to my lot to take charge of the business parts of the establishment. I have had the privilege this day of assisting in setting the type for printing of the first piece of the Book of Abraham that is to be presented to the inhabitants of the earth in the last days (1842).

The Joseph Smith Translation of the Bible

John M. Bernhisel

Elder John M. Bernhisel called at the request of Pres. Taylor and explained concerning his manuscript copy of the New Translation of the Bible, as taken from the manuscript of the Prophet Joseph Smith. Bro. Bernhisel stated: "I had great desires to see the New Translation, but did not like to ask for it; but one evening, being at Bro. Joseph's house about a year after his death, Sister Emma to my surprise asked me if I would not like to see it. I answered yes. She handed it to me the next day, and I kept it in my custody about three months. She told me it was not prepared for the press, as Joseph had designed to go through it again. I did not copy all that was translated, leaving some few additions and changes that were made in some of the books. But so far as I did copy, I did so as correctly as I could do. The markings in my Bible correspond precisely with the markings in the Prophet Joseph's Bible, so that all the books corrected in his Bible so far as I now know are marked in my Bible; but as I stated, the additions are not all made in my manuscript of those books that I did not copy (1975a, p. 118).

John M. Bernhisel

The School of the Prophets met at 1 P.M. President Young spoke of the new translation of the Bible and said it was not complete. Dr. Bernhisel testified that the Prophet told him he wished to revise it. Emma Smith let Dr. Bernhisel have the new translation to peruse it for three months; during this time the Doctor copied much of it.

Orson Pratt compared many of the sayings in the new and old translations.

George A. Smith testified that he had heard Joseph say before his death that the new translation was not complete, that he had not been able to prepare for it, and that it was probably providentially so (1975b, p. 119).

Howard Coray

One morning, I went as usual into the office to go to work. I found Joseph sitting on one side of a table and Robert B. Thompson on the opposite side, and the understanding I got was that they were examining or hunting in the manuscript of the new translation of the Bible for something on priesthood, which Joseph wished to present, or have read to the people the next conference. Well, they could not find what they wanted, and Joseph said to Thompson, "Put the manuscript [to] one side, and take some paper and I will tell you what to write." Bro. Thompson took some foolscap paper that was at his elbow and made himself ready for the business. I was seated probably six or eight feet on Joseph's left side, so that I could look almost squarely into Joseph's left eye—I mean the side of his eye. Well, the Spirit of God descended upon him, and a measure of it upon me, insomuch that I could fully realize that God, or the Holy Ghost, was talking through him. I never, neither before or since, have felt as I did on that occasion. I felt so small and humble I could have freely kissed his feet (1977, p. 344).

B. F. Cummings

[While working in the Mission Office in Independence, Missouri, Cummings visited the archives of the Reorganized Church of Jesus Christ of Latter-day Saints. Then, he says:] I was permitted to handle the manuscript [of the Joseph Smith Translation of the Bible] and scan its pages, but of course anything like a critical examination of it was out of the question within the time at my disposal. As I was turning its leaves I came to a page on which was written in a bold hand and large letters, bolder and larger than the rest of the writing on that page, this sentence, which, unless memory is at fault, I here reproduce verbatim: "The Song of Solomon is not inspired writing" (1915, p. 388).

Orson Pratt

He [Orson Pratt] mentioned that as Joseph used the Urim and Thummim in the translation of the Book of Mormon, he wondered why he did not use it in the translation of the New Testament. Joseph explained to him that the experience he had acquired while translating the Book of Mormon by the use of the Urim and Thummim had rendered him so well acquainted with the spirit of revelation and prophecy, that in the translating of the New Testament he did not need the aid that was necessary in the first instance (1871, p. 183).

Truman O. Angell: "He said, 'I'll give you work enough for twenty men.'"

Israel A. Barlow: "I shall see this man and know for myself if he is a prophet."

George Q. Cannon: "There was that about him which . . . distinguished him from all the men [I] had ever seen."

Oliver Cowdery: "On a sudden, as from the midst of eternity, the voice of the Redeemer spake peace to us, while the veil was parted and the angel of God came down clothed with glory."

Governor Thomas Ford: "It is to be feared that in course of a century, some gifted man like Paul, some splendid orator . . . [may] make the name of the martyred Joseph ring as loud, and stir the souls of men as much, as the mighty name of Christ itself."

Martin Harris: "It is not a mere belief, but is a matter of knowledge. I saw the plates and the inscriptions thereon. I saw the angel, and he showed them unto me."

Joseph L. Heywood: "I was baptized by Elder Orson Hyde, in the Mississippi River, the Prophet Joseph assisting in cutting the ice."

Mary I. Horne: "He said, . . . 'If I had a wife as small as you, when trouble came I would put her in my pocket and run.'"

Edward Hunter: "Joseph's parting words . . . were: 'You have known me for several years; say to the governor, under oath, everything good and bad you know of me.'"

Benjamin F. Johnson: "He blessed my mother and told her that not one of all her children should ever leave the Church; which, up to this, the year 1894, has been the case; and now as a family we number not less than one thousand."

Mary Ellen Kimball: "He said to Brother Rosecrans, 'If I never see you again, or if I *never come back,* remember that I love you.' This went through me like electricity."

Heber C. Kimball: "He . . . went from house to house, and from tent to tent, upon the bank of the river, healing the sick by the power of Israel's God."

Mary A. Lambert: "I never had such a feeling for mortal man as thrilled my being when my eyes first rested upon Joseph Smith."

Alfred B. Lambson *(seated right):* "The Prophet was a large man, broad-shouldered and heavy-set. There are no pictures that do justice to him."

Christopher Layton: "As he heartily grasped our hands, the fervently spoken words, 'God bless you,' sank deep into our hearts, giving us a feeling of peace such as we had never known before."

Mary Elizabeth Rollins Lightner: "We all felt that he was a man of God, for he spoke with power, and as one having authority in very deed."

Wandle Mace: "He would unravel the scriptures and explain doctrine as no other man could. What had been mystery he made so plain it was no longer mystery."

Joseph S. Murdock: "We find him to be a man of his word; he is very punctual in all his dealings."

Edward Partridge: "The forenoon was taken up in telling the visions of the preceding evening."

Orson Pratt: "An impostor might indeed predict the raising of Three Witnesses, but he could never call down an angel from heaven, in the presence of these Witnesses, to fulfill his prediction."

Parley P. Pratt: "There was something connected with the serene and steady penetrating glance of his eye, as if he would penetrate the deepest abyss of the human heart, gaze into eternity, penetrate the heavens, and comprehend all worlds."

Josiah Quincy: "What historical American of the nineteenth century has exerted the most powerful influence upon the destinies of his countrymen? . . . Joseph Smith, the Mormon Prophet."

Willard Richards: "Brother Joseph, if it is necessary that you die in this matter, and if they will take me in your stead, I will suffer for you."

Orrin Porter Rockwell: "Oh Joseph, Joseph, they have killed the only friend I ever had."

Emma Smith: "I am satisfied that no man could have dictated the writing of the [Book of Mormon] manuscript unless he was inspired. . . . It would have been improbable that a learned man could do this; and for one so ignorant and unlearned as [Joseph] was, it was simply impossible."

Hyrum Smith: "There were prophets before, but Joseph has the spirit and power of all the prophets."

Joseph F. Smith: "The greatest event that has ever occurred in the world, since the resurrection of the Son of God from the tomb and his ascension on high, was the coming of the Father and the Son to that boy Joseph Smith."

Joseph Smith III: "I never heard any quarreling or harsh language between [my father and mother]."

Lucy Mack Smith: "Joseph . . . seemed much less inclined to the perusal of books than any of the rest of our children, but far more given to meditation and deep study."

Mary Fielding Smith: "I believe I felt as much at parting with him as an own brother."

William Smith: "We never knew we were bad folks until Joseph told his vision. We were considered respectable till then, but at once people began to circulate falsehoods and stories in a wonderful way."

Eliza R. Snow: "I scrutinized his face as closely as I could without attracting his attention, and decided that his was an honest face."

Lorenzo Snow: "He was free and easy in conversation with me, making me feel perfectly at home in his presence."

William C. Staines: "I had seen him in a vision while crossing the sea, and when I saw him that day he had on the same hat and coat that I saw [in my vision]."

Edward Stevenson: "He said, 'When I speak as a man it is Joseph only that speaks. But when the Lord speaks through me, it is no more Joseph Smith who speaks; but it is God, and let all Israel hear.'"

John Taylor: "Joseph Smith, the Prophet and Seer of the Lord, has done more, save Jesus only, for the salvation of men in this world than any other man that ever lived in it."

Phoebe Carter Woodruff: "This was only a few hours after the miracle. From that day I never doubted that this was the work of God."

Wilford Woodruff: "Joseph was frank, open, and familiar."

Brigham Young: "I feel like shouting hallelujah all the time, when I think that I ever knew Joseph Smith, the Prophet."

Margaret P. Young: "It was 2 o'clock in the morning before we permitted him to retire. We wanted to listen to him all night."

5

The Ordinances and the Church

The Priesthood and Its Ordinances

Ordinances Come from God

Wilford Woodruff

Where has the power of God been since the death of Joseph? With this people. They say, these apostates, that Brigham Young organized the endowments and originated the principle of plural marriage. They're liars, every one of them, and the truth is not in them; in so far as this matter is concerned. There's Sister Bathsheba Smith, she and I both had our endowments under the hands of the Prophet Joseph Smith. I had my second anointings and sealings under his hands. There is not a single principle in this Church that he did not lay the foundation for; he called the Twelve together the last time he spoke to us, and his face shone like amber. And upon our shoulders he rolled the burden of the kingdom, and he gave us all the keys and powers and gifts to carry on this great and mighty work. He told us that he had received every key, every power, and every gift for the salvation of the living and the dead, and he said: "Upon the Twelve I seal these gifts and powers and keys from henceforth and forever. No matter what may come to me. And I lay this work upon your shoulders. Take it and bear it off, and if you don't, you'll be damned" (CD, 4:111).

Orderliness in Priesthood Administration

ORSON HYDE

[In the winter of 1832–33] One Francis C. Bishop, an elder in our church, was very anxious to be ordained a high priest, but he was not considered a proper candidate to fill the office at that time; and his urgent solicitations to be promoted to the High Priesthood confirmed the Saints in the opinion that he wanted a high station without meriting it, or without being called by the Spirit of God to that work. He was sent forth into the world to preach in the capacity and calling of an elder; but he was not long out before he declared himself to be a high priest—and that he was ordained by an angel from heaven. This made much stir in the branches of the church and also in the world. But when the news of his proceedings reached the Prophet Joseph, he called Bishop home forthwith. He was introduced into the school of the prophets, and there closely questioned upon his course. He said he was ordained by an angel to the High Priesthood, yet, on a more close examination, he crossed his own testimony and statements—became confused, and blushed with shame and guilt—he fell down upon his knees and confessed that he had lied in the name of the Lord—begged to be forgiven and cried aloud for mercy. We all forgave him, but we could not give him our confidence, for he had destroyed it. Elder Sidney Rigdon was present at that meeting, and though he has since fallen, still he knows that my statements are correct. Zebedee Coltrin was also present, and many others that I might name.

Brother Joseph observed to Bishop that he knew he had lied before he confessed it; that his declarations were not only false in themselves, but they involved a false principle. An angel, said Joseph, may administer the word of the Lord unto men, and bring intelligence to them from heaven upon various subjects; but no true angel from God will ever come to ordain any man, because they have once been sent to establish the priesthood by ordaining me thereunto; and the priesthood being once established on the earth, with power to ordain others, no heavenly messenger will ever come to interfere with that power by ordaining any more. He referred to the angel that came to Cornelius and told Cornelius to send for Peter; but if there had been no Peter with keys and power to administer, the angel might have done it himself; but as there was, the angel would not interfere. Saul was directed to go to Ananias for instruction and to be administered to by him; but if there had been no Ananias with power and authority on the earth to administer in the name of Christ, the Lord might have done it himself. You may therefore know, he is either a liar or has been imposed upon in consequence of transgression by an angel of the devil, for this priesthood shall never be taken away from this church (1846, pp. 138–39).

John Taylor

I remember a remark made on one occasion by Joseph Smith, in speaking with Bishop Partridge, who was then bishop. He was a splendid good man, as Bishop Hunter is. But he got some crooked ideas into his head; he thought he ought to manage some things irrespective of Joseph, which caused Joseph to speak rather sharply to him. Joseph said, "I wish you to understand that I am President of this Church, and I am your president, and I preside over you and all your affairs." Is that correct doctrine? Yes. It was true then and it is true today (JD, 21:36).

Wilford Woodruff

February 19 [1837]—I attended meeting at the temple. President Joseph Smith [Jr.] had been absent on business for the Church, but not half as long as Moses was in the mount away from Israel; yet many of the people in Kirtland, if they did not make a calf to worship, as did the Israelites, [apostasy] turned their hearts away from the Lord, and from his servant Joseph, and had engaged in speculation, and given way to false spirits, until they were darkened in their minds; and many were opposed to Joseph Smith, and some wished to appoint David Whitmer to lead the Church in his stead. In the midst of this cloud of dark spirits, Joseph returned to Kirtland, and this morning arose in the stand. He appeared much depressed; but soon the Spirit of God rested upon him, and he addressed the assembly in great plainness for about three hours, and put his enemies to silence. When he arose he said, "I am still the President, Prophet, Seer, Revelator, and Leader of the Church of Jesus Christ. God, and not man, has appointed and placed me in this position, and no man or set of men have power to remove me, or appoint another in my stead; and those who undertake this, if they do not speedily repent, will burn their fingers and go to hell." He reproved the people sharply for their sins, darkness, and unbelief. The power of God rested upon him, and bore testimony that his sayings were true (1865, p. 183).

Ordinances of Apostate Religion

Daniel H. Wells

I heard the Prophet Joseph Smith state once in Nauvoo that whether "Mormonism" was right or wrong, the people were just as well without as with the ordinances taught and administered by the sectarians of the day (JD, 12:72).

The Ordinances of the Gospel

Anointings

Joseph Smith

At early candle-light I met with the Presidency at the west school room, in the temple, to attend to the ordinance of anointing our heads with holy oil; also the Councils of Kirtland and Zion met in the two adjoining rooms, and waited in prayer while we attended to the ordinance. I took the oil in my left hand, Father Smith being seated before me, and the remainder of the Presidency encircled him round about. We then stretched our right hands towards heaven, and blessed the oil, and consecrated it in the name of Jesus Christ.

We then laid our hands upon our aged Father Smith, and invoked the blessings of heaven. I then anointed his head with the consecrated oil, and sealed many blessings upon him. The Presidency then in turn laid their hands upon his head, beginning at the oldest, until they had all laid their hands upon him, and pronounced such blessings upon his head, as the Lord put into their hearts, all blessing him to be our Patriarch, to anoint our heads, and attend to all duties that pertain to that office. The Presidency then took the seat in their turn, according to their age, beginning at the oldest, and received their anointing and blessing under the hands of Father Smith. And in my turn, my father anointed my head, and sealed upon me the blessings of Moses, to lead Israel in the latter days, even as Moses led him in days of old; also the blessings of Abraham, Isaac, and Jacob. All of the Presidency laid their hands upon me, and pronounced upon my head many prophecies and blessings, many of which I shall not notice at this time. But as Paul said, so say I, let us come to visions and revelations (HC, 2:379–80).

Consecration of Oil

Mosiah Hancock

Sometimes after our annual conference, the Prophet and others brought oil to our house to be consecrated! And it was my father's fortune to be kind to the poor, to preach the gospel, to guard the Prophet, and to work on the temple (n.d., p. 25).

Endowment

Wandle Mace

During these labors [of preparing to go West] I was called to the temple to receive my endowments and sealings, as Joseph said, "Those whose names are on the books showing their labors for the temple shall have the first claim." President Brigham Young and the Twelve were very particular to carry out his instructions; they saw that those who spent their whole time in these labors received the reward of their diligence by giving them a great endowment (n.d. [b], p. 194).

Bathsheba W. Smith

Soon after my husband's return [fall 1843] we were blessed by receiving our endowments and were sealed under the holy law of celestial marriage which was revealed July 12th, 1843. I heard the Prophet Joseph charge the Twelve with the duty and responsibility of administering the ordinances of endowment and of sealing for the living and the dead. I met many times with Brother Joseph and others who had received their endowments, in company with my husband, in an upper room dedicated for that purpose, and prayed with them repeatedly in those meetings (n.d., pp. 8–9).

Marriage

Benjamin F. Johnson

In the evening [Joseph Smith] called me and my wife to come and sit down, for he wished to marry us according to the law of the Lord. I thought it a joke, and said I should not marry my wife again unless she courted me, for I did it all the first time. He chided my levity, told me he was in earnest, and so it proved, for we stood up and were sealed by the Holy Spirit of Promise.

This occurrence is referred to in the life of Joseph Smith as "Spending the evening in giving counsel to Brother Johnson and wife" (1947, p. 96).

Priesthood Blessings

JANE J. BLACK

The leading brethren of the Church loved this noble woman. The Prophet Joseph Smith blessed and set her apart to administer to her sex as long as she lived, with a promise of success in her labors. During her life she brought more than 3,000 babies into the world, and never lost a mother or baby. This was according to a promise Pres. Young gave her as he was ready to start to the Valleys. He said to her, "Jane, if you will try and live up to the counsel the Prophet Joseph gave you, I promise you will never lose a mother or baby" (n.d. [b]).

MARGARETTE BURGESS

The Prophet Joseph was often at my father's house. Some incidents which I recollect of him made deep impressions on my child-mind. One morning when he called at our house, I had a very sore throat. It was much swollen and gave me great pain. He took me up in his lap, and gently anointed my throat with consecrated oil and administered to me, and I was healed. I had no more pain nor soreness (1892, p. 66).

SARAH ANN HAMSON

The family moved to Ohio and then to Nauvoo where they went to hear the elders speak and the Prophet Joseph explain the principles of the gospel. One time at an outdoor meeting when the Prophet was speaking, a man was accidentally shot through the arm by a gun that he was leaning on, and the Prophet stepped over to him and asked for a bandage. He bound the arm and blessed the man and in a few days, he was alright again (ca. 1931).

NEWEL KNIGHT

October the 14th [1832] my eldest son Samuel was born. [My wife] Sally's health was very poor, she was naturally a feeble woman, and having passed through many afflictions her sufferings were severe. Previous to Samuel's birth she had been unfortunate, and the doctors had told her she could not live and give birth to a living child. The Prophet Joseph while on a visit to my house blessed her and promised her the desire of her heart. She never doubted Joseph's word, and when her son was born, she blessed him, and desired to have him named Samuel, for she had asked him of the Lord (n.d.).

George Reynolds

While residing in Kirtland, Elder Reynolds Cahoon had a son born to him. One day when President Joseph Smith was passing his door he called the Prophet in and asked him to bless and name the baby. Joseph did so and gave the boy the name of Mahonri Moriancumer. When he had finished the blessing, he laid the child on the bed, and turning to Elder Cahoon he said, "The name I have given your son is the name of the Brother of Jared; the Lord has just shown (or revealed) it to me." Elder William F. Cahoon, who was standing near, heard the Prophet make this statement to his father; and this was the first time the name of the Brother of Jared was known in the Church in this dispensation (1892, p. 282).

Mephibosheth Sirrine

At an early age, he [Mephibosheth] became acquainted with the young prophet, Joseph Smith, the man who claimed to have received visitation of heavenly beings; who restored the gospel of Jesus Christ and the priesthood of God giving him the right to act in his name and do His work here upon the earth. Both of these boys were good athletes and became fast friends, often wrestling together to test each other's strength.

While "Bosha" [Mephibosheth] was living in New York State near the Prophet's home he became very ill and was too weak to rise from his bed. The prophet visited him and called him to go out and preach the gospel in these words, "Bosha, get up. I have a mission for you."

Mephibosheth replied, "Brother Joseph, I am so weak I can hardly raise my head, but if you will get me a bite to eat and have your wife pack my suitcase, I will leave on my mission." He also requested that the Prophet anoint his head with consecrated oil and give him a special health blessing.

This the Prophet proceeded to do and promised him in the name of the Lord that it would not be but a few minutes until he would be walking as well as ever, [and] that when he got to the end of his mission trek, permission would be granted him to speak in a school-house and that he would have a large audience. He told of how a lady and her daughter would be present, and at the close of the meeting they would walk down the aisle and invite him to stay at their home and to have dinner there.

This was fulfilled as it had been promised. When he was opening the meeting, he observed a lady and her daughter walk down the aisle and seat themselves near the front of the large audience, and the girl took a tablet as the Prophet had also predicted, and began to take down his sermon in shorthand. After the people had left the building, they remained and came forward to invite Mephibosheth to dinner that evening and to stay at their home as long as he was in that part of the country. Later, he married this young woman who became the mother of his first three children, namely Theodore C., Parley P. and Helen Sirrine. This was a great testimony to Mephibosheth Sirrine. He recognized the prophetic power of the Prophet, Joseph Smith (n.d.).

Zina D. H. Young

Jan. 2nd, 1889—Today is the birthday of my firstborn son, Zebulon Jacobs, who [was born] Sunday, Jan. 2, 1842, about sunrise . . . in Nauvoo, Hancock Co., Illinois. Joseph Smith came with Brother Dimick B. Huntington and blessed me after I was taken sick [and] said all would be well. The next day he came in and blessed the boy, [and] said he should be a Patriarch, Priest, and King; just give him time to grow up. This gave me comfort and strength to exercise faith (1889).

Sacrament

Joseph Smith

The council adjourned to the day following, March 1st, when, after attending the funeral of Seth Johnson, several who had recently been baptized were confirmed, and the sacrament was administered to the Church. Previous to the administration, I spoke of the propriety of this institution in the Church, and urged the importance of doing it with acceptance before the Lord, and asked, How long do you suppose a man may partake of this ordinance unworthily, and the Lord not withdraw His Spirit from him? How long will he thus trifle with sacred things, and the Lord not give him over to the buffetings of Satan until the day of redemption! The Church should know if they are unworthy from time to time to partake, lest the servants of God be forbidden to administer it. Therefore our hearts ought to be humble, and we to repent of our sins, and put away evil from among us (HC, 2:204).

Settings Apart

Ann G. Carling

While living in Nauvoo, the Prophet Joseph Smith laid his hands on Ann's head and set her apart as a midwife, telling her that she would be successful in caring for the sick if she would use herbs exclusively in her work. Some years later in Utah she became known as the "herb doctor." She had an herb garden and prepared her own tea and medicine (1963, 6:429).

Harriet M. Johnson

Before the death of the Prophet Joseph Smith, he set apart Harriet Johnson as midwife, and between then and the time she died she helped bring into the world about four thousand babies (1963, 6:431).

Washing of Feet

Orson Pratt

When the temple was built, the Lord did not see proper to reveal all the ordinances of the endowments, such as we now understand. He revealed little by little. No rooms were prepared for washings; no special place prepared for the anointings, such as you understand, and such as you comprehend at that period of the history of the Church! Neither did we know the necessity of the washings, such as we now receive. It is true, our hands were washed, our faces, and our feet. The Prophet Joseph was commanded to gird himself with a towel, doing this in the temple. What for? That the first elder might witness to our Father and God, that we were clean from the blood of that wicked generation, that then lived [see D&C 88:138]. We had gone forth according to our best ability, to publish glad tidings of great joy, for thousands of miles, upon this continent. After this we were called in, and this washing of hands and feet was to testify to

God that we were clean from the blood of this generation. The holy anointing was placed upon the heads of his servants, but not the full development of the endowments in the anointing. These administrations in the Kirtland Temple were revealed, little by little, corresponding with what I have already been saying, that the Lord does not give the fullness at once, but imparts to us according to his own will and pleasure (JD, 19:16).

Joseph Smith

On the 23rd of January [1833], we again assembled in conference; when, after much speaking, singing, praying, and praising God, all in tongues, we proceeded to the washing of feet (according to the practice recorded in the 13th chapter of John's Gospel), as commanded of the Lord. Each elder washed his own feet first, after which I girded myself with a towel and washed the feet of all of them, wiping them with the towel with which I was girded. Among the number, my father presented himself, but before I washed his feet, I asked of him a father's blessing, which he granted by laying his hands upon my head, in the name of Jesus Christ, and declaring that I should continue in the Priest's office until Christ comes. At the close of the scene, Brother Frederick G. Williams, being moved upon by the Holy Ghost, washed my feet in token of his fixed determination to be with me in suffering, or in journeying, in life or in death, and to be continually on my right hand; in which I accepted him in the name of the Lord.

I then said to the elders, As I have done so do ye; wash ye, therefore, one another's feet; and by the power of the Holy Ghost I pronounced them all clean from the blood of this generation; but if any of them should sin willfully after they were thus cleansed, and sealed up unto eternal life, they should be given over unto the buffetings of Satan until the day of redemption. Having continued all day in fasting, and prayer, and ordinances, we closed by partaking of the Lord's supper. I blessed the bread and wine in the name of the Lord, when we all ate and drank, and were filled; then we sang a hymn, and the meeting adjourned (HC, 1:323–24).

Wilford Woodruff

[April 6, 1837] The Presidency of the Church, the Twelve Apostles, and other quorums, met in solemn assembly, and sealed upon our heads

our washings, anointings, and blessings, with a loud shout of hosannah to God and the Lamb; the Spirit of the Lord rested upon us. After spending three hours in the upper room, the quorums repaired to the lower court; the vails were lowered, and the ordinance of washing of feet was administered. Elder H. [Heber] C. Kimball washed my feet, and pronounced blessings upon me. After this ordinance, the vails of the temple were rolled up, and President Joseph Smith [Jr.,] addressed the elders for three hours, clothed with the Spirit and power of God. He unbosomed his feelings in the house of his friends, and gave much instruction. He urged upon us the absolute necessity of giving strict heed to his teachings and counsel, and the revelations of the Lord to the Church, and be wise in all things, that Zion and her stakes may be redeemed and established, no more to be thrown down. He said that the kings of the earth would yet come to behold the glory of Zion, and that great and glorious blessings would be bestowed upon the Saints in the last days. . . .

The house was again filled at candlelight. President [Joseph] Smith [Jr.] requested the elders to speak their feelings freely, and sing, exhort, and pray, as the Spirit should give utterance. The meeting continued during the whole night; many of the gifts were poured out upon the people; at break of day we were dismissed (1865, pp. 264–65).

Church Organization and Structure

First Presidency

Joseph Smith

"Doctor" Hurlburt was ordained an elder; after which Elder Rigdon expressed a desire that himself and Brother Frederick G. Williams should be ordained to the offices to which they had been called, viz., those of Presidents of the High Priesthood, and to be equal in holding the keys of the kingdom with Brother Joseph Smith, Jun., according to the revelation given on the 8th of March, 1833. Accordingly I laid my hands on Brothers Sidney and Frederick, and ordained them to take part with me in holding the keys of this last kingdom, and to assist in the Presidency of the High Priesthood, as my counselors; after which I exhorted the brethren to faithfulness and diligence in keeping the commandments of

God, and gave much instruction for the benefit of the Saints, with a promise that the pure in heart should see a heavenly vision; and after remaining a short time in secret prayer, the promise was verified; for many present had the eyes of their understanding opened by the Spirit of God, so as to behold many things. I then blessed the bread and wine, and distributed a portion to each. Many of the brethren saw a heavenly vision of the Savior, and concourses of angels, and many other things, of which each one has a record of what he saw (HC, 1:334–35).

Apostles

Heber C. Kimball

When Jesus lived on the earth, he ordained and organized a Quorum of Twelve Apostles, and said to them, "I have laid the foundation, and you must build the house." Joseph Smith did the same; he made choice of Twelve Apostles, and ordained them, and said, "I have laid the foundation, and you may build upon it, you may rear the house;" and these very persons are the ones who will lead you through into the celestial world, and they will be at your head all the time (JD, 3:20–21).

Joseph E. Taylor

I presume the Latter-day Saints have heard President Taylor tell the story that during the days of the Prophet Joseph Smith the latter called upon President Taylor, Orson Hyde, and some others to write a constitution for the Church. Having received the appointment they applied themselves diligently to frame the instrument, and from time to time they reported to one another and compared notes. But there was always something that could not be accepted, could not be passed upon. Brother Joseph, after a while, asked, "Well, Brother Taylor, have you got that constitution prepared?"

"No, sir."

"What is the reason?"

"Because we cannot write it; we cannot agree upon the constitution."

"Well," said Joseph, "I knew you could not. Ye are my constitution—as Twelve Apostles—ye are the living oracles." That is what he meant. "The word of the Lord shall proceed from you, and that, too, in keeping with the circumstances and conditions of the people, and you shall have the inspiration of Almighty God given to you to give counsel suited to them" (CD, 5:22–23; see, for comparison, John Taylor, JD, 18:330).

Wilford Woodruff

While in the ministry there [Fox Islands] I received a letter from Joseph Smith, the prophet of God, in which he told me that the Lord had given him a revelation, and named to me the persons that were called to fill the places of those who had fallen. My name was among them. He said that he wanted me to gather up the Saints I had baptized and bring them to Zion. What were the circumstances? I was on an island of the sea. There was not a horse or an ox on the island. There was not a man or a woman that knew how to harness a horse. I told one of the brethren, who had some money, that we must furnish a train of horses, wagons, harness, etc., and he proposed to advance the money for that purpose. He went with me and we bought about fifty horses; and then I had to match these horses, and get harness to fit them. I went to a wagon-maker and engaged twenty or twenty-five wagons. I did this in order to prepare the people to go with me, according to the words of the Prophet. I arranged everything, agreed with this brother to furnish the money, and left in advance with the understanding that they were to leave the first day of September. The letter to me was dated the first of August. I went to Maine, as my wife was there with her first child. I waited for this company to come to me, but they did not come till the first of October. We had them to travel from Maine to Missouri through snow, rain, and mud. However, we passed through it all, and got up there, according to the commandment of the Lord to me (CR, Oct. 1897, p. 46).

Brigham Young

After we returned from Missouri, my brother Joseph Young and myself had been singing after preaching in a meeting; and when the meeting was dismissed, Brother Joseph Smith said, "Come, go down to my house with me." We went and sung to him a long time, and talked with him. He then opened the subject of the Twelve and Seventies for the first time I ever thought of it. He said, "Brethren, I am going to call out Twelve Apostles. I think we will get together, by-and-by, and select Twelve Apostles, and select a Quorum of Seventies from those who have been up to Zion, out of the camp boys." In 1835, the last of January or in February, or about that time, we held our meetings from day to day, and

Brother Joseph called out Twelve Apostles at that time. He had a revelation when we were singing to him. Those who were acquainted with him knew when the spirit of revelation was upon him, for his countenance wore an expression peculiar to himself while under that influence. He preached by the spirit of revelation, and taught in his council by it, and those who were acquainted with him could discover it at once, for at such times there was a peculiar clearness and transparency in his face. He followed up that revelation until he organized the Church, and so along until the baptism of the dead was revealed (JD, 9:89).

Seventies

Joseph Young

Under the heading "A Scrap of History," President Joseph Young writes as follows in relation to the organization of the Seventies: "On the 8th day of February, in the year of our Lord, 1835, the Prophet Joseph Smith called Elders Brigham Young and Joseph Young to the chamber of his residence in Kirtland, Ohio; it being the Sabbath day. After they were seated and he had made some preliminaries, he proceeded to relate a vision he had seen, in regard to the state and condition of those elders who died in Zion's Camp in Missouri. He said: 'Brethren, I have seen those men who died of the cholera in our camp; and the Lord knows, if I get a mansion as bright as theirs, I ask no more.' At this relation he wept, and for some time could not speak because of his tender feelings in memory of his brethren. When he had somewhat relieved himself, he resumed the conversation, and addressing himself to Brother Brigham Young he said: 'I wish you to notify all the brethren living in branches within a reasonable distance from this place, to meet at a general conference on Saturday next. I shall then and there appoint twelve special witnesses to open the door of the gospel to foreign nations, and you (speaking to Brother Brigham) will be one of them.'" The prophet, according to the narrator, then explained the duties of the Twelve Apostles, after which he turned to Joseph Young and said with much earnestness: "Brother Joseph, the Lord has made you President of the Seventies."

Upon the 28th of the month the first quorum of Seventy were chosen and ordained, under the hands of the Prophet and other Church leaders. Joseph Young was the second name upon the list, and he was one of the original Seven Presidents of that body. Soon afterwards he succeeded to the first or senior place, which he retained to the end of his life, thus realizing the Prophet's forecast concerning him. Not long after the organization of this quorum the Prophet said in the course of an address to them: "Brethren, some of you are angry with me because you did not fight in Missouri; but let me tell you, God did not want you to fight. He could not organize his kingdom, with twelve men to open the gospel door to the nations of the earth, and with seventy men under their direction to follow in their tracks, unless he took them from a body of men who had offered their lives, and who had made as great a sacrifice as did Abraham. Now the Lord has got his Twelve and his Seventy, and there will be other quorums of Seventies called, who will make the sacrifice, and those who will not make their sacrifices and their offerings now will make them hereafter" (1904, 4:443–44).

Patriarchs

BRIGHAM YOUNG

At the time that Zion's Camp, as it is called, went up to Missouri in 1834, so far as I am aware, Joseph had never received any intimation as to there being a patriarch in the Church. On our return home from Missouri, my brother Joseph Young, while conversing with me, asked if it would be right for our father to give us a blessing. Said he—"I feel just as though I want my father to give me a patriarchal blessing." When we reached Kirtland we talked with Joseph on the subject, and he said, "Certainly," and finally we appointed a day, and Brother Joseph, the Prophet, came to where we met and ordained my father a Patriarch, and he was the first man ordained to the office of Patriarch in the Church, and he blessed his children; and soon after this Joseph ordained his father a patriarch and his father called his children together and blessed them. Then Joseph had another revelation, that a record would be kept, and when this was revealed to him, he then had his father call his house together again, and blessed them over, and a record was kept of it. This is to show you, and especially those who have no experience in the Church, how the Lord has led this people along (JD, 18:240–41).

Note: While there is no reason to doubt the general sense of what Brigham Young says here—that following Zion's Camp the Prophet ordained his father a patriarch, who in turn gave blessings to Brigham and Joseph Young—our records show that the Prophet's father, Joseph Smith Sr., was ordained a Patriarch on Dec. 18, 1833, and as such was the first Patriarch ordained in this dispensation (see HC, 4:190).

High Councils (and Disciplinary Councils)

Heber C. Kimball

During my stay here [Kirtland] and on the 17th February 1834, a general council of twenty-four high priests assembled at the house of Joseph Smith, Jr., by revelation, and proceeded to organize the High Council of the Church of Christ, which was to consist of twelve high priests. The number composing the council who voted in the name of and for the church in appointing these councilors were forty-three, as follows; nine high priests, seventeen elders, four priests, and thirteen members. During this time I received much precious instruction concerning the order of the kingdom (1845a, p. 771).

George A. Smith

Mankind is capable of a great many extravagances; we very well remember the time when a very zealous man named Hawley arraigned Joseph Smith before bishop's counsel in Kirtland, and charged him with having forfeited his office as a prophet of God because he had not prohibited the aged sisters from wearing caps. I attended the council, which was held very late, and the man there advocated that he [Joseph] was cut off from the Church, for God had cut him off from the Church, as well as from his Apostleship, because he had suffered the men to wear little cushions on the shoulders of their coat sleeves. It being then fashionable to wear a little cotton on the shoulders, and in consequence of some of the brethren wearing such coats, the prophet of God was cut off from the Church by this man, and persecuted as an impostor, and another was placed in his stead.

That man was possessed of such wisdom as man could reasonably manifest, yet he was so perfectly full of folly and of his own traditions and notions he had fancied over in his own head, that seemingly it was impossible for him to understand anything better; he was blinded, and lifted his hand against the prophet of God. Instances of this kind have been continually accumulating, and it is one of the most perfect illustrations of the sayings of the Prophet, that He [God] would sift His people as with a sieve. It has been a constant sifting from the time we entered the Church up to the present (JD, 2:362).

Bishops

Brigham Young

June 1 [1839]—A conference was held in Quincy; President Joseph Smith presided. He informed the seventies it was not the will of God that they should appoint, or have committees to take care of their poor, but that bishops were the authorities that God had specially appointed for that purpose; which counsel was immediately responded to (1968, p. 42).

Relief Society

Nancy N. Tracy

The work on the [Nauvoo] temple was progressing, elders were being sent out to the nations to preach the gospel, emigrants from different parts flocked in, and everything prospered. About this time the Relief Society was organized with Emma Smith, president, with two counselors, and Eliza R. Snow, secretary. This was for the relief of the poor and for every noble purpose that came within woman's sphere of action. I united with this society. There was much valuable instruction given in these meetings. Sometimes Emma would bring the Prophet in to give instructions. One in particular, I remember; he opened the meeting by prayer. He was so full of the Spirit of the Holy Ghost that his frame shook and his face shone and looked almost transparent. This was about the time that the order of the celestial marriage was given by revelation to him. He had taught it to a few who would hear it, but I heard him say at one time when he was preaching (turning to those that sat behind him), "If I should reveal to these, my Brethren, who now seem to be my bosom friends, what God has revealed to me, they would be the first to seek my life." And it was so. Even when this law of celestial marriage was taught, these very men, William Marks, the Laws, and others, turned vipers against him (n.d. [a], pp. 24–25).

WILFORD WOODRUFF

Now I want to say a few words concerning our Relief Societies. They were organized by the Prophet Joseph Smith, in Nauvoo, at an early day; and he took great interest in the organization of that society. And he knew by the spirit of inspiration, what result that organization would have in the Church, and he saw by the spirit of inspiration the necessity of that society. And now they are all through these mountains, in every ward (CD, 3:425).

Sunday School

MARY ANN WINTERS

One Sunday morning early in June, 1844, I was at a meeting in the grove east on Mulholland Street, when Brother Joseph arose and said he wanted all the children that could, to bring their testaments and hymn books and meet there the next Sabbath and have a Sunday School. He said, "I don't know as I will be here—I will if I can, but Brother Stephen Goddard will be here and take charge of you, won't you, Brother Goddard?" Brother Goddard assented, and then Brother Joseph called for teachers, and a number volunteered. He spoke at some length on the importance of this move, and as far as I know this was the first Sunday School in the history of the Church. I attended the next Sabbath and my teacher was Sister Clara Chase. I cannot remember of meeting but twice in the Sunday School when those awful days came that terminated in the martyrdom of Brother Joseph and Hyrum Smith (1916c, p. 641).

The Law of Common Consent

WANDLE MACE

Conference convened within the walls of the [Nauvoo] temple on the 6th day of April 1843. The meeting called to order in the usual way Joseph arose and said, "One object of this conference was to ascertain the standing of the First Presidency, which he would do by presenting himself for trial." He asked if they were satisfied with him to preside over the whole church, or would they have another. Said he, "If I have done anything that ought to injure my character, reputation, or standing or have dishonored our religion by any means, in the sight of men or angels, or in the sight of men and women, I am sorry for it, and if you will forgive me, I will endeavor to do so no more. I do not know that I have done anything of the kind; but if I have, come forward and tell me of it, I want you to come boldly and frankly, and tell me of it, and if not, ever after hold your peace."

A motion was made and seconded that "President Joseph Smith continue President of the whole church." After a few minutes silence the motion was put by Brigham Young, President of the Twelve, when one vast sea of hands was raised, the motion being carried unanimously.

Joseph returned his thanks to the Saints for the manifestation of their confidence and said, he "would serve them according to the best ability God should give him." He said, he did not know anything against the Twelve or he would present them for trial (n.d. [b], pp. 80–81).

JOHN TAYLOR

You will recollect that about the 19th of January, 1841, a revelation was given defining the various positions of men called to act in the priesthood [D&C 124]. First, the Lord gave to the Church Hyrum Smith to be Patriarch, then Joseph Smith, Jun., to be Prophet, Seer, and Revelator to the people, and Sidney Rigdon and William Law for his counselors, Brigham Young as President of the Twelve, which Twelve he called by name—then the high priests, seventies, and elders—then again the bishops and lesser priesthood. Now, says he, at the next general conference present this organization to the conference for its acceptance or rejection. At the next conference the various quorums were presented in that form and the people voted as quorums and with uplifted hands. Some of these men that the Lord had named, however, were rejected: One man named Hicks, and another Bishop Ripley. John E. Page, one of the Quorum of the Twelve, was also rejected, but after a hearing was afterwards restored. The Prophet Joseph told the people to vote in that manner, as the majority of the several quorums would form a quorum or authority that would be decisive. This manner of voting was observed at Far West also; and even after Joseph's death this same rule was observed, though not with the same unanimity as at our general conference (JD, 19:139–40).

6

Historical Items

The Vermont and Palmyra Years (1813–1830)

Joseph's Leg Operation (1813)

Lucy Mack Smith

Joseph, our third son, having recovered from the typhus fever, after something like two weeks' sickness, one day screamed out while sitting in a chair, with a pain in his shoulder, and, in a very short time he appeared to be in such agony that we feared the consequences would prove to be something very serious. We immediately sent for a doctor. When he arrived and had examined the patient, he said that it was his opinion that this pain was occasioned by sprain. But the child declared this could not be the case as he had received no injury in any way whatever, but that a severe pain had seized him all at once, of the cause of which he was entirely ignorant.

Notwithstanding the child's protestations, still the physician insisted that it must be a sprain, and consequently he anointed his shoulder with some bone linament, but this was of no advantage to him, for the pain continued the same after the anointing as before.

When two weeks of extreme suffering had elapsed, the attendant physician concluded to make closer examination, whereupon he found that a large fever sore had gathered between his breast and shoulder. He immediately lanced it, upon which it discharged fully a quart of matter.

As soon as the sore had discharged itself the pain left it, and shot like lightning (using his own terms) down his side into the marrow of the bone of his leg and soon became very severe. My poor boy, at this, was almost in despair, and he cried out, "Oh, father, the pain is so severe, how can I bear it!"

His leg soon began to swell and he continued to suffer the greatest agony for the space of two weeks longer. During this period I carried him much of the time in my arms in order to mitigate his suffering as much as possible; in consequence of which I was taken very ill myself. The anxiety of mind that I experienced, together with physical over-exertion, was too much for my constitution, and my nature sank under it.

Hyrum, who was rather remarkable for his tenderness and sympathy, now desired that he might take my place. As he was a good, trusty boy, we let him do so, and, in order to make the task as easy for him as possible, we laid Joseph upon a low bed and Hyrum sat beside him, almost day and night for some considerable length of time, holding the affected part of his leg in his hands and pressing it between them, so that his afflicted brother might be enabled to endure the pain which was so excruciating that he was scarcely able to bear it.

At the end of three weeks, we thought it advisable to send again for the surgeon. When he came he made an incision of eight inches, on the front side of the leg, between the knee and the ankle. This relieved the pain in a great measure, and the patient was quite comfortable until the wound began to heal, when the pain became as violent as ever.

The surgeon was called again, and he this time enlarged the wound, cutting the leg even to the bone. It commenced healing the second time, and as soon as it began to heal it also began to swell again, which swelling continued to rise till we deemed it wisdom to call a council of surgeons; and when they met in consultation they decided that amputation was the only remedy.

Soon after coming to this conclusion, they rode up to the door and were invited into a room apart from the one in which Joseph lay. They being seated, I addressed them thus: "Gentlemen, what can you do to save my boy's leg?" They answered, "We can do nothing; we have cut it open to the bone and find it so affected that we consider his leg incurable and that amputation is absolutely necessary in order to save his life."

This was like a thunderbolt to me. I appealed to the principal surgeon, saying, "Dr. Stone, can you not make another trial? Can you not, by cutting around the bone, take out the diseased part, and perhaps that which is sound will heal over, and by this means you will save his leg? You will not, you must not, take off his leg, until you try once more. I will not consent to let you enter his room until you make me this promise."

After consulting a short time with each other, they agreed to do as I had requested, then went to see my suffering son. One of the doctors, on approaching his bed, said, "My poor boy, we have come again." "Yes," said Joseph, "I see you have; but you have not come to take off my leg, have you, sir?" "No," replied the surgeon, "it is your mother's request that we make one more effort, and that is what we have now come for."

The principal surgeon, after a moment's conversation, ordered cords to be brought to bind Joseph fast to a bedstead; but to this Joseph objected. The doctor, however, insisted that he must be confined, upon which Joseph said very decidedly, "No, doctor, I will not be bound, for I can bear the operation much better if I have my liberty." "Then," said Dr. Stone, "will you drink some brandy?"

"No," said Joseph, "not one drop."

"Will you take some wine?" rejoined the doctor. "You must take something, or you can never endure the severe operation to which you must be subjected."

"No," exclaimed Joseph, "I will not touch one particle of liquor, neither will I be tied down; but I will tell you what I will do—I will have my father sit on the bed and hold me in his arms, and then I will do whatever is necessary in order to have the bone taken out." Looking at me, he said, "Mother, I want you to leave the room, for I know you cannot bear to see me suffer so; father can stand it, but you have carried me so much, and watched over me so long, you are almost worn out." Then looking up into my face, his eyes swimming in tears, he continued. "Now, mother, promise me that you will not stay, will you? The Lord will help me, and I shall get through with it."

To this request I consented, and getting a number of folded sheets, and laying them under his leg, I retired, going several hundred yards from the house in order to be out of hearing.

The surgeons commenced operating by boring into the bone of his leg, first on one side of the bone where it was affected, then on the other side, after which they broke it off with a pair of forceps or pincers. They thus took away large pieces of bone. When they broke off the first piece, Joseph screamed out so loudly, that I could not forbear running to him. On my entering the room, he cried out, "Oh, mother, go back, go back; I do not want you to come in—I will try to tough it out, if you will go away."

When the third piece was taken away, I burst into the room again—and oh, my God! what a spectacle for a mother's eye! The wound torn open, the blood still gushing from it, and the bed literally covered with blood. Joseph was pale as a corpse, and large drops of sweat were rolling down his face, whilst upon every feature was depicted the utmost agony!

I was immediately forced from the room, and detained until the operation was completed; but when the act was accomplished, Joseph put upon a clean bed, the room cleared of every appearance of blood, and the instruments which were used in the operation removed, I was permitted again to enter.

Joseph immediately commenced getting better, and from this onward, continued to mend until he became strong and healthy. When he had so far recovered as to be able to travel, he went with his uncle, Jesse Smith, to Salem, for the benefit of his health, hoping the sea-breezes would be of service to him, and in this he was not disappointed.

Having passed through about a year of sickness and distress, health again returned to our family, and we most assuredly realized the blessing; and indeed, we felt to acknowledge the hand of God, more in preserving our lives through such a tremendous scene of affliction, than if we had, during this time, seen nothing but health and prosperity (1958, pp. 54–58).

Overview of Events and Life in Palmyra (1816–1830)

Newel Knight

On the first day of June, 1830, the first conference was held by the Church, at Fayette, New York. Our number consisted of about thirty, besides many others who came to learn of our principles, or were already believers, but had not been baptized. . . .

Soon after conference Joseph Smith . . . came to Colesville to make us a visit. There were many in our neighborhood who believed and were anxiously waiting for an opportunity to be baptized. Meeting was appointed for the Sabbath, and on Saturday afternoon we erected a dam across a stream which was close by, with the intention of baptizing those who applied on Sunday. But during the night a mob collected and tore away the dam....

Early on Monday morning we were on the alert, and before our enemies were aware of it, Oliver Cowdery proceeded to baptize Emma Smith, Hezekiah Peck and wife, Joseph Knight and wife, ... Levi Hall, Polly Knight, and Julia Stringham. But before the baptism was entirely finished, the mob began to collect again. We retired to my father's house, and the mob, which numbered about fifty, surrounded the house, raging with anger, and apparently wishing to commit violence against us. So violent and troublesome were they that the brethren were obliged to leave my father's house, and they succeeded in reaching mine. The mob, who soon found where they had gone, followed them, and it was only by great prudence on our part and help from our Heavenly Father that they were kept from laying violent hands upon us.

A meeting had been appointed for the evening to confirm those who had been baptized in the morning. The time appointed had arrived, and our friends had nearly all collected together, when, to our great surprise and sorrow, the constable came and arrested Brother Joseph Smith, Jun., on a warrant charging him with being a disorderly person, and of setting the country in an uproar by preaching the Book of Mormon.

The constable, soon after he had arrested Joseph, told him that the plan of those who had got out the warrant for his arrest was to get him into the hands of the mob who were now lying in ambush for him, and that he, the constable, was determined to save Joseph from them, as he found him to be a different person to what he had been represented. This proved true, for they had not proceeded far from the house when the wagon in which Joseph and the constable were riding was surrounded by the mob, who seemed only to await some signal from the constable. But to their great discomfiture, he gave the horses the whip and was soon out of their reach.

As the constable was driving briskly along, one of the wagon wheels came off, which accident left them almost in the hands of the mob who had pursued them closely. But the constable was an expert man and managed to get the wheel on again before the mob overtook him, and soon left them in the rear once more.

He drove on to the town of South Bainbridge, Chenango County, where he lodged Joseph in an upper room of a tavern; and in order that all might be safe for himself and Joseph, he slept during the night with his feet against the door, and kept a loaded gun by him (Joseph occupied a bed in the same room), and declared that if they were unlawfully molested he would fight for Joseph and defend him to the utmost of his ability.

On the following day a court was convened for the purpose of investigating the charges which had been made against Joseph Smith, Jun. On account of the many scandalous reports which had been put in circulation, a great excitement prevailed. My father, Joseph Knight, Sen., did not let the opportunity pass of doing all in his power to assist this persecuted boy. He went to two of his neighbors, James Davidson and John Reid, Esqs., respectable farmers who were well versed in the laws of their country, and retained them in behalf of Joseph during his trial.

The trial commenced among a crowded multitude of spectators. . . . Among the witnesses called up against Joseph was one Josiah Stoal, a gentleman for whom Joseph formerly worked. He was examined as follows:

Question—"Did not the prisoner, Joseph Smith, have a horse from you?"

Answer—"Yes."

Q.—"Did he not go to you and tell you an angel had appeared unto him and told him to get the horse from you?"

A.—"No, he told me no such thing."

Q.—"Well, how did he get the horse from you?"

A.—"He bought it from me the same as any other man would do."

Q.—"Have you had your pay?"

A.—"That is not your business."

The question being repeated, the witness replied, "I hold his note for the price of the horse, which I consider as good as the money; for I am well acquainted with Joseph Smith, Jun., and know him to be honest, and, if he wishes, I am ready to let him have another horse on the same terms."

Mr. Jonathan Thompson was next called and examined.

Question—"Has not the prisoner, Joseph Smith, Jun., had a yoke of oxen of you?"

Answer—"Yes."

Q.—"Did he not obtain them from you by telling you that he had had a revelation to the effect that he was to have them?"

A.—"No, he did not mention a word of the kind concerning the oxen; he purchased them the same as any other man would."

After several more similar attempts the court was detained for a time in order that two young ladies, daughters of Josiah Stoal, with whom Joseph had at times kept company, might be sent for, in order, if possible, to elicit something from them which could be made a pretext against Joseph.

The young ladies came and were each examined as to his character and conduct in general, but in particular as to his behavior towards them in public and private. They both bore such testimony in Joseph's favor as to leave his enemies without a cause for complaint. Several attempts were made to prove something against Joseph, and even circumstances which were alleged to have taken place in Broome County were brought forward. But these Joseph's lawyers would not admit against him, in consequence of which his persecutors managed to detain the court until they had succeeded in obtaining a warrant from Broome County. This warrant they served upon him at the very moment he had been acquitted by the court.

The constable who served this second warrant upon Joseph had no sooner arrested him than he began to abuse him. So heartless was he that, although Joseph had been kept all day in court without anything to eat since the morning, he hurried him off to Broome County, a distance of about fifteen miles, before allowing him to eat. The constable took him to a tavern where were gathered a number of men who used every means to abuse, ridicule, and insult him. They spit upon him, pointed their fingers at him, saying, "Prophesy! prophesy!" Thus did they imitate those who crucified the Savior of mankind, not knowing what they did.

The tavern was but a short distance from Joseph's own house. He wished to spend the night with his wife, offering to give any bail desired for his appearance. But this was denied him. He applied for something to eat. The constable ordered him some crusts of bread and some water, which was the only fare he received that night. At length he retired to bed. The constable made him lie next to the wall. He then laid himself down, threw his arms around Joseph, as if fearing that he intended to escape; and in this manner was Joseph compelled to spend the night.

Next day he was brought before the magistrate's court of Colesville, Broome County, and placed on trial. His friends and lawyers were again at his side, and his former persecutors were arrayed against him with the rage and fury of demons visible upon their countenances, and manifested in their actions. Many witnesses were again examined, some of whom swore to the most palpable falsehoods, just as those had done who appeared against him the previous day. But they contradicted themselves so plainly that the court would not admit their testimony. Others were called who showed by their zeal that they were willing to prove anything against him. But all they could do was to tell some things that they had heard somebody else say about him.

They proceeded for a considerable time in this frivolous and vexatious manner, when finally I was called upon and examined by Lawyer Seymour, who had been sent for specially for this occasion. One lawyer, Burch, was also retained on the prosecution. But Mr. Seymour seemed to be a more zealous Presbyterian, and seemed more anxious and determined that the people should not be deluded by any one professing godliness and not denying the power thereof.

As soon as I had been sworn, Mr. Seymour proceeded to interrogate me as follows:

Question—"Did the prisoner, Joseph Smith, Jun., cast the devil out of you?"

Answer—"No, sir."

Question—"Why, have you not had the devil cast out of you?"

Answer—"Yes, sir."

Question—"And had not Joseph Smith some hand in it being done?"

Answer—"Yes, sir."

Question—"And did he not cast him out of you?"

Answer—"No, sir. It was done by the power of God, and Joseph Smith was the instrument in the hands of God on this occasion. He commanded him to come out of me in the name of Jesus Christ."

Question—"And are you sure it was the devil?"

Answer—"Yes, sir."

Question—"Did you see him after he was cast out of you?"

Answer—"Yes sir, I saw him."

Question—"Pray, what did he look like?"

(Here one of the lawyers on the part of the defense told me I need not answer that question.) I replied: "I believe, I need not answer you that question, but I will do it if I am allowed to ask you one, and you can answer it. Do you, Mr. Seymour, understand the things of the Spirit?"

"No," answered Mr. Seymour. "I do not pretend to such big things."

"Well, then," I replied, "it will be of no use for me to tell you what the devil looked like, for it was a spiritual sight and spiritually discerned, and, of course, you would not understand it were I to tell you of it."

The lawyer dropped his head, while the loud laugh of the audience proclaimed his discomfiture.

Mr. Seymour now addressed the court and in a long and violent harangue endeavored to blacken the character of Joseph, and bring him in guilty of the charges preferred against him.

Messrs. Davidson and Reid followed on Joseph's behalf. They held forth in true colors the nature of the prosecution, the malignity of intention, and the apparent disposition of the prosecution to persecute their client rather than to do him justice. They took up the different arguments that had been brought forward by the lawyers for the prosecution, and having shown their utter futility and misapplication they proceeded to scrutinize the evidence which had been adduced, and each in his turn thanked God that he had been engaged in so good a cause as that of defending a man whose character stood so well the test of such a strict investigation.

In fact these men, although not regular lawyers, were, upon this occasion, able to put to silence their opponents, and convince the court that Joseph Smith, Jun., was innocent. They spoke like men inspired of God, while those who were arrayed against Joseph trembled under the sound of their voices and shook before them as criminals before the bar of justice. Disappointment and shame were depicted on the faces of the assembled multitude, who now began to learn that nothing could be sustained against Joseph.

The constable, who had arrested Joseph and treated him in so cruel and heartless a manner, came forward and apologized and asked his forgiveness for the ill-treatment he had given him. So much was this man changed that he told Joseph the mob had resolved if the court acquitted him that they would take him, tar and feather him, and ride him on a rail; and further, that if Joseph wished, he would lead him out another way, so that he could escape in safety.

After all the efforts of the people and court to sustain the charges brought against Joseph proved an entire failure, he was discharged and succeeded in making good his escape from the mob through the instrumentality of his new friend, the constable. . . .

After a few days the Prophet, accompanied by Oliver Cowdery, came to my house, intending to confirm those who had been baptized. These servants of God had scarcely arrived when the mob began to collect, and so violent were they that it was thought best for Joseph and Oliver to make their escape lest they should suffer at the hands of our enemies. They left without taking any refreshment, the mob closely pursuing them, and it was ofttimes as much as Joseph and Oliver could do to escape them. However, by traveling all night, excepting a short time when they were forced to lie down and rest themselves under a tree, alternately watching and sleeping, they managed to get beyond the reach of their pursuers (1969, pp. 52–61).

Wandle Mace

Almost as soon as the father [Joseph Smith Sr.] and mother [Lucy Smith] of the Prophet Joseph Smith set their feet upon the hospitable shore of Illinois, I became acquainted with them. I frequently visited them and listened with intense interest as they related the history of the rise of the Church in every detail.

With tears they could not withhold, they narrated the story of the persecution of their boy, Joseph, which commenced when he was about fourteen years old, or from the time the angel first visited him. Not only was the boy, Joseph, persecuted but the aged father was harassed and imprisoned on false charges until finally driven from Missouri in the depth of winter he contracted disease from exposure, from which he never recovered.

In these conversations, mother [Lucy] Smith, as she was familiarly called, related much of their family history. She told how their family would all be seated around the room while they all listened to Joseph with the greatest interest as he taught them the pure principles of the gospel as revealed to him by the angels, and of his glorious vision of the Father and the Son, when the father said to him as he pointed to his companion, "This is my beloved Son, hear Him."

She said, "During the day our sons would endeavor to get through their work as early as possible, and say, 'Mother, have supper early, so we can have a long evening to listen to Joseph.' Sometimes Joseph would describe the appearance of the Nephites, their mode of dress and warfare, their implements of husbandry, etc., and many things he had seen in vision. Truly ours was a happy family, although persecuted by preachers, who declared there was no more vision, the canon of scripture was full, and no more revelation was needed." But Joseph had seen a vision and must declare it.

Oh, how many happy hours I have spent with these good old folks.

They were as honest and true as it was possible for mortals to be; and they exemplify the words of the Apostle who said, "All who will live godly in Christ Jesus, shall suffer persecution" [2 Tim. 3:21] (n.d. [a]).

Orrin Porter Rockwell

Orrin Porter Rockwell was a pioneer from the day that Joseph received his first vision or visitation by holy beings; from his own statement made to me [Elizabeth Roundy] in 1875 when he came to me to write the history of his life. He stated that Joseph Smith's father and mother used to come to his father's house and tell his parents of the wonderful things that were being revealed to their son Joseph. He said he used to watch for their coming and plead with his mother to let him stay up to keep the pine torch burning, as that was the only means they used to illuminate their dwelling. When they spoke of getting means to print the Book of Mormon Porter determined to help, and as he had no other way he went after his day's work was done and picked berries by moonlight and in the early morning and sold the berries and gave Joseph the money to help with the printing. He also gathered wood [and] hauled it to town and sold it and used the means for the same purpose. No man loved Joseph the Prophet more than O. P. Rockwell. He was not one having the advantage of education but his heart was devoted to the cause of truth. He would not have hesitated to have given his life for Joseph at any time. He accompanied Joseph with others when he went to Washington to ask for redress of President Van Buren; also went with Joseph and Hyrum when they started to come West. He was sent by Joseph to his wife Emma with a message and through that some brethren went with him to see the Prophet and patriarch and persuaded them to return, which he always spoke of with regret and manifestations of grief (n.d.).

Orlando Saunders

Mr. Saunders is a man seventy-eight years old [in March 1881]; a fair type of the intelligent New York farmer; seemingly well-to-do in this world's goods; and quite active for a man of his years; and withal, has an honest and thoughtful face.

Entering upon conversation with reference to our business, Mr. Saunders at once said:

"Well, you have come to a poor place to find out anything. I don't know anything against these men, myself." (Evidently judging that we wanted to get something against them, only.)

"Were you acquainted with the Smiths, Mr. Saunders?"

"Yes, sir; I knew all of the Smith family well. They have all worked for me many a day. They were very good people. Young Joe (as we called him then) has worked for me, and he was a good worker."

"In what respect did they differ from other people, if at all?"

"I never noticed that they were different from other neighbors. They were the best family in the neighborhood in case of sickness; one was at my house nearly all the time when my father died. I always thought them honest. They were owing me some money when they left here. One of them came back in about a year and paid me."

"How were they as to habits of drinking and getting drunk?"

"Everybody drank a little in those days, and the Smiths with the rest; they never got drunk to my knowledge."

" . . . How well did you know young Joseph Smith?"

"Oh, just as well as one could, very well. He has worked for me many a time, and been about my place a great deal. He stopped with me many a time, when through here, after they went west to Kirtland. He was always a gentleman when about my place."

"What did you know about his finding that book, or the plates in the hill over here?"

"He always claimed that he saw the angel and received the book; but I don't know anything about it. Have seen it, but never read it as I know of; didn't care anything about it."

"Well; you seem to differ a little from a good many of the stories told about these people."

"I have told you just what I know about them, and you will have to go somewhere else for a different story" (1881).

EMMA HALE SMITH

In an interview conducted in February, 1879, by Joseph Smith III, the son of Joseph and Emma Smith, the following questions and answers were given. Also present during the interview were a Bishop Rogers, Elders W. W. Blair, H. A. Stebbins, Emma's husband, Lewis C. Bidamon, and "a few others," all of whom were members of the Reorganized Church of Jesus Christ of Latter day Saints. The interview was conducted in Nauvoo,

Ill., the questions having been written and agreed upon prior to the interview.

Question.—Who performed the marriage ceremony for Joseph Smith and Emma Hale? When? Where?

Answer.—I was married at South Bainbridge, New York; at the house of Squire Tarbell, by him, when I was in my 22nd or 23rd year.

We here suggested that Mother Smith's *History* gave the date of the marriage as January 18th, 1827. To this she replied:

I think the date correct. My certificate of marriage was lost many years ago, in some of the marches we were forced to make.

In answer to a suggestion by us that she might mistake about who married father and herself; and that it was rumored that it was Sidney Rigdon, or a Presbyterian clergyman, she stated:

It was not Sidney Rigdon, for I did not see him for years after that. It was not a Presbyterian clergyman. I was visiting at Mr. Stowell's, who lived in Bainbridge, and saw your father there. I had no intention of marrying when I left home; but, during my visit at Stowell's, your father visited me there. My folks were bitterly opposed to him; and, being importuned by your father, aided by Mr. Stowell, who urged me to marry him, and preferring to marry him to any other man I knew, I consented. We went to Squire Tarbell's and were married. Afterwards, when father found that I was married, he sent for us. The account in Mother Smith's *History* is substantially correct as to date and place. Your father bought your uncle Jesse's [Hale] place, off father's farm, and we lived there till the Book of Mormon was translated; and I think published. I was not in Palmyra long.

Question.—How many children did you lose, mother, before I was born?

Answer.—There were three. I buried one in Pennsylvania, and a pair of twins in Ohio.

Question.—Who were the twins that died?

Answer.—They were not named.

Question.—Who were the twins that you took to raise?

Answer.—I lost twins. Mrs. Murdock had twins and died. Bro. [John] Murdock came to me and asked me to take them, and I took the babes. Joseph died at eleven months. They were both sick when your father was mobbed. The mob who tarred and feathered him left the door open when they went out with him, the child relapsed and died. Julia lived, though weaker than the boy.

Question.—When did you first know Sidney Rigdon? Where?

Answer.—I was residing at Father Whitmer's when I first saw Sidney Rigdon. I think he came there.

Question.—Was this before or after the publication of the Book of Mormon?

Answer.—The Book of Mormon had been translated and published some time before. Parley P. Pratt had united with the Church before I knew Sidney Rigdon, or heard of him. At the time the Book of Mormon was translated there was no church organized, and Rigdon did not become acquainted with Joseph and me till after the Church was established in 1830. How long after that I do not know, but it was some time.

Question.—Who were scribes for father when translating the Book of Mormon?

Answer.—Myself, Oliver Cowdery, Martin Harris, and my brother, Reuben Hale.

Question.—Was Alva Hale one?

Answer.—I think not. He may have written some; but if he did, I do not remember it. . . .

Question.—Had he [Joseph] not a book or manuscript from which he read [when translating], or dictated to you?

Answer.—He had neither manuscript nor book to read from.

Question.—Could he not have had, and you not know it?

Answer.—If he had had anything of the kind he could not have concealed it from me.

Question.—Are you sure that he had the plates at the time you were writing for him?

Answer.—The plates often lay on the table without any attempt at concealment, wrapped in a small linen table cloth, which I had given him to fold them in. I once felt of the plates, as they thus lay on the table, tracing their outline and shape. They seemed to be pliable like thick paper, and would rustle with a metallic sound when the edges were moved by the thumb, as one does sometimes thumb the edges of a book.

Question.—Where did father and Oliver Cowdery write?

Answer.—Oliver Cowdery and your father wrote in the room where I was at work.

Question.—Could not Father have dictated the Book of Mormon to you, Oliver Cowdery, and the others who wrote for him, after having first written it, or having first read it out of some book?

Answer.—Joseph Smith (and for the first time she used his name direct, having usually used the words, "your father," or "my husband") could neither write nor dictate a coherent and well-worded letter, let alone dictating a book like the Book of Mormon. And, though I was an active participant in the scenes that transpired, and was present during the translation of the plates, and had cognizance of things as they transpired, it is marvelous to me, "a marvel and a wonder," as much so as to any one else.

Question.—I should suppose that you would have uncovered the plates and examined them?

Answer.—I did not attempt to handle the plates, other than I have told you, nor uncover them to look at them. I was satisfied that it was the work of God, and therefore did not feel it to be necessary to do so.

Major Bidamon here suggested: Did Mr. Smith forbid your examining the plates?

Answer.—I do not think he did. I knew that he had them, and was not specially curious about them. I moved them from place to place on the table, as it was necessary in doing my work.

Question.—Mother, what is your belief about the authenticity, or origin of the Book of Mormon?

Answer.—My belief is that the Book of Mormon is of divine authenticity—I have not the slightest doubt of it. I am satisfied that no man could have dictated the writing of the manuscript unless he was inspired; for, when [I was] acting as his scribe, your father would dictate to me hour after hour; and when returning after meals, or after interruptions, he would at once begin where he had left off, without either seeing the manuscript or having any portion of it read to him. It would have been improbable that a learned man could do this; and, for one so ignorant and unlearned as he was, it was simply impossible.

Question.—What was the condition of feeling between you and father?

Answer.—It was good.

Question.—Were you in the habit of quarreling?

Answer.—No. There was no necessity of any quarreling. He knew that I wished for nothing but what was right; and, as he wished for nothing else, we did not disagree. He usually gave some heed unto what I had to say. It was quite a grievous thing to many that I had any influence with him. . . .

Question.—By whom were you baptized? Do you remember?

Answer.—I think by Oliver Cowdery, at Bainbridge.

Question.—You say you were married at South Bainbridge, and have used the word Bainbridge. Were they one and the same town?

Answer.—No. There was Bainbridge and South Bainbridge; some distance apart; how far I don't know. I was in South Bainbridge (1879, pp. 289–90).

George A. Smith

Forty-seven times he was arraigned before the tribunals of law, and had to sustain all the expense of defending himself in those vexatious suits, and was every time acquitted. He was never found guilty but once. I have been told, by Patriarch Emer Harris, that on a certain occasion he was brought before a magistrate in the state of New York, and charged with having cast out devils; the magistrate, after hearing the witnesses, decided that he was guilty, but as the statutes of New York did not provide a punishment for casting out devils, he was acquitted (JD, 2:213).

Lucy Mack Smith

When the time had nearly arrived for the last payment to be made [on the Smith home], and when my husband was about starting for Mr. Stoal's and Mr. Knight's in order to get the money to make the same, Joseph called my husband and myself aside and said, "I have been very lonely ever since Alvin died and I have concluded to get married, and if you have no objections to my uniting myself in marriage with Miss Emma Hale, she would be my choice in preference to any other woman I have ever seen." We were pleased with his choice and not only consented to his marrying her, but requested him to bring her home with him and live with us (1958, p. 93).

John Stafford

[John Stafford] is now a retired physician, being too aged and infirm to practice. Answering a question as to the character of Joseph Smith, he said:

"He was a real clever, jovial boy. What [Pomeroy] Tucker said about them was false, absolutely. My father, William Stafford, was never connected with them in any way. The Smiths, with others, were digging for money before Joe got the plates. My father had a stone, which some thought they could look through, and old Mrs. Smith came there after it one day, but never got it. Saw them digging one time for money (this was three or four years before the Book of Mormon was found), the Smiths and others. The old man and Hyrum were there, I think, but Joseph was not there. The neighbors used to claim Sally Chase could look at a stone she had, and see money. Willard Chase used to dig when she found where the money was. Don't know as anybody ever found any money."

"What was the character of Smith, as to his drinking?"

"It was common for everybody to drink, and to have drink in the field; one time Joe, while working for some one after he was married, drank too much boiled cider. He came in with his shirt torn; his wife felt bad about it, and when they went home, she put her shawl on him."

"Had he been fighting and drunk?"

"No; he had been scuffling with some of the boys. Never saw him fight; have known him to scuffle; would do a fair day's work if hired out to a man; but were poor managers."

"What about the black sheep your father let them have?"

"I have heard that story, but don't think my father was there at the time they say Smith got the sheep. I don't know anything about it."

"You were living at home at the time, and it seems you ought to know if they got a sheep, or stole one, from your father?"

"They never stole one, I am sure; they may have got one sometime."

"Well, Doctor, you know pretty well whether that story is true or not, that Tucker tells. What do you think of it?"

"I don't think it is true. I would have heard more about it, that is [if it were] true. I lived a mile from the Smiths. They were peaceable. The old woman had a great deal of faith that their children were going to do something great. Joe was quite illiterate. After they began to have school at their house, he improved greatly."

"Did they have school in their own house?"

"Yes, sir, they had school in their house, and studied the Bible."

"Who was their teacher?"

"They did not have any teacher; they taught themselves."

" . . . If young Smith was as illiterate as you say, Doctor, how do you account for the Book of Mormon?"

"Well, I can't; except that Sidney Rigdon was connected with them."

"What makes you think he was connected with them?"

"Because I can't account for the Book of Mormon any other way."

"Was Rigdon ever around there before the Book of Mormon was published?"

"No, not as we could ever find out. Sidney Rigdon was never there, that Hurlburt, or Howe, or Tucker could find out."

"Well, you have been looking out for the facts a long time, have you not, Doctor?"

"Yes, I have been thinking and hearing about it for the last fifty years, and lived right among all their old neighbors there most of the time."

"And no one has ever been able to trace the acquaintance of Rigdon and Smith, until after the Book of Mormon was published, and Rigdon was proselyted by Parley P. Pratt, in Ohio?"

"Not that I know of" (1881).

Thomas H. Taylor

To our inquiries if he was acquainted with the Smiths, and the early settlers throughout that part sometimes called Mormons, Mr. Taylor said: "Yes, I knew them very well. They were very nice men, too. The only trouble was they were ahead of the people; and the people, as in every such case, turned out to abuse them, because they had the manhood to stand for their own convictions. I have seen such work all through life."

"What did the Smiths do that the people abused them so?"

"They did not do anything. Why! these rascals at one time took Joseph Smith and ducked him in the pond that you see over there, just because he preached what he believed, and for nothing else. And if Jesus Christ had been there, they would have done the same to Him. Now I don't believe like he did; but every man has a right to his religious opinions, and to advocate his views, too. If people don't like it, let them come out and meet him on the stand, and show his error. Smith was always ready to exchange views with the best men they had."

"Why didn't they like Smith?"

"To tell the truth, there was something about him they could not understand. Some way he knew more than they did, and it made them mad."

"But a good many tell terrible stories, about them being rogues, and liars, and such things. How is that?"

"Oh! they are a set of d——d liars. I have had a home here, and been here, except when on business, all my life—ever since I came to this country—and I know these fellows. They make these lies on Smith, because they love a lie better than the truth. I can take you to a great many old settlers here who will substantiate what I say, and if you want to go, just come around to my place across the street there, and I'll go with you."

"Well, that is very kind, Mr. Taylor, and fair; if we have time we will call around and give you the chance; but we are first going to see these fellows who, so rumor says, know so much against them."

"All right; but you will find they don't know anything against those men when you put them down to it. They could never sustain anything against Smith."

"Do you think Smith ever got any plates out of the hill he claimed to?"

"Yes; I rather think he did. Why not he find something as well as anybody else. Right over here, in Illinois and Ohio, in mounds there, they have discovered copper plates since, with hieroglyphics all over them; and quite a number of the old settlers around here testified that Smith showed the plates to them—they were good, honest men, and what is the sense of saying they lied. Now, I never saw the Book of Mormon—don't know anything about it, nor care; and don't know as it was ever translated from the plates. You have heard about the Spaulding romance; and some claim that it is nothing but the books of the Bible that were rejected by the compilers of the Bible; but all this don't prove that Smith never got any plates" (1881).

The First Vision (Spring 1820)

Allen Coates

"Joseph Smith (Jr.) raked and bound [that is, raking and binding hay] [for] my grandfather when he was in the cradle on the folks homestead on a little outright east of where our residence was."

The Smiths "they came here awful poor people from out toward Victor somewhere. I didn't know too much about them beyond that, but he [Joseph, Jr.] was a poor boy. . . ."

" . . . And Grandpa, at that time they were having revival meetings in the Methodist Church and my grandfather invited Joseph Smith, the boy, to go up with him, you see. And, a great revival, trying to experience both things and he got interested and excited and involved in the meeting so that when he went home he had some kind of a dream or vision or something.

And, Grandfather, a great man, talked religion any [?], while he was working, see. And he got the boy interested And he said, "Are you ready to go to a meeting with me?" Well, the boy agreed to it right away because everything looked bright in that way to him and he was getting on the road somewheres where he ought to be. And so they went over to the meeting and he got so interested in it, he caught the spirit sometime. And he had a vision afterwards but it didn't seem to be what you'd think a person would get out of a revival hardly. But he claimed he was led into some orchard, they call it the sacred orchard, you know, the Mormons do, out near Palmyra."

" . . . (Joseph) was a good boy to work. I heard that. Oh yes, there was nothing lazy about him. He was up and coming and looking to get ahead and he got more inspiration from my old grandfather" (1974).

Joseph Curtis

In the spring of 1835 [October 1834] Joseph Smith and company with his father and mother and some others came to Michigan and paid us a visit. In a meeting [he] stated the reason why he preached the doctrine he did. I will state a few things according to my memory. As a revival of some of the sects was going on, some of his father's family joined in the revival. Himself being quite young, [and] he feeling an anxiety to be religious, [and] his mind [being] somewhat troubled, this scripture came to his mind, which says, "If a man lacks wisdom, let him ask of God, who giveth liberally and upbraideth not." Believing it, he went with a determination to obtain [wisdom], to enquire of the Lord himself. After some struggle the Lord manifested to him that the different sects were wrong; also that the Lord had a great work for him to do. It worried his mind; he told his father, [and] his father told him to do as the Lord manifested. [He] had other manifestations . . . [and he] saw an angel with a view of this hill Cumorah and the plates of gold; [he then] had certain instructions, got the plates by the assistance of the Urim and Thummim, translated them by the gift and power of God. . . . [He] also stated he [had] done nothing more than he was commanded to do; for this his name was cast out as evil; for this he was persecuted (1881).

Orson Pratt

When he was thus praying he saw a light which appeared to be approaching him from the heavens. As it came nearer it seemed to grow brighter until it settled upon the tops of the trees. He thought it would consume the leaves of the trees; but it gradually descended and rested upon him. His mind was immediately caught away. He saw in this light two glorious personages, one of whom spoke to him, pointing to the other, saying, "This is my beloved Son, hear ye him." This was a glorious vision given to this boy. When these persons interrogated him to know what he desired, he answered and said, "Lord, show me which is the true church." He was then informed by one of these personages that there was no true church upon the face of the whole earth (JD, 14:141).

William Smith

The people in our neighborhood were very much stirred up with regard to religious matters by the preaching of a Mr. Lane, an elder of the Methodist Church, and celebrated throughout the country as a "great revival preacher."

My mother, who was a very pious woman and much interested in the welfare of her children, both here and hereafter, made use of every means which her parental love could suggest, to get us engaged in seeking for our soul's salvation, or (as the term then was) "in getting religion." She prevailed on us to attend the meetings, and almost the whole family became interested in the matter, and seekers after truth. I attended the meetings with the rest, but being quite young and inconsiderate, did not take so much interest in the matter as the older ones did. This extraordinary excitement prevailed not only in our neighborhood but throughout the whole country. It extended from the Methodists to the Baptists, from them to the Presbyterians; and so on until finally, almost all the sects became engaged in it; and it became quite the fashion to "get religion." My mother continued her importunities and exertions to interest us in the importance of seeking for the salvation of our immortal souls, until almost all of the family became either converted or seriously inclined (1883, pp. 6–7).

William Smith

"What caused Joseph to ask for guidance as to what church he ought to join," asked Brother Briggs.

"Why, there was a joint revival in the neighborhood between the Baptists, Methodists, and Presbyterians and they had succeeded in stirring up quite a feeling, and after the meeting the question arose which church should have the converts. Rev. Stockton was the president of the meeting and suggested that it was their meeting and under their care and they had a church there and they ought to join the Presbyterians, but as father did not like Rev. Stockton very well, our folks hesitated, and the next evening a Rev. Mr. Lane of the Methodists preached a sermon on 'what church shall I join?' And the burden of his discourse was to ask God, using as a text 'If any of you lack wisdom, let him ask of God, who giveth to all men liberally. . . .' And of course when Joseph went home and was looking over the text he was impressed to do just what the preacher had said, and going out in the woods with child-like, simple trusting faith believing that God meant just what He said, he kneeled down and prayed; and the time having come for the reorganization of His church, God was pleased to show him that he should join none of these churches but if faithful he should be chosen to establish the true Church" (1891).

William Smith

It will be remembered that just before the angel appeared to Joseph there was an unusual revival in the neighborhood. It spread from town to town, from city to city, from county to county, and from state to state. My mother attended those meetings, and being much concerned about the spiritual welfare of the family, she persuaded them to attend the meetings. Finally my mother, one sister, my brothers Samuel and Hyrum became Presbyterians. Joseph and myself did not join; I had not sown all my wild oats. At the close of these meetings the different ministers began to beat around to see how many converts they could get to join their respective churches. All said, "Come and join us, we are right." . . . And here let me say, that it was at the suggestion of the Rev. M_____, that my brother asked of God. He said, "Ask of God." It was the church of Christ he was seeking for, what all should seek. God promised to give knowledge to all who lacked it, if they would ask. Accordingly he went and bowed in prayer to God. While he was engaged in prayer, he saw a pillar of fire descending. Saw it reach the top of the trees. He was overcome, became unconscious, did not know how long he remained in this condition, and when he came to himself, the great light was about him, and he was told by the personage whom he saw descend with the light, not to join any of the churches (1884, p. 643).

Edward Stevenson

In 1834 Joseph Smith the Prophet preached with such power as had not there ever before been witnessed in this nineteenth century. The brother of the Prophet, Hyrum, also the father of them, Joseph Senior, were with him. Let me as a living witness speak of the moving, stirring sensation created in this town [that is, Pontiac,] and surrounding country of the then territory of Michigan. The Church was only in its infancy then, and much less evil spoken of; less opposition was met and fewer lies were in circulation respecting the Saints. Infidelity was scarcely thought of or spoken of, and skepticism very rare in that period. Consequently there were more who were willing to listen, reflect upon and digest the new doctrines, and eventually to obey it.

There have been alterations and improvements made regarding the schoolhouse, but these are the exact premises where people thronged in large numbers, more than could be able to find even standing space, in and around the house. Not the least disturbance or resistance was offered until Satan came also; but the good word had taken deep root, as seed sown on good ground, which could not be rooted out. I can very well remember many of the words of the boy Prophet as they were uttered in simplicity, but with a power which was irresistible to all present, although at that time I could not understand how it was that so few comparatively obeyed it. Three elder brothers of mine, as well as our neighbors, repeatedly in my hearing spoke highly of the new doctrines—that they were scriptural, so plainly set forth, and that, too, with such force as never before was experienced in this section of country. Here are some of the Prophet's words, as uttered in the schoolhouse. With uplifted hand he said: "I am a witness that there is a God, for I saw Him in open day, while praying in a silent grove, in the spring of 1820." He further testified that God, the Eternal Father, pointing to a separate personage, in the likeness of Himself, said: "This is my Beloved Son; hear ye Him." O how these words thrilled my entire system, and filled me with joy unspeakable to behold one who, like Paul the apostle of olden time, could with boldness testify that he had been in the presence of Jesus Christ!

The young Prophet further said that in 1823, three years after his first vision, while praying in his father's house (I have been so highly favored of the Lord as to have been in the very house where the servant of God said he was fervently praying), when suddenly the house was filled with light brighter than the noon-day sun, in the midst of which there stood an angel, who said he was sent from the presence of God, as a messenger to him. The angel instructed him regarding a marvelous work that God was about to bring to pass, and that he, Joseph, was the one who was selected to be God's servant and mouthpiece to bring about and establish the great and marvelous work. "Three times," said the young man, "did this angel continue his visits during the same night, each time repeating the same instructions, only extending some little, and quoting several passages of scripture relating to the great work which was to come forth." In closing the last visit the angel invited the boy to meet him on a neighboring hill, two miles away from his father's house, where he would give him still further instructions and permit him to see a book of gold plates containing a history of two nations who had previously inhabited this great land of America. So plainly was this made known that on the next day Joseph said he was able to find the exact place, and met the angel as requested.

More than two hours were occupied during that evening meeting, and so absorbing and interesting was the discourse that no one seemed to be weary, or to realize so much time had been consumed. A succession of meetings were held, in which the Prophet was joined, and very interestingly, too, by the three witnesses to the Book of Mormon. During his visit to this branch the Prophet testified that he was instructed to organize a Church after the pattern of the Church which Jesus organized, with twelve Apostles, seventies, elders, gifts, and blessings, with signs following, as found recorded in the sixteenth chapter of Mark, which he read and explained; adding that God had fulfilled the words of John the Revelator, "And I saw another angel fly in the midst of heaven, having the everlasting gospel to preach unto them that dwell on the earth, and to every nation, and kindred, and tongue, and people. Saying with a loud voice, Fear God, and give glory to him; for the hour of his judgment is come." The angel had done his work; the true Church was set up with, first Apostles, secondarily Prophets, with gifts, etc.; "And as a servant of God," said Joseph, "I promise you, inasmuch as you will repent and be baptized for the remission of your sins, you shall receive the Holy Ghost, and speak with tongues, and the signs shall follow you, and by this you may test me as a prophet sent of God" (1894a, pp. 443–45).

CHARLES L. WALKER

[February 2, 1893] Brother John Alger said while speaking of the Prophet Joseph Smith, that when he, John, was a small boy he heard the Prophet Joseph relate his vision of seeing the Father and the Son, [and] that God touched his eyes with his finger and said, "Joseph, this is my Beloved Son, hear Him." As soon as the Lord had touched his eyes with

his finger he immediately saw the Savior. After meeting, a few of us questioned him about the matter, and he told us at the bottom of the meeting house steps that he was in the house of Father Smith in Kirtland when Joseph made this declaration, and that Joseph while speaking of it put his finger to his right eye, suiting the action with the words so as to illustrate and at the same time impress the occurrence on the minds of those unto whom he was speaking. We enjoyed the conversation very much, as it was something that we had never seen in church history or heard of before (1980, 1:755–56).

Note: It was mid-May 1831 that Father Smith moved onto a farm in Kirtland which had been purchased by the Prophet Joseph, and it was on 22 January 1838 that Mother Smith gave the Prophet's cousin, Elias Smith, power of attorney to sell all their Kirtland holdings. Thus we suppose that it was somewhere between May 1831 and January 1838 that the above-mentioned account of the First Vision occurred. Since John Alger was born 11 November 1820 he would have been between ten and a half and eighteen years of age. As Alger describes himself as "a small boy," we are left to guess that Joseph's expressions were made closer to 1831 than 1838. The observation that the Father appeared first, and then the Son, accords with Joseph Smith's 1835 account of the First Vision (see Backman, 1971, p. 159).

Witnesses to the Book of Mormon

Oliver Cowdery

Oliver Cowdery, after his excommunication in Far West, April 11th, 1838, engaged in law business and practiced for some years as a lawyer in Michigan, but he never denied the truth of the Book of Mormon. On the contrary, he seems to have used every opportunity he had to bear testimony of its divine origin. While in Michigan, a gentleman, on a certain occasion, addressed him as follows: "Mr. Cowdery, I see your name attached to this book. If you believe it to be true, why are you in Michigan?" The gentleman then read the names of the Three Witnesses and asked: "Mr. Cowdery, do you believe this book?" "No, sir," was the reply. "Very well," continued the gentleman, "but your name is attached to it, and you declare here (pointing to the book) that you saw an angel, and also the plates, from which the book purports to be translated; and now you say you don't believe it. Which time did you tell the truth?" Oliver Cowdery replied with emphasis, "My name is attached to that book, and what I there have said is true. I did see this; I know I saw it, and faith has nothing to do with it, as a perfect knowledge has swallowed up the faith which I had in the work, knowing, as I do, that it is true."

At a special conference held at Kanesville, Iowa, October 21st, 1848, Oliver Cowdery was present and made the following remarks:

"Friends and Brethren.—My name is Cowdery, Oliver Cowdery. In the early history of this Church I stood identified with her, and one in her councils. True it is that the gifts and callings of God are without repentance; not because I was better than the rest of mankind was I called; but to fulfill the purposes of God, He called me to a high and holy calling.

"I wrote, with my own pen, the entire Book of Mormon (save a few pages) as it fell from the lips of the Prophet Joseph Smith, as he translated it by the gift and power of God, by the means of the Urim and Thummim, or, as it is called by that book, 'holy interpreters.' I beheld with my eyes, and handled with my hands, the gold plates from which it was transcribed. I also saw with my eyes and handled with my hands the 'holy interpreters.' That book is true. Sidney Rigdon did not write it; Mr. Spaulding did not write it; I wrote it myself as it fell from the lips of the Prophet. It contains the everlasting gospel, and came forth to the children of men in fulfillment of the revelations of John, where he says he saw an angel come with the everlasting gospel to preach to every nation, kindred, tongue, and people. It contains principles of salvation; and if you, my hearers, will walk by its light and obey its precepts, you will be saved with an everlasting salvation in the kingdom of God on high. Brother Hyde has just said that it is very important that we keep and walk in the true channel, in order to avoid the sandbars. This is true. The channel is here. The holy priesthood is here.

"I was present with Joseph when an holy angel from God came down from heaven and conferred on us, or restored, the lesser or Aaronic Priesthood, and said to us, at the same time, that it should remain upon the earth while the earth stands.

"I was also present with Joseph when the higher or Melchisedek Priesthood was conferred by holy angels from on high. This priesthood we then conferred on each other, by the will and commandment of God. This priesthood, as was then declared, is also to remain upon the earth until the last remnant of time. This holy priesthood, or authority, we then conferred upon many, and is just as good and valid as though God had done it in person.

"I laid my hands upon that man—yes, I laid my right hand upon his head (pointing to Brother Hyde), and I conferred upon him this priesthood, and he holds that priesthood now. He was also called through me, by the prayer of faith, an Apostle of the Lord Jesus Christ."

Soon afterwards Oliver Cowdery was rebaptized, but while making preparations to come to Utah, he was suddenly stricken with death in Richmond, Mo., March 3rd, 1850. Elder Phinehas H. Young, who was present when he died, testifies:

His last moments were spent in bearing testimony of the truth of the gospel revealed through Joseph Smith, and the power of the holy priesthood, which he had received through his administration (CD, 2:164–65).

Martin Harris

The Prophet Joseph Smith, and Oliver Cowdery and David Whitmer and myself, went into a little grove to pray to obtain a promise that we should behold it with our natural eyes, that we could testify of it to the world. We prayed two or three times and at length an angel stood before Oliver and showed them the plates, but I had gone off by myself for I knew it was me that was keeping the angel from appearing. In my desperation I asked the Prophet seer to kneel down with me and to pray for me also that I may also see the plates, and we did kneel down and pray. Immediately, the angel stood before me and said, "Look" and when I glanced at the angel, I fell, but I stood on my feet and saw the angel turn the leaves of gold and I said, "It is enough, my Lord and my God." I then heard the voice of God say, "The book is true and translated correctly" (n.d., pp. 1–6).

Joseph B. Noble

I formed an acquaintance with Mary A. Beman. . . . My first introduction to this young woman was at McMillons, my place of boarding. She was teaching school in the neighborhood. Her father, Alvah Beman, lived about 2 1/2 miles distance. [He was] a man well off as to houses and land and goods of this world, and very highly esteemed among men for his word. This man was well acquainted with the Smith family before the coming forth of the Book of Mormon and was with Joseph [and] at one time assisted him in hiding the plates from a mob. He was permitted to handle the plates with a thin cloth covering them (n.d. [c], p. 3).

Joseph Smith

Not many days after the above commandment was given, we four, viz., Martin Harris, David Whitmer, Oliver Cowdery, and myself, agreed to retire into the woods, and try to obtain, by fervent and humble prayer, the fulfilment of the promises given in the above revelation—that they should have a view of the plates. We accordingly made choice of a piece of woods convenient to Mr. Whitmer's house, to which we retired, and having knelt down, we began to pray in much faith to Almighty God to bestow upon us a realization of these promises.

According to previous arrangement, I commenced prayer to our Heavenly Father, and was followed by each of the others in succession. We did not at the first trial, however, obtain any answer or manifestation of divine favor in our behalf. We again observed the same order of prayer, each calling on and praying fervently to God in rotation, but with the same result as before.

Upon this, our second failure, Martin Harris proposed that he should withdraw himself from us, believing, as he expressed himself, that his presence was the cause of our not obtaining what we wished for. He accordingly withdrew from us, and we knelt down again, and had not been many minutes engaged in prayer, when presently we beheld a light above us in the air, of exceeding brightness; and behold, an angel stood before us. In his hands he held the plates which we had been praying for these to have a view of. He turned over the leaves one by one, so that we could see them, and discern the engravings thereon distinctly. He then addressed himself to David Whitmer, and said, "David, blessed is the Lord, and he that keeps His commandments;" when, immediately afterwards, we heard a voice from out of the bright light above us, saying, "These plates have been revealed by the power of God, and they have been translated by the power of God. The translation of them which you have seen is correct, and I command you to bear record of what you now see and hear."

I now left David and Oliver, and went in pursuit of Martin Harris, whom I found at a considerable distance, fervently engaged in prayer. He soon told me, however, that he had not yet prevailed with the Lord, and earnestly requested me to join him in prayer, that he also might realize the same blessings which we had just received. We accordingly joined in prayer, and ultimately obtained our desires, for before we had yet finished, the same vision was opened to our view, at least it was again opened to me, and I once more beheld and heard the same things; whilst at the same moment, Martin Harris cried out, apparently in an ecstasy of joy, "'Tis enough; 'tis enough; mine eyes have beheld; mine eyes have beheld;" and jumping up, he shouted, "Hosanna," blessing God, and otherwise rejoiced exceedingly (HC, 1:54–55).

William Smith

[The following is from an interview conducted by "E. C. Briggs and others" of the Reorganized Church, with William Smith:]

"I did not see [the plates] uncovered, but I handled them and hefted them while wrapped in a tow frock and judged them to have weighed about sixty pounds. I could tell they were plates of some kind and that they were fastened together by rings running through the back. Their size was as described in mother's history.

" . . . Father and my brother Samuel saw them as I did, while in the frock. So did Hyrum and others of the family."

" . . . Didn't you want to remove the cloth and see the bare plates?" said Brother Briggs.

"No," he [William] replied, "for Father had just asked if he might not be permitted to do so, and Joseph, putting his hand on them said: 'No, I am instructed not to show them to anyone. If I do, I will transgress and lose them again.' Besides we did not care to have him break the commandments and suffer as he did before."

"Did you not doubt Joseph's testimony sometimes?" said Brother Briggs.

"No," was the reply, "We all had the most implicit confidence in what he said. He was a truthful boy. Father and mother believed him, why should not the children? I suppose if he had told crooked stories about other things we might have doubted his word about the plates, but Joseph was a truthful boy. That father and mother believed his report and suffered persecution for that belief shows that he was truthful. No, we never doubted his word for one minute" (1891).

David Whitmer

[The following interviews of David Whitmer by Orson Pratt and Joseph F. Smith took place at Richmond, Missouri, on the 7th and 8th of September, 1878. Elders Pratt and Smith had traveled east from Salt Lake City to visit historical sites of the Church. On their way they stopped at

Richmond, Missouri, to interview David Whitmer, the last surviving witness of the Book of Mormon.]

At Richmond we [Orson Pratt and Joseph F. Smith] put up at the Shaw House (before the cyclone a three-story brick building, but has been restored since the tempest, only two stories), now kept by Mr. Warren Ewing, son-in-law to the original proprietor, Mr. S. Shaw, once a freighter to Utah, now dead. On Saturday morning, September 7th, we met Mr. David Whitmer, the last remaining one of the Three Witnesses to the Book of Mormon. He is a good-sized man, seventy-three years of age last January, and well-preserved (he was born January 7, 1805). He is close-shaven, his hair perfectly white and rather thin; he has a large head and a very pleasant, manly countenance that one would readily perceive to be an index to a conscientious, honest heart. He seemed wonderfully pleased, as well as surprised, at seeing Elder Orson Pratt. Said he would not have known him—he had grown so fat and stout; he remembered him as a slender, bashful, timid boy. After a few moments conversation he excused himself, saying he would return again to see us. This meeting was in the barroom of the hotel. When he called again he was in company with Colonel Childs, a middle-aged man, and a resident of the place. By invitation we accompanied them to Mr. Whitmer's office, where we were introduced to Mr. David J. Whitmer (eldest son of David), Mr. Geo. [George] Schweich (grandson of the old gentleman), Mr. John C. Whitmer (son of Jacob Whitmer), Colonel James W. Black, of Richmond, and several others. A couple of hours were very pleasantly passed in conversation, principally on Utah matters, when we parted for dinner, agreeing to meet Mr. Whitmer again at his office at 4:30 P.M.

Agreeable to appointment, we met Mr. Whitmer and his friends at his office, but as the place was too public for private conversation and as it seemed impossible to obtain a private personal interview with David Whitmer, by himself, we invited him and such of his friends as he saw proper to fetch along, to our room in the hotel. Mr. Whitmer apologized for not inviting us to his house, as it was "wash day," and he and his wife were "worn out" with the extra labor, exposure, etc., consequent on rebuilding since the cyclone. He accepted our invitation to our room and brought with him James R. B. Vancleave, a fine-looking, intelligent, young newspaper man of Chicago, who is paying his addresses to Miss Josephine Schweich (granddaughter of David Whitmer), George Schweich (grandson), John C. Whitmer (son of Jacob), W. W. Warner, and another person whose name we did not learn. In the presence of these, the following, in substance, as noticed in Brother Joseph F. Smith's journal, is the account of the interview.

Elder O. [Orson] Pratt to D. [David] Whitmer. Can you tell the date of the bestowal of the apostleship upon Joseph, by Peter, James, and John?

D. W. I do not know; Joseph never told me. I can only tell you what I know, for I will not testify to anything I do not know.

J. F. S. [Joseph F. Smith] to D. W. Did Oliver Cowdery die here in Richmond?

D. W. Yes, he lived here, I think, about one year before his death. He died in my father's house, right here, in March, 1850. Phineas Young was here at the time.

Elder O. P. Do you remember what time you saw the plates?

D. W. It was in June, 1829—the latter part of the month, and the Eight Witnesses saw them, I think, the next day or the day after (that is, one or two days after). Joseph showed them the plates himself, but the angel showed us (the Three Witnesses) the plates, as I suppose to fulfill the words of the book itself. Martin Harris was not with us at this time; he obtained a view of them afterwards (the same day). Joseph, Oliver, and myself were together when I saw them. We not only saw the plates of the Book of Mormon but also the brass plates, the plates of the Book of Ether, the plates containing the records of the wickedness and secret combinations of the people of the world down to the time of their being engraved, and many other plates. The fact is, it was just as though Joseph, Oliver, and I were sitting just here on a log, when we were overshadowed by a light. It was not like the light of the sun nor like that of a fire, but more glorious and beautiful. It extended away round us, I cannot tell how far, but in the midst of this light about as far off as he sits (pointing to John C. Whitmer, sitting a few feet from him), there appeared as it were, a table with many records or plates upon it, besides the plates of the Book of Mormon, also the Sword of Laban, the Directors—i.e., the ball which Lehi had—and the Interpreters. I saw them just as plain as I see this bed (striking the bed beside him with his hand), and I heard the voice of the Lord, as distinctly as I ever heard anything in my life, declaring that the records of the plates of the Book of Mormon were translated by the gift and power of God.

Elder O. P. Did you see the angel at this time?

D. W. Yes; he stood before us. Our testimony as recorded in the Book of Mormon is strictly and absolutely true, just as it is there written. Before

I knew Joseph, I had heard about him and the plates from persons who declared they knew he had them, and swore they would get them from him. When Oliver Cowdery went to Pennsylvania, he promised to write me what he should learn about these matters, which he did. He wrote me that Joseph had told him his (Oliver's) secret thoughts, and all he had meditated about going to see him, which no man on earth knew, as he supposed, but himself, and so he stopped to write for Joseph.

Soon after this, Joseph sent for me (D. W.) to come to Harmony to get him and Oliver and bring them to my father's house. I did not know what to do, I was pressed with my work. I had some 20 acres to plow, so I concluded I would finish plowing and then go. I got up one morning to go to work as usual and, on going to the field, found between five and seven acres of my ground had been plowed during the night.

I don't know who did it; but it was done just as I would have done it myself, and the plow was left standing in the furrow.

This enabled me to start sooner. When I arrived at Harmony, Joseph and Oliver were coming toward me, and met me some distance from the house. Oliver told me that Joseph had informed him when I started from home, where I had stopped the first night, how I read the sign at the tavern, where I stopped the next night, etc., and that I would be there that day before dinner, and this was why they had come out to meet me; all of which was exactly as Joseph had told Oliver, at which I was greatly astonished. When I was returning to Fayette, with Joseph and Oliver, all of us riding in the wagon, Oliver and I on an old-fashioned, wooden, spring seat and Joseph behind us; while traveling along in a clear open place, a very pleasant, nice-looking old man suddenly appeared by the side of our wagon and saluted us with, "Good morning, it is very warm," at the same time wiping his face or forehead with his hand. We returned the salutation, and, by a sign from Joseph, I invited him to ride if he was going our way. But he said very pleasantly, "No, I am going to Cumorah." This name was something new to me, I did not know what Cumorah meant. We all gazed at him and at each other, and as I looked around inquiringly of Joseph, the old man instantly disappeared, so that I did not see him again.

J. F. S. Did you notice his appearance?

D. W. I should think I did. He was, I should think, about 5 feet 8 or 9 inches tall and heavy set, about such a man as James Vancleave there, but heavier; his face was as large, he was dressed in a suit of brown woolen clothes, his hair and beard were white, like Brother Pratt's, but his beard was not so heavy. I also remember that he had on his back a sort of knapsack with something in, shaped like a book. It was the messenger who had the plates, who had taken them from Joseph just prior to our starting from Harmony. Soon after our arrival home, I saw something which led me to the belief that the plates were placed or concealed in my father's barn. I frankly asked Joseph if my supposition was right, he told me it was. Some time after this, my mother was going to milk the cows, when she was met out near the yard by the same old man (judging by her description of him) who said to her: "You have been very faithful and diligent in your labors, but you are tired because of the increase in your toil; it is proper therefore that you should receive a witness that your faith may be strengthened." Thereupon he showed her the plates. My father and mother had a large family of their own; the addition to it, therefore, of Joseph, his wife Emma, and Oliver very greatly increased the toil and anxiety of my mother. And although she had never complained, she had sometimes felt that her labor was too much, or at least she was perhaps beginning to feel so. This circumstance, however, completely removed all such feelings and nerved her up for her increased responsibilities.

Elder O. P. Have you any idea when the other record will be brought forth?

D. W. When we see things in the Spirit and by the power of God they seem to be right here; the present signs of the times indicate the near approach of the coming forth of the other plates, but when it will be I cannot tell. The Three Nephites are at work among the lost tribes and elsewhere. John the Revelator is at work, and I believe the time will come suddenly, before we are prepared for it.

Elder O. P. Have you in your possession the original MSS. [manuscripts] of the Book of Mormon?

D. W. I have; they are in O. [Oliver] Cowdery's handwriting. He placed them in my care at his death, and charged me to preserve them as long as I lived; they are safe and well preserved.

J. F. S. What will be done with them at your death?

D. W. I will leave them to my nephew, David Whitmer, son of my brother Jacob, and my namesake.

Elder O. P. Would you not part with them to a purchaser?

D. W. No. Oliver charged me to keep them, and Joseph said my father's house should keep the records. I consider these things sacred, and would not part with nor barter them for money.

J. F. S. We would not offer you money in the light of bartering for the MSS., but we would like to see them preserved in some manner where they would be safe from casualties and from the caprices of men, in some institution that will not die as man does.

D. W. That is all right. While camping around here in a tent, all my effects exposed to the weather, everything in the trunk where the MSS. [manuscripts] were kept became moldy, etc., but they were preserved, not even being discolored (we supposed his camping in a tent, etc., had reference to his circumstances after the cyclone, in June last). As he and others affirm, the room in which the MSS. were kept was the only part of the house which was not demolished, and even the ceiling of that room was but little impaired. "Do you think," said Philander Page, a son of Hiram Page, one of the Eight Witnesses, "that the Almighty cannot take care of his own?"

Next day (Sunday, September 8) Mr. Whitmer invited us to his house, where, in the presence of David Whitmer, Esq. (son of Jacob), Philander Page, J. R. B. Vancleave, David J. Whitmer (son of David, the witness), George Schweich (grandson of David), Colonel Childs, and others, David Whitmer brought out the MSS. of the Book of Mormon. We examined them closely and those who knew the handwriting pronounced the whole of them, excepting comparatively few pages, to be in the handwriting of Oliver Cowdery. It was thought that these few pages were in the handwritings of Emma Smith and John and Christian Whitmer.

We found that the names of the eleven witnesses were, however, subscribed in the handwriting of Oliver Cowdery. When the question was asked Mr. Whitmer if he and the other witnesses did or did not sign the testimonies themselves, Mr. W. replied, "Each signed his own name."

"Then where are the original signatures?"

D. W. I don't know; I suppose Oliver copied them, but this I know is an exact copy.

Someone suggested that he, being the last one left of the eleven witnesses, ought to certify to this copy.

Lawyer D. Whitmer (Jacob's son) suggested that he had better reflect about it first and be very cautious.

J. F. S. suggested that perhaps there were two copies of the manuscripts, but Mr. Whitmer replied that, according to the best of his knowledge, there never was but the one copy. Herein, of course, he is evidently uninformed.

Elder O. Pratt again felt closely after the subject of procuring the MSS., but we found that nothing would move him on this point. The whole Whitmer family are deeply impressed with the sacredness of this relic. And so thoroughly imbued are they with the idea and faith that it is under the immediate protection of the Almighty that, in their estimation, not only are the MSS. themselves safe from all possible contingencies, but that they are a source of protection to the place or house in which they may be kept, and, it may be, to those who have possession of them.

Another reason why they cling to this relic is that David Whitmer has reorganized the "Church of Christ" with six elders and two priests, after the pattern of the first organization, the two priests as we suppose representing Joseph and Oliver as holding the Aaronic priesthood from the hand of John the Baptist. David and John Whitmer were two of these six elders, four others, viz. John C. Whitmer, W. W. Warner, Philander Page, and John Short, having been ordained by David and John. And as the recent death of John has diminished the number to five elders it would be interesting to know if, according to their strict construction, the vacancy can be filled.

Their creed is to preach nothing but the Bible and the Book of Mormon. Mr. Whitmer and others called on us again in the evening, at the hotel, and conversed, reiterating many things before stated. Upon inquiry, Mr. Whitmer informed us that Oliver Cowdery had told him all about his visiting the Church at Council Bluffs and of his having been rebaptized. He said, "Oliver died the happiest man I ever saw, after shaking hands with the family and kissing his wife and daughter, he said, 'Now I lay me down for the last time, I am going to my Savior,' and died immediately, with a smile on his face."

In response to some questions, Mr. Whitmer said: "Many things have been revealed which were designed only for the Church, and which the world cannot comprehend, but the Book of Mormon and those testimonies therein given were to go to all the world."

We replied, "Yes, and we have sent that book to the Danes, the Swedes, the Spanish, the Italians, the French, the German, the Welsh, and to the islands of the sea, the book even having been translated into Hindoostanee. So you see the Church has not been idle." To this he made no reply. In parting with him, he said "This may be the last time I shall ever see you in the flesh, so farewell."

This ended our interview with the last remaining witness who saw the plates of the Book of Mormon, yet not the last witness of its truth, for now such witnesses are multiplied into tens of thousands (1878, pp. 771–74).

Restoration of the Aaronic Priesthood (May 15, 1829)

Oliver Cowdery

I was present with Joseph when an holy angel from God came down from heaven and conferred on us, or restored, the lesser or Aaronic priesthood, and said to us at the time, that it should remain upon the earth while the earth stands. I was also present with Joseph when the higher or Melchizedek priesthood was conferred by the holy angel from on high. This priesthood we then conferred upon each other by the will and commandment of God (1904, pp. 941–42).

Oliver Cowdery

[Joseph Smith] was ministered unto by the angel, and by his direction he obtained the records of the Nephites, and translated by the gift and power of God. He was ordained by the angel John, unto the lesser or Aaronic priesthood, in company with myself, in the town of Harmony, Susquehanna County, Pennsylvania, on Friday, the 15th day of May, 1829; after which we repaired to the water, even to the Susquehanna River, and were baptized; he first administering unto me, and after, I to him. But before baptism our souls were drawn out in mighty prayer, to know how we might obtain the blessings of baptism and of the Holy Spirit according to the order of God; and we diligently sought for the right of the fathers, and the authority of the holy priesthood, and the power to administer the same; for we desired to be followers of righteousness, and in the possession of greater knowledge, even the knowledge of the mysteries of the kingdom of God.

Therefore we repaired to the woods, even as our father Joseph [the son of Jacob] said we should, that is, to the bush, and called upon the name of the Lord, and he answered us out of the heavens. And while we were in the heavenly vision, the angel came down and bestowed upon us this priesthood; and then, as I have said, we repaired to the water and were baptized. After this, we received the high and holy priesthood; but an account of this will be given elsewhere, or in another place (1904, p. 942).

Oliver Cowdery

[On December 18, 1833, when the Prophet gave his father a blessing, and ordained him to be the Patriarch, he also blessed others, including Oliver Cowdery. After pronouncing Oliver's blessing, Joseph said:]

These blessings [that is, those mentioned in the blessing] shall come upon him [Oliver] according to the blessings of the prophecy of Joseph in ancient days, which he said should come upon the seer of the last days and the scribe that should sit with him, and that should be ordained with him, by the hands of the angel in the bush, unto the lesser priesthood, and after receive the holy priesthood under the hands of those who had been held in reserve for a long season, even those who received it under the hands of the Messiah, while he should dwell in the flesh upon the earth, and should receive the blessings with him, even the seer of the God of Abraham, Isaac, and Jacob, saith he, even Joseph of old (1904, p. 943).

Oliver Cowdery

I have cherished a hope, and that one of my fondest, that I might leave such a character as those who might believe in my testimony, after I should be called hence, might do so, not only for the sake of the truth, but might not blush for the private character of the man who bore that testimony. I have been sensitive on this subject, I admit, but I ought to so be; you would be under the circumstances had you stood in the presence of John with our departed Brother Joseph, to receive the lesser priesthood, and in the presence of Peter, to receive the greater, and looked down through time, and witness the effects these two must produce—you would feel what you have never felt, were wicked men conspiring to lessen the effects of your testimony on man, after you should have gone to your long-sought rest. But, enough of this (1846).

Note: Oliver's testimony here is important, for from time to time there are those who suggest that the Melchizedek Priesthood was restored by the voice of God speaking "in the chamber of old Father Whitmer" (see D&C 128:21), and not by the visitation of Peter, James, and John. Yet here Oliver certifies that he stood in the presence of Peter, obviously meaning that James and John were present also. In the Patriarchal Blessing Book, under the date of October 2, 1835 (as noted above), Oliver testified that he and Joseph received the Melchizedek Priesthood "under the hands of those who . . . received it under the hands of those who received it under the hands of the Messiah, while he should dwell in the flesh upon the earth." In 1848 Oliver testified: "I was also present with Joseph when the higher or Melchisedek priesthood was conferred by the holy angel from on high" (1904, pp. 941–42).

Restoration of the Melchizedek Priesthood (ca. Spring or Summer 1829)

Addison Everett

At Colesville [Joseph] and Oliver were under arrest on charges of deceiving the people. When they were at the justice's house for trial in the evening, all were waiting for Mr. Reid, Joseph's lawyer. . . . Mr. Reid came in and said he wanted to speak to his clients in private and that the law allowed him that privilege, he believed. The judge pointed to a door to a room in the back part of the house and told them to step in there. As soon as they got into the room, the lawyer said there was a mob outside in front of the house, "and if they get hold of you they will perhaps do you bodily injury; and I think the best way for you to get out of this is to get right out there," pointing to the window and hoisting it. They got into the wood in going a few rods from the house—it was night and they traveled through brush and water and mud, fell over logs, etc., until Oliver was exhausted; then Joseph helped him along through the mud and water, almost carrying him.

They traveled all night, and just at the break of day Oliver gave out entirely and exclaimed,

"O Lord! Brother Joseph, how long have we got to endure this thing?" They sat down on a log to rest and Joseph said that at that very time Peter, James, and John came to them and ordained them to the Apostleship.

They had sixteen or seventeen miles to travel to get back to Mr. Hales, his father-in-law's, but Oliver did not complain any more of fatigue.

Now Brother Huntington I have told you what I heard Brother Joseph tell, almost the only time I ever heard him talk. It is a source of satisfaction and pleasure to me to have seen and heard the prophet of God (1890, pp. 75–76).

Restoration and Organization of the Church (1830)

David Lewis

My name is David Lewis. I am the son of Lemuel and Weighty Selecta (Stanton) Lewis and was born at Saranc, Clinton County, New York, May 5, 1818.

The first time I ever saw the Prophet Joseph he was speaking concerning his mission; that was two years before the organization of the Church. He said: "I am come to die for the Church of Jesus Christ of Latter-day Saints."* He lived at that time in Fayette, N.Y., at the place where the Church was organized.** I never lived in Pennsylvania, but passed through there while on my mission with Brother Henry H. Jacobs. I lived with my parents four miles from where the Church was organized. When I was eight years old my father had left Clinton County and located in western New York. I was at the meeting where the Church was organized, April 6, 1830. When I went to meeting to be baptized about a month after the Church was organized I remember I had two miles to go down the road and to follow a cow trail through low lands.

My recollection is that I was baptized in a small stream. The Prophet baptized me. I don't remember where the town of Colesville was, nor Waterloo. The size of the house where the Church was organized was, I should judge, about 14' by 16'. It had no floor except dirt. The village was a very small one, just a little place; I think it was on level ground.

("Do you remember hearing of Fayette?" was propounded by one of the brethren). Yes, sir, that's the place I was trying to think of, that's where the Church was first organized. The question was here asked, "David, are you tired?" He replied, "No, I never get tired of talking about the Church of Jesus Christ of Latter-day Saints." It seems to me that at the organization of the Church Joseph first laid his hands upon Oliver Cowdery and ordained him, and then Oliver ordained Joseph.

How I came to be present at the organization of the Church was, I

---

*Lewis's memory is faulty: Prior to the organization of the Church Joseph knew he would organize it, but he did not know the full name of the Church until some years after the Church was organized (see D&C 115:3–4).

**This too shows faulty memory: Two years before the Church was organized, Joseph and Emma lived with Emma's parents in Harmony, Pennsylvania. He did spend time at the Whitmer farm between June 1 and July 1, 1829, while translating the Book of Mormon.

had spoken to Joseph, about a week before that about being baptized. Joseph told me to ask my father and mother and if possible get their consent. I went home and asked my mother if she was willing that I join the Church. She answered, "What church?" I said, "Joseph's church." She said, "Yes David, you can do that if you please, but David the whole world is against them, including all the good ministers." I said, "I like the way Joseph speaks, he preaches baptism for the remission of sins, the laying on of hands for the reception of the Holy Ghost, etc."

I just went up there to see Joseph; I used to often go over to see Joseph. I cannot tell what Joseph was doing at the time of the organization of the church, excepting that he was engaged in general church work and translating the Book of Mormon. He always wore a white shirt with a ruffle on the breast about two inches wide.

Just before entering the house in which the Church was organized I heard Joseph say, "Come, let us organize the Church." He laid his hands upon the head of everybody present and confirmed them members of the Church.* There were present at that meeting, besides myself, Joseph and Hyrum Smith, Oliver Cowdery, David Whitmer, Peter Whitmer Jun., and Samuel H. Smith. The sacrament was administered upon that occasion for the first time. I attended meeting regularly every Sunday at that place until we moved to Kirtland.

I was baptized on my twelfth birthday which was May 5, 1830, just twenty-nine days after the organization of the Church. Before leaving home for the purpose of being baptized, I promised my mother that I would come right home as soon as the ceremony was performed. After the ceremony there was quite a severe thunderstorm, and Joseph asked me to remain under shelter until the storm had passed. I told him of the promise I had made to my mother. Joseph said, "You better stay till the rain is over." I said, "I have to go, Joseph, and I must go to keep my promise with my mother." Joseph then shook hands with me and asked the Lord to bless me, and he promised me that the Lord would be with me, and would take me safely home to my mother. On the way home I ran up against a big elm tree. I was frightened and thought I was lost. I cried in my fright, but soon I thought of the Prophet's words, that the Lord would guide me home in safety to my mother. I thereupon knelt down and asked the Lord to take me safely to my home and to be a lamp to my feet and a

---

*This too seems unlikely, as they had not yet been baptized.

guide to my pathway. Suddenly a light appeared which resembled the light of a coal oil lamp. I started for home and the light went ahead of me directly on the path where I walked. This light kept moving before me until I reached my home. My mother, who was looking out for me, saw it also, and it lit up her window with its rays; it went around the back door of the house and stopped there. My mother opened the door and just as soon as the door was opened the light went out. I afterwards told Joseph about the light guiding me home. He said, "David, I knew that you would get lost in the woods and that the Lord would guide you home" (1908).

Joseph Smith

Whilst the Book of Mormon was in the hands of the printer, we still continued to bear testimony and give information, as far as we had opportunity; and also made known to our brethren that we had received a commandment to organize the Church; and accordingly we met together for that purpose, at the house of Mr. Peter Whitmer, Sen., (being six in number,) on Tuesday, the sixth day of April, A.D., one thousand eight hundred and thirty. Having opened the meeting by solemn prayer to our Heavenly Father, we proceeded, according to previous commandment, to call on our brethren to know whether they accepted us as their teachers in the things of the Kingdom of God, and whether they were satisfied that we should proceed and be organized as a Church according to said commandment which we had received. To these several propositions they consented by a unanimous vote. I then laid my hands upon Oliver Cowdery, and ordained him an elder of the "Church of Jesus Christ of Latter-day Saints;" after which, he ordained me also to the office of an elder of said Church. We then took bread, blessed it, and brake it with them; also wine, blessed it, and drank it with them. We then laid our hands on each individual member of the Church present, that they might receive the gift of the Holy Ghost, and be confirmed members of the Church of Christ. The Holy Ghost was poured out upon us to a very great degree—some prophesied, whilst we all praised the Lord, and rejoiced exceedingly (HC, 1:74–78).

Lucy Mack Smith

Brothers and Sisters in the Church. I have looked around me this day [October 8, 1845] with a thankfulness and a prayer to God that every soul may be faithful that we may all enjoy the spirit of this gospel. I feel a solemnity that the tongue cannot express, nor pen write. I look back on the progress of the Church and see it just as clear as when the Church was organized. The next Wednesday after that I was baptized. I can see the rising persecution. It has been in all our hearts to help fetch forth that kingdom that it may roll forth. It seems as if it is preserved by the Spirit of God and that all the devils in hell seem to be trying to put it down, but the Lord will roll on His work. And my desire is that Brother Phineas [Young] may be blessed—and that all the blessings of heaven may rest upon you all. I want all your prayers in my trouble. When I look at my family, how they have been persecuted day and night, I suffer in that reflection. But still they are comforted. I feel pretty much the same as when the Church was first organized, and when the Nephites rejoiced over us, that the Church just arising, as they had lain and slumbered for ages. Angels fluttered over us that time. If you remain faithful the Nephites will be your brothers and sisters and will give you intelligence—and may the blessing of heaven be with you all (1845).

The Kirtland Years (1831–1838)

General Comments on Life in Kirtland

Truman O. Angell

The next day, Sunday [in the fall of 1835], meeting assembled in the temple on a loose floor which had been arranged for carpenters' benches etc., the house was partly filled, the people being seated on work benches and other things. President Joseph Smith, [Jr.,] during the meeting, arose to speak upon an order he had given to Oliver Cowdery to seek out a book for a Church Record; for such must be kept; this had been complied with, a good book had been selected, and it pleased President Smith.

The book was not paid for, but was to be returned to Painesville if it did not suit; and the Prophet said he would be glad to have the Saints donate the amount, about $12.50, and make the purchase, and keep the book; it being of good paper and thoroughly well bound. A man arose near the middle of the house and said he wanted the leaves counted to see if it would not be better to buy the paper by the ream, the difference being that we might put it in a newspaper, or something of the kind. Brother Joseph spoke out and said the devil could not raise his head there, but he would know him. I note this to show the little means with which the Church was obliged to commence the history of a people destined to become great (1967, pp. 196–97).

Philo Dibble

There was a branch of the Church raised up in Kirtland before the Prophet came there, and at the time he arrived a variety of false spirits were manifest, such as caused jumping, shouting, falling down, etc. Joseph said, as soon as he came, "God has sent me here, and the devil must leave here or I *will*." Those delusive spirits were not seen nor heard any more at that time (1892a, p. 23).

Philo Dibble

At this time Sidney Rigdon was left to preside at Kirtland and frequently preached to us. Upon one occasion he said the keys of the kingdom were taken from us. On hearing this, many of his hearers wept, and when some one undertook to dismiss the meeting by prayer he said praying would do them no good, and the meeting broke up in confusion.

Brother Hyrum [Smith] came to my house the next morning and told me all about it, and said it was false, and that the keys of the kingdom were still with us. He wanted my carriage and horses to go to the town of Hiram and bring Joseph. The word went abroad among the people immediately that Sidney [Rigdon] was going to expose "Mormonism."

Joseph came up to Kirtland a few days afterwards and held a meeting in a large barn. Nearly all the inhabitants of Kirtland turned out to hear him. The barn was filled with people, and others, unable to get inside, stood around the door as far as they could hear.

Joseph arose in our midst and spoke in mighty power, saying: "I can contend with wicked men and devils—yes, with angels. No power can pluck those keys from me, except the power that gave them to me; that was Peter, James, and John. But for what Sidney [Rigdon] has done, the devil shall handle him as one man handles another."

Thomas B. Marsh's wife went from the meeting and told Sidney [Rigdon] what Joseph had said, and he replied: "Is it possible that I have been so deceived? But if Joseph says so, it is so."

About three weeks after this, Sidney [Rigdon] was lying on his bed alone. An unseen power lifted him from his bed, threw him across the room, and tossed him from one side of the room to the other. The noise being heard in the adjoining room, his family went in to see what was the matter, and found him going from one side of the room to the other, from the effects of which Sidney was laid up for five or six weeks. Thus was Joseph's prediction in regard to him verified (1968, pp. 80–81).

Heber C. Kimball

We went and performed that journey [i.e., Zion's Camp], traveled two thousand miles in a little over three months. We walked forty miles per day when we were not hindered, we walked the entire journey there and back. Such as were designated by the Lord were permitted to return home to their families, but the single men were told by the Prophet to go and preach the gospel in the country round about. When we arrived in Kirtland, Joseph said, "Come, brethren, let us go into the stone-quarry and work for the Lord." And the Prophet went himself, in his tow frock and tow breeches, and worked at quarrying stone like the rest of us (JD, 10:165).

Elizabeth Ann Whitney

It was about this time my husband was ordained a bishop by revelation and commandment from God. . . . We had always been in the habit of entertaining our friends and acquaintances generously and hospitably, but after we received the gospel we did not feel like using our means and time in a way that would only benefit those who had an abundance of this world's means. According to our Savior's pattern and agreeably to the Prophet Joseph's and our own ideas of true charity and disinterested benevolence, we determined to make a Feast for the Poor, such as we knew could not return the same to us; the lame, the halt, the deaf, the blind, the aged and infirm.

This feast lasted three days, during which time all in the vicinity of Kirtland who would come were invited, and entertained as courteously and generously as if they had been able to extend hospitality instead of receiving it. The Prophet Joseph and his two counselors were present each day, talking, blessing, and comforting the poor, by words of encouragement and their most welcome presence; some are now living who were present at that Feast, and many have passed behind the veil. The Prophet Joseph often referred to this particular Feast during his lifetime, and testified of the great blessing he felt in associating with the meek and humble ones whom the Lord has said that "He delights to own and bless." He often said to me that it was preferable and far superior to the elegant and select parties he afterwards attended, and afforded him much more genuine satisfaction; and to me it was a feast of fat things indeed; a season of rejoicing never to be forgotten (1878c, p. 83; see HC, 2:362 for Joseph Smith's account of these events).

Mobbing in Hiram, Ohio (March 24, 1832)

Levi W. Hancock

[In early May 1832, I] lived awhile with John Reed, then went to Chagrin and stopped with Solomon for a few days, when the Prophet Joseph Smith sent for me. I went and saw him again and had a conversation with him. Heard him tell about him being mobbed in Hiram and how they pulled the hair out of his head. Then he showed me the place where they had pulled the hair out of. He said they poured Aqafortis down him, he thought. I said, "While I was in Cleveland I heard some laughing about it, who said the devil must have gotten the better of the Lord that time. I told them I thought he did once before when they killed the Son of God and his Disciples too. I did not consider that proved him an imposter." I never saw men so much confounded. I said no more but all eyes were on me while I stayed at the house (n.d. [b], p. 50).

George A. Smith

While [Ezra Booth] was in apostasy, he searched his cranium for some means to justify himself and published a series of lying letters in the *Ohio Star*, a paper printed in Ravenna. These nine letters had been republished several times as evidence against "Mormonism;" and his apostasy culminated in collecting a mob who tarred and feathered Joseph Smith, and inflicted upon his family the loss of one of its number at Hiram, Portage County, Ohio.

Joseph Smith was occupying the room of a house Brother Johnson was living in, at the same time; it was a two-story building, had steps in front. The mob surrounded the house; the twins being afflicted with measles, Joseph was lying upon a trundle bed with one of them. The mob rushed in, gathered up Joseph while in his bed, took him out in his night clothes, and carried him out on to the top of the steps. Joseph got a foot at liberty and kicked one of the men, and knocked him down off the steps, and the print of his head and shoulders were visible on the ground in the morning. Warren Waste, who was the strongest man in the western reserve, considered himself perfectly able to handle Joseph alone, but when they got hold of him Waste cried out, "Do not let him touch the ground, or he will run over the whole of us." Waste suggested in carrying him to cross his legs, for they said that would make it easier for the Prophet, but that was done in consequence of the severe pain it would give to the small of the back. He was daubed with tar, feathered, and choked, and aqua fortis poured into his mouth. Dr. Dennison had been employed to perform a surgical operation, but he declined when the time came to operate. The liquid they poured into his mouth was so powerful that it killed the grass where some of it had been scattered on the ground. Joseph is reported by the mob to have said, be merciful, when they told him to call upon his God for mercy. They immediately, as he began to pray, heard an alarm which made them think they were about to be surprised, and left suddenly.

Sidney Rigdon, who resided near by, had been dragged by the heels out of his bed at the same time, and his body stripped and a coat of tar and feathers applied. The next morning he was crazy, his head greatly inflamed and lacerated.

Joseph found his way in from the light of the house, the mob having abandoned him. While he was engaged in getting off the tar by the application of grease, soap, and other materials, Philemon Duzette, the father of our celebrated drummer, came there, and seeing the Prophet in this condition, took it as an evidence of the truth of "Mormonism," and was baptized. These circumstances exposed the life of the child, the measles struck in and caused its death, and the whole of this persecution was got up through the influence of those apostates; and it made it necessary to keep up a constant watch lest some violence should be repeated.

Luke Johnson informed us that Warren Waste was afterwards a cripple, rendered so by weakness in the small of the back, and Dr. Dennison died in the Ohio Penitentiary where he was incarcerated for procuring an abortion, which caused death; Joseph soon after located in Kirtland (JD, 11:4–6; see also Luke S. Johnson, 1864, p. 835).

Joseph Smith

On the 24th of March [1832], the twins before mentioned, which had been sick of the measles for some time, caused us to be broken of our rest in taking care of them, especially my wife. In the evening I told her she had better retire to rest with one of the children, and I would watch with the sicker child. In the night she told me I had better lie down on the trundle bed, and I did so, and was soon after awakened by her screaming murder, when I found myself going out of the door, in the hands of about a dozen men; some of whose hands were in my hair, and some had hold of my shirt, drawers, and limbs. The foot of the trundle bed was towards the door, leaving only room enough for the door to swing open. My wife heard a gentle tapping on the windows, which she then took no particular notice of (but which was unquestionably designed for ascertaining whether or not we were all asleep), and soon after the mob burst open the door and surrounded the bed in an instant, and, as I said, the first I knew I was going out of the door in the hands of an infuriated mob.

I made a desperate struggle, as I was forced out, to extricate myself, but only cleared one leg, with which I made a pass at one man, and he fell on the door steps. I was immediately overpowered again; and they swore by G—, they would kill me if I did not be still, which quieted me. As they passed around the house with me, the fellow that I kicked came to me and thrust his hand, all covered with blood, into my face, and with an exulting hoarse laugh, muttered "*Ge, gee, G—d—ye, I'll fix ye.*"

They then seized me by the throat and held on till I lost my breath. After I came to, as they passed along with me, about thirty rods from the house, I saw Elder Rigdon stretched out on the ground, whither they had dragged him by his heels. I supposed he was dead. I began to plead with them, saying, "You will have mercy and spare my life, I hope." To which they replied, "G—d—ye, call on yer God for help, we'll show ye no mercy;" and the people began to show themselves in every direction; one coming from the orchard had a plank; and I expected they would kill me, and carry me off on the plank. They then turned to the right, and went on about thirty rods further; about sixty rods from the house, and thirty from where I saw Elder Rigdon, into the meadow, where they stopped, and one said, "Simonds, Simonds" (meaning, I supposed, Simonds

Ryder), "pull up his drawers, pull up his drawers, he will take cold." Another replied: "*Ain't ye going to kill 'im? ain't ye going to kill 'im?*" when a group of mobbers collected a little way off, and said: "Simonds, Simonds, come here;" and "Simonds" charged those who had hold of me to keep me from touching the ground (as they had done all the time), lest I should get a spring upon them.

They held a council, and as I could occasionally overhear a word, I supposed it was to know whether or not it was best to kill me. They returned after a while, when I learned that they had concluded not to kill me, but to beat and scratch me well, tear off my shirt and drawers, and leave me naked. One cried, "Simonds, Simonds, *where's the tar bucket?*" "I don't know," answered one, "*where 'tis, Eli's left it.*" They ran back and fetched the bucket of tar, when one exclaimed, with an oath, "*Let us tar up his mouth;*" and they tried to force the tar-paddle into my mouth; I twisted my head around, so that they could not; and they cried out, "*G—d—ye, hold up yer head and let us give ye some tar.*" They then tried to force a vial into my mouth, and broke it in my teeth. All my clothes were torn off me except my shirt collar; and one man fell on me and scratched my body with his nails like a mad cat, and then muttered out: "*G—d—ye, that's the way the Holy Ghost falls on folks!*"

They then left me, and I attempted to rise, but fell again; I pulled the tar away from my lips, so that I could breathe more freely, and after a while I began to recover, and raised myself up, whereupon I saw two lights. I made my way towards one of them, and found it was Father Johnson's. When I came to the door I was naked, and the tar made me look as if I were covered with blood, and when my wife saw me she thought I was all crushed to pieces, and fainted. During the affray abroad, the sisters of the neighborhood had collected at my room. I called for a blanket, they threw me one, and shut the door; I wrapped it around me and went in.

In the meantime, Brother John Poorman heard an outcry across the corn field, and running that way met Father Johnson, who had been fastened in his house at the commencement of the assault by having his door barred by the mob, but on calling his wife to bring his gun, saying he would blow a hole through the door, the mob fled, and Father Johnson, seizing a club, ran after the party that had Elder Rigdon, and knocked down one man, and raised his club to level another, exclaiming, "*What are you doing here?*" when they left Elder Rigdon and turned upon Father

Johnson, who, turning to run toward his own house, met Brother Poorman coming out of the corn field; each supposing the other to be a mobber, and encounter ensued, and Poorman gave Johnson a severe blow on the left shoulder with a stick or stone, which brought him to the ground. Poorman ran immediately towards Father Johnson's, and arriving while I was waiting for the blanket, exclaimed, "I'm afraid I've killed him." Killed who? asked one; when Poorman hastily related the circumstances of the encounter near the corn field, and went into the shed and hid himself. Father Johnson soon recovered so as to come to the house, when the whole mystery was quickly solved concerning the difficulty between him and Poorman, who, on learning the facts, joyfully came from his hiding place.

My friends spent the night in scraping and removing the tar, and washing and cleansing my body; so that by morning I was ready to be clothed again. This being the Sabbath morning, the people assembled for meeting at the usual hour of worship, and among them came also the mobbers; viz.: Simonds Ryder, a Campbellite preacher and leader of the mob; one McClentic, who had his hands in my hair; one Streeter, son of a Campbellite minister; and Felatiah Allen, Esq., who gave the mob a barrel of whiskey to raise their spirits. Besides these named, there were many others in the mob. With my flesh all scarified and defaced, I preached to the congregation as usual, and in the afternoon of the same day baptized three individuals.

The next morning I went to see Elder Rigdon, and found him crazy, and his head highly inflamed, for they had dragged him by his heels, and those, too, so high from the ground that he could not raise his head from the rough, frozen surface, which lacerated it exceedingly; and when he saw me he called to his wife to bring him his razor. She asked him what he wanted of it; and he replied, to kill me. Sister Rigdon left the room, and he asked me to bring his razor; I asked him what he wanted of it, and he replied he wanted to kill his wife; and he continued delirious some days. The feathers which were used with the tar on this occasion, the mob took out of Elder Rigdon's house. After they had seized him, and dragged him out, one of the banditti returned to get some pillows; when the women shut him in and kept him a prisoner some time.

During the mobbing one of the twins contracted a severe cold, continued to grow worse until Friday, and then died. The mobbers composed of various religious parties, but mostly Campbellites, Methodists, and

Baptists, who continued to molest and menace Father Johnson's house for a long time. Elder Rigdon removed to Kirtland with his family—then sick with the measles—the following Wednesday; and, on account of the mob, he went to Chardon on Saturday, March 31st (HC, 1:261–65).

School of the Prophets (January 24, 1833—; 1834–1835)

George A. Smith

He [George A. Smith] said that the Prophet Joseph started a school there for the brethren to learn the classical language but more especially Hebrew and had hired an efficient professional linguist for that purpose and in this school they were also to learn all the common literature of the day (1869b).

Night of the Falling Stars (November 13, 1833)

Philo Dibble

On one occasion Joseph was preaching in Kirtland sometime in the fall of 1833. Quite a number of persons were present who did not belong to the Church, and one man, more bitter and skeptical than others, made note with pencil and paper of a prophecy uttered on that occasion, wherein Joseph said that "Forty days shall not pass, and the stars shall fall from heaven."

Such an event would certainly be very unusual and improbable to the natural man, and the skeptic wrote the words as a sure evidence to prove Joseph to be a false Prophet.

On the thirty-ninth day after the utterance of that prophecy a man and brother in the Church, by the name of Joseph Hancock, who is yet living in Payson, Utah, and another brother were out hunting game and got lost. They wandered about until night, when they found themselves at the house of this unbeliever, who exultingly produced this note of Joseph Smith's prophecy, and asked Brother Hancock what he thought of his Prophet now that thirty-nine days had passed and the prophecy was not fulfilled.

Brother Hancock was unmoved and quietly remarked, "There is one night left of the time, and if Joseph said so, the stars will certainly fall tonight. This prophecy will all be fulfilled."

The matter weighed upon the mind of Brother Hancock, who watched that night, and it proved to be the historical one, known in all the world as "the night of the falling of the stars."

He stayed that night at the house of the skeptical unbeliever, as it was too far from home to return by night, and in the midst of the falling of the stars he went to the door of his host and called him out to witness what he had thought impossible and the most improbable thing that could happen, especially as that was the last night in which Joseph Smith could be saved from the condemnation of "a false prophet."

The whole heavens were lit up with the falling meteors, and the countenance of the new spectator was plainly seen and closely watched by Brother Hancock, who said that he turned pale as death, and spoke not a word.

After that event the unbeliever sought the company of any Latter-day Saint. He even enticed Mormon children to keep him company at his house. Not long afterwards, too, he sent for Joseph and Hyrum to come to his house, which they did, but with no noticeable results, for I believe he never received the gospel (1892a, p. 23).

Note: Absalom Warren Smith records the following in his journal: "In the year 1833, Nov. 13th, I and my brother Elisha, were returning home from a corn husking, from Uncle James Smith's about eleven o'clock at night. I noticed in the sky numbers of stars falling from the heavens, from the southeast direction. We watched them for a few moments and they increased very fast. We were much excited over the strange experience, but we went home. The stars continued to fall, but we went to bed without informing my father of the strange phenomena, with the intention of getting up after taking a short sleep. About two o'clock in the morning I got up, and the stars or meteors, as they were called by some, caused me to call my father and the rest of the family. They were all greatly surprised at the great sight. Many of the neighbors saw it and were greatly frightened. Some said they thought the world was coming to an end. This continued till daylight, then they disappeared" (Maud Bliss Allen, 1962, pp. 24–25).

Ira Ames, for his part, recorded in his journal the following: "This fall, 13 November 1833, I witnessed the beautiful scene of the falling of the stars. I went from house to house waking up the people to have them see it. I went to Joseph's house. He was standing at the front gate with Oliver Cowdery" (see Ames, n.d., p. 6).

The Little Rock [Arkansas] Gazette, on December 11, 1833, p. 3, contained the following: "The Falling Stars—The meteoric phenomenon witnessed here on the morning of the 13th ult. was general throughout the United States. The Washington, Baltimore,

Philadelphia, and New York papers, give the same description of it, as those who witnessed it in this region, and to the north and south of us."

Joseph Smith spoke of the meteor shower as "a literal fulfillment of the word of God, as recorded in the holy Scriptures, and a sure sign that the coming of Christ is close at hand" (see HC, 1:439–40).

Joseph Smith

[*November 13, 1833*] About 4 o'clock A.M. I was awakened by Brother Davis knocking at my door, and calling on me to arise and behold the signs in the heavens. I arose, and to my great joy, beheld the stars fall from heaven like a shower of hailstones; a literal fulfilment of the word of God, as recorded in the holy Scriptures, and a sure sign that the coming of Christ is close at hand. In the midst of this shower of fire, I was led to exclaim, "How marvelous are Thy works, O Lord! I thank Thee for Thy mercy unto Thy servant; save me in Thy kingdom for Christ's sake. Amen."

The appearance of these signs varied in different sections of the country: in Zion, all heaven seemed enwrapped in splendid fireworks, as if every star in the broad expanse had been suddenly hurled from its course, and sent lawless through the wilds of ether. Some at times appeared like bright shooting meteors, with long trains of light following in their course, and in numbers resembled large drops of rain in sunshine. These seemed to vanish when they fell behind the trees, or came near the ground. Some of the long trains of light following the meteoric stars were visible for some seconds; these streaks would curl and twist up like serpents writhing. The appearance was beautiful, grand, and sublime beyond description; and it seemed as if the artillery and fireworks of eternity were set in motion to enchant and entertain the Saints, and terrify and awe the sinners of the earth. Beautiful and terrific as was the scenery, it will not fully compare with the time when the sun shall become black like sack-cloth of hair, the moon like blood, and the stars fall to the earth—Rev. 6:13 (HC, 1:439–40).

Zion's Camp (May–July 1834)

Levi W. Hancock

We had now in our camp two hundred and five (205) and truly we had seen the hand of God in our favor all the way. Once in particular, when we had camped without in the middle of February. One man [Joseph Smith] took a spade and said, "Who knows but what I can find water here" and put the spade in the ground and dug a small hole and it filled with water, good water. When this was done some said it was as much of a miracle as when Moses smote the rock and water came out. But the greatest miracle in our favor was when we had got between the two fishing rivers on a high ridge by a log meeting house. We had been told that morning by a colored woman who came to the fence where we were walking that there were three hundred men who were armed and equipped to fall on us that night and cut us off. Men came riding by who would cuss and swear that before morning we would all be in hell, for there was an army before and behind and death was our portion. Without enemy Jenkins Salisbury wanted Joseph to let him fight. "No," said he, "the Lord will give us a bramble to keep off the dogs this night."

In a short time it commenced thundering and the clouds arose and I went into the tent and lay down and knew no more till I found myself one third buried in water, the tent had blown down, and all hands gone. I soon found they had gone to the old Sanctuary for shelter, where I also went. The lightning flashed and thunder roared one continual sound and flash so connected one could hardly hear any interval between the flash and the peal of thunder as if all the marshall [martial] bands of drummers of the whole earth had assembled and was beating the bounds of war.

We lay on the benches dripping with water till daylight when we were called to go and discharge our pieces and load anew, which we did and to our astonishment two thirds, if not more, went off.

It was a pleasant morning. We got our breakfast and soon learned that the two branches of the fishing river were so high we could not cross over. The branch west had raised upwards of forty feet and all boats were gone. We turned our course northward about three miles and camped near an old acquaintance of some in our camp. Next day we were visited by a committee from the mob when Lyman Wright [Wight] exclaimed to them the cause of our coming and others spoke, which appeared to give satisfaction. After the meeting, these of the community went away and Joseph said, "Let us help this man right up his corn." We all went into the field and straightened up the corn for our friend that the stock had laid low.

I then returned to camp in the morning. My brother Joseph had taken sick, which proved to be the cholera. Joseph Smith went to pray for him and when through said that I must stand aside or I shall be smitten of the Lord. He said, "A scourge must come and I cannot help it. You have murmured in your hearts" and told them to fix for moving off. I then heard the revelation which said our sacrifice was accepted, for we had offered our lives as Abraham did (n.d. [b], pp. 56–57).

Heber C. Kimball

The same day when we had got within one mile of the Snye, we came to a very beautiful little town called Atlas. Here we found honey for the first time on our journey, that we could buy; we purchased about two thirds of a barrel. We went down to the Snye and crossed over that night in a ferry boat. We camped for the night on the bank of the Snye. There was a great excitement in the country through which we had passed, and also ahead of us; the mob threatened to stop us. Guns were fired in almost all directions through the night. Brother Joseph did not sleep much, any, but was through the camp pretty much during the night.

We pursued our journey on the 4th [of June 1834], and camped on the bank of the Mississippi River. Here we were somewhat afflicted and the enemy threatened much that we should not cross over the river out of Illinois into Missouri. It took us two days to cross the river, as we had but one ferry boat, and the river was one mile and a half wide. While some were crossing, many others spent their time in hunting and fishing, &c. When we had got over, we camped about one mile back from the little town of Louisiana, in a beautiful oak grove, which is immediately on the bank of the river. At this place there was some feelings of hostility manifested again by Sylvester Smith, in consequence of a dog growling at him while he was marching his company up to the camp, he being the last that came over the river. The next morning Brother Joseph said that he would descend to the spirit that was manifested by some of the brethren, to let them see the folly of their wickedness. He rose up and commenced speaking, by saying, "If any man insults me, or abuses me, I will stand in my own defense at the expense of my life; and if a dog growl at me, I will let him know that I am his master." At this moment Sylvester Smith, who had just returned from where he had turned out his horses to feed, came up, and hearing Brother Joseph make those remarks, said, "If that dog bites me, I'll kill him." Brother Joseph turned to Sylvester and said, "If you kill that dog, I'll whip you," and then went on to show the brethren how wicked and unchristian-like such conduct appeared before the eyes of truth and justice (1845b, pp. 788–89).

Heber C. Kimball

The next day the sheriff of that county, named Neil Gilliam, came to deliver a short address to us. We formed into companies and marched into a grove a little distance from the camp, and there formed ourselves into a circle, and sat down upon the ground. Previous to Mr. Gilliam's address he (Gilliam) said, "I have heard much concerning Joseph Smith, and I have been informed that he is in your camp; if he is here I would like to see him." Brother Joseph arose and said, "I am the man." This was the first time he was made known during the journey of one thousand miles. Mr. Gilliam then arose and gave us some instructions concerning the manners and customs of the people, their disposition, etc., and what course we should take in order to gain their favor and protection.

. . . Here Brothers Ezra Thayer and Thomas Hayes were taken sick with the cholera. We left them there, and also Brother Joseph Hancock, who had been taken with the cholera during the storm, and who was the first person attacked with it. Brother Joseph called the camp together, and told us that in consequence of the disobedience of some who had not been willing to listen to his words, but had been rebellious, God had decreed that sickness should come upon us, and we should die like sheep with the rot; and said he, "I am sorry, but I cannot help it." When he spake these things it pierced me like a dart, having a testimony that so it would be (1945, pp. 54–56).

Wilford Woodruff

When the five men entered our camp there was not a cloud to be seen in the whole heavens but as the men left the camp there was a small black cloud appeared in the northwest, and it began to unroll itself like a scroll, and in a few minutes the whole heavens were covered with a pall as black as ink. This indicated a sudden storm which soon broke upon us with wind, rain, thunder, lightning, and hail. Our beds were soon afloat and our tents blown down over our heads. We all fled into the Baptist Meeting House. As the Prophet Joseph came in shaking the water from his hat and clothing he said, "Boys, there is some meaning in this—God is in the storm." We sang praises to God and lay all night on the benches under cover, while our enemies were in the pelting storm. It was reported that the mob cavalry who fled into the school house tried to hold their horses by the bridles between the logs, but when the heavy hail struck them they all broke away, skinning the fingers of those who held them. The horses fled before the storm and were not found for several days. It was reported that the captain of the company in the school house said that they could do nothing against the d—d Mormons but what there must be a d—d hail storm or some other d—d thing to hinder them from doing anything. But they did not feel disposed to acknowledge that God was fighting our battles.

The storm was tremendous—wind and rain, hail and thunder met them in great wrath and soon softened their direful courage and frustrated all their designs to "kill Joe Smith and his army." Instead of continuing firing, which they commenced, they crowded under wagons, into hollow trees, filled one old shanty, etc., and when the storm was over their ammunition was soaked; and the party in Clay County were extremely anxious in the morning to return to Jackson County, having experienced the pitiless peltings of the storm all night. And as soon as arrangements could be made, this "forlorn hope" took the back track for Independence to join the main body of the mob, fully satisfied, as were the survivors of the company who were drowned, that when Jehovah fights, they would rather be absent. The gratification is too terrible (1838, pp. 62–65).

WILFORD WOODRUFF

Those who are here today, Brother Gates, Brother Noble, and perhaps others, who were present on that occasion, will remember the day that Joseph Smith called the camp together. We were all well. There was no disease nor sickness in our camp. But he told us what awaited us. He gave us to understand that there was to be a chastisement visit our camp. He told us the reason. He had given counsel to the brethren with regard to many things, and a number of them had disobeyed that counsel. They did not understand and appreciate fully his position and standing as a prophet of God. "Yes," says he, "you think of me as a boy, like the rest of you, but you will understand soon that I occupy a position where God governs and controls me." Those who were present know the feelings that we had. There was not a dry eye in camp. He stood upon a wagon and told us the judgments of God would visit our camp and we would be chastised.

These things came to pass. The day that we landed the destroying angel visited our camp, and, of course, there was sorrow. I do not know the number that went to the grave, but somewhere about fourteen, I think. Then we understood that we had a prophet in our midst. We knew very well that what he said would come to pass. Well, everything that was done in that camp, going and returning, a record of it, in a measure, has been kept. During that thousand miles journey the word of the Lord was given unto us, and we fully understood we were being led by a prophet of God. We realized that all the way through that mission (CD, 2:207).

Dedication of the Kirtland Temple (March 27, 1836)

Benjamin Brown

The succeeding winter, I again went up to Kirtland, to attend the dedication of the temple, and to meet with the solemn assembly that was there convened. There the Spirit of the Lord, as on the day of Pentecost, was profusely poured out. Hundreds of elders spoke in tongues, but many of them being young in the Church, and never having witnessed the manifestation of this gift before, felt a little alarmed. This caused the Prophet Joseph Smith to pray the Lord to withhold the Spirit. Joseph then instructed them on the nature of the gift of tongues, and the operation of the Spirit generally. We had a most glorious and never-to-be-forgotten time. Angels were seen by numbers present, and the first endowments were received (1853).

Joseph Smith

[After the dedicatory prayer,] I then asked the several quorums separately, and then the congregation, if they accepted the dedication prayer, and acknowledged the house dedicated. The vote was unanimous in the affirmative, in every instance.

The Lord's Supper was then administered; President Don Carlos Smith blessed the bread and the wine, which was distributed by several elders to the Church; after which I bore record of my mission, and of the ministration of angels.

President Don Carlos Smith also bore testimony of the truth of the work of the Lord in which we were engaged.

President Oliver Cowdery testified of the truth of the Book of Mormon, and of the work of the Lord in these last days.

President Frederick G. Williams arose and testified that while President Rigdon was making his first prayer, an angel entered the window and took his seat between Father Smith and himself, and remained there during the prayer.

President David Whitmer also saw angels in the house.

President Hyrum Smith made some appropriate remarks congratulating those who had endured so many toils and privations to build the house.

President Rigdon then made a few appropriate closing remarks, and a short prayer, at the close of which we sealed the proceedings of the day by shouting hosanna, hosanna, hosanna to God and the Lamb, three times, sealing it each time with amen, amen, and amen.

President Brigham Young gave a short address in tongues, and David W. Patten interpreted, and gave a short exhortation in tongues himself, after which I blessed the congregation in the name of the Lord, and the assembly dispersed a little past four o'clock, having manifested the most quiet demeanor during the whole exercise.

I met the quorums in the evening and instructed them respecting the ordinance of washing of feet, which they were to attend to on Wednesday following; and gave them instructions in relation to the spirit of prophecy, and called upon the congregation to speak, and not to fear to prophesy good concerning the Saints, for if you prophesy the falling of these hills and the rising of the valleys, the downfall of the enemies of Zion and the rising of the kingdom of God, it shall come to pass. Do not quench the Spirit, for the first one that opens his mouth shall receive the Spirit of prophecy.

Brother George A. Smith arose and began to prophesy, when a noise was heard like the sound of a rushing mighty wind, which filled the temple, and all the congregation simultaneously arose, being moved upon by an invisible power; many began to speak in tongues and prophesy; others saw glorious visions; and I beheld the temple was filled with angels, which fact I declared to the congregation. The people of the neighborhood came running together (hearing an unusual sound within, and seeing a bright light like a pillar of fire resting upon the temple), and were astonished at what was taking place. This continued until the meeting closed at eleven P.M.

The number of official members present on this occasion was four hundred and sixteen, being a greater number than ever assembled on any former occasion (HC, 2:427–28).

Sylvia Cutler Webb

One of my earliest recollections was the dedication of the Temple. My father took us up on his lap and told us why we were going and what it meant to dedicate a house to God. And although so very young at that time, I clearly remember the occasion. I can look back through the lapse of years and see as I saw then Joseph the Prophet, standing with his hands raised towards heaven, his face ashy pale, the tears running down his cheeks as he spoke on that memorable day. Almost all seemed to be in tears. The house was so crowded the children were mostly sitting on older people's laps; my sister sat on father's, I on my mother's lap. I can even remember the dresses we wore. My mind was too young at that time to grasp the full significance of it all, but as time passed it dawned more and more upon me, and I am very grateful that I was privileged to be there (1989, pp. 182–83).

Kirtland Bank Failure (1837)

George A. Smith

For several years we had used the paper of Geauga Bank at Painesville as money. A loan of a few hundred dollars was asked for by Joseph Smith, with ample security, but was refused, and Elder Reynolds Cahoon was told they would not accommodate the "Mormon Prophet," although they acknowledged the endorsers were above question, simply because it would encourage "Mormonism." So much of their specie was drawn by Joseph Smith during the three succeeding days, as greatly improved their tempers, and they said to Elder Cahoon, "Tell Mr. Smith he must stop this, and any favor he wants we are ready to accord him."

Subsequently application was made to the legislature of the state for a bank charter, the notes to be redeemed with specie and their redemption secured by real estate. The charter was denied us on the grounds that we were "Mormons," and soon a combination of apostates and outsiders caused us to leave Kirtland, the most of our property unsold; and our beautiful temple yet remains a lasting monument of our perseverance and industry. The loss sustained through this persecution was probably not less than one million dollars (JD, 13:106).

Joseph Smith

Some time previous to this I resigned my office in the "Kirtland Safety Society" [or "Bank"], disposed of my interest therein, and withdrew from the institution; being fully aware, after so long an experiment, that no institution of the kind, established upon just and righteous principles for a blessing not only to the Church but the whole nation, would be suffered to continue its operations in such an age of darkness, speculation, and wickedness. Almost all banks throughout the country, one after the other, have suspended specie payment, and gold and silver have risen in value in direct ratio with the depreciation of paper currency. The great pressure of the money market is felt in England as well as America, and bread stuffs are everywhere high (HC, 2:497).

Lucy Mack Smith

In the fall of 1836, a bank was established in Kirtland. . . . [Then] Joseph discovered that a large amount of money had been taken away by fraud, from this bank. He immediately demanded a search warrant of Esquire F. G. Williams, which was flatly refused. "I insist upon a warrant," said Joseph, "for if you will give me one, I can get the money, and if you do not, I will break you of your office." "Well, break it is, then," said Williams, "and we will strike hands upon it." "Very well," said Joseph, "from henceforth I drop you from my quorum, in the name of the Lord" (1958, pp. 240–41).

The Missouri Years (March 1838–April 1839)

General Comments on Life in Missouri

Philo Dibble

I moved to Jackson County, Missouri, from Kirtland, Ohio, in 1832, and was driven from Jackson to Clay County in 1833. Afterwards I, with others who had been driven from their homes, settled in Caldwell County.

I was privileged one day to take a stroll with the Prophet on the prairie. Difficulties and troubles were gathering thick around us as a people, and as was natural became the subject of conversation.

As we walked along I suggested to Joseph to send for General Atchison, who was then at Liberty, Clay County, forty miles distant. "He is general of the third division of the state of Missouri; not only a general, but a lawyer; and not only a lawyer, but a friend to law," I remarked.

Joseph made no reply. We soon turned about and were traveling towards home in the town of Far West.

Within half an hour after we got home, a man on the best horse in town was speeding his way towards Liberty, and before the close of the next day General Atchison was in Far West with one hundred men.

About this time a lawsuit was pending, in which Joseph was to be tried for some alleged infraction of law or mob politics, it's hard to tell which. It was agreed in some way and by some parties that this trial should take place in a grove of timber about half way between Far West and Gallatin, a little town about twenty miles distant, where there was no house. That such a place should be selected for a trial before some civil tribunal leaves room for suspicion and doubt as to the "civil" part of the performance about to take place.

General Atchison was employed by Joseph as his lawyer, and in laying his plans for the expected trial, he said to Joseph, "I want no man to go with us—you and I must go alone."

This proposition rather staggered Joseph, which was perceived by Atchison, who promptly added, "My life for yours, let it be as I want it."

Joseph consented, and they went to the woods designated as a proper place to try a prophet. There they found an armed mob in waiting. On seeing only Atchison and Joseph, the attendants at court began cursing, swearing, and threatening.

Atchison said, "Hold on, boys; if the first gun is fired there will not be one of you left."

The mob took this to signify that they were surrounded by Atchison's troops. They cooled down, let the trial proceed, in which Joseph was proven innocent of any infraction of law, and came away unmolested (1892c, p. 345).

Chapman Duncan

By this time Joseph the Prophet had come out to Adam-ondi-Ahman, Davies Country. . . . I think the next day he said to those present, Hyrum

Smith, Bishop Vinson Knight, myself, and two or three others, "Get me a spade, and I will show you the altar that Adam offered sacrifice on." I believe this was the only time Joseph was in Di-Ahman. He went about forty rods north of my house and placed the shovel with care and placed his foot on it. When he took out the shovelful of dirt it bared the stone, on the side of [the] upper edge nearly a foot deep. The dirt was two inches deep on the stone, I reckon. About four feet or more were disclosed. He did not dig to the bottom of the wall—three layers of good masonry wall put up, were unearthed. The stone looked like dressed stone, nice joints, ten inches thick, eighteen inches or more long. He came back down the slope perhaps fifteen rods. On the level, the Prophet stopped and remarked, "This place where we stood is the place where Adam gathered his posterity and blessed them, and predicted what should come to pass to later generations." The next day he returned to Far West, Lyman Wight and Bishop Knight going with him (n.d.).

Heber C. Kimball

[At Adam-ondi-Ahman] the Prophet Joseph called upon Brother Brigham, myself, and others, saying, "Brethren, come, go along with me, and I will show you something." He led us a short distance to a place where were the ruins of three altars built of stone, one above the other, and one standing a little back of the other, like unto the pulpits in the Kirtland Temple, representing the order of three grades of priesthood; "There," said Joseph, "is the place where Adam offered up sacrifice after he was cast out of the garden." The altar stood at the highest point of the bluff. I went and examined the place several times while I remained there (1945, pp. 209–10).

Daniel D. McArthur

When the Mormon boys got into Adam-ondi-Ahman, it was in the dead of the night, but the news soon went the rounds that the cannon was taken from the mob, which caused them to rejoice that the Lord had heard their prayers. So it was concluded by Joseph the Prophet and the brethren to take the cannon in the morning up on a hill to the place where old father Adam blessed his sons and fire off a few rounds. Consequently, as soon as the sun rose in the morning, the Saints collected on the spot and the cannon was prepared and loaded and fired three times, and every time it was discharged, the Saints took off their hats and shouted Hosannah to God and the Lamb. Three times the report was heard twenty-five miles distinctly (n.d., p. 7).

Lucy Mack Smith

Joseph was at our house writing a letter. While he was thus engaged, I stepped to the door, and looking towards the prairie, I beheld a large company of armed men advancing towards the city, but, as I supposed it to be training day, said nothing about it.

Presently the main body came to a halt. The officers dismounting, eight of them came into the house. Thinking they had come for some refreshment, I offered them chairs, but they refused to be seated, and, placing themselves in a line across the floor, continued standing. I again requested them to sit, but they replied, "We do not choose to sit down; we have come here to kill Joe Smith and all the 'Mormons.'"

"Ah," said I, "what has Joseph Smith done, that you should want to kill him?"

"He has killed seven men in Daviess County," replied the foremost, "and we have come to kill him, and all his Church."

"He has not been in Daviess County," I answered, "consequently the report must be false. Furthermore, if you should see him, you would not want to kill him."

"There is no doubt that the report is perfectly correct," rejoined the officer; "it came straight to us, and I believe it; and we were sent to kill the Prophet and all who believe in him, and I'll be d—d if I don't execute my orders."

"I suppose," said I, "you intend to kill me, with the rest?"

"Yes, we do," returned the officer.

"Very well," I continued, "I want you to act the gentleman about it, and do the job quick. Just shoot me down at once, then I shall be at rest; but I should not like to be murdered by inches."

"There it is again," said he. "You tell a 'Mormon' that you will kill him, and they will always tell you, 'that is nothing—if you kill us, we shall be happy.'"

Joseph, just at this moment finished his letter, and, seeing that he was at liberty, I said, "Gentlemen, suffer me to make you acquainted with Joseph Smith, the Prophet." They stared at him as if he were a spectre. He smiled, and stepping towards them, gave each of them his hand, in a manner which convinced them that he was neither a guilty criminal nor yet a hypocrite.

Joseph then sat down and explained to them the views, feelings, etc., of the Church, and what their course had been; besides the treatment which they had received from their enemies since the first. He also argued, that if any of the brethren had broken the law, they ought to be tried by the law, before anyone else was molested. After talking with them some time in this way, he said, "Mother, I believe I will go home now—Emma will be expecting me." At this two of the men sprang to their feet, and declared that he should not go alone, as it would be unsafe—that they would go with him, in order to protect him. Accordingly the three left together, and, during their absence, I overheard the following conversation among the officers, who remained at the door:

1st Officer. "Did you not feel strangely when Smith took you by the hand? I never felt so in my life."

2nd Officer: "I could not move. I would not harm a hair of that man's head for the whole world."

3rd Officer. "This is the last time you will catch me coming to kill Joe Smith, or the 'Mormons' either."

1st Officer. "I guess this is about my last expedition against this place. I never saw a more harmless, innocent appearing man than the 'Mormon' Prophet."

2nd Officer. "That story about his killing them men is all a d—d lie—there is no doubt of it; and we have had all this trouble for nothing; but they will never fool me in this way again; I'll warrant them" (1958, pp. 254–56).

Haun's Mill (October 30, 1838)

John D. Lee

The morning after the battle of Crooked River, [Brother] Haun came to Far West to consult with the Prophet concerning the policy of the removal of the settlers on Log Creek to the fortified camps. Col. [Lyman] Wight and myself were standing by when the Prophet said to him: "Move in, by all means, if you wish to save your lives." Haun replied that if the settlers left their homes all of their property would be lost, and the Gentiles would burn their houses and other buildings. The Prophet said: "You had much better lose your property than your lives, one can be replaced, the other cannot be restored; but there is no need of your losing either if you will only do as you are commanded." Haun said that he considered the best plan was for all of the settlers to move into and around the mill, and use the blacksmith's shop and other buildings as a fort in case of attack; in this way he thought they would be perfectly safe. "You are at liberty to do so if you think best," said the Prophet. Haun then departed, well satisfied that he had carried his point.

The Prophet turned to Col. Wight and said: "That man did not come for counsel, but to induce me to tell him to do as he pleased; which I did. Had I commanded them to move in here and leave their property, they would have called me a tyrant. I wish they were here for their own safety. I am confident that we will soon learn that they have been butchered in a fearful manner" (1881, pp. 78–79).

The Square at Far West (October–November 1838)

Lyman Wight

In October, 1838, after learning that Far West was surrounded by a mob, he [Lyman Wight] raised fifty-three volunteers in Adam-ondi-Ahman (twenty-five miles distant,) and repaired immediately to Far West to aid in its defense, where, with Joseph and Hyrum Smith and others, he was betrayed into the hands of his enemies, by Colonel George M. Hinkle, on the 31st; and was sentenced by a court martial to be shot the next morning (November 1) at 8 o'clock. During the evening, General Moses Wilson took him out by himself, and tried to induce him to betray Joseph Smith, and swear falsely against him; at which time the following conversation took place.

General Wilson said, "Colonel Wight, we have nothing against you, only that you are associated with Joseph Smith. He is our enemy and a damned rascal, and would take any plan he could to kill us. You are a damned fine fellow; and if you will come out and swear against him, we will spare your life, and give you any office you want; and if you don't do it, you will be shot tomorrow at 8 o'clock."

Colonel Wight replied, "General Wilson, you are entirely mistaken in your man, both in regard to myself and Joseph Smith. Joseph Smith is not an enemy to mankind, he is not your enemy; but is as good a friend as you have got. Had it not been for him, you would have been in hell long ago, for I should have sent you there by cutting your throat, and no other man but Joseph Smith could have prevented me, and you may thank him for your life. And, now, if you will give me the boys I brought from Adam-ondi-Ahman yesterday, I will whip your whole army."

Wilson said, "Wight, you are a strange man; but if you will not accept my proposal, you will be shot tomorrow morning at 8."

Colonel Wight replied, "Shoot and be damned" (1865, p. 457).

Liberty Jail (Winter 1838–1839)

Lysander Gee

My Dear Brother [Alexander McRae]: Having been acquainted with you for many years, and also having been cognizant of many matters connected with your life, and connections with the Prophet Joseph Smith, one of which I particularly figured [in] and to which I wish to call your attention, as I believe you to be the only living man at this time, besides myself, who knows of the circumstance. If you please, I wish you to endorse the same, and place it in the hands of the Church Historian; that it may be made record of, and show that, boy as I was at that time, I was true to my trust and faithful to my brethren in tribulation, as I hope I ever may be.

You will recollect that soon after Joseph Smith, Hyrum Smith, Sidney Rigdon, Lyman Wight, Caleb Baldwin, and yourself were confined in Liberty Jail, Clay Co., Missouri, Sidney Rigdon was let out on bail, soon after which preparations were made and arrangements entered into for the release of the Prophet and his fellow prisoners from their confinement and from the hands of their persecutors; to effect which purpose, a letter was prepared by you and your fellow prisoners, directed to Alanson Ripley, then residing in Far West, forty miles from Liberty, with instructions for him to furnish tools and implements sufficient to break the prison. The said letter was delivered to me by Joseph, at the lower window of, and on the south side of the jail in which you was confined, with instructions from Joseph to read the letter and then fold up the same in as small compass as possible, and if driven to a corner, to eat and swallow the same, but to carry the contents thereof and deliver the same verbally. I started immediately for Far West, traveling on foot, through mud, and wading streams in the winter time, and faithfully delivered the message to

A. Ripley and Heber C. Kimball. The result of which you will remember, and how nearly it succeeded, and no doubt would have done so, had it not have been for a little indiscretion on the part of one single man, by the name of Shoemaker. Wishing you health and yet many years to do good in this life, I am, respectfully your Brother, Lysander Gee (1879).

Ebenezer Robinson

During the winter and early spring, the prisoners at Liberty had been released except Joseph and Hyrum Smith. In April they were taken to Daviess County, where bills of indictment were found against them. They took a change of venue to another county, and the sheriff detailed a guard to accompany him in their removal. The first night the guards were allowed to get intoxicated, when the prisoners mounted two fine horses and quietly rode to Quincy, Illinois. A few weeks later the writer saw the sheriff at Quincy, making Joseph Smith, Jr., a friendly visit, and received pay for the horses (1890, p. 243).

Erastus Snow

[Shortly after December 13, 1838] I took a load of my mother-in-law's furniture, with her team, to sell at Liberty, and while there I visited, in connection with several more of my brethren, the Prophet Joseph and those confined in Liberty Jail with him. I, with four others, was locked up on a charge of attempting to liberate the Prophet Joseph. When brought up for examination a few days after, I managed my own case, pled my own cause, and was discharged. The other four employed two lawyers. All were bound over to court, and I was accepted as their bondsman. During this time Joseph prophesied that not a hair of [our] heads should be hurt, as he saw [me] pleading in court (1923, p. 107).

Note: Threats upon the lives of Erastus and those in his party made the Prophet's prophecy all the more welcome. Erastus Snow was not a trained attorney, but pled the case because the Prophet asked him to. So effective was his presentation, which he made without the assistance of an attorney, that after the trial "the attorneys flocked around him, wanting to know where he had studied law, stating that they had never heard a better plea" (Erastus Snow, 1912, 3:30–31; see also Alexander McRae, 1854).

Mercy R. Thompson

About the 1st of February, 1839, by the request of her husband, my sister [Mary Fielding Smith, wife of Hyrum Smith,] was placed on a bed in a wagon and taken a journey of about forty miles to visit him in prison [Liberty Jail]. Her infant son, Joseph F., then being about eleven weeks old. I had to accompany her, taking my own babe along, then [being] near[ly] eight months old. The weather being extremely cold, we suffered much on the journey. We arrived at the prison in the evening. We were admitted and the doors closed upon us. A *night* never to be forgotten. A *sleepless night*. I nursed the darling babes, and in the morning prepared to start for home with my afflicted sister; and as long as memory lasts will remain in my recollection the creeking hinges of that door which closed upon the noblest men on earth. Who can imagine our feelings as we traveled homewards? *But* would I sell the honor bestowed upon me of being locked up in jail with such characters for gold? No! No! (n.d.; see also Mercy R. Thompson, 1892, p. 398).

The Nauvoo Years (1839–1844)

Life in Nauvoo

Lewis Barney

One day being in company with Joseph and several others, Joseph said he needed a little money, and if he had it, he could put it to a better use than any other person in the world. I said nothing to him about it but went home and got $200.00 and went to Joseph's store. Joseph not being present and I being acquainted with Lyman Wight, said to him, "I have a little money for Brother Joseph that I wish to let him have."

Brother Wight said, "Let me take it, and I will hand it to him."

I told him to write me a receipt for it. While he was writing the receipt Brother Joseph stepped in.

I said, "Brother Joseph, I have some money for you. I was about to let Brother Wight have for you."

Joseph said, "I am the man to take it." So I handed him the $200.00, for which he gave me his note payable six months after date (n.d., pp. 22–23).

William A. Bills Sr.

I was well acquainted with the Prophet Joseph and Hyrum and their father and mother, as also William and Don Carlos Smith. We were close neighbors. Father, being a tailor, made their clothes. I used to take Joseph and Hyrum's clothes to Joseph's house. His mother once showed me the mummies; they were in appearance as natural as any other person would be after being dried up as they were. They were the color of cork sole leather, common size, five in number, if I recollect all right (n.d.).

William Black

Now, a few words about Father before coming to the valleys. He was a trusted bodyguard of the Prophet Joseph when eighteen years old. He was put to various tests and came through with flying colors. No man ever lived who loved Joseph Smith better than Father unless he had a greater capacity given him from the Lord to love.

At one time a mob general had his army assembled across the river from Nauvoo with the intention of exterminating the Mormons unless they left at once, so he decided to be sporty and serve notice on Joseph in person. Some way the Prophet got wise to this. The Prophet knew the general would come through a certain land to come to the city, so he selected six men and gave them all the same counsel, which was, "Boys, don't let him come into the city except as a prisoner." So the Prophet placed two of the men at the end of the lane where the general would enter the lane, one on either side of the road, each with a gun. At the middle way of the lane were two more men. At the end of the lane next to the city the Prophet placed uncle Robert Barrow and father.

The general rode a fine white horse. He had selected six men to go with him, all well mounted. After riding off the boat on the Nauvoo side, they rode casually along until they got near the first two guards. The captain discovered what was in the wind, and he gave the order to charge, and just before he got to the guard they stepped out in the road, threw their guns down on him, and ordered him to halt. He turned quick in his saddle and screamed to his men, "Come on boys." By this time they were past the first guard. He did the same with the second guard.

Uncle Robert said, "George, the son of B has passed all the other boys, and he is coming like hell." Father said, "Don't worry, he will stop when he gets here or I'll pick him off that horse, and I'll come close to getting all his men before they know where they are at if they offer resistance." Father gave the order, and the captain nearly pulled his horse over backwards trying to stop. Father walked up to him and said, "Captain, you are my prisoner. Throw the reins over your horse's head," which order was promptly obeyed. "Now unbuckle those six-shooters, as well as that saber. Give them to me." Father buckled that paraphernalia around himself, picked up the reins, and told the captain to tell his men to follow, which they did. Uncle Robert and father led the captain to the Prophet's office.

Father said, "Captain, get down from your horse, go in that office, and talk to a prophet of God. I will entertain your men." He sure entertained them. He told them what a bunch of cowards they were and what God had in store for them if they did not repent of their sins and cease trying to take the lives of God's other children, who had just as much right to serve God according to the dictates of their own conscience as any people who ever graced the earth.

After Father had lectured to those fellows about an hour, the captain came out of the office. It was very plain he had been crying. Father gave him his guns and saber. He went back across the river and dispersed his army. Next day it was learned that one of his men asked him how it was he passed the first two sets of guards and stopped at the last set. His reply was, "I saw shoot in that fellow's eye, and if I had disobeyed his order he would have shot hell right out of me" (n.d., pp. 16–17).

William Henrie

The Prophet Joseph Smith owned three farms in a row at Nauvoo. He sold the one in the middle to William Henrie, and from that day on as he passed by their place he would always stop in and rest and chat, and Myra would give him a glass of cold milk or buttermilk or a baked potato or a bun or cookie or whatever she had handy, and he would always bless the home and all those who dwelt there when he took his leave. William said you knew he was a true prophet of God because you could not be in his presence without feeling the influence and Spirit of God, which seemed to flow from him almost as heat does from a stove. You could not see it, but you felt it (1955, p. 4).

Wandle Mace

During the winter, the long evenings were utilized for improvement in public speaking. Lyceums or lecturing schools were opened, and it is surprising how much good was accomplished in attending a lyceum one winter; the new members at the commencement of the school would only occupy a few minutes of their time, but before the winter was gone they could occupy all the half hour allotted them, and then had scarcely time enough.

Our lyceum was composed of eighteen members. Each presided over the meeting in turn. One of the principles of the gospel was chosen as a subject, and each member spoke an half hour upon it. Three evenings was taken up with the one principle before another was touched. Six members occupied the first evening, the second evening six other members spoke upon the same subject, and the remaining six occupied the third evening; so that each one of the eighteen had equal time and opportunity to talk upon the subject.

It was very curious how the same subject would be handled by different men, each member presenting it in a manner peculiar to himself, all coming to the same conclusion by the evidence adduced from the scriptures; there was no jarring, no contention nor discord, and all were entertained, instructed, and edified. Joseph encouraged us by his presence whenever practicable, giving us instructions and assistance. He would tell the brethren to "Get into your lyceums, and investigate doctrine, and if you run against a snag, I am here, I will help you off." There were days and nights of pleasure and profit—to listen to a prophet's voice and receive instruction from one who communed with angels and received his instruction from on high when or wherever I met him, whether in the lyceum, on the street, or at home, he spoke forth words of light and intelligence for the salvation of mankind. For the approaching conference a rough floor was laid in the foundation of the [Nauvoo] temple, the walk was up about halfway of the windows of the first story (n.d. [b], pp. 79–80).

Samuel W. Richards

In the winter of 1843–44, the Prophet Joseph Smith sent to me one of the Twelve Apostles of the Church to learn if I would be one of a company of twenty-five (25) young men whom he wished to send out to pioneer the Rocky Mountains and lower California, to find a place for the Church to remove to as the persecutions were getting too strong to think of staying in that part of the country, so near the borders of the state from which we were driven, without being able to obtain any redress, or any sympathy from any source in the Union. My personal acquaintance with the Prophet up to this time was of a most endearing character, and I most freely and gladly responded to the request, and my name was enrolled as one of the chosen number. Weekly meetings were held for the purpose of instructing the company of twenty-five (25) young men thus selected. These meetings were attended by the presiding authorities, including the Prophet's counselors Sidney Rigdon and Hyrum Smith; also several of the Twelve Apostles then present in the city of Nauvoo.

I had been present at three or four of these meetings before I heard the Prophet say just what was expected of those twenty-five (25) young men who were to go on that expedition. At one of the meetings he said he wanted young men of faith who could go upon the mountains and talk with God face to face as Moses did on Mount Sinai, and learn from Him where His people should make a home. When I heard this in one of the meetings, I was very seriously affected. My first thought was to resign at once before leaving the meeting room, but after a few moments of reflection I thought I would ask my Heavenly Father before I decided the matter.

I went home and upon my knees by my bedside I prayed for some manifestation that would satisfy my mind as to what I should do. My prayer was answered. In vision I performed the entire journey successfully, and, in connection with it, I saw the future of my entire life, and also down to the end of time, when all things were restored to their Eden grandeur, purity, and excellence, for the use of man. All this was given to me as the result of responding to the wishes of the Prophet by becoming a member of that pioneer party organized to find a place for the Church in the wilds of the west. The outfit of the party was to be two animals for each man, one to ride and one to pack; a double-barreled gun, one barrel for shot and one for ball, with which we were to provide our living on the way; and each one to take no less than five-hundred dollars ($500.00) in cash with which to purchase lands to settle upon if necessary.

During the latter part of the winter the persecutions became very severe and increased almost daily. Soon after the pioneer company was fully organized and properly instructed as to what was expected of them, the Prophet Joseph left Nauvoo and with his brother Hyrum went in a westerly direction, as was supposed by some to escape the pending trouble seemingly coming upon the people; but by others it was supposed that his intention was to join the pioneer party when it should go out, and be their leader to the mountains. He was followed by those who did not feel disposed to consult his wishes in the least and was accused by them of cowardice, and as having no regard for the people in their time of trouble, but sought his own safety. Because of this accusation the plan was never carried out. He told his accusers that if his life was of no value to them it was not to himself and he would return with them, going as a lamb to the slaughter, which verily proved true.

It was well known, however, that the Prophet had perfected every necessary arrangement for the Saints to make their exodus to the mountains of the West, and as had been prophesied many times in our weekly pioneer meetings, they would become a great and a mighty people, establishing the Kingdom of God upon the earth, no more to be thrown down forever.

The removal of the Saints from Nauvoo to the Rocky Mountains was no plan originating with Brigham Young, but originating with the Prophet Joseph Smith. This I personally know. Brigham Young, at the time, was away in the East on missionary work, when these plans were being arranged under the Prophet's personal direction, assisted by his brother Hyrum, who mostly presided at the meetings of the party. At our meetings the spirit of prophecy was always strong, and on one occasion the Patriarch Hyrum Smith arose from his seat and remarked, "There has been enough said," and dismissed the meeting without further ceremony (1903).

Ebenezer Robinson

My health had so far recovered that I was able to walk from my house to the printing office, when, early in May 1840, as I was walking to the office, I received a manifestation from the Lord, such an one as I never received before or since. It seemed that a ball of fire came down from above and striking the top of my head passed down into my heart, and told me, in plain distinct language, what course to pursue and I could get the Book of Mormon stereotyped and printed. I went into the printing office, and in a few moments Brother Joseph Smith, Jr., he who translated the Book of Mormon by the gift and power of God, as I verily know, stepped into the office, when I said to him, "Brother Joseph, if you will furnish $200, and give us the privilege of printing two thousand copies of the Book of Mormon, Carlos and I will get $200 more and we will get it stereotyped and give you the plates." He dropped his face into his hand for a minute or so, when he said, "I will do it." He asked how soon we would want the money. I replied in two weeks.

Brother Carlos and I made an effort immediately to obtain our $200. We found a brother in the Church who would let us have $120 until the next April at thirty-five percent interest, the interest to be incorporated in the note, and all to draw six percent interest, if not paid when due. We consented to the terms, and got the money. A few days after, the same brother brought us $25 more, on the same terms, making $145. I took the money and put it away.

In a few days Brother Joseph Smith came to the printing office and said, "Brother Robinson, if you and Carlos get the Book of Mormon stereotyped you will have to furnish the money, as I cannot get the $200." I replied that if "he would give us the privilege of printing four thousand copies we would do it." He said he "would do that." We then made a strenuous effort to raise more money, but signally failed, and did not succeed in raising another dollar for that purpose.

We were considerably in debt to different persons, and our creditors were repeatedly pressing us for money, so that after a little time we began to draw a few dollars from the $145. We knew that it would not do to be paying thirty-five percent interest for money to pay ordinary debts with, so Carlos said to me one day in June, "Brother Robinson, you take that money and go to Cincinnati and buy some type and paper, which we must have." I said, "Yes, I will go, but I will not come home until the Book of Mormon is stereotyped," for it was as fire shut up in my bones, both day and night, that if I could only get to Cincinnati the work could be accomplished. He replied that "that was out of the question, as it could not be done with our limited means." Brother Hyrum Smith also said it could not be done, but Brother Joseph Smith did not say it could not be done when I told him, but he said, "God bless you."

Brother Joseph and I immediately went to work and compared a copy of the Kirtland edition with the first edition, by reading them entirely through, and I took one of the Kirtland edition as a copy for the stereotype edition (1890, pp. 258–59).

Note: In stereotyping, a printer makes a papier-mâché mat, which is used to cast a metal cut, which, in turn, is used for printing. With this process mats could be sent to other printers, enabling copies, or stereotypes, of the original printing to be made.

Shadrach Roundy

About the year 1840 [Roundy] removed to Nauvoo, where he served as captain of police. In times of imminent danger and persecutions he acted as special guard around the person of the Prophet Joseph. On several occasions he was on duty without intermission for many days and nights, without sleep or rest. His love for the Prophet was so great that he would have given his own life freely in defense of his beloved friend and brother. On one occasion, when the Prophet had been forewarned that he was in danger, he sent for Brother Roundy and told him to pick a trusty man to be on guard with him at his house, as a party was coming that night by water to kidnap him. Brother Roundy selected Joseph Arnold and placed him on guard at the gate, with orders to admit no one, while he himself took his beat by the river, but on hearing a noise he hastily repaired to the gate and found William Law inside the gate and others in the act of entering.

Brother Roundy, who had a hickory walking cane in his hand, quickly took hold of it at each end, and pressing it against the men forced them back outside, and then fastened the gate. William Law endeavored to explain that the men who were with him were gentlemen merchants who wanted to see the mummies. Brother Roundy replied that if they were gentlemen they should come at gentlemen's hours. William Law insisted that Brother Joseph would admit them, as they would pay $10 in pocket money, there being about forty of them; the admission being about 25 cents for each. On their agreeing not to try to enter while he was gone, Brother Roundy went to Joseph's room. The Prophet, who had overheard the conversation, told Elder Roundy to go back and tell the strangers as a messenger from him what he (Roundy) had already told them himself. Thus was the Prophet's life and property preserved by the courage and fidelity of Elder Roundy and his associate (1971, pp. 642–43).

Joseph F. Smith

I will tell you a little circumstance that I saw myself and you would think it very inappropriate of a prophet, but there were reasons for it that perhaps it would be difficult for me to explain here. I was one day playing marbles in front of the mansion with my cousin Alexander Smith. We were amusing ourselves on the sidewalk. The fence ran along within six or eight feet of the door of the mansion, and we were playing at the gate just outside the stone steps, when all of a sudden the door flew open and I looked, and there came a great, big man right off the end of Joseph Smith's foot, and he lit on the sidewalk just by the gate. I saw that myself. Well, I wondered what in the world was the matter. Since I grew to be a man, I learned that this man was there insulting the Prophet and abusing him in his own house, until the Prophet thought he had stood enough abuse from him, so he opened his door and invited him out; that he did not go as quickly as the Prophet wanted him to go, and he gave him the assistance of his boot, and helped him out.

Well, now, some biased man would say: "Why, would a prophet of God do such a thing as that!" Some would be shocked beyond measure to think that the man who beheld the face of God and the face of His son Jesus Christ—who had seen the glory that was manifested in the temple at Kirtland, when Moses, and Elias, and Elijah, and others of the prophets visited him, and Christ Himself also again—and their countenances shone as the glory of God, almost beyond the brightness of the sun—that a man who had beheld these wonderful things, and who had been entrusted with the great mission of restoring the great revelation of salvation to the earth for the last time, should be seen to kick a man out of his house that was abusing him. But he was tried beyond endurance many a time by false brethren, by false accusers, by malicious persons, by wicked men, by mobs and murderers, and evil creatures that sought his life from the day that he received his first message from God until the day they succeeded in taking his precious life from the earth. There was never a moment of his life that he was free from such things as these, being hounded, and abused, and insulted by wicked men; and he had been less a man if he had not kicked Josiah Butterfield out of his house on that day.

I saw him on another occasion standing in a wagon in the grove near the temple site in Nauvoo. Perhaps there are some here that remember the circumstance. The wind was blowing unfavorably for the speaker to be heard by the congregation from the stand. A wagon was drawn round to the windward side, and he appeared and took his position in the wagon box, and from there he addressed the people. I remember this circumstance well (CD, 5:28; see also HC, 5:316).

Joseph Smith III

I was not yet seven years old when my father [the Prophet Joseph Smith] and his family moved from Quincy to Nauvoo. Leaving Quincy in May, 1839, we removed to the vicinity of the little town of Commerce, which was located some three quarters of a mile up the Mississippi River from the home of Hugh White, whose farm Father purchased. . . .

From . . . the fall of 1839 or 1840, more or less confusion of memory obtains because of the rapidity with which events transpired. Hugh White, the river pilot from whom Father purchased the farm, had started to dig a well, but when he reached the solid rock he had desisted. Father had workmen dig into this solid stratum of rock, seeking for water, and while I was standing on the stone doorstep at the front of the house, a blast was fired in this well which threw one piece of some fifteen or twenty pounds in weight which just brushed the rim of my hat and struck a stone at my feet.

It seems to me now that it must have been about 1842 that what is called the military spirit took possession of the people at Nauvoo. One event connected with this is also vividly impressed on my mind. After the organization, the state had issued arms to some extent to the people of Nauvoo, and among them were the then fashionable horse pistols, or large pistols to be carried in holsters in front of the saddle. Father had two of these.

Loren Walker, who afterwards married Uncle Hyrum's oldest daughter, Lovina, had charge of the firearms and military accouterments. One day, while I was sleeping he cleaned these pistols, loaded them, and laid them on the bed. On waking I saw these pistols and with a boy's curiosity I took one in my hands, not thinking about their being loaded, and pointing it at the ceiling above my head, I thought, "Now if this was loaded, I could hit such a place with it," and to my astonishment, on pulling the trigger, the weapon was discharged and the bullet went through the ceiling and the roof of the house.

Father and a number of others were sitting in the room, and as some annoyance had been experienced from persecutors, the first thought was that someone had made an attempt upon Father's life. The pistol had jumped out of my hand and the plastering torn loose by the shot had fallen plentifully on the bed. The men folks rushed out of doors to discover when the shot was fired, but found nothing.

It occurred to Loren Walker where he had left his holster of pistols, and remembering that I was on the bed, he was fearful that by some means one of the weapons had been discharged and I had been hurt. So he rushed to the bed, parted the curtains, and found me staring at the hole in the ceiling, the pistol lying by me on the bed. He found I was not hurt, and it passed off as a rather laughable occurrence, a good deal like the story of the big hole that rumor said Father had dug in the Hill Cumorah. This incident can be verified by the same evidence used to support the story of the one Father dug: "The hole is still there."

. . . The rising generation was not exempt from the influence of the military spirit. A military captain by the name of Bailey, who had conceived the idea of the organization of the boys, succeeded to quite an extent, and after the Nauvoo Legion had grown to large proportions, he had at one time some six hundred of the boys under his command, divided into companies and pretty well trained.

On one of these parades Captain Bailey was out with quite a fair proportion of the older boys, and perhaps without previous understanding the young fellows armed themselves with things to produce noise, tin pans and horns, with branches of shrubs and trees, and started to march from the hill down onto the plain where the maneuvering was taking place. A scout reported to the commanding general that there was an "enemy" in force marching on them, and a detachment of horses was sent to disperse them. As they approached the boys formed in a square, and when the horsemen came pretty close, they broke out with beating their pans, waving their branches, and shouting. The horsemen retreated and the boys resumed their march. A second detachment of horsemen was sent to disperse them; but as before they formed a square and again repulsed the horsemen.

Father, being the commanding general, said to the officer of the day, "You had better summon Charlie," meaning the horse which he rode, and the officer in charge replied, "Very well, I direct you and Charlie to disperse the rebels." It may have been, as I now suppose, the spirit of sport that made the occasion notable, but Father with his horse alone, for he would not accept company, started towards the approaching band of boys. They, as before, formed a square, and when the horseman was sufficiently near, raised a great shout, waved their branches, and blew their horns; but the horse which Father rode was of a different temper and he plunged among them, scattering them right and left, and had to be forcibly restrained by his rider from tramping them down.

The horse was possessed of the spirit of the ancient war horses. He was utterly without fear.

. . . [I once saw Orrin P. Rockwell]. It was at dusk in the evening, just after the sun went down and before it was dark. I was in the door yard in the front of the house, not far from the fence on Water Street, running by the north side of the lot, when I saw him coming up the street from the hotel side. I had always been fond of him, and so I climbed over the fence and met him at the street. After I shook hands with him, he broke into tears, and sobbed out, scarcely able to speak, "Oh, Joseph, Joseph, they have killed the only friend I ever had," and for some little time he could not compose himself to talk with me coherently.

I do not remember of the breaking of the ground for the building of the temple, but I do remember the meetings in the grove on the hillside near the temple, and going there to Sunday School. Here I was a scholar in a class of about sixty boys under the teaching of Almon W. Babbitt, who as my memory now recalls him, was a kind, friendly, pleasant teacher. Whatever he may have been in after years he was then a man of good presence and quite able to teach. I remember that at the meetings there, I felt myself fortunate if I was permitted to sit with my mother or in the midst of the congregation; but generally, when Father was at home, I was taken by him upon the stand. I remember hearing George J. Adams, Parley P. Pratt, Amasa Lyman, and Orson Hyde, and my father preach from the stand in the grove. I do not remember hearing Brigham Young or others preach. They may have done so, but Father was usually the speaker. I remember the occurrence, stated by some as having taken place, that when one of the elders had preached quite a lengthy sermon, to which attention had been called, after it was delivered Father said that he had but one fault to find with it, that it was not true.

I remember when the cornerstone [of the Nauvoo Temple] was laid. The basement had been built and a rough floor laid preparatory to the assembling to witness the laying of the cornerstone, and I was on the platform with my father and others. There were too many to remember. The whole area of the building was covered, and all around it in the yard were members of the assembly standing and sitting upon benches of stone.

. . . The memories from that time to the dreaded culmination are almost like the changing views of a kaleidoscope. About the first that now occurs to my memory was the appearance of the messenger announcing the death of Father, who I think was Lorenzo Wassen, my mother's nephew, the son of Benjamin Wassen, and my mother's sister, Elizabeth. He came in covered with dust bringing the news. I remember the gathering of the crowd at the Nauvoo Mansion, and recall seeing Dr. Willard Richards on a platform erected in the frame house or building across the road from the mansion on the south side of Water Street, and the congregations of thousands who gathered to listen to him and others detailing something of the tragedy and counseling quiet resignation. I did not hear his speech, or if I did, I do not remember it, as my mother and we children were in the living room in the mansion—mother overwhelmed with her grief, and we children sympathizing as children will without fairly comprehending the importance of such an event. I remember the hours of seclusion of the family from intrusion, the gloom and the dread of the time, awaiting until the bodies were brought home, they being placed in their coffins in the southwest corner of the dining room, and the gathering of the little group (my mother and her children, my brother, Frederick Alexander, and my adopted sister, Julia Murdock, and myself). Notwithstanding the grief and the oppression of the hour, the darkness of which I can feel even now, I recall the attitude of my mother. After leaning over the coffin, she placed her hand upon the cheek of my father, and in grief-stricken accents said, "Oh! Joseph! Joseph! O my husband! My husband! Have they taken you from me at last!" Friendly hands ministered to us, and mother was assisted to her room again, and we were alone while the multitude flocked through the house, taking a last look at him who in life had been their leader and their friend. I do not know much about the cavalcade which formed, nor was I a witness to the depositing of the bodies, or the boxes supposed to contain the bodies of Father and Uncle Hyrum, in the temporary tomb, built in the hillside near the temple. I remember some of the rumors passed around as to the place the bodies were deposited, but I knew where the bodies were subsequently buried, for I was present upon one occasion when in the presence of two others, there was an opening of the place of deposit, and I saw the features of my father as they were exposed and a lock of hair was cut from his head, a portion of which I have in my possession today, in a brooch which my mother used to wear. . . .

It has been reported by those who pretended to be friends of Father, that Mother was quarrelsome and was antagonistic to my father, and frequently made trouble for him. I have this to say now, that tracing my memory back through the period of time in which my father was permitted to stay with his family, that I never heard any quarreling or harsh language between them under any circumstances, and that even disagreements between them were not conducted in a noisy or angry manner, that mother's language was quiet and temperate, and so was Father's (1910, pp. 132, 133–36, 138, 139, 142, 143, 334–38).

Samuel A. Woolley

Together with my brothers Edwin D. and John M., I started for the gathering place of the Saints in the fall of 1839, but on reaching Quincy, Ill., we met the Prophet and the Patriarch and were advised to stop at that place for the winter, which we did, and I worked at chopping and hauling wood.

... During a conference meeting held in Nauvoo in the spring of 1843 an officer came to arrest Joseph the Prophet; but in order to prevent him from doing so a number of boys, including myself, commenced whittling sticks and whistling, and every time the officer neared the house where the Prophet was, we would stand in front of him and whittle and whistle. The result of this was that he did not arrest Joseph Smith that day. During the troublous times of 1844 I served as a city guard in Nauvoo (1971, p. 781).

Nauvoo Temple (April 6, 1841)

Samuel Miles

I was present when the books, writings, etc., were deposited in the southeast cornerstone of the Nauvoo Temple. Joseph was there overseeing the selection made for deposit. Perhaps two hundred persons were collected around the place. When a Bible was presented for deposit it was thought necessary that it should be complete—containing the Apocrypha. As there seemed to be none within reach, except large, highly-prized family Bibles, Brother Reynolds Cahoon volunteered to go to his home, which was nearby, and cut out the Apocrypha from his large family Bible, which was accepted, and the Bible thus made complete. After several books, coins, periodicals, and publications had been accepted and deposited, a poem was presented [to] the Prophet to be laid away with the other things. Joseph handed it to one of the brethren requesting him to read it. When he was through Joseph said, "What does it amount to?"

"See saw, Margery Daw, Sold her bed and laid in the straw."

So the poor poem was left out in the cold (1892, p. 174).

Nancy N. Tracy

One day I looked over toward the temple and saw a large crowd gathered with some two or three women present; so I thought I would go over. I put on my bonnet and shawl and made my way over. Brother Joseph was there and seemed busily engaged over something. Finally, he looked up and saw us women. He said for the brothers to stand back and let the sisters come up. So they gave way, and we went up. In the huge chief cornerstone was cut out a square about a foot around and about as deep lined with zinc, and in it Brother Joseph had placed a Bible, a Book of Mormon, hymn book, and other church works, along with silver money that had been coined in that year. Then a lid was cemented down, and the temple was reared on the top of this. It made me think of the prophets in ancient days hiding up their records to come forth in some future generation. At any rate, it was for some wise purpose, but I never heard any explanation on it. The building progressed rapidly, and I was present when the capstone was laid and heard the last ring of the trowel. The Saints turned out en mass. The address on that occasion was pathetic and grand, being delivered by Brigham Young (n.d. [a], p. 26).

Dixon Kidnapping (June 23, 1843)

John L. Butler

In the summer before I went to Kentucky, Brother Joseph started with his wife, Emma, to visit her friends, and I expect some of the dissenters told some of the Missourians, and a mob came over and put themselves up as officers of the peace to take him to Missouri and make away with him. They were going to Stone River to see her friends and on the way they waylaid him and took him prisoner, and Emma did not know what to do, so she started back again to Nauvoo. Now these Missourians took him to a house belonging to an old man and asked him if he would let them have a room to put their prisoner. Now while they were going and after they had gotten there, there was a fellow with a revolver pointing it to Joseph's ribs, and once in a while he would give him a poke with it, until he had taken the skin off in more than one or two places.

Well, the old man heard by some of his folks that they had ill-treated their prisoner, so he thought that he would go and see the prisoner, so he went to the door, and it was fastened so that he could not get in. They were counseling together what they would do with him. I expect the old man demanded admittance, but they would not let him in, so he told them that he was coming in, or would set fire to the place and burn them up, but what would go in, so they let him in.

"A pretty thing," said he, "to keep a man out of his own house when he had kindly let you have a room to secure your prisoner in." So he asked

Joseph whether he had been ill-treated. Joseph opened his shirt bosom and showed him his side which was then bleeding, and said, "If you call that ill treatment, why I have been ill treated." The old man looked and said, "Who did it?" and Joseph said his captors. The old man said, "Gentlemen, you have abused this man shamefully and I tell you, you can't do such things in my house, and I tell you how we serve folks that don't go by the laws of the Constitution of the United States. We just take them by lynch law, and I can tell you that you must not abuse a prisoner in this part of the state or you will be very apt to know of it."

He then asked Joseph whether he had had anything to eat. He said that he had not. "Why," said the old man, "these other men have had something to eat, why did you not get some?" "Because," said Joseph, "they would not give me any." "Never mind, you shall have some." "Oh," said they, "he is only a damned Mormon." "Well," said the old man, "Mormon or no Mormon, he is a man and a citizen of the United States and he has got to have justice and he is going to have it so long as he stays with me." They then growled about something, but the old man went off to get something to eat for Joseph. He gave him something good to eat and told him that he should have a bed to sleep upon, but that those other fellers would have to find their own, for they should not sleep with him.

Joseph told him about Emma's going back to Nauvoo and that he expected someone would be along to help him out of the difficulty. The old man then told Joseph that he would keep him there until some of his friends should come to his assistance. His treatment to Joseph was very kind. If it had not been for him, I don't know how Brother Joseph would have fared, but the Lord was his guardian angel, and he would just let things go so far and no further. He softened the old man's heart so that he should have justice done him, and to bring about his purposes.

Well, at this time Emma had gone back to Nauvoo and told the brethren that Brother Joseph had been taken by a mob. I, at that time, had been ordained one of Joseph's lifeguards, so some thirty of the brethren with myself started to go to Brother Joseph and rescue him from the bloodthirsty wretches if we could. It took us some time, for we did not get on the right track for awhile. Well, we met them coming back. The old man had gone and gotten some of his friends and taken Brother Joseph and started to Nauvoo with him. The mob was taken also and brought with him, except two or three, those who abused Brother Joseph so mean; they went home the next day fearing, I expect, that the old man would bring his threats into realities, so they put for home.

Now we met Brother Joseph and his escort, and we had not been with him more than half an hour when about three hundred of the brethren came up all mounted and ready for anything that might transpire. The old man gave up Joseph after his thanking him for his hospitality and kindness to him. The brethren took the mob prisoners, and the old man and his friends wished us good day and started for home. And we started for home, too. Sister Emma sent Joseph out some clean clothes, but Joseph [saw] . . . his brethren were as dirty as he and he was not going in clean and his brethren dirty; the dust upon the road then was four or five inches deep. The folks all heard of our arrival home, and they all came out and lined the street on both sides. Brother Joseph was first and then Brother Hodge and myself, his lifeguards, and then came the officers that took him prisoner, and then the rest of the brethren. The folks, both men and women and children, were glad to see their leader again, and out of the hands of murderers; they took off their hats and bonnets and ushered him all the way up the street. Brother Joseph took off his hat and looked around upon the people and shouted, "Hosanna to God." The officers said that the people thought a good deal of him. "Yes," said Brother Joseph, "they are the best people in the world."

. . . I went home with Brother Joseph to the mansion house and saw the prisoners safely under guard. They did not know what to think; they thought that they were about done for; they thought that they would be killed; they took their trial, but Brother Joseph did not want to hurt them at all, so he let them go home and told them in the future to do unto others as they would that others should do unto them. They looked very sheepish; they went home and left us once more to ourselves, but there were lots of apostates there so that Brother Joseph could hardly not make a move without its going abroad to the mobs (1993, pp. 13, 20–21, 24–27; see also Lucy Walker Kimball, n.d.; Matilda E. Loveless, n.d.; Wandle Mace, n.d. [b], pp. 85–89; Jennie Miles, n.d.; Helen Mar Whitney, 1882a, p. 70; Andrew Jenson, 1971, p. 637; and HC, 5:439–54 for the Prophet Joseph's account).

Joseph's Last Meeting with the Twelve (March 18, 1844)

Wilford Woodruff

I remember very well the last charge that Joseph gave to the Apostles. We had as little idea that he was going from us as the Apostles of the Savior did that He was going to be taken from them. Joseph talked with us as plainly as did the Savior to His Apostles, but we did not understand that he was about to depart from us any more than the Apostles understood the Savior. Now, I have heard of other parties rising up and pretending that the Prophet Joseph Smith gave unto them a charge to lead and direct the Church of Jesus Christ of Latter-day Saints. I want to say that it is false; there is not a word of truth in it. When he delivered that charge to the Apostles he was filled with the power of God. His face was clear as amber, and the room was filled with the Spirit of God, like the holy fire. In his address he told us that he had received at the hands of the Almighty God all the keys, and powers, and priesthood, and ordinances and gifts belonging to the dispensation in which we lived. "Now," says he, "I have sealed all these blessings upon your heads, upon you Apostles of the Lamb of God, who have been chosen to bear off this Church and kingdom on the earth;" and after making this solemn proclamation to us, he said, "Now, you have got to round up your shoulders and bear off this kingdom, or you will be damned." I never shall forget that (CD, 5:188–89).

Joseph's Last Public Speech (June 18, 1844)

George Laub

Now I will relate a few words of his last address to the Nauvoo Legion while upon a small building across the street opposite his dwelling. Thus, he spoke concerning some of the brethren [who were] a whining, and he was sorry to see such proceedings. He addressed us with a lengthy discourse. I cannot remember all, but he told us that there were some men who were seeking his life with all schemes that could be devised, and if they do kill me they will shed innocent blood. He spoke concerning

Joseph Jackson by relating some of Jackson's secret wickedness, which he drew out of him, and then said he [that is, Jackson], "Now G—d—, your soul if you tell on me; I will kill you for you told me nothing, and I never told any other person besides you." And he told me that he had murdered four men and made catfish meat of them and the engagement of making bogus money and other wicked things; thus he stated that he was now colleague with the mob (n.d., p. 31).

Matilda E. Loveless

The last time I saw Joseph was the day he delivered his last public address, when he said "I call upon God and angels to witness that I have unsheathed my sword with a firm and unalterable determination that the people shall have their loyal rights, and shall be protected from mobs, violence, or my blood shall be spilt upon the ground like water and my body consigned to the silent tomb." I can remember so well that day it looked so cloudy and as though it would storm so my mother sent me to my father with his coat. I remember so well the scene and how attentive my father was [to] the remarks of Joseph, so I listened and became equally so (n.d.).

James P. Terry

I was at the last meeting where the Prophet ever spoke in public. He was dressed in his regimentals or uniform. He stood on the little frame building on the corner of the lot across the street south of the Mansion House. While speaking he said, as nearly as I can recollect, drawing his sword: "As I draw my sword here today, the sword of the Almighty is drawn in the heavens, and it will never be returned until the wrongs committed against me and the Latter-day Saints have been redressed" (1893, p. 331).

Antecedents to the Martyrdom

Benjamin Ashby

I was in my father's garden one morning the memorable June 1844 when he road past on his way to Carthage. Never shall I forget the look of deep sorrow that covered his noble countenance—that was the last time I saw him alive. He was met on the way by an officer and posse with an order from the governor for the return of the state arms and he turned back to see the order complied with. On getting into town he called Bro. J. [Joseph] B. Noble to accompany him, and with his Brother Hyrum they turned off the road, leaving the company, and took a short cut across the hills. When alone he asked Hyrum what the Spirit indicated to him. He replied that he could get no satisfactory answer. Joseph then said, "Well, if they kill me, I shall die innocent, and my blood will be required of this nation." This is as near as I remember the testimony of Brother Noble shortly before he died.

In the afternoon he went to Carthage and to his martyrdom.

I sat upon the steps of my father's house on the evening of the day that he was shot until twelve o'clock, and never did I hear before such an uproar and noise that seemed to pervade the very atmosphere—dogs howling, mingled with confused noises as though all the legions of the damned were in commotion.

Not dreaming of the tragedy that had been enacted that afternoon, I went to bed, but at the dawn of morning the sad tale was brought to our ears, and the grief and sorrow of a whole people cannot be pictured in language. For days a man, woman, or child could not be met but they were in tears for the loss of their beloved leaders. Soon the wagon containing the two brothers arrived in the city and passed down to the Mansion House, where we visited and viewed their marred features as they lay in the habiliments of the grave (n.d. [b]).

Nancy Boss

Nancy Boss was born in Davison County, North Carolina on the 26th March, 1829, daughter of Phillip and Obedience Brown Boss. Her father passed away in the year 1835, leaving grandmother with nine children—six sons and three daughters. She moved with her children to Brown County, Illinois, in 1838, where she and her family allied themselves with the Mormon Church and gathered at Nauvoo in 1842. At the time of the Prophet Joseph's death, Grandmother was employed as a servant girl at the home of Col. Williams, the man who led the mob that killed the Prophet. She cooked the dinner for the mob before they started to the jail. Knowing she was a Mormon girl, Col. Williams refused to let her leave the house. She said before she went there to work for Williams, the mob burned her mother's house.

Her mother seemed to be a person who could make friends, seemed she was loved and respected by all who knew her. They called her Aunt Biddy. One of her friends, [a] non-Mormon, warned her to get out and leave her home, as the mob intended to burn it. That night she took her children, some being quite young, and took what things they could carry, went down to the swamps to sleep, thinking it would be safe for them there. Said the mosquitoes nearly ate them up. Their home wasn't burned that night, but was burned to ashes the next night.

So grandmother and the children, that were old enough, had to seek for employment; and she was real glad to get work at Col. Williams, not knowing, of course, that he was the leader of the mob. While at Williams' home he threatened her life if she attempted to make her escape. She told how the mob carried on like so many demons, and heard them plan the martyrdom.

The night before they killed the Prophet they painted their faces black and drank whiskey, acted as if they had gone mad. She said her room was upstairs, and [as] she was sitting on the stair steps she heard Williams say, "Every nit makes a louse, let's kill her." She was so badly frightened she sat by her window and watched, did not know at what moment they would come upstairs and kill her, and likely would have done so, but her time had not come to die; she was needed in the service of the Lord.

The next night after the mob had murdered the Prophet, they came back to Col. Williams' home and they seemed very much frightened. They knew they had committed a terrible, wicked crime, and they didn't know what was going to happen to them. She said they acted like crazy men.

She, in some way, got word from her husband, Capt. James Brown, that he would be down in the woods at a certain place and would wait for her. She put a few things in a small bundle and threw them out of the window and took a bucket as though she were going after water. After she got out she dropped the bucket, took her little bundle, and made for the woods as fast as her feet would take her. She didn't know at what moment they would shoot her; no doubt prayers were being offered up for her safety. She found her cousin, mounted on his horse, and they made their escape safely (n.d.).

Anson Call

In June, 1844, Anson Call, with David Evans, was appointed to visit the leaders of the mob forces then gathering against Nauvoo, and endeavor to effect a peaceable settlement of the pending troubles. They were unsuccessful and barely escaped mob violence. They also visited Judge Thomas of the circuit court, then sitting at Knoxville, eighty miles from Nauvoo, and tried to get a change of venue by which the Prophet—accused of treason and riot—might be brought before that tribunal instead of being taken to Carthage, which town was swarming with enemies who had sworn to kill him. Judge Thomas declined to interfere, remarking that it was better one or two men should be killed than that a whole people should perish. Messrs. Call and Evans delivered this answer to Emma Smith, who promised to send it to her husband, then on the west side of the Mississippi. Willard Richards told Anson Call that this was never done.

June 24, 1844, was the last day that he saw the Prophet alive. Joseph bade farewell to the Legion near the Masonic Hall saying: "Boys, I have come to bid you good bye; I am going to leave you for a while." He turned in the saddle, raised his hand, and added, "You are my boys, and I bless you in the name of Israel's God. Be faithful and true, and you shall have your reward—farewell." He then set out for Carthage. "Sunday morning, June 28"—says Mr. Call—"O. P. Rockwell rode into Nauvoo at full speed, with the sweet dripping from his horse, shouting 'Joseph is killed—Joseph is killed; they have killed him—they have killed him!'"

A few days after the murder he visited Carthage and was shown through the jail. He saw Hyrum Smith's blood on the floor of the fatal room, and the Prophet's blood on the well curb outside the prison. He met a number of the murderers, among them Captain Robert Smith of the Carthage Greys. Says he: "I suppose I was the first man who ever testified to him that Joseph Smith was a prophet of God. He never could look me in the face afterwards" (1904, 4:143–44).

Robert Crookston Sr.

The Prophet Joseph was mayor of Nauvoo City. Some apostates published a paper with so many malicious lies about our people that the city council proclaimed it a nuisance. They then raised the hue and cry of rebellion of our people against the government and collected a mob so as to get Joseph in their power.

I was called with a number of the brethren to protect the city. I was just recovering from a spell of fever and ague. My legs were so swollen I could hardly walk the length of a block, far less travel twenty miles across a prairie half a leg deep in water about half the distance on account of heavy rains. The fever sores on my legs forbade me getting wet under any ordinary condition, but I had faith in God and the blessing of our grand old Patriarch, who promised that I should take no harm and would return in safety to my parents. We were quartered in a large brick house yet unfinished, belonging to a man by the name of Foster. Joseph reviewed the Legion that day on the flat and spoke encouragingly to them. Drawing his sword, he said that if there was a drop of blood spilt it should never again be sheathed until this nation is drenched in blood.

The last time I saw him in life he and his brother Hyrum, Brothers Taylor and Richards were on their way to Nauvoo on horseback. Joseph's horse was a pacer and the other three were trotters. He rode his horse in a kingly manner. Frocham and his wife and others were there. Brother Frocham's wife, with a look of fear on her pale face, said, "Poor Joseph. We will never see him again," and rushed into the house and threw herself on the bed and wept aloud.

Her impression was right. He and his brother were martyred the next day. Our company was dismissed. Brother Fife and I started for home alone, but we mistook the Carthage road for the Macedonia road and walked into Carthage, where we were arrested and placed in Carthage Jail under guard until morning. We were then escorted to the court house, where the judge merely asked us what we wanted there. Brother Fife had a happy thought and spoke up, saying, "We want to pass to Macedonia." The judge, turning to the clerk, said, "Write these gentlemen out a pass to Macedonia."

They had gotten what they wanted. Joseph and Hyrum were in jail, and they did not want any more Mormons around so we went home, the distance being about eight miles. We were not molested, but we overheard threats as to what would happen to the Smiths, so we went to our captain and entreated him to call out our brethren and go within a half mile of Carthage to strip off timber and lay in ambush. But he refused, saying that the governor had put the county under martial law and anyone bearing arms under his command would be liable to arrest. We told him we were willing to risk that, but he was firm in his purpose. In the afternoon the troops from Macedonia who were friendly to the Mormon prisoners were sent home. They said they would not give a button for the lives of the Smiths, but if that damned old governor had allowed them to remain they would have seen to it that the prisoners would have had a fair trial.

But the governor left them to the mercy of a mob, while they, themselves, went up to Nauvoo to argue the people about being law-abiding citizens, knowing full well that the mob at Carthage were doing their bloody work.

Brother Babbet, lawyer, came home soon after on horseback, stating that the mob had given him but five minutes to leave or they would kill him, and he fully expected that our Prophet would be killed.

When the awful tidings reached us, the people wept aloud. One could hear the sobs and crying from every quarter. They felt as though the hosts of hell were let loose to do their murderous work of extermination if possible.

The Gentiles approved of the ghastly deed and predicted that it would be the end of Mormonism (n.d.).

Isaac C. Haight

June 1 [1844]—The enemies of the Church began to rage without and hypocrites and dissenters to manifest themselves within. The Laws, Fosters, Higbees, and others got up a printing press [the *Nauvoo Expositor*] in the city and began to slander the Saints in the most shameful manner, so that the city council considered it a nuisance and ordered the mayor to call on the police and legion to abate the nuisance. It was done according to order.

June 10 [1844]—We burnt the fixtures and papers and destroyed the press. The same day the proprietors were at a meeting at Carthage to devise means to destroy our city and drive and kill the saints. This the Saints were not disposed to submit to, as the mob began to gather on every side of us, and our Lieutenant General Joseph Smith thought best for our safety to call out the Nauvoo Legion until he could get word from the governor. The legion was drilled everyday till the governor arrived at Carthage which was about the twenty-second. He ordered the legion dismissed and sent for Joseph and Hyrum to come to Carthage, or he would send the militia to bring them to be tried on charge of riot in the destruction of the press of the *Nauvoo Expositor*. They refused to go unless the governor would protect them from the fury of the mob then gathered at Carthage. The governor then pledged his end [*sic*] and the honor of the state that they would be protected. Then upon the plighted faith of the Governor [Thomas Ford] and the state of Illinois, they agreed to go to Carthage to be tried by those that had sworn to take their lives.

Therefore, on the morning of the 26th day, they in company with about twenty of their friends started for Carthage (I was one of the number) with fearful foreboding of the snare that was laid for to effect the death of the best man that was now upon the earth. The prophet was calm as a summer morning and seemed to know or have a knowledge of the fate that awaited him. Once as we were riding along he turns to Hyrum and says, "Brother Hyrum, let us go back to Nauvoo and all die together." Thus showing that he was well aware of what would befall him. But Hyrum thought best to go on.

We, therefore, proceeded until we got in about four miles of Carthage to Brother Fellows, and then we met the governor's agent with sixty armed men going to Nauvoo to demand the state arms which the state had distributed to the legion as their proportion of the arms of the state agreeable to the charter organizing the legion.

The demand was accepted by the lieutenant general, and it was agreed that we should return to Nauvoo in company with the agent and his men and collect the arms, which we did. When we got to Nauvoo the state arms were collected as soon as possible with as little noise as could be expected under existing circumstances. Joseph and Hyrum then started for Carthage accompanied only by two or three of the brethren. The Governor forbid the others to go. It was hard to part with our Beloved Prophet into the hands of his enemies (n.d. [a], pp. 13–14).

Solomon Hancock

Perhaps because of Solomon's loyalty to the Prophet, he was chosen to perform one of the last kindnesses given to Joseph Smith before his death.

Solomon's wife, Phoebe Hancock, was pregnant when once they came to Quincy, Illinois, to buy food and clothes. Solomon had promised his wife five dollars to buy clothes and other articles for the new baby, which would soon be born, and their wagon was also loaded with butter and eggs to sell in town.

But just before they arrived in Quincy, Solomon informed his wife that he felt he could not give her the five dollars after all. She was surprised—and more than a little disappointed. After all, the money was for things their baby would need.

"I'm sorry," he told her, "but I've had three strong warnings from the Spirit that I shouldn't expect to use this money for the baby."

Frustrated, Phoebe showed her husband the list of items that she had planned to buy with the money, but Solomon only told her that she should use the money from the sale of the butter and eggs to buy the most important items. She reluctantly complied, and bought all that she could with the little money she had. But she was so disappointed that on the way home she sat down on the wagon board, pulled her bonnet down to hide her face, folded her arms, and turned her back on her husband.

They had traveled only a little way when they came to a crossroads, where they were surprised to meet the Prophet Joseph Smith. To their dismay, the men with the Prophet were taking him to prison in Carthage, Illinois.

Joseph called Solomon by name and said, "Have you got five dollars?"

"Yes, I have," Solomon said.

"I knew it," Joseph responded. "I told these men we would get something to eat before we got to the Carthage Jail."

Solomon gave the Prophet the five dollars, and his guards took him on his way. Phoebe wept, and asked forgiveness for wanting the money which the Prophet needed so much for food.

Soon the Prophet and his brother were killed by a mob that stormed the prison, and Solomon's and Phoebe's grief at the death of the Prophet could be assuaged, a little bit, by the knowledge that the Spirit had called on them to aid him during his last hours (1978, p. 67).

Note: Solomon Hancock is mentioned in HC 3:225; this story, however, does not match up. Solomon and Phoebe had a son named Elijah on April 2, 1844, so it's very unlikely she was pregnant in June 1844. Apparently the person who recorded this event either placed it at the wrong time (just before the martyrdom) or with the wrong circumstance (Phoebe's pregnancy). Perhaps this encounter took place earlier in the year, nearer to Elijah's birth. Or perhaps Phoebe was not pregnant but a new mother, hoping to use the money for their newborn son.

Dennison L. Harris

In the spring of 1844 I was invited by Austin A. Cowles, who was at the time a member of the high council, to attend a secret meeting; I was also asked to invite my father. The meeting was to be held on the following Sunday, at William Law's brick house. There was another young man by the name of Robert Scott who was also invited by William Law to attend the same meeting—being intimate friends we found out during the week that both of us had been invited to attend the same meeting. I told my father about this meeting, and he went immediately to Brother Joseph, who lived some two and one half miles distant, and informed him of the same. Joseph told my father to send the boys to him, but for him (my father) not to go to the meeting nor to pay any attention to it. When Sunday morning came Robert Scott (the young man referred to as my intimate friend) and I went and saw Brother Joseph. After telling him about receiving the invitation, he instructed us to go to this meeting and pay strict attention and do the best we could to learn, and remember all the proceedings. We went. At that meeting they were counseling together and working up the system and planning how to get at things the best. They were opposed to the doctrine of plurality of wives, which was the cause of their conspiring against Joseph.

[On being asked who were present, Brother Harris said:] As near as I can recollect, William and Wilson Law, Austin Cowles, the Higbees—Francis and Chauncey, Robert Foster and [his] brother, and two of the Hickes. I am positive of those; and there were a great many others of similar character. Marks was not present at all. I think Jason W. Briggs was there; also Finche and Rollinson, merchants and enemies to the Church, were there. This was the first meeting. They were plotting how and what they could do against Joseph.

The next Sunday, we attended again, having received an invitation to come back. And when they told us to come again on the next Sabbath they told us to keep quiet what had passed at the meeting, and to say nothing to our fathers, or anybody else. We reported to Joseph the proceedings as far as they went. Joseph said: "Boys, come and see me next Sunday morning, and go on to the meeting." We did so. They went on with their arrangements, and agreed to make further arrangements during the week. They worked this up considerably that Sunday, and still gave us an invitation to attend the following week. Joseph told us to go again, this being the third Sunday, and was desirous that we should see and learn all that took place this day, for, said he, "this will be your last meeting; this will be the last time they will admit you into their council, and they will come to some determination. But be sure," he continued, "that you make no covenants nor enter into any obligation whatever with that party. Be strictly reserved, and make no promise either to conspire against me or any portion of the community. Be silent and do not take any part in their deliberations."

That day we were received and welcomed by William Law and Austin

Cowles. We passed up the alley. On each side were men on guard, armed in the same way. Before we went to this meeting Brother Joseph said to us: "Boys, this day will be their last meeting, and they may shed your blood, but I hardly think they will, as you are so young, but they may. If they do I will be a lion in their path. Don't flinch, if you have to die, die like men. You will be martyrs to the cause, and your crown can be no greater. But," said he, "again, I hardly think they will shed your blood."

We went, as I have said, to the house of meeting and passed the guards. There was a great deal of counseling going on with each other. And every little while Austin Cowles would come and sit by my side and put his arm around my neck to ascertain how I felt with regard to their proceedings, and at the same time William Law would do the same thing with Robert Scott. They talked about Joseph, denouncing him, and accusing him. We told them that we did not know anything against Joseph or about the things they were charging him with, that we were only young men, and therefore had nothing to say. They would then try to convince us by relating things to us against him, but we told them that we knew nothing about them, and did not understand them, that we had been reared in the Church and always esteemed Brother Joseph highly. Robert had been reared by William Law, and I had been a neighbor of Austin Cowles, and consequently they esteemed us as friends, and we did them. They continued to persuade us, we being the only ones who did not sympathize with their proceedings, but they failed to convert us.

Finally they went on to administer the oath to those present. Each man was required to come to the table and hold up the Bible in his right hand. When Brother Higbee would say, "Are you ready?" the man being sworn answered, "Yes." He would say, "You solemnly swear before God and all holy angels and these your brethren, by whom you are surrounded, that you will give your life, your liberty, your influence, your all for the destruction of Joseph Smith and his party, so help you God!"

Each one was sworn in that way, numbering in the neighborhood of two hundred persons, and they were all sworn before we were called upon. There were also three women brought in who testified that Joseph Smith and others—Hyrum among them—had tried to seduce them into this spiritual marriage and wanted them for their wives and also wanted to lie with them. They also made oath before this Justice, after which they were escorted out of the room, by way of the back door.

After all in the room had taken the oath but Robert and me, we were labored with by those two brethren, William Law and Austin Cowles. They sat together side by side, with Brother Cowles on one side and Brother Law on the other. Their arguments were to try to convince us that Joseph was wrong; that he was in transgression, that he was a fallen prophet, and that the Church would be destroyed except action be taken at once against him—a strong one, one that would tell, etc. We told them that we were young, that we were not members of the high council, and that we knew nothing at all about their charges. They then told us that Joseph had read the revelation on celestial marriage to the high council and that Joseph had instructed them in this revelation, and that he had tried to make them believe it. After laboring with us in this way with a view of trying to get us to take the oath, we told them we could not do it.

They then told us that they were combining and entering into a conspiracy for the protection and salvation of the Church, and that if we refused to take the oath they would have to kill us. They could not, they said, let us go out with the information that we had gained, because it would not be safe to do so. And someone spoke up and said, "Dead men tell no tales." They gathered around us and after threatening they perceived that we could not be frightened into it. They again commenced to persuade and advise us in this way: "Boys, do as we have done. You are young, you will not have anything to do in this affair, but we want that you should keep it a secret and act with us."

We then told them that we positively could not. They then said that if we did not yield to their requirement that they would have to shed our blood, and they went so far as to start us downstairs in charge of two men armed with guns [and] with bayonets, and William and Wilson Law, Austin Cowles, and one of the Fosters started down [the] stairs into the cellar. There they said they would cut our throats if we refused to take the oath. We told them positively that we would have to die then because we could not receive the oath, but that we desired to be turned loose. They said they could not turn us loose with the information that we had received, because it would not be safe to do it.

They then walked us off with one man on each side of us, armed with sword and bowie knife and two men behind us with loaded guns, cocked, with bayonets on them. We were started to the cellar, but we had not gone more than about fifteen feet when someone cried out, "Hold on, let us talk this matter over." We were stopped, when they commenced to counsel among themselves, and I distinctly remember one of them saying that our fathers knew where we were, and that if we never returned it would at once cause suspicion and lead to trouble. They became very uneasy about it, for if they shed our blood it would be dangerous for them, as it was known where we were.

Finally they concluded to let us go if we would keep our mouths shut. We were escorted out and then they hated to let us go. They took us toward the river, and still cautioned us about being silent and keeping secret everything we had heard, for, said they, if we opened our mouths about it, they would kill us anywhere—that they would consider it their duty to kill us whenever or wherever the opportunity afforded, either by night or by day. I told them it would be in our interest and to our peace and safety never to mention it to anybody. They said they were glad we could see that, and after warning us in strong terms, and before the guard left us, I saw Brother Joseph's hand from under the bank of the river.

He was beckoning us to him. They turned back but were yet watching us and listening to us, and one of us said, "Let us go toward the river." The guard made answer and said, "Yes, you better go to the river." With this we started off on the run, and we ran past where Brother Joseph was, and Brother John Scott was with him—he was one of his bodyguard. They slipped around the bank and came down to the same point where we were, and these men, the guard, went back.

We all walked down the river quite a piece, nearly a quarter [of a mile], nearly opposite Joseph's store under the bank near Joseph's residence (it was in the afternoon). We got in a little kind of wash, and were inside Joseph's enclosure where the board fence came into the river. Joseph said, "Let us sit down here." We sat down. Joseph said, "Boys, we saw the danger you were in. We were afraid you would not get out alive, but we are thankful that you got off."

He then asked us to relate the results of the meeting. We told him all that had happened. We also told him the names of those who were there. After Joseph heard us he looked very solemn indeed, and he said, "Oh brethren, you do not know what this will terminate in." He looked very solemn, and not being able to control himself he broke right out. Brother Scott rose, and putting his arm around Brother Joseph's neck, said, "Oh Brother Joseph, Brother Joseph, do you think they are going to kill you?" And they fell on each other's necks and wept bitterly for some time. We all wept.

After Joseph recovered himself, Brother John repeated the same question. Brother Joseph lifted Brother John's arms from off his neck and said, "I fully comprehend it." But he would not say that he was going to be killed. But he said in the conversation, "Brethren, I am going to leave you. I shall not be with you long; it will not be many months until I shall have to go." Brother John said, "Brother Joseph, are you going to be slain?" He never answered, but he felt very sorrowful. After considerable conversation Joseph said that he would go away and would not be known among the people for twenty years or upwards. Finally he said, "I shall go to rest," but he did not say a word about dying.

You know, Brother Joseph (here the speaker addressed himself to Brother Joseph F. Smith), that the Prophet started over the river, just before he gave himself up, to go away. It might be that he intended or meant that he would leave the place, and it might be that he knew that his life would be taken. I could not say as to that.

Before leaving, Joseph put a seal upon our mouths, and told us to tell nobody, not even our fathers, for twenty years. He cautioned us very seriously, and I did as he told me.

There was one thing which Joseph said which I have not related. He said: "They accuse me of polygamy, and of being a false prophet" and many other things which I do not now remember. "But," said he, "I am no false prophet; I am no imposter. I have had no dark revelations; I have had no revelations from the devil. I have made no revelations; I have not got anything up myself. The same God that has thus far dictated and directed me, and inspired me and strengthened me in this work, gave me this revelation and commandment on celestial and plural marriage, and the same God commanded me to obey it.

"He [God] said to me that unless I accept it and introduce it and practice it, I together with my people should be damned and cut off from this time henceforth. And they say if I do so and so they will kill me. What shall I do! What shall I do! If I do not practice it I shall be damned with all my people. If I do teach it and practice it and urge it, they say they will kill me, and I know they will. But," said he, "we have got to observe it, that it [is] an eternal principle, and that it was given to [me] by way of commandment and not by way of instruction" (1881).

Wandle Mace

On the following morning [June 23, 1844], as with Brother Hyrum Mace I was walking up the street towards Joseph's house, talking over the events of the last few days, two men came to us in a great hurry, from an opposite direction. They were very much excited over the present situation and thought it was absolutely necessary that Joseph should return. We took an opposite view of the case and did not want to see him return into the very jaws of death.

But said they, "If Joseph don't come back the governor will put the city under 'martial' law, and then nothing can be brought into the city, neither can anything be taken out, and then what will all our property be worth?" They further argued that the governor was our friend, and he would protect Joseph from all harm if he came back.

I returned answer with considerable warmth of feeling, that I did not believe it. On the contrary, I believed the governor to be in perfect harmony with the mob, and if Joseph recrossed the river, he would be murdered. I did not want him to return; what is a little property compared to his life? Joseph could in a very short time build a city and property worth more than all Hancock County; and should we, for the sake of a little property, be so selfish as to push him into the very jaws of death!

These men, Reynolds Cahoon and Hiram Kimball, then left us and turned and walked towards Joseph's house; when they reached it, and before entering, they leaned on the fence, talked together for some time, they then went into the house. We—Hyrum Mace and myself—both felt the impression that they were going to persuade Sister Emma, Joseph's wife, to write to him and prevail on him to return. This feeling came upon us so forcibly, we were very uneasy as to the result.

From O. P. Rockwell, who was one of Joseph's company, I learned our impressions were correct. He said Cahoon brought a letter to Joseph from his wife; he opened and read the letter, then handed it to his brother Hyrum and said, "I know my own business." Cahoon replied to Joseph, "You always said, if the Church would stick to you, you would stick to the church. Now trouble comes you are the first to run." Joseph made him no reply. He would not talk to him.

Hyrum read the letter and thought "we had better go back, and if we die, we will die like men." Joseph replied, "Hyrum you are my oldest brother, and if you say go back, we will go back." He said further, "If they had let me alone, there would have been no bloodshed, but now I expect to be butchered."

They accordingly recrossed the river the same night, June 23rd, and [Joseph] sent a letter to Governor Ford saying he would start for Carthage the next morning. The next morning, 24th June, Joseph had an interview with the officers of the Legion and instructed them to dismiss their men, but have them in a state of readiness, to be called upon if an emergency should occur (n.d. [b], pp. 143–45).

Sara Jane Miller

Sister Miller used to relate that as the Prophet Joseph Smith was on his way to Carthage and martyrdom, he passed the place where she as a little child of five years was playing; and taking her in his arms, he kissed her. The Prophet had been closely associated with her parents (n.d.).

Joseph F. Smith

I also remember seeing him [Joseph] riding upon his horse Charley, which this picture before us suspended upon the wall here is supposed to represent. He was dressed in his uniform, as he appears there. The last time I saw him was when he crossed the river, he and my father, from Iowa back to Nauvoo, after they had started for the Rocky Mountains; for let me tell you that the Prophet Joseph contemplated journeying to these mountains for the purpose of looking out a gathering place for the people of God. Being constantly persecuted by his enemies, he laid his plans to slip out of their grasp and way, and come out to these mountains to explore them with a view to seeking out a place where the people of God could be gathered and worship God in peace and according to the dictates of their own consciences. But some of these false brethren, of whom I have been speaking, raised the hue and cry that only a false shepherd flew from the flock when the wolves approached. He was upbraided by some of those false brethren of being a false shepherd. When that word came to him he was wounded in his feelings, and so hurt that he turned round and said: "If this is all my friends care for my life, why should I care for it?" And he returned home and went, as he said, "like a lamb to the slaughter." I saw him and my father as they were rowed in a skiff across the Mississippi River, and watched them till they landed at the bank of the river near the old *Times and Seasons* printing office, watched them as they walked up the bank of the river on to Water Street, and walked along and come into our house.

Joseph sat down while my father washed and arranged his toilet. And while Uncle Joseph was sitting there, he took me on his knee and trotted me and played with me. In a little while my father came in. Joseph says, "What is the matter with this little boy?" Father said, "Nothing, I guess."

He says, "He looks as though he hasn't a drop of blood in him." I remember it so well. Up to this time, you may remember, I had lived on milk, a good deal of it skim milk, and I suppose I was rather pale, a circumstance that arose through the prostrated condition of my mother, brought on by cruel persecutions in Missouri (CD, 5:28–29; see also HC, 5:316).

For other accounts of the events preceding the martyrdom, see Robert Crookston Sr., n.d.; George Laub, n.d.; George A. Smith, JD, 2:216–17; Job F. Smith, n.d. [a], pp. 7–8; Joseph F. Smith, 1916, pp. 57–58; Daniel H. Wells, 1904, p. 176; and Edwin D. Woolley, 1971, p. 283.

Premonitions of the Martyrdom

Mary Ann Green

Her father [William A. Green] was very much attached to the Prophet and his brethren, and often he was bowed down with grief . . . when he witnessed the life of jeopardy and persecution that they endured from day to day. The day before the Prophet Joseph and Hyrum were killed, he visited them in the jail and was received with many blessings. The day that the Prophet and Hyrum were killed, Mary's father [was] sitting by the window and looking out. Seeing the soldiers and the governor pass by, he said, "Seeing those men a coming, I fear that something will happen"—and sure enough that day they were killed. The following year her father took very ill and died, on the 15th day of July 1845 (n.d.).

William Greenhalgh

In 1841 William Greenhalgh had a dream concerning Joseph Smith, and dreamed he was on an open prairie. I saw wood houses and a large building a distance from that, like a coach house. On the side of these two wood houses I saw a company of men that looked very dark in their appearance. They seemed to [be] hollowing [hallooing] and making a noise. While this was going on, I saw a man rise up in the air above them. Then in 1842 I came to Nauvoo. [In] 1843 I went to Layart and when I came to Carthage I stood still and looked at the place and saw it was the very place I saw in my dream. My dream came to my mind when looking at it. In 1844 when Joseph Smith was martyred in Carthage, then the fulfillment of my dream came to me again (n.d.).

Note: The above is an accurate transcription of Greenhalgh's history. He begins in the third person ("In 1841 William Greenhalgh had a dream . . . and dreamed he was . . .") and moves to the first person ("I saw wood houses . . .").

Oliver B. Huntington

I have just learned from Brother Peter W. Cownover another evidence of the certainty in the Prophet's mind that he was going to Carthage to be slain as a sacrifice for the Saints.

Brother Cownover had been to Carthage in charge of prisoners arrested by the county sheriff, and when he reached that place he and the prisoners were all thrown into jail together, without judge or jury, and after they were liberated he returned to Nauvoo, and arrived just as Joseph was starting for Carthage. After usual salutations, Brother Cownover asked Joseph where he was going.

"I am going to Carthage to give myself up," was his reply.

Brother Cownover said, "If you go there they will kill you."

"I know it," replied the Prophet, "but I am going. I am going to give myself for the people, to save them" (1890c, p. 125).

William W. Phelps

In June 1844 when Joseph Smith went to Carthage and delivered himself up to Gov. Ford I accompanied him, and while on the way thither he related to me and his Brother Hyrum the following dream. He said, "While I was at Jordan's in Iowa the other night I dreamed that myself and my brother Hyrum went on board a large steamboat lying in a small bay near the great ocean. Shortly after we went on board there was an alarm of fire, and I discovered that the boat had been anchored some distance from the shore out in the bay, and that an escape from the fire in the confusion appeared hazardous. But as delay was folly, I and Hyrum jumped overboard and tried our faith at walking upon the water. At first we sank in the water nearly to our knees, but as we proceeded we increased in faith and were soon able to walk upon the water.

"Looking towards the burning boat in the east, we saw that it was drifting towards the wharf and the town with a great flame and clouds of smoke, and as if by whirlwind the town was taking fire too, so that the scene of destruction and horrors of the frightened inhabitants was terrible. We proceeded on the bosom of the mighty deep and were soon out of sight of land. The ocean was still, the rays of the sun were bright, and we forgot all the troubles of our Mother Earth.

"Just at that moment I heard the sound of a human voice, and turning round saw my brother Samuel H. approaching towards us from the east. We stopped and he came up. After a moment's conversation he informed me that he had been lonesome and had made up his mind to go with me across the mighty deep.

"We all started again and in a short time were blessed with the first sight of a city, whose silver steeples and towers were more beautiful than any that I had ever seen or heard of on earth. It stood, as it were, upon the western shore of the mighty deep we [were] walking on, and its order and glory seemed far beyond the wisdom of man. While we were gazing upon the perfection of the city, a small boat launched off from the port and almost as quick as thought came to us. In an instant they took us on board and saluted, with welcome and with music, such as is not of earth.

"The next scene on landing was more than I can describe. The greetings and the music from a thousand towers, and the light of God himself at the return of three of his sons, soothed my soul into [such] quiet and joy that I felt as if I were truly in heaven. I gazed upon the splendor. I greeted my friends.

"I awoke, and lo, it was a dream.

"While I meditated upon such a marvelous scene, I fell asleep again, and behold, I stood near the shore of the burning boat, and there was great consternation among the officers, crew, and passengers of the flaming craft, as there seemed to be much ammunition or powder on board. The alarm was given that the fire was near the magazine, and in a moment suddenly it blew up with a great noise and sank in the deep water with all on board. I then turned to the country east among the bushy openings and saw William and Wilson Law endeavoring to escape from the wild beasts of the forest, but two lions rushed out of a thicket and devoured them. I awoke again."

I will say that Joseph never told this dream again, as he was martyred about two days after. I relate from recollection as nearly as I can (n.d.).

Parley P. Pratt

A day or two previous to this circumstance I had been constrained by the Spirit to start prematurely for home, without knowing why or wherefore; and on the same afternoon I was passing on a canal boat near Utica, New York, on my way to Nauvoo. My brother, William Pratt, being then on a mission in the same state (New York), happened, providentially, to take passage on the same boat. As we conversed together on the deck, a strange and solemn awe came over me, as if the powers of hell were let loose. I was so overwhelmed with sorrow I could hardly speak; and after pacing the deck for some time in silence, I turned to my brother William and exclaimed—"Brother William, this is a dark hour; the powers of darkness seem to triumph, and the spirit of murder is abroad in the land; and it controls the hearts of the American people, and a vast majority of them sanction the killing of the innocent. My brother, let us keep silence and not open our mouths. If you have any pamphlets or books on the fullness of the gospel lock them up; show them not, neither open your mouth to the people; let us observe an entire and solemn silence, for this is a dark day, and the hour of triumph for the powers of darkness. O, how sensible I am of the spirit of murder which seems to pervade the whole land." This was June 27, 1844, in the afternoon, and as near as I can judge, it was the same hour that the Carthage mob were shedding the blood of Joseph and Hyrum Smith, and John Taylor, nearly one thousand miles distant.

My brother bid me farewell somewhere in western New York, he being on his way to a conference in that quarter, and passing on to Buffalo I took steamer for Chicago, Illinois. The steamer touched at a landing in Wisconsin, some fifty or sixty miles from Chicago, and here some new passengers came on board and brought the news of the martyrdom of Joseph and Hyrum Smith. Great excitement prevailed on board, there being a general spirit of exultation and triumph at this glorious news, as it was called, much the same as generally shown on the first receipt of the news of a great national victory in time of war.

Many passengers now gathered about me and tauntingly inquired what the Mormons would do now, seeing their prophet and leader killed.

To these taunts and questions I replied, that they would continue their mission and spread the work he had restored, in all the world. Observing that nearly all the prophets and apostles who were before had been killed, and also the Savior of the world, and yet their death did not alter the truth nor hinder its final triumph.

At this reply many of them seemed astonished, and some inquired who would succeed him, and remarked to me: "Perhaps you will be the man who will now seek to be leader of the Mormons in his stead—who are you, sir?" I replied: "I am a MAN, sir; and a MAN never triumphs and exults in the ruin of his country and the murder of the innocent." This was said in the energy of my soul, and by constraint of the Spirit, and a powerful and peculiar accent was thrown upon the word MAN each time it occurred in the sentence. This served as a sufficient rebuke, and all were silent (1985, pp. 292–93).

The Martyrdom (June 27, 1844)

James A. Armstrong

[In an affidavit, said:] During the summer of 1908 I had charge of a company of missionaries going through the South Central part of Minnesota and on one occasion after Sunday and Monday meetings in Fairbault, Minnesota, a neighbor came to the residence where we were living and asked for two Mormon missionaries to come to the deathbed of a Miss Law, sister of William Law, the one-time first counselor to Joseph Smith.

Ephraim Peterson, then from Ephraim, Utah, and I called on this party who said she was a sister of William Law. She appeared to be of sound and sane mind and in possession of all her faculties, although she was in very poor health. I would estimate she was in her eighties and very feeble, although she was very alert and keen of mind.

She stated that she had promised her brother William that she would contact some of the missionaries or some of the church authorities and make a confession for him to the effect that he, William Law, fired the shot that killed the Prophet Joseph Smith at the Carthage Jail at Carthage, Illinois.

Further affiant sayeth not.

Witness my hand and seal at Salt Lake City, Utah, this 15th day of November, 1952 (1952).

Mary Smith Norman

My father [Samuel H. Smith], at the time of his brother's arrest and imprisonment in Carthage Jail, determined to go to them at once, well knowing that their lives were in danger. He set out for Carthage, taking with him a fourteen-year-old boy who was working for him. They traveled by team and wagon, and when they neared Carthage, were met by a guard of the mob, who, apprehending his coming, had been placed there to intercept him. They allowed the boy to proceed with the team, but he was turned back. He gave the boy instructions to go direct to the Hamilton House in Carthage and there await further orders.

He then returned home as quickly as possible, purchased a horse noted for its speed, and determined to reach his brothers in time to be of assistance to them, although the hope seemed a forlorn one. He went unarmed, and as he again neared Carthage he met several people coming from there in great haste, among them a man and a woman in a buggy, of whom he asked what had happened, and received answer that "the two Smiths had been killed by the mob."

The terrible shock was too much for him, and for an instant he reeled in his saddle and they expected him to fall. Then, as the necessity of immediate action flashed across his mind, he steadied himself, saying, "God help me! I must go to them," and he again pressed forward. The mob, expecting his return and intent upon murder, were secreted in a thicket, and two men on horseback with rifles gave chase. As they emerged from the thicket, the man in the buggy gave a warning shout; my father, turning his head quickly, took in the situation at a glance and put his horse to the utmost speed, still keeping his course straight toward Carthage. His splendid horsemanship kept him somewhat out of the range of the bullets sent after him, though one passed through the top of his hat. The chase was a long and exciting one, but he finally outdistanced them and rode into Carthage and made his way to the jail, being the first to arrive there after the tragedy. The mob in the meantime had dispersed (1914).

Alfred Randall

I quote from the Journal History in the Historian's office in Salt Lake City, where it is found, that on June 24th, 1844, Alfred Randall accompanied the Prophet Joseph Smith to Carthage Jail, and it has been stated that he was one of the last to leave the jail. He was pushed down the narrow stairs backwards at the point of a bayonet.

He was in Carthage about 10 o'clock that night where the troops under Governor Ford were stationed in squads around the square. He was standing nearby when he heard one of them say: "I calculate to see old Joe Smith dead before I return." Several others said: "So do I—So do I, and I'll be d—d if I don't" was the general comment. One fellow then spoke up and said: "I shouldn't wonder if some d—d Mormon isn't hearing all we say." Another one, who stood next to Alfred said: "If I knew there was, I would run him through with my bayonet."

Alfred then wandered to another crowd and heard one say: "I guess this will be the last of Old Joe Smith and his d—d Mormons." He then went to Hambleton's [Hamilton] Hotel where Governor Ford was standing by the fence, and he heard a soldier tell Governor Ford: "The soldiers are determined to see Joe Smith dead before they leave here." Ford replied harshly: "If you know of any such plot, keep it to yourself."

Now Joseph and Hyrum Smith had planned to go westward in the hope of escaping persecution, but they were told: "Submit yourselves to be arrested and tried before the magistrate." John Taylor protested, saying that they would be murdered if they came to Carthage. But Governor Ford replied: "I pledge myself for their safety." So they returned, believing that they were under the protection of Governor Ford. Nothing could have been further from the truth. An infuriated mob filled the city, declaring that they would not leave until "Old Joe Smith" was killed.

A mob stormed the jail, and before they were dispersed, Joseph and his brother Hyrum had been murdered. Two days later, on June 29th, 1844, the bodies of the two men lay in state at the Mansion House, and from 8:00 A.M. to 5:00 P.M. a steady stream of mourners filed past the twin biers. Many and varied were the thoughts of the crowd as they took the last look at their leaders. What was now in store for this band of religious people of which Alfred Randall was a member? (n.d.).

Willard Richards

Possibly the following events occupied near three minutes, but I think only about two, and have penned them for the gratification of many friends.

Carthage, June 27, 1844.

A shower of musket balls were thrown up the stairway against the door of the prison in the second story, followed by many rapid footsteps.

While Generals Joseph and Hyrum Smith, Mr. Taylor, and myself, who were in the front chamber, closed the door of our room against the entry at the head of the stairs, and placed ourselves against it, there being no lock on the door, and no catch that was usable.

The door is a common panel, and as soon as we heard the feet at the stairs head, a ball was sent through the door, which passed between us, and showed that our enemies were desperadoes, and we must change our position.

General Joseph Smith, Mr. Taylor and myself sprang back to the front part of the room, and General Hyrum Smith retreated two-thirds across the chamber directly in front of and facing the door.

A ball was sent through the door which hit Hyrum on the side of his nose, when he fell backwards, extended at length, without moving his feet.

From the holes in his vest (the day was warm, and no one had his coat on but myself), pantaloons, drawers, and shirt, it appears evident that a ball must have been thrown from without, through the window, which entered his back on the right side, and passing through, lodged against his watch, which was in his right vest pocket, completely pulverizing the crystal and face, tearing off the hands and mashing the whole body of the watch. At the same instant the ball from the door entered his nose.

As he struck the floor he exclaimed emphatically, "I am a dead man." Joseph looked towards him and responded, "Oh, dear brother Hyrum!" and opening the door two or three inches with his left hand, discharged one barrel of a six shooter (pistol) at random in the entry, from whence a ball grazed Hyrum's breast, and entering his throat passed into his head, while other muskets were aimed at him and some balls hit him.

Joseph continued snapping his revolver round the casing of the door into the space as before, three barrels of which misfired, while Mr. Taylor with a walking stick stood by his side and knocked down the bayonets and muskets which were constantly discharging through the doorway, while I stood by him, ready to lend any assistance, with another stick, but could not come within striking distance without going directly before the muzzle of the guns.

When the revolver failed, we had no more firearms, and expected an immediate rush of the mob, and the doorway full of muskets, halfway in the room, and no hope but instant death from within.

Mr. Taylor rushed into the window, which is some fifteen or twenty feet from the ground. When his body was nearly on a balance, a ball from the door within entered his leg, and a ball from without struck his watch, a patent lever, in his vest pocket near the left breast, and smashed it into "pie," leaving the hands standing at 5 o'clock, 16 minutes, and 26 seconds, the force of which ball threw him back on the floor, and he rolled under the bed which stood by his side, where he lay motionless, the mob from the door continuing to fire upon him, cutting away a piece of flesh from his left hip as large as a man's hand, and were hindered only by my knocking down their muzzles with a stick; while they continued to reach their guns into the room, probably left handed, and aimed their discharge so far round as almost to reach us in the corner of the room to where we retreated and dodged, and then I recommenced the attack with my stick.

Joseph attempted, as the last resort, to leap the same window from whence Mr. Taylor fell, when two balls pierced him from the door, and one entered his right breast from without, and he fell outward, exclaiming, "Oh Lord, my God!" As his feet went out of the window my head went in, the balls whistling all around. He fell on his left side a dead man.

At this instant the cry was raised, "He's leaped the window!" and the mob on the stairs and in the entry ran out.

I withdrew from the window, thinking it of no use to leap out on a hundred bayonets, then around General Joseph Smith's body.

Not satisfied with this I again reached my head out of the window, and watched some seconds to see if there were any signs of life, regardless of my own, determined to see the end of him I loved. Being fully satisfied that he was dead, with a hundred men near the body and more coming round the corner of the jail, and expecting a return to our room, I rushed towards the prison door, at the head of the stairs, and through the entry from whence the firing had proceeded, to learn if the doors into the prison were open.

When near the entry, Mr. Taylor called out, "Take me." I pressed my way until I found all doors unbarred, returning instantly, caught Mr. Taylor under my arm and rushed by the stairs into the dungeon, or inner prison, stretched him on the floor and covered him with a bed in such a manner as not likely to be perceived, expecting an immediate return of the mob.

I said to Mr. Taylor, "This is a hard case to lay you on the floor, but if your wounds are not fatal, I want you to live to tell the story."

I expected to be shot the next moment, and stood before the door awaiting the onset (HC, 6:619–21).

John Taylor

Soon afterwards I was sitting at one of the front windows of the jail, when I saw a number of men, with painted faces, coming round the corner of the jail, and aiming towards the stairs. The other brethren had seen the same, for, as I went to the door, I found Brother Hyrum Smith and Dr. Richards already leaning against it. They both pressed against the door with their shoulders to prevent its being opened, as the lock and latch were comparatively useless. While in this position, the mob, who had come upstairs, and tried to open the door, probably thought it was locked, and fired a ball through the keyhole; at this Dr. Richards and Brother Hyrum leaped back from the door, with their faces towards it; almost instantly another ball passed through the panel of the door, and struck Brother Hyrum on the left side of the nose, entering his face and head. At the same instant, another ball from the outside entered his back, passing through his body and striking his watch. The ball came from the back, through the jail window, opposite the door, and must, from its range, have been fired from the Carthage Greys, who were placed there ostensibly for our protection, as the balls from the firearms, shot close by the jail, would have entered the ceiling, we being in the second story, and there never was a time after that when Hyrum could have received the latter wound. Immediately, when the ball struck him, he fell flat on his back, crying as he fell, "I am a dead man!" He never moved afterwards.

I shall never forget the feeling of deep sympathy and regard manifested in the countenance of Brother Joseph as he drew nigh to Hyrum, and, leaning over him exclaimed, "Oh! my poor, dear brother Hyrum!" He, however, instantly arose, and with a firm, quick step, and a determined expression of countenance, approached the door, and pulling the six-shooter left by Brother Wheelock from his pocket, opened the door slightly and snapped the pistol six successive times; only three of the barrels, however, were discharged. I afterwards understood that two or three were wounded by these discharges, two of whom, I am informed, died. I had in my hands a large, strong hickory stick brought there by Brother Markham, and left by him, which I had seized as soon as I saw the mob approach; and while Brother Joseph was firing the pistol, I stood close behind him. As soon as he had discharged it he stepped back, and I immediately took his place next to the door, while he occupied the one I had done while he was shooting. Brother Richards, at this time, had a knotty walking-stick in his hands belonging to me, and stood next to Brother Joseph, a little farther from the door, in an oblique direction, apparently to avoid the rake of the fire from the door. The firing of Brother Joseph made our assailants pause for a moment; very soon after, however, they pushed the door some distance open, and protruded and discharged their guns into the room, when I parried them off with my stick, giving another direction to the balls.

It certainly was a terrible scene: streams of fire as thick as my arm passed by me as these men fired, and, unarmed as we were, it looked like certain death. I remember feeling as though my time had come, but I do not know when, in any critical position, I was more calm, unruffled, and energetic, and acted with more promptness and decision. It certainly was far from pleasant to be so near the muzzles of those firearms as they belched forth their liquid flame and deadly balls. While I was engaged in parrying the guns, Brother Joseph said, "That's right, Brother Taylor, parry them off as well as you can." These were the last words I ever heard him speak on earth.

Every moment the crowd at the door became more dense, as they were unquestionably pressed on by those in the rear ascending the stairs, until the whole entrance at the door was literally crowded with muskets and rifles, which, with the swearing, shouting, and demoniacal expressions of those outside the door and on the stairs, and the firing of guns, mingled with their horrid oaths and execrations, made it look like pandemonium let loose, and was, indeed, a fit representation of the horrid deed in which they were engaged.

After parrying the guns for some time, which now protruded thicker and farther into the room, and seeing no hope of escape or protection there, as we were now unarmed, it occurred to me that we might have some friends outside, and that there might be some chance of escape in that direction, but here there seemed to be none. As I expected them every moment to rush into the room—nothing but extreme cowardice having kept them out—as the tumult and pressure increased, without any other hope, I made a spring for the window which was right in front of the jail door, where the mob was standing, and also exposed to the fire of the Carthage Greys, who were stationed some ten or twelve rods off. The weather was hot, we all of us had our coats off, and the window was raised to admit air. As I reached the window, and was on the point of leaping out, I was struck by a ball from the door about midway of my thigh, which struck the bone, and flattened out almost to the size of a quarter of a dollar, and then passed on through the fleshy part to within about half an inch of the outside. I think some prominent nerve must have been severed or injured for, as soon as the ball struck me, I fell like a bird when shot, or an ox when struck by a butcher, and lost entirely and instantaneously all power of action or locomotion. I fell upon the windowsill and cried out, "I am shot!" Not possessing any power to move, I felt myself falling outside of the window, but immediately I fell inside, from some, at that time, unknown cause. When I struck the floor my animation seemed restored, as I have seen it sometimes in squirrels and birds after being shot. As soon as I felt the power of motion I crawled under the bed, which was in a corner of the room, not far from the window where I received my wound. While on the way and under the bed I was wounded in three other places; one ball entered a little below the left knee, and never was extracted; another entered the forepart of my left arm, a little above the wrist, and, passing down by the joint, lodged in the fleshy part of my hand, about midway, a little above the upper joint of my little finger; another struck me on the fleshy part of my left hip, and tore away the flesh as large as my hand, dashing the mangled fragments of flesh and blood against the wall.

My wounds were painful, and the sensation produced was as though a ball had passed through and down the whole length of my leg. I very well remember my reflections at the time. I had a very painful idea of becoming lame and decrepit, and being an object of pity, and I felt as though I would rather die than be placed in such circumstances.

It would seem that immediately after my attempt to leap out of the window, Joseph also did the same thing, of which circumstance I have no knowledge, only from information. The first thing that I noticed was a cry that he had leaped out of the window. A cessation of firing followed, the mob rushed downstairs, and Dr. Richards went to the window. Immediately afterward I saw the doctor going towards the jail door, and as there was an iron door at the head of the stairs, adjoining our door, which led into the cells for criminals, it struck me that the doctor was going there, and I said to him, "Stop, Doctor, and take me along." He proceeded to the door and opened it, and then returned and dragged me along to a small cell prepared for criminals.

Brother Richards was very much troubled, and exclaimed, "Oh! Brother Taylor, is it possible that they have killed both Brother Hyrum and Joseph? it cannot surely be, and yet I saw them shoot them"; and elevating his hands two or three times, he exclaimed, "Oh Lord, my God, spare Thy servants!" He then said, "Brother Taylor, this is a terrible event"; and he dragged me farther into the cell, saying, "I am sorry I can not do better for you"; and, taking an old, filthy mattress, he covered me with it, and said, "That may hide you, and you may yet live to tell the tale, but I expect they will kill me in a few moments." While lying in this position I suffered the most excruciating pain.

Soon afterwards Dr. Richards came to me, informed me that the mob had precipitately fled, and at the same time confirmed my worst fears that Joseph was assuredly dead. I felt a dull, lonely, sickening sensation at the news. When I reflected that our noble chieftain, the prophet of the living God, had fallen, and that I had seen his brother in the cold embrace of death, it seemed as though there was a void or vacuum in the great field of human existence to me, and a dark gloomy chasm in the kingdom, and that we were left alone. Oh, how lonely was the feeling! How cold, barren and desolate! In the midst of difficulties he was always the first in motion; in critical positions his counsel was always sought. As our prophet he approached our God, and obtained for us his will; but now our prophet, our counselor, our general, our leader, was gone, and amid the fiery ordeal that we then had to pass through, we were left alone without his aid, and as our future guide for things spiritual or temporal, and for all things pertaining to this world, or the next, he had spoken for the last time on earth.

These reflections and a thousand others flashed upon my mind. I thought, why must the good perish, and the virtuous be destroyed? Why must God's nobility, the salt of the earth, the most exalted of the human family, and the most perfect types of all excellence, fall victims to the cruel, fiendish hate of incarnate devils?

The poignancy of my grief, I presume, however, was somewhat allayed by the extreme suffering that I endured from my wounds (1999, pp. 88–94).

Leonora C. Taylor

Joseph Smith urged Emma to go to Carthage with him. She refused on account of having chills and fever. He replied, if they did not hang me I do not know how they [will] kill me (ca. 1856).

Wilford Woodruff

I was sitting with Brigham Young in the depot in the city of Boston at the time when the two prophets were martyred. Of course we had no telegraphs and no fast reports as we have today to give communication over the land. During that period Brother Young was waiting there for a train of cars to go to Peterborough. Whilst sitting there, we were overshadowed by a cloud of darkness and gloom as great as I ever witnessed in my life under almost any circumstances in which we were placed. Neither of us knew or understood the cause until after the report of the death of the prophets was manifested to us. Brother Brigham left; I remained in Boston, and next day took passage for Fox Islands, a place I had visited some years before and baptized numbers of people and organized branches upon both those islands. My father-in-law, Ezra Carter, carried me on a wagon from Scarborough to Portland. I there engaged passage on board of a steamer. I had put my trunk on board and was just bidding my father-in-law farewell when a man came out from a shop—a shoemaker—holding a newspaper in his hand. He said, "Father Carter, Joseph and Hyrum Smith have been martyred—they have been murdered in Carthage Jail!"

As soon as I looked at the paper, the Spirit said to me that it was true. I had no time for consultation, the steamer's bell was ringing, so I stepped on board and took my trunk back to land. As I drew it off, the plank was drawn in. I told Father Carter to drive me back to Scarborough. I there took the car for Boston and arrived at that place on Saturday night.

On my arrival there I received a letter which had been sent from Nauvoo, giving us an account of the killing of the prophets. I was the only man in Boston of the Quorum of the Twelve.

I had very strange feelings, as, I have no doubt, all the Saints had. I attended a meeting on the following day in Boydston's Hall, where a vast number of the inhabitants of Boston and some three hundred Latter-day Saints had assembled. Hundreds of men came to that meeting to see what the "Mormons" were going to do now that their prophets were dead. I felt braced up; every nerve, bone, and sinew within me seemed as though made of steel. I did not shed a tear. I went into that hall, though I knew not what I was going to say to that vast audience. I opened the Bible promiscuously and opened to the words of St. John, where he saw under the altar the souls of them that were slain for the word of God and heard them cry, "How long, O Lord, holy and true, doest thou not judge and avenge our blood on them that dwell on the earth?" The Lord informed them that they must wait a little season, until their brethren were slain as they were. I spoke on those words.

Next day I met Brigham Young in the streets of Boston, he having just returned, opposite to Sister Voce's house. We reached out our hands, but neither of us was able to speak a word. We walked into Sister Voce's house. We each took a seat and veiled our faces. We were overwhelmed with grief, and our faces were soon bathed in a flood of tears. I felt then that I could talk, though I could not do so before—that is, to Brother Brigham. After we had done weeping, we began to converse together concerning the death of the prophets. In the course of the conversation, he smote his hand upon his thigh and said, "Thank God, the keys of the kingdom are here."

. . . All that President Young or myself or any member of the Quorum need have done in the matter was to have referred to the last instructions at the last meeting we had with the Prophet Joseph before starting on our mission. . . .

The Prophet Joseph, I am now satisfied, had a thorough presentiment that that was the last meeting we would hold together here in the flesh. We had had our endowments; we had had all the blessings sealed upon our heads that were ever given to the apostles or prophets on the face of the earth. On that occasion the Prophet Joseph rose up and said to us: "Brethren, I have desired to live to see this temple built. I shall never live to see it, but you will. I have sealed upon your heads all the keys of the kingdom of God. I have sealed upon you every key, power, principle that the God of heaven has revealed to me. Now, no matter where I may go or what I may do, the kingdom rests upon you."

Now, don't you wonder why we, as apostles, could not have understood that the prophet of God was going to be taken away from us? But we did not understand it. The apostles in the days of Jesus Christ could not understand what the Savior meant when He told them, "I am going away; if I do not go away the Comforter will not come!" Neither did we understand what Joseph meant. "But," he said, after having done this, "ye apostles of the Lamb of God, my brethren, upon your shoulders this kingdom rests; now you have got to round up your shoulders and bear off the kingdom." And he also made this very strange remark, "If you do not do it you will be damned" (CD, 1:291–92).

Aftermath of the Martyrdom

Reaction of Hyrum's Wife to the Martyrdom

Martha Ann Harris

I was born in Nauvoo, Ill., Hancock County, May 14th 1841, the youngest daughter of Hyrum Smith, Patriarch, who was martyred in

Carthage Jail. I am an only sister to Joseph Fielding Smith, the only two children of Mary Fielding, his [Hyrum Smith's] second wife. I was three years old when my dear father was taken from the bosom of his family and friends, when he bid them the last farewell, and he gave them the last farewell kiss.

I remember well the night that he was murdered. I had the measles and I had taken cold. It had settled on my lungs, and I could not speak above my breath. I begged my dear mother to lie down to rest once. She read the Bible a while, then walked again until the day began to dawn. Then there was a knock at the door. My mother asked who was there. The answer was, "George Grant." She opened the door and asked what news. He gave answer that Joseph and Hyrum were both murdered. My mother stepped back calmly exclaiming, "It cannot be possible, can it?" He answered, "Yes, it is too true."

She fell back against the bureau. Brother Grant took her and placed her in a chair. The news flew like wildfire through the home. The crying of agony that went through that house and the anguish and sorrow that were felt can be easier felt than described, but that will never be forgotten by those who were called to pass through it.

He was a loving and affectionate father, indulgent almost to a fault.

I remember one day Mother had made him a pair of pants and he was very proud of them. I saw him walk back and forth with his hands in his pockets. It was seldom that he was cheerful. He always looked serious and sober. I can remember many things about my beloved father.

I remember after my father's death how sad and sorrowful my darling mother used to look. She scarcely ever smiled again. If we could get her to laugh, we thought we had accomplished quite a feat. I never saw her more than smile.

Oh, how I loved my mother. I feared to displease her. I would rather burn my hand than vex my mother. I can see the sorrowful look my mother wore to this very day in my mind's eye. God bless her memory.

She worked in the temple (Nauvoo) for three weeks. I was with her all the time.

I emigrated to Salt Lake City with my widowed mother in 1848 (1881; see also 1924).

Mourning and Gloom Following the Prophet's Death

William Adams

I am not able to describe the sorrow and lamentation of the Saints in beholding the dead bodies of the Prophet and Patriarch, butchered in cold blood by assassins and murdered under the promise of protection by the governor of the state of Illinois. The curse of God must have followed him, for I saw him at the legislature in Springfield, the capital of Illinois, not as a member, but having come from Peoria where he resided, and he had not influence enough to get a door keeper elected. He looked like a poor rejected creature, and short time afterward he died a pauper and was buried by public expense in Peoria (1894).

Warren Foote

[June 28, 1844] Elihu Allen and I were working in the harvest field cutting his wheat when about three o'clock P.M. my wife came out and told us that word had just come that Joseph Smith and his brother Hyrum was shot in Carthage Jail yesterday afternoon. I said at once that "it cannot be so." Yet it so affected us that we dropped the cradle and rake and went home. We found that the word had come so straight that we could no longer doubt the truth of it. We all felt as though the powers of darkness had overcome, and that the Lord had forsaken His people. Our Prophet and Patriarch were gone. Who now is to lead the Saints? In fact we mourned "as one mourneth for his only son." Yet after all the anguish of our hearts and deep mourning of our souls, a spirit seemed to whisper, "All is well. Zion shall yet arise and spread abroad upon the earth, and the kingdoms of this world shall become the kingdom of our God and His Christ." So we felt to trust in God (n.d. [a], p. 62).

Goudy E. Hogan

I will here make mention of a circumstance that took place the 27th day of June while I, with some other boys, was out in the woods gathering wild strawberries. There came some of the neighbor's boys and brought sorrowful news that Joseph Smith was martyred, which report I had frequently heard several times before, but this time it had an impression on my mind that it was too true, and I was overcome with grief and sorrow to that degree that I went out to one side and wept like a child. I had no control over my feelings, and when I came to the house my parents were cast down with grief. A few days after, I, with my Father, went to Nauvoo after our beloved Prophet and Patriarch were buried, and the whole city of Nauvoo was in mourning. Every family was downcast and in mourning, as though every family had lost a member of their family (1945).

John M. Horner

About this time, a convention was called for the purpose of making a nomination of someone for President of the United States. The Prophet was unanimously chosen, and many delegates were appointed to electioneer in a number of the states, to endeavor to elect the Prophet president. I was sent back to New Jersey; I ordered a thousand or so of the Prophet's "Views of the Powers and Policies of the Government of the United States," printed and took these with me. One night, while speaking to a full house of attentive listeners, I invited all to speak who wished to at the close of my lecture. One gentleman got up and said: "I have one reason to give why Joseph Smith can never be president of the United States; my paper, which I received from Philadelphia this afternoon, says that he was murdered in the Carthage Jail, on June 27th." Silence reigned, the gathering quietly dispersed, but the grief and sadness of this heart was beyond the power of man to estimate (1960, 3:549).

Zina D. H. Young

It was the 27th of June, 1844, and it was rumored that Joseph was expected in from Carthage. I did not know to the contrary until I saw the governor and his guards descending the hill by the temple, a short distance from my house. Their swords glistened in the sun, and their appearance startled me, though I knew not what it foreboded. I exclaimed to a neighbor who was with me, "What is the trouble! It seems to me that the trees and the grass are in mourning!" A fearful silence pervaded the city, and after the shades of night gathered around us it was thick darkness. The lightnings flashed, the cattle bellowed, the dogs barked, and the elements wailed. What a terrible night that was to the saints, yet we knew nothing of the dark tragedy which had been enacted by the assassins at Carthage.

The morning dawned; the sad news came [to some]; but as yet I had not heard of the terrible event. I started to go to Mother Smith's on an errand. As I approached I saw men gathered around the door of the mansion. A few rods from the house I met Jesse P. Harmon. "Have you heard the news?" he asked. "What news?" I inquired. "Joseph and Hyrum are dead!" Had I believed it, I could not have walked any further. I hastened to my brother, Dimick. He was sitting in his house, mourning and weeping aloud as only strong men can weep. All was confirmed in a moment. My pen cannot utter my grief nor describe my sorrow. But after awhile a change came, as though the released spirits of the departed sought to comfort us in that hour of dreadful bereavement.

"The healer was there, pouring balm on my heart,

"And wiping the tears from my eyes;

"He was binding the chain that was broken in twain,

"And fastening it firm in the skies" (1877, pp. 326–27).

Spiritual Witnesses of the Martyrdom

Anson Call

[Shortly after the Prophet's martyrdom] I had a dream or a vision which I will relate.

I was traveling by myself in a lonely place till I came to a new field about three acres in size. I went to the door of the house. I discovered Joseph in the house standing in the middle of the floor. I sprang and clinched him by the hand. I threw my arms around him and kissed him and said "Joseph, I thought you was dead." He said, "I am." I said, "This is certainly Joseph." He said, "Yes, it is Joseph. Take your seat and I will tell you all about it." I seated myself and then discovered I was in a congregation of saints whom I was acquainted with.

Joseph then said, "Brethren, I have been killed in Carthage Jail, and it will not make any difference with you, if you do as you are told. I shall continue to govern and control this kingdom as I have hitherto done. The keys of this kingdom were committed to me. I hold them and I shall continue to hold them worlds without end. I am dead and I am out of the power of my enemies. I am now where I can do you good. Be no longer troubled, be faithful, be diligent. Do as you are told, and you shall see the salvation of God."

I then discovered myself sitting in the bed. I spoke to my wife and told her what I had seen and heard and let her heart be comforted, for we should yet see good days and prevail over our enemies. I then commenced comforting my intimate brethren and told them what I had seen and heard (1839).

Note: See D&C 90:2–3 where the Lord told the Prophet the keys of the kingdom would not be taken from him, "while thou art in this world, neither in the world to come." See also D&C 112:15.

Elisha H. Davis Jr.

My father, Elisha H. Davis, and Orson Hyde were together in a house in New York (both on missions). I do not remember the owner's name. Orson Hyde, . . . was lying on a couch asleep with his face to the wall. My father was writing at a table when Orson Hyde was startled and jumped up and exclaimed, "Oh, Brother Davis, they have murdered the Prophet," which proved true. Afterwards Brother Hyde was called home by President Young and my father left in charge of the work of the Lord (1916).

Caring for the Martyrs' Bodies

Edward Hunter

Brother Hunter and his companions reached Nauvoo June 27, 1844, the very day that Joseph and Hyrum Smith were murdered in Carthage Jail. "Next day," says his narrative, "their bodies were brought from Carthage to Nauvoo. We formed two lines to receive them; I was placed at the extreme right, to wheel in after the bodies and march to the Mansion. As we passed the temple, there were crowds of mourners there, lamenting the great loss of our Prophet and Patriarch. The scene was enough to almost melt the soul of man.

"Mr. Brewer, myself, and others took Brother Joseph's body into the Mansion House. When we went to the wagon to get the corpse, Colonel Brewer, a U.S. officer, taking up the Prophet's coat and hat, which were covered with blood and dirt, said, 'Mr. Hunter, look here; vengeance and death await the perpetrators of this deed.' At midnight Brothers Dimick B. Huntington, G. Goldsmith, William Huntington, and myself carried the body of Joseph from the Mansion House to the Nauvoo House, and put him and Hyrum in one grave.

"Their death was hard to bear. Our hope was almost gone, not knowing then that Joseph had prepared for the kingdom to go on, by delivering the keys to the Twelve and rolling off the burden from his shoulders on to theirs. Great sorrow prevailed in the hearts of the people. President Brigham Young and the rest of the Twelve were away" (1971, p. 231).

Viewing the Martyrs' Bodies

Mary A. Rich

My father was at the mansion all night, doing what he could to help them. In the morning he came up early and told me that if I would get up I could go down, as he had gotten permission for me to see Joseph and Hyrum Smith as they lay at their home. I went down, saw them, and laid my hand on Joseph's forehead. The blood was oozing out of the wound in his shoulder, and the sheet that was around him was stained with blood. Still he looked very natural; Hyrum had been shot in the face and therefore he did not look very natural. The funeral was held at one o'clock that day. The Saints were all allowed to go and view the remains after they were dressed (n.d., p. 17).

Lucy Meserve Smith

That evening the murder was committed at Carthage, such a barking and howling of dogs, and bellowing of cattle all over the city of Nauvoo, I have never heard before or since. News came the next morning of the awful tragedy. In the afternoon I repaired to the mansion and there witnessed the awful scene, the Prophet and Patriarch laying in their gore with kettles of bloody water and cloths standing near, while every man, woman, and child were in tears. I forbear to say more on the subject (1888–89).

Eliza R. Snow

The awful tragedy of the 27th of June, 1844, is a livid, burning, scathing stain on our national escutcheon. To look upon the noble, lifeless forms of those brothers, Joseph and Hyrum Smith, lying side by side, after having been brought home from Carthage, where they had been slaughtered in their manhood and in their innocence, was a sight that might well appall the heart of a true American citizen: but, what it was for loving wives and children, the loyal heart may feel, but let *language keep silence!* (1944b, p. 210).

EUNICE B. SNOW

On the last day which [Joseph Smith] spent in Nauvoo, he passed our house with his brother Hyrum, both riding. My mother and I were standing in the dooryard, and as he passed he bowed with uplifted hat to my mother. Hyrum seemed like one in a dream, sad and despondent, taking no notice of anyone. They were on their way to the Carthage Jail, and it was the last time I saw the Prophet alive. Shortly after this, my father came home and told my mother that the Prophet and his brother had been murdered, whereupon my mother exclaimed, "How can it be possible? Will the Lord allow anything like that?"

Immediately she sank back in her chair and fainted. When she came to herself, my father lamented the fact with her.

Lucy Mack Smith, Emma Hale Smith, my mother, and I together viewed the bodies, and I shall never forget the impression made upon me when the Prophet's mother saw the bodies of her dead sons. Falling on her knees and clasping her hands, she cried out. "O God, why were my noble sons permitted to be martyred?"

Then controlling herself with a mighty effort, she said, "Thy will, not mine, O Lord, be done" (1910b).

Joseph's Burial

EDWIN RUSHTON

Father's acquaintance with and admiration for the Prophet grew rapidly, and there developed an intimate friendship between them. The Rushton family often serenaded the Prophet.

After the martyrdom, Father was one of four who took part in the second burial of the Prophet, to preserve the body from the hands of ruthless, designing men. Joseph Smith had prepared a burial vault for the Smith family, and when persecution became alarming he came to Father and requested him, in the event the Prophet was killed, to see that the remains of the Smith family were put into this vault.

When Joseph Smith was on his way to Carthage for the last time, Father was standing nearby when Joseph said to his wife, "Emma, can you train my sons to walk in their father's footsteps?"

She answered, "Oh, Joseph, you are coming back."

Father says Joseph asked the same question three times, and that

Emma gave the same answer each time. The Prophet then rode away to Carthage and his death (1974, pp. 170–71).

The Transfiguration of Brigham Young (August 8, 1844)

Benjamin Ashby

Bro. Willard Richards was the only one of the Twelve Apostles who was in Nauvoo. John Taylor, being wounded, remained in Carthage. Soon the Twelve began to return, also Sidney Rigdon, who endeavored to have himself elected as Guardian of the Church. I was present when he made his silly and boastful speech about leading the Church back to Pittsburgh and twirling the nose of Queen Victoria, &c., &c. Too foolish to be worth remembering! I did not know Rigdon when he was in the spirit of his calling and cannot say what manner of man he was, but when I knew him he had lost the favor of God, and he was as dry sticks in his preaching.

I was in the congregation when the question of the succession to the leadership of the Church was before the people, and I solemnly assert and testify that the last time I saw the features, the gestures, and heard the sound of the voice of Joseph Smith was when the form, voice, and countenance of Brigham Young was transfigured before the congregation so that he appeared like Joseph Smith in every particular. Thus the Lord showed the people that the mantle of Joseph had been bestowed upon Brigham (n.d. [b]).

Jane J. Black

With the death of the Prophet Joseph, there grew conflicts and dissentions over the right to Church leadership. It was a time to try the faith of each member, and many fell away. Many were hoping the church was finished. Sidney Rigdon, Joseph's former counselor, claimed that no one could be a prophet and [take] Joseph's place by mere appointment; the people must wait for God to call a prophet. A meeting was called for August 8th, to decide the matter of a "Guardian," as most of the Apostles were now back home. When Brigham Young, president of the Quorum of the Twelve, started to speak, Jane suddenly sat up electrified! Her back tingled. Her heart raced; she hardly breathed. Joseph Smith's voice spoke to them! She sat up straighter to see better. Brigham seemed taller, as tall as their slain Seer. She strained forward. . . . Yes, he even looked like their slain Prophet. Shocked, dazed she sat, feeling more than hearing, listening to the whisperings within her, and that familiar voice once again. She wasn't alone in her perception . . . for turning tear-brimmed eyes around her she saw others wiping their eyes; some of the brethren on the stand cried unashamedly. The Prophet to succeed Joseph had been chosen! The family of William and Jane remained staunch and true to the leadership of Brigham Young from that moment on (n.d. [b], p. 7).

Robert T. Burton

In time it became the question who was going to lead the people. One said, "follow me," and another, "follow me," until some of the people became confused. Most of the Apostles and leading elders were absent on missions. I was well acquainted with the Prophet. I was imperfectly acquainted with Brigham Young. When Brigham Young returned, and arose in the congregation and began to speak, I arose from my seat, as did hundreds of others, to look at Joseph. His voice, his language, every expression seemed to come from Joseph himself. It was a testimony to many hundreds of the Latter-day Saints that from that time to the present has never left their memories for a moment. By it God communicated to His people who the successor of Joseph was. It has been a great comfort to me. I speak it here in all soberness and thoughtfulness that I rose to my feet to look upon Joseph Smith because I thought I heard his voice, and felt his spirit and the influence that he had (CD, 5:31).

William Carbine

I was nine years old when the Prophet was martyred. I well remember the excitement at that time. The people hardly knew what to do. The Prophet was gone and Sidney Rigdon wanted a guardian put in for the Church. Brother Thomas Grover, one of the High Council, spoke and told the people not to be in a hurry: the Twelve would be home soon and they would tell the people what to do. When Brigham Young came home he held a meeting, at which time the mantle of Joseph fell on him. It was a manifestation to let the people know who was to lead the Church. His looks and ways were like the Prophet. I, as a boy, was quite well acquainted with the Prophet. I was sitting with my mother in the meeting and I thought it was the Prophet and told my mother so. There are a good many who have heard my mother tell this (1963, p. 204).

Homer Duncan

At the special meeting held at Nauvoo, after Joseph Smith's death—at the time that the mantle of the prophet of the Lord fell upon Brigham Young—I sat listening to someone speaking, with my head down, my face hid in the palms of my hands and my elbows resting on my knees. While [I was] in this position, Brigham Young came to the stand and commenced to speak with the voice of Joseph the Prophet. Being so well acquainted with the Prophet's voice, I nearly sprang from my seat, through astonishment; but I sat and heard the Prophet Joseph's voice as long as Brigham was speaking. Not only did the voice of Brigham sound like that of Joseph, but the very gestures of his right hand, when he was saying anything very positive, reminded me of Joseph. My decision was then made as to who should lead the Church: for surely the mantle of Joseph had fallen upon Brigham (1971, p. 625).

Mary D. Ensign

I was at the meeting when [Sidney Rigdon] stood in his carriage and harangued the people for three hours. He thought it his place to lead them. The saints did not know what to do. It seemed as though everything was at a standstill. The meeting was held in a large grove at that time one afternoon. There was an immense crowd in attendance. Meeting was opened as usual and Brigham Young stepped to the stand. It seemed as though the Prophet was before us and had been resurrected. People craned their necks to get a better view of him, he so resembled the Prophet in looks and speech. Surely the mantle of the Prophet had fallen on Brigham. I remember as well what father said on our way home after the meeting. "They need not hunt any farther. Brigham Young is the man" (n.d., p. 3).

Samuel K. Gifford

Previous to the death of the Prophet, Brigham Young, who was president of the Twelve, and Heber C. Kimball were on their way to Quincy, stopped at the Morley settlement, and preached in the Hickory Grove.

As President Young arose from his seat to speak to the people, a sudden change came over him before my eyes. And he stood there to all appearance as the Prophet Joseph Smith himself. He stood the same as Joseph, and every motion of his body and his voice and manner of delivery was truly that of Joseph Smith. I did not understand the meaning of it, for Joseph was still living, and I did not suppose the Lord would suffer his enemies to take his life (n.d.).

Rachel R. Grant

After the Prophet's death, when Sidney Rigdon came to Nauvoo and spoke, he thought that it was his right and privilege to be President of the Church. President Young jumped right up on the seat and spoke. If you had had your eyes shut, you would have thought it was the Prophet. In fact, he looked like him, his very countenance seemed to change, and he spoke like him (1905, p. 550).

William Greenhalgh

In a few days Sidney Rigdon came up to Nauvoo with a pretended revelation saying the Lord had sent him as a guardian to act for Joseph. He then told the people if they did not accept of him, God would reject them as a people, with their dead, and he was to return to Pittsburgh where God would raise up a people at Pittsburgh for him. Then with uplifted hands he called on God and angels to bear him witnesses and he appointed again the next day to speak to them and see if the people would accept of him.

Just at this time came home Brigham Young and Heber C. Kimball. On the morning following, Brigham Young ordered the people to bring a wagon to the south side of the congregation so that the people could all hear what he had to say. Sidney Rigdon spoke a little and then Brigham rose and said, "I would to God there were not such a hurrying spirit here." He spoke with such power and the voice of Joseph sounded through him so plain that the people who could not see him thought it was Joseph come again. Even those that could not see him knew that it was the voice of Joseph speaking through Brigham Young. Now my wife, who was sitting close by me, was not able to turn her head. She asked me if that was Joseph? I told her no, but that it was Joseph speaking through Brigham. To me this was a living testimony that the mantle had fallen from Joseph on Brigham. From this time on many wanted to wheel off and part from the Saints. But Brigham forbade them and told them that the flock must not be scattered (n.d.).

Lorenzo H. Hatch

I was a young man, being but eighteen years old, 1500 miles from home. The question in my mind was, who would lead the Church now that the Prophet Joseph Smith was gone. About a month later a letter came from my uncle, Jeremiah Hatch, who had married a daughter of Sidney Rigdon. He claimed that the Lord had called Sidney Rigdon to lead the Church. I was at the house of one of my cousins in the town of Bristol, Vermont. It was about noon. I stood in the middle of the sitting room reading the letter to my cousin, when a voice plain and distinct said, "Brigham Young is the man God has chosen to fill the vacancy." I so declared to my cousin. My father had gone to the Great Beyond and Brigham Young was a father to me all the remainder of his life (1994, p. 7).

Drusilla D. Hendricks

The prophets were killed on Thursday, June 27, 1844. I could well bear witness to the feelings of the brethren, who were on missions at that time, for my feelings were such that I prayed the Lord to take them from me—it was more than I could stand. Then the load was made lighter, according to my prayer, so that I could attend to my business.

Sister Booth and I came home together; we started Friday, June 28. We did not know that the Prophets were killed, only by our feelings, until we got out about six miles and met another boat. They hailed each other and then we were told who was killed, saying they had the hour and minute that he was killed. Then from the captain to the last hand on deck came running to us with the news to see how we felt. We could not have felt worse. When we reached home everything was in mourning.

It was not long before Sidney Rigdon called a meeting in order to present his claims to the presidency of the Church. Some of the Twelve had returned from their missions, and the day the meeting was held and while it was in session, Brigham Young (president of the Quorum of the Twelve Apostles) and others slipped up to the stand and said nothing until Sidney Rigdon was through; he was standing near the center of the audience in a wagon, as the meeting was in the Bowery. Then Pres. Brigham Young began to speak. I jumped up to look and see if it was not Brother Joseph, for surely it was his voice and gestures. Every Latter-day Saint could easily see upon whom the priesthood descended, for Brigham Young held the keys. Sidney Rigdon led off a few, but where are they now? They have dwindled, many in unbelief, and have come to naught (n.d.).

William Henrie

When the meeting was called to choose a new leader of the Church, William and his four sons, Daniel, James, Joseph, and Samuel were all present, and they listened to the claims of all who thought they should preside at the Church's head, but when Brigham Young got up and spoke and the mantle of Joseph Smith fell upon him, they all testified that there was no question or any room left for doubt in the minds of all those present, for as Daniel said, "As he began to talk he sounded like the Prophet, and he took on the appearance of the Prophet until we thought it was the Prophet reincarnated. We thought he had really come back to us. We were never more wide awake in our lives, and yet there was his apparition before our eyes. It was a soul-stirring experience."

Many years later Marian, son of James, in talking to his father about it, said "Oh, Father, I think you were just having an illusionation." James brought one fist down hard into the other hand with a bang and said "Illusi—hell! I saw with my own eyes and heard with my own ears. I was not asleep, or dreaming, and I was not alone. We all saw it, and heard it, and felt the Spirit present. We marveled over it and talked of nothing else for days."

It was the final thing that convinced Daniel that the Latter-day Saints church was true and divinely inspired. He went down and was baptized in the Mississippi River July 16, 1845 (1955, pp. 4–5).

Emily S. Hoyt

We were in Nashville [Iowa] when the mob murdered Joseph and Hiram. We went to Nauvoo and saw their earthly forms, which the mob had laid low. Joseph had been shot a little above the eyebrows, in the center between them, almost as if with a good aim; his face was mild and pleasant; even in death [he] looked good. Hiram had been shot in the neck and the blood had settled rather more; he was a noble-looking form. The appearance of true greatness could not be denied. We returned from that melancholy scene heart sickened and sorrowful cast down but not in despair. The Twelve [were] away, most of them. But [they] returned as soon as possible. We were summoned over the river again and went to hear what was wanted. Brigham Young, then president of the Twelve, had returned home.

The people were convened in the Old Bowery where Joseph had last spoken to the people. Sidney Rigdon made a speech and claimed to have authority to lead the Church. Others had similar claims. None appeared reasonable to me. The last one arose. It was the then president of the Twelve, Brigham Young. He spoke to the people altogether in a different style from any of those who had preceded him. A cloud of witnesses arose after Brigham Young had sat down and testified to the truth of what he had said. President Brigham Young arose from his seat the second time and addressed the audience.

I had been well acquainted with Joseph the latter part of his life. We had been at his home many times and Joseph, Hiram, and families felt at home with us. From a place of retreat before the Illinois mob, Joseph sent to S. P. [Samuel Pierce, her husband] for money to aid him in escaping for a time from the grasp of his ungodly pursuers. S. P. sent the money and they had the power in their own hands to go any place they might choose. They consulted and deliberated. Emma, Joseph's wife, wanted her husband and his brother Hiram to give themselves up; she called them cowards, etc. Joseph said if it would save the people he was willing to be sacrificed.

After everything was ready for them to get away, Joseph said he would go and give himself up to the state authorities. The governor was pledged to protect them. Joseph said he felt that it might be like a lamb going to the slaughter. The result of his counsel is well known. They returned and were murdered.

The Latter-day Saints were apparently left without a leader. But the God of heaven, who had said it was his business to provide for his saints, sent President Brigham Young home just in time, and clothed him not with "the mantle of Elijah" but the spirit and power which had rested on Joseph. I was an eye, and ear, witness. The manner of reasoning, the expression of the countenance, the sound of the voice thrilled my whole soul. My own eyes had beheld Joseph's murdered body. My own hands had felt death's icy coldness on his once noble forehead. I knew that Joseph was dead. And yet I often startled and involuntarily looked at the stand to see if it was not Joseph. It was not; it was Brigham Young, and if any one doubts the right of Brigham to manage affairs for the saints, all I have to say to them is *this*. "Get the Spirit of God and know for yourselves. The Lord will provide for his own! Has the word of the Lord ever failed?" The Lord will provide for his own. Brigham Young will not live forever, clothed with mortality. But He who rules in heaven and on earth will control all things by the counsel of his own will. Saints will live (n.d., pp. 20–22).

Benjamin F. Johnson

I do further bear as a testimony, faithful and true, to the Church and to all the world, that at a conference of the whole Church, at Nauvoo, [on August 8, 1844,] subsequent to the Prophet's death and return of the absent Apostles, that I sat in the assembly near to President Rigdon, closely attentive to his appeal to the conference to recognize and sustain his claim as "Guardian for the Church." And I was perhaps, to a degree, forgetful of what I knew to be the rights and duties of the apostleship, and as he closed his address and sat down, my back was partly turned to the seat occupied by Apostle Brigham Young and other Apostles, when suddenly, and as from heaven, I heard the voice of the Prophet Joseph, that thrilled my whole being, and quickly turning around I saw in the transfiguration of Brigham Young, the tall, straight, and portly form of the Prophet Joseph Smith, clothed in a sheen of light, covering him to his feet; and I heard the real and perfect voice of the Prophet, even to the whistle, as in years past caused by the loss of a tooth said to have been broken out by the mob at Hiram. This view, or vision, although but for seconds, was to me as vivid and real as the glare of lightning or the voice of thunder from the heavens, and so deeply was I impressed with what I saw and heard in this transfiguration, that for years I dared not publicly tell what was given me of the Lord to see. But when in later years I did publicly bear this testimony, I found that others would testify to having seen and heard the same. But to what proportion of the congregation who were present I could never know. But I know this, my testimony is true.

The Prophet's lost tooth, to which I alluded was, as generally understood, broken out by the mob at Hiram while trying to pry open his mouth to strangle him with acid, which from [that] time until the tooth was replaced by a dentist neighbor a year or so previous to his death . . . [caused] a whistle-like sound to accompany all his public speaking, which I again plainly heard at the time of which I write (1903).

Zadok K. Judd

Right here I might relate another circumstance that to me was a sufficient testimony of the truth of the gospel. I had for years been more or less acquainted with the Prophet Joseph Smith. I had many, many times heard him preach; had heard him talk with others in common conversation. I had known his voice as well as I do that of my most intimate friend. At the time of his martyrdom in June, I was in Springfield, Illinois. This circumstance I am going to relate happened late in the fall or early winter [1844]. The people had usually convened for meeting in a little grove near the temple. A bowery had been built, and seats arranged to accommodate all. A good place for summer meeting. In the meantime the building of the temple had progressed; the roof was on, the windows were in, the floor was laid, but no seats arranged. It was a cold, wet Sunday and a drizzling rain. The meeting had been adjourned from the grove to the temple, for there people could get shelter. While waiting for the people to gather and also for the hour of meeting, Brigham Young, Heber C. Kimball and some others of the Quorum of the Twelve had come to an upper room or a kind of gallery and seemed to be passing and repassing an open door and window and from the position I had chosen, which was next to the wall and near the stand, I could see them very plainly, and although I knew Joseph was dead, I could scarcely make myself believe he was not there. His look, his motion, his walk, were precisely like that of Joseph, and yet it was Brigham Young, and when he came to and commenced to speak to the people his voice was like Joseph's.

In the meantime people had gathered in, and standing huddled close together made such an immense weight on the floor that the propping under the center gave way and let the floor settle a few inches, which caused quite a panic among the people, and some tried to rush for the door, but the loud voice of the Prophet Joseph soon restored quiet, and only a few were hurt by being pushed down and stepped on. No damage was done, only a few broken windows. The change of voice and appearance I could not account for only that the mantle of Joseph had fallen on Brigham Young (n.d.).

Jerome B. Kempton

(During the meeting held on August 8, 1844,) Brigham Young spoke in favor of sustaining the Quorum of the Twelve as the presidency of the church. He said, "I do not ask you to take my counsel or advice alone, but every one of you act for yourselves." Jerome and [his wife] Maria were present at the meeting where Brigham Young's voice and looks, as he stood speaking to the people, seemed to take on the appearance of the Prophet. Everyone saw it, heard it, and felt the spirit of the Prophet. "The resemblance was so real that Maria fainted and had to be carried out." They trusted Brigham Young and accepted him as their divinely appointed leader, president, and spiritual guide with the other Apostles (1985, p. 28).

Heber C. Kimball

In a grove some little distance east of the temple, . . . I was among the number that was obliged to stand, it being impossible for half of the congregation to be seated. . . . I can bear witness, with hundreds of others who stood that day under the sound of Brigham's voice, of the wonderful and startling effect that it had upon us. If Joseph had risen from the dead and stood before them, it could hardly have made a deeper or more lasting impression. It was the very voice of Joseph himself. This was repeatedly spoken of by the Latter-day Saints. And surely it was a most powerful and convincing testimony to them that he was the man, instead of Sidney Rigdon, that was destined to become the "great leader," and upon whose shoulders the mantle of Joseph had fallen (1883).

Catherine T. Leishman

The next year, 1844, the Prophet was martyred in the Carthage Jail. That memorable day was the saddest of all days for the Saints. I was then about twelve years of age and was a living witness to these trying scenes.

I have heard the Prophet speak many times. I have played and also gone to school with his children. I saw the men bring the bodies of Joseph and Hyrum, his brother, home after they were killed, and I looked upon their dead faces as they lay in their coffins and was a witness to all the trying scenes that followed. The Saints were now as a flock without a shepherd. Apostles and missionaries were called home. The Saints were soon called to the temple and the great question as to who should be their leader was settled. Then Brigham Young was chosen to fill the vacancy of our beloved Prophet. I saw Brigham Young rise to take his place as President of our Church and testify that he appeared to me and others to be Joseph the Prophet himself in person and voice, and I exclaimed "Oh, the Prophet Joseph is resurrected." My sister Rachel said, "No, that is Brother Brigham Young" (n.d., p. 3).

William B. Pace

Sidney Rigdon spent what seemed to me several hours, haranguing the people on the importance of making him their leader, after which

Brigham Young arose and said only a word, when it was observed by the whole congregation that the mantle of "Joseph" was upon him, in word, gesture, and general appearance.

The people arose en-masse to their feet, astonished, as it appeared that Joseph had returned and was speaking to the people. I was small and got upon a bench that I might more fully witness the "phenomena." There was no longer any question as to who was the leader (n.d.).

Jane S. Richards

The newly wedded pair [that is, Jane and Franklin D. Richards] took up their abode at Nauvoo, where, on the 2nd of December, 1843, their first child was born. She was a bright and beautiful spirit and was named Wealthy Lovisa, after both her grandmothers. With this child in her arms, Mrs. Richards attended the special meeting held on the 8th of August, 1844, where President Brigham Young stood transfigured before the congregation, many of whom in consequence recognized him as the lawful successor to the Prophet Joseph Smith. Mrs. Richards is a living witness to the marvelous manifestation. She was sitting in the meeting and had bent over to pick up a small plaything dropped by her little daughter when President Young uttered the first words of his address. His voice was that of the Prophet. On hearing it, she was so startled that she dropped the article she had just taken from the floor, and on looking up beheld the form and features of the martyred Seer (1904, pp. 581–82).

William Watkins

A meeting was appointed for August 8th [1844], by which time Brigham Young and most of the other apostles had returned home. It was at this meeting Sidney Rigdon made a lengthy and tedious speech presenting his claims, telling the people what wonderful things he had planned for them. It was a solemn time, for he was a man who on account of his experience and talents had been sustained as Joseph's counselor by the people, although contrary to the Prophet's wish for some time past, but the darkness was soon dispelled, for Brigham Young explained before the people on that day the order of the priesthood. He was filled with the power of the Holy Ghost. He stood before the people as the Prophet Joseph Smith often had done and we heard the voice of the true shepherd, for he spoke with the voice of Joseph. His manner and appearance were like unto Joseph's and it was manifested to all those present upon whom the responsibility rested to carry on the work of God and lead the Saints.

I sat in that assembly and did not realize for a time but that I was still listening to the Prophet Joseph, so great and marvelous was the manner in which the manifestation before the entire congregation was made, that when the proposition was placed before the people to decide whom they would sustain as the leader of the Church, the Twelve Apostles with Brigham Young as their president were almost unanimously sustained (n.d. [a], p. 3).

John Welch

I was well acquainted with the Prophet Joseph Smith and heard him speak both in public and in private many times. I was present at the meeting in the grove at Nauvoo August 8th, 1844, when Sidney Rigdon made the claim that it was his right to assume the leadership and presidency of the church. I saw Brigham Young, then the president of the Twelve Apostles, stand up to speak to the people, and he spoke with the voice of Joseph Smith; and I further declare and testify that he, Brigham Young, had the appearance of the Prophet Joseph Smith while he, Brigham Young, was talking; that I was convinced then, and have never doubted in all the intervening years from that time up to the present, that Brigham Young was the right man and the man chosen of God to lead the Church (1902).

Note: Attached to this typewritten deposition in the handwriting of Heber Boden is the following note: "John Welch is my grandfather. He and his wife, my grandmother, Eliza Billington Welch, have both frequently borne this testimony to me. [Signed] Heber Wallace Boden, Dec. 17, 1933."

Eliza Westover

The question was a general one, "What shall we do without a leader and prophet?" I was fifteen years old and felt so sad. I was to meeting when Sidney Rigdon declared himself our true prophet and leader. Very few responded to the call. I am happy to say none of my father's family felt that he was. Soon after, President Young came from the east where he was on a mission. I was to meeting when he said he was our prophet and seer. When he spoke it was in Brother Joseph's voice. I gave a jump off my seat and said, "Our prophet has come to life. We have our president back."

I looked up and there stood Brother Joseph just as plain as I ever saw him alive. For a minute I heard Brother Joseph's voice and saw his features;

then a mist seemed to pass from Brother Brigham's face and go up; then there stood Brother Brigham talking to us.

Hundreds saw the same thing that I did, but not all that were present (1916).

Alzina Willis

A special meeting was called, to be held on Thurs., August 8, 1844. The members of the church were all urged to attend. Among others, Brigham Young addressed the great multitude of saints assembled there. He spoke with great power. When he first arose to speak, we were greatly astonished. President Young stood transfigured before us, and we beheld the Prophet, Joseph Smith, and heard his voice as plainly as ever we did when he was living among us. My father and mother were there in attendance. I turned to my Mama and said, "Mama, I thought the Prophet was dead?" Mama answered and said, "He is, Alzina, and this is the way our Heavenly Father has told us who is to be our next leader and Prophet."

I was eleven years old at the time (1973, p. 45).

Mary Ann Winters

I was at the great meeting when the mantle of Brother Joseph rested upon Brother Brigham until his whole being seemed changed and his voice was like that of the Prophet. The people around me [rose] to their feet to get a better chance to hear and see; I and my little companion of the day, Julia Felsaw, being small of stature, stood upon the benches that we, too, might behold the wonderful transformation; and I know that from that time on, the power of that change remained with Brother Brigham Young as long as he lived on the earth. The faithful and honest-hearted were quick to discern the right and took up the armor of the gospel anew, rallied round the faithful Brigham, whose rightful leadership had been plainly shown to them, and went to work with renewed zeal to whatever he pointed out to do (1916c, p. 642).

Wilford Woodruff

[Brigham] then asked if they wanted the Twelve Apostles to step forth and magnify their calling and build up the Church and establish the kingdom of God in all the earth. "All who do, raise your right hand," and almost every soul in that congregation voted; and when Brigham Young arose and commenced speaking, as has been said, if my eyes had not been so I could see, if I had not seen him with my own eyes, there is no one that could have convinced me that it was not Joseph Smith speaking. It was as the voice and face of Joseph Smith; and anyone can testify to this who was acquainted with these two men (CD, 2:383–84).

Selected Biographical Registry

Adams, William (1822–1901). Born in Ireland; emigrated to the United States in 1842–1843; lived with the Saints in Nauvoo; worked as a stonecutter on the Nauvoo Temple; went west with the Saints in 1849; served missions in Pennsylvania and Iron County, Utah; later became a counselor to the president of the San Juan Stake.

Allen, Lucy (1815–1908). The daughter of Isaac Morley; born in Kirtland, Ohio; married Joseph Stewart Allen in 1835; went to Utah with the Saints.

Alley, Lydia Ann (1828–1909). Family accepted the gospel when Lydia was about aged three and living in Salem, Massachusetts; they later moved to Nauvoo. Lydia married Daniel H. Wells; had six children; after moving to Utah, served in the Thirteenth Ward Relief Society and the Salt Lake Primary Association; worked as an officiator in the Salt Lake Temple.

Allred, William (1819–1901). Was fifteen when he first met the Prophet; was with him in Missouri and Nauvoo; went west with the Saints; is buried in St. Charles, Idaho.

Anderson, William (1809–1846). After periods of religious doubt, concluded he would trust the Bible. He prayed, and the Spirit manifested to him an apostasy had occurred; baptized in August 1841; received a patriarchal blessing from Hyrum Smith.

Angell, Polly Ann Johnson (1813–1876 [or 1878]). Born in Riga, Monroe County, New York; married Truman O. Angell in September 1832; went west with the Saints.

Angell, Truman O. (1810–1887). Brother-in-law to Brigham Young; worked on Kirtland and Nauvoo Temples; later became Church Architect; supervised construction of the Salt Lake Temple.

Selected Biographical Registry

Armstrong, James Arthur (1883–1969). Born in Sanpete County, Utah; served a mission in Minnesota, where he met the sister of William Law.

Ashby, Benjamin (1828–1907). Baptized in December 1841 in Nauvoo; was a member of the Nauvoo Legion; later raised crops at Winter Quarters; went west with the Saints; in 1853 served a mission to Great Britain.

Ball, Thomas (1822–1905). Joined the Church in England; emigrated to Utah in 1869; became patriarch of the Summit Stake; also served as counselor to William Cluff, president of the Summit Stake; served a mission to England from 1876 to 1878.

Barlow, Israel A. (1806–1883). Ordained a seventy in 1835 by the Prophet Joseph Smith; in 1839 was one of the first Latter-day Saints to settle in Nauvoo; in 1848 came to Utah with Brigham Young company; buried in Bountiful, Utah.

Bellows, John F. (1825–1894). Baptized in May 1843; came to Utah in 1850 with the Stephen Markham company; served in the Utah War; buried in Payson, Utah.

Bigler, Henry William (1815–1900). Baptized in 1837; gathered with the Saints in Nauvoo; became a member of the Mormon Battalion; discovered gold at Sutter's Fort after the Battalion march ended; served as mission president of the Sandwich Islands; served two missions in the United States; became a temple worker in St. George during his later years.

Bills, William Andrew (1835–1915). Moved with family to Nauvoo in the spring of 1839; in 1846 started for the west with the body of the Saints; settled in Little Cottonwood in Salt Lake County; was a babe in his mother's arms when the mob threatened to kill Joseph and Hyrum Smith in Far West, Missouri; preserved memories of his father, John Bills, who as a tailor made clothes for Joseph and Hyrum and superintended the making of the uniforms for the first company of the Nauvoo Legion.

Black, George (1823–1872). Baptized in 1840; at age eighteen became one of Joseph Smith's bodyguards; went west with the Saints; a veteran of the Black Hawk War; received his patriarchal blessing from Joseph Smith Sr.

Black, George David (1841–1912). Parents were converts; went west with the Saints; married Mary Hunt; established himself in northern Utah and Idaho; served as a member of the Bannock Stake high council; was Sunday School superintendent in Wilford, Idaho.

Black, Jane Johnston (1801–1890). Born in Lisborn, Ireland; as a young woman she gained some distinction as a preacher of the gospel; heard the Mormon elders preach in 1835; baptized in January 1839 by William Clayton; set apart as a midwife by Joseph Smith; delivered over three thousand babies without losing either a mother or child; after the martyrdom, John Taylor called for her to nurse the wounds he received at Carthage and to testify to the Lord of what took place there.

Boice, James (b. 1814). Born in Fredericksburg, Upper Canada; married Jean Hearns in 1833; baptized the same year; in 1837 they migrated to Kirtland, Ohio; migrated west with the main body of the Saints.

Boss, Nancy (1829–1888). Born in Lexington, North Carolina; baptized in 1841; married David Rawson in 1849; bore him ten children; went west; settled in Weber County, Utah.

Brown, Benjamin (1794–1878). Born in Queensbury, Washington County, New York; married in 1819; joined the Church in part because of an inspired vision; delayed his baptism for one year, waiting for his wife to be converted; present at dedication of Kirtland Temple; served missions to New York, the Eastern States, Nova Scotia, Mississippi, and Great Britain; served as the first bishop of the Salt Lake Fourth Ward.

Browning, Charilla Abbot (1829–1914). Baptized in Nauvoo in 1843; married David Browning Sr.; was mother to eight children; migrated to Utah with the Saints; lived in Ogden; taught school and sang in the Ogden Tabernacle Choir.

Bullock, Lucy Clayton (1820–1879). One of the first Latter-day Saint converts in England; baptized in 1837; married Thomas Bullock; mother to six children; driven from their Nauvoo home by the mob in 1846; went west, stopping first at Winter Quarters; settled in the Salt Lake Valley; served as a ward Relief Society president and a midwife.

Burgess, Harrison (1814–1883). Born in Putnam, Washington County, New York; baptized in 1832; member of Zion's Camp; ordained to First Quorum of the Seventy in 1835; bishop in Pine Valley, Utah.

Burgess, Margarette [Margaret] (1837–1919). Born in Indiana County, Pennsylvania; baptized about 1845; went west with the Saints; died in St. George, Utah.

Burnett, Peter H. (1807–1895). A nonmember of the Church living in Missouri at the time of the Missouri troubles; had memories of Joseph

Smith, Sidney Rigdon, and others; went west; became the first governor of the state of California.

Butler, John Lowe (1808–1860). Baptized in 1835; victim of the Missouri persecutions; served several missions; in Nauvoo was ordained a bodyguard to the Prophet Joseph Smith; an officiator in the Nauvoo Temple; bishop in Spanish Fork; kept an extensive journal, which appears to be one of the sources from which Joseph Smith's clerks and scribes compiled his history.

Cahoon, William F. (1813–1897). Baptized while living in Kirtland; served as a member of the First Quorum of the Seventy in 1835; worked on the Kirtland Temple; married by the Prophet Joseph Smith to Nancy Gibbs in 1836; member of Zion's Camp; served several missions; played the brass drum in the Nauvoo Legion Band; left with the Saints for the west; arrived in the Salt Lake Valley in September 1849.

Call, Anson (1810–1890). Baptized in 1834; suffered at the hands of mobs; friend of Joseph Smith; well remembered for recording Joseph's 1842 prophecy that the Saints would flee to the Rocky Mountains; went west with the Saints; represented Millard County in Utah legislature; founded Call's Fort; served as counselor to William R. Smith in Davis Stake presidency.

Callister, Caroline Smith (1820–1895). Daughter of John and Clarissa Smith and cousin of the Prophet Joseph Smith; married Thomas Callister in 1845; mother of seven children.

Cannon, Angus M. (1834–1915). Born in Liverpool, England; emigrated with his family to Nauvoo; baptized in September 1844; later went west; managed *Deseret News;* became mayor of St. George, Utah; served as president of the Salt Lake Stake; later ordained a patriarch.

Cannon, George Q. (1827–1901). Born in Liverpool, England; emigrated with his family to Nauvoo; baptized in 1840; came to Utah in 1847 with John Taylor company; served missions in the Sandwich Islands and England; ordained an apostle in 1860; served as a first counselor in the First Presidency to Presidents John Taylor, Wilford Woodruff, and Lorenzo Snow.

Carbine, William (1835–1921). Born in Cairo, Green County, New York; left Nauvoo with his family for the west in the spring of 1846; his father died en route; served in both the Walker War and Black Hawk War; served in bishoprics and on stake high councils.

Carling, Ann Green (1799 [or 1802]–1893). Born in Lugwardine, Herefordshire, England; married John Dutson in 1826; second marriage to John Carling in 1844 while in Nauvoo; endowed in the Nauvoo Temple; went west with the Saints; died in Fillmore, Utah.

Carter, Jared (1801–1849). Born in Benson, Rutland County, Vermont; joined the Church and ordained an elder in 1831; served missions in eastern states, New York, Michigan, Massachusetts, Connecticut, and Vermont. Served on high council in Kirtland, Ohio, and Far West, Missouri; member of committee overseeing construction of Kirtland Temple; disfellowshipped at Nauvoo; promised to return to Church; died in DeKalb County, Illinois.

Chidester, John (1809–1893). Born in Pompey, Onondaga County, New York; baptized in Michigan in June 1832; joined Zion's Camp in 1834; ordained a seventy in 1837; served a mission to Michigan in 1842; built and operated a ferry boat across the Mississippi River when the Saints were expelled from Nauvoo in 1846; went west; a carpenter, millwright, wheelwright, and farmer; helped colonize Washington County, Utah, where he later died.

Clark, Sarah T. (1831–1918). Born in Bedfordshire, England; endowed February 1846 in Nauvoo Temple; married Joseph Clark in 1849; died in Provo, Utah.

Clawson, Margaret Judd (1831–1912). Born in Ontario, Canada; married Hiram B. Clawson in 1852; lived in Nauvoo as a youth; went west with the Saints; lived at Winter Quarters in 1849; mother of Rudger Clawson, who became president of the Quorum of the Twelve Apostles.

Clayton, William (1814–1879). Born in Lancashire, England; baptized in England in October 1837; ordained high priest in 1838; missionary to England in 1840; recorder and clerk of Nauvoo Temple in 1842; succeeded Willard Richards as clerk to Joseph Smith from 1842 until the Prophet's death; recorded the revelation on celestial marriage; several items from his journal have been included in the Doctrine and Covenants; wrote the hymn, "Come, Come Ye Saints."

Coates, Allen (b. 1794). In 1802 moved with his family to the Palmyra region; claimed memories of Joseph Smith and the Smith family; not a member of the Church.

Coltrin, Zebedee (1804–1887). Born in Ovid, Seneca County, New York; baptized in Ohio in January 1831; attended School of the Prophets in Kirtland; member of Zion's Camp in 1834; member of the First Council of the Seventy in 1837; served a mission to Michigan in 1844; endowed in Nauvoo Temple in 1845; ordained a patriarch during Utah years.

Coray, Howard (1817–1908). Born in Dansville, Steuben County, New York; baptized in 1840; a clerk for Joseph Smith; assigned to compile a Church history; helped Lucy Mack Smith write her history of the Prophet; served missions to Pennsylvania and the Southern States; a farmer, bookkeeper, schoolteacher, and county assessor; once owned a molasses factory; died in Utah.

Cowdery, Oliver (1806–1850). Joseph Smith's scribe for much of the translation of the Book of Mormon; present when John the Baptist restored the Aaronic Priesthood; present when Peter, James, and John restored the Melchizedek Priesthood; one of the Three Witnesses to the Book of Mormon; by revelation commanded to select original members of the Quorum of the Twelve; present when Moses, Elias, and Elijah restored priesthood keys; associate president of the Church; excommunicated in April 1838; rebaptized 12 November 1848.

Cox, Elias (1835–1917). Born in Putnam, Indiana; baptized in 1844; went west with his family; in Utah, served as bishop, high councilor; member of the Utah State constitutional convention in 1882.

Crookston, Robert Sr. (1821–1916). Born in Fife, Scotland; emigrated to the United States; married Ann Welch at Winter Quarters, Nebraska; fathered eleven children; helped procure stone for the Salt Lake Temple; worked on Logan Temple and Tabernacle; died as a high priest in Logan, Utah.

Crosby, Caroline (1807–1884). Born in Warwick, Franklin County, Maine; baptized in 1835; lived in Kirtland and Nauvoo; moved to Utah in 1848 with the main body of the Saints; served a mission with her husband, Jonathan, to Society Islands (Tahiti); member of Relief Society presidency in Beaver, Utah, in 1868; died in Beaver, Utah.

Crosby, Jesse (1820–1895). Born in Yarmouth, Nova Scotia, Canada; baptized in 1838; ordained a seventy in 1840; endowed in 1846 in Nauvoo Temple; served missions in the eastern states, Michigan, the southern states, and Canada; worked on Nauvoo Temple; in Nauvoo, a close neighbor and friend of Joseph Smith; among the first of the pioneers to reach the Salt Lake Valley in 1847; buried in Panguitch, Utah.

Cummings, B. F. (1855–1918). Born in Ogden, Weber County, Utah; a child of Mormon pioneers of 1847; lawyer; Utah state legislator; served missions to the eastern and central sates; founding editor of *Liahona: The Elder's Journal,* published in Independence, Missouri; widely known as expert genealogist.

Curtis, Joseph (1818–1883). Born in Comeata, Erie, Pennsylvania;

endured mob persecutions in Far West, Missouri; married Sara (Sally) Ann Reed on 1 January 1846 in Nauvoo; went west with the Saints; died in Payson, Utah.

Curtis, Levi (birth and death dates unavailable). Lived in Nauvoo; went west; settled in Springville, Utah.

Decker, Isaac (1799–1873). Born in Tycanic, Columbia County, New York; married Harriet Page Wheeler in 1820; fathered six children; called on a mission during Missouri persecutions; ordained a high priest; endowed in December 1845 in Nauvoo Temple; traveled to Salt Lake in the Brigham Young company of 1847.

Dibble, Philo (1806–1895). Born in Peru, Berkshire County, Massachusetts; baptized in October 1830; wounded by the mob in Missouri and miraculously healed; endowed in Nauvoo Temple; went west; settled in Springville, Utah; maintained a journal during life of Joseph Smith, and mentions frequent contact with him.

Duncan, Chapman (1812–1900). Born in Bath, Grafton County, New Hampshire; baptized on 25 December 1832; ordained a seventy; endowed in Nauvoo Temple on 1 January 1846; served missions to Vermont, Virginia, and China; fought the crickets in Salt Lake until the gulls came; buried in Lyman, Utah.

Duncan, Homer (1815–1906). Born in Barnet, Caledonia County, Vermont; great-grandson of American Revolutionary War hero General Israel Putnam; baptized on 9 August 1838 at Adam-ondi-Ahman, Missouri, after seeing a vision of Orson Pratt and Lyman E. Johnson preaching and baptizing; ordained a seventy in 1839; received patriarchal blessing from Joseph Smith Sr.; served missions to New York, Canada, Texas, and the British Isles; crossed the plains eleven times with ox teams; buried in the Salt Lake City Cemetery.

Eccles, Henry (1823–1874). Joined the Church in Manchester, Lancaster, England; emigrated to the United States; settled in Nauvoo with the Saints; befriended Joseph Smith; tarred and feathered by a mob for his defense of Joseph Smith; a master marble worker; went west with the Saints.

Ensign, Mary D. (1833–1920). Born in Bellville, Wayne Country, Michigan; baptized in 1841; married Martin Luther Ensign in 1852; mother of nine children; endowed at the Endowment House in Salt Lake City in 1857; buried in Brigham City, Utah.

Everett, Addison (1805–1885). Born in Wallhall, Ulster County, New York; baptized in 1837; ordained a bishop in Nauvoo; entered Salt Lake Valley on 24 July 1847 with the Brigham Young company; drove

Brigham's ox teams during the trek; bishop of the Eighth Ward in Salt Lake City from 1848 to 1860; died in St. George, Utah.

Everett, Schuyler (1835–1924). Born in New York, New York; son of Addison and Eliza Ann Everett; baptized in 1843 in the Mississippi River; endowed in the Endowment House in Salt Lake City in 1861; buried in St. George, Utah.

Foote, Warren (1817–1903). Born in Dryden, Tampskins County, New York; read entire Bible three times before age sixteen; visited Joseph Smith in Kirtland in 1837; baptized in 1842; ordained a seventy in 1844; endowed in Nauvoo Temple in 1846; buried in Glendale, Utah.

Ford, Thomas (1800–1850). Born in Uniontown, Fayette County, Pennsylvania; an accomplished attorney; became judge to Circuit Court in Illinois from 1835 to 1837; worked for the Galena District in 1839; appointed to Illinois Supreme Court in 1841; resigned to run for governor; held office from 1842 to 1846; lied to Joseph Smith about providing state protections during Joseph's confinement at Carthage; died in Peoria; buried at public expense.

Fox, Jesse W. (1819–1894). Born in Adams, Jefferson County, New York; baptized in 1844; ordained by President John Taylor as a seventy and later a high priest; arrived in Nauvoo just in time to see the bodies of Joseph and Hyrum Smith; crossed plains; taught at the University of Deseret with Orson Pratt; surveyed and set the stakes for the Salt Lake, Manti, and Logan Temples; his funeral was conducted in the Assembly Hall; buried in the Salt Lake City Cemetery.

Freeze, Lillie (1855–1936 [or 1937]). Born in Salt Lake City; charter member and first general secretary of the Primary Association; served in Relief Society, Young Women's Mutual Improvement Association, and on mission boards; wrote extensively in Church publications like the *Deseret News, Children's Friend, Woman's Exponent, Improvement Era,* and *Liahona;* married James P. Freeze; mother of four children.

Gee, Lysander (1818–1894). Born in Austinburgh, Ashtabula, Ohio; baptized in 1840; ordained a seventy and, later, a high priest; was a plasterer, carpenter, justice of the peace, and attorney; helped carry out a failed plan designed to enable Joseph Smith to escape from Liberty Jail; buried in Tooele, Utah.

Gilbert, John H. (1802–1895). Born in Richmond, Ontario County, New York; learned printer's trade in Canandaigua, New York; moved to Palmyra in 1824; formed partnership with Pomeroy Tucker and published the *Wayne Sentinel* from 1824 to 1827; when Egbert B.

Grandin purchased the *Sentinel* he hired Gilbert to assist in the print shop, in which Gilbert printed the Book of Mormon, inserting much of the punctuation into the manuscript copy; never joined the Church.

Grant, Jedediah Morgan (1816–1856). Born in New York; baptized in 1833 by John F. Boynton; went on Zion's Camp march in 1834; worked on Kirtland Temple; ordained a seventy in 1835 by Joseph Smith; led a company of Saints to Utah in 1847; first mayor of Salt Lake City; served as a counselor to Brigham Young; noted as a convincing public speaker.

Grant, Rachel Ridgeway (1820–1907). Born in Hornerstown, Monmouth County, New Jersey; baptized in 1840; received patriarchal blessing in 1843 from Hyrum Smith; went west, arriving in 1853; mother of Heber J. Grant, who was born nine days before the death of his father, Jedediah Morgan Grant; served as president of the Relief Society in the Thirteenth Ward for thirty-five years; died in Salt Lake City.

Greenhalgh, William (1811–1882). Born in Bolton, Lancashire, England; baptized in 1840; later ordained a seventy; endowed in Nauvoo Temple in 1846; saw events of the martyrdom in an inspired dream or vision before they took place; buried in Santaquin, Utah.

Greer, Catherine (1837–1927 [or 1929]). Born in Dresden, Tennessee; baptized in 1853; had memories of Joseph and Hyrum Smith visiting her parent's home in her youth.

Haight, Isaac C. (1813–1886). Born in Windham, Greene County, New York; baptized on 3 March 1839; ordained a seventy; received patriarchal blessing from Hyrum Smith in 1843; endowed in Nauvoo Temple in December 1845; member of Nauvoo City Police; joined Saints in exodus west; mayor of Cedar City; stake president; representative to state legislative assembly in Fillmore, Utah; died in Thatcher, Arizona.

Hale, Aroet (1828–1911). Born in Dover, Strafford County, New Hampshire; baptized in 1837; endowed in Nauvoo Temple; drummer boy in Nauvoo Legion at time of the martyrdom; served in the first bishopric in Grantsville, Tooele County; served for twenty-four years on high council of the Tooele Stake; buried in Grantsville, Utah.

Hale, Jesse (1792–1874). Born in Harmony, Susquehannah County, Pennsylvania; older brother of Emma Hale Smith, wife of the Prophet Joseph Smith; married Mary McKune in 1815; owned the home at

Harmony where Joseph and Emma lived for a time and where parts of the Book of Mormon were translated; later moved to Illinois.

Hamson, Sarah Ann (1828–1903 [or 1905]). Born in Carlisle, Cumberland County, Pennsylvania; baptized in 1842; endowed in Nauvoo Temple in 1846; married George Frederick Hamson; mother of twelve children.

Hancock, Levi W. (1803–1882). Born in Springfield, Hampden County, Massachusetts; baptized in 1830; member of Zion's Camp in 1834; appointed a president of the First Quorum of the Seventy in 1835; lived with Saints in Missouri and Nauvoo; member of Nauvoo Legion and Mormon Battalion; ordained a patriarch in 1872; died in Washington, Utah.

Hancock, Mosiah (1834–1907). Born in Kirtland; as a youth knew Joseph Smith in Missouri and Nauvoo; member of Nauvoo whistling and whittling brigade; helped colonize and build southern Utah and Arizona; fought in Black Hawk War; died in Hubbard, Arizona.

Harmon, Jesse P. (1795–1877). Born in Rupert, Bennington County, Vermont; baptized in 1838; received patriarchal blessing from Hyrum Smith in 1843; came to Utah in October 1848 with the Heber C. Kimball company; a colonel in the Utah Nauvoo Legion; died in Holden, Utah.

Harper, John (1812–1863). Born in Belfast, Ireland; baptized in 1841, came to Nauvoo in 1843; worked on Nauvoo House and Nauvoo Temple; member of Nauvoo Legion; a president in stake seventies quorum; died in Washington, Utah.

Harris, Dennison (1825–1885). Born in Windham, Pennsylvania; son of Emer Harris; nephew of Martin Harris; baptized in 1842; ordained high priest and bishop; remembered for courageous interaction with mob in behalf of Joseph Smith; died in Monroe, Utah.

Harris, Martha Ann Smith (1841–1943). Born in Nauvoo; daughter of Hyrum and Mary Fielding Smith; married William Jasper Harris in Endowment House, Salt Lake City; mother of eleven children; died in Provo, Utah.

Harris, Martin (1783–1875). Born in Easttown, Saratoga County, New York; respected landowner and farmer in Palmyra; paid printing costs for publication of Book of Mormon; wife lost 116 pages of translation; one of the Three Witnesses to the Book of Mormon; member of Zion's Camp and Kirtland high council; excommunicated; rebaptized; died in Clarkston, Utah.

Hatch, Ira Stearns (1800 [or 1801, 1802, 1803]–1869). Born in Win-chester, New Hampshire; ordained a seventy in Nauvoo; died in Bountiful, Utah.

Hatch, Lorenzo Hill (1826–1910). Born in Lincoln, Addison County, Vermont; baptized in 1840; ordained a seventy and, later, a patriarch; served missions to Indiana, Vermont, Arizona, and New Mexico; worked on Nauvoo Temple; member of the Idaho state legislature; died in Logan, Utah.

Hendricks, Drusilla (1810–1881). Born in Sumner, Tennessee; married James Hendricks; endowed in Nauvoo Temple; had premonition of injury to her husband; later a mob musket shot crippled him at Battle of Crooked River, paralyzing him from the neck down; nursed and cared for husband, helping him cross the plains; he became a bishop; died in Richmond, Utah.

Henrie, William (1799–1883). Born in Marrietta, Lancaster County, Pennsylvania; a farmer, miller, and owner of livestock and a lumber mill; heard gospel preached by Samuel Smith and Parley P. Pratt; baptized in 1842; endowed in 1846 in Nauvoo Temple; ordained a high priest; went to Utah in 1847; died in Bountiful, Utah.

Hess, John W. (1824–1903). Born in Franklin County, Pennsylvania; baptized in 1834; remembers the Prophet staying in his father's home; ordained a seventy, high priest, bishop, and patriarch; an orderly sergeant in Nauvoo Legion; worked on Nauvoo Temple; endowed in Nauvoo Temple; president of Davis Stake; died and buried in Farmington, Utah.

Hickman, William A. (1815–1883). In 1834, fed members of Zion's Camp when they passed through his property in Missouri; later joined the Church; went to the Prophet's assistance when Joseph was arrested in 1841; participated in Battle of Nauvoo in 1846; served as bishop's counselor; lost the spirit of the gospel; excommunicated for murder and other crimes.

Hogan, Goudy E. (1829–1898). Born in Tinsprestifield, Thelemarken, Norway; baptized in 1843; as a teen sat on the stand behind the Prophet when Joseph spoke at the 1844 April conference; emigrated to Utah in 1848; ordained a high priest and bishop; buried in Richmond, Utah.

Holbrook, Joseph (1806–1885). Born in Florence, Oneida County, New York; a farmer, carpenter, and judge; baptized in 1833; joined Zion's Camp; wounded at Battle of Crooked River; member of Nauvoo Police; served as counselor in bishopric; member of the Utah legislature; buried in Bountiful, Utah.

Holden, Edwin (1807–1894). Born in New Salem, Franklin County, Massachusetts; rode fifteen miles on horseback to meet Joseph Smith; endowed in Nauvoo Temple; buried in Provo, Utah.

Horne, Joseph (1811 [or 1812]–1897). Born in London, England; baptized in 1836; ordained a seventy and a high priest; a farmer, mason, and merchant; went west in Edward Hunter's company; counselor in bishopric, high councilor, and patriarch; married Mary Isabella Hale; father of twenty-five children; buried in Salt Lake City, Utah.

Horner, John M. (1821–1907). Born in Monmouth County, New Jersey; a farmer, teacher, bricklayer, and miner; baptized in 1840 by Erastus Snow; went to California on the ship *Brooklyn;* earned great sums and gave generous support to missionaries; lost half a million dollars; died in the Sandwich Islands.

Hoyt, Emily Smith (1806–1893). Born in Royalton [or Tunbridge], Vermont; daughter of Asael Smith and cousin to Joseph Smith; endowed in Nauvoo Temple; married Samuel Pierce Hoyt; went west with the body of the Saints.

Hunter, Edward (1793–1883). Born in Newton, Delaware County, Pennsylvania; a merchant and farmer; baptized in 1840; Joseph Smith preached in his home while in Chester County, Pennsylvania; bishop in Nauvoo; portions of D&C 127 and 128 revealed while Joseph Smith was hiding in Hunter's home; Presiding Bishop of the Church from 1851 to 1883; died in Salt Lake City, Utah.

Huntington, Oliver B. (1823–1909). Born in Watertown, Jefferson County, New York; baptized in 1836 in Kirtland, Ohio; ordained a high priest and patriarch; a farmer, bee inspector, stock raiser, schoolteacher, and school trustee; his personal journal is a rich source of information on Joseph Smith, whom he knew well; traveled to Utah in the Brigham Young company; served a mission to England; died in Springville, Utah.

Hyde, Orson (1805–1878). Born in Oxford, New Haven County, Connecticut; taught by Sidney Rigdon in 1831; missionary companion of Samuel H. Smith in 1832; clerk to First Presidency in 1833; member of Zion's Camp; member of the Council of the Twelve Apostles from 1835 to 1878; dedicated Israel for the return of the Jews in 1841; associate judge for the Utah State Supreme Court; member of the territorial legislature and president of Utah State Senate; died in Sanpete County, Utah.

James, Jane (b. 1821). Walked two thousand miles to meet Joseph Smith, much of journey with bare feet; of African-American descent; went west with Saints to Utah; died a faithful member of the Church.

Jenson, Andrew (1850–1941). Born in Torslev, Denmark; as a youth kept a journal of crossing the plains; wrote the first foreign-language Church book published in Utah; set apart as a historian in the Church Historian's Office; traveled widely, gathering historical data; died in Salt Lake City.

Johnson, Benjamin F. (1818–1905). Born in Pomfret, Chatagua County, New York; baptized in 1835 in Kirtland, Ohio; established close friendship with Joseph Smith; made bricks for Kirtland Temple; lived with Saints in Missouri, Nauvoo, and western United States; served as secretary to Joseph Smith; assigned to visit Emma Smith to persuade her to go west; ordained a seventy, bishop, and patriarch; died in Mesa, Arizona.

Johnson, Evaline Jewell Burdick (b. ca. 1830). Moved to Kirtland with her parents in early the 1830s; had childhood memories of meeting the Prophet Joseph Smith.

Johnson, Joel Hills (1802–1882). Born in Grafton, Worcester, Massachusetts; baptized in 1831; owned sawmill; inventor; present at dedication of Kirtland Temple; traveled to Utah in Willard Richards company; served missions to Iowa, Nebraska, Ohio, and New York; served as a bishop, high councilor, patriarch, and stake president; present when the Word of Wisdom was revealed; wrote the hymn "High On the Mountain Top"; buried in Kane, Utah.

Johnson, Luke S. (1803–1861). Born in Pomfret, Windsor County, Vermont; baptized in 1831; ordained an elder and high priest; ordained an apostle in 1835; excommunicated in 1838; rebaptized in 1846; endowed in 1854 in Salt Lake City; ordained a bishop in St. John, Tooele County, Utah; died in the home of his brother-in-law, Orson Hyde.

Jones, William E. (1817–1898). Born in Parish of Gold, Flint, Wales; a schoolteacher and bricklayer; baptized in 1841; came across the Atlantic to Nauvoo in 1842; active in Church affairs in Utah; buried in Gunlock, Utah.

Judd, Zadok Knapp (1827–1909). Born in Leeds, Ontario, Canada; baptized in 1836 in Canada; ordained a seventy and a bishop; received patriarchal blessing from Joseph Smith Sr.; endowed in Nauvoo Temple in 1846; a tailor and farmer; traveled to Utah in 1848 with the Mormon Battalion contingent; buried in Kanab, Utah.

Kempton, Jerome B. (1820–1899). Born in Fort Ann, Washington

County, New York; ordained a seventy; endowed in 1846 in Nauvoo Temple; father of twenty-three children; went west, settled in Salt Lake and Manti; buried in Blackfoot, Idaho.

Keys, Celia Anzenette/Anjenette (b. ca. 1836). Born in Clay County, Missouri; daughter of Elisha and Joanna Keys; married Alma K. Taylor of Clay County, ca. 1857.

Kimball, Heber C. (1801–1868). Born in Sheldon, Franklin County, Vermont; married Vilate Murray in 1822; converted in 1832; member of Zion's Camp in 1834; ordained to the Council of the Twelve Apostles in 1835; opened missionary work in Great Britain in 1837; served as counselor to Brigham Young from 1847 to 1868; died in Salt Lake City, Utah.

Kimball, Vilate Murray (1806–1867). Born in Florida, Montgomery County, New York; married Heber C. Kimball in 1822; baptized in 1832; endowed in 1845 in Nauvoo Temple; died and buried in Salt Lake City, Utah.

Knight, Catherine M'Guire (b. 1833 [or 1836]). Born in Georgetown, Lancaster County, Pennsylvania; daughter of William Wells and Charlotte Ann Ash (or Bobb) McGuire (or M'Guire).

Knight, Joseph Sr. (1772–1847). Born in Oakham, Worcester, Massachusetts; married Polly Peck ca. 1795; Joseph Smith used his buggy to retrieve gold plates from Cumorah; Church grew up around Knight family in Colesville, New York; helped pioneer Latter-day Saint settlement of Independence, Missouri; died while at Mt. Pisgah, Iowa, preparing to go west.

Knight, Lydia Goldthwaite Bailey (1812–1884). Born in Sutton, Worcester County, Massachusetts; married Calvin Bailey in 1828; he later deserted her; joined Church in 1833 in Canada because of the preaching of Joseph Smith; moved to Kirtland in 1835; married Newel Knight; moved to Missouri and later Nauvoo; went west to Salt Lake Valley; died in St. George, Utah.

Knight, Newel (1800–1847). Born in Marlborough, Windham County, Vermont; joined Church in Colesville, New York, a convert of Joseph Smith; moved to Kirtland and, in 1831, to Missouri; expelled from Jackson County in 1833; member of high councils in Clay County, Far West, and Nauvoo; his first wife, Sally Coburn, died in Missouri in 1834; worked on Kirtland Temple; boarded at home of Hyrum Smith; met and married Lydia Goldthwaite Bailey; died during flight from Nauvoo.

Lambert, Charles (1816–1892). Born in Kirk Deighton, Yorkshire,

England; baptized in 1843; stonecutter; worked on Nauvoo Temple, later endowed there; he and Mary Cannon were married by John Taylor; fought in Battle of Nauvoo in September 1846; built house at Winter Quarters; senior president of 23rd Quorum of Seventies for forty-three years; built one of first adobe houses in Salt Lake Valley; member of Salt Lake police force; served a mission to England; died in Granger, Utah.

Lambert, Mary Alice Cannon (1828–1920). Born in Liverpool, England; baptized in 1840; married Charles Lambert in November 1844; mother of six children; buried in Salt Lake City, Utah.

Lambson, Alfred Boaz (1820–1905). Born in Roylton, Niagara County, New York; visited Nauvoo, met Joseph Smith, and was baptized; married Melissa Jane Bigler; wheelwright who repaired eighty-five wheels in one night at Winter Quarters; father-in-law of Joseph F. Smith; died and buried in Salt Lake City, Utah.

Lamoreaux, Andrew (1812–1855). Born in Pickering, York, Ontario Canada; baptized in Canada in 1837; moved to Nauvoo; in 1852 called by Brigham Young to preside over French mission; translated pamphlets and Doctrine and Covenants into French; took sick and died in St. Louis, Missouri.

Laub, George (1840–1880). Born in Earl, Lancaster County, Pennsylvania; baptized in 1842; penned the earliest written account of the transfiguration of Brigham Young; emigrated to Utah in 1852; helped colonize St. George in 1863 at Brigham Young's request; a joiner and a foreman for the building of the St. George Tabernacle; died in St. George, Utah.

Layton, Christopher (1821–1898). Born in Thorncote, Bedfordshire, England; baptized in 1842; emigrated to the United States in 1843; served as a guard for Nauvoo Temple; member of Mormon Battalion; dug gold at Sutter's Fort; a butcher; a director for Utah Central Railroad; a seventy, patriarch, and stake president; died in Kaysville, Utah.

Leavitt, Dudley (1830–1908). Born in province of Quebec, Canada; baptized in 1838; farmer; missionary companion of Jacob Hamblin to Indians; served as a branch president; buried at Bunkerville, Nevada.

Leavitt, Sarah Sturdevant (1798–1878). Born in Lime, Grafton County, New Hampshire; married Jeremiah Leavitt in 1817; mother to nine children; gained testimony by hearing the testimony of a sister-in-law and reading Parley P. Pratt's *A Voice of Warning;* baptized in Kirtland,

Ohio; joined Saints in Nauvoo; husband died on journey west; settled in Tooele, and later Washington County, Utah.

Lee, John D. (1812–1877). Born in Kaskaskia, Randolph County, Illinois; baptized in 1837; ordained a seventy at Far West; served missions to Tennessee and Kentucky; a major in Nauvoo Legion; colonized in southern Utah; died in Mountain Meadows, Utah.

Leech, James (b. 1815). Born in Pilling Lane, Lancashire, England; baptized in Nauvoo, Illinois, in November 1841; associated with the Church in Illinois and Utah.

Leishman, Catherine Thomas (1834–1927). Born in Rockingham, Richmond County, North Carolina; moved to Knox County, Mississippi, in 1835; joined the Church in 1844; moved to Nauvoo in 1843; rented home from Joseph Smith; lived in Cedar Valley, Utah; moved to Cache County; lived in Logan and Wellsville.

Lewis, David (b. 1818). Born in Saranac, Clinton County, New York, or Potsdam, St. Lawrence County, New York; present at the organization of the Church on 6 April 1830; baptized by the Prophet Joseph Smith; lived in Kirtland, went west with the Saints; served a mission to New York City.

Lightner, Mary Elizabeth Rollins (1818–1913). Born in Lima, Livingston County, New York; baptized in 1830 in Kirtland, Ohio; appears to have been the first person in Kirtland to read the Book of Mormon; in Liberty, Missouri, rescued some sheets of the Book of Commandments when mob destroyed the print shop; made shirts and taught school and painting; married Adam Lightner, who never joined the Church; went west with the Saints.

Linder, Usher F. (1809–1876). Illinois attorney who had some memories of Joseph Smith; non-Latter-day Saint.

Littlefield, Lyman O. (1819–1893). Baptized in 1834; member of Zion's Camp in 1834; worked in offices of *Nauvoo Neighbor* and *Times and Seasons;* served missions to Illinois and Alabama; published an account of the martyrdom; died in Smithfield, Utah.

Loveless, Matilda (1829–1909). Born in Nashville, Tennessee; moved with her parents to Nauvoo in 1840; present at laying of capstone of Nauvoo Temple and dedication; married James Washington Loveless in 1847; drove a team across the plains; arrived in Utah in 1851; settled in Provo, Utah.

Lovell, John (1812–1881). Born in Worroc, Somerset, England; baptized in 1837 after hearing the preaching of John Taylor and others; a stonemason; worked on Nauvoo Temple; ordained a seventy and high priest; driven by mob from Nauvoo; settled with wife in Iowa; she died from exposure; crossed the plains in 1852; died in Oak City, Utah.

Lyman, Amasa M. (1813–1877). Born in Grafton, New Hampshire; married Louisa Maria Tanner in June 1835 in Kirtland; subsequent marriages to Cynthia Wright, Rosannah Reynolds, and Paulina Phelps; ordained an apostle in 1842; deprived of apostleship in 1867; excommunicated in 1870; died in Fillmore, Utah.

Lyman, Asa (1785–1844 [or 1847]). Born in Lebanon, New London, Connecticut; married Sarah (Sally) Davis; ordained a high priest; endowed in Nauvoo Temple.

Lyman, Paulina (1827–1912). Born in Tazewell, Illinois; daughter of Morris Phelps; baptized in 1835 or 1837; married Amasa M. Lyman in 1846 in the Nauvoo Temple; mother of seven children.

Mace, Wandle (1809–1890). Born in Johnstown, Montgomery County, New York; baptized in 1837 or 1838 by Parley P. Pratt; a farmer, inventor, millwright, and owner of a carriage business; started an iron foundry in Nauvoo; served missions to the Catskill Mountains and Missouri; went to Utah in 1859; worked on St. George Temple.

Martineau, Susan (1836–1818). Born in Kirtland, Ohio; daughter of Joel Hills Johnson; baptized in 1844; watched Nauvoo Temple burn; married James Henry Martineau; went west; almost kidnapped by Indians; lived at Big Cottonwood; moved to Iron County.

Mather, Frederic G. (1844–1925). A late nineteenth century essayist; wrote for newspapers and magazines such as *Harper's New Monthly Magazine, The Century, The Atlantic Monthly,* and *The North American Review;* visited Palmyra and central Pennsylvania in 1880 to interview individuals who said they knew Joseph Smith; relied on anti-Mormon literature to write several essays on Joseph Smith and the Church; the tone of his writing is critical, condescending, and filled with ridicule.

Maughan, William (1834–1905). Born in Alston, Cumberland, England; baptized in Nauvoo in 1851; ordained an elder, high priest, bishop, and patriarch; drove ox team to Utah in 1850; served a mission to Great Britain; buried in Wellsville, Utah.

McArthur, Daniel D. (1820–1903). Born in Holland, Erie County, New York; baptized in 1838; ordained a seventy, high priest, bishop, and patriarch; lived in Kirtland and Missouri; moved to Nauvoo in 1844; farmer; went to Utah in 1848; served a mission to Great Britain.

McLaughlin, Harriet C. (1834–1907). Born in Sparta, Livingston

County, New York; baptized in 1843, perhaps the last child publicly baptized by Joseph Smith; came west with pioneers in 1847.

McGuire, William Wells (1809–1887). Born in Chester, Delaware County, Pennsylvania; baptized in 1839; married Charlotte Ann Ash (or Bobb); father of three children.

Merrill, Marriner W. (1832–1906). Born in Sackville, New Brunswick, Canada; at age nine saw a vision of the Saints going west; joined the Church ten years later; went to Salt Lake in 1853; served a mission to Nova Scotia and New Brunswick; counselor to stake president; served as stake president; member of Brigham Young College Board; father of forty-five children; ordained an apostle in 1889 by Wilford Woodruff; died in Richmond, Utah.

Miles, Samuel (1826–1910). Born in Attica, Genesee County, New York; baptized in 1836; present at laying of cornerstone of Far West Temple on 4 July 1838; attended University of Nauvoo; taught by Professor Orson Pratt; joined Mormon Battalion; a farmer and schoolteacher; served a mission to California; served as a high councilor, Sunday School superintendent, and patriarch; died in St. George, Utah.

Miller, Henry W. (1807–1885). Born in Lexington, Green County, New York; a carpenter, builder, lawyer, farmer, and stock raiser; baptized in 1839; gathered timber for Nauvoo House and Nauvoo Temple; appointed by a general conference of the Church to gather funds for Nauvoo Temple; served as president of the Freedom Stake, Adams County, Illinois; traveled to Utah in 1850 in the Orson Hyde company; served as a high councilor; member of the Mormon Battalion; served a mission to the Cherokee nation; colonized in southern Utah; died in Farmington, Utah.

Miller, Sara Jane Rich (1839–1926). Born in Burton or Quincy, Adams County, Illinois; daughter of Charles C. and Sara DeArmond Rich; member of the Nauvoo Third Ward.

Millet, Artemus (1790–1874). Born in Westmoreland, Cheshire County, New Hampshire; a builder, farmer, and stonemason; converted by Brigham Young in 1833; worked on Kirtland and Nauvoo Temples; traveled to Utah in 1850; died in Scipio, Utah.

Moore, Calvin W. (1827 [or 1829]–1908). Born in Palmer, Hampden County, Massachusetts; baptized in 1835 or 1838 at Kirtland; member of the Mormon Battalion; came to Utah with the battalion in 1848; bishop of Lawrence Ward, Emery Stake, Utah; buried in Castledale, Utah.

Moore, Reverend George (1811–1847). Born in Sudbury, Middlesex

County, Massachusetts; graduate of Harvard Divinity School; Unitarian minister; served as Unitarian missionary and pastor in Quincy, Illinois, at time Latter-day Saints were in Nauvoo; made several visits to Nauvoo, recording his impressions in his diary, including a "short but pleasant" visit with Joseph Smith.

Neff, John (1794–1869). Born in Strasburgh, Lancaster County, Pennsylvania; baptized in 1844; arrived with his family at Nauvoo in 1846, just in time to be driven across the Mississippi River by the mob; went to Winter Quarters; a wealthy man who used his wealth to help the poor and the Saints to gather to Zion; arrived in the Salt Lake Valley in October 1847; built first flouring mill of its kind in Utah; buried in Salt Lake City, Utah.

Nelson, William G. (1833–1922). Born in Mt. Vernon, Illinois; baptized by the Prophet Joseph Smith in 1841 or 1842; crossed the plains to Utah in 1850; served missions to Mississippi and Illinois; among first settlers in Franklin, Idaho, where he was later buried.

Noble, Joseph B. (1810–1900). Born in Egremont, Berkshire County, Massachusetts; baptized in 1832; married Mary Adeline Beman; taught by Brigham Young and Heber C. Kimball; ordained a seventy, bishop, high councilor, and patriarch; a miller; member of Zion's Camp in 1834; when sick, miraculously healed by Joseph Smith; member of the First Quorum of the Seventy; came to Utah in 1847 with the Jedediah M. Grant company; buried in Bountiful, Utah.

Noble, Mary A. (1810–1851). Born in Livonia, Livingston County, New York; daughter of Alva Beman; became a teacher; as a youth remembered serving a meal to the Prophet Joseph Smith; wife of Joseph B. Noble; died in Salt Lake City, Utah.

Norman, Mary Bailey Smith (1837–1916). Daughter of the Prophet Joseph Smith's brother Samuel Harrison Smith and his wife, Mary Bailey.

Oakley, John (1819–1890). Born in Flatlands, Kings County, New York; baptized in 1840; received patriarchal blessing from Hyrum Smith; endowed in Nauvoo Temple; ordained a seventy; a clerk and farmer; buried in Snowflake, Arizona.

Osborn, David (1807–1892). Born in Greenbrier County, West Virginia; baptized in 1835; went west with the Saints; buried in Montpelier, Idaho.

Pace, William B. (1832–1907). Born in Murfeesboro, Rutherford County, Tennessee; baptized in 1839 or 1840; joined Mormon Battalion at age fourteen with his father; went west; settled in Payson, and later Provo, Utah; served a mission to the Indians in 1855; member of the Utah State Legislature; died and buried in Provo, Utah.

Palmer, James (1829–1905). Born in Dymock, Gloucestershire, England; baptized in 1840, a convert of Wilford Woodruff; served missions to Wales and England; ordained a seventy; did masonry work on Nauvoo House; buried in Grantsville, Utah.

Palmer, Mrs. (birth and death dates unavailable). Early resident of Palmyra-Manchester area; possibly lived in Monroe, Sevier County, Utah, with her daughter who taught in the Presbyterian schools.

Partridge, Edward W. (1793–1840). Born in Pittsfield, Berkshire County, Massachusetts; converted by missionaries while living in Painesville, Ohio, in 1830; first bishop of the Church in 1831; sent to oversee settlement of Saints in Jackson County, Missouri; served missions to the Eastern States and New England; called to be a bishop of Nauvoo Upper Ward in 1839; died in Nauvoo, Illinois.

Phelps, Laura Clark (1808–1842). Born in Connecticut; married Morris C. Phelps on 12 April 1825 in Macedonia, Hancock, Illinois; mother of five children; joined the Church in 1831; moved to Jackson County during winter of 1831 and 1832; driven by mob from their home in 1833, moved to Clay County; taught school and practiced obstetrics; supported her family while husband confined in Richmond Jail with Joseph Smith; buried in Nauvoo.

Phippen, James (1819–1908). Born in Springfield, Clark County, Ohio; baptized in 1839; harness maker; member of Nauvoo Third Ward; ordained a seventy; married Julia Adelia Pratt in 1845; father of eight children; buried in Oakley, Idaho.

Pomeroy, Sarah Matilda Colborn (1834–1926). Born in Rose, Wayne County, New York; married Francis M. Pomeroy; mother of six children; died in Mesa, Arizona.

Potter, Amasa (1833–1911). Born in Avon, Lorraine County, Ohio; baptized in 1847; a farmer, laborer, and hotel manager; crossed the plains in 1848; served a mission to Australia; worked in the Manti Temple; buried in Payson, Utah.

Pratt, Orson (1811–1881). Born in Hartford, Washington County, New York; a writer, teacher, surveyor, and historian; performed 4,000-mile missionary journey with Lyman Johnson in 1832; member of Zion's Camp in 1834; ordained an apostle in 1835; entered Salt Lake Valley in 1847; presided over British Mission; dedicated Scotland to missionary work; appointed Church Historian in 1874; died in Salt Lake City, Utah.

Selected Biographical Registry

Pratt, Parley Parker (1807–1857). Born in Burlington, Otsego County, New York; a farmer, editor, legislator, and prolific writer; married Thankful Halsey in 1827; served a mission to Lamanites in 1830; member of Zion's Camp in 1834; ordained an apostle in 1835; jailed with the Prophet at Richmond, Missouri; served missions to England (1839) and South America (1851 to 1852); presided over Church in New York City from 1844 to 1845; murdered in Van Buren, Arkansas.

Quincy, Josiah (1772–1864). Born in Boston, Massachusetts; lawyer; member of Massachusetts State Senate; Speaker of the Massachusetts State House of Representatives; U.S. representative from Massachusetts; judge of Boston Municipal Court; mayor of Boston; president of Harvard University; visited Nauvoo and Joseph Smith in spring 1844; died in Quincy, Massachusetts; not a member of the Church.

Randall, Alfred (1811–1891). Born in Bridgewater, Oneida County, New York; a carpenter and farmer; heard Governor Thomas Ford tell mob not to speak of their murderous intentions; among those who accompanied Joseph and Hyrum to Carthage Jail; served two missions to Sandwich Islands; buried in Ogden, Utah.

Reynolds, George (1842–1909). Born in London; baptized in May 1856; in 1863 called as secretary and emigration clerk of European Mission; arrived in Utah in 1865; member of the First Council of the Seventy; served as secretary to the First Presidency for forty-three years; regent for University of Deseret; prolific author; wrote *Complete Concordance of Book of Mormon;* served as test case before U.S. Supreme Court on plural marriage.

Rich, Mary A. (1829–1912). Born in Peoria, Tazewell County, Illinois; baptized in 1839; married Charles C. Rich; mother of ten children; as a young child Joseph Smith put her on his knee and blessed her; gave Joseph a drink of water en route to Carthage; endowed in Nauvoo Temple.

Richards, Franklin D. (1821–1899). Born in Richmond, Berkshire County, Massachusetts; baptized in 1838; ordained a seventy, high priest, and apostle; served several missions; Church Historian for ten years; probate judge of Weber County from 1869 to 1883; member of the territorial legislature; regent at University of Deseret; brigadier general of Nauvoo Legion; buried in Ogden, Utah.

Richards, Jane Snyder (1823–1912). Born in Pamelia Four Corners, Jefferson County, New York; married Franklin D. Richards in 1842;

member of Relief Society in Nauvoo; left Nauvoo for Utah in 1846: "We were among the last to go"; on general Relief Society board in Salt Lake; Utah representative to National Council of Women in 1891.

Richards, Samuel W. (1824–1909). Born in Richmond, Berkshire, Massachusetts; baptized in 1838; a farmer and city councilor; worked on Nauvoo Temple; served a mission to Great Britain; regent at University of Deseret; president of European Mission; ordained a patriarch; buried in Salt Lake City, Utah.

Riggs, John (1812–1892). Born in Oxford, New Haven, Connecticut; worked on Kirtland Temple and attended dedication; present when David Patten was wounded at Battle of Crooked River; studied medicine under Frederick G. Williams; ordained a seventy; moved to Utah in 1851; buried in Provo, Utah.

Riser, George Christian (1818 [or 1819]–1892). Born in Kornwestheim, Wuerttemberg, Germany; baptized in 1842; a farmer and shoemaker; received patriarchal blessing from Hyrum Smith; president of German Mission from 1845 to 1855; arrested and imprisoned for preaching the gospel; buried in Salt Lake City, Utah.

Robinson, Ebenezer (1816–1891). Born in Floyd, Oneida County, New York; Church clerk and recorder; clerk to high council in Missouri in 1831; publisher and coeditor of *Times and Seasons;* left Nauvoo; joined with Sidney Rigdon and later joined RLDS Church; became a follower of David Whitmer in 1888.

Robinson, Joseph Lee (1811–1893). Born in Shaftsbury, Bennington County, Vermont; baptized in 1836; built wagons during 1845 and 1846 for trip west; ordained an elder, high priest, bishop, and patriarch; chair maker; crossed the plains in 1848; elected justice of peace for Davis County; buried in Farmington, Utah.

Rockwell, Orrin Porter (1813–1878). Born in Belchertown, Hampshire County, Massachusetts; at age four, his family moved to Manchester, New York, where he was befriended by Joseph Smith; baptized on 6 April 1830; went to Missouri in 1831; accompanied Joseph Smith to Washington, D.C., seeking redress for wrongs against Saints in Missouri; accused, imprisoned, and acquitted in 1842 of making assassination attempt against life of Missouri Governor Lilburn W. Boggs; deputy marshal in Utah; died in Salt Lake City, Utah.

Rollins, James Henry (1816–1899). Born in Lima, Livingston County, New York; baptized in Jackson County, Missouri, in 1832; had vision of Joseph Smith prior to meeting him; became a bishop in Utah.

Rushton, Edwin (1824–1904). Born in Leek, Staffordshire, England; baptized in 1840; a farmer, miller, whip sawyer, and stockman; ordained a seventy and high priest; came to Utah with the John Brown company in 1851; buried in Salt Lake City, Utah.

Salisbury, Catherine Smith (1812–1900). Born in Lebanon, Grafton County, New Hampshire; younger sister of the Prophet Joseph Smith; baptized by David Whitmer on 9 June 1830; married Jenkins Salisbury in 1831; after death of her husband in 1856, she remained at Plymouth, Hancock County, Illinois; affiliated with RLDS Church.

Salisbury, Herbert S. (1879–1964). Son of Don C. Salisbury; grandson of Catherine Smith Salisbury; city engineer and county surveyor when living in Carthage, Illinois; Assistant Church Historian for RLDS Church; president of Graceland College, Lamoni, Iowa.

Saunders, Orlando (b. ca. 1803). Palmyra resident; contemporary of the Prophet Joseph Smith; gave some testimony of knowing Joseph Smith; interviewed by E. L. and William H. Kelley of RLDS Church in March 1881.

Scott, Jacob (1782–1845). Born in Londonberry, Ireland; married Sarah Warnock in 1804; father of eight children; baptized in 1837; farmer; died in Nauvoo, Illinois, in 1845.

Searles, Asa (b. 1810). Boyhood schoolmate of young Joseph Smith, perhaps at the Palmyra Academy; by adulthood had moved to Lee County, Illinois.

Sirrine, Mephibosheth (1811–1848). Born in Putnam County, New York; served missions to Michigan and England; presided for a short time over all the Eastern States branches of the Church; in 1848 traveled west on the steamboat *Niagara;* died of consumption at the mouth of the Ohio River.

Smith, Bathsheba W. (1822–1910). Born in Shinnston, Harrison, West Virginia; baptized in 1837; married George A. Smith in 1841; experienced persecutions in Missouri; witnessed death of David W. Patten; ordinance worker in Nauvoo Temple, Endowment House in Salt Lake, and in Logan Temple; charter member of Relief Society; general Relief Society president; died in Salt Lake City, Utah.

Smith, Emma Hale (1804–1879). Born in Harmony, Susquehanna County, Pennsylvania; married Joseph Smith in 1827; helped with early translation of Book of Mormon; directed by revelation to compile hymns for worship services; first Relief Society president in 1842; remained in Illinois after the martyrdom; married Lewis Bidamon in 1847; died in Nauvoo.

Selected Biographical Registry

Smith, George A. (1817–1875). Born in Potsdam, St. Lawrence County, New York; farmer; cousin of the Prophet Joseph Smith; baptized in 1832; member of Zion's Camp in 1835; appointed to the First Quorum of the Seventy in 1835; ordained an apostle in 1839; served a mission to England; member of Nauvoo Legion; appointed Church Historian in 1854; counselor to Brigham Young; died in Salt Lake City, Utah.

Smith, Job F. (1828–1913). Born in Deerhurst, Gloucester, England; baptized in 1840; endowed in Nauvoo Temple; traveled to Utah with the Brigham Young company in 1848; helped colonize Utah and Arizona.

Smith, Joseph F. (1838–1918). Born in Far West, Missouri; son of Hyrum and Mary Fielding Smith; nephew of the Prophet; walked to Salt Lake Valley with his widowed mother; served missions to Sandwich Islands and England; ordained an apostle in 1866; in 1868 set apart as member of the Quorum of the Twelve at age twenty-eight; counselor to Presidents John Taylor, Wilford Woodruff, and Lorenzo Snow; sixth President of the Church; died in Salt Lake City, Utah.

Smith, Lucy Mack (1775–1856). Mother of the Prophet Joseph Smith; born in Gilsum, New Hampshire; married Joseph Smith Sr. in 1796; mother of eight sons and three daughters; led a group of Saints from Palmyra to Kirtland, Ohio, in 1831; moved with the Saints to Kirtland, Far West, and Nauvoo, where she died; dictated *History of Joseph Smith* to Martha Jane Coray.

Smith, Lucy Meserve (1817–1892). Born in Newry, Oxford County, Maine; baptized in 1837; worked for Emma Smith from 1844 to 1845; married George A. Smith; mother of two children; settled in Provo, Utah; served as Relief Society president.

Smith, Mary Fielding (1801–1852). Born in Honidon, Bedforshire, England; emigrated to Toronto, Canada, in 1832; heard the gospel preached by Parley P. Pratt; baptized in 1836; moved to Kirtland; married Hyrum Smith in 1837; sponsored the Sisters Penny Subscription, which raised money for nails and glass for Nauvoo Temple; crossed the plains with the Saints; buried in the Salt Lake City Cemetery.

Smith, William (1811–1893). Brother of the Prophet Joseph Smith; born in Royalton, Windsor County, Vermont; member of Zion's Camp in 1834; ordained an apostle in 1835; represented Hancock County in the Illinois state legislature in 1842; editor of Nauvoo newspaper,

The Wasp, in 1842; appointed presiding patriarch in 1845; excommunicated in 1845; joined RLDS Church; died in Osterdock, Iowa.

Snow, Eliza R. (1804–1887). Born in Becket, Berkshire County, Massachusetts; baptized in 1835; a teacher, poetess, and seamstress; tutored the Prophet's children in his home; secretary to Relief Society in 1842; secretary of the first Relief Society in Nauvoo; second general Relief Society president; authored hymns, including "Oh My Father"; died in Salt Lake City, Utah.

Snow, Erastus (1818–1888). Born in St. Johnsbury, Caledonia County, Vermont; baptized in 1833; served missions in Pennsylvania, New York, Vermont, New Hampshire, Ohio, Maryland, Virginia, Denmark, and Scandinavia; participant in Kirtland Temple dedication in 1836; member of Iowa high council in 1839; a counselor in the Salt Lake Stake presidency in 1848; founder of St. George, Utah, in 1861; buried in Salt Lake City, Utah.

Snow, Eunice Billings (1830–1914). Born in Mentor Lake, Ohio; daughter of Titus Billings and Diantha Morley; went to school with the Prophet's children; endowed in Nauvoo Temple.

Snow, Lorenzo (1814–1901). Born in Mantua, Portage County, Ohio; studied at Oberlin College; first heard the Prophet speak in 1831; baptized in 1836 by John F. Boynton; confirmed by Hyrum Smith; served missions to Ohio, Kentucky, Illinois, England, Italy, and Sandwich Islands; ordained an apostle in 1849; in 1849 gathered funds to help the poor emigrate; printed Book of Mormon in Italian; visited Palestine with George A. Smith from 1872 to 1873; set apart as fifth President of the Church in 1898; died in Brigham City, Utah.

Stafford, John (birth and death dates unavailable). Physician; neighbor of Smith family in Palmyra; interviewed by E. L. and William H. Kelley of RLDS Church in March 1881.

Staines, William C. (1818–1881). Born in Higham Ferrers, Northampton, England; baptized in 1841; merchant; agent for Brigham Young in 1870; saw the Prophet in a vision before he met him; saw Brigham Young transfigured.

Stevenson, Edward (1821–1897). Born in Gibralter, Spain; emigrated to America in 1827; heard Jared Carter and Joseph Woods preach the gospel in Michigan; baptized in 1833; crossed the Atlantic nine times to serve missions in the United States, Canada, and Europe; member of the First Council of the Seventy; crossed plains in 1847, then seventeen more times to help others.

Stowell, William R. (1822–1901). Born in Solon, Cortland, New York; a farmer, carpenter, miller, gristmill operator, and soldier; baptized in 1833; went to New York to advocate presidential candidacy of Joseph Smith in 1844; went to Utah in 1850; buried in Colonia Juarez, Chihuahua, Mexico.

Taggart, George Washington (1816–1893). Born in Sharon, Hilsboro County, New Hampshire; married Harriet Bruce in Nauvoo in 1843; she died in February 1845; married Fannie Parks in July 1845 in Nauvoo; died in Richville, Utah.

Tanner, John (1788–1850). Born in Hopkinton, Washington, Rhode Island; converted by the preaching of Jared and Simeon Carter; baptized in 1833; ordained a high priest; wealthy, but always willing to help others; endowed in Nauvoo Temple; died in South Cottonwood, Salt Lake City, Utah.

Taylor, John (1808–1887). Born in Milnthorpe, Westmoreland County, England; emigrated to Toronto, Canada, in 1829; married Leonora Cannon in 1833; heard Parley P. Pratt preach the gospel in 1836; ordained an apostle in 1838; member of Nauvoo city council and Nauvoo Legion; editor of *Nauvoo Neighbor* and *Times and Seasons;* at Carthage during martyrdom, where he was shot with five musket balls; served missions to England and France; third President of the Church; died in Kaysville, Utah.

Taylor, Joseph (1825–1900). Born in Bowling Green, Warren County, Kentucky; baptized in 1835; endowed in Nauvoo Temple in 1846; private in Company A of Mormon Battalion; member of the First Quorum of the Seventy; buried in Ogden, Weber County, Utah.

Taylor, Joseph E. (1839–1913). Born in Horsham, Sussex, England; undertaker and casket maker; a high priest and patriarch; second counselor to president of Salt Lake Stake for twenty-eight years; served missions to Nebraska, Iowa, and Illinois; died in Salt Lake City, Utah.

Taylor, Leonora Cannon (1796–1868). Born in Peel, Isle of Man, England; sister of George Q. Cannon; married John Taylor in 1833; mother of five children; influenced by an inspired dream to join the Church in 1836; endowed in Nauvoo Temple.

Taylor, Thomas H. (birth and death dates unavailable). Neighbor of the Smith family in Manchester, New York; engaged in several early American reform movements; interviewed by E. L. and William H. Kelley of the RLDS Church in March 1881.

Taylor, William (1823–1910). Born in Hale, Westmoreland, England; emigrated to Canada; heard Parley P. Pratt preach; baptized in 1841; emigrating to Missouri, mob obstructions detained Taylor family in

Warsaw, Illinois, where they later met Joseph Smith; brother to President John Taylor; died in Holladay, Utah.

Terry, James P. (1813–1918). Born in Albion, Ontario, Canada; a farmer, school trustee, and road supervisor; baptized in 1840; driven from Missouri by Governor Boggs' extermination order; removed to Nauvoo and then to Utah, arriving in 1849; served missions to Canada and United States; died in Hinckley, Utah.

Thomas, Martha (1808–1895). Born in North Gallatin, Sumner County, Tennessee; her father was killed in the War of 1812; taught and baptized in 1835 by Wilford Woodruff; endowed in Nauvoo Temple; crossed plains in 1849.

Thompson, Mercy Rachel (1807–1893). Born in Honidon, Bedfordshire, England; emigrated to Canada in 1832 with her brother Joseph and sister Mary; baptized in 1836; rode in wagon from Far West to visit the Prophet and Hyrum in Liberty Jail; ordinance worker in Nauvoo Temple; gave $800 to Perpetual Emigration Fund; her husband, Robert B. Thompson, was a private secretary to the Prophet Joseph Smith; died in Salt Lake City, Utah.

Tracy, Nancy (1816–1902). Born in Henderson, Jefferson County, New York; converted in 1832 by the preaching of David W. Patten; baptized in May 1834; joined the Relief Society; served a mission to New York with her husband in 1844; crossed the plains in 1850; died in Ogden, Utah.

Tyler, Daniel (1816–1906). Born in Sempronius, Cayuga County, New York; baptized in 1832 or 1833; served a mission to England in 1854; later presided over Swiss, Italian, French, and German missions; marched with the Mormon Battalion; buried in Beaver, Utah.

Walker, Charles L. (1832–1904). Born in Leek, Stafford County, England; emigrated to the United States in 1849; worked in St. Louis and Kentucky to earn money to help his parents emigrate; arrived in Salt Lake Valley in 1855; worked for his brother-in-law, Parley P. Pratt; blacksmith; called to settle in Dixie Cotton Mission; lived in St. George for forty years; composed many poems and hymns, including "Dearest Children, God Is Near You"; died in St. George, Utah.

Walker, William Holmes (1820–1908). Born in Peacham, Caledonia, Vermont; baptized in 1835; ordained a seventy, high priest, and patriarch; member of the Mormon Battalion; served a mission to South Africa; worked in Logan and Salt Lake Temples; died and buried in Lewiston, Idaho.

Wasson, Lorenzo (b. ca. 1818–1857). Born in Amboy, Lee County,

Illinois; son of Emma Smith's sister and brother-in-law, Elizabeth and Benjamin Wasson; moved to Illinois in 1836; joined the Church in 1842; married Marietta Crocker in 1843; died in Amboy, Illinois.

Watkins, William (1827–1911). Born in London, England; a teacher, farmer, merchant, and bookkeeper; baptized in 1841; emigrated to Nauvoo in 1842; served a political mission to Kentucky in 1844; went to Utah in 1852; served as elder's quorum president, counselor to stake president, and patriarch; died and buried in Brigham City, Utah.

Welch, John (1823–1910). Born in Brampton, Derbyshire, England; baptized in 1841; endowed in Nauvoo Temple; served as patriarch; died in Paradise, Utah; buried in Brigham City, Utah.

Westover, Eliza (1829–1923). Born in Holliston, Middlesex County, Massachusetts; daughter of John and Judith Haven; baptized in 1842; married Charles Westover in October 1849; endowed in Nauvoo Temple in January 1846.

Westover, Mary (1836–1932). Moved to Illinois in 1838 with her family; moved to Nauvoo in 1842; passed through Winter Quarters; arrived in the Salt Lake Valley in 1847; married Charles Westover; appears to be the same person as Mary C. Westover, who gave her recollections of Joseph Smith in *Young Woman's Journal* 17 (1906).

Whitmer, David (1805–1888). Born near Harrisburg, Dauphin County, Pennsylvania; one of the Three Witnesses to the Book of Mormon; first baptized by Joseph Smith in June 1829; rebaptized for admission into the Church on 6 April 1830; appointed president of the Church in Missouri in 1834; apostatized and excommunicated in 1838; always true to testimony of Book of Mormon; elected mayor of Richmond, Missouri, where he lived and died.

Whitney, Helen Mar (1828–1896). Born in Mendon, Monroe County, New York; daughter of Heber C. and Vilate Murray Kimball; married Horace Kimball Whitney in 1843; endowed in Nauvoo Temple.

Wight, Lyman (1796–1858). Born in Fairfield, Herkimer County, New York; farmer; married Harriet Bention in 1823; baptized by Oliver Cowdery in 1830; driven from Jackson County in 1833; member of Zion's Camp in 1834; member of high council in Clay County, Missouri; imprisoned with Joseph Smith at Liberty Jail; ordained an apostle in 1841; moved to Texas in 1845; excommunicated in 1848; died in Dexter, Texas.

Wilcox, Walter (1821–1910). Born in Dorchester, Suffolk County, Massachusetts; baptized in June 1844; lawyer; went west with Saints;

practiced law in Utah; temple worker in Salt Lake Temple; died and buried in Salt Lake City, Utah.

Williams, Zilpha (1815–1889). Born in Hillborough, New Hampshire; daughter of Samuel and Mary Baker Cilley; married Almond McCumber Williams in Erie, Pennsylvania, in 1833; endowed in Nauvoo Temple; died in Walla Walla, Washington.

Willis, Alzina (1834–1910). Born in Tunkhannock, Wyoming County, Pennsylvania; daughter of Cornelius Peter Lott and Dermelia Darrow; married William Sidney Smith Willis in 1852.

Winters, Mary Ann (1833–1912). Born in Bethel, Oxford County, Maine; her father died the same year she was born; her mother married Parley P. Pratt.

Woodland, John (1776–1869). Born in Princess Ann County, Virginia; a farmer and cooper; married Ruth McGhee in 1813; Ruth died in 1818; married Celia Stapleford (or Steepleford) in 1818; father of sixteen children; baptized in 1835; endured Missouri persecutions; buried in Willard, Utah.

Woolley, Edwin D. (1807–1881). Born in East Bradford, Chester County, Pennsylvania; a farmer and merchant; married Mary Wickersham in 1831; moved to Illinois in 1839; ordained a high priest by Joseph Smith in 1838; crossed the plains to Utah in 1848; served as Brigham Young's personal business manager; served as a bishop; died in Salt Lake City, Utah.

Woolley, Samuel A. (1825–1900). Born in Newlin, Columbia County, Pennsylvania; heard gospel preached by George A. Smith and Lorenzo Barnes in 1836; moved to Nauvoo in 1840; member of Nauvoo whistling and whittling brigade; first person to quarry stone for Nauvoo Temple; served a mission to Hindustan from 1852 to 1855; served as a bishop; attended dedication of Salt Lake Temple; died in his home in Salt Lake City, Utah.

Workman, Andrew (1824–1909). Born in Carlisle, Nicholas County, Kentucky; a farmer and sawmill worker; baptized in 1839; part of evacuation from Nauvoo; joined Mormon Battalion; died in Virgin City, Utah.

Young, Brigham (1801–1877). Born in Whitingham, Windham County, Vermont; a carpenter, painter, and glazier; baptized in 1832; member of Zion's Camp in 1834; ordained an apostle in 1835; served a mission to England in 1839; directed Mormon exodus from Missouri in 1839, and from Nauvoo from 1846 through 1848; set apart as second President of the Church in 1848; governor of Utah; died in Salt Lake City, Utah.

Young, Emily Partridge (1824–1899). Born in Painseville, Geauga County, Ohio; daughter of Edward and Lydia Partridge; baptized in 1832 by John Corrill; endured Missouri persecutions; went west with the Saints; married Joseph Smith; later married Brigham Young, bearing him seven children.

Young, Joseph (1797–1881). Born in Hopkinton, Middlesex County, Massachusetts; first heard the gospel taught by his brother, Brigham Young; member of Zion's Camp in 1834; second man called to the First Council of the Seventy in 1835; witnessed Haun's Mill Massacre; one of first settlers in Nauvoo; crossed the plains in 1850; served a mission to England in 1870; died in Salt Lake City, Utah.

Young, Lorenzo Dow (1807–1895). Born in Smyrna, Chenango County, New York; brother to Brigham Young; married Persis Goodall in 1826; baptized in 1832; member of Zion's Camp in 1834; supervised plastering of Kirtland Temple; arrived in the Salt Lake Valley in 1847; served as a bishop and patriarch; died in Salt Lake City, Utah.

Young, Margaret P. (1823–1907). Born in Ashton, Delaware County, Pennsylvania; daughter of Robert and Hannah Peirce; married Morris Whiteside in 1844; received patriarchal blessing from Hyrum Smith; endowed in Nauvoo Temple, later married Brigham Young.

Bibliography

Items are listed alphabetically, according to author and year of publication. Where an author has more than one item appearing in a given year, items are lettered chronologically to the degree possible. Hence: "Clawson, Margaret. 1919a." "Clawson, Margaret. 1919b." etc. Where the entry has no date, such entries read, for example, "Mace, Wandle. n.d. [a]." and "Mace, Wandle. n.d. [b]." to distinguish one entry from another. Because reference to a collection often gives inadequate information to clearly identify a source, items in collections are identified by an author's name. For example: "Angell, Truman O. 1967. 'Autobiography.' In Kate B. Carter, comp., Our Pioneer Heritage, 20 vols., *Salt Lake City, Utah: Daughters of the Utah Pioneers, 1958–77, 10:196–99." Since the quotations in the book are listed by the person who first recorded the reminiscence, rather than the person who recorded it for publication (unless the two are the same), some of the references are repeated in this bibliography. For example, Orson F. Whitney's* History of Utah *is listed multiple times because he often quoted others who remembered Joseph—but it is listed not under Orson F. Whitney but under the names of those whom he quotes. LDS Church Archives and LDS Family History Library are located in Salt Lake City, Utah. Spelling and punctuation of the titles of unpublished materials have been standardized. This bibliography contains information for both the book and the accompanying CD-ROM.*

Adams, Henry. 1952. *Charles Francis Adams Visits the Mormons in 1844.* Boston, Mass. N.p.

Adams, Mary F. 1906. "Joseph Smith, the Prophet." *Young Woman's Journal* 17, no. 12 (December): 538.

Adams, William. 1894. "History of William Adams, Written by Himself." January 1894. Typescript copy. BYU Special Collections. Harold B. Lee Library, Provo, Utah.

Alexander, Alvah. 1906. "Joseph Smith, the Prophet." *Young Woman's Journal* 17, no. 12 (December): 541.

Allen, Andrew J. 1958. "From the Journal of A. J. Allen." In Kate B. Carter, comp., *Our Pioneer Heritage,* 20 vols., Salt Lake City, Utah: Daughters of the Utah Pioneers, 1958–77, 1:102.

Allen, Charles Hopkins. n.d. Untitled Manuscript. Mormon Biography File. LDS Church Archives.

Allen, Daniel. n.d. "Daniel Allen Journal." LDS Church Archives.

Allen, James B. 1976. "A Dialogue between Wilford Woodruff and Lyman Wight." *BYU Studies* 17, no. 1 (autumn): 110–11.

Allen, Lucy D. 1906. "Joseph Smith, the Prophet." *Young Woman's Journal* 17, no. 12 (December): 537–38.

Allen, Maud Bliss. 1962. *Absalom Wamsley Smith, His Ancestry and Descendants.* Salt Lake City, Utah: N.p.

Alley, Lydia Ann. 1971. "Alley, Lydia Ann." In Andrew Jenson, *LDS Biographical Encyclopedia,* 4 vols., Salt Lake City, Utah: Western Epics, 2:511.

Allred, James. ca. 1905. In Eliza M. A. Munson, "Early Pioneer History," Mormon Biography File, LDS Church Archives.

Allred, Wiley. 1892. "Recollections of the Prophet Joseph Smith." *Juvenile Instructor* 27, no. 8 (15 April): 255–56.

Allred, William Moore. 1883. "Reminiscences and Diary, 1883." Holograph. LDS Church Archives.

———. 1892. "Recollections of the Prophet Joseph Smith." *Juvenile Instructor* 27, no. 15 (1 August): 471–72.

Alvord, Samuel Morgan. 1908. *A Genealogy of the Descendants of Alexander Alvord, An Early Settler of Windsor, Conn. and Northampton, Mass.* Webster. N. Y.: A. D. Andrews, Printer.

Ames, Ira. n.d. "Journal of Ira Ames." Typescript copy. Copies in private family possession.

Ames, Ira, et. al. 1834. *Evening and Morning Star* 2, no. 23 (August): 182.

Anderson, Karl. 1989. *Joseph Smith's Kirtland: Eyewitness Accounts.* Salt Lake City, Utah: Deseret Book.

Anderson, William. 1969. "A Boy's Love: A Man's Devotion." In "Eventful Narratives," in *Classic Experiences and Adventures,* Salt Lake City, Utah: Bookcraft.

Andrus, Hyrum L., and Helen Mae Andrus. 1974. *They Knew the Prophet.* Salt Lake City, Utah: Bookcraft.

Angell, Truman O. n.d. "Journal of Truman O. Angell." Typescript copy. BYU Special Collections. Harold B. Lee Library, Provo, Utah.

———. 1967. "Autobiography." In Kate B. Carter, comp., *Our Pioneer Heritage,* 20 vols., Salt Lake City, Utah: Daughters of the Utah Pioneers, 1958–77, 10:196–99.

Anonymous. 1897. Under the signature of "Oak Leaf." In Letters to the Editor, *Juvenile Instructor* 32, no. 19 (1 October): 611–13.

Appleby, William. 1848–1856. *Autobiography and Journal 1848–1856.* Holograph. LDS Church Archives.

Armstrong, James A. 1952. "James Arthur Armstrong (1883–1969) Affidavit." LDS Church Archives.

Ashby, Benjamin. n.d. [a]. "Autobiography of Benjamin Ashby." LDS Church Archives.

———. n.d. [b]. "Benjamin Ashby Autobiography." Copy of holograph. BYU Special Collections. Harold B. Lee Library, Provo, Utah.

———. n.d. [c]. "Writing of Benjamin Ashby (1828–1907)." Typescript copy. LDS Church Archives.

Atwood, Millen. 1842. "Reminiscences and Diary, July 1842–June 1844." Typescript copy. LDS Church Archives.

———. 1904. "Millen Atwood." In Orson F. Whitney, *History of Utah,* 4 vols., Salt Lake City, Utah: G. Q. Cannon & Sons Co., 4:55.

Backman, Milton. 1971. *Joseph Smith's First Vision.* Salt Lake City, Utah: Bookcraft.

Ball, Jonah. 1843a. "Jonah R. Ball to Harvey Howard of Shutesbury, Mass., January, 1843." LDS Church Archives.

———. 1843b. "Jonah R. Ball to Harvey Howard of Shutesbury, Mass., May 19, 1843." LDS Church Archives.

Ball, Thomas. n.d. In Joseph S. Ball, "The Life of Patriarch Thomas Ball," Mormon Biography File, LDS Church Archives.

Ballantyne, Richard. 1989. In Conway B. Sonne, *Knight of the Kingdom,* Salt Lake City, Utah: Deseret Book.

Barlow, Israel A. 1968. In Ora Haven Barlow, *The Israel Barlow Story and Mormon Mores,* Salt Lake City, Utah: Publishers Press.

Barney, Edson. n.d. "Biographical Sketch of Edson Barney." LDS Church Archives.

———. 1892. "Recollections of the Prophet Joseph Smith." *Juvenile Instructor* 27, no. 8 (15 April): 256.

Barney, Lewis. n.d. "Autobiography of Lewis Barney." Typescript copy. BYU Special Collections. Harold B. Lee Library, Provo, Utah.

———. ca. 1888. "Lewis Barney Reminiscences (ca. 1888)." LDS Church Archives.

Barton, Eliza Anderson. 1963. "Eliza Anderson Barton." In Kate B. Carter, comp., *Our Pioneer Heritage,* 20 vols., Salt Lake City, Utah: Daughters of the Utah Pioneers, 1958–77, 6:509.

Bates, Jane Woolf. n.d. "A Biographical Sketch of Jane Elizabeth Hyde Molen Together with a Part of Her Family Background." Mormon Biography File. LDS Church Archives.

Baum, Mary Ann. n.d. "Grandparents of Hannetta Ann Davis Loveless, on Her Mother's Side." LDS Church Archives.

Beecher, Maureen Ursenbach, ed. 1979. "'All Things Move in Order in the City': The Nauvoo Diary of Zina Diantha Huntington Jacobs." *BYU Studies* 19, no. 3 (spring): 291–93.

Bellows, John F. 1892. "Recollections of the Prophet Joseph Smith." *Juvenile Instructor* 27, no. 20 (15 October): 641–42.

Belnap, Adeline K. n.d. In Lola B. Coolbear, "The Life Story of Adeline Knight Belnap," typescript copy, BYU Special Collections, Harold B. Lee Library, Provo, Utah.

Belnap, Gilbert. n.d. "Gilbert Belnap Autobiography." BYU Special Collections. Harold B. Lee Library, Provo, Utah.

Benbow, John. n.d. "Life Sketch of Ellen Benbow Carter." LDS Church Archives.

Benson, Ezra T. 1855. Deseret Theological Institute, Minutes of 23 May 1855. LDS Church Archives.

———. 1945a. "Ezra Benson Autobiography." *Instructor* 80, no. 2 (February): 56.

———. 1945b. "Ezra Benson Autobiography." *Instructor* 80, no. 3 (March): 103.

———. 1945c. "Ezra Benson Autobiography." *Instructor* 80, no. 5 (May): 213–14.

Bernhisel, John M. ca. 1881. Washington Franklin Anderson. "Reminiscences of John M. Bernhisel." LDS Church Archives.

———. 1904. "John Milton Bernhisel." In Orson F. Whitney, *History of Utah*, 4 vols., Salt Lake City, Utah: G. Q. Cannon & Sons Co., 4:664–65.

———. 1912. In David M. Bernhisel, "Dr. John Milton Bernhisel," *Utah Genealogical and Historical Magazine* 3 (October): 173–77.

———. 1975a. Journal History. 20 June 1868. LDS Church Archives.

———. 1975b. L. John Nuttall's Diary. 10 September 1879. BYU Special Collections. Harold B. Lee Library, Provo, Utah.

Bessey, Anthony Wayne. 1904. "Anthony Wayne Bessey." In Orson F. Whitney, *History of Utah*, 4 vols., Salt Lake City, Utah: G. Q. Cannon & Sons Co., 4:408.

Bigelow, Mary. n.d. "Autobiography of Mary Bigelow." Typescript copy. LDS Church Archives.

Bigler, Henry W. 1892. "Recollections of the Prophet Joseph Smith." *Juvenile Instructor* 27, no. 5 (1 March): 151–52.

Bigler, Jacob G. n.d. "A Short Sketch of the Life of Jacob G. Bigler." Mormon Biography File. LDS Church Archives.

Bills, William A. Sr. n.d. "Family History of William Andrew Bills Sr." Copies in private family possession.

Bishop David Evans Family Association, Lehi, Utah. 1972. *Bishop David Evans and His Family.* Provo, Utah: J. Grant Stevenson.

Black, George David Jr. n.d. "A History of Mary McCrea Black Brown and George David Black and Mary Hunt Black." Mormon Biography File. LDS Church Archives.

Black, Jane J. n.d. [a]. "Biographical Sketch of William 'Young' Black and Jane Johnston Black by Geniel Robertson." Typescript copy. Daughters of the Utah Pioneers, Salt Lake City, Utah.

———. n.d. [b]. "Life Story of Edward L. Black the son of George Black who was the son of William Y. Black and Jane Johnson as written by Himself." Copies in private family possession.

———. 1963. "Jane Johnston Black." In Kate B. Carter, comp., *Our Pioneer Heritage,* 20 vols., Salt Lake City, Utah: Daughters of the Utah Pioneers, 1958–77, 6:427.

Black, Susan Easton. 1984–88. *Membership of The Church of Jesus Christ of Latter-day Saints, 1830–1848.* 50 vols. Provo, Utah: Brigham Young University, Religious Studies Center.

———. 1997. *Who's Who in the Doctrine and Covenants.* Salt Lake City, Utah: Bookcraft.

Black, William. n.d. "Life Story of Edward L. Black the son of George Black who was the son of William Y. Black and Jane Johnson as written by Himself." Copies in private family possession.

Blanchard, Jerusha W. 1922. In Nellie S. Bean, "Reminiscences of the Granddaughter of Hyrum Smith," *Relief Society Magazine* 9, no. 1 (January): 8.

Blodget (Blodgett), Newman Greenleaf. n.d. "Newman Greenleaf Blodgett Family History." Typescript copy. Copies in private family possession.

Boice, James. 1931. "Biography of James Boice, written by his granddaughter Rachel Boyce Olson, and read at the family reunion April 7, 1931, at Lovell Wyoming." Mormon Biograpny File. LDS Church Archives.

Boltin, Curtis Edwin. n.d. *Reminiscences and Journal.* LDS Church Archives.

Boss, Nancy. n.d. In Samantha D. R. Rose, "Short Sketch of My Mother's Life," Mormon Biography File, LDS Church Archives; also in "A Copy of the History of Delana (Rawson) Rose," in "History of Daniel H. Rosen," LDS Church Archives.

Bowen, Cynthia Harrington Durphy [Durfey]. 1996–1997. In Lynne Watkins Jorgensen, "The Mantle of the Prophet Joseph Passes to Brother Brigham: A Collective Spiritual Witness," *BYU Studies* 36, no. 4 (fall): 155.

Bracken, James B. 1881. "Statement of James Bracken, Nov. 6, 1881." LDS Church Archives.

———. 1892. "Recollections of the Prophet Joseph Smith." *Juvenile Instructor* 27, no. 7 (1 April): 203.

Bracken, Levi. n.d. "Levi Bracken Family History." Mormon Biography File. LDS Church Archives.

Brown, Benjamin. 1853. *Testimonies for the Truth: A Record of Manifestations of the Power of God, Miraculous and Providential, Witnessed in the Travels and Experience of Benjamin Brown, High Priest in The Church of Jesus Christ of Latter-day Saints, Pastor of the London, Reading, Kent, and Essex Conferences.* Liverpool: S. W. Richards.

Brown, John. n.d. "Sketch of the Life of John Brown, Written by Himself." Mormon Biography File. LDS Church Archives.

Brown, Lorenzo. 1823–1846. "Lorenzo Brown Journal, vol. 1, (1823–1846)." Typescript copy. BYU Special Collections. Harold B. Lee Library, Provo, Utah.

———. 1880. "Sayings of Joseph by Those Who Knew Him at Different Times." LDS Church Archives.

Brown, Mary B. n.d. "Mary McRee Black Brown." Mormon Biography File. LDS Church Archives.

Browning, Charilla A. 1904. "Charilla Abbot Browning." In Orson F. Whitney, *History of Utah,* 4 vols., Salt Lake City, Utah: G. Q. Cannon & Sons Co., 4:592.

Brunson, Peter L. n.d. "Seymour Brunson." Typescript copy. BYU Special Collections. Harold B. Lee Library, Provo, Utah.

Bryce, Wyona, and John T. Matt[?]. n.d. "Life Story of John Taylor." Mormon Biography File. LDS Church Archives.

Buckwalter, Henry Shuler. 1971. "Buckwalter, Henry Shuler." In Andrew Jenson, *LDS Biographical Encyclopedia,* 4 vols., Salt Lake City, Utah: Western Epics, 1:604.

Bullock, Clara Fullmer. n.d. "Life Story of Benjamin Bullock, III." LDS Church Archives.

Bullock, Lucy Clayton. 1942. In Flora Reynolds, "My Grandmother's History, Read in Daughters of Utah Pioneers Camp, Jan. 14, 1942," typescript copy, Daughters of Utah Pioneers, Salt Lake City, Utah.

———. 1965. "Lucy Clayton Bullock." In Kate B. Carter, comp., *Our Pioneer Heritage,* 20 vols., Salt Lake City, Utah: Daughters of the Utah Pioneers, 1958–77, 8:287–88.

Bullock, Thomas. n.d. [a]. "Biographical Sketch of Thomas Bullock." LDS Church Archives.

———. n.d. [b]. "Thomas Bullock, In Memory of the Murdered Prophet Joseph Smith 1844," LDS Church Archives.

Bunnell, Stephen Ithamar. n.d. [a]. "A Dream—From the Life of Stephen I. Bunnell." Mormon Biography File. LDS Church Archives.

———. n.d. [b]. "Stephen Ithamar Bunnell." Mormon Biography File. LDS Church Archives.

Burbank, Daniel Mark. 1814–94. "Autobiography of Daniel Mark Burbank, 1814–1894." LDS Church Archives.

Burbank, Sarah. 1924. "Account of the Life of Sarah Burbank, Written at Richfield, Utah, March 13, 1924." Mormon Biography File. LDS Church Archives.

Burgess, Harrison. 1969. "Sketch of a Well-Spent Life." In "Labors in the Vineyard," in *Classic Experiences and Adventures,* Salt Lake City, Utah: Bookcraft.

Burgess, Margarette [Margaret]. 1892. "Recollections of the Prophet Joseph Smith" *Juvenile Instructor* 27, no. 2 (15 January): 66–67.

———. 1918. "Mothers in Israel: Margaret McIntire Burgess." *Relief Society Magazine* 5, no. 1 (January): 14.

Burgess, Mariah Pulsipher. 1963. "Personal Diary of Mariah Pulsipher Burgess." In Terry and Nora Lund, *The Pulsipher Family History Book.* N.p.

Burgess, William. 1985. "William Burgess, Autobiography." In Kenneth Glyn Hales, ed. and comp., *Windows: A Mormon Family,* Tucson, Ariz.: Skyline Printing.

Burkett, George Jr. n.d. "Some History of George Burkett Jr., (account written at his own dictation)." Mormon Biography File. LDS Church Archives.

Burnett, Peter H. 1946. *An Old California Pioneer.* Oakland, Calif.: Biobooks.

Burnham, Wallace Kendall. n.d. In Lydia Stanley Burnham, "Life Sketch of Wallace Kendall Burnham," Mormon Biography File, LDS Church Archives.

Burton, Rachel Fielding. n.d. "Autobiography of Rachel Fielding Burton." LDS Church Archives.

Burton, Robert Taylor. n.d. "Statement of Robert T. Burton." LDS Church Archives.

———. 1905. "Statement Concerning the Transfiguration." 28 July 1905. Typescript copy. LDS Church Archives.

Bushman, Martin B. n.d. "Martin B. Bushman." Mormon Biography File. LDS Church Archives.

———. 1842. "Martin Bushman to Leonard Pinkle, Dec. 18, 1842." LDS Church Archives.

Butler, Caroline. 1993. William G. Hartley. *My Best for the Kingdom: History and Autobiography of John Lowe Butler, a Mormon Frontiersman.* Salt Lake City, Utah: Aspen Books.

Butler, John L. 1993. "John Lowe Butler Autobiography, Long Version." William G. Hartley *My Best for the Kingdom: History and Autobiography of John Lowe Butler, a Mormon Frontiersman.* Salt Lake City, Utah: Aspen Books. See also "Autobiography of John Lowe Butler." Typescript copy. BYU Special Collections. Harold B. Lee Library, Provo, Utah.

Butterfield, Jacob Kemp. 1836. "Jacob K. Butterfield to Widow Persis Butterfield, Nov. 11, 1836." LDS Church Archives.

———. 1837. "Jacob Kemp Butterfield to Persis Butterfield, May 10, 1837." LDS Church Archives.

Cahoon, William F. n.d. "Autobiography and Family Record." LDS Church Archives.

———. 1892. "Recollections of the Prophet Joseph Smith." *Juvenile Instructor* 29, no. 16 (15 August): 492–93.

———. 1960. "William Cahoon, Autobiography." In Stella Shurtleff Cahoon and Brent Farrington Cahoon, *Reynolds Cahoon and His Stalwart Sons,* Salt Lake City, Utah: Paragon Press.

Call, Anson. n.d. "Statement of Anson Call, Salt Lake City, Utah." LDS Church Archives.

———. 1838. "Anson Call, Manuscript Journal, Summer 1838." Cited in Robert J. Matthews, *A Plainer Translation,* Provo, Utah: BYU Press, 1975.

———. 1839. "The Life and Record of Anson Call, Commenced in 1839." Typescript copy. Huntington Library, San Marino, California. See also holograph 30, LDS Church Archives.

———. 1904. "Anson Call." In Orson F. Whitney, *History of Utah,* 4 vols., Salt Lake City, Utah: G. Q. Cannon & Sons Co., 4:143–44.

———. 1962. "'Sketch of the Life of Anson Call' Taken from the original diary of Anson Call, recopied by Lorna B. Schlote, great-grand daughter, Feb. 1962." LDS Church Archives.

Call, Chester. n.d. Untitled Manuscript. Mormon Biography File. LDS Church Archives.

Callister, Caroline S. n.d. "Incidents in the Life of Caroline Smith Callister." Mormon Biography File. LDS Church Archives.

Cannon, Angus M. 1906. "Joseph Smith, the Prophet." *Young Woman's Journal* 17, no. 12 (December): 546–47.

Cannon, David Henry Sr. 1922. "A History of the Cannon Family as Given by David H. Cannon at a Meeting of the Daughters of the Pioneers Held at St. George, Utah, February 19, 1922." Typescript copy. Daughters of the Utah Pioneers, Salt Lake City, Utah.

Cannon, George Q. 1870. "Joseph Smith, the Prophet," *Juvenile Instructor* 5, no. 22 (29 October): 174–75.

———. 1894. "Topics of Our Times." *Juvenile Instructor* 29, no. 23 (1 December): 746.

———. 1964. *Life of Joseph Smith the Prophet.* Salt Lake City, Utah: Deseret Book, 1964.

Cannon, Joseph J. 1905. "Joseph Smith, the Hero." *Young Woman's Journal* 16, no. 12 (December): 560–61.

Carbine, William. 1963. "William Van Orden Carbine." In Kate B. Carter, comp., *Our Pioneer Heritage,* 20 vols., Salt Lake City, Utah: Daughters of the Utah Pioneers, 1958–77, 6:204.

Cardon, Joseph E., and Samuel O. Bennion. 1930. *Testimonies of the Divinity of The Church of Jesus Christ of Latter-day Saints, by its Leaders.* Independence, Mo.: Zion's Press.

Carling, Ann G. 1963. "Ann Green Dutson Carling." In Kate B. Carter, comp., *Our Pioneer Heritage,* 20 vols., Salt Lake City, Utah: Daughters of the Utah Pioneers, 1958–77.

Carter, Dominicus. n.d. Untitled Biographical Sketch. LDS Church Archives.

Carter, Jared. n.d. "Journal of Jared Carter." Typescript copy. LDS Church Archives.

Carter, Kate B. 1939–51. *Heart Throbs of the West.* 12 vols. Salt Lake City, Utah: Daughters of the Utah Pioneers.

———. 1952–57. *Treasures of Pioneer History.* 6 vols. Salt Lake City, Utah: Daughters of the Utah Pioneers.

———. 1958–77. *Our Pioneer Heritage.* 20 vols. Salt Lake City, Utah: Daughters of the Utah Pioneers.

Chamberlain, Ellen Carling. n.d. "Asenath E. Browning and Isaac Vanwagoner Carling, a Sketch." LDS Church Archives.

Chase, Isaac. n.d. "History of Isaac Chase." Mormon Biography File. LDS Church Archives.

Cheney, Aaron Lindon. n.d. "History of Elam Cheney." Copies in private family possession.

Cheney, Elam. n.d. "Our Cheney Family History." Copies in private family possession.

———. 1906. "Joseph Smith, the Prophet." *Young Woman's Journal* 17, no. 12 (December): 539–40.

Cheney, Nathan B. n.d. "Descriptive Narrative of the Lives of our Great Grand Parents, Nathan Calhoun and Eliza Beebe Cheney." Typescript copy. LDS Church Archives.

———. 1844. "Nathan Cheney to Mr. Charles Beebe, Sandusky Cattauraugus Co., N.Y., June 28–29, 1844." LDS Church Archives.

Cheney, Talitha Garlik Avery. 1969. "Baptized in the Mississippi by the Prophet." In Kate B. Carter, comp., *Our Pioneer Heritage,* 20 vols., Salt Lake City, Utah: Daughters of Utah Pioneers, 1958–77, 12:202.

Chidester, John M. 1892. "Recollections of the Prophet Joseph Smith." *Juvenile Instructor* 27, no. 5 (1 March): 151.

Clark, Mary Stevenson. n.d. "Autobiography of Mary Stevenson Clark." LDS Church Archives.

Clark, Sara T. n.d. In Samuel R. Brown, "Sketch of the Life of Sara T. Clark, by Samuel R. Brown," LDS Church Archives.

Clawson, Hiram B. 1881. "Hiram B. Clawson." *Tullidge's Quarterly Magazine* 1, no. 4 (July): 678.

Clawson, Margaret. 1919a. "Mothers of Our Leaders: Rambling Reminiscences of Margaret Gay Judd Clawson." *Relief Society Magazine* 6, no. 5 (May): 259, 261.

———. 1919b. "Mothers of Our Leaders: Rambling Reminiscences of Margaret Gay Judd Clawson." *Relief Society Magazine* 6, no. 6 (June): 317–20.

Clayton, William. 1840. "William Clayton to 'Beloved Brothers and Sisters,' Dec. 10, 1840." LDS Church Archives.

———. 1843. *William Clayton's Nauvoo Diaries and Personal Writings.* Edited by Robert C. Fillerup. 23 May 1843. htpp://www.code-co.com/rcf/mhistdoc/clayton.htm.

———. 1845. *History of the Nauvoo Temple.* LDS Church Archives.

———. 1874. "Sworn statement of William Clayton, February 16, 1874." In Andrew Jenson, ed., *The Historical Record* 6 (1887): 224.

———. 1921. *William Clayton's Journal: A Daily Record of the Journey of the Original Company of "Mormon" Pioneers from Nauvoo, Ill., to the Valley of the Great Salt Lake.* Salt Lake City, Utah: The Clayton Family Association and the Deseret News Press.

———. 1978. "The Historian's Corner." *BYU Studies* 18, no. 3 (spring): 477.

Cleland, Robert G., and Juanita Brooks, ed. 1983. *A Mormon Chronicle: The Diaries of John D. Lee, 1848–1877.* 2 vols. Salt Lake City, Utah: University of Utah Press.

Cloward, James Mason. n.d. "Grandparents of Hannetta Ann Davis Loveless, on Her Mother's Side," LDS Church Archives.

Cluff, Harvey Harris. n.d. "Autobiography of Harvey Harris Cluff." Typescript copy. BYU Special Collections. Harold B. Lee Library, Provo, Utah.

Coates, Allen. 1974. "Notes from Oral History Conducted Feb. 13, 1974 of Allen

Wesley Coates by Gordon C. Thomasson, in Shortsville, New York." BYU Special Collections. Harold B. Lee Library, Provo, Utah.

Cole, Zula Rich. 1960. "Ashbel, His Wife and Children." In Kate B. Carter, comp., *Our Pioneer Heritage,* 20 vols., Salt Lake City, Utah: Daughters of the Utah Pioneers, 1958–77, 3:528.

Collected Discourses. 1886–98. Edited by Brian H. Stuy. 5 vols. Burbank, California, and Woodland Hills, Utah: B. H. S. Publishing, 1987–92.

Coltrin, Zebedee. 1866–1898. "The Papers of Zebedee Coltrin." In E. Cecil McGavin, *The Record of the Spanish Fork Branch,* 29 April 1866 to 1 December 1898, LDS Church Archives.

———. 1878. "Zebedee Coltrin Address, Minutes of the High Priest Meeting, Spanish Fork, Utah, February 5, 1878." LDS Church Archives.

———. 1883a. "Statement of Zebedee Coltrin." Minutes, 3 October 1883, Salt Lake School of the Prophets. LDS Church Archives.

———. 1883b. "Statement of Zebedee Coltrin." Minutes, 11 October 1883, Salt Lake School of the Prophets. LDS Church Archives.

Conference Report. Salt Lake City, Utah: The Church of Jesus Christ of Latter-day Saints, 1880–2003.

Conkling, J. Christopher. 1979. *A Joseph Smith Chronology.* Salt Lake City, Utah: Deseret Book.

Conover, Peter Wilson. n.d. "Biographical Sketch of the Life of Peter Wilson Conover." LDS Church Archives.

Cook, Lyndon W. 1981. *The Revelations of the Prophet Joseph Smith.* Salt Lake City, Utah: Deseret Book.

Cook, Lyndon W., and Milton Backman. 1985. *Kirtland Elder's Quorum Record 1836–1841.* Provo, Utah: Grandin Book Co.

Coray, Howard. n.d. "Diary [Autobiography] of Howard Coray, 1821–1881." BYU Special Collections. Harold B. Lee Library, Provo, Utah.

———. 1889. "Howard Cory to Martha Jane Lewis, Aug. 2, 1889." LDS Church Archives.

———. 1977. In Dean C. Jessee, "Howard Coray's Recollections of Joseph Smith," *BYU Studies* 17, no. 3 (spring): 343–46.

Coray, Martha Jane Knowlton. 1882. "Obituaries." *Woman's Exponent* 10, no. 17 (1 February): 133.

Corrill, John. 1839. *A Brief History of the Church of Christ of Latter Day Saints (Commonly Called Mormons), Including an Account of their Doctrine and Discipline, with the Reasons of the Author for Leaving the Church.* St. Louis: N.p.

Cottam, Thomas. 1892. "Recollections of the Prophet Joseph Smith." *Juvenile Instructor* 27, no. 2 (15 January): 65.

Cowdery, Oliver. 1834. "Oliver Cowdery to John Whitmer, 1 Jan., 1834." Huntington Library, San Marino, California.

———. 1835. "Oliver Cowdery to William Frye, December 22, 1835." Huntington Library, San Marino, California.

———. 1846. "Oliver Cowdery to Phineas Young, March 23, 1846." LDS Church Archives.

———. 1904. In Joseph Fielding Smith, "Restoration of the Melchizedek Priesthood," *Improvement Era* 7, no. 12 (October): 941–43.

Cowley, Matthias F. n.d. [a]. "A Life Sketch of Emily Maria Cheney Fose and Her Parents." LDS Church Archives.

———. n.d. [b]. "Matthias Cowley Autobiography." LDS Church Archives.

———. 1964. *Wilford Woodruff: History of His Life and Labors.* Salt Lake City, Utah: Bookcraft.

Cox, Elias. 1906. "Joseph Smith, the Prophet." *Young Woman's Journal* 17, no. 12 (December): 544.

Cox, Henrietta. n.d. "(Biography of) Henrietta Janes Cox." LDS Church Archives.

———. 1892. "Recollections of the Prophet Joseph Smith." *Juvenile Instructor* 27, no. 7 (1 April): 203.

Cox, Martha C. n.d. "Martha Cragun Cox (1852–1932) Autobiography, 1928–1930." LDS Church Archives.

Crary, Christopher G. 1893. *Pioneer and Personal Reminiscences.* Marshalltown, Iowa: Marshall Printing Company.

Croft, Noel. ca. 1972. "Heber J. Grant to Samuel Marshall Ellis, April 5, 1932." Noel B. Croft Collection. LDS Church Archives.

Crookston, Robert Sr. n.d. "Autobiography of Robert Crookston Senior." LDS Church Archives.

Crosby, Caroline B. 1851. "Memoirs Begun at Tubuai, Society Islands, 1851." Holograph. LDS Church Archives.

———. 1982. "Caroline Barnes Crosby: Autobiography (1807–1882)." In Kenneth W. Godfrey, Audrey M. Godfrey, and Jill Mulvey Derr, *Women's Voices: An Untold History of the Latter-day Saints 1830–1900,* Salt Lake City, Utah: Deseret Book, 46–57.

Crosby, Jesse W. n.d. [a]. "Jesse Wentworth Crosby Autobiography (1820–1869)." Typescript copy. BYU Special Collections. Harold B. Lee Library, Provo, Utah.

———. n.d. [b]. "LaFayette C. Lee, Notebook." LDS Church Archives.

Cummings, Annette A. 1906. "Joseph Smith, the Prophet." *Young Woman's Journal* 17, no. 12 (December): 538.

Cummings, B. F. 1915. "The Prophet's Last Letters." *Improvement Era* 18, no. 5 (March): 388–89.

Cummings, Sarah. n.d. "Sketch of Career of Joseph Stacy Murdock." Mormon Biography File. LDS Church Archives.

Curtis, George. n.d. [a]. "Biography of George Curtis." LDS Church Archives.

———. n.d. [b]. "Zacheus Curtis." Mormon Biography File. LDS Church Archives.

Curtis, Joseph. 1881. "History of Joseph Curtis, son of Nahum & Millicent Curtis, which was born Dec. 24, 1818, in the Town of Coneatea, Erie Co., Penn." LDS Church Archives.

Curtis, Levi. 1892. "Recollections of the Prophet Joseph Smith." *Juvenile Instructor* 27, no. 12 (15 June): 385–86.

Dalley, William. n.d. "Biography of William Dalley, As Hyrum and Mayhew Dalley remember their father, written by Alvin D. Wilcock." LDS Church Archives.

Dana, Charles Root. 1847. "Journals 1847." Microfilm of holograph. LDS Church Archives.

Davis, Elisha H. Jr. 1916. "Statement of Elisha Hildebrand Davis Jr., 1916." LDS Church Archives.

Day, Henry. n.d. "Life of Henry Day." LDS Church Archives.

Decker, Isaac. 1870. "Statement Made by Isaac Decker." 21 September 1870. LDS Church Archives.

Dibble, Philo. 1892a. "Recollections of the Prophet Joseph Smith." *Juvenile Instructor* 27, no. 1 (1 January): 22–23.

———. 1892b. "Recollections of the Prophet Joseph Smith." *Juvenile Instructor* 27, no. 10 (15 May): 303–4.

———. 1892c. "Recollections of the Prophet Joseph Smith." *Juvenile Instructor* 27, no. 11 (1 June): 345.

———. 1968. "Philo Dibble Autobiography (1806–c.1843)." In "Early Scenes in Church History," *Four Faith Promoting Classics,* Salt Lake City, Utah: Bookcraft.

Dodge, Enoch E. 1906. "Joseph Smith, the Prophet." *Young Woman's Journal* 17, no. 12 (December): 544–45.

Draper, William. 1886. "Life Of William Draper—Born in Richmond, Frontanact County, Canada, April 24th 1807; Died in Freedom, Sanpete County, Utah, May 28th 1886." LDS Church Archives.

Driggs, Olivia Pratt. 1924. "Olivia Pratt Driggs." *Relief Society Magazine* 11, no. 8 (August): 387.

Duncan, Chapman. n.d. "Extract from the Journal of Chapman Duncan." LDS Church Archives.

Duncan, Homer. 1971. "Duncan, Homer." In Andrew Jenson, *LDS Biographical Encyclopedia,* 4 vols., Salt Lake City, Utah: Western Epics, 1:625.

Dursterler, Linda M., and Dallin Oaks. 1987. "The William Hyrum Oaks and Janett Bethers Family." LDS Family History Library.

Eccles, Henry. n.d. "Henry Eccles Family Group Sheet." Mormon Biography File. LDS Church Archives.

Ehat, Andrew F. 1983. "Joseph Smith's Introduction to Temple Ordinances and the 1844 Mormon Succession Question." Master's thesis. Provo, Utah: Brigham Young University.

Ehat, Andrew F., and Lyndon Cook. 1980. *The Words of Joseph Smith: The Contemporary Accounts of the Nauvoo Discourses of the Prophet Joseph.* Provo, Utah: BYU Religious Studies Center.

Ellsworth, Edmund. ca. 1892. "Autobiography [ca. 1892]." Holograph. LDS Church Archives.

BIBLIOGRAPHY

Ensign, Mary D. n.d. "Biography of Mary Dunn Ensign, daughter of Simeon Adams Dunn and Adaline Rawson Dunn." LDS Church Archives.

Epperson, Mary Jane Robey. 1906. "Joseph Smith, the Prophet." *Young Woman's Journal* 17, no. 12 (December): 540–41.

Everett, Addison. n.d. "Sayings of Joseph by Those Who Knew Him at Different Times." LDS Church Archives.

———. 1890. "Words and Incidents of the Prophet Joseph's Life." *Young Woman's Journal* 2, no. 2 (November): 75–77.

Everett, Schuyler. n.d. "Biography of Schuyler Everett." Microfilm of holograph. Utah Historic Records Survey, Federal Writers' Project (WPA). Provo, Utah: BYU Library.

Fairbanks, Susan. 1844. "Susan Mandeville Fairbanks to Elizabeth Ann Mandeville in Pompton Plaines, New Jersey, July 17, 1844." LDS Church Archives.

Fausett [Fawsett], Mary Ann Shelton. n.d. "The Biography of Mary Ann Shelton Fausett (Written by her grandson, William L. Van Wagoner, and revised and handed in by her great grand-daughter, H. Margarette Hair Hanson)." LDS Church Archives.

Fawsett, William. 1892. "Recollections of the Prophet Joseph Smith." *Juvenile Instructor* 27, no. 2 (15 January): 66.

Fielding, Joseph. 1979. In Andrew F. Ehat, "'They Might Have Known That He Was Not a Fallen Prophet'—The Nauvoo Journal of Joseph Fielding," *BYU Studies* 19, no. 2 (winter): 144–57.

Fife, Elizabeth Watts. 1918. "Unusual Mothers: Elizabeth Watts Fife, Mother of Eighteen Children." *Relief Society Magazine* 10, no. 10 (October): 562.

Fisher, James Madison. 1906. "Typescript of Journal of James Madison Fisher [1906]." In "History and Genealogy of Jesse, Joseph, and James Madison Fisher and Evaline McLean," compiled by Lucy Elizabeth Fisher Brown, microfilm, LDS Family History Library.

Foote, David. 1971. "Foote, David." In Andrew Jenson, *LDS Biographical Encyclopedia,* 4 vols., Salt Lake City, Utah: Western Epics, 1:376.

Foote, Warren. n.d. [a]. "Autobiography of Warren Foote." Typescript copy. BYU Special Collections. Harold B. Lee Library, Provo, Utah.

———. n.d. [b]. "Diary of Warren Foote." In *Foote Genealogical History,* n.p. Copies in private family possession.

Ford, Thomas. 1854. *History of Illinois, From its Commencement as a State in 1818 to 1847.* Chicago: S. C. Griggs & Co.

Forsgren, John E. 1945. "John E. Forsgren." In Kate B. Carter, comp., *Heart Throbs of the West,* 12 vols., Salt Lake City, Utah: Daughters of the Utah Pioneers, 1939–51, 6:38–39.

Fox, Jessie W. 1890. "A Russian Naval Station." *Juvenile Instructor* 25, no. 6 (25 March): 162.

———. 1904. "Jessie Williams Fox." In Orson F. Whitney, *History of Utah,* 4 vols., Salt Lake City, Utah: G. Q. Cannon & Sons Co., 4:347.

Freeze, Lillie. 1890. "Remarks at the Y. L. M. I. Conference of Box Elder Stake." *Young Woman's Journal* 2, no. 2 (November): 81.

Fullmer, John S. 1843. "John S. Fullmer to Josiah Stowell Jr., Feb. 17, 1843, in Elmyra, N.Y." LDS Church Archives.

Gardner, Chloe Louise Snow. n.d. "Brief Sketch of the Life of Sally Adams Snow." Mormon Biography File. LDS Church Archives.

Garn, Daniel. 1934. "Sketch of the life of Daniel Garn, A Utah Pioneer of 1847, As told by his son, Philip Garn, February 15, 1934." LDS Church Archives.

Garner, David. n.d. Untitled Manuscript. Mormon Biography File. LDS Church Archives.

Garner, Harriet Erminie Black. n.d. "Mary Hunt Black Biographical Sketch." Typescript copy. LDS Church Archives.

Garner, Mary Field. n.d. "Autobiographical Sketch of Mary Field Garner, 1836–1943." LDS Church Archives.

Gates, Susa Young. 1930. *The Life Story of Brigham Young*. New York: The MacMillan Company.

Gee, Lysander. 1879. "Lysander Gee to Alexander McRae, 2 April 1879." LDS Church Archives.

Gem, The. 1829. *The Gem, of Literature and Science* (Rochester, N.Y.) 1, no. 9 (5 September): 70.

———. 1830. *The Gem, A Semi-Monthly Literary and Miscellaneous Journal* (Rochester, N.Y.) 2, no. 17 (25 December): 135.

Gibson, Jacob. n.d. "The Book of the Generations of Jacob Gibson 1849–1881." LDS Church Archives.

Gifford, Mervin Leroy. 1975. "Stephen Markham: Man of Valor." Master's thesis. Provo, Utah: Brigham Young University.

Gifford, Samuel Kendall. n.d. *A Short Biography of Samuel Kendall Gifford, son of Alpheus and Anna Nash Gifford, born Nov. 11, 1821 at Milo, Yates County, New York. Dictated by himself and written by Hannah Jane Gifford, a grand-daughter.* LDS Church Archives.

———. 1893. "Recollections of the Prophet Joseph Smith." *Juvenile Instructor* 28, no. 1 (1 January): 15.

Gilbert, John H. 1893. "Memorandum." 8 September 1893. Typescript copy. BYU Special Collections. Harold B. Lee Library, Provo, Utah.

Gleason, John Streator. n.d. "History of John Streator Gleason." Mormon Biography File. LDS Church Archives.

Glines, James Harvey. 1845–1899. "Reminiscences and Diary, March 1845—December, 1899." Holograph. LDS Church Archives.

Godfrey, Donald G., and Brigham Y. Card. 1993. *The Diaries of Charles Ora Card: The Canadian Years 1886–1903*. Salt Lake City, Utah: University of Utah Press.

Grant, Jedediah Morgan. 1996. In Davis Bitton, *Images of the Prophet Joseph Smith*, Salt Lake City, Utah: Aspen Books.

Grant, Rachel R. 1905. "Joseph Smith, the Prophet." *Young Woman's Journal* 16, no. 12 (December): 550.

Green, Mary Ann. n.d. "History Taken from Record of Irene Louise Peterson Elmer Marriott, North Weber, Ogden, Weber Utah." LDS Church Archives.

Greene, John Portentius. 1839. *Facts Relative to the Expulsion of the Mormons or Latter-day Saints, from the State of Missouri, under the "Exterminating Order."* Cincinnati: R. P. Brooks.

Greenhalgh, William. n.d. "The History and Life of William Greenhalgh, son of Robert and Ellen Greenhalgh, Born July 29, 1811, in Bregmat (Brightmat) (Near Belton, Lanceshire, England)." Typescript copy from "The History and Life of William Greenhalgh." In a journal written in his own hand. Copies in private family possession.

Greer, Catherine E. n.d. "Anecdotes and Reminiscences of Her Life as Related by Grandma Ellen C. Greer." LDS Church Archives.

Griffin, Charles Emerson. n.d. "Autobiography of Charles Emerson Griffin." LDS Church Archives.

Griffon, Dawnell Hatton. n.d. *Kiss the Babies for Me: A Story of an Allred Family*. Copies in private family possession.

Groves, Elisha Hurd. n.d. "An Account of the Life of Elisha Hurd Groves." Mormon Biography File. LDS Church Archives.

Gunn, Stanley R. 1962. *Oliver Cowdery: Second Elder and Scribe*. Salt Lake City, Utah: Bookcraft.

Gurley, Zenos H. 1885. "Questions Asked of David Whitmer at his Home in Richmond, Ray County, Missouri, Jan. 21, 1885, by Zenos H. Gurley." LDS Church Archives.

Guymon, Noah Thomas. n.d. "Typescript Notes from the Journal of Noah Thomas Guymon." Copies in private family possession.

Haight, Isaac C. n.d. [a]. "Autobiography of Isaac C. Haight." Typescript copy. BYU Special Collections. Harold B. Lee Library, Provo, Utah.

———. n.d. [b]. "A Brief Sketch of the Life of Isaac C. Haight." LDS Church Archives.

Hale, Aroet L. n.d. "Autobiography of Aroet Lucious Hale." Typescript copy. BYU Special Collections. Harold B. Lee Library, Provo, Utah.

Hale, Jesse. 1845. "Jesse Hale to Emma Smith, March 30, 1845." LDS Church Archives.

Hales, Kenneth Glyn, ed. and comp. 1985. *Windows: A Mormon Family*. Tucson, Ariz.: Skyline Printing.

Hall, Thomas. 1893. "Recollections of the Prophet Joseph Smith." *Juvenile Instructor* 28, no. 1 (1 January): 14–15.

Hamblin, Jacob. n.d. "Journal 8." Typescript copy. Microfilm. LDS Church Archives.

———. 1881. In James A. Little, *Jacob Hamblin: A Narrative of His Personal Experience, as Frontiersman, Missionary to the Indians and Explorer,* Salt Lake City, Utah: Juvenile Instructor Office.

Hammond, Joseph. n.d. "History of James Deans and Susanna Hammond, compiled by Rita C. Lee, a great-granddaughter." LDS Church Archives.

Hamson, Sarah Ann. ca. 1931. "(Biography of) Sarah Ann Smith Hamson." LDS Church Archives.

Hancock, Joseph. n.d. "Joseph Hancock (Original Pioneer)." Mormon Biography File. LDS Church Archives.

Hancock, Levi W. n.d. [a]. "Handwritten Statement by Levi Ward Hancock (1803–1882) [n.d.]." LDS Church Archives.

———. n.d. [b]. "The Levi Hancock Autobiography." Typescript copy. BYU Special Collections. Harold B. Lee Library, Provo, Utah.

Hancock, Mosiah. n.d. Amy E. Baird, Victoria Jackson, and Laura L. Wassell, comp. "Autobiography of Mosiah Hancock (1834–1865)." Typescript copy. BYU Special Collections. Harold B. Lee Library, Provo, Utah.

Hancock, Solomon. 1978. "Erastus and Francis Hancock, An Informal Family History." Cited in Spencer J. Palmer, "Five Dollars for Joseph Smith," *Ensign* 8, no. 4 (April): 67.

Harding, Glen F. 1973. "A Record of the Ancestry and Descendants of John Jacob Zundel, Known as Jacob Zundel." LDS Family History Library.

Harmon, Jesse P. n.d. "A Sketch of the Life of Ansil Perse Harmon by Jane Harmon Pratt (a daughter of Ansel Perse Harmon)." LDS Church Archives.

Harper, John. n.d. "History of John Harper, written by Himself." Mormon Biography File. LDS Church Archives.

———. ca. 1861. "Record Made by John Harper." LDS Church Archives.

Harris, Clinton. 1857. In George A. Smith, "Notes of a Conversation . . . 1857," LDS Church Archives.

Harris, Dennison L. 1881. "Verbal Statement of Bishop Dennison L. Harris to President Joseph F. Smith in the Presence of Elder Franklin Spener, at the house of Bishop Dorius of Ephraim, San Pete County, Utah, on Sunday Afternoon, May 15, 1881, and reported by George F. Gibbs." LDS Church Archives.

Harris, Louisa H. n.d. In Silas A. Harris, "A Brief Sketch of Louisa Hall Harris," Mormon Biography File, LDS Church Archives.

Harris, Martha Ann. 1881. "Statement of Martha Ann Smith Harris, Provo City, March 22, 1881." LDS Church Archives.

———. 1924. In Richard P. Harris, "Martha Ann Smith Harris," *Relief Society Magazine* 11, no. 1 (January): 12.

———. 1991. "Martha Ann's Vision." *Joseph Smith Sr. Family Reunion News* 10, no. 1 (5 March): 4.

Harris, Martin. n.d. In Ole A. Jensen, "Testimony of Martin Harris (One of the Witnesses of the Book of Mormon)," BYU Special Collections, Harold B. Lee Library, Provo, Utah.

———. 1886. In Edward Stevenson, "The Three Witnesses to the Book of Mormon," *Latter-day Saints' Millennial Star* 48, no. 25 (21 June): 389–91.

Harvey, Isaac Julian. 1839. "Isaac Julian Harvey to Mrs. Sarah Harvey, 26 April 1839." LDS Church Archives.

Hatch, Abram. 1904. "Abram Hatch." In Orson F. Whitney, *History of Utah,* 4 vols., Salt Lake City, Utah: G. Q. Cannon & Sons Co.

Hatch, Ira S. n.d. "Biography of Ranson Hatch." LDS Church Archives.

———. 1984. In Richard Ira Elkins, "PU-AM-EY: Ira Hatch, Indian Missionary, 1835–1909," Bountiful, Utah: n.p., 1984, 1990, LDS Family History Library.

———. 1988. In Lula Campbell and the Hatch Family Historical Committee, "Wandering Home: Stories and Memories of Ira Stearns Hatch, Meltiar Hatch, and John Henry Hatch, and their Wives and Children, With Historical-Genealogical and Biographical Data on their Ancestry and Descendants," LDS Family History Library.

Hatch, Lorenzo H. n.d. "Autobiography of Lorenzo Hill Hatch (1826–1846)." Typescript copy. BYU Special Collections. Harold B. Lee Library, Provo, Utah.

———. 1994. "The Journal of Lorenzo Hill Hatch." In Dale Hatch, "Jeremiah Hatch and Family History," LDS Family History Library.

Hatch, Orin. n.d. In Spencer Fearnley Hatch, *Patriarch Orin Hatch, 1830–1906: A Biography,* n.p.

Hayden, Amos S. 1875. *Early History of the Disciples in the Western Reserve.* Cincinnati: Chase & Hall, Publishers.

Hendricks, Drusilla D. n.d. "Historical Sketch of James Hendricks & Drusilla Dorris Hendricks." LDS Church Archives.

Hendrix, Daniel. 1897. "The Origin of Mormonism." *St. Louis Globe–Democrat,* 21 February 1897, 34.

Henrie, James. 1902. "A Short Sketch of the Life of James Henrie, Son of William and Myra Mayall Henrie." Dictated to his sister Effie Heywood, 15 April 1902. Copies in private family possession.

Henrie, William. n.d. In Thelma Miller Bigbee, "Stories of the Associations of the William Henry Family with the Prophet Joseph Smith as Told to Me by My Aunt Mary Henrie Cooper. Written by Thelma Miller Bigbee," LDS Church Archives.

———. 1955. In Callie O. Morley, "History of William and Myra Mayall Henrie, Pioneers of 1847 and 1847," Delta, West Millard County, Utah, October 1955, LDS Church Archives.

———. 1974. Rhea A. S. Anderson. "My Pioneer Heritage." 15 January 1974. Copies in private family possession.

Herrick, Lester James. 1904. "Lester James Herrick." In Orson F. Whitney, *History of Utah,* 4 vols., Salt Lake City, Utah: G. Q. Cannon & Sons Co., 4:286.

Heslop, Mary Owen. 1996. "Jeremiah Hatch: The Life and Times of an Extraordinary Man." LDS Family History Library.

Hess, John W. 1892. "Recollections of the Prophet Joseph Smith." *Juvenile Instructor* 27, no. 10 (15 May): 302–3.

Heywood, Joseph L. n.d. "Diary of Joseph L. Heywood, 1815–1910." Typescript copy. BYU Special Collections. Harold B. Lee Library, Provo, Utah.

———. 1971. "Heywood, Joseph Leland." In Andrew Jenson, *LDS Biographical Encyclopedia,* 4 vols., Salt Lake City, Utah: Western Epics, 1:646.

Hickenlooper, William H. 1971. "Hickenlooper, William Hainey." In Andrew Jenson, *LDS Biographical Encyclopedia,* 4 vols., Salt Lake City, Utah: Western Epics, 1:609.

Hickman, William A. n.d. "Sketch of the Life of William A. Hickman." LDS Church Archives.

Higbee, Isaac. 1864. "Items from the Journal of Isaac Higbee, May 24, 1864." LDS Church Archives.

Higgins, Nelson. n.d. "Nelson Higgins." Mormon Biography File. LDS Church Archives.

Hill, Isaac. n.d. "History of Isaac Hill from His Personal Diary." Copied by Geneva M. Wilding. Salt Lake City, Utah. Copies in private family possession.

Hillman, Silas. n.d. In Ellen Jane Koyle Rose, "History of Adlina Hillman Koyle," copies in private family possession.

Hinckley, Arza Erastus. n.d. "Life Sketch of Arza Erastus Hinckley." LDS Church Archives.

Hinman, Henry Lyman. 1910. "Henry Lyman Hinman to Susa Y. Gates, Oct. 22, 1910." LDS Church Archives.

Hofheins, Jacob. n.d. "Family History of Jacob Hofheins." LDS Church Archives.

Hogan, Goudy E. 1945. "History of Goudy E. Hogan." Typescript copy. BYU Special Collections. Harold B. Lee Library, Provo, Utah.

Holbrook, Joseph. n.d. "Autobiography of Joseph Holbrook (1806–1846)." Typescript copy. BYU Special Collections. Harold B. Lee Library, Provo, Utah.

Holbrook, S. 1844. "S. Holbrook to S. D. Cowles, July 1, 1844." LDS Church Archives.

Holdaway, Joseph Alma. n.d. "Autobiography of Joseph Alma Holdaway." LDS Church Archives.

Holden, Edwin. 1892. "Recollections of the Prophet Joseph Smith." *Juvenile Instructor* 27, no. 5 (1 March): 153.

Horne, Joseph Jr. 1989. "The Journal of Joseph Horne, Junior, 1858–1861, Including His Life Summary." Transcribed by Stephen D. Robison. LDS Family History Library.

Horne, Mary I. 1951. "The Prophet Joseph Smith: The Testimony of Sister M. Isabella Horne." *Relief Society Magazine* 38, no. 3 (March): 158–60.

———. 1982. In Lyneve Wilson Kramer and Eva Durant Wilson, "Mary Isabella Hales Horne," *Ensign* 12, no. 8 (August): 63–66.

———. 1985. "Mary Hales Autobiography." In Kenneth Glyn Hales, ed. and comp., *Windows: A Mormon Family,* Tucson, Ariz.: Skyline Printing.

Horner, John M. 1960. "From the Autobiography of John M. Horner." In Kate B.

Carter, comp., *Our Pioneer Heritage,* 20 vols., Salt Lake City, Utah: Daughters of the Utah Pioneers, 1958–77, 3:549.

Houston, James. n.d. "Religious History of Grandfather James Houston, born 1817." Mormon Biography File. LDS Church Archives.

Hovey, Joseph Grafton. n.d. "Autobiography of Joseph Grafton Hovey (1812–1847)." Typescript copy. BYU Special Collections. Harold B. Lee Library, Provo, Utah.

Hoyt, Emily S. n.d. "Reminiscences and Diaries of Emily Smith Hoyt, 1851–1893." LDS Church Archives. Quoted by permission of Jonathan Dibble and family.

Hubbard, Marshall Moore. n.d. [a]. "Brief Genealogical Sketch of Sister Percia Cornelia Grover Bunnell and her parents." Mormon Biography File. LDS Church Archives.

———. n.d. [b]. "Hubbard, Marshall Moore." Typescript copy. LDS Church Archives.

Huffaker, Lewis Albert. n.d. "Lewis Albert Huffaker." LDS Church Archives.

Hulet, Sylvanus Cyrus. n.d. "A Sketch of the Lives of Sylvanus Cyrus Hulet and Catherine Stoker Hulet." LDS Church Archives.

Hunter, Edward. 1904. "Edward Hunter." In Orson F. Whitney, *History of Utah,* 4 vols., Salt Lake City, Utah: G. Q. Cannon & Sons Co.

———. 1971. "Hunter, Edward." In Andrew Jenson, *LDS Biographical Encyclopedia,* 4 vols., Salt Lake City, Utah: Western Epics, 1:229–30.

Huntington, Dimick Baker. 1904. "Dimick Baker Huntington." In Orson F. Whitney, *History of Utah,* 4 vols., Salt Lake City, Utah: G. Q. Cannon & Sons Co., 4:210.

Huntington, Oliver B. n.d. [a]. "Autobiography of Oliver B. Huntington (1823–1839)." Typescript copy. BYU Special Collections. Harold B. Lee Library, Provo, Utah.

———. n.d. [b]. "History of the Life of Oliver B. Huntington, Written by Himself 1878–1900." Typescript copy. BYU Special Collections. Harold B. Lee Library, Provo, Utah.

———. 1890a. "Words and Incidents of the Prophet Joseph's Life." *Young Woman's Journal* 2, no. 2 (November): 75–77.

———. 1890b. "Words and Incidents of the Prophet Joseph's Life." *Young Woman's Journal* 2, no. 3 (December): 124–25.

———. 1890c. "Letter to the Editor (Susa Gates)." *Young Woman's Journal* 2, no. 3 (December): 125.

———. 1891a. "To the Editor." *Young Woman's Journal* 2, no. 5 (February): 225–26.

———. 1891b. "Prophecy." *Young Woman's Journal* 2, no. 7 (April): 314–15.

———. 1891c. "Sayings of Joseph Smith." *Young Woman's Journal* 2, no. 3 (May): 366.

———. 1891d. "Words and Incidents of the Prophet Joseph's Life." *Young Woman's Journal* 2, no. 10 (July): 466–68.

———. 1893. "Sayings of the Prophet Joseph Smith." *Young Woman's Journal* 4, no. 7 (April): 320–21.

———. 1896. "Recollections of 'Diahman.'" *Juvenile Instructor* 31, no. 3 (1 February): 83–85.

———. 1902. "An Incident in Zion's Camp." *Juvenile Instructor* 37, no. 1 (1 January): 20–21.

———. 1960. "William Cahoon, Autobiography." In Stella Shurtleff and Brent Farrington Cahoon, eds. *Reynolds Cahoon and His Stalwart Sons,* Salt Lake City, Utah: Paragon Press.

Hyde, Elizabeth H. B. 1912. "Elizabeth H. B. Hyde." *Utah Genealogical and Historical Magazine* 3 (October): 207–8.

Hyde, Marinda N. Johnson. 1877. "Marinda Hyde Autobiography." In Edward W. Tullidge, *Women of Mormondom,* New York: Tullidge & Crandall, 403–6.

Hyde, Mary Ann. 1880. "Mrs. M[ary] A[ann] P[rice] Hyde Autobiography, Springville, Utah, May 20, 1880." Bancroft Library, University of California, Berkeley; see also Microfilm of holograph. LDS Church Archives.

Hyde, Orson. 1846. "Although Dead, Yet he Speaketh." *Latter-day Saints' Millennial Star* 8, no. 9 (20 November): 138–39.

———. 1864. "History of Orson Hyde." *Latter-day Saints' Millennial Star* 26, no. 49 (3 December): 774–76.

———. 1869. "Remarks," given 6 October 1869. *Deseret News Semi-Weekly,* 16 November 1869.

———. 1913. "Orson Hyde." *Utah Genealogical and Historical Magazine* 4 (April): 55–64.

Hyde, William. n.d. "The Private Journal of William Hyde." BYU Special Collections. Harold B. Lee Library, Provo, Utah.

Illinois Democratic Press. 1852. "The Mormons." *New York Daily Times,* 28 September 1852, 6.

Isom, Alice Parker. n.d. "Memoirs of Alice Parker Isom." LDS Church Archives.

Jackson, Levi. n.d. "A Short Sketch of the Life of Levi Jackson." LDS Church Archives.

Jackson, Mary E. Miller. 1960. "John Kittleman and His Family." In Kate B. Carter, comp., *Our Pioneer Heritage,* 20 vols., Salt Lake City, Utah: Daughters of the Utah Pioneers, 1958–77, 3:559.

Jacob, Norton. n.d. [a]. "Autobiography of Norton Jacob (1804–1847)." Typescript copy. BYU Special Collections. Harold B. Lee Library, Provo, Utah.

———. n.d. [b]. "Reminiscences and Journal (May 1844–Jan.)." LDS Church Archives.

James, Jane. 1905. "Joseph Smith, the Prophet." *Young Woman's Journal* 16, no. 12 (December): 551–53.

Jenkins, David. 1841. "David Jenkins to Leonard Pinkle, Sept. 28 [1841?]." LDS Church Archives.

Jenson, Andrew. 1971. *LDS Biographical Encyclopedia.* 4 vols. Salt Lake City, Utah: Western Epics.

Johnson, Aaron. 1997. "Aaron Johnson." In Susan Easton Black, *Who's Who in the Doctrine and Covenants,* Salt Lake City, Utah: Bookcraft.

Johnson, Benjamin F. 1903. "Benjamin F. Johnson to George S. Gibbs, 1903." LDS Church Archives. Also in E. Dale LeBaron, "Benjamin Franklin Johnson: Colonizer, Public Servant, and Church Leader," master's thesis, Provo, Utah: Brigham Young University, 1967, 325–46.

———. 1947. *Benjamin F. Johnson, My Life's Review.* Independence, Mo.: Zion's Printing and Publishing Company.

Johnson, Evaline B. 1906. "Joseph Smith, the Prophet." *Young Woman's Journal* 17, no. 12 (December): 545.

Johnson, Harriet M. 1963. "Harriet Matilda Daniel Johnson." In Kate B. Carter, comp., *Our Pioneer Heritage,* 20 vols., Salt Lake City, Utah: Daughters of the Utah Pioneers, 1958–77, 6:431.

Johnson, Isabella M. n.d. "Isaac Russell." Mormon Biography File. LDS Church Archives.

Johnson, Joel H. n.d. [a]. "Life of Joel H. Johnson." Mormon Biography File. LDS Church Archives.

———. n.d. [b]. "Selections from the Autobiography of Joel Hills Johnson, (1802–1868)." Typescript copy. BYU Special Collections. Harold B. Lee Library, Provo, Utah.

———. 1881. *Voice from the Mountains, Being a Testimony of the Truth of the Gospel of Jesus Christ, as Revealed by the Lord to Joseph Smith Jr.* Salt Lake City, Utah: Juvenile Instructor.

Johnson, Luke S. 1864. "History of Luke Johnson." *Latter-day Saints' Millennial Star* 26, no. 53 (31 December): 834–36.

———. 1865. "History of Luke Johnson." *Latter-day Saints' Millennial Star* 27, no. 1 (7 January): 5–7.

Johnson, Philo. 1894. Untitled manuscript, 18 April 1894. LDS Church Archives.

Johnson, Speedy Brown Ellsworth. 1894. "Sketch of the Life of Speedy Brown Ellsworth Johnson." In Philo Johnson, untitled manuscript, 18 April 1894, LDS Church Archives.

Jones, Dan. 1855. "The Martyrdom of Josephand Hyrum Smith." Written by Dan Jones to Thomas Bullock, 20 January 1855. LDS Church Archives.

Jones, Jacob. n.d. [a]. In Helen D. O'Connor, "Jacob Jones—Biography of a Pioneer," LDS Church Archives.

———. n.d. [b]. "Testimony of Jacob Jones." LDS Church Archives.

Jones, James Naylor. n.d. Untitled manuscript. Mormon Biography File. LDS Church Archives.

Jones, William E. 1892. "Recollections of the Prophet Joseph Smith." *Juvenile Instructor* 27, no. 2 (15 January): 65–66.

Journal History. LDS Church Archives.

Journal of Discourses. 26 vols. London: Latter-day Saints' Book Depot, 1854–86.

Judd, Zadoc K. n.d. "Autobiography of Zadoc Knapp Judd." Typescript copy. BYU Special Collections. Harold B. Lee Library, Provo, Utah.

Kartchner, William Decatur. 1963. "William Decatur Kartchner." In Kate B. Carter, comp., *Our Pioneer Heritage*, 20 vols., Salt Lake City, Utah: Daughters of the Utah Pioneers, 1958–77, 6:335.

Kay, John Moburn. 1904. "John Moburn Kay." In Orson F. Whitney, *History of Utah*, 4 vols., Salt Lake City, Utah: G. Q. Cannon & Sons Co., 4:452.

Kearnes, Emma M. Guymon. n.d. "A Brief History of Emma M. Guymon Kearnes." LDS Church Archives.

Kelley, William H. 1992. Milton V. Backman Jr. and Richard O. Cowan. *Joseph Smith and the Doctrine and Covenants*. Salt Lake City, Utah: Deseret Book.

Kelsey, Easton. n.d. "Sayings of Joseph by Those Who Knew Him at Different Times." LDS Church Archives.

Kelsey, Eli Brazee. n.d. "History of the Life of Eli Brazee Kelsey, as Written by Cecil Kelsey Mills of Magna, Utah, Granddaughter of Eli B. Kelsey and Letitia Sheets, His First Wife." LDS Church Archives.

Kempton, Jerome B. 1985. Margarite Kimpton Stevens and Jan Stevens Lockard, *Kempton/Kimpton Families: Life and Lineage of Jerome B. Kempton*. Stevenson's Genealogy Center, Provo, Utah.

Kendall, Elizabeth C. 1960. In Bertha M. Linebarger, "Elizabeth Clements Kendall," in Kate B. Carter, comp., *Our Pioneer Heritage*, 20 vols., Salt Lake City, Utah: Daughters of the Utah Pioneers, 1958–77, 3:112.

Kesler, Frederick. n.d. "A Statement on the Back of One of the Photographs of Bishop Frederick Kesler, Given by Him to His Daughter Clara Olivia Kesler." LDS Church Archives.

———. 1952. "Reminiscences, by Donnette Smith Kesler, the Wife of Alonzo Pratt Kesler." Elbert C. Kirkham Company, Salt Lake City, Utah, 1952. Multilithed.

———. 1988. In Kimberly Day, "Frederick Kesler, Utah Craftsman," *Utah Historical Quarterly* 56, no. 1 (winter): 57–58.

Keys, Celia Anzenette/Anjenette. n.d. May Taylor Tiffany, *History of H. H. Taylor and Eliza Jane Bird Taylor*. Copies in private family possession.

Kimball, Heber C. 1845a. "Extracts from H. C. Kimball's Journal." *Times and Seasons* 6, no. 1 (15 January): 770–73.

———. 1845b. "Extracts from H. C. Kimball's Journal." *Times and Seasons* 6, no. 2 (4 February): 787–90.

———. 1845c. "Extracts from H. C. Kimball's Journal." *Times and Seasons* 6, no. 3 (15 February): 803–5.

———. 1862. "Remarks, President Heber C. Kimball, Feb. 9, 1862." *Deseret News*, 5 November 1862, 1.

———. 1864a. "Heber C. Kimball Journal." *Latter-day Saints' Millennial Star* 26, no. 34 (20 August): 535–36.

———. 1864b. "Heber C. Kimball Journal." *Latter-day Saints' Millennial Star* 26, no. 35 (27 August): 550–52.

———. 1864c. "Heber C. Kimball Journal." *Latter-day Saints' Millennial Star* 26, no. 36 (3 September): 568–69.

———. 1864d. "Heber C. Kimball Journal." *Latter-day Saints' Millennial Star* 26, no. 38 (17 September): 598–600.

———. 1880. In Helen Mar Whitney, "Heber C. Kimball Journal," in "Life Incidents," *Woman's Exponent* 9, no. 3 (1 July): 18.

———. 1883. In Helen Mar Whitney, "Scenes in Nauvoo after the Martyrdom of the Prophet and Patriarch," *Woman's Exponent* 11, no. 17 (1 February): 130.

———. 1945. In Orson F. Whitney, *Life of Heber C. Kimball,* Salt Lake City, Utah: Stevens and Wallis, Inc.

Kimball, Lucy Walker. n.d. "A Brief Biographical Sketch of the Life and Labors of Lucy Walker Kimball." LDS Church Archives.

———. 1888. "Lucy Walker Kimball." In Lyman Omer Littlefield, "Reminiscences of Latter-day Saints," Logan, Utah: The Utah Journal Co., 42–44.

———. 1905. "Joseph Smith, the Prophet." *Young Woman's Journal* 16, no. 12 (December): 548–49.

Kimball, Mary Ellen. 1892. "Recollections of the Prophet Joseph Smith." *Juvenile Instructor* 27, no. 16 (15 August): 490–91.

Kimball, Sarah M. 1883. *Woman's Exponent* 12, no. 7 (1 September): 51. Also in Hyrum L. Andrus and Helen Mae Andrus, *They Knew the Prophet,* Salt Lake City, Utah: Bookcraft, 1974, 130.

Kimball, Vilate M. 1877. "Vilate Kimball Autobiography (1806–1837)." In Edward W. Tullidge, *Women of Mormondom,* New York: Tullidge & Crandall, 107–9.

King, Culbert. n.d. Untitled Manuscript. Mormon Biography File. LDS Church Archives.

King, Thomas Rice. 1877. *Genealogy of the King Family, Utah Territory, 1877.* LDS Church Archives.

Kingsbury, Joseph Corroden. 1846. "History of Joseph Corroden Kingsbury. Copied from his own handwriting in his little books where he kept his diary by his granddaughter Roselia Meservy Watson. As written by his own hand 1846, 1847, 1849, 1850 and later." Mormon Biography File. LDS Church Archives.

Kirtland Council Minute Book. n.d. LDS Church Archives. Also published as Fred C. Collier, *Kirtland Council Book.* Salt Lake City, Utah: Collier's Publishing Co., 1996.

Kittleman, Elizabeth Jane. 1960. In Mary E. Miller Jackson, "John Kittleman and His Family," in Kate B. Carter, comp., *Our Pioneer Heritage,* 20 vols., Salt Lake City, Utah: Daughters of the Utah Pioneers, 1958–77, 3:559.

Knapp, Stephen Boughton. 1905. "Memorandum, April 1905." LDS Church Archives.

Knight, Catherine. 1918. "Catherine M'Guire Knight." In "Unusual Mothers," *Relief Society Magazine* 5, no. 10 (October): 554–55.

Knight, Joseph Jr. 1974. "Joseph Knight Jr." In Hyrum L. Andrus and Helen Mae

Andrus, *They Knew the Prophet,* Salt Lake City, Utah: Bookcraft. Also in "Joseph Knight Jr., Folder," LDS Church Archives.

Knight, Joseph Sr. 1976. In Dean C. Jessee, "Joseph Knight's Recollection of Early Mormon History," *BYU Studies* 16, no. 4 (winter): 29–39.

———. 1997. "Joseph Knight Sr." In Susan Easton Black, *Who's Who in the Doctrine and Covenants,* 167.

Knight, LaFayette. 1843. "Extracts from a Letter Written by LaFayette Knight, from Carthage, Ill., Dec. 21, 1843." LDS Church Archives.

Knight, Lydia B. n.d. "Lydia Knight's Life, Written by her Great Granddaughter, Wilma S. Hawkins." Mormon Biography File. LDS Church Archives.

———. 1883. Susa Young Gates. *Lydia Knight's History.* Salt Lake City, Utah: Juvenile Instructor's Office.

———. 1974. In Hyrum L. Andrus and Helen Mae Andrus, *They Knew the Prophet,* Salt Lake City, Utah: Bookcraft.

Knight, Newel. n.d. "Autobiography and Journal of Newel Knight, 1800–1847." LDS Church Archives.

———. 1969. "Newel Knight's Journal." In "Scraps of Biography," in *Classic Experiences and Adventures,* Salt Lake City, Utah: Bookcraft.

———. 1974. In Hyrum L. Andrus and Helen Mae Andrus, *They Knew the Prophet,* Salt Lake City, Utah: Bookcraft.

Knight, Samuel Eli. n.d. "Sketch of Samuel Knight." Mormon Biography File. LDS Church Archives.

———. 1892. "Recollections of the Prophet Joseph Smith." *Juvenile Instructor* 27, no. 20 (15 October): 641.

Lake, Philomena [Philomela] Smith. 1936. "'Philomena Smith Lake.' In 'Sketch of James Lakes Life.' Written 26 August 1936 by S. C. Richardson, and copied 29 August 1949 by Mary Ellen Lake Jarvis," Mormon Biography File, LDS Church Archives.

Lambert, Charles. n.d. "Autobiography of Charles Lambert (1816–1892)." LDS Church Archives.

Lambert, Mary A. n.d. "My Mother: Mary Alice Cannon Lambert, Pioneer of Nauvoo, Ill., and a Utah Pioneer of 1849." Mormon Biography File. LDS Church Archives.

———. 1905. "Joseph Smith, the Prophet." *Young Woman's Journal* 16, no. 12 (December): 554.

Lambson, Alfred B. 1915. "Alfred Boaz Lambson." *Utah Genealogical and Historical Magazine* 6 (July): 147–148.

———. 1952. "Reminiscences, by Donnette Smith Kesler, the Wife of Alonzo Pratt Kesler." Elbert C. Kirkham Company, Salt Lake City, Utah, 1952. Multilithed.

Lamoreaux, Andrew. 1971. "Lamoreaux, Andrew." In Andrew Jenson, *LDS Biographical Encyclopedia,* 4 vols., Salt Lake City, Utah: Western Epics, 3:666.

Lapham, Fayette. 1870. "Interview with the Father of Joseph Smith, the Mormon Prophet." *The Historical Magazine* 17 (May): 305–9.

Laub, George. n.d. "George Laub Autobiography." Typescript copy. BYU Special Collections. Harold B. Lee Library, Provo, Utah. Also in Eugene England, ed., "George Laub's Nauvoo Journal," *BYU Studies* 18, no. 2 (winter 1978): 157–58.

Layton, Christopher. 1911. *Autobiography of Christopher Layton*. Edited by John Q. Cannon. Salt Lake City, Utah: The Deseret News.

Leany, William. n.d. "Autobiography of William Leany." BYU Special Collections. Harold B. Lee Library, Provo, Utah.

Leavitt, Dudley. 1893. "Recollections of the Prophet Joseph Smith." *Juvenile Instructor* 28, no. 1 (1 January): 16.

Leavitt, Sarah S. 1919. "History of Sarah Studevant Leavitt (1798–1847)." Edited by Juanita L. Pulsipher. N.p.

Lee, John D. 1881. *Mormonism Unveiled*. St. Louis, Mo.: N. D. Thompson & Co.

———. 1938. *Journals of John D. Lee 1846–47 and 1859*. Edited by Charles Kelley. Salt Lake City, Utah: Western Printing Company, 1938.

Leech, James. 1892. "Recollections of the Prophet Joseph Smith." *Juvenile Instructor* 27, no. 5 (1 March): 152–53.

Leishman, Catherine T. n.d. "Catherine Thomas Leishman. Autobiographical Sketch." LDS Church Archives.

Leithead, James. 1901. "Life and Labors of James Leithead." Written 25 January 1901. Mormon Biography File. LDS Church Archives.

Lewis, David. 1908. "Testimony Taken in the Presence of Andrew Jenson, Hiram B. Clawson, Martin S. Lindsay, Stokey Anderson, and M. Minerva Jenson, Historian's Office, September 10, 1908." Mormon Biography File. LDS Church Archives.

Lewis, James. n.d. "Autobiography of James Lewis." Mormon Biography File. LDS Church Archives.

Lightner, Mary Elizabeth Rollins. 1905a. "Mary Elizabeth Lightner, Address at Brigham Young University, April 14, 1905." Typescript copy. BYU Special Collections. Harold B. Lee Library, Provo, Utah.

———. 1905b. "Testimony." *Young Woman's Journal* 16, no. 12 (December): 556–57.

———. 1926. "Mary Elizabeth Rollins Lightner." *Utah Genealogical and Historical Magazine* 17 (July): 193–205.

———. 1936. In Elsie E. Barrett, "Mary Elizabeth Rollins Lightner," typescript biographical sketch, Huntington Library, San Marino, California.

Linder, Usher F. 1879. *Reminiscences of the Early Bench and Bar of Illinois*. Chicago: The Legal News Company.

Little, James A. 1893. "Biography of William Rufus Rogers Stowell, 1893." LDS Church Archives.

Littlefield, Louisa. 1892. "Recollections of the Prophet Joseph Smith." *Juvenile Instructor* 27, no. 1 (1 January): 24.

Littlefield, Lyman O. 1888. "Autobiography (1819–1848)." *Reminiscences of Latter-day Saints*. Logan, Utah: The Utah Journal Co.

———. 1892a. "The Prophet Joseph Smith in Zion's Camp." *Juvenile Instructor* 27, no. 1 (1 January): 56–57.

———. 1892b. "Recollections of the Prophet Joseph Smith." *Juvenile Instructor* 27, no. 2 (15 January): 64–65.

———. 1892c. "The Prophet Joseph Smith in Zion's Camp." *Juvenile Instructor* 27, no. 4 (15 February): 108–11.

Lott, Cornelius Peter. 1973. In Lorraine W. Silcox, "Zina-Forget-Me-Not: A Biographical Story." Sacramento, Calif.: N.p. Copies in private family possession.

Lovell, John. n.d. "History of John Lovell." Mormon Biography File. LDS Church Archives.

Loveless, John. n.d. "Autobiography of John Loveless." Mormon Biography File. LDS Church Archives. See also "Autobiography of John Loveless," in Kate B. Carter, comp., *Our Pioneer Heritage*, 20 vols., Salt Lake City, Utah: Daughter of Utah Pioneers, 1958–77, 12:221–26.

Loveless, Matilda E. n.d. "Grandmother Loveless." Mormon Biography File. LDS Church Archives.

Luddington, Elam. 1845. "A Short History of Elam Luddington's Life, and Travels on Missions, Oct. 16, 1845." Mormon Biography File. LDS Church Archives.

Lundwall, Nels Benjamin. 1915. "Lundwall, Nels Benjamin, 1884–1969: Correspondence, 1915." LDS Church Archives.

Lyman, Asa. 1847. "11 Sept. 1847 Death of Asa Lyman Reported by G. A. S. George A. Smith." Mormon Biography File. LDS Church Archives.

Lyman, Amasa M. 1832. Journal History, 24 August 1832. LDS Church Archives.

———. 1865a. "Amasa Lyman's History." *Latter-day Saints' Millennial Star* 27, no. 30 (29 July): 472–73.

———. 1865b. "Amasa Lyman's History." *Latter-day Saints' Millennial Star* 27, no. 31 (5 August): 487–89.

Lyman, Paulina. 1902. "Paulina Lyman, Affidavit, 31 July 1902." LDS Church Archives.

Lyman, Paulina Phelps. 1963. "Pauline Phelps Lyman." In Kate B. Carter, comp., *Our Pioneer Heritage*, 20 vols., Salt Lake City, Utah: Daughters of the Utah Pioneers, 1958–77, 6:432.

Lyon, T. Edgar. 1977–1978. "Recollections of 'Old Nauvooers': Memories from Oral History." *BYU Studies* 18, no. 2 (winter 1977–1978): 144–49.

Mace, Hiram. 1896. *Deseret Evening News*, 21 September 1896. Cited in "Autobiography of Hiram Mace," Mormon Biography File, LDS Church Archives.

Mace, Wandle. n.d. [a]. *The Journal of Wandle Mace*. Huntington Library, San Marino, California.

———. n.d. [b]. "Autobiography of Wandle Mace." Typescript copy. BYU Special Collections. Harold B. Lee Library, Provo, Utah.

———. 1964. *The Diary of Wandle Mace.* Salt Lake City, Utah: Genealogical Society of Utah.

Mack, Almira. n.d. "Benjamin Mack." Mormon Biography File. LDS Church Archives.

Marsh, Thomas Baldwin. 1864a. "History of Thomas B. Marsh." *Latter-day Saints' Millennial Star* 26, no. 24 (11 June): 375–76. Also in *Deseret News,* 24 March 1858.

———. 1864b. "History of Thomas B. Marsh." *Latter-day Saints' Millennial Star* 26, no. 25 (18 June): 390–92.

———. 1864c. "History of Thomas B. Marsh." *Latter-day Saints' Millennial Star* 26, no. 26 (25 June): 406.

Martin, Moses. 1834. Journal History. 20 May 1834. LDS Church Archives.

Martineau, Susan Ellen Johnson. 1906. "Joseph Smith, the Prophet." *Young Woman's Journal* 17, no. 12 (December): 541–42.

Mather, Frederic G. 1880. "The Early Days of Mormonism." *Lippincott's Monthly Magazine* 26 (August): 210.

Matthews, Robert J. 1975. *A Plainer Translation.* Provo, Utah: BYU Press.

Maughan, Mary Ann Weston. 1959. "Journal of Mary Ann Weston Maughan." In Kate B. Carter, comp., *Our Pioneer Heritage,* 20 vols., Salt Lake City, Utah: Daughters of the Utah Pioneers, 1958–77, 2:363–66.

Maughan, Peter. 1904. "Peter Maughan." In Orson F. Whitney, *History of Utah,* 4 vols., Salt Lake City, Utah: G. Q. Cannon & Sons Co., 4:140.

Maughan, William H. 1986. *William Harrison Maughan Family History.* Providence, Utah: Keith W. Watkins & Sons, Inc.

Mayer, George. n.d. "A Sketch of the Life of George Mayer," Mormon Biography File. LDS Church Archives.

McArthur, Daniel D. n.d. "Autobiography of Daniel D. McArthur (1820–1846)." Typescript copy. BYU Special Collections. Harold B. Lee Library, Provo, Utah.

———. 1892. "Recollections of the Prophet Joseph Smith." *Juvenile Instructor* 27, no. 4 (15 February): 128–29.

McBride, Reuben. n.d. "Statement." LDS Church Archives.

———. 1833–1834. "Journal of Reuben McBride." Microfilm of holograph. LDS Church Archives.

———. 1886. "Reuben McBride to Martha McBride Kimball, November, 1886." Photocopy of holograph. Nauvoo Restoration, Inc., Files, Nauvoo, Illinois.

McConkie, Bruce R. 1966a. "Are General Authorities Human?" LDS Institute of Religion, University of Utah, Salt Lake City, Utah, 28 October 1968.

———. 1966b. *Mormon Doctrine.* Salt Lake City, Utah: Bookcraft.

McDonald, John. n.d. "Short Sketch of the Life of John McDonald." Handwritten. Mormon Biography File. LDS Church Archives.

McDonald, William. n.d. "Autobiography of William McDonald." Mormon Biography File. LDS Church Archives.

McGuire, William W. 1886. "Statement to Andrew Jenson from W. W. McGuire, June 25, 1886." Mormon Biography File. LDS Church Archives.

McIntire, William P. n.d. *Minute Book of William Paterson McIntire.* LDS Church Archives.

McIntyre, Myron, and Noel R. Barton, ed. 1966. *Christopher Layton.* Salt Lake City, Utah: Publishers Press, by Christopher Layton Family Organization, 1966.

McKee, Persis M. Sweat. n.d. "The Life of Persis M. Sweat McKee." LDS Church Archives.

McLaughlin, Harriet C. 1926. In May McLaughlin Tanner, "Early History of Harriet Louisa Chase McLaughlin, 1926," LDS Church Archives.

McLelland, Thomas. n.d. "Thomas McLelland." Mormon Biography File. LDS Church Archives.

McLellin, William E. 1832a. "William McLellin to Relatives, 4 Aug 1832." Used by permission of Community of Christ Archives, Independence, Missouri.

———. 1832b. "William McLellin to Samuel McLellin, 4 Aug 1832." Used by permission of Community of Christ Archives, Independence, Missouri.

———. 1848. *Ensign of Liberty of the Church of Christ.* Kirtland, Ohio: [s.n.], 1847–1849.

———. 1882. "Letter from Elder W. H. Kelley." *Saints' Herald* 29, no. 5 (1 March): 67.

———. 1994. *The Journals of William E. McLellin 1831–1836.* Edited by Jan Shipps and John W. Welch. Provo, Utah.: BYU Studies, Brigham Young University, and Urbana and Chicago, Ill.: University of Illinois Press.

———. 1997. "William E. McLellin." In Susan Easton Black, *Who's Who in the Doctrine and Covenants,* Salt Lake City, Utah: Bookcraft, 190–93.

McRae, Alexander. 1854. "Letter to *Deseret News,* October 9, 1854." In Joseph Smith, *History of The Church of Jesus Christ of Latter-day Saints,* edited by B. H. Roberts, 7 vols., 2d ed., Salt Lake City, Utah: The Church of Jesus Christ of Latter-day Saints, 1932–51, 3:256.

Mendenhall, William. n.d. "William Mendenhall Memorandum." LDS Church Archives.

Merrill, Clarance. 1966. "Clarance Merrill, Pioneer." In Kate B. Carter, comp., *Our Pioneer Heritage,* 20 vols., Salt Lake City, Utah: Daughters of the Utah Pioneers, 1958–77, 9:319–20.

Merrill, Franklin. n.d. "Franklin Merrill." Mormon Biography File. LDS Church Archives.

Merrill, Mariner Wood. 1971. "Merrill, Mariner W." In Andrew Jenson, *LDS Biographical Encyclopedia,* 4 vols., Salt Lake City, Utah: Western Epics, 1:156.

Merrill, Philemon Christopher. ca. 1890. "Philemon Christopher Merrill." Mormon Biography File. LDS Church Archives.

Merrill, Rhoda Eldridge. 1963. "Rhoda Eldridge Merrill." In Kate B. Carter, comp., *Our Pioneer Heritage,* 20 vols., Salt Lake City, Utah: Daughters of the Utah Pioneers, 1958–77, 6:519–20.

Miles, Jennie B. n.d. "William P. McIntire." Mormon Biography File. LDS Church Archives.

Miles, Samuel. 1892. "Recollections of the Prophet Joseph Smith." *Juvenile Instructor* 27, no. 6 (15 March): 173–74.

———. 1971. "Miles, Samuel." In Andrew Jenson, *LDS Biographical Encyclopedia*, 4 vols., Salt Lake City, Utah: Western Epics, 1:536–37.

Miller, George. 1917. In H. W. Mills, "De Tal Palo Tal Astilla," *Annual Publications—The Historical Society of Southern California* 10 (1917): 86–172.

———. 1997. "George Miller." In Susan Easton Black, *Who's Who in the Doctrine and Covenants*, Salt Lake City, Utah: Bookcraft, 195–96.

Miller, Henry William. n.d. [a] "Henry W. Miller." Mormon Biography File. LDS Church Archives.

———. n.d. [b] "The Life Story of Henry William Miller, compiled by Arnold D. Miller Jr., His Grandson." Mormon Biography File. LDS Church Archives.

———. 1952. "William Henry Miller." In Kate B. Carter, comp., *Treasures of Pioneer History*, 6 vols., Salt Lake City, Utah: Daughters of the Utah Pioneers, 1952–57, 1:448.

Miller, Sara Jane R. n.d. "Sara Jane Rich Miller." Mormon Biography File. LDS Church Archives.

———. 1906. "Ben E. Rich to Heman C. Smith." 20 November 1906. LDS Church Archives.

Millet, Artemus. n.d. "Journal of Artemus Millet Written by Himself." LDS Church Archives.

Miner, Moroni. n.d. "Moroni Miner." Mormon Biography File. LDS Church Archives.

Moesser, Joseph H. n.d. "A Sketch of the Life of Joseph Hyrum Moesser." Mormon Biography File. LDS Church Archives.

Monson, Roxie la Preal Clap. n.d. "Biography of James Chauncey Snow." Mormon Biography File. LDS Church Archives.

Moon, Hugh. n.d. "The Book of the Life of Hugh Moon." Mormon Biography File. LDS Church Archives.

Moore, Calvin W. 1892. "Recollections of the Prophet Joseph Smith." *Juvenile Instructor* 27, no. 1 (15 April): 255.

Moore, George. 1982. In Donald Q. Cannon, "Reverend George Moore Comments on Nauvoo, the Mormons, and Joseph Smith," *Western Illinois Regional Studies* 5 (spring): 8, 10–11.

Moore, Joseph Webber. n.d. "Joseph Webber Moore." Mormon Biography File. LDS Church Archives.

Morris, George. 1816–1849. "George Morris Autobiography, 1816–1849." Typescript copy. BYU Special Collections. Harold B. Lee Library, Provo, Utah.

Morris, Rob. 1861. *The Biography of Eli Bruce, Sheriff of Niagara County, New York*. Louisville, Ky.: Morris & Monsarrat, 266–67.

Morrison, Richard W. 1956. "History of John and Sarah Mark Morrison, of Their

Travels from Ireland to Franklin, Idaho." Written 10 October 1956. Mormon Biography File. LDS Church Archives.

Moses, Julian. 1904. "Julian Moses." In Orson F. Whitney, *History of Utah*, 4 vols., Salt Lake City, Utah: G. Q. Cannon & Sons Co., 4:325.

Munson, Eliza M. A. n.d. "Early Pioneer History." Mormon Biography File. LDS Church Archives.

Murdock, John. n.d. "John Murdock Journal." Typescript copy. BYU Special Collections. Harold B. Lee Library, Provo, Utah.

Murdock, John Riggs. 1904. "John Riggs Murdock." In Orson F. Whitney, *History of Utah*, 4 vols., Salt Lake City, Utah: G. Q. Cannon & Sons Co., 4:190–91.

Murdock, Joseph S. n.d. In Sarah Cummings, "Sketch of Career of Joseph Stacy Murdock," Mormon Biography File, LDS Church Archives.

———. 1844. "Joseph Stacey Murdock to John Dougless, East Hamilton, N.Y., Jan. 24, 1844." LDS Church Archives.

Murphy, Emanuel M. 1860. *History of Brigham Young.* 30 December 1860. LDS Church Archives.

———. 1980. "A Short History of Emanuel Masters Murphy, by a Granddaughter." In Don E. Norton, *Emanuel Masters Murphy 1809–1871, Ancestry, Life, Children*, Provo, Utah: Stevenson's Genealogical Center.

Neff, John. n.d. "Neff History." Mormon Biography File. LDS Church Archives.

———. 1904. "John Neff." In Orson F. Whitney, *History of Utah*, 4 vols., Salt Lake City, Utah: G. Q. Cannon & Sons Co., 4:105.

Neff, John III. n.d. "John Neff History." Mormon Biography File. LDS Church Archives.

Nelson, Leland R. 1979. *The Journal of Joseph: The Personal History of a Modern Prophet.* Mapleton, Utah: Council Press.

Nelson, Thomas Billington. n.d. "A Sketch of the Life of Thomas Billington Nelson." Mormon Biography File. LDS Church Archives.

Nelson, William Goforth. n.d. "William Goforth Nelson." Mormon Biography File. LDS Church Archives.

———. 1906. "Joseph Smith, the Prophet." *Young Woman's Journal* 17, no. 12 (December): 542–43.

———. 1977. "Autobiography of William Goforth Nelson." In Davis Bitton, *Guide to Mormon Diaries and Autobiographies,* Provo, Utah: BYU Press.

Nickerson, Eliphalet Seneca Sullivan. n.d. "Family Record of Caroline Stewart." Microfilm of holograph. LDS Church Archives.

Nickerson, Freeman. n.d. "Freeman Nickerson." Mormon Biography File. LDS Church Archives.

Noble, Joseph B. n.d. [a]. "Autobiographical Sketch of Jos. Bates Noble." Mormon Biography File. LDS Church Archives.

———. n.d. [b]. "Joseph Bates Noble Autobiography." BYU Special Collections. Harold B. Lee Library, Provo, Utah.

———. n.d. [c]. "A Journal or Diary of Joseph Bates Noble 1810–1834." Typescript copy. BYU Special Collections. Harold B. Lee Library, Provo, Utah.

———. 1880. "Early Scenes in Church History." *Juvenile Instructor* 15, no. 10 (15 March): 112.

Noble, Mary A. n.d. [a]. "A History of Mary A. Noble." Holograph. BYU Special Collections. Harold B. Lee Library, Provo, Utah.

———. n.d. [b]. "A Journal of Mary A. Noble." In "Joseph Bates Noble Autobiography," BYU Special Collections, Harold B. Lee Library, Provo, Utah.

Noble, Susan Hammond Ashby. n.d. "A Sketch of the Life of Susan Hammond Ashby Noble by Her Daughter Louisa Adeline." Mormon Biography File. LDS Church Archives.

Norman, Mary Bailey Smith. 1914. "Reminiscences, June 24, 1914." LDS Church Archives.

Nye, Ephraim H. n.d. "Ephraim H. Nye Biographical Information." LDS Church Archives. See also Edwin F. Parry. *Stories about Joseph Smith the Prophet.* Salt Lake City, Utah: Deseret News Press, 1951, 100–102.

Oakley, John. n.d. *John Oakley Journal.* LDS Church Archives.

Oaks, Dallin H., and Marvin S. Hill. 1979. *Carthage Conspiracy: The Trial of the Accused Assassins of Joseph Smith.* Urbana, Ill.: University of Illinois Press.

Oaks, Sarah Ann Wood. 1906. *Vernal (Utah) Express.* Saturday, 3 March 1906, 1. Also in Linda M. Dursteler and Dallin H. Oaks, "The William Hyrum Oaks and Janett Bethers Family," LDS Family History Library.

Ockey, Edward. n.d. "A Short Account of the Life of Edward Ockey." Mormon Biography File. LDS Church Archives.

Openshaw, Rose. n.d. "The History of Morris Phelps." Mormon Biography File. LDS Church Archives.

Osborn [Osborne], David. n.d. "Autobiography of David Osborn." Typescript copy. BYU Special Collections. Harold B. Lee Library, Provo, Utah.

———. 1892. "Recollections of the Prophet Joseph Smith." *Juvenile Instructor* 27, no. 6 (15 March): 173.

Owens, James Clark Jr. n.d. In Irene Webb Merrill, "James Clark Owens," Mormon Biography File, LDS Church Archives.

Pace, James. n.d. "Biography of James Pace." Mormon Biography File. LDS Church Archives.

Pace, Lucinda. n.d. In Erma Pace Peterson, "Biography of Lucinda Gibson Strickland Pace," in Gordon H. Wright, "History of James Pace, Born June 15, 1811—Died April 6, 1888," LDS Family History Library.

Pace, William B. n.d. "William Pace Autobiography." Typescript copy. BYU Special Collections. Harold B. Lee Library, Provo, Utah.

Pack, Julia Ives. 1966. "Julia Ives Pack Autobiography." In Kate B. Carter, comp., *Our Pioneer Heritage,* 20 vols., Salt Lake City, Utah: Daughters of the Utah Pioneers, 1958–77, 9:450.

Pack, Ward Eaton. 1937. "Sketch of the Life of Julia Ives Pack, Utah Pioneer of 1847.

Prepared by her Granddaughter, Myrtle Pack Ure." Daughters of the Utah Pioneers, Salt Lake City, Utah.

Packard, Nephi. 1904. "Nephi Packard." In Orson F. Whitney, *History of Utah*, 4 vols., Salt Lake City, Utah: G. Q. Cannon & Sons Co., 4:518.

Packard, Noah. n.d. "Noah Packard Autobiography." Typescript copy. BYU Special Collections. Harold B. Lee Library, Provo, Utah.

———. 1997. "Noah Packard." In Susan Easton Black, *Who's Who in the Doctrine and Covenants*, Salt Lake City, Utah: Bookcraft, 205.

Page, John E. 1865. "History of John E. Page." *Latter-day Saints' Millennial Star* 27, no. 7 (18 February): 103.

Palmer, James. n.d. "Reminiscences." LDS Church Archives.

Palmer, Mrs. n.d. "Stories from Notebook of Martha Cox, Grandmother of Fern Cox Anderson." LDS Church Archives.

Parker, John Davis. 1880. "Affidavit, Sept. 3, 1880." LDS Church Archives.

Parker, Joseph Falconer. n.d. "Joseph Falconer Parker (1841–1936) Collection 1848–1935." LDS Church Archives.

Parrish, Caddie Rich. n.d. "Abel Morgan Sargent." Mormon Biography File. LDS Church Archives.

Partridge, Edward. 1958. In Lucy Mack Smith, *History of Joseph Smith*, Salt Lake City, Utah: Bookcraft.

Patten, George. n.d. "A Short Sketch of the Life of Geo[rge] Patten." Mormon Biography File. LDS Church Archives.

———. n.d. "Statement." Mormon Biography File. LDS Church Archives.

———. 1971. "Patten, George." In Andrew Jenson, *LDS Biographical Encyclopedia*, 4 vols., Salt Lake City, Utah: Western Epics, 2:157.

Patten, Joanna Hollister. n.d. "A Biographical Sketch of the Life of Joanna Hollister Patten." Mormon Biography File. LDS Church Archives.

Pay, Mary Goble. 1974. "Death Strikes the Handcart Company." In Richard H. Cracroft and Neal E. Lambert, *A Believing People: Literature of the Latter-day Saints*, Provo, Utah: BYU Press, 143–150.

Peart, Jacob. n.d. "Autobiographical Sketch of Jacob Peart." Mormon Biography File. LDS Church Archives.

Peart, Jacob Haldon. 1904. "Jacob Peart." In Orson F. Whitney, *History of Utah*, 4 vols., Salt Lake City, Utah: G. Q. Cannon & Sons Co., 4:383.

———. n.d. "History of Jacob Haldon Peart." Mormon Biography File. LDS Church Archives.

Peirce, Eli Harvey. n.d. "Eli Harvey Peirce." Mormon Biography File. LDS Church Archives.

Perry, Orin Alonzo. 1904. "Orin Alonzo Perry." In Orson F. Whitney, *History of Utah*, 4 vols., Salt Lake City, Utah: G. Q. Cannon & Sons Co., 4:440.

Perry, Philander Jackson. n.d. "Biographical Sketch of Philander Jackson Perry." Mormon Biography File. LDS Church Archives.

Perry, Sylvester Lyman. n.d. "Sylvester Lyman Perry." Mormon Biography File. LDS Church Archives.

Peterson, Erma Pace. n.d. "Biography of Lucinda Gibson Strickland Pace." In Gordon H. Wright, "History of James Pace, Born June 15, 1811—Died April 6, 1888," LDS Family History Library.

Phelps, Morris Calvin. n.d. "Laura Clark." Mormon Biography File. LDS Church Archives.

Phelps, William W. n.d. "Joseph Smith's Last Dream." LDS Church Archives.

———. 1835a. Journal History. 2 June 1835. LDS Church Archives.

———. 1835b. "William Phelps Letter, 19–20 July 1835." In Leah Y. Phelps, "Letters of Faith from Kirtland," in *Improvement Era* 45, no. 8 (August 1942): 529.

———. 1940. "Letters of W. W. Phelps." *Utah Genealogical and Historical Magazine* 31 (January): 26.

Phillips, Edward. 1889. In Sylvia Phillips, "Biographical Sketch of Edward Phillips, Written by Sylvia Phillips in 1889 from Dictation," Mormon Biography File, LDS Church Archives.

———. 1904. "Edward Phillips." In Orson F. Whitney, *History of Utah,* 4 vols., Salt Lake City, Utah: G. Q. Cannon & Sons Co., 4:385–86.

Phillips, Hannah Simmonds. n.d. In Hannah Maria Phillips Layton, "Brief Sketch of the Life of Hannah Simmonds Phillips," Mormon Biography File, LDS Church Archives.

Phippen, James W. 1892. "Recollections of the Prophet Joseph Smith." *Juvenile Instructor* 27, no. 1 (1 January): 24.

———. 1906. "Joseph Smith, the Prophet." *Young Woman's Journal* 17, no. 12 (December): 540.

Pomeroy, Sarah M. 1906. "Joseph Smith, the Prophet." *Young Woman's Journal* 17, no. 12 (December): 538–39.

Porter, Larry C., and Susan Easton Black, ed. 1988. *The Prophet Joseph Smith: Essays on the Life and Mission of Joseph Smith.* Salt Lake City, Utah: Deseret Book.

Porter, Nathan Tanner. ca. 1879. "Reminiscences." Microfilm of holograph. LDS Church Archives.

Potter, Amasa. n.d. "Amasa Potter Life History (Written by a Son of Amasa Potter)." Mormon Biography File. LDS Church Archives.

———. 1857. "Reminiscences and Journal of Amasa Potter, Jan. 1857—Jan. 1910." Microfilm of holograph. LDS Church Archives.

———. 1894. "A Reminiscence of the Prophet Joseph Smith." *Juvenile Instructor* 29, no. 4 (15 February): 131–32.

Poulson, P. W. 1878. "P. W. Poulson to Editors of *The Deseret News.*" *Deseret News,* 16 August 1878, 2.

Pratt, Orson. 1871. "Minutes of the School of the Prophets in Salt Lake City, January 14, 1871." LDS Church Archives. Cited in Robert J. Matthews, "The Prophet Translates the Bible by the Spirit of Revelation," in Larry C. Porter and Susan

Easton Black, ed., *The Prophet Joseph Smith: Essays on the Life and Mission of Joseph Smith,* Salt Lake City, Utah: Deseret Book, 1988.

———. 1975. *The Orson Pratt Journals.* Compiled by Elden J. Watson. Salt Lake City: Elden Jay Watson, Publisher.

———. 1979. "Orson Pratt to Parley P. Pratt, 1853." LDS Church Archives. Cited in Anonymous, *John Lathrop (1584–1653): Reformer, Sufferer, Pilgrim, Man of God,* Salt Lake City, Utah: Institute of Family Research.

Pratt, Parley P. 1952. In Parker Pratt Robison, *Writings of Parley Parker Pratt.* Salt Lake City, Utah: Parker Pratt Robison.

———. 1965. *Key to the Science of Theology.* Salt Lake City, Utah: Deseret Book.

———. 1985. *Autobiography of Parley P. Pratt.* Salt Lake City, Utah: Deseret Book.

Preston, Harriet A. 1920. "A Moment of Peace." *Relief Society Magazine* 7, no. 1 (January): 17–19.

Pugmire, Budge. 1961. "William Budge—Captain." In Kate B. Carter, comp., *Our Pioneer Heritage,* 20 vols., Salt Lake City, Utah: Daughters of the Utah Pioneers, 1958–77, 4:63.

Pugmire, Jonathan. n.d. "Jonathan Pugmire." Mormon Biography File. LDS Church Archives.

Pulsipher, John. n.d. "John Pulsipher Autobiography." BYU Special Collections. Harold B. Lee Library, Provo, Utah.

Pulsipher, Sariah Robbins. 1906. "Joseph Smith, the Prophet." *Young Woman's Journal* 17, no. 12 (December): 545–46.

Pulsipher, Zerah. n.d. "Autobiography of Zerah Pulsipher." Typescript copy. BYU Special Collections. Harold B. Lee Library, Provo, Utah.

———. 1950. "Early Life and Ministry of Zerah Pulsipher." In N. B. Lundwall, *Faith Like the Ancients,* 2 vols., Manti, Utah: Mountain Valley Publishers.

Quincy, Josiah. 1857. "The Mormons and Their Prophet—Mr. Quincy's Lecture." *New York Daily Times,* 14 January 1857, 4.

———. 1883. *Figures of the Past from the Leaves of Old Journals.* Boston: Roberts Brothers.

Quincy Whig. 1840. *Quincy (Illinois) Whig,* 17 October 1840, 1. Also in Milton R. Hunter, *Pearl of Great Price Commentary,* Salt Lake City, Utah: Stevens and Wallis, Inc., 1948, 16.

Ralphs, Sarah Johnson. n.d. "Thomas Ralphs and Sarah Johnson Ralphs, Pioneers of 1849." Mormon Biography File. LDS Church Archives.

Randall, Alfred. n.d. "My Grandfather Alfred Randall." Mormon Biography File. LDS Church Archives.

Rawson, Eliza Jane Cheney. n.d. "A Biographical Sketch on the Life of Eliza Jane Cheney Rawson." Mormon Biography File. LDS Church Archives.

Rawson, Horace Strong. n.d. "A Short Sketch of Biography of Horace S. Rawson." Mormon Biography File. LDS Church Archives.

Reed, Ira. n.d. "Ira Reed." Mormon Biography File. LDS Church Archives.

Remington, Lydia Ripley Badger. n.d. "Life Sketch of Mrs. Lydia R. Badger Remington." Mormon Biographical File. LDS Church Archives.

Reynolds, George. 1891. "Lessons from the Life of Nephi." *Juvenile Instructor* 26, no. 15 (1 August): 476–77.

———. 1892. "The Jaredites, Part II." *Juvenile Instructor* 27, no. 9 (1 May): 282. Also cited in *Improvement Era* 8, no. 9 (July 1905): 704–5.

Reynolds, John. 1879. *My Own Times.* Chicago, Ill.: Chicago Historical Society, Fergus Printing Company.

Rich, Ben E. 1908. "Benjamin Erastus Rich [1855–1913] Correspondence, 1881–1908." LDS Church Archives.

Rich, Emmeline Grover. 1906. "Joseph Smith, the Prophet." *Young Woman's Journal* 17, no. 12 (December): 543.

Rich, Mary A. n.d. "The Life of Mary A. Rich." Typescript copy. BYU Special Collections. Harold B. Lee Library, Provo, Utah.

Rich, Sara DeArmon Pea. n.d. "Autobiography of Sarah DeArmon Rich." Compiled by Alice M. Rich. Typescript copy. BYU Special Collections. Harold B. Lee Library, Provo, Utah.

Richards, Jane S. 1880. "Reminiscences of Mrs. F. D. [Jane Snyder] Richards." San Fransisco, 1880. Bancroft Library, University of California, Berkeley.

———. 1904. "Jane Snyder Richards." In Orson F. Whitney, *History of Utah,* 4 vols., Salt Lake City, Utah: G. Q. Cannon & Sons Co., 4:581–82.

———. 1905. "Joseph Smith, the Prophet." *Young Woman's Journal* 16, no. 12 (December): 550.

Richards, John Kenny. n.d. "An History of the Richards Family by Joseph Hill Richards, September 7, 1923." Mormon Biography File. LDS Church Archives.

Richards, Louisa Lulu Greene. 1904. "Louisa Lula Greene Richards." In Orson F. Whitney, *History of Utah,* 4 vols., Salt Lake City, Utah: G. Q. Cannon & Sons Co., 4:598.

Richards, Samuel W. n.d. "What Joseph Smith Looked Like." From a note found in an old book belonging to Samuel W. Richards, LDS Church Archives.

———. 1903. "Samuel W. Richards Affidavit, Sworn Dec. 11, 1903." LDS Church Archives.

———. 1907. "Joseph Smith, the Prophet." *Young Woman's Journal* 18, no. 12 (December): 537–39.

Richards, Willard. 1865. "History of Willard Richards." *Latter-day Saints' Millennial Star* 27, no. 9 (4 March): 133–36.

———. 1997. In Susan Easton Black, *Who's Who in the Doctrine and Covenants,* Salt Lake City, Utah: Bookcraft.

Ricks, Sara Beriah Fiske Allen. n.d. "A Brief Sketch of the Life of Sarah Beriah Fiske Allen Ricks." Mormon Biography File. LDS Church Archives.

Riggs, John. n.d. *Autobiographical Sketch.* LDS Church Archives.

———. 1884. "Dr. John Riggs." In "History of Provo," *Tullidge's Quarterly Magazine* 3, no. 3 (July): 282–83.

Riser, George C. n.d. "Reminiscences of George Christian Riser 1818–1892." LDS Church Archives.

Roberts, Brigham Henry. 1930. *A Comprehensive History of The Church of Jesus Christ of Latter-day Saints, Century One.* 6 vols. Salt Lake City, Utah: The Church of Jesus Christ of Latter-day Saints.

———. 1963. *The Life of John Taylor.* Salt Lake City, Utah: Bookcraft.

Robey, Jeremiah Sr. 1951. "Jeremiah Robey, Sr." In Kate B. Carter, comp., *Heart Throbs of the West,* 12 vols., Salt Lake City, Utah: Daughters of the Utah Pioneers, 1939–51, 12:394.

Robinson, Ebenezer. 1890. "Autobiography (1832–1843)." In *The Return, vols. 1–3* (1888–1890), 58, 115, 149, 206, 243, 258–59.

Robinson, Joseph L. n.d. "Historical Record of Joseph Lee Robinson." Mormon Biography File. LDS Church Archives.

———. 1974. In Hyrum L. Andrus and Helen Mae Andrus, *They Knew the Prophet,* Salt Lake City, Utah: Bookcraft.

Rockwell, Orrin Porter. n.d. "Elizabeth D. E. Roundy to President Spencer Clawson, President [of the] Semi Centennial Jubilee Committee." Mormon Biography File. LDS Church Archives.

———. 1966. In Harold Schindler, *Orrin Porter Rockwell: Man of God, Son of Thunder,* Salt Lake City, Utah: University of Utah Press.

Rockwood, Albert P. 1971. "Rockwood, Albert P." In Andrew Jenson, *LDS Biographical Encyclopedia,* 4 vols., Salt Lake City, Utah: Western Epics, 1:194.

Rogers, Aurelia S. 1898. *Life Sketches of Orson Spencer and Others, and History of Primary Work.* Salt Lake City, Utah: George Q. Cannon & Sons Company.

Rogers, David White. 1839. "Statement 1 Feb. 1839." LDS Church Archives.

Rogers, Thomas Edward. 1915. "Thomas Rogers." 11 November 1915. Mormon Biography File. LDS Church Archives.

———. 1967. "The Minuteman." In Kate B. Carter, comp., *Our Pioneer Heritage,* 20 vols., Salt Lake City, Utah: Daughters of the Utah Pioneers, 1958–77, 10:95.

Rollins, James H. n.d. "A Life Sketch of James Henry Rollins (1816–1839)." Typescript copy. BYU Special Collections. Harold B. Lee Library, Provo, Utah.

Rose, Abraham. 1964. "From His Records." In Kate B. Carter, comp., *Our Pioneer Heritage,* 20 vols., Salt Lake City, Utah: Daughters of the Utah Pioneers, 7:234–35.

Rosenthall, Vernice Gold. n.d. "Biography of Martin Horton Peck." Mormon Biography File. LDS Church Archives.

Ross, Ellen Jane Koyle. n.d. "John Hyrum Koyle, Senior." Personal history. Copies in private family possession.

Roundy, Shadrach. n.d. "Shadrach Roundy." Mormon Biography File. LDS Church Archives.

———. 1971. "Roundy, Shadrach." In Andrew Jenson, *LDS Biographical Encyclopedia,* 4 vols., Salt Lake City, Utah: Western Epics, 1:642–43.

Rushton, Edwin. n.d. "Edwin Rushton Statement." LDS Church Archives.

———. 1974. "Edwin Rushton (Related by His Son)." In Hyrum L. Andrus and Helen Mae Andrus, *They Knew the Prophet*. Salt Lake City, Utah: Bookcraft.

Russell, Isaac. n.d. In Isabella M. Johnson, "Isaac Russell," Mormon Biography File, LDS Church Archives.

Rust, George Smith. n.d. "Brief Biographical Sketch of George Smith Rust." Mormon Biography File. LDS Church Archives.

Rust, William W. n.d. "William Walker Rust." Mormon Biography File. LDS Church Archives.

Saint Louis Weekly Reveille. 1844. Monday Morning (15 July), 7.

Salisbury, Herbert S. 1945. "Things the Prophet's Sister Told Me." 30 June 1945. Typescript copy. LDS Church Archives.

Salisbury, Catherine S. 1865. "Katherine Salisbury to 'Dear Nephews' John, Joseph F., and Samuel H. B. Smith, Sept. 11, 1865." BYU Special Collections. Harold B. Lee Library, Provo, Utah.

———. 1881. "Katherine Smith Salisbury, Affidavit, 15 April 1881." Artificial Collection, Community of Christ Archives, Independence, Missouri. Published in *Saints' Herald* 28, no. 11 (1 June): 169. Also cited in Dan Vogel, comp., *Early Mormon Documents*. Salt Lake City, Utah: Signature Books, 1996, 1:519–20.

———. 1886. "Katherine Salisbury to Dear Sisters, 10 March 1886." *Saints' Herald* 33, no. 17 (1 May): 260. Also in Dan Vogel, comp., *Early Mormon Documents*. Salt Lake City, Utah: Signature Books, 1996, 1:521–22.

———. 1891. In Warren Lovel Van Dine, "Biographical Sketch of Catherine Smith Salisbury," *Carthage Republican,* 16 May 1891, microfilm, LDS Church Archives.

———. 1945. In Herbert S. Salisbury, "Things the Prophet's Sister Told Me," 30 June 1945, typescript copy, LDS Church Archives.

Sanderson, Henry Weeks. n.d. "History of Henry Weeks Sanderson." LDS Church Archives.

Sanderson, James. n.d. "James Sanderson." Typescript copy. LDS Church Archives.

Saunders, Orlando. 1881. In William H. Kelley and E. L. Kelley, "Interview with Orlando Saunders and Dr. John Stafford, March, 1881," *Saints' Herald* 28, no. 11 (1 June): 165. Also in *Juvenile Instructor* 17, no. 19 (1 October 1882): 301–2.

Scott, Jacob. 1842a)."Jacob Scott to Mary Warnock, February 28, 1842." LDS Church Archives. Used by permission of Community of Christ Archives, Independence, Missouri.

———. 1842b. "Jacob Scott to Mary Warnock, March 24, 1842." LDS Church Archives. Used by permission of Community of Christ Archives, Independence, Missouri.

———. 1844. "Jacob Scott to Mary Warnock, January 5, 1844." LDS Church Archives.

Searles, Asa. 1893. *Recollections of the Pioneers of Lee County (Illinois)*. Edited by Seraphina G. Smith. Dixon, Ill.: I. A. Kennedy.

Seeley, Clarissa Jane Wilcox. 1988. In Montell and Kathryn Seely, *Seely History,* Provo, Utah: Community Press.

Sessions, Perrigrine. 1904. "Perrigrine Sessions." In Orson F. Whitney, *History of Utah,* 4 vols., Salt Lake City, Utah: G. Q. Cannon & Sons Co., 4:103.

Sewell, James. n.d. "James Sewell Notebook (1853–1886)." LDS Church Archives.

Shirts, Ambrose. 1958. "History of Peter Shirts (Shurtz) and His Descendants." Copies in private family possession.

Shirts [Shurtz], Peter. n.d. "Peter Shirts (Shurtz)." Mormon Biography File. LDS Church Archives.

Shurtliff, Luman Andros. n.d. "Biographical Sketch of the Life of Luman Andros Shurtliff." Typescript copy. BYU Special Collections. Harold B. Lee Library, Provo, Utah.

Sirrine, Mephibosheth. n.d. In Warren L. Sirrine, "The Life of George Warren Sirrine," Mormon Biography File, LDS Church Archives.

Smith, Bathsheba W. n.d. "Autobiography of Bathsheba W. Smith." Typescript copy. BYU Special Collections. Harold B. Lee Library, Provo, Utah.

———. 1844. "Bathsheba W. Smith to George A. Smith." 6 July 1844. In Kenneth W. Godfrey, Audrey M. Godfrey, and Jill Mulvay Derr, *Women's Voices: An Untold History of the Latter-day Saints, 1830–1900,* Salt Lake City, Utah: Deseret Book, 1982, 132.

———. 1892. "Recollections of the Prophet Joseph Smith." *Juvenile Instructor* 27, no. 11 (1 June): 344–45.

———. 1905. "Joseph Smith, the Prophet." *Young Woman's Journal* 16, no. 12 (December): 549–50.

Smith, Elias. n.d. In Sarah C. Thomas, comp. *Elias Smith Journals 1804–1888,* 3 vols. LDS Church Archives.

———. 1971. "Smith, Elias." In Andrew Jenson, *LDS Biographical Encyclopedia,* 4 vols., Salt Lake City, Utah: Western Epics, 1:720.

Smith, Emma Hale. 1879. Joseph Smith III, "Last Testimony of Sister Emma." *Saints' Herald* 26, no. 19 (1 October): 289–90.

———. 1884. In E. C. Briggs, "Brother Joseph Smith," *Saints' Herald* 31, no. 25 (21 June): 396–97.

Smith, George A. n.d. "Memoirs of George A. Smith." Typescript copy. BYU Special Collections. Harold B. Lee Library, Provo, Utah.

———. 1869a. *Deseret News,* 30 June 1869, 247–48.

———. 1869b. *Deseret Theological School American Fork City Record Book, 1868–1869.* LDS Church Archives.

———. 1938. In Joseph Fielding Smith, *Life of Joseph F. Smith,* Salt Lake City, Utah: Deseret Book.

Smith, Hyrum. 1832–33. "Hyrum Smith Diary, 18 Nov. 1832–18 April 1833." BYU Special Collections. Harold B. Lee Library, Provo, Utah.

———. 1835–38. "Hyrum Smith Book of Records 1835–38." BYU Special Collections. Harold B. Lee Library, Provo, Utah.

Smith, Israel A. 1955. "The Inspired Version." *Saints' Herald* (14 November): 5–7, 21. Also cited in Robert J. Matthews, *A Plainer Translation,* Provo, Utah: BYU Press, 1975, 100.

Smith, Jesse Nathaniel. 1834–1906. "Autobiography and Journal of Jesse Nathaniel Smith 1834–1906." LDS Church Archives.

———. 1892. "Recollections of the Prophet Joseph Smith." *Juvenile Instructor* 27, no. 1 (1 January): 23–24.

———. 1894. "Jesse Nathaniel Smith (1834–1906) Statement 15 February 1894." LDS Church Archives.

Smith, Job F. n.d. [a]. *Diary of Job Smith, a Pioneer of Nauvoo, Ill., and Utah,* Typescript copy. Huntington Library, San Marino, California.

———. n.d. [b]. "My Recollections of the Prophet During the Last Year of His Life, from a Manuscript Written by Job Smith." LDS Church Archives.

Smith, John. n.d. *Journal Entries from the Journal of John Smith.* BYU Special Collections. Harold B. Lee Library, Provo, Utah.

Smith, John L. 1832. "Journals of John Lyman Smith, Born November 17, 1832, Son of John Smith, a Cousin to the Prophet Joseph Smith." Microfilm of holograph. LDS Church Archives.

———. 1892. "Recollections of the Prophet Joseph Smith." *Juvenile Instructor* 27, no. 6 (15 March): 172–73.

Smith, Joseph. 1976. *Teachings of the Prophet Joseph Smith.* Compiled by Joseph Fielding Smith. Salt Lake City, Utah: Deseret Book.

Smith, Joseph III. 1909. "Joseph Smith III to John Smith, Patriarch, Dec. 20, 1909." BYU Special Collections. Harold B. Lee Library, Provo, Utah.

———. 1910. "What Do I Remember of Nauvoo?" *Journal of History* 3, no. 2 (April): 132, 133–136, 138, 139, 142, 143, 334–38. Lamoni, Iowa: Reorganized Church of Jesus Christ of Latter-day Saints.

Smith, Joseph F. 1898. "Shall We Record Testimony?" *Improvement Era* 1, no. 5 (March): 372.

———. 1910. *Liahona* 7, no. 47 (14 May): 752–53. Also cited in Preston Nibley, *Faith Promoting Stories,* Independence, Mo.: Zion's Printing and Publishing Co., c.1943, 7–8.

———. 1916. "Boyhood Reflections of President Joseph F. Smith." *Utah Genealogical and Historical Magazine* 7 (April): 53–58.

———. 1918. Conference Report of The Church of Jesus Christ of Latter day Saints, October 1918.

———. 1968. In Hugh Nibley, "A New Look at the Pearl of Great Price, Part I: Challenge and Response (Continued)," *Improvement Era* 71, no. 3 (March): 17–18.

———. 1981. "Joseph F. Smith to E. Wesley Smith, June 17, 1909." In Hyrum M. Smith III and Scott G. Kenney, *From Prophet to Son,* Salt Lake City, Utah: Deseret Book, 111.

Smith, Joseph F., John R. Winder, and Anthon H. Lund. 1909. "The Origin of Man." *Improvement Era* 13, no. 1 (November): 75–81.

Smith, Joseph Fielding. 1967. *Doctrines of Salvation*. Compiled by Bruce R. McConkie. 3 vols. Salt Lake City, Utah: Bookcraft.

Smith, Lucy Mack. 1845. "Lucy Mack Smith Remarks." October Conference. LDS Church Archives. Also in Joseph Smith, *History of the Church of Jesus Christ of Latter-day Saints*, edited by B. H. Roberts, 7 vols., 2d ed., Salt Lake City, Utah: The Church of Jesus Christ of Latter-day Saints, 1932–51, 7:470–472.

———. 1892. In Samuel W. Richards, "Duty of Marriage," *The Contributor* 13, no. 4 (February): 165–68.

———. 1920. "Minutes of a Meeting of the Richards and Young Families held in Nauvoo, Ill., Jan. 8, 1845." *Utah Genealogical and Historical Magazine* 11 (July): 116–17.

———. 1958. *History of Joseph Smith*. Salt Lake City, Utah: Bookcraft.

Smith, Lucy Meserve. 1888–89. "The Papers of Lucy M. Smith, wife of George A. Smith, Daughter of Josiah Smith and Lucy Misserve Smith." Handwritten copy with one or two word changes. LDS Church Archives. Also in "Original Historical Narrative of Lucy Meserve Smith, Salt Lake City, Utah, August 14, 1888–9, Written by Herself," Mormon Biography File, LDS Church Archives.

———. 1892. "Recollections of the Prophet Joseph Smith." *Juvenile Instructor* 27, no. 15 (1 August): 470–71.

Smith, Mary Fielding. ca. 1837a. "Mary Fielding to Mercy Thompson, circa Sept. 1, 1837." In Kenneth W. Godfrey, Audrey M. Godfrey, and Jill Mulvay Derr, *Woman's Voices: An Untold History of the Latter-day Saints, 1830–1900*, Salt Lake City, Utah: Deseret Book, 1982, 64–67.

———. ca. 1837b. "Mary Fielding to Robert B. and Mercy Thompson, circa Oct. 7, 1837." In Kenneth W. Godfrey, Audrey M. Godfrey, and Jill Mulvay Derr, *Woman's Voices: An Untold History of the Latter-day Saints, 1830–1900*, Salt Lake City, Utah: Deseret Book, 1982, 67–68.

———. ca. 1837c. "Mary Fielding Smith to Mercy R. Thompson." Circa November 1837. In "A Valuable Document," *Young Woman's Journal* 2, no. 8 (May 1891): 378–79.

Smith, Ruby K. n.d. "Margaret Gay Judd Clawson." Mormon Biography File. LDS Church Archives.

Smith, Willard G. n.d. In Cordelia Smith Reeder Ellingford, "Biography of Willard Gilbert Smith," Mormon Biography File, LDS Church Archives.

Smith, William. 1865. "History of William Smith." *Latter-day Saints' Millennial Star* 27, no. 1 (7 January): 7–8.

———. 1883. *William Smith on Mormonism*. Lamoni, Iowa: Herald Steam Book and Job Office.

———. 1884. "The Old Soldier's Testimony." *Saints' Herald* 31, no. 40 (4 October): 643–44.

———. 1891. "Another Testimony." *Deseret Evening News*, 20 January 1891.

———. 1894. "William B. Smith's Last Statement." *Zion's Ensign,* 13 January 1894, 6.

Smoot, Margaret S. n.d. *Autobiography.* Bancroft Library, University of California, Berkeley, California. See also microfilm of holograph, LDS Church Archives.

Snow, Eliza R. 1880a. "R. S. Reports." *Woman's Exponent* 9, no. 7 (1 September): 54.

———. 1880b. In M. F. C. Morrison and A. Louise Hasler, "Report of the Meeting Held in Mt. Pleasant, San Pete County, August 7, 1880," *Woman's Exponent* 9, no. 9 (1 October): 71.

———. 1884. *Biography and Family Record of Lorenzo Snow.* Salt Lake City, Utah: Deseret News Co., Printers.

———. 1916. "The Mother of Mothers in Israel: Eliza R. Snow." *Relief Society Magazine* 3, no. 4 (April): 184.

———. 1944a. "Sketch of My Life." *Relief Society Magazine* 31, no. 3 (March): 131–34. Also in *Eliza R. Snow: An Immortal,* Salt Lake City, Utah: Nicholas G. Morgan Sr. Foundation, 1957.

———. 1944b. "Sketch of My Life." *Relief Society Magazine* 31, no. 4 (April): 207–13.

———. 1944c. "Sketch of My Life." *Relief Society Magazine* 31, no. 9 (September): 504.

———. 1978. In Chris R. Arrington,"The Finest of Fabrics: Mormon Women and the Silk Industry in Early Utah," in *Utah Historical Quarterly* 46, no. 4 (fall): 378. Originally found in *Deseret News,* 1 August 1876.

Snow, Erastus. 1923. In Franklin R. Snow, "Autobiography of Erastus Snow," *Utah Genealogical and Historical Magazine* 14 (April): 106–10.

———. 1912. "Erastus Snow." *Utah Genealogical and Historical Magazine* 3 (January): 30–31.

Snow, Eunice B. 1910a. "A Sketch of the Life of Eunice Billings Snow." *Woman's Exponent* 39, no. 2 (August): 13–14. Also cited in Hyrum L. Andrus and Helen Mae Andrus, *They Knew the Prophet,* Salt Lake City, Utah: Bookcraft, 1974, 152–53.

———. 1910b. "A Sketch of the Life of Eunice Billings Snow." *Woman's Exponent* 39, no. 3 (September): 22–23. Also cited in Hyrum L. Andrus and Helen Mae Andrus, *They Knew the Prophet,* Salt Lake City, Utah: Bookcraft, 1974, 152–53.

Snow, James Chaney. n.d. "Journal of James Chaney Snow, 1817–1837." LDS Church Archives.

———. 1971. "Snow, James Chaney." In Andrew Jenson, *LDS Biographical Encyclopedia,* 4 vols., Salt Lake City, Utah: Western Epics, 1:795.

Snow, Lorenzo. 1919. In LeRoi C. Snow, "Devotion to a Divine Inspiration," *Improvement Era* 22, no. 8 (June): 656. Also in Thomas C. Romney, *The Life of Lorenzo Snow,* Salt Lake City, Utah: S.U.P. Memorial Foundation, 1955, 35.

———. 1937. In LeRoi C. Snow, "How Lorenzo Snow Found God," *Improvement Era* 40, no. 2 (February): 82–84, 105.

Somerville, William. n.d. [a]. "History of William Somerville." In Oscar W. McConkie, Memorabilia. Copies in private family possession.

———. n.d. [b]. In Loras Burke Tangren, "A Record of William Somerville, Son of Andrew Somerville and Margaret Fuller, born near Lanarchshire, Scotland, April 4, 1817," LDS Church Archives.

Speirs, Adam. 1904. "Adam Speirs." In Orson F. Whitney, *History of Utah,* 4 vols., Salt Lake City, Utah: G. Q. Cannon & Sons Co., 4:555.

Speirs, Harriet. 1927. "A Biography of William Strong, a Member of the Mormon Battalion," June–July 1927. Mormon Biography File. LDS Church Archives.

Sperry, Charles. n.d. "A Sketch of the Life and History of Charles Sperry, the Son of Jay Sperry and Mary Lamont Who were Married April 26, 1810." LDS Church Archives.

Spilsbury, George. 1904. "George Spilsbury." In Orson F. Whitney, *History of Utah,* 4 vols., Salt Lake City, Utah: G. Q. Cannon & Sons Co., 4:400.

Stafford, John. 1881. In William H. Kelley and E. L. Kelley, "Interview with Orlando Saunders and Dr. John Stafford, March, 1881," *Saints' Herald* 28, no. 11 (1 June): 165. Also in *Juvenile Instructor* 17, no. 19 (1 October 1882): 301–2.

Staines, William C. 1891. "Reminiscences of William C. Staines." *The Contributor* 12, no. 4 (February): 121–23.

———. 1904. "William C. Staines." In Orson F. Whitney, *History of Utah,* 4 vols., Salt Lake City, Utah: G. Q. Cannon & Sons Co., 4:117–18. Also in "William Staines," Mormon Biography File, LDS Church Archives.

Steed, Laura Lucinda Reed. 1971. "Steed, Laura." In Andrew Jenson, *LDS Biographical Encyclopedia,* 4 vols., Salt Lake City, Utah: Western Epics, 3:247–48.

Stevens, Lyman. n.d. "History of Lyman Stevens." Mormon Biography File. LDS Church Archives.

Stevenson, Edward. 1877. Journal History. 23 December 1877. LDS Church Archives.

———. 1878a. Journal History. 7 January 1878. LDS Church Archvies.

———. 1878b. "Edward Stevenson to the Editors of the *Salt Lake Herald,* 21 January 1878."

———. 1894a. "The Home of My Boyhood." *Juvenile Instructor* 29, no. 14 (15 July): 443–45.

———. 1894b. "Incidents of My Early Life." *Juvenile Instructor* 29, no. 18 (15 September): 570.

———. 1904. "Edward Stevenson." In Orson F. Whitney, *History of Utah,* 4 vols., Salt Lake City, Utah: G. Q. Cannon & Sons Co., 4:115.

———. 1974. In Hyrum L. Andrus and Helen Mae Andrus, *They Knew the Prophet,* Salt Lake City, Utah: Bookcraft,

Stevenson, Joseph Grant. 1955. "The Life of Edward Stevenson." Master's thesis. Provo, Utah: Brigham Young University.

Stewart, Andrew Jackson. 1908. "Scraps from an Old Timer's Journal." LDS Church Archives.

Stoddard, Charles H. 1949. In Hannah R. Stoddard, "Hannah Rebecca Larson Stoddard, Affidavit, Oct. 15, 1949," LDS Church Archives.

Stout, Allen Joseph. n.d. "Journal of Allen Joseph Stout (1815–1848)." Typescript copy. BYU Special Collections. Harold B. Lee Library, Provo, Utah.

Stout, Hosea. n.d. "Diary of Hosea Stout (1844–1870)." 8 vols. Typescript copy. BYU Special Collections. Harold B. Lee Library, Provo, Utah, 1:6–7, 23.

———. 1887. "Statement by Hosea Stout, Sept. 1887." LDS Church Archives.

Stout, Wayne. 1941. "Allen Joseph Stout: A Great Champion of Mormonism." Mormon Biography File. LDS Church Archives.

———. 1941. "Asenath Slafter Janes." LDS Church Archives.

Stowell, William Rufus Rogers. 1893. In James A. Little, "Biography of William Rufus Rogers Stowell, 1893," LDS Church Archives.

Strickland, Lucinda Gibson. n.d. "Biography of Lucinda Gibson Strickland." LDS Church Archives.

Strong, Ezra. 1882. "Ezra Strong Notebook (ca. 1882–1884)." LDS Church Archives.

Taggart, George W. 2001. In Ronald O. Barney, "'A Man That You Could Not Help Likeing,' Joseph Smith and Nauvoo Portrayed in a Letter by Susannah and George Taggart," *BYU Studies* 40, no. 2 (2001): 165–79.

Taggart, Richmond. 1833. "Rev. Richmond Taggart to Rev. R. Goings, March 2, 1833." LDS Church Archives.

Tanner, John. n.d. "John Tanner." Mormon Biography File. LDS Church Archives.

———. 1904. "Joseph Smith Tanner." In Orson F. Whitney, *History of Utah,* 4 vols., Salt Lake City, Utah: G. Q. Cannon & Sons Co., 4:379.

Tanner, Mary Jane Mount. 1972. "'Personal History of Mary Jane Mount Tanner (Wife of Myron Tanner).' Taken in part from her diary and memoirs abridged with notes by Grace Tanner Anderson (daughter). Copied from the original in possession of Katherine Tanner Carter, January 1972." Typescript copy. BYU Special Collections, Harold B. Lee Library, Provo, Utah.

Tanner, Nathan. n.d. "Incidents in the Life of Nathan Tanner." Typescript copy. Mormon Biography File. LDS Church Archives.

———. 1904. "Nathan Tanner." In Orson F. Whitney, *History of Utah,* 4 vols., Salt Lake City, Utah: G. Q. Cannon & Sons Co., 4:635–36.

Taylor, Elmer. 1904. "Elmer Taylor." In Orson F. Whitney, *History of Utah,* 4 vols., Salt Lake City, Utah: G. Q. Cannon & Sons Co., 4:380.

Taylor, John. 1880. "R. S. Reports." *Woman's Exponent* 9, no. 7 (1 September): 53–54.

———. 1999. *Witness to the Martyrdom: John Taylor's Personal Account of the Last Days of the Prophet Joseph Smith.* Edited by Mark H. Taylor. Salt Lake City, Utah: Deseret Book.

Taylor, Joseph E. 1892. "Recollections of the Prophet Joseph Smith." *Juvenile Instructor* 27, no. 7 (1 April): 202–3.

Taylor, Leonora C. ca. 1856. "Statement by Leonora Cannon Taylor, ca. 1856." LDS Church Archives.

Taylor, Pleasant Green. n.d. "Pleasant Green Taylor." Mormon Biography File. LDS Church Archives.

Taylor, Thomas H. 1881. In William H. Kelley and E. L. Kelley, "Interview with Orlando Saunders and Dr. John Stafford, March, 1881," *Saints' Herald* 28, no. 11 (1 June): 165. Also in *Juvenile Instructor* 17, no. 19 (1 October 1882): 299–302.

Taylor, William. 1906. "Joseph Smith, the Prophet." *Young Woman's Journal* 17, no. 12 (December): 547–48.

Telford, Effie Lenore. n.d. "History of John Telford." Mormon Biography File. LDS Church Archives.

Terrel, William. 1902. "William Terrel, Statement January 3, 1902." LDS Church Archives.

Terry, Jael. n.d. "Biographical Sketch of Jael Terry." Mormon Biography File. LDS Church Archives.

Terry, James P. 1893. "Recollections of the Prophet Joseph Smith." *Juvenile Instructor* 28, no. 10 (15 May): 331–32.

Thomas, Martha. 1927. "Martha Pane Jones Thomas Autobiography (1812–1847)." In *Daniel Stillwell Thomas Family History*, Salt Lake City, Utah: Kate Woodhouse Kirkham, 23–35.

Thompson, Mary Jane. 1906. "Joseph Smith, the Prophet." *Young Woman's Journal* 17, no. 12 (December): 541.

Thompson, Mercy Rachel. n.d. "Autobiographical Sketch." LDS Church Archives.

———. 1892. "Recollections of the Prophet Joseph Smith." *Juvenile Instructor* 27, no. 13 (1 July): 398–400.

Thompson, Sherwood R. 1841. "Sherwood R. Thompson to Eunice E. Thompson, January 14, 1841." LDS Church Archives.

Tippets, John H. n.d. "John H. Tippets." Mormon Biography File. LDS Church Archives.

Tolton, Mary Ann Tomlinson. 1887. In John Franklin Tolton, "Memories of the Life of John Franklin Tolton: A Brief Record of the Family and Other Matters," Commenced 23 August 1887, Mormon Biography File, LDS Church Archives.

Tracy, Nancy N. n.d. [a]. "Life History of Nancy Naomi Alexander Tracy, Written by Herself." Typescript copy. BYU Special Collections. Harold B. Lee Library, Provo, Utah.

———. n.d. [b]. *Narrative*. Bancroft Library, University of California, Berkeley. See also Microfilm of holograph. LDS Church Archives.

Tripp, Enoch Bartlett. 1904. "Enoch Bartlett Trip." In Orson F. Whitney, *History of Utah*, 4 vols., Salt Lake City, Utah: G. Q. Cannon & Sons Co., 4:490–91.

Tullidge, Edward W. 1866. "Views of Mormonism." *New York Galaxy*, 1 Oct. 1866, 209–14.

———. 1877. *Women of Mormondom*. New York: Tullidge & Crandall.

Turnbow, Samuel. ca. 1876. "The Journal of Samuel Turnbow." Typescript copy. BYU Special Collections. Harold B. Lee Library, Provo, Utah.

Tyler, Daniel. 1892a. "Recollections of the Prophet Joseph Smith." *Juvenile Instructor* 27, no. 3 (1 February): 93–95.

———. 1892b. "Recollections of the Prophet Joseph Smith." *Juvenile Instructor* 27, no. 4 (15 February): 127–28.

———. 1892c. "Recollections of the Prophet Joseph Smith." *Juvenile Instructor* 27, no. 16 (15 August): 491–92.

———. 1893. "Recollections of the Prophet Joseph Smith." *Juvenile Instructor* 28, no. 10 (15 May): 331–32.

———. 1969. "Incidents of Experience." In "Scraps of Biography," in *Classic Experiences and Adventures,* Salt Lake City, Utah: Bookcraft.

Van Orden, Peter Edmund. n.d. "Incidents in the Life of William Van Orden, My Grandfather." Mormon Biography File. LDS Church Archives.

Vogel, Dan. 1996. *Early Mormon Documents.* Vol. 1. Salt Lake City, Utah: Signature Books.

Vogel, George William. n.d. "Life History of George Wm. Vogel." Mormon Biography File. LDS Church Archives.

Waldram, Julia Carbine. n.d. "LDS Temples: Henry W. Miller and Elmira Pond Miller." 16 October 1870. Daughters of the Utah Pioneers, Salt Lake City, Utah.

Walker, Charles L. 1980. In A. Karl Larson and Katharine Miles Larson, *Diary of Charles Lowell Walker,* 2 vols., Logan, Utah: Utah State University Press.

Walker, Kyle. 2002. "Katherine Smith Salisbury's Recollections of Joseph's Meetings with Moroni." *BYU Studies* 41, no. 3 (2002): 5–17.

Walker, William H. 1943. *The Life Incidents and Travels of Elder William Holmes Walker, and His Association with Joseph Smith, the Prophet.* N.p.: Elizabeth Jane Walker Piepgrass.

Wall, Nancy Haws. n.d. In Garth D. Mangum, *William Madison Wall, His Life and Family,* n.p.

Wall, William Madison. n.d. "Life Sketch of William Madison Wall." Mormon Biography File. LDS Church Archives.

Wasson, Lorenzo D. 1841. "Lorenzo Wasson to David Hale, Feb. 1841." With an addendum by Joseph Smith. LDS Church Archives.

Watkins, William. n.d. [a]. "Autobiography of William Watkins." Typescript copy. BYU Special Collections. Harold B. Lee Library, Provo, Utah.

———. n.d. [b]. "History of William Lampard Watkins." Mormon Biography File. LDS Church Archives.

Watson, Elden J. 1971. *Manuscript History of Brigham Young 1846–1847.* Salt Lake City, Utah: Eldon J. Watson, Publisher.

Webb, Sylvia Cutler. 1915. "The Autobiography of Sylvia C. Webb." *Saints' Herald* 62, no. 12 (24 March): 289–93.

Weed, Harriet. 1883. *Autobiography of Thurlow Weed.* Boston: Houghton, Mifflin & Co.

Welch, John. n.d. "John Welch and Eliza Billington Welch." Mormon Biography File. LDS Church Archives.

———. 1902. "John Welch Deposition, July 5, 1902." LDS Church Archives.

Wells, Daniel H. 1904. "Daniel H. Wells." In Orson F. Whitney, *History of Utah*, 4 vols., Salt Lake City, Utah: G. Q. Cannon & Sons Co.

Wells, Emmeline B. 1904. "Emmeline B. Woodward Wells." In Orson F. Whitney, *History of Utah*, 4 vols., Salt Lake City, Utah: G. Q. Cannon & Sons Co., 4:587.

———. 1905. "Joseph Smith, the Prophet." *Young Woman's Journal* 16, no. 12 (December): 554–56.

———. 1919. "President Emmeline B. Wells." *Relief Society Magazine* 6, no. 8 (August): 459–60.

Wells, Lydia Ann Alley. 1923. "A Sketch of the Life of Lydia A. Alley Wells, by Herself." *Relief Society Magazine* 10, no. 7 (July): 324.

Wells, Susan Hannah Alley. 1923. "Susan Hannah Alley Wells." *Relief Society Magazine* 10, no. 7 (July): 322.

Westover, Eliza. 1916. "Eliza Westover to Lewis B. Westover." 16 July 1916. LDS Church Archives.

Westover, Leona S. 1961. "Warren Walling—Captain." In Kate B. Carter, comp., *Our Pioneer Heritage*, 20 vols., Salt Lake City, Utah: Daughters of the Utah Pioneers, 1958–77, 4:49.

Westover, Mary C. 1906. "Joseph Smith, the Prophet." *Young Woman's Journal* 17, no. 12 (December): 545.

Westover, Mary E. Shumway, and Eva Westover. n.d. "The History of Mary E. Shumway Westover." Mormon Biography File. LDS Church Archives.

Whitaker, Elizabeth Mills. 1937. "Called by Death—Beloved Utah Pioneer Passes away in Centerville, Utah." *Deseret News*, 8 June 1937.

White, Catherine Foutz. 1971. "White, Catherine Foutz." In Andrew Jenson, *LDS Biographical Encyclopedia*, 4 vols., Salt Lake City, Utah: Western Epics, 2:736–37.

White, Evander J. n.d. "Evander J. White." Mormon Biography File. LDS Church Archives.

White, Joel William. n.d. "Autobiographical Sketch of the Life of Joel William White 1831–1910." LDS Church Archives.

White, John Stout. n.d. "A Pioneer Story Told by a Pioneer (Mrs. J. H. Hess)." LDS Church Archives.

Whitmer, David. 1878. In Orson Pratt, "Report of Elders Orson Pratt and Joseph F. Smith," *Latter-day Saints' Millennial Star* 40, no. 49 (9 December): 769–74.

———. 1884. In E. C. Briggs, "Brother Joseph Smith," *Saints' Herald* 31, no. 25 (21 June): 396–97.

———. 1885. "Questions Asked of David Whitmer at His Home in Richmond, Ray County, Missouri, Jan. 21, 1885, by Zenos H. Gurley." LDS Church Archives.

———. 1887. *An Address to All Believers in Christ by a Witness to the Divine Authenticity of the Book of Mormon*. Richmond, Mo.: David Whitmer, Publisher.

Whitmer, John. n.d. *The Book of John Witmer.* Typescript copy. BYU Special Collections. Harold B. Lee Library, Provo, Utah.

Whitney, Elizabeth Ann. 1878a. "A Leaf from an Autobiography." *Woman's Exponent* 7, no. 7 (1 September): 51.

———. 1878b. "A Leaf from an Autobiography." *Woman's Exponent* 7, no. 9 (1 October): 71.

———. 1878c. "A Leaf from an Autobiography." *Woman's Exponent* 7, no. 11 (1 November): 83.

———. 1878d. "A Leaf from an Autobiography." *Woman's Exponent* 7, no. 12 (15 November): 91.

———. 1878e. "A Leaf from an Autobiography." *Woman's Exponent* 7, no. 14 (15 December): 105.

———. 1879. "A Leaf from an Autobiography." *Woman's Exponent* 7, no. 18 (15 February): 191.

Whitney, Helen Mar. 1880a. "Early Reminiscences." *Woman's Exponent* 9, no. 1 (1 June): 5.

———. 1880b. "Life's Incidents." *Woman's Exponent* 9, no. 3 (1 July): 18.

———. 1880c. "Life's Incidents." *Woman's Exponent* 9, no. 5 (1 August): 39.

———. 1881a. "Life's Incidents." *Woman's Exponent* 9, no. 17 (1 February): 190.

———. 1881b. "Heber C. Kimball Journal." In "Life Incidents," *Woman's Exponent* 10, no. 2 (15 June): 9.

———. 1881c. "Scenes in Nauvoo." *Woman's Exponent* 10, no. 5 (1 August): 34. Also in Stanley B. Kimball, "Heber C. Kimball and Family, the Nauvoo Years," *BYU Studies* 15, no. 4 (summer 1975): 447–79.

———. 1881d. "Scenes in Nauvoo." *Woman's Exponent* 10, no. 6 (15 August): 42.

———. 1881e. "Scenes and Incidents in Nauvoo." *Woman's Exponent* 10, no. 11 (1 November): 83.

———. 1881f. "Scenes and Incidents in Nauvoo." *Woman's Exponent* 10, no. 12 (15 November): 94, 159.

———. 1882a. "Scenes and Incidents in Nauvoo." *Woman's Exponent* 11, no. 4 (15 July): 26. Also in Stanley B. Kimball, "Heber C. Kimball and Family, the Nauvoo Years," *BYU Studies* 15, no. 4 (summer 1975): 447–79.

———. 1882b. "Scenes and Incidents in Nauvoo." *Woman's Exponent* 11, no. 8 (15 September): 68, 70–71, 161.

———. 1882c. "Scenes and Incidents in Nauvoo." *Woman's Exponent* 11, no. 12 (15 November): 90.

———. 1882d. "Heber C. Kimball Letters, 1844." *Woman's Exponent* 11, no. 13 (1 December 1882): 98.

———. 1883. "Scenes and Incidents in Nauvoo." *Woman's Exponent* 11, no. 15 (1 January): 114.

———. 1905. In Orson F. Whitney, *The Mormon Prophet's Tragedy,* Salt Lake City, Utah: Deseret News.

Whitney, Horace K. n.d. "Horace K. Whitney." Mormon Biography File. LDS Church Archives.

Whitney, Newell K. 1904. "Newell K. Whitney." In Orson F. Whitney, *History of Utah,* 4 vols., Salt Lake City, Utah: G. Q. Cannon & Sons Co.

Whitney, Orson F. 1904. *History of Utah.* 4 vols. Salt Lake City, Utah: George Q. Cannon & Sons, Co.

Widstoe, Osborne J. P. 1911. "Hyrum Smith, Patriarch." *Utah Genealogical and Historical Magazine* 2 (April): 60.

Wight, Lyman. 1865. "Lyman Wight History." *Latter-day Saints' Millennial Star* 27, no. 29 (22 July): 455–57.

Wight, Orange L. 1903. "Recollections of Orange L. Wight." Typescript copy. BYU Special Collections. Harold B. Lee Library, Provo, Utah.

Wilcox, Maria Wealthy. 1905. "Joseph Smith, the Prophet." *Young Woman's Journal* 16, no. 12 (December): 553–54.

Wilding, George. n.d. "Statement of Henry David Wilding." Mormon Biography File. LDS Church Archives.

Wilds, Belle Congress. 1918."A Short Biography of Mrs. Rhoda Eldridge Merrill." *Relief Society Magazine* 5, no. 4 (September): 491.

Wilkinson, Susan Hough Conrad. 1844. "Susan Hough Conrad Wilkinson to Mary Woolley, August 5, 1844." LDS Church Archives.

Willden, Boyd, and Lilly Zufelt Willden. 1998. *Life Stories of Charles Zufelt and Dolly Mae DeLuche, with Their Descendants and Ancestors,* 301–2. Privately printed, 1998. LDS Family History Library.

Williams, Ezra Granger. n.d. "Biographical Sketch of the Life of Dr. Ezra Granger Williams by His Daughter, Lucy Godfrey." Mormon Biography File. LDS Church Archives.

Williams, Frederick G. n.d. "Notes on the Life of Frederick G. Williams, One Time Counselor to the Prophet Joseph Smith." LDS Church Archives.

Williams, Rebecca Swain. n.d. In Lucy E. Godfrey, "Biographical Sketch of Rebecca Swain Williams, Wife of Dr. Frederick Granger Williams and Mother of Dr. Ezra Granger Williams," Mormon Biography File, LDS Church Archives.

Williams, Samuel Otho. 1844. "Samuel Otho Williams to John, July 10, 1844." LDS Church Archives.

Williams, Sylvia C. 1973. *Journal of Warren G. Child.* Copies in private family possession.

Williams, Zilpa B. 1845. "Zilpha Williams to Samuel Cilley, July 16, 1845." LDS Church Archives.

Willis, Alzina. 1973. In Lorraine W. Silcox, "Zina-Forget-Me-Not: A Biographical Story," Sacramento, Calif: N.p. Copies in private family possession.

Wilson, George Christian. n.d. "History of Lewis Dunbar Wilson." Mormon Biography File. LDS Church Archives.

Wilson, Lewis Dunbar Jr. n.d. "Lewis Dunbar Wilson Jr." Mormon Biography File. LDS Church Archives.

Winters, Hiram. n.d. Untitled Manuscript. Mormon Biography File. LDS Church Archives.

Winters, Mary Ann. 1905. "Joseph Smith, the Prophet." *Young Woman's Journal* 16, no. 12 (December): 557–58.

———. 1916a. "An Autobiographical Sketch of the Life of the Late Mary Ann Stearns Winters, Daughter of Mary Ann Stearns Pratt." In "Mary Ann Frost Stearns Pratt," *Relief Society Magazine* 3, no. 8 (August): 428.

———. 1916b. "Mothers in Israel: Autobiographical Sketch of Mary Ann Stearns Winters." *Relief Society Magazine* 3, no. 10 (October): 574–81.

———. 1916c. "Mothers in Israel: Autobiography of Mary A. S. Winters." *Relief Society Magazine* 3, no. 11 (November): 641–42.

Woodland, John. n.d. "Biographical Sketch of John and Celia Steepleford Woodland." LDS Church Archives.

Woodruff, Phoebe Carter. 1877. "Address to the Ladies of Utah, Delivered in January 1870." In Edward W. Tullidge, *Women of Mormondom*. New York: Tullidge & Crandall, 399.

———. 1880. "Autobiographic Sketch of Phebe Woodruff, Salt Lake City, 1880." Bancroft Library, University of California, Berkeley. See also Microfilm of holograph. LDS Church Archives.

Woodruff, Wilford. 1838. "History of the Travels of Zion's Camp, Led by the Prophet Joseph Smith from Kirtland, Ohio, to Clay County, Missouri, in the Spring of 1838. Written by Wilford Woodruff, Assistant Historian, who was a member of Zion's Camp." LDS Church Archives.

———. 1842. "Wilford Woodruff, Daily Journal and History, February 19, 1842." Cited in Milton R. Hunter, *Pearl of Great Price Commentary*. Salt Lake City, Utah: Stevens and Wallis, Inc., 1948.

———. 1865a. "History of Wilford Woodruff." *Latter-day Saints' Millennial Star* 27, no.12 (25 March): 182–83.

———. 1865b. "History of Wilford Woodruff." *Latter-day Saints' Millennial Star* 27, no. 17 (29 April): 263–65.

———. 1865c. "History of Wilford Woodruff." *Latter-day Saints' Millennial Star* 27, no. 21 (27 May): 326–28.

———. 1865d. "History of Wilford Woodruff." *Latter-day Saints' Millennial Star* 27, no. 24 (17 June): 375–76.

———. 1894a. "Remarks of President Wilford Woodruff, June 24, 1894 at the Temple Workers Excursion, Brigham City, Utah." Cited in "Family Record of Eliza Smith Somerville." LDS Church Archives.

———. 1894b. In George Q. Cannon, "Topics of Our Times," *Juvenile Instructor* 29, no. 23 (1 December): 746.

Woodruff, Wilford Jr. 1971. "Woodruff, Wilford Jr." In Andrew Jenson, *LDS Biographical Encyclopedia,* 4 vols., Salt Lake City, Utah: Western Epics, 1:616.

Woodward, Mariah. 1906. "Joseph Smith, the Prophet." *Young Woman's Journal* 17, no. 12 (December): 543–44.

Woolley, Samuel A. ca. 1885. "History of Samuel Amos Woolley, Written by His Daughter, Florence Woolley Russell." Mormon Biography File. LDS Church Archives.

———. 1971. "Woolley, Samuel A." In Andrew Jenson, *LDS Biographical Encyclopedia,* 4 vols., Salt Lake City, Utah: Western Epics, 1:781.

Woolf, John Anthony. n.d. "John Anthony Woolf Sr." Mormon Biography File. LDS Church Archives.

Woolley, Edwin D. 1971. "Woolley, Edwin D." In Andrew Jenson, *LDS Biographical Encyclopedia,* 4 vols., Salt Lake City, Utah: Western Epicss, 1:631–32.

Workman, Andrew. 1892. "Recollections of the Prophet Joseph Smith." *Juvenile Instructor* 27, no. 20 (15 October): 641.

Workman, Sariah A. 1906. "Joseph Smith, the Prophet." *Young Woman's Journal* 17, no. 12 (December): 542.

York, Asa Bartlett. n.d. "Asa Bartlett York." Mormon Biography File. LDS Church Archives.

Young, Brigham. 1844. "Brigham Young to Vilate Young, Aug. 11, 1844." LDS Church Archives.

———. 1845. "Minutes of a Meeting of the Richards and Young Families Held in Nauvoo, Ill., Jan. 8, 1845." *Utah Genealogical and Historical Magazine* 11 (July 1920): 107–11.

———. 1849. "Brigham Young Remarks, 16 Feb. 1849." LDS Church Archives.

———. 1850a. "Brigham Young Remarks, 8 April 1850." LDS Church Archives.

———. 1850b. "Brigham Young Remarks, 7 October 1850." Typescript copy. LDS Church Archives.

———. 1855. "Deseret Theological Institute, Minutes of (2 May) 1855." LDS Church Archives.

———. 1862. "Remarks on August 31, 1862." *Deseret News,* 22 October 1862.

———. 1866. "Remarks by President Brigham Young at the Semi Annual Conference, Great Salt Lake City, Oct. 8, 1866." LDS Church Archives.

———. 1874. "Discourse by President Brigham Young, June 21, 1874." *Deseret News,* 1 July 1874, 340–41.

———. 1968. In Elden J. Watson, *Manuscript History of Brigham Young 1801–1844,* Salt Lake City, Utah: Eldon J. Watson, Publisher.

Young, Emily Partridge. 1885. "Autobiography of Emily D. P. Young." *Woman's Exponent* 14, no. 5 (1 August): 37–38.

———. 1897. "Statement Written June 27, 1897." LDS Church Archives.

Young, John R. 1920. *Memoirs of John R. Young, Utah Pioneer 1847.* Salt Lake City, Utah: The Deseret News.

Young, Joseph. 1845. "Minutes of a Meeting of the Richards and Young Families Held in Nauvoo, Ill., Jan. 8, 1845." *Utah Genealogical and Historical Magazine* 11 (July 1920): 108–11.

———. 1880. "Joseph Young Sr. to Lewis Harvey, 16 November 1880." LDS Church Archives.

———. 1904. "Joseph Young." In Orson F. Whitney, *History of Utah,* 4 vols., Salt Lake City, Utah: G. Q. Cannon & Sons Co.

Young, Lorenzo D. 1946. In James A. Little, "Biography of Lorenzo Dow Young," *Utah Historical Quarterly* 14, no. 1 (January): 43–52.

Young, Margaret Pierce. n.d. "Margaret Pierce Young (1823–1907) Journal Excerpts." LDS Church Archives.

Young, Zina D. H. 1877. In Edward W. Tullidge, *Women of Mormondom,* New York: Tullidge & Crandall.

———. 1889. "Zina D. H. Young, Diary 1889." LDS Church Archives.

———. 2000. In Martha Sonntag Bradley and Mary Brown Firmage Woodward, *Four Zinas,* Salt Lake City, Utah: Signature Books.

Zundel, Abigail Abbott. 1973. "History of Abigail Abbott Zundel." In Glen F. Harding, "A Record of the Ancestry and Descendants of John Jacob Zundel, Known as Jacob Zundel," LDS Family History Library.

Zundel, Emma Maria. 1973. "History of Emma Maria Zundel (1836–1926)." In Glen F. Harding, "A Record of the Ancestry and Descendants of John Jacob Zundel, Known as Jacob Zundel," LDS Family History Library.

Zundel, John Jacob. 1973. "George Harding to Phebe [Harding], circa 1910." In Glen F. Harding, "A Record of the Ancestry and Descendants of John Jacob Zundel, Known as Jacob Zundel," LDS Family History Library.

Index

Aaronic Priesthood. *See* Priesthood
Abraham, book of, 259–60
Abundance, prophecy of, 173
Accounts: bias in, 10–11; accuracy of, 16–17
Accusations, Joseph Smith on, 92
Adam and Eve, vision of, 187
Adam, altar of, 349–50
Adamic language, 170
Adams, Mary F., 54–55
Adams, William, 425; on mourning martyrdom, 405
Adulterer, 178
Age, memory and, 11–12
Alcohol, selling, on Sunday, 54–55
Allen, Lucy, 425
Alley, Lydia Ann, 425
Allred, William, 425
Altar, 349–50
Ames, Ira, 339
Anderson, William, 425
Angel(s): ministering of, 194–97; Joseph Smith chastised by, 242–43; ordinances and, 270–71; Kirtland Temple dedication and, 345–47
Angell, Polly Ann Johnson, 425
Angell, Truman O., 425; on Joseph Smith as leader, 48–49; on Church record, 330–31
Animals, respecting, 54
Anointing, 272

Apocrypha, 112
Apostasy: prophecy on, 141, 148–49; Joseph Smith asserts power against, 271
Apostatizing, Joseph Smith on, 118
Apostles: prophecy on, 153–54; revelation to, 216–17; organization of, 280–82; Joseph Smith's last meeting with, 373, 403
Apron, Joseph Smith wears, 87
Arm: healing of Elsa Johnson's, 122–23; priesthood blessing heals, 274
Armstrong, James A., 426; on sister of William Law, 393
Army: spirit, 249–50; mob, in Nauvoo, 357–58
Arrest(s): of Joseph Smith, 81–82; Joseph Smith escapes, by revelation, 214–15; of Joseph Smith in Colesville, 292–98; whittling saves Joseph Smith from, 368–69
Ashby, Benjamin, 426; corrected by Joseph Smith, 90; on martyrdom, 374–75; on transfiguration of Brigham Young, 411
Atchison, General, 348–49
Attorney, Erastus Snow as, 355
Ax, sharpening, 42
Axeltree, Joseph Smith repairs, 117

Index

Baby: Joseph Smith borrows, 70–71; Phoebe Hancock promised five dollars for, 380–81
Bail, Anson Call serves as Joseph Smith's, 81–82
Baldwin, Caleb, 354–55
Ball, Thomas, 426
Barlow, Israel A., 426; on meeting Joseph Smith, 105; on Oliver Cowdery's vision, 185–86; on grandfather's escape from mob, 218–19; on grandfather's obedience, 224–25
Barney, Lewis, 356
Battles, prophecy on, 134–35
Bellows, John F., 426
Belnap, Adeline K., 251–52
Beman, Alvah, 315
Bennett, John C., 135
Bernhisel, John M.: occupation of, 1; Joseph Smith Bible translation and, 265–66
Bias, in accounts, 10–11
Bible: Joseph Smith reads entire, 210; Joseph Smith translation of, 265–67; Nauvoo Temple cornerstone and, 369–70
Bigler, Henry W., 426; on Joseph Smith and prayer, 221–22
Bills, William A., 426; on Smith family in Nauvoo, 356–57
Biographical registry, 425–54
Bishop, Francis C., 270–71
Bishops, organization of, 285
Black, George, 426
Black, George David, 426
Black, Jane J., 2, 427; strength of, 19; priesthood blessing given to, 274; on transfiguration of Brigham Young, 411–12
Black, William, 357–58
Blanchard, Jerusha W., 259
Blessing(s): for Benjamin F. Johnson, 63–64; Joseph Smith and, 84–85; faith in time of, 115; faith and, 211–12; enjoying, 212; revelation and, 218; priesthood, 274–76
Bloodshed, 178; vision of, 189–90
Boat: dream of, 193–94; sunk by angel, 195–96
Bodies: Brigham Young on, 217; of Hyrum and Joseph Smith, 408–10
Boice, James, 427
Boldness, of Joseph Smith, 42–43
Book of Martyrs, 112
Book of Mormon: conversion and, 5–6; Joseph Smith blesses Mary Elizabeth Rollins Lightner for having, 85; printing of, 232–36; Martin Harris pays Joseph Smith to translate, 247–48; Sidney Rigdon and, 248, 304–6; hired girl and translation of, 248–49; Orrin Porter Rockwell's help in printing, 299; interview with Emma Hale Smith on, 300–304; witnesses to, 313–24; attempted stereotyping of, 361–62. *See also* Golden plates
Book, for Church record, 330–31
Borrowing, 65
Boss, Nancy, 427; on martyrdom, 375–76
Bread and butter, 85
Bread, prophecy on, 113, 151–52, 162–63
Brother of Jared, 275
Brother, Joseph Smith helps boy looking for, 57
Brown, Benjamin, 427; healing of, 121; on Kirtland Temple dedication, 345
Brown, Lorenzo, 210
Browning, Charilla Abbot, 427
Bullock, Lucy Clayton, 427
Burdens, Joseph Smith's patience with, 80–81
Burgess, Harrison, 427; witnesses vision, 186
Burgess, Margarette, 427; on Joseph

Index

Smith's love of children, 70–71; priesthood blessing given to, 274
Burial, of Joseph Smith, 410–11
Burnett, Peter H., 427; on Joseph Smith, 28–29
Burton, Robert T., 412
Butler, Caroline, 20
Butler, John L., 428; counseled to leave house, 93–94; promised healthy house, 98–99; on Dixon kidnapping, 370–72
Butterfield, Jacob, 5
Butterfield, Josiah, 363–64

Cahoon, Reynolds: Joseph Smith names son of, 275; convinces Joseph Smith to go to Carthage, 386–88
Cahoon, William F., 428; on humility of Joseph Smith, 67–68; on Joseph Smith's digging well, 128; on prophecy for Saints going to Missouri, 131–32
Calf, 55
California, dream about, 52–53
Call, Anson, 428; as Joseph Smith's bail, 81–82; Pearl of Great Price and, 259–60; on martyrdom, 376–77; sees Joseph Smith after martyrdom, 407–8
Callister, Caroline S., 428; on Joseph Smith's humor, 85; on faith of Joseph Smith, 113
Campbellite minister, 177–78
Cane, 56
Cannon, 350–51
Cannon, Angus M., 428; on preaching of Joseph Smith, 197–98
Cannon, George Q., 428; quotes Joseph Smith, 14; meets Joseph Smith, 105; on prophecy of Civil War, 132
Carbine, William, 428; on transfiguration of Brigham Young, 412–13

Carling, Ann Green, 2, 428; set apart as midwife, 277
Carriage, overthrowing of, 161–62
Carter, Jared, 429; Joseph Smith heals child of, 118; prophecy about mission of, 132
Carthage Jail. *See* Martyrdom
Cat's paw, 111
Celestial marriage: revelation about, 211–12, 259; as ordinance, 273–74
Chandler, Michael H., 261–62
Character, of Joseph Smith, 37–41
Charity, Joseph Smith on, 92
Charlie, 366
Chase, Phoebe, 2
Chase, Sylvia, 121–22
Cheney, Elam, 29
Chidester, John M., 429; on spiritual sensitivity of Joseph Smith, 100
Childbearing, prophecy about, 135
Children: Joseph Smith's love for, 70–74; pray for safety of Joseph Smith, 116–17
Cholera: Joseph Smith tries to heal, 116; Artemus Millet healed of, 124–25; revelation about, 254; obedience and, 343
Church of Jesus Christ of Latter-day Saints, The: structure of, 279–87; restoration and organization of, 327–30
Church record, 330–31
Civil War, 102–4; prophecy of, 132, 134–35, 172; fulfilling of prophecy and, 155–56
Clark, Sarah T., 429; on preaching of Joseph Smith, 198
Clark, William O., 92
Clark, Wycom, 161–62
Clawson, Margaret, 429; on Joseph Smith's friendliness, 43
Clayton, William, 259, 429; healing of, 122
Clothing, Mary I. Horne mends Joseph Smith's, 100–101

INDEX

Coach, Joseph Smith stops runaway, 61–62
Coates, Allen, 429; on First Vision, 307–8
Colborn, Thomas, 66–67
Colesville, arrest and trial of Joseph Smith in, 292–98
Coltrin, Zebedee, 429; on rebuking evil spirits, 181; visions of, 186–87; on Joseph Smith after revelation, 252
Common Consent, law of, 286–87
Compassion, of Joseph Smith, 54–55
Conrad, Sally Heller, 248–49
Consecration of oil, 273
Constitution: accuracy of quote about, 13; Joseph Smith on, 80; of Church, 280–81
Consumption, Lorenzo D. Young healed of, 126–27
Conversation, Joseph Smith and, 63
Cook, Squire, 205
Coray, Howard, 430; on Joseph Smith as friend, 43–45; on Joseph Smith as leader, 49–50; on Joseph Smith's knowledge, 111; on preaching of Joseph Smith, 198–99; on Joseph Smith's receiving revelation, 266
Cornerstone: prophecy about, 168–69; of Nauvoo Temple, 369–70
Correcting others, Joseph Smith and, 90–94
Corrill, John, 120–21
Counsel, of Joseph Smith, 93–94
Courage: of early Saints, 19; of Joseph Smith, 61–63
Cowdery, Oliver, 430; as record keeper, 17; weakened by vision, 185–86; sees Adam and Eve, 187; printing of Book of Mormon and, 232–36; wants Joseph Smith to change revelation, 257–58; as witness to Book of Mormon, 313–15; on restoration of Aaronic Priesthood, 324–26

Cowdery, Warren, 1
Cownover, Peter W., 390
Cox, Elias, 430; on faith of Joseph Smith, 113
Cox, Martha C., 210–11
Crookston, Robert Sr., 430; on martyrdom, 377–79
Crosby, Caroline B., 430; on journey of Frederick G. Williams' daughter, 219
Crosby, Jesse W., 430; on misquotation of Joseph Smith, 9; on Joseph Smith and temporal concerns, 41–42; on Joseph Smith's honesty, 65; on introspection of Joseph Smith, 94–95; on Joseph Smith and opinions, 99
Cummings, B. F., 430; on Joseph Smith Bible translation, 267
Curtis, Joseph, 430; on First Vision, 308
Curtis, Levi, 431; on healing of William D. Huntington, 128–30

Danger, prophecy about deliverance from, 153
Davis, Elisha H., Jr., 408
Dead, prophecy about fear of the, 144
Debt: Joseph Smith forgives, 57–58; Joseph Smith repays, 66–67; Parley P. Pratt chastised for, 176–77
Decker, Isaac, 431; on destruction of gentiles, 132–33
Destruction: of Olmsted Johnson, 158; of eastern states, 166
Devotion, of Joseph Smith, 98
Dibble, Philo, 431; on healing of Elsa Johnson, 122–23; prophecy about safety of, 133–34; on receiving revelation, 252–53; on Kirtland, 331–32; on falling stars, 338–40; on Missouri trial of Joseph Smith, 348–49
Discernment, 174–81

Disciplinary councils, organization of, 284–85
Discouragement, 83
Disease, Satan and, 120–21
Ditch, 76–77
Dixon kidnapping, 370–72
Doctrine and Covenants, 251–59
Donner Party, 157
Douglas, Stephen A., 136–37, 142–43
Dream, 192–94; Brigham Young's, about sheep, 52–53; as premonition of martyrdom, 389–91
Dress: of angels, 196–97; disciplinary council and, 284–85
Duncan, Chapman, 431; on altar of Adam, 349–50
Duncan, Homer, 431; on transfiguration of Brigham Young, 413

Early Saints, 1–6, 19–20
Eastern states, prophecy about destruction of, 166
Eccles, Henry, 431
Education: of early Saints, 4–5; of Joseph Smith, 250
Egyptian record: Illinois Democratic Press on, 39–40; Joseph Smith corrects woman on, 91–92; Jerusha W. Blanchard on, 259; Sarah S. Leavitt on, 260; Warren Foote on, 260; William W. Phelps on, 260–61; Orson Pratt on obtaining, 261–62; translation of, 262–65; Joseph Smith on obtaining, 263–64; publishing of, 265; William Law uses, as excuse, 362–63. *See also* Pearl of Great Price
Emerson, Ralph Waldo, on slavery, 103
Emotion, memory and, 20–21
Employee, Joseph Smith defends, 99–100
Endowment, 273

Enemies, prophecy about, 154–55, 161
England: Joseph Smith foresees work in, 112; prophecy on war and, 134–35
Ensign, Mary D., 431; on prophecy of measles, 134; on transfiguration of Brigham Young, 413
Ensign Peak, 212–13
Everett, Addison, 431; on Joseph Smith and miracles, 130; on restoration of Melchizedek Priesthood, 326
Everett, Schuyler, 432; on kindness of Joseph Smith, 55
Evil spirits: rebuking, 181–83, 187–89; in Kirtland, 331. *See also* Satan

Fabric, 162
Fairbanks, Susan, 4
Faith: of Saints, 102; of Joseph Smith, 113–18; in trials, 115; exercising, contrary to will of God, 116; revelations and lack of, 211–12
Falling stars, 338–40
Families, missionary work and, 3–4
Far West, 353–54; prophecy on cornerstone in, 168–69
Farm, Saints have faith in buying, 113–14
Farr, Lorin, 2
Feast for the Poor, 332–33
Feeling sorry, five dollars and, 60
Feet, washing of, 277–79
Fever sore, healing of, 123
Fight, Joseph Smith breaks up, 92–93
First meetings, with Joseph Smith, 105–10
First Presidency, organization of, 279–80
First Vision, 307–13; repeated accounts of, 17–18
"Fishing River Revelation," 254
Fits, 150

Index

Five dollars: Joseph Smith gives, 60; girls give Joseph Smith, 64–65; Solomon Hancock gives Joseph Smith, 380–81

Flour, 65

Foote, Warren, 432; on Egyptian record, 260; on mourning martyrdom, 405

Ford, Thomas, 432; on Joseph Smith, 29–30; to hear good and bad about Joseph Smith, 66; martyrdom and, 394–95; after martyrdom, 405

Fordham, Elijah, 119

Forgiveness, 94–95; Joseph Smith and, 228

Fox, Jesse W., 432; on prophecy of wars, 134–35

Free speech, 99

Free thinker, 205

Freeze, Lillie, 432; on prophecy about childbearing, 135

Friend(s): of Joseph Smith, 1–3; Joseph Smith as, 43–48

Funeral: Joseph Smith plans, 58–59; prayer to calm storm at, 117

Gee, Lysander, 432; on Liberty Jail, 354–55

Geese, 208

Gentiles, prophecy on destruction of, 132–33

German, Joseph Smith speaks in, 184

Gifford, Samuel K., 413–14

Gifts, spiritual, 184

Gilbert, Algernon Sidney, 2

Gilbert, John H., 432; on printing of Book of Mormon, 232–36

Goats, Brigham Young's dream about, 52–53

Golden plates: translation of, 236–37; hiding places of, 237; obtaining, 238–42, 247; in Hill Cumorah, 250–51. *See also* Book of Mormon

Gospel, prophecy on spreading of, 156–57, 167–68

Gossip, forgiving, 94–95

Government, Joseph Smith on United States, 80

Grandin, Egbert, 232–36

Grant, Jedediah M., 433; misquotes Joseph Smith, 13; on happiness, 114

Grant, Rachel R., 433; on Joseph Smith, 30–31; on transfiguration of Brigham Young, 414

Gratitude, of Joseph Smith, 63–65

Green, Mary Ann, 389

Green, William A., 389

Greene, John P., 184

Greenhalgh, William, 433; has premonition of martyrdom, 389–90; on transfiguration of Brigham Young, 414

Greer, Catherine, 135, 433

Guards, Joseph Smith chastises, 90–91

Guns: cannot shoot Joseph Smith, 73–74; prophecy on obtaining, 164–65; Joseph Smith III plays with, 365

Haight, Isaac C., 433; on martyrdom, 379–80

Hair: prophecy about, 155; discerning angels by, 196

Hale, Aroet L., 433; on character of Joseph Smith, 37–38; on curse of John C. Bennett, 135

Hale, Jesse, 433; on Joseph Smith's love for Saints, 75

Hamson, Sarah Ann, 434; on priesthood blessing, 274

Hancock, Levi W., 434; on prophecy about Brigham Young, 136; on visions and rebuking evil spirits, 187–89; dreams and, 192; on Hiram mobbing, 333; on Zion's Camp, 340–42

Hancock, Mosiah, 434; on Joseph Smith's playfulness, 82; on consecration of oil, 273

INDEX

Hancock, Solomon, 380–81
Hand, healing of William Clayton's, 122
Handkerchief, 121–22
Happiness, Joseph Smith on, 114
Harding, Stephen S., 2
Harmon, Jesse P., 434; on prophecy about *Nauvoo Expositor,* 136
Harper, John, 434; healing of, 118–19
Harris, Clinton, 123
Harris, Dennison L., 434; on martyrdom, 381–86
Harris, Louisa Hall, 19
Harris, Martha Ann Smith, 434; on Mary Fielding Smith's reaction to martyrdom, 403–4
Harris, Martin, 434; handling snakes and, 91; discerns Savior, 174–75; printing of Book of Mormon and, 232–36; pays Joseph Smith to translate Book of Mormon, 247–48; as witness to Book of Mormon, 315
Hatch, Abram, 248
Hatch, Ira S., 434; gives Joseph Smith money, 219–20
Hatch, Lorenzo H., 435; knows Brigham Young will be president, 415
Haun's Mill Massacre, 226–27, 352–53
Healing: performed by Joseph Smith, 23–24, 118–27; of Benjamin F. Johnson, 84; of William D. Huntington, 128–30; prophecy about, of Jacob Scott, 156; of Brigham Young, 171; of Margarette Burgess, 274; of Mephibosheth Sirrine, 275–76
Heaven, John the Revelator and, 212
Hebrew, 338; Joseph Smith encourages learning, 63
Hendricks, Drusilla D., 435; on transfiguration of Brigham Young, 415–16

Henrie, Daniel, 416
Henrie, James, 11
Henrie, William, 435; wrestles Joseph Smith, 11; on Joseph Smith in Nauvoo, 358; on transfiguration of Brigham Young, 416
Herbs, as medicine, 126
Hess, John W., 435; on character of Joseph Smith, 38
Heywood, Joseph L., 199
Hickenlooper, William H., 174
Hickman, William A., 435; on openness of Joseph Smith, 80
High Councils, organization of, 284–85
Hill Cumorah, large room in, 250–51
Hiram, Ohio, mobbing in, 333–38
Hired girl, in house of David Whitmer, 248–49
Hogan, Goudy E., 435; on Joseph Smith, 38–39; on mourning martyrdom, 405–6
Holbrook, Joseph, 435; on industriousness of Joseph Smith, 69
Holden, Edwin, 436; on Joseph Smith and temporal concerns, 42
Holiness, of Joseph Smith, 96
Holy Ghost: Orson Hyde believes space is filled with, 93; following, 214
Honesty, of Joseph Smith, 65–67
Horne, Joseph, 436
Horne, Mary I.: on Joseph Smith as leader, 50; Joseph Smith's humor and, 85; on spiritual sensitivity of Joseph Smith, 100–101
Horner, John M., 436; prophecy of abundance for, 173; on mourning martyrdom, 406
Horse(s): Joseph Smith calms frightened, 61–62; Joseph Smith discusses, 95; prophecy about, 157–58; prophecy fulfilled through, 158–59; of Joseph Smith, 366
House: John L. Butler promised

healthy, 98–99; John Woodland builds, 179–80
Houston, James, 5
Hoyt, Emily S., 436; on transfiguration of Brigham Young, 416–18
Humility, of Joseph Smith, 50–51, 65, 67–69, 94–95, 286–87, 332
Humor, of Joseph Smith, 85–89
Hunter, Edward, 436; to tell Governor Ford truth, 66; on bodies of Hyrum and Joseph Smith, 408–9
Huntington, Dimick, 139–41
Huntington, Oliver B., 436; on prophecy about Stephen A. Douglas, 136–37; on prophecy about Missouri, 137–38; on prophecy about Rocky Mountains, 138–39; on prophecy about Dimick Huntington, 139–41; on vision of Rocky Mountains, 189; on hired girl and translation of Book of Mormon, 248–49; on premonition of martyrdom, 390
Huntington, William D., 128–30
Hurricane, 154
Hurry, 215–16
Hyde, Orson, 436; occupation of, 2; receives correction, 10, 93; quotes Joseph Smith, 13; believes space is filled with Holy Ghost, 93; on prophecies, 141; on priesthood order, 270–71; as spiritual witness to martyrdom, 408

Illinois Democratic Press, 39–40
Indians, 55–56; prophecy about mission to, 140–41; Joseph Smith speaks in tongues to, 183. *See also* Lamanite
Industriousness, of Joseph Smith, 69–70
Ingersoll, Peter, 3
Iniquity, preachers searching for, 180–81

Interpretation of tongues, 185
Introspection, of Joseph Smith, 94–95

Jackson, Joseph, 373–74
Jail: prophecy about, 160; Brother Markham escapes from, 221
James, Jane, 436; on Joseph Smith, 31
Jenson, Andrew, 437; on prophecy about Stephen A. Douglas, 142–43
Jerusalem: prophecy about Orson Hyde and, 141; prophecy on, 145; prophecy about Eliza R. Snow and, 162
Jesus Christ: woman asks Joseph Smith if he claims to be, 95–96; first miracle of, 130; Joseph Smith on gospel of, 131; visits meeting, 174–75; Zebedee Coltrin sees, 186–87
Jews, Joseph Smith jokes about gathering of, 87–88
John the Revelator: vision of, 189, 210–11; revelation about, 212
Johnny cake, 115–16
Johnson, Benjamin F., 437; on gratitude of Joseph Smith, 63–64; receives blessing from Joseph Smith, 84; on humor of Joseph Smith, 86; Joseph Smith counsels, to take wife, 101; on revelations, 253; on celestial marriage, 273–74; on transfiguration of Brigham Young, 418
Johnson, Elsa, 122–23
Johnson, Evaline B., 437; on Joseph Smith's love for children, 71–72
Johnson, Harriet M., 2; set apart as midwife, 277
Johnson, Joel H., 437; on Word of Wisdom, 253–54
Johnson, Luke S., 437; occupation of, 1
Johnson, Olmsted, 158
Jones, Dan, 2
Jones, Jacob: on Joseph Smith, 31; on

Index

Joseph Smith speaking in tongues, 183
Jones, William E., 437; on boldness of Joseph Smith, 42–43
Josephites, 149
Journey, Joseph Smith foresees easy, 220
Judd, Zadok K., 437; on transfiguration of Brigham Young, 418–19
Justice, 176–77

Kempton, Jerome B., 437; on transfiguration of Brigham Young, 419–20
Kendall, Elizabeth C., 2; prophecy about, 144
Kesler, Frederick, 4
Keys: Sidney Rigdon on, 331–32; Joseph Smith holds, 407–8
Keys, Celia A., 438; on kindness of Joseph Smith, 55–56
Kidnapping, Dixon, 370–72
Kimball, Heber C., 438; occupation of, 2; on humility of Joseph Smith, 68; on positive attitude of Joseph Smith, 83; on humor of Joseph Smith, 86; on faith, 115; on Joseph Smith's healing others, 123–24; prophecies about, 144–45; struggles with Satan in England, 174; on visions, 189–90; on preaching of Joseph Smith, 199–200; on revelations given to Joseph Smith, 211–12; on "Fishing River Revelation," 254; on organization of Apostles, 280; on organization of High Council, 284; on work in Kirtland, 332; on Zion's Camp, 342–43; on altar of Adam, 350; on transfiguration of Brigham Young, 420
Kimball, Mary Ellen, 75–76
Kimball, Vilate M., 438; on spirit armies, 249–50

Kindness, of Joseph Smith, 54–55, 76–77
Kingsberry, Joseph C., 259
Kirtland Bank, failure of, 347–48
Kirtland Council Minute Book, 254–55
Kirtland, Ohio, life in, 330–33
Kirtland Temple: vision of, 190, 191–92; washing and anointing in, 277–78; dedication of, 345–47
Knight, Catherine M'Guire, 438; on gratitude of Joseph Smith, 64–65
Knight, Joseph Jr., 236–37
Knight, Joseph Sr., 438; Joseph Smith gives cane to, 56
Knight, Lydia B., 438; on Joseph Smith, 31; speaks in tongues, 183–84; on preaching of Joseph Smith, 200–201
Knight, Newel, 438; on Joseph Smith, 31; devil cast out of, 181–83; on revelation on sacrament, 255; on Sally Coburn's priesthood blessing, 274–75; on Colesville arrest and trial of Joseph Smith, 292–98
Knight, Sally Coburn, 274–75
Knight, Vinson: to buy farm, 113–14; revelation about, 251–52; Pearl of Great Price and, 259–60
Knowledge, of Joseph Smith, 111–12, 217

Lamanite: skeleton of, 159–60; prophecy about gospel and, 167–68. *See also* Indians
Lambert, Charles, 438
Lambert, Mary A., 105–6, 439
Lambson, Alfred B., 439; prophecy about, 145–46
Lamoreaux, Andrew, 439; prophecy about, 146
Lapham, Fayette, 2
Laub, George, 439; on prophecy about Missouri, 147; on Joseph Smith's last public speech, 373–74

Law of Common Consent, 286–87
Law, William: cannot shoot Joseph Smith, 73–74; tries to kidnap Joseph Smith, 176; tries to enter Joseph Smith's property, 362–63; holds secret meetings, 381–86; sister of, 393
Layton, Christopher, 439
Leader, Joseph Smith as, 48–54
Learning, Joseph Smith encourages, 63
Leavitt, Dudley, 439; on preaching of Joseph Smith, 202
Leavitt, Sarah S., 439; on prophecy about rich man, 147–48; on Egyptian record, 260
Lee, John D., 440; on Joseph Smith, 32; on gift of memory, 224; on wrestling and Joseph Smith, 225–26; on Haun's Mill Massacre, 352–53
Leech, James, 440; on Joseph Smith's kindness, 76–77
Leg: Joseph Smith breaks Howard Coray's, 43–44; Brother Whitney breaks, 119–20; healing of Clinton Harris's, 123; operation on Joseph Smith's, 289–92
Leishman, Catherine T., 440; on Joseph Smith's love for Saints, 77; on transfiguration of Brigham Young, 420
Levitation, of Newel Knight, 181–83
Lewis, David, 440; on organization of Church, 327–29
Liberty Jail, 354–56
Life, prophecy about preserving, 154
Light of God, 114
Lightner, Mary Elizabeth Rollins, 440; on Joseph Smith's love for Saints, 77–78; receives blessing from Joseph Smith, 85; on prophecy of apostasy, 148–49; on prophecy of future of Church, 149; on prophecy of martyrdom, 149–50; interpretation of tongues and, 185; on revelation about John the Revelator, 212
Linder, Usher F., 440
Literacy, of early Saints, 4–5
Little Rock Gazette, The, 339–40
Littlefield, Lyman O., 440; on Joseph Smith, 32; on Joseph Smith's love for children, 72–73; on testimonies of Joseph Smith and Sidney Rigdon, 98
Lord, prophecy about seeing, 152
Loveless, Matilda E., 440; on Joseph Smith's last public speech, 374
Lovell, John, 440; on Joseph Smith as man, 95
Lyceums, 358–59
Lyman, Amasa M., 441; on revelation of Joseph Smith, 212
Lyman, Asa, 441; prophecy about, 150
Lyman, Paulina, 441; on prophecy about Rocky Mountains, 150–51

Mace, Wandle, 441; on Joseph Smith as friend, 45–46; on Joseph Smith's conversations, 63; on attempt to kidnap Joseph Smith, 176; on preaching of Joseph Smith, 202–3; on receiving endowment, 273; on law of Common Consent, 286–87; on Smith family, 298–99; on lyceums, 358–59; on martyrdom, 386–88
Mahonri Moriancumer, 275
Man, Joseph Smith as, 95–96
Mansion House, Joseph Smith kicks man out of, 99–100
Mantle of Joseph. *See* Transfiguration, of Brigham Young
Markham, Brother, 221
Marriage. *See* Celestial marriage
Martineau, Susan, 441; on Joseph Smith's good humor, 87
Martyrdom: prophecy about, 149–50, 152, 156, 172; Joseph Smith III on, 366–68; Benjamin Ashby on,

374–75; events preceding, 374–89; Anson Call on, 376–77; Robert Crookston Sr. on, 377–79; Isaac C. Haight on, 379–80; Solomon Hancock on, 380–81; Dennison L. Harris on, 381–86; Wandle Mace on, 386–88; Joseph F. Smith on, 388–89; premonitions of, 389–93, 401, 403; of Hyrum and Joseph Smith, 393–403; Mary Fielding Smith's reaction to, 403–4; mourning, 405–7; spiritual witnesses of, 407–8

Mather, Frederic G., 441; on Joseph Smith's good humor, 87

Maughan, William H., 441; on preaching of Joseph Smith, 203

McArthur, Daniel D., 441; on Joseph Smith's good humor, 87; on prophecies, 151; on cannon, 350–51

McConkie, Bruce R., 7–9

McGuire, William W., 442; on preaching of Joseph Smith, 203

McLaughlin, Harriet C., 441

McLellin, William E., 2; revelations and, 255–58

McRae, Alexander, 354–55

Measles, 134

Medicine, herbs as, 126

Meetings, secret, 381–86

Melchizedek Priesthood. *See* Priesthood

Memory: age and, 11–12, 20–22; gift of, 224

Mental quickness, of Joseph Smith, 78–79

Mercantile business, 102

Merrill, Marriner W., 442

Merrill, Philemon C., 4–5

Mesmerism, 123

Methodist minister, 78–79

Michael, vision of, 179

Midwife, 277

Miles, Samuel, 442; on Nauvoo Temple cornerstone, 369

Military spirit, 365–66

Miller, Henry W., 442; building of Nauvoo temple and, 151–52

Miller, Sara Jane, 442; Joseph Smith kisses, 388

Millet, Artemus, 442; healing of, 124–25

Miracles: of Joseph Smith, 128–31; Joseph Smith asked about Jesus', 130

Misfortune, prophecy about, 158–59

Misquotation, 7–9; of Joseph Smith, 11, 13–15

Mission: of Andrew Lamoreaux, 146; of Wilford Woodruff, 169; of Brigham Young, 172; of John R. Young, 173; of Joseph Young, 173–74; advice for George A. Smith's, 222; Wilford Woodruff to continue on, 228–29; from Zion's Camp, 332

Missionaries, persecution of, 157

Missionary work, 3–4; Book of Mormon and, 5–6; Joseph Smith and, 97–98; in England, 112

Missouri: safety for Saints going to, 131–32; prophecy about, 137–38, 147, 153; improvements in, 155–56; comments on life in, 348–52

Missouri Compromise, 102–4

Mob: Joseph Smith stands up to, 62–63; John L. Butler escapes, 93–94; Joseph Smith inspired to escape, 100; prophecy about, 157; taking guns from, 164–65; storm holds back, 199–200, 343–44; Joseph Smith preaches against, 204; Israel A. Barlow escapes, 218–19; Joseph Smith saves golden plates from, 243–47; in Hiram, 333–38; at Zion's Camp, 340–43; Joseph Smith's Missouri trial and, 348–49;

517

INDEX

stopped in Nauvoo, 357–58; martyrdom and, 375–76; chases Samuel H. Smith, 393–94
Mobocrats, 88
Moesser, Joseph H., 73
Money, faith in, 113–14
Moore, Calvin W., 442; on kindness of Joseph Smith, 56
Moore, Reverend George, 442
Morey, Elder, 65
Moriancumer, Mahonri, 275
Mourning, deaths of Hyrum and Joseph Smith, 405–7
Mud, children stuck in, 70–71
Mummies. *See* Egyptian record
Murdock, John, 152
Murdock, Joseph S., 66
Mush, 77–78

Names, prophecy on, 172
Nauvoo: Susan Fairbanks on, 4; Parley P. Pratt jokes with Joseph Smith in, 88–89; fighting in, 92–93; prophecy about apostate going to, 166–67; mob stopped in, 357–58; Joseph Smith in, 358; lyceums in, 358–59; exodus planned in, 359–61; stereotyping of Book of Mormon in, 361–62; William Law tries to enter Joseph Smith's property in, 362–63; Joseph Smith kicks man out of house in, 363–64; military spirit in, 365–66; preaching in, 367
Nauvoo Expositor, 379–80; prophecy about, 136
Nauvoo Temple, 369–70; cutting wood for, 151–52; Joseph Smith III on, 367
Neff, John, 443; on prophecy of martyrdom, 152
Nelson, William G., 443; on prophecy about sickness, 152–53
Nickerson, Mr., 200–201
Noble, Joseph B., 443; on Hebrew classes, 63; on voices of angels, 195; on witness to Book of Mormon, 315
Noble, Mary A., 443; on Joseph Smith's preaching, 19; meets Joseph Smith, 106
Norman, Mary Smith, 443; on Samuel H. Smith and martyrdom, 393–94
Nye, Ephraim H., 57

Oakley, John, 443; on Joseph Smith as man, 95
Obedience: receiving revelation and, 217; Joseph Smith and, 224–27; Haun's Mill Massacre and, 226–27; cholera and, 343
Occupations, of Joseph Smith's friends, 1–3
Officers, sent to kill Joseph Smith, 351–52
Oil, consecration of, 273
"O My Father," 213
Openness, of Joseph Smith, 80
Opinion: Lorenzo D. Young encouraged to give, 53–54; prophecy and, 99
Ordinances: divinity of, 269; of apostate religions, 272; of gospel, 272–79
Orton, Roger, 186
Osborn, David, 443; on Joseph Smith, 19; on prophecy about Missouri, 153

Pace, William B., 443; on transfiguration of Brigham Young, 420–21
Page, John, 2
Palmer, James, 444; testimony of, 19; on Joseph Smith, 33
Palmer, Mrs., 27–28, 444
Parker, Sally, 237
Partridge, Edward W., 271, 444; on industriousness of Joseph Smith, 69–70

518

Index

Patience, of Joseph Smith, 80–81
Patriarchs, organization of, 283–84
Pay, Mary Goble, 22
Pearl of Great Price, 259–65. *See also* Egyptian record
Perfection, Joseph Smith on demanding, 95
Persecution: of missionaries, 157; Joseph Smith preaches on, 199–200; of Joseph Smith, 306–7, 333–38
Perseverance, of Joseph Smith, 81–82, 118
Phelps, Laura Clark, 444
Phelps, William W.: occupation of, 2; chastises Parley P. Pratt, 176–77; on Egyptian record, 260–61; premonition of martyrdom and, 390–91
Phippen, James W., 444; on playfulness of Joseph Smith, 82–83
Physical descriptions, of Joseph Smith, 28–37
Playfulness, of Joseph Smith, 82–83
Pocket, wife in, 85
Poem, Nauvoo Temple cornerstone and, 369
Politics, Joseph Smith and, 102–4
Pomeroy, Sarah M., 444; on honesty of Joseph Smith, 66–67
Positive attitude, of Joseph Smith, 83
Potter, Amasa, 444; on meeting Joseph Smith, 106–7; on calming of storm, 130; will be delivered from danger, 153; on speaking in tongues, 184
Pratt, Orson, 444; on prophecy about Apostles, 153–54; on vision of Kirtland Temple, 190; revelation given for, 257; on obtaining Egyptian record, 261–62; on Urim and Thummim and Bible translation, 267; on washing and anointing, 277–78; on First Vision, 308–9
Pratt, Parley P., 445; on Joseph Smith, 33–34; arrives in Nauvoo, 88–89; on Joseph Smith chastising guards, 90–91; on Joseph Smith as normal man, 95–96; on healing of Elijah Fordham, 119; on healing of Chloe Smith, 125; on prophecy about preserving life, 154; W. W. Phelps chastises, 176–77; awakened by angel, 195; on preaching of Joseph Smith, 203–4; on dictation of revelations, 257; has premonition of martyrdom, 391–93
Prayer: family, of Joseph Smith, 98; to avoid whipping, 115; Johnny cake and, 115–16; of children for safety of Joseph Smith, 116–17; to calm storm, 117; Newel Knight and vocal, 181–83; preaching of Joseph Smith and, 198; Joseph Smith and, 221–24; postures for, 222; of wicked man, 222; using caution in, 222–23; family, 223; revelation and, 254–55
Preachers, search for iniquity, 180–81
Preaching: of Joseph Smith, 197–209; in Nauvoo, 367
President of United States, Joseph Smith wanted as, 406
Preston, Harriet A., 131
Priesthood: administration, 270–71; blessings, 274–76; restoration of Aaronic, 324–26; restoration of Melchizedek, 326
Promises, of Joseph Smith, 98–99
Prophecy: of Joseph Smith, 24; for Howard Coray to find companion, 44–45; of safety for Saints going to Missouri, 131–32; about Jared Carter's mission, 132; of Civil War, 132, 172; of destruction of gentiles, 132–33; about safety of Philo Dibble, 133–34; of measles, 134; of conversion of Catherine E. Greer's mother, 135; of curse of John C. Bennett, 135; about Brigham

Young, 136; about *Nauvoo Expositor,* 136; about Stephen A. Douglas, 136–37, 142–43; about Missouri, 137–38, 147, 153; about Rocky Mountains, 138–39, 150–51, 167–68; about Dimick Huntington, 139–41; about Orson Hyde and Jerusalem, 141; about riches, 141; about apostasy, 141, 148–49; about Elizabeth C. Kendall's fear of the dead, 144; about Queen of England, 144–45; about Jerusalem, 145; about Alfred B. Lambson, 145–46; about future leaders of Church, 149; about martyrdom, 149–50, 152, 156, 172; about fits, 150; about twelve years, 151; about bread, 151–52, 162–63; about seeing Lord, 152; about sickness, 152–53; about being delivered from danger, 153; about Apostles, 153–54; about preserving lives of prisoners, 154; about storms and hurricanes, 154; about enemies, 154–55; about splinters, 154–55; about hair, 155; about improvements in Missouri, 155–56; about recovery of Jacob Scott, 156; about spreading of gospel, 156–57, 167–68; about mobs, 157; about persecution of missionaries, 157; about horse, 157–58; about destruction of Olmsted Johnson, 158; about misfortunes of Saints, 158–59; about Lamanite skeleton, 159–60; about jail, 160; about scourge, 160; about wickedness of people, 160–61; about escaping enemies, 161; about curse of Wycom Clark, 161–62; about Eliza R. Snow's visiting Jerusalem, 162; about fabric, 162; about safety of John Taylor, 163; about obtaining guns, 164–65; about rain, 165–66; about destruction of eastern states, 166; about apostate going to Nauvoo, 166–67; about Lamanites and gospel, 167–68; about cornerstone, 168–69; about mission of Wilford Woodruff, 169; about Adamic language, 170; about safety of Brigham and Joseph Young, 170–71; about healing of Brigham Young, 171; about mission of Brigham Young, 172; about names, 172; of abundance, 173; about mission of John R. Young, 173; about mission of Joseph Young, 173–74

Prophet: opinions of, 10; Joseph Smith as, 89–90; Joseph Smith on being, 96; Israel A. Barlow can recognize, 105

Public speaking, 358–59; Joseph Smith and, 68

Punctuation, of Book of Mormon, 234

Purity, of Joseph Smith, 96

Queen of England, 144–45

Quincy, Josiah, 445; on Joseph Smith, 34; on mental quickness of Joseph Smith, 78–79

Rain: prophecy about, 165–66; Joseph Smith preaches in, 205–6

Randall, Alfred, 445; on martyrdom, 394–95

Rattlesnakes, 54

Rebuking evil spirits, 181–83, 187–89

Record keeping, 22–23

Relief Society, organization of, 285–86

Revelation: Joseph Fielding Smith on accepting, 15–16; angels contradicting previous, 196; Joseph Smith preaches about, 197–98; given to Joseph Smith, 210–18; lack of faith and, 211–12; continuing, 212; to Apostles, 216–17; obedience and receiving, 217; Joseph Smith and Sidney Rigdon

Index

receive, 252–53; Benjamin F. Johnson on, 253; about cholera, 254; prayer and, 254–55; about sacrament, 255; scribe for, 256; dictating and writing, 256–57; Oliver Cowdery wants Joseph Smith to change, 257–58; William E. McLellin attempts to write false, 258; about celestial marriage, 259

Reynolds, George, 445; on brother of Jared's name, 275

Reynolds, Governor, 222–23

Rich man, prophecy about, 147–48

Rich, Mary A., 445; on viewing bodies of Hyrum and Joseph Smith, 409

Richards, Franklin D., 445; on prophecy of storms, 154; on continuing revelation, 212

Richards, Jane S., 445; on Joseph Smith, 34–35; on transfiguration of Brigham Young, 421

Richards, Samuel W., 446; on expedition to Rocky Mountains, 359–61

Richards, Willard: occupation of, 1; on Book of Mormon, 5; on martyrdom, 395–97

Riches, prophecy about, 141

Ride, Joseph Smith refuses to give, 178

Rigdon, Sidney: has feelings against Heber C. Kimball, 86; dresses up truth, 87; Joseph Smith on, 87; testimony of, 98; tries to stop wrestling, 225–26; on writing Book of Mormon, 248; receives revelation, 252–53; as scribe for revelations, 256–57; Book of Mormon and, 304–6; says keys taken from Joseph Smith, 331–32; persecution of, 335–38; Liberty Jail and, 354–55. *See also* Transfiguration, of Brigham Young

Riggs, John, 446; on Frederick G. Williams' seeing angel, 196; on translation of Egyptian record, 262–63

Righteous indignation, 99–100

Riser, George C., 446; on Joseph Smith's good humor, 87–88

Robinson, Ebenezer, 446; baptism of, 97–98; on prophecy of splinters, 154–55; on preaching of Joseph Smith, 204; on escape from Liberty Jail, 355; attempts to stereotype Book of Mormon, 361–62

Robinson, George W., 2

Robinson, Joseph L., 446; on preaching of Joseph Smith, 204

Rockwell, Orrin Porter, 446; Joseph Smith pays for release of, 45–46; on prophecy of hair, 155; love of, for Joseph Smith, 299

Rocky Mountains: prophecy about, 138–39, 150–51, 167–68; vision of, 189; as idea originating with Joseph Smith, 359–61; as gathering place, 388–89

Rollins, James H., 446; has vision of Joseph Smith, 220

Roundy, Shadrach, 362–63

Rushton, Edwin, 447; on Joseph Smith's good humor, 88; on burial of Joseph Smith, 410–11

Russia, 134–35

Sabbath, 180–81, 225–26

Sacrament: revelation about, 255; as ordinance, 276–77

Sacrifice, Joseph Smith tests faith with, 102

Saints: Joseph Smith's love for, 75–78; faith of, 102

Salisbury, Catherine Smith, 447; on prophecy about Missouri, 155–56; on obtaining golden plates, 238

Salisbury, Herbert S., 447; on Joseph Smith, 35

Satan: disease and, 120–21; struggling

with, 174; appearing as angel, 196. *See also* Evil spirits

Saunders, Orlando, 447; on Smith family, 299–300

School of the Prophets, 338

Scott, Jacob, 447; prophecy about recovery of, 156; on preaching of Joseph Smith, 204

Scourge, prophecy about, 160

Scribe, for revelation, 256

Scriptures: correction of, 231–32; writing, 231–32

Searles, Asa, 447; on Joseph Smith, 35–36

Seership, 218–21

Servant girl, 375–76

Settings apart, 277

Seventies, organization of, 282–83

Sheep, dream about, 52–53

Sickness: prophecy about, 152–53, 160; of Brigham Young, 171

Sign, 177–78

Sirrine, Mephibosheth, 447; receives priesthood blessing, 275–76

Skeleton, 159–60

Slavery, 102–4; Joseph Smith helps buy child out of, 54–55

Smells, angels and, 194

Smith family: Fayette Lapham on, 2; Wandle Mace on, 298–99; Orlando Saunders on, 299–300; John Stafford on, 304–6; William A. Bills Sr. on, in Nauvoo, 356–57

Smith, Absalom Warren, 339

Smith, Bathsheba W., 447; on prophecy about martyrdom, 156; on receiving endowment, 273

Smith, Chloe, 125

Smith, Don Carlos, 126

Smith, Emma Hale, 447; on education of Joseph Smith, 250; interview on Joseph Smith and Book of Mormon with, 300–304; Lucy Mack Smith on marriage of, 304

Smith, George A., 448; on positive attitude of Joseph Smith, 83; heals Saints, 126; on prophecies, 156–57; on asking for sign, 177–78; on preaching of Joseph Smith, 205; on revelations, 212–13; on prayer and Joseph Smith, 222; on disciplinary council, 284–85; on trials of Joseph Smith, 304; on Hiram mobbing, 333–35; on School of Prophets, 338; on failure of Kirtland Bank, 347–48

Smith, Hyrum: has vision in temple, 186; printing of Book of Mormon and, 232–36; Liberty Jail and, 354–55; martyrdom of, 393–403; mourning death of, 405–7; body of, 408–10

Smith, Job F., 448; on prophecy about mobbers, 157; on preaching of Joseph Smith, 205

Smith, John, 212; on Joseph Smith, 36

Smith, John L.: on prayer for Johnny cake, 115–16; on prophecy about horse, 157–58

Smith, Joseph:

Character and personality of: friends of, 1–3; opinions of, 9; on opinions of prophets, 10; wrestling and accuracy of accounts, 10–11; misquotations of, 11, 13–15; on Constitution, 13; as record keeper, 17; as teacher, 18–19, 54; followers of, 19–20; as speaker, 21; on Spirit and memory, 21; in his youth, 27–28; as worker, 28; physical descriptions of, 28–37; character of, 37–41; crowd parts for, 38–39; temporal concerns and, 41–42; boldness of, 42–43; as friend, 43–48; arranges release of O. P. Rockwell, 45–46; stays with Taylor family, 46–48; as leader, 48–54; humility of, 50–51, 65, 67–69, 94–95, 286–87, 332; kindness of,

54–55, 76–77; forgives debts, 57–58; plans funeral for Robert B. Thompson, 58–59; not a merchant, 60–61; courage of, 61–63; stands up to mob, 62–63; conversation and, 63; encourages learning, 63; gratitude of, 63–65; man refuses to bow to, 65; honesty of, 65–67; wants Governor Ford to know good and bad, 66; answers questions of teacher, 67–68; public speaking and, 68; accepts counsel of Brigham Young, 68–69; industriousness of, 69–70; borrows baby, 70–71; love of, for children, 70–74; love of, for Saints, 75–78; mental quickness of, 78–79; Methodist minister and, 78–79; on United States government, 80; openness of, 80; patience of, 80–81; arrests of, 81–82; perseverance of, 81–82, 118; playfulness of, 82–83; positive attitude of, 83; blessing others and, 84–85; wit and good humor of, 85–89; on Sydney Rigdon's speaking, 87; as prophet, 89–90; chastises prison guards, 90–91; correcting others and, 90–94; inspired counsel of, 93–94; introspection of, 94–95; on perfection, 95; as man, 95–96; holiness of, 96; on prophets, 96; on purity, 96; missionary work and, 97–98; devotion of, 98; testimony of, 98; promises of, 98–99; on prophecy and opinion, 99; righteous indignation and, 99–100; spiritual sensitivity of, 100–101; faith of Saints and, 102; politics and, 102–4; first meetings with, 105–10; knowledge of, 111–12; distinguishes truth in scripture, 112

and gifts of the Spirit:
healing performed by, 23–24, 118–27, 128–30; prophecies of, 24; faith of, 113–18; on happiness, 114; repairs axeltree, 117; healing of, 119–20; tells Don Carlos and George A. Smith to heal Saints, 126; digs well in rock, 128; miracles performed by, 128–31; calms storm, 130; on Jesus Christ's first miracle, 130; blesses well, 131; on Jesus Christ's gospel, 131; borrows money, 174; on struggles with Satan, 174; discernment and, 174–81; William Law tries to kidnap, 176; Campbellite Minister and, 177–78; on bloodshed, 178; on signs and adulterers, 178; refuses ride to man, 178; confirms vision of Michael, 179; jumps on Sabbath, 180–81; discerns men seeking his blood, 181; casts devil out of Newel Knight, 181–83; speaks in tongues to Indians, 183; reads German Bible, 184; has vision in temple, 186; has vision, 187–89; vision of Rocky Mountains and, 189; has vision of war, 189–90; visions of, 190–92; dreams of, 192–94; voices of angels and, 195; preaching of, 197–209; preaches against mob, 204; undercover name of, 205; knows Lorenzo Snow wants to be baptized, 207–8; receives revelation about Bible, 210; speaks with John the Revelator, 210–11; revelations given to, 210–18; ancestry of, 212; shows Brigham Young Ensign Peak, 212–13; escapes arrest by revelations, 214–15; ordained before coming here, 215; visits Wilford Woodruff after martyrdom, 215–16; says his knowledge is from Lord, 217; tells Israel A. Barlow not to spend night, 218–19; seership of, 218–21; foresees journey of Frederick G. Williams's daughter,

219; knows Ira S. Hatch, 219–20; foresees easy journey, 220; knows of James H. Rollins' vision, 220; foresees safe escape of Brother Markham, 221; should remember sister, 221; on prayer, 221–22; prayer and, 221–24; will receive what he asks, 222–23; Daniel Tyler on prayer of, 223–24; gift of memory and, 224; obedience and, 224–27; tells men to wrestle on Sabbath, 225–26; on Haun's Mill Massacre, 226–27; forgiveness and, 228; tells Wilford Woodruff to continue on mission, 228–29

prophecies of, regarding:
Missouri, 131–32, 137–38, 147, 153, 155–56; mission of Jared Carter, 132; Civil War, 132, 172; destruction of gentiles, 132–33; safety of Philo Dibble, 133–34; measles, 134; battles, 134–35; conversion, 135; curse of John C. Bennett, 135; childbearing, 135; Brigham Young, 136, 170, 171, 172; *Nauvoo Expositor,* 136; Stephen A. Douglas, 136–37, 142–43; Rocky Mountains, 138–39, 150–51; Dimick Huntington, 139–41; Orson Hyde and Jerusalem, 141; riches, 141; apostasy, 141, 148–49; Elizabeth C. Kendall, 144; Heber C. Kimball's seeing Queen of England, 144–45; Heber C. Kimball and Jerusalem, 145; use of Alfred B. Lambson, 145–46; death of Andrew Lamoreaux, 146; curse of rich man, 147–48; future leaders of Church, 149; martyrdom, 149–50, 152, 156, 172; fits, 150; next twelve years, 151; John Murdock's seeing Lord, 152; sickness, 152–53; Amasa Potter, 153; Apostles, 153–54; hurricanes, 154; preservation of lives, 154; safety of Orrin Porter Rockwell, 155; recovery of Jacob Scott, 156; spreading of gospel, 156–57, 167–68; destruction of mobs, 157; persecution of missionaries, 157; scare of horse, 157–58; destruction of Olmsted Johnson, 158; misfortune of Saints, 158–59; identity of skeleton, 159–60; jail, 160; scourge, 160; wickedness of people, 160–61; escaping enemies, 161; curse of Wycom Clark, 161–62; Eliza R. Snow's visit to Jerusalem, 162; fabric in Zion, 162; John Tanner, 162–63; safety of John Taylor, 163; obtaining guns from mob, 164–65; rain, 165–66; destruction of eastern states, 166; Brank will not go to Nauvoo, 166–67; cornerstone, 168–69; mission of Wilford Woodruff, 169; Adamic language, 170; safety of Brigham and Joseph Young, 170–71; John M. Horner, 173; mission of John R. Young, 173; mission of Joseph Young, 173–74; falling stars, 338–40; safety for lawyers, 355

and scriptures:
corrects scripture, 231–32; on Urim and Thummim, 232; attempts to get plates, 238–42; chastised by angel, 242–43; saves golden plates from enemies, 243–47; receives money to translate Book of Mormon, 247–48; education of, 250; receives revelation about Vinson Knight, 251–52; Philo Dibble on revelation and, 252–53; tells Saints to pray for revelation, 254–55; receives revelation for Orson Pratt, 257; will not change revelation, 257–58; reads Book of

Index

Abraham to Anson Call and Vinson Knight, 259–60; on obtaining Egyptian record, 263–64; Bible translation of, 265–67; Howard Coray on revelation and, 266; asserts authority as president, 271; on anointing, 272; on ordinances of apostate religions, 272

and ordinances and the Church: priesthood blessings given by, 274–76; on sacrament as ordinance, 276–77; washes feet, 278; on ordaining First Presidency, 279–80; on organization of Church, 329; Sidney Rigdon says keys taken from, 331–32

and historical items: leg operation of, 289–92; Colesville arrest and trial of, 292–98; Orrin Porter Rockwell's love for, 299; interview with Emma Hale Smith on, 300–304; Lucy Mack Smith on marriage of, 304; trials of, 304; persecution of, 306–7, 333–38; on witnesses to Book of Mormon, 316–17; prophesies safe return of David Lewis to his mother, 327–29; on Hiram mobbing, 335–38; finds water at Zion's Camp, 340–41; on Kirtland Temple dedication, 345–47; on failure of Kirtland Bank, 348; Missouri trial of, 348–49; altar of Adam and, 349–50; officers sent to kill, 351–52; Haun's Mill Massacre and, 352–53; Lyman Wight will not testify falsely against, 353–54; Liberty Jail and, 354–55; receives money from Lewis Barney, 356; in Nauvoo, 358; exodus to Rocky Mountains and, 359–61; William Law tries to enter property of, 362–63; kicks Josiah Butterfield out of house, 363–64; disperses army, 365–66; horse of, 366; kept from being arrested by whittling, 368–69; last meeting of, with Apostles, 373, 403; last public speech of, 373–74; Dennison L. Harris spies for, 381–86; betrayal of, 388–89; has premonition of martyrdom, 390–91, 401, 403; gunshot that killed, 393; martyrdom of, 393–403; mourning death of, 405–7; wanted for President of United states, 406; visits Anson Call after martyrdom, 407–8; body of, 408–10; burial of, 410–11; whistle of, 418

Smith, Joseph F., 448; on quoting prophets, 7; on kindness of Joseph Smith, 57–58; on preaching of Joseph Smith, 205–6; on revelation about celestial marriage, 259; on translation of Egyptian record, 264–65; on Joseph Smith's kicking man out of house, 363–64; on martyrdom, 388–89

Smith, Joseph Fielding, 15–16

Smith, Joseph III: interviews Emma Hale Smith, 300–304; Nauvoo memories of, 364–68; on martyrdom, 366–68

Smith, Joseph Sr.: on prophecy about Rocky Mountains, 138–39; anointing of, 272

Smith, Lucy Mack, 448; on Joseph Smith and golden plates, 238–47; on Joseph Smith's leg operation, 289–92; on Joseph Smith's marrying Lucy Hale Smith, 304; on organization of Church, 329–30; on officers sent to kill Joseph Smith, 351–52; reaction of, to martyrdom, 410

Smith, Lucy Meserve, 448; on Joseph Smith's love for children, 73; on meeting Joseph Smith, 107; on

INDEX

viewing bodies of Hyrum and Joseph Smith, 409
Smith, Mary Fielding, 448; goes to Liberty Jail, 355–56; reaction of, to martyrdom, 403–4
Smith, Robert, 212
Smith, Samuel H., 393–94
Smith, Vienna, 221
Smith, William, 448; on industriousness of Joseph Smith, 70; on obtaining golden plates, 247; on First Vision, 309–10; as witness to Book of Mormon, 317
Snakes, Martin Harris and, 91
Snow, Eliza R., 449; occupation of, 2; on prophecies of Joseph Smith, 162; receiving revelation and, 213; on viewing bodies of Hyrum and Joseph Smith, 409
Snow, Erastus, 449; Liberty Jail and, 355
Snow, Eunice B., 449; on Joseph Smith, 36, 40–41; on viewing bodies of Hyrum and Joseph Smith, 410
Snow, Lorenzo, 449; on Joseph Smith, 36–37; on preaching of Joseph Smith, 206–7; baptism of, 207–8
Snowball fight, 83
Soldiers, spirit, 249–50
Somerville, William, 116–17
Song of Solomon, 267
Speaker, Joseph Smith as, 21
Speaking in tongues, 183–85, 186–87; Kirtland Temple dedication and, 345
Speech, Joseph Smith's last public, 373–74
Spilsbury, George, 3
Spirit of God, 215–16
Spirit, memory and, 21–22
Spirit soldiers, 249–50
Splinters, prophecy about, 154–55
Spy, of Joseph Smith, 381–86
Squirrel, 54

Stafford, John, 449; on Smith family, 304–6
Staines, William C., 449; on meeting Joseph Smith, 107
Stars, falling, 338–40
Stereotyping, of Book of Mormon, 361–62
Stevenson, Edward, 449; on playfulness of Joseph Smith, 83; on Joseph Smith as prophet, 89–90; on knowledge of Joseph Smith, 112; on First Vision, 310–12
Stoddard, Charles H., 73–74
Store: Truman O. Angell to build, 48–49; Joseph Smith's not keeping, 60–61; Joseph Smith tests faith with, 102
Storm: will not hurt Saints, 113; prayers to calm, 117; Joseph Smith calms, 130; prophecy about, 154; dream of, 193–94; holds back mob, 199–200; at Zion's Camp, 343–44
Storytelling, 7–9
Stout, Allen, 210–11
Stowell, William R., 301, 449
Structure, of The Church of Jesus Christ of Latter-day Saints, 279–87
Suit, prophecy and, 136–37
Sunday School, organization of, 286
Sword of Laban, 250–51

Taggart, George W., 450; on Joseph Smith, 37
Tanner, John, 450; gives Joseph Smith $2,000, 162–63
Taylor, Father, 134–35
Taylor, John, 450; has vision, 3; quotes Joseph Smith, 14; on Joseph Smith as leader, 51; on courage of Joseph Smith, 62–63; prophecy about, 163; revelation on Holy Ghost for, 214; on family prayer, 223; on writing scripture, 231; on priesthood order, 271; on law of Common Consent, 287;

526

martyrdom and, 393–403; on martyrdom, 397–401
Taylor, Joseph, 450; on prophecy about John Taylor, 163
Taylor, Joseph E., 450; on organization of Apostles, 280–81
Taylor, Leonora C., 450; on premonition of martyrdom, 401
Taylor, Thomas H., 450; on Joseph Smith, 306–7
Taylor, William, 450; on Joseph Smith as friend, 46–48
Teacher: Joseph Smith as, 54; Joseph Smith answers questions of, 67–68
Teapot, 19
Temple: blessings for builders of, 63–64; Heber C. Kimball encourages building of, 83
Temporal concerns, Joseph Smith and, 41–42
Terry, James P., 451; on preaching of Joseph Smith, 208; on Joseph Smith's last public speech, 374
Testimony, of Joseph Smith, 98
Thomas, Martha, 451; on visions, 192; on Joseph Smith's receiving revelation, 214
Thompson, Mercy Rachel, 451; on kindness of Joseph Smith, 58–59; on Liberty Jail, 355–56
Thompson, Robert B., 58–59
Toast, to mobocrats, 88
Tongues: speaking in, 183–85, 186–87, 345; interpretation of, 185
Tornado, prophecy about, 154
Tracy, Nancy N., 451; on Relief Society, 285; on Nauvoo Temple Cornerstone, 369–70
Transfiguration, of Brigham Young, 411–24
Trial(s): Joseph Smith receives inspiration for, 100–101; faith in, 115; of Joseph Smith in Colesville, 292–98; of Joseph Smith, 304
Truth, Sidney Rigdon dresses up, 87

Twelve years, prophecy about, 151
Tyler, Daniel, 451; on prophecies of Joseph Smith, 165–66; on mother's vision, 179; on prayer of Joseph Smith, 223–24; on forgiveness and Joseph Smith, 228; on correction of scripture, 231–32
Tyler, Elizabeth Comins, 179

Urim and Thummim: Joseph Smith on, 232; Bible translation and, 267

Vision(s), 185–92; of John Taylor, 3; of John Murdock, 152; of Michael, 179; of James H. Rollins, 220; of Samuel W. Richards, 360
Voices, of angels, 195

Wagon, Joseph Smith foresees turning over of, 219
Walker, Charles L., 451; on First Vision, 312–13
Walker, William H., 451; on devotion of Joseph Smith, 98; on righteous indignation, 99–100; on revelations given to Joseph Smith, 214–15
War: prophecy of, 172; vision of, 189–90
Washing of feet, 277–79
Wasson, Lorenzo D., 451; on kindness of Joseph Smith, 59–60
Watch, man sells wife for, 87
Water: Joseph Smith finds, 128, 340–41; dream of, 193–94
Waterloo, 134–35
Watkins, William, 452; on transfiguration of Brigham Young, 421–22
Webb, Sylvia Cutler, 347
Weight, Joseph Smith tries to gain, 85
Welch, John, 452; on transfiguration of Brigham Young, 422
Well: Joseph Smith digs, 128; Joseph Smith blesses, 131
Wells, Daniel H., 272

INDEX

Wells, Emmeline B., 107–9
Westover, Eliza, 452; on transfiguration of Brigham Young, 422–23
Westover, Mary C., 452; on prayer to calm storm, 117
Wheat, prophecy about, 147–48
Whip, 224–25
Whipping, prayer to avoid, 115
Whistle, of Joseph Smith, 418
Whitehorse Prophecy, The, 15
Whitmer, David, 452; as qualified witness, 11; hired girl in house of, 248–49; as witness to Book of Mormon, 317–24
Whitney, Elizabeth Ann: on prophecy of destruction of eastern states, 166; on Feast for the Poor, 332–33
Whitney, Helen Mar, 452
Whitney, Newel K.: occupation of, 2; on meeting Joseph Smith, 109; healing of, 119–20
Whittling, 368–69
Wickedness, prophecy about, 160–61
Wife: man sells, for watch, 87; Joseph Smith counsels Benjamin F. Johnson to take, 101
Wight, Lyman, 452; John Corrill enters complaint against, 120–21; rebukes evil spirits, 181; will not testify falsely against Joseph Smith, 353–54; Liberty Jail and, 354–55
Wight, Orange L., 166–67
Wilcox, Walter, 452
Will of God, exercising faith contrary to, 116
Williams, Colonel, 375–76
Williams, Frederick G.: occupation of, 1; sees angel, 196
Williams, Zilpha, 453; on preaching of Joseph Smith, 208
Willis, Alzina, 453; on transfiguration of Brigham Young, 423
Wilson, General, 353–54
Wind, prayer to stop, 215–16

Windows, vision about temple, 191–92
Wine, revelation about sacrament, 255
Winters, Mary Ann, 453; on humor of Joseph Smith, 88–89; on preaching of Joseph Smith, 208; on organization of Sunday School, 286; on transfiguration of Brigham Young, 423
Wit, of Joseph Smith, 85–89
Witnesses: qualified and unqualified, 11; accuracy of accounts of, 16–17; to Book of Mormon, 313–24; spiritual, of martyrdom, 407–8
Women, revelations and, 213
Wood: Joseph Smith's playfulness gathering, 82; for Nauvoo Temple, 151–52
Woodland, John, 453; builds house, 179–80
Woodruff, Wilford: occupation of, 2; on meeting Joseph Smith, 110; on prophecy about spreading of gospel, 167–68; on prophecy about cornerstone, 168–69; prophecy about mission of, 169; on Joseph Smith's jumping on Sabbath, 180–81; on men seeking Joseph Smith's blood, 181; on being saved by angels, 197; on revelations given to Joseph Smith, 215–17; sick on mission, 228–29; on publishing of Pearl of Great Price, 265; on divinity of ordinances, 269; on Joseph Smith's asserting authority, 271; on washing of feet, 278–79; on organization of Apostles, 281; on Relief Society, 286; on storm at Zion's Camp, 343–44; on chastisement of Zion's Camp, 344–45; on Joseph Smith's last meeting with Apostles, 373; on martyrdom, 401–3; on transfiguration of Brigham Young, 423–24

Woolley, Edwin D., 453; Joseph Smith tests faith of, 102
Woolley, Samuel A., 453; keeps Joseph Smith from being arrested, 368–69
Word of Wisdom, 252, 253–54
Work, Joseph Smith and, 28
Workman, Andrew, 453; on kindness of Joseph Smith, 60
Works, Angeline, 125–26
World, as Jesus Christ's first miracle, 130
Wrestling: accuracy of accounts and, 10–11; kindness of Joseph Smith and, 56; Joseph Smith starts, on Sabbath, 225–26

"Yankee doodle do it," 83
Young, Brigham, 453; occupation of, 2; receives correction, 10; on Constitution, 13; on Joseph Smith as leader, 52–53; on Joseph Smith's not keeping a store, 60–61; Joseph Smith accepts counsel of, 68–69; on Joseph Smith's arrests, 81–82; on Joseph Smith's correcting Orson Hyde, 93; on Joseph Smith as normal man, 96; on faith of Joseph Smith, 117–18; prophecy about, 136; on prophecies of Joseph Smith, 170–72; prophecy about healing of, 171; speaks in tongues, 184; has vision of Ensign Peak, 212–13; on bodies, 217; on revelations given to Joseph Smith, 217–18; on Urim and Thummim, 232; on room in Hill Cumorah, 250–51; on organization of Apostles, 281–82; on organization of patriarchs, 283–84; on organization of bishops, 285; transfiguration of, 411–24
Young, Emily Partridge, 454; on patience of Joseph Smith, 80–81
Young, John R., 173
Young, Joseph, 454; prophecy about safety of, 170–71; prophecy about mission of, 173–74; on organization of Seventies, 282–83
Young, Lorenzo D., 454; on Joseph Smith as leader, 53–54; healing of, 126–27
Young, Margaret P., 208–9, 454
Young, Zina D. H.: receives priesthood blessing, 276; on mourning martyrdom, 406–7
Youth: Joseph Smith in his, 27–28; Joseph Smith's love for, 70–74

Zelph, 159–60
Zion, loyalty to, 228–29
Zion's Camp, 340–45